Course	Corporate Finance
Course Number	**BUSI 408**

Chip Snively

University of North Carolina

Kenan Flagler School of Business

http://create.mheducation.com

ISBN-10: 1121682715   ISBN-13: 9781121682719

Contents

Credits

Overview

CHAPTER 1

Introduction to Corporate Finance

Compensation of corporate executives in the United States continues to be a hot button issue. It is widely viewed that CEO pay has grown to exorbitant levels (at least in some cases). In July 2010, the Dodd–Frank *Wall Street Reform and Consumer Protection Act* became law. The "say on pay" portion of the bill requires that, beginning in January 2011, corporations with a market value over $75 million must allow a nonbinding shareholder vote on executive pay. (Note that because the bill applies to corporations, it does not give voters a "say on pay" for U.S. representatives and senators.)

▲ For updates on the latest happenings in finance, visit www.rwjcorporatefinance.blogspot.com

Specifically, the measure allows shareholders to approve or disapprove a company's executive compensation plan. Because the bill is nonbinding, it does not permit shareholders to veto a compensation package and does not place limits on executive pay. In February 2011, the shareholders of Beazer Homes USA and Jacobs Engineering Group became the first shareholders to vote against executive compensation under the new law. One analyst expected that these two companies would not be alone. He predicted that at least 50 companies would receive negative shareholder votes during 2011.

Understanding how a corporation sets executive pay, and the role of shareholders in that process, takes us into issues involving the corporate form of organization, corporate goals, and corporate control, all of which we cover in this chapter.

1.1 What Is Corporate Finance?

Suppose you decide to start a firm to make tennis balls. To do this you hire managers to buy raw materials, and you assemble a workforce that will produce and sell finished tennis balls. In the language of finance, you make an investment in assets such as inventory, machinery, land, and labor. The amount of cash you invest in assets must be matched by an equal amount of cash raised by financing. When you begin to sell tennis balls, your firm will generate cash. This is the basis of value creation. The purpose of the firm is to create value for you, the owner. The value is reflected in the framework of the simple balance sheet model of the firm.

THE BALANCE SHEET MODEL OF THE FIRM

Suppose we take a financial snapshot of the firm and its activities at a single point in time. Figure 1.1 shows a graphic conceptualization of the balance sheet, and it will help introduce you to corporate finance.

The assets of the firm are on the left side of the balance sheet. These assets can be thought of as current and fixed. *Fixed assets* are those that will last a long time, such as buildings. Some fixed assets are tangible, such as machinery and equipment. Other fixed assets are intangible, such as patents and trademarks. The other category of assets, *current assets,* comprises those that have short lives, such as inventory. The tennis balls that your firm has made, but has not yet sold, are part of its inventory. Unless you have overproduced, they will leave the firm shortly.

Figure 1.1
The Balance Sheet
Model of the Firm

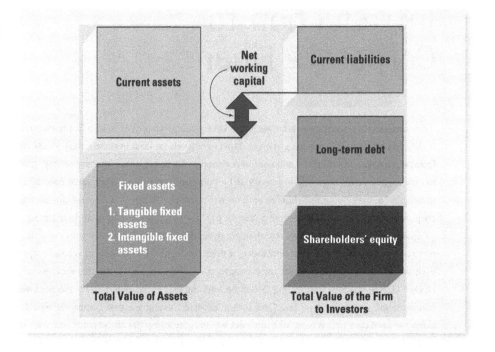

Before a company can invest in an asset, it must obtain financing, which means that it must raise the money to pay for the investment. The forms of financing are represented on the right side of the balance sheet. A firm will issue (sell) pieces of paper called *debt* (loan agreements) or *equity shares* (stock certificates). Just as assets are classified as long-lived or short-lived, so too are liabilities. A short-term debt is called a *current liability.* Short-term debt represents loans and other obligations that must be repaid within one year. Long-term debt is debt that does not have to be repaid within one year. Shareholders' equity represents the difference between the value of the assets and the debt of the firm. In this sense, it is a residual claim on the firm's assets.

From the balance sheet model of the firm, it is easy to see why finance can be thought of as the study of the following three questions:

1. In what long-lived assets should the firm invest? This question concerns the left side of the balance sheet. Of course the types and proportions of assets the firm needs tend to be set by the nature of the business. We use the term **capital budgeting** to describe the process of making and managing expenditures on long-lived assets.

2. How can the firm raise cash for required capital expenditures? This question concerns the right side of the balance sheet. The answer to this question involves the firm's **capital structure,** which represents the proportions of the firm's financing from current and long-term debt and equity.

3. How should short-term operating cash flows be managed? This question concerns the upper portion of the balance sheet. There is often a mismatch between the timing of cash inflows and cash outflows during operating activities. Furthermore, the amount and timing of operating cash flows are not known with certainty. Financial managers must attempt to manage the gaps in cash

flow. From a balance sheet perspective, short-term management of cash flow is associated with a firm's **net working capital.** Net working capital is defined as current assets minus current liabilities. From a financial perspective, short-term cash flow problems come from the mismatching of cash inflows and outflows. This is the subject of short-term finance.

THE FINANCIAL MANAGER

For current issues facing CFOs, see www.cfo.com.

In large firms, the finance activity is usually associated with a top officer of the firm, such as the vice president and chief financial officer, and some lesser officers. Figure 1.2 depicts a general organizational structure emphasizing the finance

Figure 1.2
Hypothetical
Organization Chart

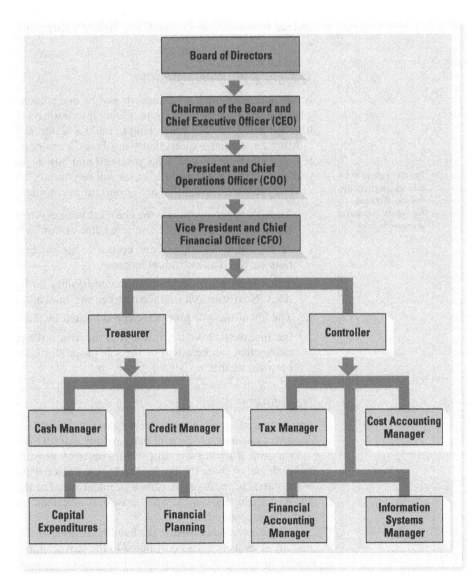

activity within the firm. Reporting to the chief financial officer are the treasurer and the controller. The treasurer is responsible for handling cash flows, managing capital expenditure decisions, and making financial plans. The controller handles the accounting function, which includes taxes, cost and financial accounting, and information systems.

1.2   The Corporate Firm

The firm is a way of organizing the economic activity of many individuals. A basic problem of the firm is how to raise cash. The corporate form of business—that is, organizing the firm as a corporation—is the standard method for solving problems encountered in raising large amounts of cash. However, businesses can take other forms. In this section we consider the three basic legal forms of organizing firms, and we see how firms go about the task of raising large amounts of money under each form.

THE SOLE PROPRIETORSHIP

A **sole proprietorship** is a business owned by one person. Suppose you decide to start a business to produce mousetraps. Going into business is simple: You announce to all who will listen, "Today, I am going to build a better mousetrap."

Most large cities require that you obtain a business license. Afterward, you can begin to hire as many people as you need and borrow whatever money you need. At year-end all the profits and the losses will be yours.

Here are some factors that are important in considering a sole proprietorship:

For more about small business organization, see the "Business Formation" section at **www.nolo.com**.

1. The sole proprietorship is the cheapest business to form. No formal charter is required, and few government regulations must be satisfied for most industries.
2. A sole proprietorship pays no corporate income taxes. All profits of the business are taxed as individual income.
3. The sole proprietorship has unlimited liability for business debts and obligations. No distinction is made between personal and business assets.
4. The life of the sole proprietorship is limited by the life of the sole proprietor.
5. Because the only money invested in the firm is the proprietor's, the equity money that can be raised by the sole proprietor is limited to the proprietor's personal wealth.

THE PARTNERSHIP

Any two or more people can get together and form a **partnership.** Partnerships fall into two categories: (1) general partnerships and (2) limited partnerships.

In a *general partnership* all partners agree to provide some fraction of the work and cash and to share the profits and losses. Each partner is liable for all of the debts of the partnership. A partnership agreement specifies the nature of the arrangement. The partnership agreement may be an oral agreement or a formal document setting forth the understanding.

Limited partnerships permit the liability of some of the partners to be limited to the amount of cash each has contributed to the partnership. Limited partnerships usually require that (1) at least one partner be a general partner and (2) the limited partners do not participate in managing the business. Here are some things that are important when considering a partnership:

1. Partnerships are usually inexpensive and easy to form. Written documents are required in complicated arrangements. Business licenses and filing fees may be necessary.

2. General partners have unlimited liability for all debts. The liability of limited partners is usually limited to the contribution each has made to the partnership. If one general partner is unable to meet his or her commitment, the shortfall must be made up by the other general partners.

3. The general partnership is terminated when a general partner dies or withdraws (but this is not so for a limited partner). It is difficult for a partnership to transfer ownership without dissolving. Usually all general partners must agree. However, limited partners may sell their interest in a business.

4. It is difficult for a partnership to raise large amounts of cash. Equity contributions are usually limited to a partner's ability and desire to contribute to the partnership. Many companies, such as Apple, Inc., start life as a proprietorship or partnership, but at some point they choose to convert to corporate form.

5. Income from a partnership is taxed as personal income to the partners.

6. Management control resides with the general partners. Usually a majority vote is required on important matters, such as the amount of profit to be retained in the business.

It is difficult for large business organizations to exist as sole proprietorships or partnerships. The main advantage to a sole proprietorship or partnership is the cost of getting started. Afterward, the disadvantages, which may become severe, are (1) unlimited liability, (2) limited life of the enterprise, and (3) difficulty of transferring ownership. These three disadvantages lead to (4) difficulty in raising cash.

THE CORPORATION

Of the forms of business enterprises, the **corporation** is by far the most important. It is a distinct legal entity. As such, a corporation can have a name and enjoy many of the legal powers of natural persons. For example, corporations can acquire and exchange property. Corporations can enter contracts and may sue and be sued. For jurisdictional purposes the corporation is a citizen of its state of incorporation (it cannot vote, however).

Starting a corporation is more complicated than starting a proprietorship or partnership. The incorporators must prepare articles of incorporation and a set of bylaws. The articles of incorporation must include the following:

1. Name of the corporation.

2. Intended life of the corporation (it may be forever).

3. Business purpose.

4. Number of shares of stock that the corporation is authorized to issue, with a statement of limitations and rights of different classes of shares.

5. Nature of the rights granted to shareholders.

6. Number of members of the initial board of directors.

The bylaws are the rules to be used by the corporation to regulate its own existence, and they concern its shareholders, directors, and officers. Bylaws range from the briefest possible statement of rules for the corporation's management to hundreds of pages of text.

In its simplest form, the corporation comprises three sets of distinct interests: the shareholders (the owners), the directors, and the corporation officers (the top management). Traditionally, the shareholders control the corporation's direction, policies, and activities. The shareholders elect a board of directors, who in turn select top management. Members of top management serve as corporate officers and manage the operations of the corporation in the best interest of the shareholders. In closely held corporations with few shareholders, there may be a large overlap among the shareholders, the directors, and the top management. However, in larger corporations, the shareholders, directors, and the top management are likely to be distinct groups.

The potential separation of ownership from management gives the corporation several advantages over proprietorships and partnerships:

1. Because ownership in a corporation is represented by shares of stock, ownership can be readily transferred to new owners. Because the corporation exists independently of those who own its shares, there is no limit to the transferability of shares as there is in partnerships.

2. The corporation has unlimited life. Because the corporation is separate from its owners, the death or withdrawal of an owner does not affect the corporation's legal existence. The corporation can continue on after the original owners have withdrawn.

3. The shareholders' liability is limited to the amount invested in the ownership shares. For example, if a shareholder purchased $1,000 in shares of a corporation, the potential loss would be $1,000. In a partnership, a general partner with a $1,000 contribution could lose the $1,000 plus any other indebtedness of the partnership.

Limited liability, ease of ownership transfer, and perpetual succession are the major advantages of the corporate form of business organization. These give the corporation an enhanced ability to raise cash.

There is, however, one great disadvantage to incorporation. The federal government taxes corporate income (the states do as well). This tax is in addition to the personal income tax that shareholders pay on dividend income they receive. This is double taxation for shareholders when compared to taxation on proprietorships and partnerships. Table 1.1 summarizes our discussion of partnerships and corporations.

To find out more about LLCs, visit **www.incorporate. com**.

Today all 50 states have enacted laws allowing for the creation of a relatively new form of business organization, the limited liability company (LLC). The goal of this entity is to operate and be taxed like a partnership but retain limited liability for owners, so an LLC is essentially a hybrid of partnership and corporation. Although states have differing definitions for LLCs, the more important scorekeeper is the Internal Revenue Service (IRS). The IRS will consider an LLC a corporation, thereby subjecting it to double taxation, unless it meets certain specific criteria. In essence, an LLC cannot be too corporation-like, or it will be treated as one by the IRS. LLCs have become common. For example, Goldman, Sachs and Co., one of Wall Street's last remaining partnerships, decided to convert from a private partnership to an LLC (it later "went public," becoming a publicly held corporation). Large accounting firms and law firms by the score have converted to LLCs.

Chapter 1 Introduction to Corporate Finance

7

Table 1.1 **A Comparison of Partnerships and Corporations**

	Corporation	Partnership
Liquidity and marketability	Shares can be exchanged without termination of the corporation. Common stock can be listed on a stock exchange.	Units are subject to substantial restrictions on transferability. There is usually no established trading market for partnership units.
Voting rights	Usually each share of common stock entitles the holder to one vote per share on matters requiring a vote and on the election of the directors. Directors determine top management.	Some voting rights by limited partners. However, general partners have exclusive control and management of operations.
Taxation	Corporations have double taxation: Corporate income is taxable, and dividends to shareholders are also taxable.	Partnerships are not taxable. Partners pay personal taxes on partnership profits.
Reinvestment and dividend payout	Corporations have broad latitude on dividend payout decisions.	Partnerships are generally prohibited from reinvesting partnership profits. All profits are distributed to partners.
Liability	Shareholders are not personally liable for obligations of the corporation.	Limited partners are not liable for obligations of partnerships. General partners may have unlimited liability.
Continuity of existence	Corporations may have a perpetual life.	Partnerships have limited life.

A CORPORATION BY ANOTHER NAME . . .

The corporate form of organization has many variations around the world. The exact laws and regulations differ from country to country, of course, but the essential features of public ownership and limited liability remain. These firms are often called *joint stock companies*, *public limited companies*, or *limited liability companies*, depending on the specific nature of the firm and the country of origin.

Table 1.2 gives the names of a few well-known international corporations, their countries of origin, and a translation of the abbreviation that follows each company name.

Table 1.2 **International Corporations**

Company	Country of Origin	Type of Company	
		In Original Language	Interpretation
Bayerische Motoren Werke (BMW) AG	Germany	Aktiengesellschaft	Corporation
Red Bull GmBH	Austria	Gesellschaft mit Beschränkter Haftung	Limited liability company
Rolls-Royce PLC	United Kingdom	Public limited company	Public Ltd. Company
Shell UK Ltd.	United Kingdom	Limited	Corporation
Unilever NV	Netherlands	Naamloze Vennootschap	Joint stock company
Fiat SpA	Italy	Società per Azioni	Joint stock company
Volvo AB	Sweden	Aktiebolag	Joint stock company
Peugeot SA	France	Société Anonyme	Joint stock company

In Their Own Words

SKILLS NEEDED FOR THE CHIEF FINANCIAL OFFICERS OF eFINANCE.COM

Chief strategist: CFOs will need to use real-time financial information to make crucial decisions fast.

Chief deal maker: CFOs must be adept at venture capital, mergers and acquisitions, and strategic partnerships.

Chief risk officer: Limiting risk will be even more important as markets become more global and hedging instruments become more complex.

Chief communicator: Gaining the confidence of Wall Street and the media will be essential.

SOURCE: *BusinessWeek,* August 28, 2000, p. 120.

1.3 The Importance of Cash Flows

The most important job of a financial manager is to create value from the firm's capital budgeting, financing, and net working capital activities. How do financial managers create value? The answer is that the firm should:

1. Try to buy assets that generate more cash than they cost.
2. Sell bonds and stocks and other financial instruments that raise more cash than they cost.

Thus, the firm must create more cash flow than it uses. The cash flows paid to bondholders and stockholders of the firm should be greater than the cash flows put into the firm by the bondholders and stockholders. To see how this is done, we can trace the cash flows from the firm to the financial markets and back again.

The interplay of the firm's activities with the financial markets is illustrated in Figure 1.3. The arrows in Figure 1.3 trace cash flow from the firm to the financial

Figure 1.3
Cash Flows between the Firm and the Financial Markets

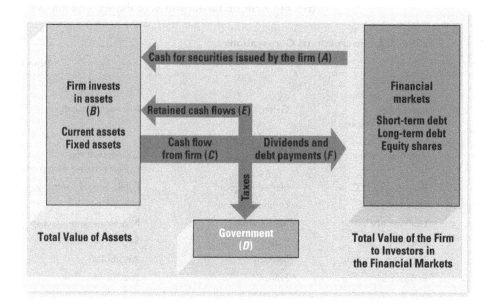

markets and back again. Suppose we begin with the firm's financing activities. To raise money, the firm sells debt and equity shares to investors in the financial markets. This results in cash flows from the financial markets to the firm (*A*). This cash is invested in the investment activities (assets) of the firm (*B*) by the firm's management. The cash generated by the firm (*C*) is paid to shareholders and bondholders (*F*). The shareholders receive cash in the form of dividends; the bondholders who lent funds to the firm receive interest and, when the initial loan is repaid, principal. Not all of the firm's cash is paid out. Some is retained (*E*), and some is paid to the government as taxes (*D*).

Over time, if the cash paid to shareholders and bondholders (*F*) is greater than the cash raised in the financial markets (*A*), value will be created.

Identification of Cash Flows   Unfortunately, it is sometimes not easy to observe cash flows directly. Much of the information we obtain is in the form of accounting statements, and much of the work of financial analysis is to extract cash flow information from accounting statements. The following example illustrates how this is done.

EXAMPLE 1.1

Accounting Profit versus Cash Flows   The Midland Company refines and trades gold. At the end of the year, it sold 2,500 ounces of gold for $1 million. The company had acquired the gold for $900,000 at the beginning of the year. The company paid cash for the gold when it was purchased. Unfortunately it has yet to collect from the customer to whom the gold was sold. The following is a standard accounting of Midland's financial circumstances at year-end:

The Midland Company Accounting View Income Statement Year Ended December 31	
Sales	$1,000,000
−Costs	−900,000
Profit	$ 100,000

By generally accepted accounting principles (GAAP), the sale is recorded even though the customer has yet to pay. It is assumed that the customer will pay soon. From the accounting perspective, Midland seems to be profitable. However, the perspective of corporate finance is different. It focuses on cash flows:

The Midland Company Financial View Income Statement Year Ended December 31	
Cash inflow	$ 0
Cash outflow	−900,000
	−$ 900,000

The perspective of corporate finance is interested in whether cash flows are being created by the gold trading operations of Midland. Value creation depends on cash flows. For Midland, value creation depends on whether and when it actually receives $1 million.

Timing of Cash Flows   The value of an investment made by a firm depends on the timing of cash flows. One of the most important principles of finance is that individuals prefer to receive cash flows earlier rather than later. One dollar received today is worth more than one dollar received next year.

EXAMPLE 1.2

Cash Flow Timing   The Midland Company is attempting to choose between two proposals for new products. Both proposals will provide additional cash flows over a four-year period and will initially cost $10,000. The cash flows from the proposals are as follows:

Year	New Product A	New Product B
1	$ 0	$ 4,000
2	0	4,000
3	0	4,000
4	20,000	4,000
Total	$20,000	$16,000

At first it appears that new product A would be best. However, the cash flows from proposal B come earlier than those of A. Without more information, we cannot decide which set of cash flows would create the most value for the bondholders and shareholders. It depends on whether the value of getting cash from B up front outweighs the extra total cash from A. Bond and stock prices reflect this preference for earlier cash, and we will see how to use them to decide between A and B.

Risk of Cash Flows   The firm must consider risk. The amount and timing of cash flows are not usually known with certainty. Most investors have an aversion to risk.

EXAMPLE 1.3

Risk   The Midland Company is considering expanding operations overseas. It is evaluating Europe and Japan as possible sites. Europe is considered to be relatively safe, whereas operating in Japan is seen as very risky. In both cases the company would close down operations after one year.

     After doing a complete financial analysis, Midland has come up with the following cash flows of the alternative plans for expansion under three scenarios—pessimistic, most likely, and optimistic:

	Pessimistic	Most Likely	Optimistic
Europe	$75,000	$100,000	$125,000
Japan	0	150,000	200,000

If we ignore the pessimistic scenario, perhaps Japan is the best alternative. When we take the pessimistic scenario into account, the choice is unclear. Japan appears to be riskier, but it also offers a higher expected level of cash flow. What is risk and how can it be defined? We must try to answer this important question. Corporate finance cannot avoid coping with risky alternatives, and much of our book is devoted to developing methods for evaluating risky opportunities.

1.4 The Goal of Financial Management

Assuming that we restrict our discussion to for-profit businesses, the goal of financial management is to make money or add value for the owners. This goal is a little vague, of course, so we examine some different ways of formulating it to come up with a more precise definition. Such a definition is important because it leads to an objective basis for making and evaluating financial decisions.

POSSIBLE GOALS

If we were to consider possible financial goals, we might come up with some ideas like the following:

- Survive.
- Avoid financial distress and bankruptcy.
- Beat the competition.
- Maximize sales or market share.
- Minimize costs.
- Maximize profits.
- Maintain steady earnings growth.

These are only a few of the goals we could list. Furthermore, each of these possibilities presents problems as a goal for the financial manager.

For example, it's easy to increase market share or unit sales: All we have to do is lower our prices or relax our credit terms. Similarly, we can always cut costs simply by doing away with things such as research and development. We can avoid bankruptcy by never borrowing any money or never taking any risks, and so on. It's not clear that any of these actions are in the stockholders' best interests.

Profit maximization would probably be the most commonly cited goal, but even this is not a precise objective. Do we mean profits this year? If so, then we should note that actions such as deferring maintenance, letting inventories run down, and taking other short-run cost-cutting measures will tend to increase profits now, but these activities aren't necessarily desirable.

The goal of maximizing profits may refer to some sort of "long-run" or "average" profits, but it's still unclear exactly what this means. First, do we mean something like accounting net income or earnings per share? As we will see in more detail in the next chapter, these accounting numbers may have little to do with what is good or bad for the firm. We are actually more interested in cash flows. Second, what do we mean by the long run? As a famous economist once remarked, in the long run, we're all dead! More to the point, this goal doesn't tell us what the appropriate trade-off is between current and future profits.

The goals we've listed here are all different, but they tend to fall into two classes. The first of these relates to profitability. The goals involving sales, market share, and cost control all relate, at least potentially, to different ways of earning or increasing profits. The goals in the second group, involving bankruptcy avoidance, stability, and safety, relate in some way to controlling risk. Unfortunately, these two types of goals are somewhat contradictory. The pursuit of profit normally involves some element of risk, so it isn't really possible to maximize both safety and profit. What we need, therefore, is a goal that encompasses both factors.

THE GOAL OF FINANCIAL MANAGEMENT

The financial manager in a corporation makes decisions for the stockholders of the firm. So, instead of listing possible goals for the financial manager, we really need to answer a more fundamental question: From the stockholders' point of view, what is a good financial management decision?

If we assume that stockholders buy stock because they seek to gain financially, then the answer is obvious: Good decisions increase the value of the stock, and poor decisions decrease the value of the stock.

From our observations, it follows that the financial manager acts in the shareholders' best interests by making decisions that increase the value of the stock. The appropriate goal for the financial manager can thus be stated quite easily:

The goal of financial management is to maximize the current value per share of the existing stock.

The goal of maximizing the value of the stock avoids the problems associated with the different goals we listed earlier. There is no ambiguity in the criterion, and there is no short-run versus long-run issue. We explicitly mean that our goal is to maximize the *current* stock value.

If this goal seems a little strong or one-dimensional to you, keep in mind that the stockholders in a firm are residual owners. By this we mean that they are entitled only to what is left after employees, suppliers, and creditors (and everyone else with legitimate claims) are paid their due. If any of these groups go unpaid, the stockholders get nothing. So if the stockholders are winning in the sense that the leftover, residual portion is growing, it must be true that everyone else is winning also.

Because the goal of financial management is to maximize the value of the stock, we need to learn how to identify investments and financing arrangements that favorably impact the value of the stock. This is precisely what we will be studying. In the previous section we emphasized the importance of cash flows in value creation. In fact, we could have defined *corporate finance* as the study of the relationship between business decisions, cash flows, and the value of the stock in the business.

A MORE GENERAL GOAL

If our goal is as stated in the preceding section (to maximize the value of the stock), an obvious question comes up: What is the appropriate goal when the firm has no traded stock? Corporations are certainly not the only type of business; and the stock in many corporations rarely changes hands, so it's difficult to say what the value per share is at any particular time.

Business ethics are considered at **www.business-ethics.com**.

As long as we are considering for-profit businesses, only a slight modification is needed. The total value of the stock in a corporation is simply equal to the value of the owners' equity. Therefore, a more general way of stating our goal is as follows: Maximize the value of the existing owners' equity.

With this in mind, we don't care whether the business is a proprietorship, a partnership, or a corporation. For each of these, good financial decisions increase the value of the owners' equity, and poor financial decisions decrease it. In fact, although we choose to focus on corporations in the chapters ahead, the principles we develop apply to all forms of business. Many of them even apply to the not-for-profit sector.

Finally, our goal does not imply that the financial manager should take illegal or unethical actions in the hope of increasing the value of the equity in the firm. What we mean is that the financial manager best serves the owners of the business by identifying goods and services that add value to the firm because they are desired and valued in the free marketplace.

1.5 The Agency Problem and Control of the Corporation

We've seen that the financial manager acts in the best interests of the stockholders by taking actions that increase the value of the stock. However, in large corporations ownership can be spread over a huge number of stockholders.[1] This dispersion of ownership arguably means that management effectively controls the firm. In this case, will management necessarily act in the best interests of the stockholders? Put another way, might not management pursue its own goals at the stockholders' expense? In the following pages we briefly consider some of the arguments relating to this question.

AGENCY RELATIONSHIPS

The relationship between stockholders and management is called an *agency relationship*. Such a relationship exists whenever someone (the principal) hires another (the agent) to represent his or her interests. For example, you might hire someone (an agent) to sell a car that you own while you are away at school. In all such relationships there is a possibility of a conflict of interest between the principal and the agent. Such a conflict is called an **agency problem.**

Suppose you hire someone to sell your car and you agree to pay that person a flat fee when he or she sells the car. The agent's incentive in this case is to make the sale, not necessarily to get you the best price. If you offer a commission of, say, 10 percent of the sales price instead of a flat fee, then this problem might not exist. This example illustrates that the way in which an agent is compensated is one factor that affects agency problems.

MANAGEMENT GOALS

To see how management and stockholder interests might differ, imagine that a firm is considering a new investment. The new investment is expected to favorably impact the

---

[1] In many countries other than the U.S. and the U.K., publicly traded companies are usually controlled by one or more large shareholders. Moreover, in countries with limited shareholder protection, when compared to countries with strong shareholder protection like the U.S. and the U.K., large shareholders may have a greater opportunity to impose agency costs on the minority shareholders. See, for example, "Investor Protection and Corporate Valuation," by Rafael La Porta, Florencio Lopez-De-Silanes, Andrei Shleifer, and Robert Vishny, *Journal of Finance* 57 (2002), pp. 1147–1170; and "Cash Holdings, Dividend Policy, and Corporate Governance: A Cross-Country Analysis," by Lee Pinkowitz, René M. Stulz, and Rohan Williamson, *Journal of Applied Corporate Finance,* Vol. 19, No. 1 (2007), pp. 81–87. They show that a country's investor protection framework is important to understanding firm cash holdings and dividend payout. For example, they find that shareholders do not highly value cash holdings in firms in countries with low investor protection when compared to firms in the U.S. where investor protection is high.

In the basic corporate governance setup, the shareholders elect the board of directors who in turn appoint the top corporate managers, such as the CEO. The CEO is usually a member of the board of directors. One aspect of corporate governance we do not talk much about is the issue of an independent chair of a firm's board of directors. However, in a large number of U.S. corporations, the CEO and the board chair are the same person. In "U.S. Corporate Governance: Accomplishments and Failings, A Discussion with Michael Jensen and Robert Monks" (moderated by Ralph Walkling), *Journal of Applied Corporate Finance,* Vol. 20, No. 1 (Winter 2008), the point is made that combining the CEO and board chair positions can contribute to poor corporate governance. Both Jensen and Monks give an edge to the U.K. in governance partially because over 90 percent of U.K. companies are chaired by outside directors and not the CEO. This is a contentious issue confronting many U.S. corporations. For example, in May 2008, 19 institutional investors, including some of ExxonMobil's largest shareholders and members of the founding Rockefeller family, supported a resolution to split the jobs of CEO and board chair. About 40 percent of the shareholders voted for the split.

share value, but it is also a relatively risky venture. The owners of the firm will wish to take the investment (because the stock value will rise), but management may not because there is the possibility that things will turn out badly and management jobs will be lost. If management does not take the investment, then the stockholders may lose a valuable opportunity. This is one example of an *agency cost.*

More generally, the term *agency costs* refers to the costs of the conflict of interest between stockholders and management. These costs can be indirect or direct. An indirect agency cost is a lost opportunity, such as the one we have just described.

Direct agency costs come in two forms. The first type is a corporate expenditure that benefits management but costs the stockholders. Perhaps the purchase of a luxurious and unneeded corporate jet would fall under this heading. The second type of direct agency cost is an expense that arises from the need to monitor management actions. Paying outside auditors to assess the accuracy of financial statement information could be one example.

It is sometimes argued that, left to themselves, managers would tend to maximize the amount of resources over which they have control or, more generally, corporate power or wealth. This goal could lead to an overemphasis on corporate size or growth. For example, cases in which management is accused of overpaying to buy up another company just to increase the size of the business or to demonstrate corporate power are not uncommon. Obviously, if overpayment does take place, such a purchase does not benefit the stockholders of the purchasing company.

Our discussion indicates that management may tend to overemphasize organizational survival to protect job security. Also, management may dislike outside interference, so independence and corporate self-sufficiency may be important goals.

DO MANAGERS ACT IN THE STOCKHOLDERS' INTERESTS?

Whether managers will, in fact, act in the best interests of stockholders depends on two factors. First, how closely are management goals aligned with stockholder goals? This question relates, at least in part, to the way managers are compensated. Second, can managers be replaced if they do not pursue stockholder goals? This issue relates to control of the firm. As we will discuss, there are a number of reasons to think that, even in the largest firms, management has a significant incentive to act in the interests of stockholders.

Managerial Compensation   Management will frequently have a significant economic incentive to increase share value for two reasons. First, managerial compensation, particularly at the top, is usually tied to financial performance in general and often to share value in particular. For example, managers are frequently given the option to buy stock at a bargain price. The more the stock is worth, the more valuable is this option. In fact, options are often used to motivate employees of all types, not just top management. According to *The Wall Street Journal,* in 2010, Michael White, CEO of DIRECTV, made $1,448,000 in salary and $31.2 million in bonuses tied to financial performance. As we mentioned, many firms also give managers an ownership stake in the company by granting stock or stock options. In 2010, the total compensation for Leslie Moonves, CEO of CBS, was reported by *The Wall Street Journal* to be just under $54 million. His base salary was $3.53 million with annual incentives of $27.55 million, stock option grants of $14.9 million, restricted stock grants of $4 million, and performance awards of $4 million. Although there are many critics of the high level of CEO compensation, from the stockholders' point of view, sensitivity of compensation to firm performance is usually more important.

The second incentive managers have relates to job prospects. Better performers within the firm will tend to get promoted. More generally, managers who are successful in pursuing stockholder goals will be in greater demand in the labor market and thus command higher salaries.

In fact, managers who are successful in pursuing stockholder goals can reap enormous rewards. During 2010, the median compensation for CEOs at the largest 350 U.S. companies was $9.3 million. The best-paid executive in 2010 was Philippe Dauman, the CEO of media giant Viacom; according to *The Wall Street Journal*, he made about $84.3 million. By way of comparison, TV star Oprah Winfrey made $315 million, and moviemaker James Cameron made about $210 million.[2]

Control of the Firm Control of the firm ultimately rests with stockholders. They elect the board of directors, who, in turn, hire and fire management.

An important mechanism by which unhappy stockholders can replace existing management is called a *proxy fight*. A proxy is the authority to vote someone else's stock. A proxy fight develops when a group solicits proxies in order to replace the existing board and thereby replace existing management. In 2002, the proposed merger between HP and Compaq triggered one of the most widely followed, bitterly contested, and expensive proxy fights in history, with an estimated price tag of well over $100 million.

Another way that management can be replaced is by takeover. Firms that are poorly managed are more attractive as acquisitions than well-managed firms because a greater profit potential exists. Thus, avoiding a takeover by another firm gives management another incentive to act in the stockholders' interests. Unhappy prominent shareholders can suggest different business strategies to a firm's top management. This was the case with Carl Icahn and computer chip designer Mentor Graphics. Carl Icahn specializes in takeovers. His ownership stake in Mentor Graphics reached 14.7 percent in 2011, making him a particularly important (and unhappy) shareholder. He offered to buy the entire company, but, in March 2011, the board of directors rejected his $1.9 billion bid, arguing that it undervalued the company and its prospects. In response, Icahn sponsored three candidates for Mentor's board of directors, all of whom were elected in May 2011.

Conclusion The available theory and evidence are consistent with the view that stockholders control the firm and that stockholder wealth maximization is the relevant goal of the corporation. Even so, there will undoubtedly be times when management goals are pursued at the expense of the stockholders, at least temporarily.

STAKEHOLDERS

Our discussion thus far implies that management and stockholders are the only parties with an interest in the firm's decisions. This is an oversimplification, of course. Employees, customers, suppliers, and even the government all have a financial interest in the firm.

---

[2]This raises the issue of the level of top management pay and its relationship to other employees. According to *The New York Times*, the average CEO compensation was greater than 180 times the average employee compensation in 2007 and only 90 times in 1994. However, there is no precise formula that governs the gap between top management compensation and that of employees.

Taken together, these various groups are called **stakeholders** in the firm. In general, a stakeholder is someone other than a stockholder or creditor who potentially has a claim on the cash flows of the firm. Such groups will also attempt to exert control over the firm, perhaps to the detriment of the owners.

1.6 Regulation

Until now, we have talked mostly about the actions that shareholders and boards of directors can take to reduce the conflicts of interest between themselves and management. We have not talked about regulation.[3] Until recently the main thrust of federal regulation has been to require that companies disclose all relevant information to investors and potential investors. Disclosure of relevant information by corporations is intended to put all investors on a level information playing field and, thereby to reduce conflicts of interest. Of course, regulation imposes costs on corporations and any analysis of regulation must include both benefits and costs.

THE SECURITIES ACT OF 1933 AND THE SECURITIES EXCHANGE ACT OF 1934

The Securities Act of 1933 (the 1933 Act) and the Securities Exchange Act of 1934 (the 1934 Act) provide the basic regulatory framework in the United States for the public trading of securities.

The 1933 Act focuses on the issuing of new securities. Basically, the 1933 Act requires a corporation to file a registration statement with the Securities and Exchange Commission (SEC) that must be made available to every buyer of a new security. The intent of the registration statement is to provide potential stockholders with all the necessary information to make a reasonable decision. The 1934 Act extends the disclosure requirements of the 1933 Act to securities trading in markets after they have been issued. The 1934 Act establishes the SEC and covers a large number of issues including corporate reporting, tender offers, and insider trading. The 1934 Act requires corporations to file reports to the SEC on an annual basis (Form 10K), on a quarterly basis (Form 10Q), and on a monthly basis (Form 8K).

As mentioned, the 1934 Act deals with the important issue of insider trading. Illegal insider trading occurs when any person who has acquired nonpublic, special information (i.e., inside information) buys or sells securities based upon that information. One section of the 1934 Act deals with insiders such as directors, officers, and large shareholders, while another deals with any person who has acquired inside information. The intent of these sections of the 1934 Act is to prevent insiders or persons with inside information from taking unfair advantage of this information when trading with outsiders.

To illustrate, suppose you learned that ABC firm was about to publicly announce that it had agreed to be acquired by another firm at a price significantly greater than its current price. This is an example of inside information. The 1934 Act prohibits you from buying ABC stock from shareholders who do not have this information. This prohibition would be especially strong if you were the CEO of the ABC firm. Other

---

[3]At this stage in our book, we focus on the regulation of corporate governance. We do not talk about many other regulators in financial markets such as the Federal Reserve Board. In Chapter 8, we discuss the nationally recognized statistical rating organizations (NRSROs) in the U.S. These include Fitch Ratings, Moody's, and Standard & Poor's. Their ratings are used by market participants to help value securities such as corporate bonds. Many critics of the rating agencies blame the 2007–2009 subprime credit crisis on weak regulatory oversight of these agencies.

kinds of a firm's inside information could be knowledge of an initial dividend about to be paid, the discovery of a drug to cure cancer, or the default of a debt obligation.

A recent example of insider trading involved Raj Rajaratnam, the founder of the hedge fund Galleon Group. He was charged with gathering inside information from friends at numerous companies. For example, a government wiretap picked up a conversation in which Rajaratnam said, "I heard yesterday from somebody who's on the board of Goldman Sachs that they are going to lose $2 per share. The Street has them making $2.50." He was arrested in October 2009 and, in May 2011, was convicted of 14 counts of securities fraud and conspiracy to commit securities fraud.

SARBANES-OXLEY

In response to corporate scandals at companies such as Enron, WorldCom, Tyco, and Adelphia, Congress enacted the Sarbanes-Oxley Act in 2002. The act, better known as "Sarbox," is intended to protect investors from corporate abuses. For example, one section of Sarbox prohibits personal loans from a company to its officers, such as the ones that were received by WorldCom CEO Bernie Ebbers.

One of the key sections of Sarbox took effect on November 15, 2004. Section 404 requires, among other things, that each company's annual report must have an assessment of the company's internal control structure and financial reporting. The auditor must then evaluate and attest to management's assessment of these issues. Sarbox also creates the Public Companies Accounting Oversight Board (PCAOB) to establish new audit guidelines and ethical standards. It requires public companies' audit committees of corporate boards to include only independent, outside directors to oversee the annual audits and disclose if the committees have a financial expert (and if not, why not).

Sarbox contains other key requirements. For example, the officers of the corporation must review and sign the annual reports. They must explicitly declare that the annual report does not contain any false statements or material omissions; that the financial statements fairly represent the financial results; and that they are responsible for all internal controls. Finally, the annual report must list any deficiencies in internal controls. In essence, Sarbox makes company management responsible for the accuracy of the company's financial statements.

Of course, as with any law, there are costs. Sarbox has increased the expense of corporate audits, sometimes dramatically. In 2004, the average compliance cost for large firms was $4.51 million. By 2007, the average compliance cost had fallen to $1.7 million, so the burden seems to be dropping, but it is still not trivial, particularly for a smaller firm. This added expense has led to several unintended results. For example, in 2003, 198 firms delisted their shares from exchanges, or "went dark," and about the same number delisted in 2004. Both numbers were up from 30 delistings in 1999. Many of the companies that delisted stated the reason was to avoid the cost of compliance with Sarbox.[4]

A company that goes dark does not have to file quarterly or annual reports. Annual audits by independent auditors are not required, and executives do not have to certify the accuracy of the financial statements, so the savings can be huge. Of course, there are costs. Stock prices typically fall when a company announces it is going dark. Further, such companies will typically have limited access to capital markets and usually will have a higher interest cost on bank loans.

---

[4]But in "Has New York Become Less Competitive in Global Markets? Evaluating Foreign Listing Choices Over Time" *Journal of Financial Economics,* Volume 91, Issue 3, March 2009, pp. 253–77, Craig Doidge, Andrew Karolyi, and René Stulz find that the decline in delistings is not directly related to Sarbanes-Oxley. They conclude that most New York delisting was because of mergers and acquisitions, distress, and restructuring.

Sarbox has also probably affected the number of companies choosing to go public in the United States. For example, when Peach Holdings, based in Boynton Beach, Florida, decided to go public in 2006, it shunned the U.S. stock markets, instead choosing the London Stock Exchange's Alternative Investment Market (AIM). To go public in the United States, the firm would have paid a $100,000 fee, plus about $2 million to comply with Sarbox. Instead, the company spent only $500,000 on its AIM stock offering.

 ◄ To test your mastery of this material, take a quiz at mhhe. com/rwj

Summary and Conclusions

This chapter introduced you to some of the basic ideas in corporate finance:

1. Corporate finance has three main areas of concern:
   a. *Capital budgeting:* What long-term investments should the firm take?
   b. *Capital structure:* Where will the firm get the long-term financing to pay for its investments? Also, what mixture of debt and equity should it use to fund operations?
   c. *Working capital management:* How should the firm manage its everyday financial activities?
2. The goal of financial management in a for-profit business is to make decisions that increase the value of the stock, or, more generally, increase the market value of the equity.
3. The corporate form of organization is superior to other forms when it comes to raising money and transferring ownership interests, but it has the significant disadvantage of double taxation.
4. There is the possibility of conflicts between stockholders and management in a large corporation. We called these conflicts *agency problems* and discussed how they might be controlled and reduced.
5. The advantages of the corporate form are enhanced by the existence of financial markets.

Of the topics we've discussed thus far, the most important is the goal of financial management: maximizing the value of the stock. Throughout the text we will be analyzing many different financial decisions, but we will always ask the same question: How does the decision under consideration affect the value of the stock?

Concept Questions

1. **Agency Problems** Who owns a corporation? Describe the process whereby the owners control the firm's management. What is the main reason that an agency relationship exists in the corporate form of organization? In this context, what kinds of problems can arise?

2. **Not-for-Profit Firm Goals** Suppose you were the financial manager of a not-for-profit business (a not-for-profit hospital, perhaps). What kinds of goals do you think would be appropriate?

3. **Goal of the Firm** Evaluate the following statement: Managers should not focus on the current stock value because doing so will lead to an overemphasis on short-term profits at the expense of long-term profits.

www.mhhe.com/rwj

4. **Ethics and Firm Goals**   Can the goal of maximizing the value of the stock conflict with other goals, such as avoiding unethical or illegal behavior? In particular, do you think subjects like customer and employee safety, the environment, and the general good of society fit in this framework, or are they essentially ignored? Think of some specific scenarios to illustrate your answer.

5. **International Firm Goal**   Would the goal of maximizing the value of the stock differ for financial management in a foreign country? Why or why not?

6. **Agency Problems**   Suppose you own stock in a company. The current price per share is $25. Another company has just announced that it wants to buy your company and will pay $35 per share to acquire all the outstanding stock. Your company's management immediately begins fighting off this hostile bid. Is management acting in the shareholders' best interests? Why or why not?

7. **Agency Problems and Corporate Ownership**   Corporate ownership varies around the world. Historically, individuals have owned the majority of shares in public corporations in the United States. In Germany and Japan, however, banks, other large financial institutions, and other companies own most of the stock in public corporations. Do you think agency problems are likely to be more or less severe in Germany and Japan than in the United States?

8. **Agency Problems and Corporate Ownership**   In recent years, large financial institutions such as mutual funds and pension funds have become the dominant owners of stock in the United States, and these institutions are becoming more active in corporate affairs. What are the implications of this trend for agency problems and corporate control?

9. **Executive Compensation**   Critics have charged that compensation to top managers in the United States is simply too high and should be cut back. For example, focusing on large corporations, Larry Ellison of Oracle has been one of the best-compensated CEOs in the United States, earning about $130 million in 2010 alone and over $1 billion during the 2006–2010 period. Are such amounts excessive? In answering, it might be helpful to recognize that superstar athletes such as Tiger Woods, top earners in the entertainment field such as James Cameron and Oprah Winfrey, and many others at the top of their respective fields earn at least as much, if not a great deal more.

10. **Goal of Financial Management**   Why is the goal of financial management to maximize the current share price of the company's stock? In other words, why isn't the goal to maximize the future share price?

CHAPTER 2

Financial Statements and Cash Flow

A write-off by a company frequently means that the value of the company's assets has declined. For example, in 2010, Bank of America announced a total of $34 billion in write-offs for bad loans. In addition, the company announced a $10.5 billion write-off because recent legislation had reduced the value of its credit card business. The write-offs made by Bank of America during 2010 followed write-offs of $33.7 billion in 2009 and $16.2 billion in 2008. Of course, Bank of America was not alone. Moody's Investor Services estimated that banks had written off $476 billion during 2009 and 2010, and it expected bank write-offs of $286 billion during 2011.

So did stockholders in these banks lose hundreds of billions of dollars (or more) because of the write-offs? The answer is probably not. Understanding why ultimately leads us to the main subject of this chapter: that all-important substance known as *cash flow*.

2.1 The Balance Sheet

ExcelMaster
coverage online

This section will introduce cell formatting and trace dependents and precedents.

The **balance sheet** is an accountant's snapshot of a firm's accounting value on a particular date, as though the firm stood momentarily still. The balance sheet has two sides: On the left are the *assets* and on the right are the *liabilities* and *stockholders' equity*. The balance sheet states what the firm owns and how it is financed. The accounting definition that underlies the balance sheet and describes the balance is:

$$\text{Assets} \equiv \text{Liabilities} + \text{Stockholders' equity}$$

We have put a three-line equality in the balance equation to indicate that it must always hold, by definition. In fact, the stockholders' equity is *defined* to be the difference between the assets and the liabilities of the firm. In principle, equity is what the stockholders would have remaining after the firm discharged its obligations.

Table 2.1 gives the 2012 and 2011 balance sheet for the fictitious U.S. Composite Corporation. The assets in the balance sheet are listed in order by the length of time it normally would take an ongoing firm to convert them into cash. The asset side depends on the nature of the business and how management chooses to conduct it. Management must make decisions about cash versus marketable securities, credit versus cash sales, whether to make or buy commodities, whether to lease or purchase items, the types of business in which to engage, and so on. The liabilities and the stockholders' equity are listed in the order in which they would typically be paid over time.

The liabilities and stockholders' equity side reflects the types and proportions of financing, which depend on management's choice of capital structure, as between debt and equity and between current debt and long-term debt.

When analyzing a balance sheet, the financial manager should be aware of three concerns: liquidity, debt versus equity, and value versus cost.

Table 2.1   The Balance Sheet of the U.S. Composite Corporation

U.S. COMPOSITE CORPORATION
Balance Sheet
2012 and 2011
($ in millions)

Assets	2012	2011	Liabilities (Debt) and Stockholders' Equity	2012	2011
Current assets:			Current liabilities:		
Cash and equivalents	$ 140	$ 107	Accounts payable	$ 213	$ 197
Accounts receivable	294	270	Notes payable	50	53
Inventory	269	280	Accrued expenses	223	205
Other	58	50	Total current liabilities	$ 486	$ 455
Total current assets	$ 761	$ 707	Long-term liabilities:		
Fixed assets:			Deferred taxes	$ 117	$ 104
Property, plant, and equipment	$1,423	$1,274	Long-term debt*	471	458
Less accumulated depreciation	550	460	Total long-term liabilities	$ 588	$ 562
Net property, plant, and equipment	873	814	Stockholders' equity:		
Intangible assets and others	245	221	Preferred stock	$ 39	$ 39
Total fixed assets	$1,118	$1,035	Common stock ($1 par value)	55	32
			Capital surplus	347	327
			Accumulated retained earnings	390	347
			Less treasury stock†	26	20
			Total equity	$ 805	$ 725
Total assets	$1,879	$1,742	Total liabilities and stockholders' equity‡	$1,879	$1,742

*Long-term debt rose by $471 million − $458 million = $13 million. This is the difference between $86 million new debt and $73 million in retirement of old debt.

†Treasury stock rose by $6 million. This reflects the repurchase of $6 million of U.S. Composite's company stock.

‡U.S. Composite reports $43 million in new equity. The company issued 23 million shares at a price of $1.87. The par value of common stock increased by $23 million, and capital surplus increased by $20 million.

Annual and quarterly financial statements for most public U.S. corporations can be found in the EDGAR database at **www.sec.gov**.

LIQUIDITY

Liquidity refers to the ease and quickness with which assets can be converted to cash (without significant loss in value). *Current assets* are the most liquid and include cash and assets that will be turned into cash within a year from the date of the balance sheet. *Accounts receivable* are amounts not yet collected from customers for goods or services sold to them (after adjustment for potential bad debts). *Inventory* is composed of raw materials to be used in production, work in process, and finished goods. *Fixed assets* are the least liquid kind of assets. Tangible fixed assets include property, plant, and equipment. These assets do not convert to cash from normal business activity, and they are not usually used to pay expenses such as payroll.

Some fixed assets are not tangible. Intangible assets have no physical existence but can be very valuable. Examples of intangible assets are the value of a trademark or the value of a patent. The more liquid a firm's assets, the less likely the firm is to experience problems meeting short-term obligations. Thus, the probability that a firm will avoid financial distress can be linked to the firm's liquidity. Unfortunately, liquid assets frequently have lower rates of return than fixed assets; for example, cash generates no investment income. To the extent a firm invests in liquid assets, it sacrifices an opportunity to invest in more profitable investment vehicles.

DEBT VERSUS EQUITY

Liabilities are obligations of the firm that require a payout of cash within a stipulated period. Many liabilities involve contractual obligations to repay a stated amount and interest over a period. Thus, liabilities are debts and are frequently associated with nominally fixed cash burdens, called *debt service,* that put the firm in default of a contract if they are not paid. *Stockholders' equity* is a claim against the firm's assets that is residual and not fixed. In general terms, when the firm borrows, it gives the bondholders first claim on the firm's cash flow.[1] Bondholders can sue the firm if the firm defaults on its bond contracts. This may lead the firm to declare itself bankrupt. Stockholders' equity is the residual difference between assets and liabilities:

$$\text{Assets} - \text{Liabilities} \equiv \text{Stockholders' equity}$$

This is the stockholders' share in the firm stated in accounting terms. The accounting value of stockholders' equity increases when retained earnings are added. This occurs when the firm retains part of its earnings instead of paying them out as dividends.

VALUE VERSUS COST

The accounting value of a firm's assets is frequently referred to as the *carrying value* or the *book value* of the assets.[2] Under **generally accepted accounting principles (GAAP),** audited financial statements of firms in the United States carry the assets at cost.[3] Thus the terms *carrying value* and *book value* are unfortunate. They specifically say "value," when in fact the accounting numbers are based on cost. This misleads many readers of financial statements to think that the firm's assets are recorded at true market values. *Market value* is the price at which willing buyers and sellers would trade the assets. It would be only a coincidence if accounting value and market value were the same. In fact, management's job is to create value for the firm that exceeds its cost.

Many people use the balance sheet, but the information each may wish to extract is not the same. A banker may look at a balance sheet for evidence of accounting liquidity and working capital. A supplier may also note the size of accounts payable and therefore the general promptness of payments. Many users of financial statements, including managers and investors, want to know the value of the firm, not its cost. This information is not found on the balance sheet. In fact, many of the true resources of the firm do not appear on the balance sheet: good management, proprietary assets, favorable economic conditions, and so on. Henceforth, whenever we speak of the value of an asset or the value of the firm, we will normally mean its market value.

The home page for the Financial Accounting Standards Board (FASB) is **www.fasb.org**.

---

[1]Bondholders are investors in the firm's debt. They are creditors of the firm. In this discussion, the term *bondholder* means the same thing as *creditor.*

[2]Confusion often arises because many financial accounting terms have the same meaning. This presents a problem with jargon for the reader of financial statements. For example, the following terms usually refer to the same thing: *assets minus liabilities, net worth, stockholders' equity, owners' equity, book equity,* and *equity capitalization.*

[3]Generally, GAAP requires assets to be carried at the lower of cost or market value. In most instances, cost is lower than market value. However, in some cases when a fair market value can be readily determined, the assets have their value adjusted to the fair market value.

So, for example, when we say the goal of the financial manager is to increase the value of the stock, we usually mean the market value of the stock not the book value.

With the increasing globalization of business, there has been a growing need to make accounting standards more comparable across countries. In recent years, U.S. accounting standards have become more closely tied to International Financial Reporting Standards (IFRS). In particular, the Financial Accounting Standards Board, which is in charge of GAAP policies, and the International Accounting Standards Board, in charge of IFRS polices, have been working towards convergence of policies by June 2011. A decision about full adoption of IFRS by U.S.–based companies is expected to follow afterwards.

For more information about IFRS, check out the website **www.ifrs.org**.

EXAMPLE 2.1

Market Value versus Book Value   The Cooney Corporation has fixed assets with a book value of $700 and an appraised market value of about $1,000. Net working capital is $400 on the books, but approximately $600 would be realized if all the current accounts were liquidated. Cooney has $500 in long-term debt, both book value and market value. What is the book value of the equity? What is the market value?

We can construct two simplified balance sheets, one in accounting (book value) terms and one in economic (market value) terms:

COONEY CORPORATION
Balance Sheets
Market Value versus Book Value

Assets			Liabilities and Shareholders' Equity		
	Book	**Market**		**Book**	**Market**
Net working capital	$ 400	$ 600	Long-term debt	$ 500	$ 500
Net fixed assets	700	1,000	Shareholders' equity	600	1,100
	$1,100	$1,600		$1,100	$1,600

In this example, shareholders' equity is actually worth almost twice as much as what is shown on the books. The distinction between book and market values is important precisely because book values can be so different from market values.

2.2 The Income Statement

ExcelMaster
coverage online

The **income statement** measures performance over a specific period—say a year. The accounting definition of income is:

$$\text{Revenue} - \text{Expenses} \equiv \text{Income}$$

If the balance sheet is like a snapshot, the income statement is like a video recording of what the people did between two snapshots. Table 2.2 gives the income statement for the U.S. Composite Corporation for 2012.

The income statement usually includes several sections. The operations section reports the firm's revenues and expenses from principal operations. One number of particular importance is earnings before interest and taxes (EBIT), which summarizes earnings before taxes and financing costs. Among other things, the nonoperating section of the income statement includes all financing costs, such as interest expense. Usually a second section reports as a separate item the amount of taxes

Table 2.2
The Income Statement of the U.S. Composite Corporation

U.S. COMPOSITE CORPORATION Income Statement 2012 ($ in millions)	
Total operating revenues	$2,262
Cost of goods sold	1,655
Selling, general, and administrative expenses	327
Depreciation	90
Operating income	$ 190
Other income	29
Earnings before interest and taxes (EBIT)	$ 219
Interest expense	49
Pretax income	$ 170
Taxes	84
Current: $71	
Deferred: 13	
Net income	$ 86
Addition to retained earnings:	$ 43
Dividends:	43

NOTE: There are 29 million shares outstanding. Earnings per share and dividends per share can be calculated as follows:

$$\text{Earnings per share} = \frac{\text{Net income}}{\text{Total shares outstanding}}$$
$$= \frac{\$86}{29}$$
$$= \$2.97 \text{ per share}$$

$$\text{Dividends per share} = \frac{\text{Dividends}}{\text{Total shares outstanding}}$$
$$= \frac{\$43}{29}$$
$$= \$1.48 \text{ per share}$$

levied on income. The last item on the income statement is the bottom line, or net income. Net income is frequently expressed per share of common stock—that is, earnings per share.

When analyzing an income statement, the financial manager should keep in mind GAAP, noncash items, time, and costs.

GENERALLY ACCEPTED ACCOUNTING PRINCIPLES

Revenue is recognized on an income statement when the earnings process is virtually completed and an exchange of goods or services has occurred. Therefore, the unrealized appreciation from owning property will not be recognized as income. This provides a device for smoothing income by selling appreciated property at convenient times. For example, if the firm owns a tree farm that has doubled in value, then, in a year when its earnings from other businesses are down, it can raise overall earnings by selling some trees. The matching principle of GAAP dictates that revenues be matched with expenses. Thus, income is reported when it is earned, or accrued, even though no cash flow has necessarily occurred (for example, when goods are sold for credit, sales and profits are reported).

NONCASH ITEMS

The economic value of assets is intimately connected to their future incremental cash flows. However, cash flow does not appear on an income statement. There are several **noncash items** that are expenses against revenues but do not affect cash flow. The most important of these is *depreciation*. Depreciation reflects the accountant's estimate of the cost of equipment used up in the production process. For example, suppose an asset with a five-year life and no resale value is purchased for $1,000. According to accountants, the $1,000 cost must be expensed over the useful life of the asset. If straight-line depreciation is used, there will be five equal installments, and $200 of depreciation expense will be incurred each year. From a finance perspective, the cost of the asset is the actual negative cash flow incurred when the asset is acquired (that is, $1,000, *not* the accountant's smoothed $200-per-year depreciation expense).

Another noncash expense is *deferred taxes*. Deferred taxes result from differences between accounting income and true taxable income.[4] Notice that the accounting tax shown on the income statement for the U.S. Composite Corporation is $84 million. It can be broken down as current taxes and deferred taxes. The current tax portion is actually sent to the tax authorities (for example, the Internal Revenue Service). The deferred tax portion is not. However, the theory is that if taxable income is less than accounting income in the current year, it will be more than accounting income later on. Consequently, the taxes that are not paid today will have to be paid in the future, and they represent a liability of the firm. This shows up on the balance sheet as deferred tax liability. From the cash flow perspective, though, deferred tax is not a cash outflow.

In practice, the difference between cash flows and accounting income can be quite dramatic, so it is important to understand the difference. For example, consider Euro Disney, operator of Disneyland Paris. For the first half of 2011, Euro Disney reported a net loss of €99.5 million. Sounds bad, but Euro Disney also reported a *positive* cash flow of €6.4 million, a difference of about €106 million!

TIME AND COSTS

It is often useful to visualize all of future time as having two distinct parts, the *short run* and the *long run*. The short run is the period in which certain equipment, resources, and commitments of the firm are fixed; but the time is long enough for the firm to vary its output by using more labor and raw materials. The short run is not a precise period that will be the same for all industries. However, all firms making decisions in the short run have some fixed costs—that is, costs that will not change because of fixed commitments. In real business activity, examples of fixed costs are bond interest, overhead, and property taxes. Costs that are not fixed are variable. Variable costs change as the output of the firm changes; some examples are raw materials and wages for laborers on the production line.

In the long run, all costs are variable. Financial accountants do not distinguish between variable costs and fixed costs. Instead, accounting costs usually fit into a classification that distinguishes product costs from period costs. Product costs are the total production costs incurred during a period—raw materials, direct labor, and manufacturing overhead—and are reported on the income statement as cost of goods sold. Both variable and fixed costs are included in product costs. Period costs are costs that are allocated to a time period; they are called *selling, general,* and *administrative expenses*. One period cost would be the company president's salary.

---

[4]One situation in which taxable income may be lower than accounting income is when the firm uses accelerated depreciation expense procedures for the IRS but uses straight-line procedures allowed by GAAP for reporting purposes.

2.3 Taxes

ExcelMaster
coverage online

This section will introduce
LOOKUP.

Taxes can be one of the largest cash outflows a firm experiences. In 2010, according to the Department of Commerce, total corporate profits before taxes in the United States were about $1.68 trillion, and taxes on corporate profits were about $470 billion or about 28 percent of pretax profits. The size of the firm's tax bill is determined by the tax code, an often amended set of rules. In this section, we examine corporate tax rates and how taxes are calculated.

If the various rules of taxation seem a little bizarre or convoluted to you, keep in mind that the tax code is the result of political, not economic, forces. As a result, there is no reason why it has to make economic sense. To put the complexity of corporate taxation into perspective, General Electric's 2006 tax return required 24,000 pages, far too much to print. The electronically filed return ran 237 megabytes.

CORPORATE TAX RATES

Corporate tax rates in effect for 2011 are shown in Table 2.3. A peculiar feature of taxation instituted by the Tax Reform Act of 1986 and expanded in the 1993 Omnibus Budget Reconciliation Act is that corporate tax rates are not strictly increasing. As shown, corporate tax rates rise from 15 percent to 39 percent, but they drop back to 34 percent on income over $335,000. They then rise to 38 percent and subsequently fall to 35 percent.

According to the originators of the current tax rules, there are only four corporate rates: 15 percent, 25 percent, 34 percent, and 35 percent. The 38 and 39 percent brackets arise because of "surcharges" applied on top of the 34 and 35 percent rates. A tax is a tax, however, so there are really six corporate tax brackets, as we have shown.

AVERAGE VERSUS MARGINAL TAX RATES

In making financial decisions, it is frequently important to distinguish between average and marginal tax rates. Your **average tax rate** is your tax bill divided by your taxable income—in other words, the percentage of your income that goes to pay taxes. Your **marginal tax rate** is the tax you would pay (in percent) if you earned one more dollar. The percentage tax rates shown in Table 2.3 are all marginal rates. Put another way, the tax rates apply to the part of income in the indicated range only, not all income.

The difference between average and marginal tax rates can best be illustrated with a simple example. Suppose our corporation has a taxable income of $200,000. What is the tax bill? Using Table 2.3, we can figure our tax bill like this:

Table 2.3
Corporate Tax Rates

Taxable Income	Tax Rate
$ 0– 50,000	15%
50,001– 75,000	25
75,001– 100,000	34
100,001– 335,000	39
335,001–10,000,000	34
10,000,001–15,000,000	35
15,000,001–18,333,333	38
18,333,334+	35

$$
\begin{aligned}
.15(\$\ 50{,}000) &= \$\ 7{,}500 \\
.25(\$\ 75{,}000 - 50{,}000) &= \ 6{,}250 \\
.34(\$100{,}000 - 75{,}000) &= \ 8{,}500 \\
.39(\$200{,}000 - 100{,}000) &= \underline{\ 39{,}000} \\
&\ \ \ \$61{,}250
\end{aligned}
$$

Our total tax is thus $61,250.

The IRS has a great website: **www.irs.gov**.

In our example, what is the average tax rate? We had a taxable income of $200,000 and a tax bill of $61,250, so the average tax rate is $61,250/200,000 = 30.625\%$. What is the marginal tax rate? If we made one more dollar, the tax on that dollar would be 39 cents, so our marginal rate is 39 percent.

EXAMPLE 2.2

Deep in the Heart of Taxes   Algernon, Inc., has a taxable income of $85,000. What is its tax bill? What is its average tax rate? Its marginal tax rate?

From Table 2.3, we see that the tax rate applied to the first $50,000 is 15 percent; the rate applied to the next $25,000 is 25 percent; and the rate applied after that up to $100,000 is 34 percent. So Algernon must pay $.15 \times \$50{,}000 + .25 \times 25{,}000 + .34 \times (85{,}000 - 75{,}000) = \$17{,}150$. The average tax rate is thus $\$17{,}150/85{,}000 = 20.18\%$. The marginal rate is 34 percent because Algernon's taxes would rise by 34 cents if it had another dollar in taxable income.

Table 2.4 summarizes some different taxable incomes, marginal tax rates, and average tax rates for corporations. Notice how the average and marginal tax rates come together at 35 percent.

With a *flat-rate* tax, there is only one tax rate, so the rate is the same for all income levels. With such a tax, the marginal tax rate is always the same as the average tax rate. As it stands now, corporate taxation in the United States is based on a modified flat-rate tax, which becomes a true flat rate for the highest incomes.

In looking at Table 2.4, notice that the more a corporation makes, the greater is the percentage of taxable income paid in taxes. Put another way, under current tax law, the average tax rate never goes down, even though the marginal tax rate does. As illustrated, for corporations, average tax rates begin at 15 percent and rise to a maximum of 35 percent.

Normally, the marginal tax rate will be relevant for financial decision making. The reason is that any new cash flows will be taxed at that marginal rate. Because financial

Table 2.4
Corporate Taxes and Tax Rates

(1) Taxable Income	(2) Marginal Tax Rate	(3) Total Tax	(3)/(1) Average Tax Rate
$ 45,000	15%	$ 6,750	15.00%
70,000	25	12,500	17.86
95,000	34	20,550	21.63
250,000	39	80,750	32.30
1,000,000	34	340,000	34.00
17,500,000	38	6,100,000	34.86
50,000,000	35	17,500,000	35.00
100,000,000	35	35,000,000	35.00

Table 2.5
Average Corporate
Tax Rates

Industry	Number of Companies	Average Tax Rate
Electric utilities (Eastern U.S.)	24	33.8%
Trucking	33	32.7
Railroad	15	27.4
Securities brokerage	30	20.5
Banking	481	17.5
Medical supplies	264	11.2
Internet	239	5.9
Pharmaceutical	337	5.6
Biotechnology	121	4.5

decisions usually involve new cash flows or changes in existing ones, this rate will tell us the marginal effect of a decision on our tax bill.

There is one last thing to notice about the tax code as it affects corporations. It's easy to verify that the corporate tax bill is just a flat 35 percent of taxable income if our taxable income is more than $18.33 million. Also, for the many midsize corporations with taxable incomes in the range of $335,000 to $10,000,000, the tax rate is a flat 34 percent. Because we will usually be talking about large corporations, you can assume that the average and marginal tax rates are 35 percent unless we explicitly say otherwise.

We should note that we have simplified the U.S. tax code for presentation purposes. In actuality, the tax code is much more complex, with various tax deductions and loopholes allowed for certain industries, as well as the taxation of multinational companies. In reality, recent evidence shows that the average tax rate can be far from 35 percent for many companies. Table 2.5 shows average tax rates for several industries. As you can see, the average tax rate ranges from 33.8 percent for electric utilities to 4.5 percent for biotechnology firms.

Before moving on, we should note that the tax rates we have discussed in this section relate to federal taxes only. Overall tax rates can be higher if state, local, and any other taxes are considered.

2.4 Net Working Capital

ExcelMaster
coverage online

This section will introduce referencing across worksheets.

Net working capital is current assets minus current liabilities. Net working capital is positive when current assets are greater than current liabilities. This means the cash that will become available over the next 12 months will be greater than the cash that must be paid out. The net working capital of the U.S. Composite Corporation is $275 million in 2012 and $252 million in 2011.

	Current assets ($ millions)	−	Current liabilities ($ millions)	=	Net working capital ($ millions)
2012	$761	−	$486	=	$275
2011	707	−	455	=	252

In addition to investing in fixed assets (i.e., capital spending), a firm can invest in net working capital. This is called the **change in net working capital.** The change in net working capital in 2012 is the difference between the net working capital in 2012 and 2011—that is, $275 million − $252 million = $23 million. The change in net working capital is usually positive in a growing firm.

2.5 Financial Cash Flow

ExcelMaster
coverage online

Perhaps the most important item that can be extracted from financial statements is the actual **cash flow** of the firm. An official accounting statement called the *statement of cash flows* helps to explain the change in accounting cash and equivalents, which for U.S. Composite is $33 million in 2012. (See Section 2.6.) Notice in Table 2.1 that cash and equivalents increase from $107 million in 2011 to $140 million in 2012. However, we will look at cash flow from a different perspective: the perspective of finance. In finance, the value of the firm is its ability to generate financial cash flow. (We will talk more about financial cash flow in a later chapter.)

The first point we should mention is that cash flow is not the same as net working capital. For example, increasing inventory requires using cash. Because both inventories and cash are current assets, this does not affect net working capital. In this case, an increase in inventory is associated with decreasing cash flow.

Just as we established that the value of a firm's assets is always equal to the combined value of the liabilities and the value of the equity, the cash flows received from the firm's assets (that is, its operating activities), CF(A), must equal the cash flows to the firm's creditors, CF(B), and equity investors, CF(S):

$$CF(A) \equiv CF(B) + CF(S)$$

The first step in determining cash flows of the firm is to figure out the *cash flow from operations*. As can be seen in Table 2.6, operating cash flow is the cash flow generated by business activities, including sales of goods and services. Operating cash flow

Table 2.6

Financial Cash Flow of the U.S. Composite Corporation

U.S. COMPOSITE CORPORATION **Financial Cash Flow** **2012** **($ in millions)**	
Cash flow of the firm	
Operating cash flow	$238
(Earnings before interest and taxes plus depreciation minus taxes)	
Capital spending	−173
(Acquisitions of fixed assets minus sales of fixed assets)	
Additions to net working capital	−23
Total	$ 42
Cash flow to investors in the firm	
Debt	$ 36
(Interest plus retirement of debt minus long-term debt financing)	
Equity	6
(Dividends plus repurchase of equity minus new equity financing)	
Total	$ 42

reflects tax payments, but not financing, capital spending, or changes in net working capital:

	$ in millions
Earnings before interest and taxes	$219
Depreciation	90
Current taxes	−71
Operating cash flow	$238

Another important component of cash flow involves *changes in fixed assets*. For example, when U.S. Composite sold its power systems subsidiary in 2012, it generated $25 million in cash flow. The net change in fixed assets equals the acquisition of fixed assets minus the sales of fixed assets. The result is the cash flow used for capital spending:

Acquisition of fixed assets	$198	
Sales of fixed assets	−25	
Capital spending	$173	($149 + 24 = Increase in property, plant, and equipment + Increase in intangible assets)

We can also calculate capital spending simply as:

$$\begin{aligned} \text{Capital spending} &= \text{Ending net fixed assets} - \text{Beginning net fixed assets} \\ &\quad + \text{Depreciation} \\ &= \$1{,}118 - 1{,}035 + 90 \\ &= \$173 \end{aligned}$$

Cash flows are also used for making investments in net working capital. In U.S. Composite Corporation in 2012, *additions to net working capital* are:

Additions to net working capital	$23

Note that this $23 million is the change in net working capital we previously calculated. Total cash flows generated by the firm's assets are then equal to:

Operating cash flow	$238
Capital spending	−173
Additions to net working capital	− 23
Total cash flow of the firm	$ 42

The total outgoing cash flow of the firm can be separated into cash flow paid to creditors and cash flow paid to stockholders. The cash flow paid to creditors represents a regrouping of the data in Table 2.6 and an explicit recording of interest expense. Creditors are paid an amount generally referred to as *debt service*.

Debt service is interest payments plus repayments of principal (that is, retirement of debt).

An important source of cash flow is the sale of new debt. U.S. Composite's long-term debt increased by $13 million (the difference between $86 million in new debt and $73 million in retirement of old debt).[5] Thus, an increase in long-term debt is the net effect of new borrowing and repayment of maturing obligations plus interest expense:

Cash Flow Paid to Creditors ($ in millions)	
Interest	$ 49
Retirement of debt	73
Debt service	122
Proceeds from long-term debt sales	−86
Total	$ 36

Cash flow paid to creditors can also be calculated as:

$$\begin{aligned}
\text{Cash flow paid to creditors} &= \text{Interest paid} - \text{Net new borrowing}\\
&= \text{Interest paid} - (\text{Ending long-term debt}\\
&\quad - \text{Beginning long-term debt})\\
&= \$49 - (471 - 458)\\
&= \$36
\end{aligned}$$

Cash flow of the firm also is paid to the stockholders. It is the net effect of paying dividends plus repurchasing outstanding shares of stock and issuing new shares of stock:

Cash Flow to Stockholders ($ in millions)	
Dividends	$43
Repurchase of stock	6
Cash to stockholders	49
Proceeds from new stock issue	−43
Total	$ 6

In general, cash flow to stockholders can be determined as:

$$\begin{aligned}
\text{Cash flow to stockholders} &= \text{Dividends paid} - \text{Net new equity raised}\\
&= \text{Dividends paid} - (\text{Stock sold}\\
&\quad - \text{Stock repurchased})
\end{aligned}$$

To determine stock sold, first notice that the common stock and capital surplus accounts went up by a combined $23 + 20 = $43, which implies that the company sold $43 million worth of stock. Second, treasury stock went up by $6, indicating that the

---

[5]New debt and the retirement of old debt are usually found in the "notes" to the balance sheet.

company bought back $6 million worth of stock. Net new equity is thus $43 − 6 = $37. Dividends paid were $43 million, so the cash flow to stockholders was:

$$\text{Cash flow to stockholders} = \$43 - (43 - 6) = \$6,$$

which is what we previously calculated.

Some important observations can be drawn from our discussion of cash flow:

1. Several types of cash flow are relevant to understanding the financial situation of the firm. **Operating cash flow,** defined as earnings before interest plus depreciation minus taxes, measures the cash generated from operations not counting capital spending or working capital requirements. It is usually positive; a firm is in trouble if operating cash flow is negative for a long time because the firm is not generating enough cash to pay operating costs. **Total cash flow of the firm** includes adjustments for capital spending and additions to net working capital. It will frequently be negative. When a firm is growing at a rapid rate, spending on inventory and fixed assets can be higher than operating cash flow.

2. Net income is not cash flow. The net income of the U.S. Composite Corporation in 2012 was $86 million, whereas cash flow was $42 million. The two numbers are not usually the same. In determining the economic and financial condition of a firm, cash flow is more revealing.

A firm's total cash flow sometimes goes by a different name, **free cash flow.** Of course, there is no such thing as "free" cash (we wish!). Instead, the name refers to cash that the firm is free to distribute to creditors and stockholders because it is not needed for working capital or fixed asset investments. We will stick with "total cash flow of the firm" as our label for this important concept because, in practice, there is some variation in exactly how free cash flow is computed. Nonetheless, whenever you hear the phrase "free cash flow," you should understand that what is being discussed is cash flow from assets that can be distributed to investors. While we are not in the naming game, we frequently use the name *distributable cash flow.*

2.6 The Accounting Statement of Cash Flows

ExcelMaster
coverage online

As previously mentioned, there is an official accounting statement called the *statement of cash flows*. This statement helps explain the change in accounting cash, which for U.S. Composite is $33 million in 2012. It is very useful in understanding financial cash flow.

The first step in determining the change in cash is to figure out cash flow from operating activities. This is the cash flow that results from the firm's normal activities in producing and selling goods and services. The second step is to make an adjustment for cash flow from investing activities. The final step is to make an adjustment for cash flow from financing activities. Financing activities are the net payments to creditors and owners (excluding interest expense) made during the year.

The three components of the statement of cash flows are determined next.

CASH FLOW FROM OPERATING ACTIVITIES

To calculate cash flow from operating activities we start with net income. Net income can be found on the income statement and is equal to $86 million. We now need to add back noncash expenses and adjust for changes in current assets and liabilities (other than cash and notes payable). The result is cash flow from operating activities. Notes payable will be included in the financing activities section.

U.S. COMPOSITE CORPORATION
Cash Flow from Operating Activities
2012
($ in millions)

Net income	$ 86
Depreciation	90
Deferred taxes	13
Change in assets and liabilities	
Accounts receivable	−24
Inventories	11
Accounts payable	16
Accrued expense	18
Other	−8
Cash flow from operating activities	**$202**

CASH FLOW FROM INVESTING ACTIVITIES

Cash flow from investing activities involves changes in capital assets: acquisition of fixed assets and sales of fixed assets (i.e., net capital expenditures). The result for U.S. Composite is shown here:

U.S. COMPOSITE CORPORATION
Cash Flow from Investing Activities
2012
($ in millions)

Acquisition of fixed assets	−$198
Sales of fixed assets	25
Cash flow from investing activities	**−$173**

CASH FLOW FROM FINANCING ACTIVITIES

Cash flows to and from creditors and owners include changes in equity and debt:

U.S. COMPOSITE CORPORATION
Cash Flow from Financing Activities
2012
($ in millions)

Retirement of long-term debt	−$73
Proceeds from long-term debt sales	86
Change in notes payable	−3
Dividends	−43
Repurchase of stock	−6
Proceeds from new stock issue	43
Cash flow from financing activities	**$ 4**

Table 2.7
Statement of
Consolidated
Cash Flows of the
U.S. Composite
Corporation

U.S. COMPOSITE CORPORATION
Statement of Cash Flows
2012
($ in millions)

Operations	
Net income	$ 86
Depreciation	90
Deferred taxes	13
Changes in assets and liabilities	
Accounts receivable	−24
Inventories	11
Accounts payable	16
Accrued expenses	18
Other	−8
Total cash flow from operations	$202
Investing activities	
Acquisition of fixed assets	−$198
Sales of fixed assets	25
Total cash flow from investing activities	−$173
Financing activities	
Retirement of long-term debt	−$ 73
Proceeds from long-term debt sales	86
Change in notes payable	−3
Dividends	−43
Repurchase of stock	−6
Proceeds from new stock issue	43
Total cash flow from financing activities	$ 4
Change in cash (on the balance sheet)	$ 33

The statement of cash flows is the addition of cash flows from operations, cash flows from investing activities, and cash flows from financing activities, and is produced in Table 2.7. When we add all the cash flows together, we get the change in cash on the balance sheet of $33 million.

There is a close relationship between the official accounting statement called the statement of cash flows and the total cash flow of the firm used in finance. Going back to the previous section, you should note a slight conceptual problem here. Interest paid should really go under financing activities, but unfortunately that is not how the accounting is handled. The reason is that interest is deducted as an expense when net income is computed. As a consequence, a primary difference between the accounting cash flow and the financial cash flow of the firm (see Table 2.6) is interest expense.

2.7 Cash Flow Management

One of the reasons why cash flow analysis is popular is the difficulty in manipulating, or spinning, cash flows. GAAP accounting principles allow for significant subjective decisions to be made regarding many key areas. The use of cash flow as a metric to evaluate a company comes from the idea that there is less subjectivity involved, and, therefore, it is harder to spin the numbers. But several recent examples have shown that companies can still find ways to do it.

Tyco used several ploys to alter cash flows. For example, the company purchased more than $800 million of customer security alarm accounts from dealers. The cash flows from these transactions were reported in the financing activity section of the accounting statement of cash flows. When Tyco received payments from customers, the cash inflows were reported as operating cash flows. Another method used by Tyco was to have acquired companies prepay operating expenses. In other words, the company acquired by Tyco would pay vendors for items not yet received. In one case, the payments totaled more than $50 million. When the acquired company was consolidated with Tyco, the prepayments reduced Tyco's cash outflows, thus increasing the operating cash flows.

Dynegy, the energy giant, was accused of engaging in a number of complex "round-trip trades." The round-trip trades essentially involved the sale of natural resources to a counterparty, with the repurchase of the resources from the same party at the same price. In essence, Dynegy would sell an asset for $100, and immediately repurchase it from the buyer for $100. The problem arose with the treatment of the cash flows from the sale. Dynegy treated the cash from the sale of the asset as an operating cash flow, but classified the repurchase as an investing cash outflow. The total cash flows of the contracts traded by Dynegy in these round-trip trades totaled $300 million.

Adelphia Communications was another company that apparently manipulated cash flows. In Adelphia's case, the company capitalized the labor required to install cable. In other words, the company classified this labor expense as a fixed asset. While this practice is fairly common in the telecommunications industry, Adelphia capitalized a higher percentage of labor than is common. The effect of this classification was that the labor was treated as an investment cash flow, which increased the operating cash flow.

◄ To test your mastery of this material, take a quiz at mhhe. com/rwj

In each of these examples, the companies were trying to boost operating cash flows by shifting cash flows to a different heading. The important thing to notice is that these movements don't affect the total cash flow of the firm, which is why we recommend focusing on this number, not just operating cash flow.

Summary and Conclusions

Besides introducing you to corporate accounting, the purpose of this chapter has been to teach you how to determine cash flow from the accounting statements of a typical company.

1. Cash flow is generated by the firm and paid to creditors and shareholders. It can be classified as:
   a. Cash flow from operations.
   b. Cash flow from changes in fixed assets.
   c. Cash flow from changes in working capital.
2. Calculations of cash flow are not difficult, but they require care and particular attention to detail in properly accounting for noncash expenses such as depreciation and deferred taxes. It is especially important that you do not confuse cash flow with changes in net working capital and net income.

Concept Questions

1. **Liquidity**   True or false: All assets are liquid at some price. Explain.

2. **Accounting and Cash Flows**   Why might the revenue and cost figures shown on a standard income statement not represent the actual cash inflows and outflows that occurred during a period?

3. **Accounting Statement of Cash Flows**   Looking at the accounting statement of cash flows, what does the bottom line number mean? How useful is this number for analyzing a company?

4. **Cash Flows**   How do financial cash flows and the accounting statement of cash flows differ? Which is more useful for analyzing a company?

5. **Book Values versus Market Values**   Under standard accounting rules, it is possible for a company's liabilities to exceed its assets. When this occurs, the owners' equity is negative. Can this happen with market values? Why or why not?

6. **Cash Flow from Assets**   Why is it not necessarily bad for the cash flow from assets to be negative for a particular period?

7. **Operating Cash Flow**   Why is it not necessarily bad for the operating cash flow to be negative for a particular period?

8. **Net Working Capital and Capital Spending**   Could a company's change in net working capital be negative in a given year? (*Hint:* Yes.) Explain how this might come about. What about net capital spending?

9. **Cash Flow to Stockholders and Creditors**   Could a company's cash flow to stockholders be negative in a given year? (*Hint:* Yes.) Explain how this might come about. What about cash flow to creditors?

10. **Firm Values**   Referring back to the Bank of America example at the beginning of the chapter, note that we suggested that Bank of America's stockholders probably didn't suffer as a result of the reported loss. What do you think was the basis for our conclusion?

Questions and Problems

BASIC
(Questions 1–10)

1. **Building a Balance Sheet**   Bishop, Inc., has current assets of $5,700, net fixed assets of $27,000, current liabilities of $4,400, and long-term debt of $12,900. What is the value of the shareholders' equity account for this firm? How much is net working capital?

2. **Building an Income Statement**   Travis, Inc., has sales of $387,000, costs of $175,000, depreciation expense of $40,000, interest expense of $21,000, and a tax rate of 35 percent. What is the net income for the firm? Suppose the company paid out $30,000 in cash dividends. What is the addition to retained earnings?

3. **Market Values and Book Values**   Klingon Cruisers, Inc., purchased new cloaking machinery three years ago for $9.5 million. The machinery can be sold to the Romulans today for $6.5 million. Klingon's current balance sheet shows net fixed assets of $5.2 million, current liabilities of $2.4 million, and net working capital of $800,000. If all the current assets were liquidated today, the company would receive $2.6 million cash. What is the book value of Klingon's assets today? What is the market value?

Chapter 2   Financial Statements and Cash Flow   37

4. **Calculating Taxes**   The Locker Co. had $273,000 in taxable income. Using the rates from Table 2.3 in the chapter, calculate the company's income taxes. What is the average tax rate? What is the marginal tax rate?

5. **Calculating OCF**   Ranney, Inc., has sales of $18,700, costs of $10,300, depreciation expense of $1,900, and interest expense of $1,250. If the tax rate is 40 percent, what is the operating cash flow, or OCF?

6. **Calculating Net Capital Spending**   Gordon Driving School's 2011 balance sheet showed net fixed assets of $1.42 million, and the 2012 balance sheet showed net fixed assets of $1.69 million. The company's 2012 income statement showed a depreciation expense of $145,000. What was Gordon's net capital spending for 2012?

7. **Building a Balance Sheet**   The following table presents the long-term liabilities and stockholders' equity of Information Control Corp. one year ago:

Long-term debt	$ 65,000,000
Preferred stock	4,000,000
Common stock ($1 par value)	15,000,000
Accumulated retained earnings	135,000,000
Capital surplus	45,000,000

During the past year, Information Control issued 10 million shares of new stock at a total price of $58 million, and issued $35 million in new long-term debt. The company generated $9 million in net income and paid $2 million in dividends. Construct the current balance sheet reflecting the changes that occurred at Information Control Corp. during the year.

8. **Cash Flow to Creditors**   The 2011 balance sheet of Anna's Tennis Shop, Inc., showed long-term debt of $1.45 million, and the 2012 balance sheet showed long-term debt of $1.52 million. The 2012 income statement showed an interest expense of $127,000. What was the firm's cash flow to creditors during 2012?

9. **Cash Flow to Stockholders**   The 2011 balance sheet of Anna's Tennis Shop, Inc., showed $490,000 in the common stock account and $3.4 million in the additional paid-in surplus account. The 2012 balance sheet showed $525,000 and $3.7 million in the same two accounts, respectively. If the company paid out $275,000 in cash dividends during 2012, what was the cash flow to stockholders for the year?

10. **Calculating Cash Flows**   Given the information for Anna's Tennis Shop, Inc., in the previous two problems, suppose you also know that the firm's net capital spending for 2012 was $945,000 and that the firm reduced its net working capital investment by $87,000. What was the firm's 2012 operating cash flow, or OCF?

INTERMEDIATE
(Questions 11–23)

11. **Cash Flows**   Ritter Corporation's accountants prepared the following financial statements for year-end 2012:
   a. Explain the change in cash during 2012.
   b. Determine the change in net working capital in 2012.
   c. Determine the cash flow generated by the firm's assets during 2012.

RITTER CORPORATION Income Statement 2012	
Revenue	$750
Expenses	565
Depreciation	90
Net income	$ 95
Dividends	$ 75

RITTER CORPORATION Balance Sheets December 31		
	2012	**2011**
Assets		
Cash	$ 65	$ 55
Other current assets	170	165
Net fixed assets	390	370
Total assets	$625	$590
Liabilities and Equity		
Accounts payable	$125	$115
Long-term debt	145	140
Stockholders' equity	355	335
Total liabilities and equity	$625	$590

12. **Financial Cash Flows** The Stancil Corporation provided the following current information:

Proceeds from long-term borrowing	$17,000
Proceeds from the sale of common stock	4,000
Purchases of fixed assets	21,000
Purchases of inventories	1,900
Payment of dividends	14,500

Determine the cash flows from the firm and the cash flows to investors of the firm.

13. **Building an Income Statement** During the year, the Senbet Discount Tire Company had gross sales of $1.06 million. The firm's cost of goods sold and selling expenses were $525,000 and $215,000, respectively. Senbet also had notes payable of $800,000. These notes carried an interest rate of 7 percent. Depreciation was $130,000. Senbet's tax rate was 35 percent.
   a. What was Senbet's net income?
   b. What was Senbet's operating cash flow?

14. **Calculating Total Cash Flows** Schwert Corp. shows the following information on its 2012 income statement: sales = $185,000; costs = $98,000; other expenses = $6,700; depreciation expense = $16,500; interest expense = $9,000; taxes = $19,180; dividends = $9,500. In addition, you're told that the firm issued $7,550 in new equity during 2012 and redeemed $7,100 in outstanding long-term debt.
   a. What is the 2012 operating cash flow?
   b. What is the 2012 cash flow to creditors?
   c. What is the 2012 cash flow to stockholders?
   d. If net fixed assets increased by $26,100 during the year, what was the addition to net working capital (NWC)?

15. **Using Income Statements** Given the following information for O'Hara Marine Co., calculate the depreciation expense: sales = $41,000; costs = $26,400; addition to retained earnings = $4,900; dividends paid = $1,570; interest expense = $1,840; tax rate = 35 percent.

16. **Residual Claims** Huang, Inc., is obligated to pay its creditors $10,900 very soon.
   a. What is the market value of the shareholders' equity if assets have a market value of $12,400?
   b. What if assets equal $9,600?

17. **Marginal versus Average Tax Rates**   (Refer to Table 2.3.) Corporation Growth has $86,000 in taxable income, and Corporation Income has $8,600,000 in taxable income.
    a. What is the tax bill for each firm?
    b. Suppose both firms have identified a new project that will increase taxable income by $10,000. How much in additional taxes will each firm pay? Why is this amount the same?

18. **Net Income and OCF**   During 2012, Raines Umbrella Corp. had sales of $630,000. Cost of goods sold, administrative and selling expenses, and depreciation expenses were $470,000, $95,000, and $140,000, respectively. In addition, the company had an interest expense of $70,000 and a tax rate of 35 percent. (Ignore any tax loss carryback or carryforward provisions.)
    a. What is Raines's net income for 2012?
    b. What is its operating cash flow?
    c. Explain your results in (a) and (b).

19. **Accounting Values versus Cash Flows**   In Problem 18, suppose Raines Umbrella Corp. paid out $34,000 in cash dividends. Is this possible? If spending on net fixed assets and net working capital was zero, and if no new stock was issued during the year, what was the change in the firm's long-term debt account?

20. **Calculating Cash Flows**   Cusic Industries had the following operating results for 2012: sales = $19,900; cost of goods sold = $14,200; depreciation expense = $2,700; interest expense = $670; dividends paid = $650. At the beginning of the year, net fixed assets were $15,340, current assets were $4,420, and current liabilities were $2,470. At the end of the year, net fixed assets were $16,770, current assets were $5,135, and current liabilities were $2,535. The tax rate for 2012 was 40 percent.
    a. What is net income for 2012?
    b. What is the operating cash flow for 2012?
    c. What is the cash flow from assets for 2012? Is this possible? Explain.
    d. If no new debt was issued during the year, what is the cash flow to creditors? What is the cash flow to stockholders? Explain and interpret the positive and negative signs of your answers in (a) through (d).

 21. **Calculating Cash Flows**   Consider the following abbreviated financial statements for Weston Enterprises:

WESTON ENTERPRISES 2011 and 2012 Partial Balance Sheets					
Assets			**Liabilities and Owners' Equity**		
	2011	2012		2011	2012
Current assets	$ 936	$1,015	Current liabilities	$ 382	$ 416
Net fixed assets	4,176	4,896	Long-term debt	2,160	2,477

WESTON ENTERPRISES 2012 Income Statement	
Sales	$12,380
Costs	5,776
Depreciation	1,150
Interest paid	314

a. What is owners' equity for 2011 and 2012?
b. What is the change in net working capital for 2012?
c. In 2012, Weston Enterprises purchased $2,160 in new fixed assets. How much in fixed assets did Weston Enterprises sell? What is the cash flow from assets for the year? (The tax rate is 40 percent.)
d. During 2012, Weston Enterprises raised $432 in new long-term debt. How much long-term debt must Weston Enterprises have paid off during the year? What is the cash flow to creditors?

www.mhhe.com/rwj

40   Part I   Overview

Use the following information for Ingersoll, Inc., for Problems 22 and 23 (assume the tax rate is 34 percent):

	2011	2012
Sales	$ 7,835	$ 8,409
Depreciation	1,125	1,126
Cost of goods sold	2,696	3,060
Other expenses	639	534
Interest	525	603
Cash	4,109	5,203
Accounts receivable	5,439	6,127
Short-term notes payable	794	746
Long-term debt	13,460	16,050
Net fixed assets	34,455	35,277
Accounts payable	4,316	4,185
Inventory	9,670	9,938
Dividends	956	1,051

22. **Financial Statements** Draw up an income statement and balance sheet for this company for 2011 and 2012.

23. **Calculating Cash Flow** For 2012, calculate the cash flow from assets, cash flow to creditors, and cash flow to stockholders.

CHALLANGE
(Questions 24–26)

24. **Cash Flows** You are researching Time Manufacturing and have found the following accounting statement of cash flows for the most recent year. You also know that the company paid $98 million in current taxes and had an interest expense of $48 million. Use the accounting statement of cash flows to construct the financial statement of cash flows.

TIME MANUFACTURING Statement of Cash Flows ($ in millions)	
Operations	
Net income	$173
Depreciation	94
Deferred taxes	19
Changes in assets and liabilities	
Accounts receivable	−18
Inventories	22
Accounts payable	17
Accrued expenses	−9
Other	3
Total cash flow from operations	$301
Investing activities	
Acquisition of fixed assets	−$215
Sale of fixed assets	23
Total cash flow from investing activities	−$192

Financing activities	
Retirement of long-term debt	−$162
Proceeds from long-term debt sales	116
Change in notes payable	6
Dividends	−86
Repurchase of stock	−13
Proceeds from new stock issue	44
Total cash flow from financing activities	**−$ 95**
Change in cash (on balance sheet)	**$ 14**

25. **Net Fixed Assets and Depreciation**   On the balance sheet, the net fixed assets (NFA) account is equal to the gross fixed assets (FA) account, which records the acquisition cost of fixed assets, minus the accumulated depreciation (AD) account, which records the total depreciation taken by the firm against its fixed assets. Using the fact that NFA = FA − AD, show that the expression given in the chapter for net capital spending, $NFA_{end} - NFA_{beg} + D$ (where D is the depreciation expense during the year), is equivalent to $FA_{end} - FA_{beg}$.

26. **Tax Rates**   Refer to the corporate marginal tax rate information in Table 2.3.

a. Why do you think the marginal tax rate jumps up from 34 percent to 39 percent at a taxable income of $100,001, and then falls back to a 34 percent marginal rate at a taxable income of $335,001?

b. Compute the average tax rate for a corporation with exactly $335,001 in taxable income. Does this confirm your explanation in part (a)? What is the average tax rate for a corporation with exactly $18,333,334? Is the same thing happening here?

c. The 39 percent and 38 percent tax rates both represent what is called a tax "bubble." Suppose the government wanted to lower the upper threshold of the 39 percent marginal tax bracket from $335,000 to $200,000. What would the new 39 percent bubble rate have to be?

Excel Master It!

Using Excel to find the marginal tax rate can be accomplished using the VLOOKUP function. However, calculating the total tax bill is a little more difficult. Below we have shown a copy of the IRS tax table for an individual for 2011 (the income thresholds are indexed to inflation and change through time).

If taxable income is over --	But not over --	The tax is:
$ 0	$ 8,500	10% of the amount over $0
8,500	34,500	$850 plus 15% of the amount over $8,500
34,500	83,600	$4,750 plus 25% of the amount over $34,500
83,600	174,400	$17,025 plus 28% of the amount over $83,600
174,400	379,150	$42,449 plus 33% of the amount over $174,400
379,150		$110,016.50 plus 35% of the amount over $379,150

In reading this table, the marginal tax rate for taxable income less than $8,500 is 10 percent. If the taxable income is between $8,500 and $34,500, the tax bill is $850 plus the marginal taxes. The marginal taxes are calculated as the taxable income minus $8,500 times the marginal tax rate of 15 percent.

a. Create a tax table for corporate taxes similar to the individual tax table shown above.
b. For a given taxable income, what is the marginal tax rate?
c. For a given taxable income, what is the total tax bill?
d. For a given taxable income, what is the average tax rate?

CASH FLOWS AT WARF COMPUTERS, INC.

Warf Computers, Inc., was founded 15 years ago by Nick Warf, a computer programmer. The small initial investment to start the company was made by Nick and his friends. Over the years, this same group has supplied the limited additional investment needed by the company in the form of both equity and short- and long-term debt. Recently the company has developed a virtual keyboard (VK). The VK uses sophisticated artificial intelligence algorithms that allow the user to speak naturally and have the computer input the text, correct spelling and grammatical errors, and format the document according to preset user guidelines. The VK even suggests alternative phrasing and sentence structure, and it provides detailed stylistic diagnostics. Based on a proprietary, very advanced software/hardware hybrid technology, the system is a full generation beyond what is currently on the market. To introduce the VK, the company will require significant outside investment.

Nick has made the decision to seek this outside financing in the form of new equity investments and bank loans. Naturally, new investors and the banks will require a detailed financial analysis. Your employer, Angus Jones & Partners, LLC, has asked you to examine the financial statements provided by Nick. Here are the balance sheet for the two most recent years and the most recent income statement:

WARF COMPUTERS
Balance Sheet
($ in thousands)

	2012	2011		2012	2011
Current assets			Current liabilities		
Cash and equivalents	$ 348	$ 301	Accounts payable	$ 314	$ 294
Accounts receivable	551	514	Notes payable	85	79
Inventories	493	510	Accrued expenses	190	308
Other	71	60	Total current		
Total current assets	$1,463	$1,385	liabilities	$ 589	$ 681
Fixed assets			Long-term liabilities		
Property, plant, and			Deferred taxes	$ 254	$ 124
equipment	$3,191	$2,446	Long-term debt	907	883
Less accumulated			Total long-term		
depreciation	1,031	840	liabilities	$1,161	$1,007
Net property, plant, and			Stockholders' equity		
equipment	$2,160	$1,606	Preferred stock	$ 16	$ 16
Intangible assets and others	610	545	Common stock	97	97
Total fixed assets	$2,770	$2,151	Capital surplus	611	599
			Accumulated retained earnings	1,904	1,233
			Less treasury stock	145	97
			Total equity	$2,483	$1,848
Total assets	$4,233	$3,536	Total liabilities and shareholders' equity	$4,233	$3,536

Nick has also provided the following information: During the year the company raised $175,000 in new long-term debt and retired $151,000 in long-term debt. The company also sold $12,000 in new stock and repurchased $48,000 in stock. The company purchased $1,140,000 in fixed assets and sold $330,000 in fixed assets.

WARF COMPUTERS Income Statement ($ in thousands)	
Sales	$5,813
Cost of goods sold	3,430
Selling, general, and administrative expense	652
Depreciation	191
Operating income	$1,540
Other income	58
EBIT	$1,598
Interest expense	105
Pretax income	$1,493
Taxes	597
Current: $467	
Deferred: 130	
Net income	$ 896
Dividends	$ 225
Retained earnings	$ 671

Angus has asked you to prepare the financial statement of cash flows and the accounting statement of cash flows. He has also asked you to answer the following questions:

1. How would you describe Warf Computers' cash flows?
2. Which cash flow statement more accurately describes the cash flows at the company?
3. In light of your previous answers, comment on Nick's expansion plans.

CHAPTER 3

Financial Statements Analysis and Financial Models

▲ For updates on the latest happenings in finance, visit www. rwjcorporatefinance. blogspot.com

The price of a share of common stock in green tractor manufacturer John Deere closed at about $88 on May 13, 2011. At that price, John Deere had a price–earnings (PE) ratio of 17. That is, investors were willing to pay $17 for every dollar in income earned by John Deere. At the same time, investors were willing to pay $9, $13, and $27 for each dollar earned by Ford, Coca-Cola, and Google, respectively. At the other extreme were Bank of America and United States Steel. Both had negative earnings for the previous year, but Bank of America was priced at about $12 per share and United States Steel at about $45 per share. Because they had negative earnings, their PE ratios would have been negative, so they were not reported. At the same time, the typical stock in the S&P 500 Index of large company stocks was trading at a PE of about 14, or about 14 times earnings, as they say on Wall Street.

Price—earnings comparisons are examples of the use of financial ratios. As we will see in this chapter, there are a wide variety of financial ratios, all designed to summarize specific aspects of a firm's financial position. In addition to discussing how to analyze financial statements and compute financial ratios, we will have quite a bit to say about who uses this information and why.

3.1 Financial Statements Analysis

ExcelMaster coverage online

This section will introduce absolute references IF and SUM IF functions.

In Chapter 2, we discussed some of the essential concepts of financial statements and cash flows. This chapter continues where our earlier discussion left off. Our goal here is to expand your understanding of the uses (and abuses) of financial statement information.

A good working knowledge of financial statements is desirable simply because such statements, and numbers derived from those statements, are the primary means of communicating financial information both within the firm and outside the firm. In short, much of the language of business finance is rooted in the ideas we discuss in this chapter.

Clearly, one important goal of the accountant is to report financial information to the user in a form useful for decision making. Ironically, the information frequently does not come to the user in such a form. In other words, financial statements don't come with a user's guide. This chapter is a first step in filling this gap.

STANDARDIZING STATEMENTS

One obvious thing we might want to do with a company's financial statements is to compare them to those of other, similar companies. We would immediately have a problem, however. It's almost impossible to directly compare the financial statements for two companies because of differences in size.

For example, Ford and GM are obviously serious rivals in the auto market, but GM is larger, so it is difficult to compare them directly. For that matter, it's difficult even to compare financial statements from different points in time for the same company if the company's size has changed. The size problem is compounded if we try to compare GM and, say, Toyota. If Toyota's financial statements are denominated in yen, then we have size *and* currency differences.

To start making comparisons, one obvious thing we might try to do is to somehow standardize the financial statements. One common and useful way of doing this is to work with percentages instead of total dollars. The resulting financial statements are called **common-size statements.** We consider these next.

COMMON-SIZE BALANCE SHEETS

For easy reference, Prufrock Corporation's 2011 and 2012 balance sheets are provided in Table 3.1. Using these, we construct common-size balance sheets by expressing each item as a percentage of total assets. Prufrock's 2011 and 2012 common-size balance sheets are shown in Table 3.2.

Notice that some of the totals don't check exactly because of rounding errors. Also notice that the total change has to be zero because the beginning and ending numbers must add up to 100 percent.

In this form, financial statements are relatively easy to read and compare. For example, just looking at the two balance sheets for Prufrock, we see that current assets were 19.7 percent of total assets in 2012, up from 19.1 percent in 2011. Current

Table 3.1

PRUFROCK CORPORATION
Balance Sheets as of December 31, 2011 and 2012
($ in millions)

Assets	2011	2012
Current assets		
Cash	$ 84	$ 98
Accounts receivable	165	188
Inventory	393	422
Total	$ 642	$ 708
Fixed assets		
Net plant and equipment	$2,731	$2,880
Total assets	$3,373	$3,588
Liabilities and Owners' Equity		
Current liabilities		
Accounts payable	$ 312	$ 344
Notes payable	231	196
Total	$ 543	$ 540
Long-term debt	$ 531	$ 457
Owners' equity		
Common stock and paid-in surplus	$ 500	$ 550
Retained earnings	1,799	2,041
Total	$2,299	$2,591
Total liabilities and owners' equity	$3,373	$3,588

Table 3.2

PRUFROCK CORPORATION Common-Size Balance Sheets December 31, 2011 and 2012			
Assets	**2011**	**2012**	**Change**
Current assets			
Cash	2.5%	2.7%	+ .2%
Accounts receivable	4.9	5.2	+ .3
Inventory	11.7	11.8	+ .1
Total	19.1	19.7	+ .6
Fixed assets			
Net plant and equipment	80.9	80.3	− .6
Total assets	100.0%	100.0%	.0%
Liabilities and Owners' Equity			
Current liabilities			
Accounts payable	9.2%	9.6%	+ .4%
Notes payable	6.8	5.5	−1.3
Total	16.0	15.1	− .9
Long-term debt	15.7	12.7	−3.0
Owners' equity			
Common stock and paid-in surplus	14.8	15.3	+ .5
Retained earnings	53.3	56.9	+3.6
Total	68.1	72.2	+4.1
Total liabilities and owners' equity	100.0%	100.0%	.0%

liabilities declined from 16.0 percent to 15.1 percent of total liabilities and equity over that same time. Similarly, total equity rose from 68.1 percent of total liabilities and equity to 72.2 percent.

Overall, Prufrock's liquidity, as measured by current assets compared to current liabilities, increased over the year. Simultaneously, Prufrock's indebtedness diminished as a percentage of total assets. We might be tempted to conclude that the balance sheet has grown "stronger."

COMMON-SIZE INCOME STATEMENTS

Table 3.3 describes some commonly used measures of earnings. A useful way of standardizing the income statement shown in Table 3.4 is to express each item as a percentage of total sales, as illustrated for Prufrock in Table 3.5.

This income statement tells us what happens to each dollar in sales. For Prufrock, interest expense eats up $.061 out of every sales dollar, and taxes take another $.081. When all is said and done, $.157 of each dollar flows through to the bottom line (net income), and that amount is split into $.105 retained in the business and $.052 paid out in dividends.

These percentages are useful in comparisons. For example, a relevant figure is the cost percentage. For Prufrock, $.582 of each $1.00 in sales goes to pay for goods sold. It would be interesting to compute the same percentage for Prufrock's main competitors to see how Prufrock stacks up in terms of cost control.

Table 3.3
Measures of Earnings

Investors and analysts look closely at the income statement for clues on how well a company has performed during a particular year. Here are some commonly used measures of earnings (numbers in millions).

Net Income	The so-called bottom line, defined as total revenue minus total expenses. Net income for Prufrock in the latest period is $363 million. Net income reflects differences in a firm's capital structure and taxes as well as operating income. Interest expense and taxes are subtracted from operating income in computing net income. Shareholders look closely at net income because dividend payout and retained earnings are closely linked to net income.
EPS	Net income divided by the number of shares outstanding. It expresses net income on a per share basis. For Prufrock, the EPS = (Net income)/(Shares outstanding) = $363/33 = $11.
EBIT	Earnings before interest expense and taxes. EBIT is usually called "income from operations" on the income statement and is income before unusual items, discontinued operations or extraordinary items. To calculate EBIT, operating expenses are subtracted from total operations revenues. Analysts like EBIT because it abstracts from differences in earnings from a firm's capital structure (interest expense) and taxes. For Prufrock, EBIT is $691 million.
EBITDA	Earnings before interest expense, taxes, depreciation, and amortization. EBITDA = EBIT + depreciation and amortization. Here amortization refers to a noncash expense similar to depreciation except it applies to an intangible asset (such as a patent), rather than a tangible asset (such as a machine). The word amortization here does not refer to the payment of debt. There is no amortization in Prufrock's income statement. For Prufrock, EBITDA = $691 + $276 = $967 million. Analysts like to use EBITDA because it adds back two noncash items (depreciation and amortization) to EBIT and thus is a better measure of before-tax operating cash flow.

Sometimes these measures of earnings are preceded by the letters LTM, meaning the last twelve months. For example, LTM EPS is the last twelve months of EPS and LTM EBITDA is the last twelve months of EBITDA. At other times, the letters TTM are used, meaning trailing twelve months. Needless to say, LTM is the same as TTM.

Table 3.4

PRUFROCK CORPORATION
2012 Income Statement
($ in millions)

Sales		$2,311
Cost of goods sold		1,344
Depreciation		276
Earnings before interest and taxes		$ 691
Interest paid		141
Taxable income		$ 550
Taxes (34%)		187
Net income		$ 363
Dividends	$121	
Addition to retained earnings	242	

Table 3.5

PRUFROCK CORPORATION Common-Size Income Statement 2012		
Sales		100.0%
Cost of goods sold		58.2
Depreciation		11.9
Earnings before interest and taxes		29.9
Interest paid		6.1
Taxable income		23.8
Taxes (34%)		8.1
Net income		15.7%
Dividends	5.2%	
Addition to retained earnings	10.5	

3.2 Ratio Analysis

ExcelMaster
coverage online

This section will introduce
conditional formatting.

Another way of avoiding the problems involved in comparing companies of different sizes is to calculate and compare **financial ratios.** Such ratios are ways of comparing and investigating the relationships between different pieces of financial information. We cover some of the more common ratios next (there are many others we don't discuss here).

One problem with ratios is that different people and different sources frequently don't compute them in exactly the same way, and this leads to much confusion. The specific definitions we use here may or may not be the same as ones you have seen or will see elsewhere. If you are using ratios as tools for analysis, you should be careful to document how you calculate each one; and, if you are comparing your numbers to those of another source, be sure you know how their numbers are computed.

We will defer much of our discussion of how ratios are used and some problems that come up with using them until later in the chapter. For now, for each ratio we discuss, several questions come to mind:

Go to
**www.reuters.com/
finance/stocks**
and find the financials
link to examine
comparative ratios
for a huge number of
companies.

1.   How is it computed?
2.   What is it intended to measure, and why might we be interested?
3.   What is the unit of measurement?
4.   What might a high or low value be telling us? How might such values be misleading?
5.   How could this measure be improved?

Financial ratios are traditionally grouped into the following categories:

1.   Short-term solvency, or liquidity, ratios.
2.   Long-term solvency, or financial leverage, ratios.
3.   Asset management, or turnover, ratios.
4.   Profitability ratios.
5.   Market value ratios.

We will consider each of these in turn. In calculating these numbers for Prufrock, we will use the ending balance sheet (2012) figures unless we explicitly say otherwise.

SHORT-TERM SOLVENCY OR LIQUIDITY MEASURES

As the name suggests, short-term solvency ratios as a group are intended to provide information about a firm's liquidity, and these ratios are sometimes called *liquidity measures*. The primary concern is the firm's ability to pay its bills over the short run without undue stress. Consequently, these ratios focus on current assets and current liabilities.

For obvious reasons, liquidity ratios are particularly interesting to short-term creditors. Because financial managers are constantly working with banks and other short-term lenders, an understanding of these ratios is essential.

One advantage of looking at current assets and liabilities is that their book values and market values are likely to be similar. Often (though not always), these assets and liabilities just don't live long enough for the two to get seriously out of step. On the other hand, like any type of near-cash, current assets and liabilities can and do change fairly rapidly, so today's amounts may not be a reliable guide to the future.

Current Ratio   One of the best-known and most widely used ratios is the *current ratio*. As you might guess, the current ratio is defined as:

$$\text{Current ratio} = \frac{\text{Current assets}}{\text{Current liabilities}} \qquad (3.1)$$

For Prufrock, the 2012 current ratio is:

$$\text{Current ratio} = \frac{\$708}{\$540} = 1.31 \text{ times}$$

Because current assets and liabilities are, in principle, converted to cash over the following 12 months, the current ratio is a measure of short-term liquidity. The unit of measurement is either dollars or times. So, we could say Prufrock has $1.31 in current assets for every $1 in current liabilities, or we could say Prufrock has its current liabilities covered 1.31 times over. Absent some extraordinary circumstances, we would expect to see a current ratio of at least 1; a current ratio of less than 1 would mean that net working capital (current assets less current liabilities) is negative.

The current ratio, like any ratio, is affected by various types of transactions. For example, suppose the firm borrows over the long term to raise money. The short-run effect would be an increase in cash from the issue proceeds and an increase in long-term debt. Current liabilities would not be affected, so the current ratio would rise.

EXAMPLE 3.1

Current Events   Suppose a firm were to pay off some of its suppliers and short-term creditors. What would happen to the current ratio? Suppose a firm buys some inventory. What happens in this case? What happens if a firm sells some merchandise?

The first case is a trick question. What happens is that the current ratio moves away from 1. If it is greater than 1, it will get bigger, but if it is less than 1, it will get smaller. To see this, suppose the firm has $4 in current assets and $2 in current liabilities for a current ratio of 2. If we use $1 in cash to reduce current liabilities, the new current ratio is ($4 − 1)/($2 − 1) = 3. If we reverse the original situation to $2 in current assets and $4 in current liabilities, the change will cause the current ratio to fall to 1/3 from 1/2.

The second case is not quite as tricky. Nothing happens to the current ratio because cash goes down while inventory goes up—total current assets are unaffected.

In the third case, the current ratio would usually rise because inventory is normally shown at cost and the sale would normally be at something greater than cost (the difference is the markup). The increase in either cash or receivables is therefore greater than the decrease in inventory. This increases current assets, and the current ratio rises.

Finally, note that an apparently low current ratio may not be a bad sign for a company with a large reserve of untapped borrowing power.

Quick (or Acid-Test) Ratio   Inventory is often the least liquid current asset. It's also the one for which the book values are least reliable as measures of market value because the quality of the inventory isn't considered. Some of the inventory may later turn out to be damaged, obsolete, or lost.

More to the point, relatively large inventories are often a sign of short-term trouble. The firm may have overestimated sales and overbought or overproduced as a result. In this case, the firm may have a substantial portion of its liquidity tied up in slow-moving inventory.

To further evaluate liquidity, the *quick,* or *acid-test, ratio* is computed just like the current ratio, except inventory is omitted:

$$\text{Quick ratio} = \frac{\text{Current assets} - \text{Inventory}}{\text{Current liabilities}} \qquad (3.2)$$

Notice that using cash to buy inventory does not affect the current ratio, but it reduces the quick ratio. Again, the idea is that inventory is relatively illiquid compared to cash.

For Prufrock, this ratio in 2012 was:

$$\text{Quick ratio} = \frac{\$708 - 422}{\$540} = .53 \text{ times}$$

The quick ratio here tells a somewhat different story than the current ratio because inventory accounts for more than half of Prufrock's current assets. To exaggerate the point, if this inventory consisted of, say, unsold nuclear power plants, then this would be a cause for concern.

To give an example of current versus quick ratios, based on recent financial statements, Walmart and Manpower, Inc., had current ratios of .89 and 1.12, respectively. However, Manpower carries no inventory to speak of, whereas Walmart's current assets are virtually all inventory. As a result, Walmart's quick ratio was only .27, and Manpower's was 1.12, the same as its current ratio.

Cash Ratio   A very short-term creditor might be interested in the *cash ratio:*

$$\text{Cash ratio} = \frac{\text{Cash}}{\text{Current liabilities}} \qquad (3.3)$$

You can verify that this works out to be .18 times for Prufrock.

LONG-TERM SOLVENCY MEASURES

Long-term solvency ratios are intended to address the firm's long-run ability to meet its obligations or, more generally, its financial leverage. These ratios are sometimes called *financial leverage ratios* or just *leverage ratios.* We consider three commonly used measures and some variations.

Total Debt Ratio   The *total debt ratio* takes into account all debts of all maturities to all creditors. It can be defined in several ways, the easiest of which is this:

$$\text{Total debt ratio} = \frac{\text{Total assets} - \text{Total equity}}{\text{Total assets}}$$

$$= \frac{\$3,588 - 2,591}{\$3,588} = .28 \text{ times} \qquad (3.4)$$

Chapter 3 Financial Statements Analysis and Financial Models **51**

In this case, an analyst might say that Prufrock uses 28 percent debt.[1] Whether this is high or low or whether it even makes any difference depends on whether capital structure matters, a subject we discuss in a later chapter.

Prufrock has $.28 in debt for every $1 in assets. Therefore, there is $.72 in equity (=$1 − .28) for every $.28 in debt. With this in mind, we can define two useful variations on the total debt ratio, the *debt–equity ratio* and the *equity multiplier:*

The online U.S. Small Business Administration has more information about financial statements, ratios, and small business topics at **www.sba.gov**.

$$\text{Debt–equity ratio} = \text{Total debt/Total equity}$$
$$= \$.28/\$.72 = .39 \text{ times} \tag{3.5}$$

$$\text{Equity multiplier} = \text{Total assets/Total equity}$$
$$= \$1/\$.72 = 1.39 \text{ times} \tag{3.6}$$

The fact that the equity multiplier is 1 plus the debt–equity ratio is not a coincidence:

$$\text{Equity multiplier} = \text{Total assets/Total equity} = \$1/\$.72 = 1.39 \text{ times}$$
$$= (\text{Total equity} + \text{Total debt})/\text{Total equity}$$
$$= 1 + \text{Debt–equity ratio} = 1.39 \text{ times}$$

The thing to notice here is that given any one of these three ratios, you can immediately calculate the other two, so they all say exactly the same thing.

Times Interest Earned Another common measure of long-term solvency is the *times interest earned* (TIE) *ratio.* Once again, there are several possible (and common) definitions, but we'll stick with the most traditional:

$$\text{Times interest earned ratio} = \frac{\text{EBIT}}{\text{Interest}}$$
$$= \frac{\$691}{\$141} = 4.9 \text{ times} \tag{3.7}$$

As the name suggests, this ratio measures how well a company has its interest obligations covered, and it is often called the *interest coverage ratio.* For Prufrock, the interest bill is covered 4.9 times over.

Cash Coverage A problem with the TIE ratio is that it is based on EBIT, which is not really a measure of cash available to pay interest. The reason is that depreciation and amortization, noncash expenses, have been deducted out. Because interest is most definitely a cash outflow (to creditors), one way to define the *cash coverage ratio* is:

$$\text{Cash coverage ratio} = \frac{\text{EBIT} + (\text{Depreciation and amortization})}{\text{Interest}}$$
$$= \frac{\$691 + 276}{\$141} = \frac{\$967}{\$141} = 6.9 \text{ times} \tag{3.8}$$

The numerator here, EBIT plus depreciation and amortization, is often abbreviated EBITDA (earnings before interest, taxes, depreciation, and amortization). It is a basic measure of the firm's ability to generate cash from operations, and it is frequently used as a measure of cash flow available to meet financial obligations.

---

[1]Total equity here includes preferred stock, if there is any. An equivalent numerator in this ratio would be (Current liabilities + Long-term debt).

More recently another long-term solvency measure is increasingly seen in financial statement analysis and in debt covenants. It uses EBITDA and interest bearing debt. Specifically, for Prufrock:

$$\frac{\text{Interest bearing debt}}{\text{EBITDA}} = \frac{\$196 \text{ million} + 457 \text{ million}}{\$967 \text{ million}} = .68 \text{ times}$$

Here we include notes payable (most likely notes payable is bank debt) and long-term debt in the numerator and EBITDA in the denominator. Values below 1 on this ratio are considered very strong and values above 5 are considered weak. However a careful comparison with other comparable firms is necessary to properly interpret the ratio.

ASSET MANAGEMENT OR TURNOVER MEASURES

We next turn our attention to the efficiency with which Prufrock uses its assets. The measures in this section are sometimes called *asset management* or *utilization ratios*. The specific ratios we discuss can all be interpreted as measures of turnover. What they are intended to describe is how efficiently, or intensively, a firm uses its assets to generate sales. We first look at two important current assets: inventory and receivables.

Inventory Turnover and Days' Sales in Inventory   During the year, Prufrock had a cost of goods sold of $1,344. Inventory at the end of the year was $422. With these numbers, *inventory turnover* can be calculated as:

$$\begin{aligned}\text{Inventory turnover} &= \frac{\text{Cost of goods sold}}{\text{Inventory}} \\ &= \frac{\$1,344}{\$422} = 3.2 \text{ times}\end{aligned} \tag{3.9}$$

In a sense, we sold off, or turned over, the entire inventory 3.2 times during the year. As long as we are not running out of stock and thereby forgoing sales, the higher this ratio is, the more efficiently we are managing inventory.

If we know that we turned our inventory over 3.2 times during the year, we can immediately figure out how long it took us to turn it over on average. The result is the average *days' sales in inventory:*

$$\begin{aligned}\text{Days' sales in inventory} &= \frac{365 \text{ days}}{\text{Inventory turnover}} \\ &= \frac{365}{3.2} = 114 \text{ days}\end{aligned} \tag{3.10}$$

This tells us that, roughly speaking, inventory sits 114 days on average before it is sold. Alternatively, assuming we used the most recent inventory and cost figures, it will take about 114 days to work off our current inventory.

For example, in May 2011, sales of General Motors (GM) trucks could have used a pickup. At that time, the company had a 111-day supply of pickups. These numbers mean that at the then-current rate of sales, it would have taken GM 111 days to deplete the available supply. A 60-day supply is considered normal in the industry. Fortunately, GM only had a 52-day supply of crossovers and a 48-day supply of cars. Of course, the days in inventory are lower for better-selling models. For example, also in May 2011, the Lexus CT 200h only had a 7-day inventory period and the Hyundai Elantra had an 8-day supply.

Receivables Turnover and Days' Sales in Receivables   Our inventory measures give some indication of how fast we can sell products. We now look at how fast we collect on those sales. The *receivables turnover* is defined in the same way as inventory turnover:

$$\text{Receivables turnover} = \frac{\text{Sales}}{\text{Accounts receivable}}$$

$$= \frac{\$2{,}311}{\$188} = 12.3 \text{ times} \qquad (3.11)$$

Loosely speaking, we collected our outstanding credit accounts and lent the money again 12.3 times during the year.[2]

This ratio makes more sense if we convert it to days, so the *days' sales in receivables* is:

$$\text{Days' sales in receivables} = \frac{365 \text{ days}}{\text{Receivables turnover}}$$

$$= \frac{365}{12.3} = 30 \text{ days} \qquad (3.12)$$

Therefore, on average, we collect on our credit sales in 30 days. For obvious reasons, this ratio is frequently called the *average collection period* (ACP). Also note that if we are using the most recent figures, we can also say that we have 30 days' worth of sales currently uncollected.

EXAMPLE 3.2

Payables Turnover   Here is a variation on the receivables collection period. How long, on average, does it take for Prufrock Corporation to *pay* its bills? To answer, we need to calculate the accounts payable turnover rate using cost of goods sold. We will assume that Prufrock purchases everything on credit.

The cost of goods sold is $1,344, and accounts payable are $344. The turnover is therefore $1,344/$344 = 3.9 times. So, payables turned over about every 365/3.9 = 94 days. On average, then, Prufrock takes 94 days to pay. As a potential creditor, we might take note of this fact.

Total Asset Turnover   Moving away from specific accounts like inventory or receivables, we can consider an important "big picture" ratio, the *total asset turnover* ratio. As the name suggests, total asset turnover is:

$$\text{Total asset turnover} = \frac{\text{Sales}}{\text{Total assets}}$$

$$= \frac{\$2{,}311}{\$3{,}588} = .64 \text{ times} \qquad (3.13)$$

In other words, for every dollar in assets, we generated $.64 in sales.

EXAMPLE 3.3

More Turnover   Suppose you find that a particular company generates $.40 in annual sales for every dollar in total assets. How often does this company turn over its total assets?

The total asset turnover here is .40 times per year. It takes 1/.40 = 2.5 years to turn assets over completely.

---

[2]Here we have implicitly assumed that all sales are credit sales. If they were not, we would simply use total credit sales in these calculations, not total sales.

PROFITABILITY MEASURES

The three types of measures we discuss in this section are probably the best-known and most widely used of all financial ratios. In one form or another, they are intended to measure how efficiently the firm uses its assets and how efficiently the firm manages its operations.

Profit Margin   Companies pay a great deal of attention to their *profit margins:*

$$\text{Profit margin} = \frac{\text{Net income}}{\text{Sales}}$$

$$= \frac{\$363}{\$2,311} = 15.7\%$$

$$(3.14)$$

This tells us that Prufrock, in an accounting sense, generates a little less than 16 cents in net income for every dollar in sales.

EBITDA Margin   Another commonly used measure of profitability is the EBITDA margin. As mentioned, EBITDA is a measure of before-tax operating cash flow. It adds back noncash expenses and does not include taxes or interest expense. As a consequence, EBITDA margin looks more directly at operating cash flows than does net income and does not include the effect of capital structure or taxes. For Prufrock, EBITDA margin is:

$$\frac{\text{EBITDA}}{\text{Sales}} = \frac{\$967 \text{ million}}{\$2,311 \text{ million}} = 41.8\%$$

All other things being equal, a relatively high margin is obviously desirable. This situation corresponds to low expense ratios relative to sales. However, we hasten to add that other things are often not equal.

For example, lowering our sales price will usually increase unit volume but will normally cause margins to shrink. Total profit (or, more importantly, operating cash flow) may go up or down, so the fact that margins are smaller isn't necessarily bad. After all, isn't it possible that, as the saying goes, "Our prices are so low that we lose money on everything we sell, but we make it up in volume"?[3]

Margins are very different for different industries. Grocery stores have a notoriously low profit margin, generally around 2 percent. In contrast, the profit margin for the pharmaceutical industry is about 13 percent. So, for example, it is not surprising that recent profit margins for Kroger and Pfizer were about 1.4 percent and 12.6 percent, respectively.

Return on Assets   *Return on assets* (ROA) is a measure of profit per dollar of assets. It can be defined several ways,[4] but the most common is:

$$\text{Return on assets} = \frac{\text{Net income}}{\text{Total assets}}$$

$$= \frac{\$363}{\$3,588} = 10.1\%$$

$$(3.15)$$

---

[3]No, it's not.

[4]For example, we might want a return on assets measure that is neutral with respect to capital structure (interest expense) and taxes. Such a measure for Prufrock would be:

$$\frac{\text{EBIT}}{\text{Total assets}} = \frac{\$691}{\$3,588} = 19.3\%$$

This measure has a very natural interpretation. If 19.3 percent exceeds Prufrock's borrowing rate, Prufrock will earn more money on its investments than it will pay out to its creditors. The surplus will be available to Prufrock's shareholders after adjusting for taxes.

Return on Equity   *Return on equity* (ROE) is a measure of how the stockholders fared during the year. Because benefiting shareholders is our goal, ROE is, in an accounting sense, the true bottom-line measure of performance. ROE is usually measured as:

$$\text{Return on equity} = \frac{\text{Net income}}{\text{Total equity}}$$
$$= \frac{\$363}{\$2,591} = 14\%$$

(3.16)

Therefore, for every dollar in equity, Prufrock generated 14 cents in profit; but, again, this is correct only in accounting terms.

Because ROA and ROE are such commonly cited numbers, we stress that it is important to remember they are accounting rates of return. For this reason, these measures should properly be called *return on book assets* and *return on book equity*. In addition, ROE is sometimes called *return on net worth*. Whatever it's called, it would be inappropriate to compare the result to, for example, an interest rate observed in the financial markets.

The fact that ROE exceeds ROA reflects Prufrock's use of financial leverage. We will examine the relationship between these two measures in the next section.

MARKET VALUE MEASURES

Our final group of measures is based, in part, on information not necessarily contained in financial statements—the market price per share of the stock. Obviously, these measures can be calculated directly only for publicly traded companies.

We assume that Prufrock has 33 million shares outstanding and the stock sold for $88 per share at the end of the year. If we recall that Prufrock's net income was $363 million, then we can calculate that its earnings per share were:

$$\text{EPS} = \frac{\text{Net income}}{\text{Shares outstanding}} = \frac{\$363}{33} = \$11$$

(3.17)

Price–Earnings Ratio   The first of our market value measures, the *price–earnings* or *PE ratio* (or multiple), is defined as:

$$\text{PE ratio} = \frac{\text{Price per share}}{\text{Earnings per share}}$$
$$= \frac{\$88}{\$11} = 8 \text{ times}$$

(3.18)

In the vernacular, we would say that Prufrock shares sell for eight times earnings, or we might say that Prufrock shares have, or "carry," a PE multiple of 8.

Because the PE ratio measures how much investors are willing to pay per dollar of current earnings, higher PEs are often taken to mean that the firm has significant prospects for future growth. Of course, if a firm had no or almost no earnings, its PE would probably be quite large; so, as always, care is needed in interpreting this ratio.

Market-to-Book Ratio   A second commonly quoted measure is the *market-to-book ratio:*

$$\text{Market-to-book ratio} = \frac{\text{Market value per share}}{\text{Book value per share}}$$
$$= \frac{\$88}{\$2,591/33} = \frac{\$88}{\$78.5} = 1.12 \text{ times}$$

(3.19)

Notice that book value per share is total equity (not just common stock) divided by the number of shares outstanding.

Book value per share is an accounting number that reflects historical costs. In a loose sense, the market-to-book ratio therefore compares the market value of the firm's investments to their cost. A value less than 1 could mean that the firm has not been successful overall in creating value for its stockholders.

Market Capitalization The market capitalization of a public firm is equal to the firm's stock market price per share multiplied by the number of shares outstanding. For Prufrock, this is:

$$\text{Price per share} \times \text{Shares outstanding} = \$88 \times 33 \text{ million} = \$2,904 \text{ million}$$

This is a useful number for potential buyers of Prufrock. A prospective buyer of all of the outstanding shares of Prufrock (in a merger or acquisition) would need to come up with at least $2,904 million plus a premium.

Enterprise Value Enterprise value is a measure of firm value that is very closely related to market capitalization. Instead of focusing on only the market value of outstanding shares of stock, it measures the market value of outstanding shares of stock plus the market value of outstanding interest bearing debt less cash on hand. We know the market capitalization of Prufrock but we do not know the market value of its outstanding interest bearing debt. In this situation, the common practice is to use the book value of outstanding interest bearing debt less cash on hand as an approximation. For Prufrock, enterprise value is (in millions):

$$\begin{aligned} \text{EV} &= \text{Market capitalization} + \text{Market value of interest bearing debt} - \text{Cash} \\ &= \$2,904 + (\$196 + 457) - \$98 = \$3,459 \text{ million} \end{aligned} \tag{3.20}$$

The purpose of the EV measure is to better estimate how much it would take to buy all of the outstanding stock of a firm and also to pay off the debt. The adjustment for cash is to recognize that if we were a buyer the cash could be used immediately to buy back debt or pay a dividend.

Enterprise Value Multiples Financial analysts use valuation multiples based upon a firm's enterprise value when the goal is to estimate the value of the firm's total business rather than just focusing on the value of its equity. To form an appropriate multiple, enterprise value is divided by EBITDA. For Prufrock, the enterprise value multiple is:

$$\frac{\text{EV}}{\text{EBITDA}} = \frac{\$3,459 \text{ million}}{\$967 \text{ million}} = 3.6 \text{ times}$$

The multiple is especially useful because it allows comparison of one firm with another when there are differences in capital structure (interest expense), taxes, or capital spending. The multiple is not directly affected by these differences.

Similar to PE ratios, we would expect a firm with high growth opportunities to have high EV multiples.

This completes our definition of some common ratios. We could tell you about more of them, but these are enough for now. We'll leave it here and go on to discuss some ways of using these ratios instead of just how to calculate them. Table 3.6 summarizes some of the ratios we've discussed.

Table 3.6   Common Financial Ratios

I. Short-Term Solvency, or Liquidity, Ratios

$$\text{Current ratio} = \frac{\text{Current assets}}{\text{Current liabilities}}$$

$$\text{Quick ratio} = \frac{\text{Current assets} - \text{Inventory}}{\text{Current liabilities}}$$

$$\text{Cash ratio} = \frac{\text{Cash}}{\text{Current liabilities}}$$

II. Long-Term Solvency, or Financial Leverage, Ratios

$$\text{Total debt ratio} = \frac{\text{Total assets} - \text{Total equity}}{\text{Total assets}}$$

$$\text{Debt–equity ratio} = \text{Total debt/Total equity}$$

$$\text{Equity multiplier} = \text{Total assets/Total equity}$$

$$\text{Times interest earned ratio} = \frac{\text{EBIT}}{\text{Interest}}$$

$$\text{Cash coverage ratio} = \frac{\text{EBITDA}}{\text{Interest}}$$

III. Asset Utilization, or Turnover, Ratios

$$\text{Inventory turnover} = \frac{\text{Cost of goods sold}}{\text{Inventory}}$$

$$\text{Days' sales in inventory} = \frac{365 \text{ days}}{\text{Inventory turnover}}$$

$$\text{Receivables turnover} = \frac{\text{Sales}}{\text{Accounts receivable}}$$

$$\text{Days' sales in receivables} = \frac{365 \text{ days}}{\text{Receivables turnover}}$$

$$\text{Total asset turnover} = \frac{\text{Sales}}{\text{Total assets}}$$

$$\text{Capital intensity} = \frac{\text{Total assets}}{\text{Sales}}$$

IV. Profitability Ratios

$$\text{Profit margin} = \frac{\text{Net income}}{\text{Sales}}$$

$$\text{Return on assets (ROA)} = \frac{\text{Net income}}{\text{Total assets}}$$

$$\text{Return on equity (ROE)} = \frac{\text{Net income}}{\text{Total equity}}$$

$$\text{ROE} = \frac{\text{Net income}}{\text{Sales}} \times \frac{\text{Sales}}{\text{Assets}} \times \frac{\text{Assets}}{\text{Equity}}$$

V. Market Value Ratios

$$\text{Price–earnings ratio} = \frac{\text{Price per share}}{\text{Earnings per share}}$$

$$\text{Market-to-book ratio} = \frac{\text{Market value per share}}{\text{Book value per share}}$$

$$\text{EV multiple} = \frac{\text{Enterprise value}}{\text{EBITDA}}$$

EXAMPLE 3.4

Consider the following 2010 data for Lowe's Companies and Home Depot (billions except for price per share):

	Lowe's Company, Inc.	The Home Depot, Inc.
Sales	$48.8	$68.0
EBIT	$ 3.2	$ 5.8
Net income	$ 2.0	$ 3.3
Cash	$ 0.7	$ 0.5
Depreciation	$ 1.6	$ 1.6
Interest bearing debt	$ 6.5	$ 8.7
Total assets	$33.7	$40.1
Price per share	$25	$37
Shares outstanding	1.3	1.6
Shareholder equity	$18.1	$18.9

(continued)

1. Determine the profit margin, ROE, market capitalization, enterprise value, PE multiple, and EV multiple for both Lowe's and Home Depot.

	Lowe's Company, Inc.	The Home Depot, Inc.
Equity multiplier	33.7/18.1 = 1.9	40.1/18.9 = 2.1
Total asset turnover	48.8/33.7 = 1.4	68.0/40.1 = 1.7
Profit margin	2.0/48.8 = 4.1%	3.3/68.0 = 4.9%
ROE	2.0/18.1 = 11.0%	3.3/18.9 = 17.5%
Market capitalization	1.3 × 25 = $32.5 billion	1.6 × 37 = $67.4 billion
Enterprise value	(1.3 × 25) + 6.5 − .7 = $38.3 billion	(1.6 × 37) + 8.7 − .5 = $67.4 billion
PE multiple	25/1.54 = 16.3	37/2.1 = 17.9
EBITDA	3.2 + 1.6 = $4.8	5.8 + 1.6 = $7.4
EV multiple	38.3/4.80 = 8.0	67.4/7.4 = 9.1

2. How would you describe these two companies from a financial point of view? Overall, they are similarly situated. In 2010, Home Depot had a higher ROE (partially because of a higher total asset turnover and a higher profit margin), but Lowe's had slightly lower PE and EV multiples. Both companies' PE multiples were somewhat above the general market, indicating possible future growth prospects.

3.3 The DuPont Identity

ExcelMaster
coverage online

This section will introduce text boxes, shapes, and lines.

As we mentioned in discussing ROA and ROE, the difference between these two profitability measures reflects the use of debt financing or financial leverage. We illustrate the relationship between these measures in this section by investigating a famous way of decomposing ROE into its component parts.

A CLOSER LOOK AT ROE

To begin, let's recall the definition of ROE:

$$\text{Return on equity} = \frac{\text{Net income}}{\text{Total equity}}$$

If we were so inclined, we could multiply this ratio by Assets/Assets without changing anything:

$$\text{Return on equity} = \frac{\text{Net income}}{\text{Total equity}} = \frac{\text{Net income}}{\text{Total equity}} \times \frac{\text{Assets}}{\text{Assets}}$$

$$= \frac{\text{Net income}}{\text{Assets}} \times \frac{\text{Assets}}{\text{Total equity}}$$

Notice that we have expressed the ROE as the product of two other ratios—ROA and the equity multiplier:

$$\text{ROE} = \text{ROA} \times \text{Equity multiplier} = \text{ROA} \times (1 + \text{Debt-equity ratio})$$

Looking back at Prufrock, for example, we see that the debt-equity ratio was .39 and ROA was 10.12 percent. Our work here implies that Prufrock's ROE, as we previously calculated, is:

$$\text{ROE} = 10.12\% \times 1.39 = 14\%$$

The difference between ROE and ROA can be substantial, particularly for certain businesses. For example, based on recent financial statements, U.S. Bancorp has an ROA of only 1.11 percent, which is actually fairly typical for a bank. However, banks tend to borrow a lot of money, and, as a result, have relatively large equity multipliers. For U.S. Bancorp, ROE is about 11.2 percent, implying an equity multiplier of 10.1.

We can further decompose ROE by multiplying the top and bottom by total sales:

$$\text{ROE} = \frac{\text{Sales}}{\text{Sales}} \times \frac{\text{Net income}}{\text{Assets}} \times \frac{\text{Assets}}{\text{Total equity}}$$

If we rearrange things a bit, ROE is:

$$\text{ROE} = \underbrace{\frac{\text{Net income}}{\text{Sales}} \times \frac{\text{Sales}}{\text{Assets}}}_{\text{Return on assets}} \times \frac{\text{Assets}}{\text{Total equity}} \qquad (3.21)$$

$$= \text{Profit margin} \times \text{Total asset turnover} \times \text{Equity multiplier}$$

What we have now done is to partition ROA into its two component parts, profit margin and total asset turnover. The last expression of the preceding equation is called the **DuPont identity** after the DuPont Corporation, which popularized its use.

We can check this relationship for Prufrock by noting that the profit margin was 15.7 percent and the total asset turnover was .64. ROE should thus be:

$$\begin{aligned} \text{ROE} &= \text{Profit margin} \times \text{Total asset turnover} \times \text{Equity multiplier} \\ &= 15.7\% \quad\;\; \times \quad\;\; .64 \quad\;\; \times \quad\;\; 1.39 \\ &= 14\% \end{aligned}$$

This 14 percent ROE is exactly what we had before.

The DuPont identity tells us that ROE is affected by three things:

1.   Operating efficiency (as measured by profit margin).
2.   Asset use efficiency (as measured by total asset turnover).
3.   Financial leverage (as measured by the equity multiplier).

Weakness in either operating or asset use efficiency (or both) will show up in a diminished return on assets, which will translate into a lower ROE.

Considering the DuPont identity, it appears that the ROE could be leveraged up by increasing the amount of debt in the firm. However, notice that increasing debt also increases interest expense, which reduces profit margins, which acts to reduce ROE. So, ROE could go up or down, depending. More important, the use of debt financing has a number of other effects, and, as we discuss at some length in later chapters, the amount of leverage a firm uses is governed by its capital structure policy.

Table 3.7   The DuPont Breakdown for Yahoo! and Google

Yahoo!

Twelve Months Ending	ROE	=	Profit Margin	×	Total Asset Turnover	×	Equity Multiplier
12/10	9.8%	=	19.5%	×	.424	×	1.19
12/09	4.8	=	9.3	×	.433	×	1.20
12/08	3.8	=	5.9	×	.527	×	1.22

Google

Twelve Months Ending	ROE	=	Profit Margin	×	Total Asset Turnover	×	Equity Multiplier
12/10	18.4%	=	29.0%	×	.507	×	1.25
12/09	18.1	=	27.6	×	.584	×	1.12
12/08	14.9	=	19.4	×	.686	×	1.12

The decomposition of ROE we've discussed in this section is a convenient way of systematically approaching financial statement analysis. If ROE is unsatisfactory by some measure, then the DuPont identity tells you where to start looking for the reasons.[5]

Yahoo! and Google are among the best-known Internet companies. They provide good examples of how DuPont analysis can be useful in helping to ask the right questions about a firm's financial performance. The DuPont breakdowns for Yahoo! and Google are summarized in Table 3.7. As shown, in 2010, Yahoo! had an ROE of 9.8 percent, up from its ROE in 2008 of 3.8 percent. In contrast, in 2010, Google had an ROE of 18.4 percent, up from its ROE in 2008 of 14.9 percent. Given this information, how is it possible that Google's ROE could be so much higher than the ROE of Yahoo! during this period of time, and what accounts for the increase in Yahoo!'s ROE?

Inspecting the DuPont breakdown, we see that Yahoo! and Google have very comparable asset turnover and financial leverage. However, Yahoo!'s profit margin increased from 5.9 percent to 19.5 percent. Meanwhile, Google's profit margin was 29.0 percent in 2010, up from 19.4 percent two years before. What can account for Google's advantage over Yahoo! in profit margins? Operating efficiencies can come from higher volumes, higher prices, and/or lower costs. Regardless of the source, it is clear that the big difference in ROE between the two firms can be attributed to the difference in profit margins.

PROBLEMS WITH FINANCIAL STATEMENT ANALYSIS

We continue our chapter by discussing some additional problems that can arise in using financial statements. In one way or another, the basic problem with financial statement analysis is that there is no underlying theory to help us identify which quantities to look at and to guide us in establishing benchmarks.

As we discuss in other chapters, there are many cases in which financial theory and economic logic provide guidance in making judgments about value and risk. Little

---

[5]Perhaps this is a time to mention Abraham Briloff, a well-known financial commentator who famously remarked that "financial statements are like fine perfume; to be sniffed but not swallowed."

such help exists with financial statements. This is why we can't say which ratios matter the most and what a high or low value might be.

One particularly severe problem is that many firms are conglomerates, owning more or less unrelated lines of business. GE is a well-known example. The consolidated financial statements for such firms don't really fit any neat industry category. More generally, the kind of peer group analysis we have been describing is going to work best when the firms are strictly in the same line of business, the industry is competitive, and there is only one way of operating.

Another problem that is becoming increasingly common is that major competitors and natural peer group members in an industry may be scattered around the globe. The automobile industry is an obvious example. The problem here is that financial statements from outside the United States do not necessarily conform to GAAP. The existence of different standards and procedures makes it difficult to compare financial statements across national borders.

Even companies that are clearly in the same line of business may not be comparable. For example, electric utilities engaged primarily in power generation are all classified in the same group. This group is often thought to be relatively homogeneous. However, most utilities operate as regulated monopolies, so they don't compete much with each other, at least not historically. Many have stockholders, and many are organized as cooperatives with no stockholders. There are several different ways of generating power, ranging from hydroelectric to nuclear, so the operating activities of these utilities can differ quite a bit. Finally, profitability is strongly affected by the regulatory environment, so utilities in different locations can be similar but show different profits.

Several other general problems frequently crop up. First, different firms use different accounting procedures—for inventory, for example. This makes it difficult to compare statements. Second, different firms end their fiscal years at different times. For firms in seasonal businesses (such as a retailer with a large Christmas season), this can lead to difficulties in comparing balance sheets because of fluctuations in accounts during the year. Finally, for any particular firm, unusual or transient events, such as a one-time profit from an asset sale, may affect financial performance. Such events can give misleading signals as we compare firms.

3.4 Financial Models

ExcelMaster
coverage online

Financial planning is another important use of financial statements. Most financial planning models output pro forma financial statements, where pro forma means "as a matter of form." In our case, this means that financial statements are the form we use to summarize the projected future financial status of a company.

A SIMPLE FINANCIAL PLANNING MODEL

We can begin our discussion of financial planning models with a relatively simple example. The Computerfield Corporation's financial statements from the most recent year are shown below.

Unless otherwise stated, the financial planners at Computerfield assume that all variables are tied directly to sales and current relationships are optimal. This means that all items will grow at exactly the same rate as sales. This is obviously oversimplified; we use this assumption only to make a point.

COMPUTERFIELD CORPORATION
Financial Statements

Income Statement		Balance Sheet			
Sales	$1,000	Assets	$500	Debt	$250
Costs	800			Equity	250
Net income	$ 200	Total	$500	Total	$500

Suppose sales increase by 20 percent, rising from $1,000 to $1,200. Planners would then also forecast a 20 percent increase in costs, from $800 to $800 × 1.2 = $960. The pro forma income statement would thus look like this:

Pro Forma
Income Statement

Sales	$1,200
Costs	960
Net income	$ 240

The assumption that all variables will grow by 20 percent lets us easily construct the pro forma balance sheet as well:

Pro Forma Balance Sheet

Assets	$600 (+100)	Debt	$300 (+50)
		Equity	300 (+50)
Total	$600 (+100)	Total	$600 (+100)

Notice we have simply increased every item by 20 percent. The numbers in parentheses are the dollar changes for the different items.

Now we have to reconcile these two pro forma statements. How, for example, can net income be equal to $240 and equity increase by only $50? The answer is that Computerfield must have paid out the difference of $240 − 50 = $190, possibly as a cash dividend. In this case dividends are the "plug" variable.

Suppose Computerfield does not pay out the $190. In this case, the addition to retained earnings is the full $240. Computerfield's equity will thus grow to $250 (the starting amount) plus $240 (net income), or $490, and debt must be retired to keep total assets equal to $600.

With $600 in total assets and $490 in equity, debt will have to be $600 − 490 = $110. Because we started with $250 in debt, Computerfield will have to retire $250 − 110 = $140 in debt. The resulting pro forma balance sheet would look like this:

Planware provides insight into cash flow forecasting at www.planware.org.

Pro Forma Balance Sheet

Assets	$600 (+100)	Debt	$110 (−140)
		Equity	490 (+240)
Total	$600 (+100)	Total	$600 (+100)

In this case, debt is the plug variable used to balance projected total assets and liabilities.

This example shows the interaction between sales growth and financial policy. As sales increase, so do total assets. This occurs because the firm must invest in net working capital and fixed assets to support higher sales levels. Because assets are growing, total liabilities and equity, the right side of the balance sheet, will grow as well.

The thing to notice from our simple example is that the way the liabilities and owners' equity change depends on the firm's financing policy and its dividend policy. The growth in assets requires that the firm decide on how to finance that growth. This is strictly a managerial decision. Note that in our example the firm needed no outside funds. This won't usually be the case, so we explore a more detailed situation in the next section.

THE PERCENTAGE OF SALES APPROACH

In the previous section, we described a simple planning model in which every item increased at the same rate as sales. This may be a reasonable assumption for some elements. For others, such as long-term borrowing, it probably is not: The amount of long-term borrowing is set by management, and it does not necessarily relate directly to the level of sales.

In this section, we describe an extended version of our simple model. The basic idea is to separate the income statement and balance sheet accounts into two groups, those that vary directly with sales and those that do not. Given a sales forecast, we will then be able to calculate how much financing the firm will need to support the predicted sales level.

The financial planning model we describe next is based on the **percentage of sales approach.** Our goal here is to develop a quick and practical way of generating pro forma statements. We defer discussion of some "bells and whistles" to a later section.

The Income Statement   We start out with the most recent income statement for the Rosengarten Corporation, as shown in Table 3.8. Notice that we have still simplified things by including costs, depreciation, and interest in a single cost figure.

Rosengarten has projected a 25 percent increase in sales for the coming year, so we are anticipating sales of $1,000 \times 1.25 = $1,250. To generate a pro forma income statement, we assume that total costs will continue to run at $800/1,000 = 80 percent of sales. With this assumption, Rosengarten's pro forma income statement is as shown in Table 3.9. The effect here of assuming that costs are a constant percentage of sales is to assume that the profit margin is constant. To check this, notice that the profit

Table 3.8

ROSENGARTEN CORPORATION Income Statement		
Sales		$1,000
Costs		800
Taxable income		$ 200
Taxes (34%)		68
Net income		$ 132
Dividends	$44	
Addition to retained earnings	88	

Table 3.9

ROSENGARTEN CORPORATION
Pro Forma Income Statement

Sales (projected)	$1,250
Costs (80% of sales)	1,000
Taxable income	$ 250
Taxes (34%)	85
Net income	$ 165

margin was $132/1,000 = 13.2 percent. In our pro forma statement, the profit margin is $165/1,250 = 13.2 percent; so it is unchanged.

Next, we need to project the dividend payment. This amount is up to Rosengarten's management. We will assume Rosengarten has a policy of paying out a constant fraction of net income in the form of a cash dividend. For the most recent year, the **dividend payout ratio** was:

$$\text{Dividend payout ratio} = \text{Cash dividends/Net income} \quad (3.22)$$
$$= \$44/132 = 33\ 1/3\%$$

We can also calculate the ratio of the addition to retained earnings to net income:

$$\text{Addition to retained earnings/Net income} = \$88/132 = 66\ 2/3\%$$

This ratio is called the **retention ratio** or **plowback ratio,** and it is equal to 1 minus the dividend payout ratio because everything not paid out is retained. Assuming that the payout ratio is constant, the projected dividends and addition to retained earnings will be:

$$\text{Projected dividends paid to shareholders} = \$165 \times 1/3 = \$\ 55$$
$$\text{Projected addition to retained earnings} = \$165 \times 2/3 = \underline{\ 110}$$
$$\underline{\underline{\$165}}$$

The Balance Sheet To generate a pro forma balance sheet, we start with the most recent statement, as shown in Table 3.10.

On our balance sheet, we assume that some items vary directly with sales and others do not. For those items that vary with sales, we express each as a percentage of sales for the year just completed. When an item does not vary directly with sales, we write "n/a" for "not applicable."

For example, on the asset side, inventory is equal to 60 percent of sales (= $600/1,000) for the year just ended. We assume this percentage applies to the coming year, so for each $1 increase in sales, inventory will rise by $.60. More generally, the ratio of total assets to sales for the year just ended is $3,000/1,000 = 3, or 300 percent.

This ratio of total assets to sales is sometimes called the **capital intensity ratio.** It tells us the amount of assets needed to generate $1 in sales; the higher the ratio is, the more capital intensive is the firm. Notice also that this ratio is just the reciprocal of the total asset turnover ratio we defined previously.

For Rosengarten, assuming that this ratio is constant, it takes $3 in total assets to generate $1 in sales (apparently Rosengarten is in a relatively capital-intensive business). Therefore, if sales are to increase by $100, Rosengarten will have to increase total assets by three times this amount, or $300.

Table 3.10

ROSENGARTEN CORPORATION
Balance Sheet

Assets			Liabilities and Owners' Equity		
	$	Percentage of Sales		$	Percentage of Sales
Current assets			Current liabilities		
Cash	$ 160	16%	Accounts payable	$ 300	30%
Accounts receivable	440	44	Notes payable	100	n/a
Inventory	600	60	Total	$ 400	n/a
Total	$1,200	120	Long-term debt	$ 800	n/a
Fixed assets			Owners' equity		
Net plant and equipment	$1,800	180	Common stock and paid-in surplus	$ 800	n/a
			Retained earnings	1,000	n/a
			Total	$1,800	n/a
Total assets	$3,000	300%	Total liabilities and owners' equity	$3,000	n/a

On the liability side of the balance sheet, we show accounts payable varying with sales. The reason is that we expect to place more orders with our suppliers as sales volume increases, so payables will change "spontaneously" with sales. Notes payable, on the other hand, represents short-term debt such as bank borrowing. This will not vary unless we take specific actions to change the amount, so we mark this item as "n/a."

Similarly, we use "n/a" for long-term debt because it won't automatically change with sales. The same is true for common stock and paid-in surplus. The last item on the right side, retained earnings, will vary with sales, but it won't be a simple percentage of sales. Instead, we will explicitly calculate the change in retained earnings based on our projected net income and dividends.

We can now construct a partial pro forma balance sheet for Rosengarten. We do this by using the percentages we have just calculated wherever possible to calculate the projected amounts. For example, net fixed assets are 180 percent of sales; so, with a new sales level of $1,250, the net fixed asset amount will be $1.80 \times \$1,250 = \$2,250$, representing an increase of $\$2,250 - 1,800 = \$450$ in plant and equipment. It is important to note that for items that don't vary directly with sales, we initially assume no change and simply write in the original amounts. The result is shown in Table 3.11. Notice that the change in retained earnings is equal to the $110 addition to retained earnings we calculated earlier.

Inspecting our pro forma balance sheet, we notice that assets are projected to increase by $750. However, without additional financing, liabilities and equity will increase by only $185, leaving a shortfall of $750 - 185 = \$565$. We label this amount *external financing needed* (EFN).

Rather than create pro forma statements, if we were so inclined, we could calculate EFN directly as follows:

$$EFN = \frac{\text{Assets}}{\text{Sales}} \times \Delta\text{Sales} - \frac{\text{Spontaneous liabilities}}{\text{Sales}} \times \Delta\text{Sales} - PM$$
$$\times \text{Projected sales} \times (1 - d)$$

$$(3.23)$$

Table 3.11

ROSENGARTEN CORPORATION Partial Pro Forma Balance Sheet					
Assets			**Liabilities and Owners' Equity**		
	Next Year	Change from Current Year		Next Year	Change from Current Year
Current assets			Current liabilities		
Cash	$ 200	$ 40	Accounts payable	$ 375	$ 75
Accounts receivable	550	110	Notes payable	100	0
Inventory	750	150	Total	$ 475	$ 75
Total	$1,500	$300	Long-term debt	$ 800	$ 0
Fixed assets			Owners' equity		
Net plant and equipment	$2,250	$450	Common stock and paid-in surplus	$ 800	$ 0
			Retained earnings	1,110	110
			Total	$1,910	$110
Total assets	$3,750	$750	Total liabilities and owners' equity	$3,185	$185
			External financing needed	$ 565	$565

In this expression, "ΔSales" is the projected change in sales (in dollars). In our example projected sales for next year are $1,250, an increase of $250 over the previous year, so ΔSales = $250. By "Spontaneous liabilities," we mean liabilities that naturally move up and down with sales. For Rosengarten, the spontaneous liabilities are the $300 in accounts payable. Finally, *PM* and *d* are the profit margin and dividend payout ratios, which we previously calculated as 13.2 percent and 33 1/3 percent, respectively. Total assets and sales are $3,000 and $1,000, respectively, so we have:

$$EFN = \frac{\$3,000}{1,000} \times \$250 - \frac{\$300}{1,000} \times \$250 - .132 \times \$1,250 \times \left(1 - \frac{1}{3}\right) = \$565$$

In this calculation, notice that there are three parts. The first part is the projected increase in assets, which is calculated using the capital intensity ratio. The second is the spontaneous increase in liabilities. The third part is the product of profit margin and projected sales, which is projected net income, multiplied by the retention ratio. Thus, the third part is the projected addition to retained earnings.

A Particular Scenario   Our financial planning model now reminds us of one of those good news–bad news jokes. The good news is we're projecting a 25 percent increase in sales. The bad news is this isn't going to happen unless Rosengarten can somehow raise $565 in new financing.

This is a good example of how the planning process can point out problems and potential conflicts. If, for example, Rosengarten has a goal of not borrowing any additional funds and not selling any new equity, then a 25 percent increase in sales is probably not feasible.

Table 3.12

ROSENGARTEN CORPORATION
Pro Forma Balance Sheet

Assets			Liabilities and Owners' Equity		
	Next Year	Change from Current Year		Next Year	Change from Current Year
Current assets			Current liabilities		
Cash	$ 200	$ 40	Accounts payable	$ 375	$ 75
Accounts receivable	550	110	Notes payable	325	225
Inventory	750	150	Total	$ 700	$300
Total	$1,500	$300	Long-term debt	$1,140	$340
Fixed assets			Owners' equity		
Net plant and equipment	$2,250	$450	Common stock and paid-in surplus	$ 800	$ 0
			Retained earnings	1,110	110
			Total	$1,910	$110
Total assets	$3,750	$750	Total liabilities and owners' equity	$3,750	$750

If we take the need for $565 in new financing as given, we know that Rosengarten has three possible sources: short-term borrowing, long-term borrowing, and new equity. The choice of some combination among these three is up to management; we will illustrate only one of the many possibilities.

Suppose Rosengarten decides to borrow the needed funds. In this case, the firm might choose to borrow some over the short term and some over the long term. For example, current assets increased by $300 whereas current liabilities rose by only $75. Rosengarten could borrow $300 − 75 = $225 in short-term notes payable and leave total net working capital unchanged. With $565 needed, the remaining $565 − 225 = $340 would have to come from long-term debt. Table 3.12 shows the completed pro forma balance sheet for Rosengarten.

We have used a combination of short- and long-term debt as the plug here, but we emphasize that this is just one possible strategy; it is not necessarily the best one by any means. We could (and should) investigate many other scenarios. The various ratios we discussed earlier come in handy here. For example, with the scenario we have just examined, we would surely want to examine the current ratio and the total debt ratio to see if we were comfortable with the new projected debt levels.

3.5 External Financing and Growth

ExcelMaster
coverage online

This section will introduce
data tables and graphing.

External financing needed and growth are obviously related. All other things staying the same, the higher the rate of growth in sales or assets, the greater will be the need for external financing. In the previous section, we took a growth rate as given, and then we determined the amount of external financing needed to support that growth. In this section, we turn things around a bit. We will take the firm's financial policy as given and then examine the relationship between that financial policy and the firm's ability to finance new investments and thereby grow.

We emphasize that we are focusing on growth not because growth is an appropriate goal; instead, for our purposes, growth is simply a convenient means of examining the interactions between investment and financing decisions. In effect, we assume that the use of growth as a basis for planning is just a reflection of the very high level of aggregation used in the planning process.

EFN AND GROWTH

The first thing we need to do is establish the relationship between EFN and growth. To do this, we introduce the simplified income statement and balance sheet for the Hoffman Company in Table 3.13. Notice that we have simplified the balance sheet by combining short-term and long-term debt into a single total debt figure. Effectively, we are assuming that none of the current liabilities vary spontaneously with sales. This assumption isn't as restrictive as it sounds. If any current liabilities (such as accounts payable) vary with sales, we can assume that any such accounts have been netted out in current assets. Also, we continue to combine depreciation, interest, and costs on the income statement.

Suppose the Hoffman Company is forecasting next year's sales level at $600, a $100 increase. Notice that the percentage increase in sales is $100/500 = 20 percent. Using the percentage of sales approach and the figures in Table 3.13, we can prepare a pro forma income statement and balance sheet as in Table 3.14. As Table 3.14 illustrates, at a 20 percent growth rate, Hoffman needs $100 in new assets. The projected addition to retained earnings is $52.8, so the external financing needed, EFN, is $100 − 52.8 = $47.2.

Table 3.13

HOFFMAN COMPANY
Income Statement and Balance Sheet

Income Statement

Sales		$500
Costs		400
Taxable income		$100
Taxes (34%)		34
Net income		$ 66
Dividends	$22	
Addition to retained earnings	44	

Balance Sheet

Assets			Liabilities and Owners' Equity		
	$	Percentage of Sales		$	Percentage of Sales
Current assets	$200	40%	Total debt	$250	n/a
Net fixed assets	300	60	Owners' equity	250	n/a
Total assets	$500	100%	Total liabilities and owners' equity	$500	n/a

Table 3.14

| HOFFMAN COMPANY |
| Pro Forma Income Statement and Balance Sheet |

Income Statement

Sales (projected)	$600.0
Costs (80% of sales)	480.0
Taxable income	$120.0
Taxes (34%)	40.8
Net income	$ 79.2
Dividends	$26.4
Addition to retained earnings	52.8

Balance Sheet

Assets			Liabilities and Owners' Equity		
	$	Percentage of Sales		$	Percentage of Sales
Current assets	$240.0	40%	Total debt	$250.0	n/a
Net fixed assets	360.0	60	Owners' equity	302.8	n/a
Total assets	$600.0	100%	Total liabilities and owners' equity	$552.8	n/a
			External financing needed	$ 47.2	n/a

Notice that the debt–equity ratio for Hoffman was originally (from Table 3.13) equal to $250/250 = 1.0. We will assume that the Hoffman Company does not wish to sell new equity. In this case, the $47.2 in EFN will have to be borrowed. What will the new debt–equity ratio be? From Table 3.14, we know that total owners' equity is projected at $302.8. The new total debt will be the original $250 plus $47.2 in new borrowing, or $297.2 total. The debt–equity ratio thus falls slightly from 1.0 to $297.2/302.8 = .98.

Table 3.15 shows EFN for several different growth rates. The projected addition to retained earnings and the projected debt–equity ratio for each scenario are also given (you should probably calculate a few of these for practice). In determining the debt–equity ratios, we assumed that any needed funds were borrowed, and we also

Table 3.15
Growth and Projected EFN for the Hoffman Company

Projected Sales Growth	Increase in Assets Required	Addition to Retained Earnings	External Financing Needed, EFN	Projected Debt–Equity Ratio
0%	$ 0	$44.0	−$44.0	.70
5	25	46.2	−21.2	.77
10	50	48.4	1.6	.84
15	75	50.6	24.4	.91
20	100	52.8	47.2	.98
25	125	55.0	70.0	1.05

Figure 3.1
Growth and
Related Financing
Needed for the
Hoffman Company

assumed any surplus funds were used to pay off debt. Thus, for the zero growth case the debt falls by $44, from $250 to $206. In Table 3.15, notice that the increase in assets required is simply equal to the original assets of $500 multiplied by the growth rate. Similarly, the addition to retained earnings is equal to the original $44 plus $44 times the growth rate.

Table 3.15 shows that for relatively low growth rates, Hoffman will run a surplus, and its debt–equity ratio will decline. Once the growth rate increases to about 10 percent, however, the surplus becomes a deficit. Furthermore, as the growth rate exceeds approximately 20 percent, the debt–equity ratio passes its original value of 1.0.

Figure 3.1 illustrates the connection between growth in sales and external financing needed in more detail by plotting asset needs and additions to retained earnings from Table 3.15 against the growth rates. As shown, the need for new assets grows at a much faster rate than the addition to retained earnings, so the internal financing provided by the addition to retained earnings rapidly disappears.

As this discussion shows, whether a firm runs a cash surplus or deficit depends on growth. Microsoft is a good example. Its revenue growth in the 1990s was amazing, averaging well over 30 percent per year for the decade. Growth slowed down noticeably over the 2000–2006 period, but, nonetheless, Microsoft's combination of growth and substantial profit margins led to enormous cash surpluses. In part because Microsoft paid few dividends, the cash really piled up; in 2011, Microsoft's cash and short-term investment horde exceeded $50 billion.

FINANCIAL POLICY AND GROWTH

Based on our discussion just preceding, we see that there is a direct link between growth and external financing. In this section, we discuss two growth rates that are particularly useful in long-range planning.

The Internal Growth Rate   The first growth rate of interest is the maximum growth rate that can be achieved with no external financing of any kind. We will call this the **internal growth rate** because this is the rate the firm can maintain with internal financing only. In Figure 3.1, this internal growth rate is represented by the point where the two lines cross. At this point, the required increase in assets is exactly equal to the addition to retained earnings, and EFN is therefore zero. We have seen that this happens when the growth rate is slightly less than 10 percent. With a little algebra (see Problem 28 at the end of the chapter), we can define this growth rate more precisely as:

$$\text{Internal growth rate} = \frac{\text{ROA} \times b}{1 - \text{ROA} \times b} \quad (3.24)$$

where ROA is the return on assets we discussed earlier, and b is the plowback, or retention, ratio also defined earlier in this chapter.

For the Hoffman Company, net income was $66 and total assets were $500. ROA is thus $66/500 = 13.2 percent. Of the $66 net income, $44 was retained, so the plowback ratio, b, is $44/66 = 2/3. With these numbers, we can calculate the internal growth rate as:

$$\begin{aligned}\text{Internal growth rate} &= \frac{\text{ROA} \times b}{1 - \text{ROA} \times b} \\ &= \frac{.132 \times (2/3)}{1 - .132 \times (2/3)} \\ &= 9.65\% \end{aligned}$$

Thus, the Hoffman Company can expand at a maximum rate of 9.65 percent per year without external financing.

The Sustainable Growth Rate   We have seen that if the Hoffman Company wishes to grow more rapidly than at a rate of 9.65 percent per year, external financing must be arranged. The second growth rate of interest is the maximum growth rate a firm can achieve with no external *equity* financing while it maintains a constant debt–equity ratio. This rate is commonly called the **sustainable growth rate** because it is the maximum rate of growth a firm can maintain without increasing its overall financial leverage.

There are various reasons why a firm might wish to avoid equity sales. For example, new equity sales can be expensive because of the substantial fees that may be involved. Alternatively, the current owners may not wish to bring in new owners or contribute additional equity. Why a firm might view a particular debt–equity ratio as optimal is discussed in later chapters; for now, we will take it as given.

Based on Table 3.15, the sustainable growth rate for Hoffman is approximately 20 percent because the debt–equity ratio is near 1.0 at that growth rate. The precise value can be calculated as follows (see Problem 28 at the end of the chapter):

$$\text{Sustainable growth rate} = \frac{\text{ROE} \times b}{1 - \text{ROE} \times b} \quad (3.25)$$

This is identical to the internal growth rate except that ROE, return on equity, is used instead of ROA.

For the Hoffman Company, net income was $66 and total equity was $250; ROE is thus $66/250 = 26.4 percent. The plowback ratio, b, is still 2/3, so we can calculate the sustainable growth rate as:

$$\begin{aligned}\text{Sustainable growth rate} &= \frac{\text{ROE} \times b}{1 - \text{ROE} \times b} \\ &= \frac{.264 \times (2/3)}{1 - .264 \times (2/3)} \\ &= 21.36\% \end{aligned}$$

Thus, the Hoffman Company can expand at a maximum rate of 21.36 percent per year without external equity financing.

EXAMPLE 3.5

Sustainable Growth   Suppose Hoffman grows at exactly the sustainable growth rate of 21.36 percent. What will the pro forma statements look like?

At a 21.36 percent growth rate, sales will rise from $500 to $606.8. The pro forma income statement will look like this:

HOFFMAN COMPANY
Pro Forma Income Statement

Sales (projected)	$606.8
Costs (80% of sales)	485.4
Taxable income	$121.4
Taxes (34%)	41.3
Net income	$ 80.1
Dividends	$26.7
Addition to retained earnings	53.4

We construct the balance sheet just as we did before. Notice, in this case, that owners' equity will rise from $250 to $303.4 because the addition to retained earnings is $53.4.

HOFFMAN COMPANY
Pro Forma Balance Sheet

Assets	$	Percentage of Sales	Liabilities and Owners' Equity	$	Percentage of Sales
Current assets	$242.7	40%	Total debt	$250.0	n/a
Net fixed assets	364.1	60	Owners' equity	303.4	n/a
Total assets	$606.8	100%	Total liabilities and owners' equity	$553.4	n/a
			External financing needed	$ 53.4	n/a

As illustrated, EFN is $53.4. If Hoffman borrows this amount, then total debt will rise to $303.4, and the debt–equity ratio will be exactly 1.0, which verifies our earlier calculation. At any other growth rate, something would have to change.

Determinants of Growth   Earlier in this chapter, we saw that the return on equity, ROE, could be decomposed into its various components using the DuPont identity. Because ROE appears so prominently in the determination of the sustainable growth rate, it is obvious that the factors important in determining ROE are also important determinants of growth.

From our previous discussions, we know that ROE can be written as the product of three factors:

$$\text{ROE} = \text{Profit margin} \times \text{Total asset turnover} \times \text{Equity multiplier}$$

If we examine our expression for the sustainable growth rate, we see that anything that increases ROE will increase the sustainable growth rate by making the top bigger and the bottom smaller. Increasing the plowback ratio will have the same effect.

Putting it all together, what we have is that a firm's ability to sustain growth depends explicitly on the following four factors:

1. *Profit margin:* An increase in profit margin will increase the firm's ability to generate funds internally and thereby increase its sustainable growth.

2. *Dividend policy:* A decrease in the percentage of net income paid out as dividends will increase the retention ratio. This increases internally generated equity and thus increases sustainable growth.

3. *Financial policy:* An increase in the debt–equity ratio increases the firm's financial leverage. Because this makes additional debt financing available, it increases the sustainable growth rate.

4. *Total asset turnover:* An increase in the firm's total asset turnover increases the sales generated for each dollar in assets. This decreases the firm's need for new assets as sales grow and thereby increases the sustainable growth rate. Notice that increasing total asset turnover is the same thing as decreasing capital intensity.

The sustainable growth rate is a very useful planning number. What it illustrates is the explicit relationship between the firm's four major areas of concern: its operating efficiency as measured by profit margin, its asset use efficiency as measured by total asset turnover, its dividend policy as measured by the retention ratio, and its financial policy as measured by the debt–equity ratio.

EXAMPLE 3.6

Profit Margins and Sustainable Growth The Sandar Co. has a debt–equity ratio of .5, a profit margin of 3 percent, a dividend payout ratio of 40 percent, and a capital intensity ratio of 1. What is its sustainable growth rate? If Sandar desired a 10 percent sustainable growth rate and planned to achieve this goal by improving profit margins, what would you think?

ROE is .03 × 1 × 1.5 = 4.5 percent. The retention ratio is 1 − .40 = .60. Sustainable growth is thus .045(.60)/[1 − .045(.60)] = 2.77 percent.

For the company to achieve a 10 percent growth rate, the profit margin will have to rise. To see this, assume that sustainable growth is equal to 10 percent and then solve for profit margin, PM:

$$.10 = PM(1.5)(.6)/[1 − PM(1.5)(.6)]$$
$$PM = .1/.99 = 10.1\%$$

For the plan to succeed, the necessary increase in profit margin is substantial, from 3 percent to about 10 percent. This may not be feasible.

Given values for all four of these, there is only one growth rate that can be achieved. This is an important point, so it bears restating:

If a firm does not wish to sell new equity and its profit margin, dividend policy, financial policy, and total asset turnover (or capital intensity) are all fixed, then there is only one possible growth rate.

74   **Part I**   Overview

Table 3.16
Summary of Internal and Sustainable Growth Rates

I. Internal Growth Rate

$$\text{Internal growth rate} = \frac{\text{ROA} \times b}{1 - \text{ROA} \times b}$$

where

ROA = Return on assets = Net income/Total assets

   b = Plowback (retention) ratio

   = Addition to retained earnings/Net income

The internal growth rate is the maximum growth rate that can be achieved with no external financing of any kind.

II. Sustainable Growth Rate

$$\text{Sustainable growth rate} = \frac{\text{ROE} \times b}{1 - \text{ROE} \times b}$$

where

   ROE = Return on equity = Net income/Total equity

   b = Plowback (retention) ratio

   = Addition to retained earnings/Net income

The sustainable growth rate is the maximum growth rate that can be achieved with no external equity financing while maintaining a constant debt–equity ratio.

One of the primary benefits of financial planning is that it ensures internal consistency among the firm's various goals. The concept of the sustainable growth rate captures this element nicely. Also, we now see how a financial planning model can be used to test the feasibility of a planned growth rate. If sales are to grow at a rate higher than the sustainable growth rate, the firm must increase profit margins, increase total asset turnover, increase financial leverage, increase earnings retention, or sell new shares.

The two growth rates, internal and sustainable, are summarized in Table 3.16.

A NOTE ABOUT SUSTAINABLE GROWTH RATE CALCULATIONS

Very commonly, the sustainable growth rate is calculated using just the numerator in our expression, ROE $\times$ b. This causes some confusion, which we can clear up here. The issue has to do with how ROE is computed. Recall that ROE is calculated as net income divided by total equity. If total equity is taken from an ending balance sheet (as we have done consistently, and is commonly done in practice), then our formula is the right one. However, if total equity is from the beginning of the period, then the simpler formula is the correct one.

In principle, you'll get exactly the same sustainable growth rate regardless of which way you calculate it (as long as you match up the ROE calculation with the right formula). In reality, you may see some differences because of accounting-related complications. By the way, if you use the average of beginning and ending equity (as some advocate), yet another formula is needed. Also, all of our comments here apply to the internal growth rate as well.

In Their Own Words

ROBERT C. HIGGINS ON SUSTAINABLE GROWTH

Most financial officers know intuitively that it takes money to make money. Rapid sales growth requires increased assets in the form of accounts receivable, inventory, and fixed plant, which, in turn, require money to pay for assets. They also know that if their company does not have the money when needed, it can literally "grow broke." The sustainable growth equation states these intuitive truths explicitly.

Sustainable growth is often used by bankers and other external analysts to assess a company's creditworthiness. They are aided in this exercise by several sophisticated computer software packages that provide detailed analyses of the company's past financial performance, including its annual sustainable growth rate.

Bankers use this information in several ways. Quick comparison of a company's actual growth rate to its sustainable rate tells the banker what issues will be at the top of management's financial agenda. If actual growth consistently exceeds sustainable growth, management's problem will be where to get the cash to finance growth. The banker thus can anticipate interest in loan products. Conversely, if sustainable growth consistently exceeds actual, the banker had best be prepared to talk about investment products because management's problem will be what to do with all the cash that keeps piling up in the till.

Bankers also find the sustainable growth equation useful for explaining to financially inexperienced small business owners and overly optimistic entrepreneurs that, for the long-run viability of their business, it is necessary to keep growth and profitability in proper balance.

Finally, comparison of actual to sustainable growth rates helps a banker understand why a loan applicant needs money and for how long the need might continue. In one instance, a loan applicant requested $100,000 to pay off several insistent suppliers and promised to repay in a few months when he collected some accounts receivable that were coming due. A sustainable growth analysis revealed that the firm had been growing at four to six times its sustainable growth rate and that this pattern was likely to continue in the foreseeable future. This alerted the banker that impatient suppliers were only a symptom of the much more fundamental disease of overly rapid growth, and that a $100,000 loan would likely prove to be only the down payment on a much larger, multiyear commitment.

Robert C. Higgins is Professor of Finance at the University of Washington. He pioneered the use of sustainable growth as a tool for financial analysis.

3.6 Some Caveats Regarding Financial Planning Models

Financial planning models do not always ask the right questions. A primary reason is that they tend to rely on accounting relationships and not financial relationships. In particular, the three basic elements of firm value tend to get left out—namely, cash flow size, risk, and timing.

Because of this, financial planning models sometimes do not produce output that gives the user many meaningful clues about what strategies will lead to increases in value. Instead, they divert the user's attention to questions concerning the association of, say, the debt–equity ratio and firm growth.

The financial model we used for the Hoffman Company was simple—in fact, too simple. Our model, like many in use today, is really an accounting statement generator at heart. Such models are useful for pointing out inconsistencies and reminding us of financial needs, but they offer little guidance concerning what to do about these problems.

In closing our discussion, we should add that financial planning is an iterative process. Plans are created, examined, and modified over and over. The final plan will be

76   **Part I**   Overview

a result negotiated between all the different parties to the process. In fact, long-term financial planning in most corporations relies on what might be called the Procrustes approach.[6] Upper-level management has a goal in mind, and it is up to the planning staff to rework and to ultimately deliver a feasible plan that meets that goal.

The final plan will therefore implicitly contain different goals in different areas and also satisfy many constraints. For this reason, such a plan need not be a dispassionate assessment of what we think the future will bring; it may instead be a means of reconciling the planned activities of different groups and a way of setting common goals for the future.

◀ To test your mastery of this material, take a quiz at mhhe. com/rwj

However it is done, the important thing to remember is that financial planning should not become a purely mechanical exercise. If it does, it will probably focus on the wrong things. Nevertheless, the alternative to planning is stumbling into the future. Perhaps the immortal Yogi Berra (the baseball catcher, not the cartoon character), said it best: "Ya gotta watch out if you don't know where you're goin'. You just might not get there."[7]

---

[6]In Greek mythology, Procrustes is a giant who seizes travelers and ties them to an iron bed. He stretches them or cuts off their legs as needed to make them fit the bed.

[7]We're not *exactly* sure what this means, either, but we like the sound of it.

Summary and Conclusions

This chapter focuses on working with information contained in financial statements. Specifically, we studied standardized financial statements, ratio analysis, and long-term financial planning.

1. We explained that differences in firm size make it difficult to compare financial statements, and we discussed how to form common-size statements to make comparisons easier and more meaningful.

2. Evaluating ratios of accounting numbers is another way of comparing financial statement information. We defined a number of the most commonly used ratios, and we discussed the famous DuPont identity.

3. We showed how pro forma financial statements can be generated and used to plan for future financing needs.

After you have studied this chapter, we hope that you have some perspective on the uses and abuses of financial statement information. You should also find that your vocabulary of business and financial terms has grown substantially.

Concept Questions

1. **Financial Ratio Analysis**   A financial ratio by itself tells us little about a company because financial ratios vary a great deal across industries. There are two basic methods for analyzing financial ratios for a company: Time trend analysis and peer group analysis. In time trend analysis, you find the ratios for the company over some period, say five years, and examine how each ratio has changed over this period. In peer group analysis, you compare a company's financial ratios to those of its peers.

Chapter 3 Financial Statements Analysis and Financial Models   **77**

Why might each of these analysis methods be useful? What does each tell you about the company's financial health?

2. **Industry-Specific Ratios** So-called "same-store sales" are a very important measure for companies as diverse as McDonald's and Sears. As the name suggests, examining same-store sales means comparing revenues from the same stores or restaurants at two different points in time. Why might companies focus on same-store sales rather than total sales?

3. **Sales Forecast** Why do you think most long-term financial planning begins with sales forecasts? Put differently, why are future sales the key input?

4. **Sustainable Growth** In the chapter, we used Rosengarten Corporation to demonstrate how to calculate EFN. The ROE for Rosengarten is about 7.3 percent, and the plowback ratio is about 67 percent. If you calculate the sustainable growth rate for Rosengarten, you will find it is only 5.14 percent. In our calculation for EFN, we used a growth rate of 25 percent. Is this possible? (*Hint:* Yes. How?)

5. **EFN and Growth Rate** Broslofski Co. maintains a positive retention ratio and keeps its debt–equity ratio constant every year. When sales grow by 20 percent, the firm has a negative projected EFN. What does this tell you about the firm's sustainable growth rate? Do you know, with certainty, if the internal growth rate is greater than or less than 20 percent? Why? What happens to the projected EFN if the retention ratio is increased? What if the retention ratio is decreased? What if the retention ratio is zero?

6. **Common-Size Financials** One tool of financial analysis is common-size financial statements. Why do you think common-size income statements and balance sheets are used? Note that the accounting statement of cash flows is not converted into a common-size statement. Why do you think this is?

7. **Asset Utilization and EFN** One of the implicit assumptions we made in calculating the external funds needed was that the company was operating at full capacity. If the company is operating at less than full capacity, how will this affect the external funds needed?

8. **Comparing ROE and ROA** Both ROA and ROE measure profitability. Which one is more useful for comparing two companies? Why?

9. **Ratio Analysis** Consider the ratio EBITD/Assets. What does this ratio tell us? Why might it be more useful than ROA in comparing two companies?

10. **Return on Investment** A ratio that is becoming more widely used is return on investment. Return on investment is calculated as net income divided by long-term liabilities plus equity. What do you think return on investment is intended to measure? What is the relationship between return on investment and return on assets?

Use the following information to answer the next five questions: A small business called The Grandmother Calendar Company began selling personalized photo calendar kits. The kits were a hit, and sales soon sharply exceeded forecasts. The rush of orders created a huge backlog, so the company leased more space and expanded capacity, but it still could not keep up with demand. Equipment failed from overuse and quality suffered. Working capital was drained to expand production, and, at the same time, payments from customers were often delayed until the product was shipped. Unable to deliver on orders, the company became so strapped for cash that employee paychecks began to bounce. Finally, out of cash, the company ceased operations entirely three years later.

11. **Product Sales** Do you think the company would have suffered the same fate if its product had been less popular? Why or why not?

12.   **Cash Flow**   The Grandmother Calendar Company clearly had a cash flow problem. In the context of the cash flow analysis we developed in Chapter 2, what was the impact of customers not paying until orders were shipped?

13.   **Corporate Borrowing**   If the firm was so successful at selling, why wouldn't a bank or some other lender step in and provide it with the cash it needed to continue?

14.   **Cash Flow**   Which was the biggest culprit here: Too many orders, too little cash, or too little production capacity?

15.   **Cash Flow**   What are some actions a small company like The Grandmother Calendar Company can take (besides expansion of capacity) if it finds itself in a situation in which growth in sales outstrips production?

Questions and Problems

connect

www.mhhe.com/rwj

BASIC
(Questions 1–10)

1.   **DuPont Identity**   If Jares, Inc., has an equity multiplier of 1.55, total asset turnover of 1.75, and a profit margin of 4.3 percent, what is its ROE?

2.   **Equity Multiplier and Return on Equity**   Nuber Company has a debt–equity ratio of .80. Return on assets is 9.7 percent, and total equity is $735,000. What is the equity multiplier? Return on equity? Net income?

3.   **Using the DuPont Identity**   Y3K, Inc., has sales of $2,700, total assets of $1,310, and a debt–equity ratio of 1.20. If its return on equity is 15 percent, what is its net income?

4.   **EFN**   The most recent financial statements for Martin, Inc., are shown here:

Income Statement		Balance Sheet			
Sales	$37,300	Assets	$127,000	Debt	$ 30,500
Costs	25,800			Equity	96,500
Taxable income	$ 11,500	Total	$127,000	Total	$127,000
Taxes (34%)	3,910				
Net income	$ 7,590				

Assets and costs are proportional to sales. Debt and equity are not. A dividend of $2,500 was paid, and Martin wishes to maintain a constant payout ratio. Next year's sales are projected to be $42,300. What external financing is needed?

5.   **Sales and Growth**   The most recent financial statements for Fontenot Co. are shown here:

Income Statement		Balance Sheet			
Sales	$54,000	Current assets	$ 31,000	Long-term debt	$ 68,000
Costs	39,300	Fixed assets	118,000	Equity	81,000
Taxable income	$14,700	Total	$149,000	Total	$149,000
Taxes (34%)	4,998				
Net income	$ 9,702				

Assets and costs are proportional to sales. The company maintains a constant 30 percent dividend payout ratio and a constant debt–equity ratio. What is the maximum increase in sales that can be sustained assuming no new equity is issued?

6. **Sustainable Growth** If the Layla Corp. has a 13 percent ROE and a 20 percent payout ratio, what is its sustainable growth rate?

7. **Sustainable Growth** Assuming the following ratios are constant, what is the sustainable growth rate?

Total asset turnover = 2.20
Profit margin = 7.4%
Equity multiplier = 1.40
Payout ratio = 40%

8. **Calculating EFN** The most recent financial statements for Bradley, Inc., are shown here (assuming no income taxes):

Income Statement		Balance Sheet			
Sales	$6,500	Assets	$17,400	Debt	$ 8,400
Costs	5,320			Equity	9,000
Net income	$1,180	Total	$17,400	Total	$17,400

Assets and costs are proportional to sales. Debt and equity are not. No dividends are paid. Next year's sales are projected to be $7,280. What is the external financing needed?

9. **External Funds Needed** Cheryl Colby, CFO of Charming Florist Ltd., has created the firm's pro forma balance sheet for the next fiscal year. Sales are projected to grow by 10 percent to $420 million. Current assets, fixed assets, and short-term debt are 20 percent, 75 percent, and 15 percent of sales, respectively. Charming Florist pays out 30 percent of its net income in dividends. The company currently has $120 million of long-term debt and $48 million in common stock par value. The profit margin is 9 percent.

    a. Construct the current balance sheet for the firm using the projected sales figure.
    b. Based on Ms. Colby's sales growth forecast, how much does Charming Florist need in external funds for the upcoming fiscal year?
    c. Construct the firm's pro forma balance sheet for the next fiscal year and confirm the external funds needed that you calculated in part (b).

10. **Sustainable Growth Rate** The Steiben Company has an ROE of 13.1 percent and a payout ratio of 40 percent.

    a. What is the company's sustainable growth rate?
    b. Can the company's actual growth rate be different from its sustainable growth rate? Why or why not?
    c. How can the company increase its sustainable growth rate?

INTERMEDIATE
(Questions 11–23)

11. **Return on Equity** Firm A and Firm B have debt–total asset ratios of 35 percent and 55 percent and returns on total assets of 9 percent and 7 percent, respectively. Which firm has a greater return on equity?

12. **Ratios and Foreign Companies** Prince Albert Canning PLC had a net loss of £37,543 on sales of £345,182. What was the company's profit margin? Does the fact that these figures are quoted in a foreign currency make any difference? Why? In dollars, sales were $559,725. What was the net loss in dollars?

13. External Funds Needed   The Optical Scam Company has forecast a 15 percent sales growth rate for next year. The current financial statements are shown here:

Income Statement		
Sales		$30,400,000
Costs		26,720,000
Taxable income		$ 3,680,000
Taxes		1,288,000
Net income		$ 2,392,000
Dividends	$ 956,800	
Addition to retained earnings	1,435,200	

Balance Sheet			
Assets		**Liabilities and Equity**	
Current assets	$ 7,200,000	Short-term debt	$ 6,400,000
		Long-term debt	4,800,000
Fixed assets	17,600,000		
		Common stock	$ 3,200,000
		Accumulated retained earnings	10,400,000
		Total equity	$13,600,000
Total assets	$24,800,000	Total liabilities and equity	$24,800,000

a. Using the equation from the chapter, calculate the external funds needed for next year.

b. Construct the firm's pro forma balance sheet for next year and confirm the external funds needed that you calculated in part (a).

c. Calculate the sustainable growth rate for the company.

d. Can Optical Scam eliminate the need for external funds by changing its dividend policy? What other options are available to the company to meet its growth objectives?

14. Days' Sales in Receivables   A company has net income of $265,000, a profit margin of 9.3 percent, and an accounts receivable balance of $145,300. Assuming 80 percent of sales are on credit, what is the company's days' sales in receivables?

15. Ratios and Fixed Assets   The Le Bleu Company has a ratio of long-term debt to total assets of .35 and a current ratio of 1.25. Current liabilities are $950, sales are $5,780, profit margin is 9.4 percent, and ROE is 18.2 percent. What is the amount of the firm's net fixed assets?

16. Calculating the Cash Coverage Ratio   Titan Inc.'s net income for the most recent year was $8,320. The tax rate was 34 percent. The firm paid $1,940 in total interest expense and deducted $2,730 in depreciation expense. What was Titan's cash coverage ratio for the year?

17. DuPont Identity   The DuPont identity presented in the chapter is commonly referred to as the three-factor DuPont identity. Another common way that the DuPont identity is expressed is the five-factor model, which is:

$$\text{ROE} = \frac{\text{Net income}}{\text{EBT}} \times \frac{\text{EBT}}{\text{EBIT}} \times \frac{\text{EBIT}}{\text{Sales}} \times \frac{\text{Sales}}{\text{Total assets}} \times \frac{\text{Total assets}}{\text{Equity}}$$

Chapter 3   Financial Statements Analysis and Financial Models   **81**

Derive the five-factor DuPont identity (EBT is earnings before tax, but after interest). What does each term measure?

18. **Common-Size and Common–Base Year Financial Statements** In addition to common-size financial statements, common–base year financial statements are often used. Common–base year financial statements are constructed by dividing the current year account value by the base year account value. Thus, the result shows the growth rate in the account. Using the following financial statements, construct the common-size balance sheet and common–base year balance sheet for the company. Use 2011 as the base year.

JARROW CORPORATION 2011 and 2012 Balance Sheets					
Assets			**Liabilities and Owners' Equity**		
	2011	**2012**		**2011**	**2012**
Current assets			Current liabilities		
Cash	$ 8,014	$ 9,954	Accounts payable	$ 40,898	$ 45,884
Accounts receivable	20,453	22,937	Notes payable	17,464	17,035
Inventory	36,822	41,797	Total	$ 58,362	$ 62,919
Total	$ 65,289	$ 74,688	Long-term debt	$ 24,000	$ 31,000
Fixed assets			Owners' equity		
Net plant and equipment	$215,370	$243,340	Common stock and paid-in surplus	$ 38,000	$ 39,200
			Retained earnings	160,297	184,909
			Total	$198,297	$224,109
Total assets	$280,659	$318,028	Total liabilities and owners' equity	$280,659	$318,028

Use the following information for Problems 19, 20, and 22:

The discussion of EFN in the chapter implicitly assumed that the company was operating at full capacity. Often, this is not the case. For example, assume that Rosengarten was operating at 90 percent capacity. Full-capacity sales would be $1,000/.90 = $1,111. The balance sheet shows $1,800 in fixed assets. The capital intensity ratio for the company is

Capital intensity ratio = Fixed assets/Full-capacity sales = $1,800/$1,111 = 1.62

This means that Rosengarten needs $1.62 in fixed assets for every dollar in sales when it reaches full capacity. At the projected sales level of $1,250, it needs $1,250 × 1.62 = $2,025 in fixed assets, which is $225 lower than our projection of $2,250 in fixed assets. So, EFN is only $565 − 225 = $340.

19. **Full-Capacity Sales** Thorpe Mfg., Inc., is currently operating at only 90 percent of fixed asset capacity. Current sales are $725,000. How much can sales increase before any new fixed assets are needed?

20. **Fixed Assets and Capacity Usage** For the company in the previous problem, suppose fixed assets are $690,000 and sales are projected to grow to $830,000. How much in new fixed assets are required to support this growth in sales?

21. **Calculating EFN** The most recent financial statements for Moose Tours, Inc., appear below. Sales for 2012 are projected to grow by 20 percent. Interest expense will remain constant; the tax rate and the dividend payout rate will also remain constant. Costs, other expenses, current assets, fixed assets, and accounts payable increase spontaneously with sales. If the firm is operating at full capacity and no new debt or equity is issued, what external financing is needed to support the 20 percent growth rate in sales?

MOOSE TOURS, INC. 2011 Income Statement	
Sales	$836,100
Costs	650,700
Other expenses	17,100
Earnings before interest and taxes	$168,300
	12,600
Interest expense	$155,700
Taxable income	54,495
Taxes	$101,205
Net income	
Dividends	$30,300
Addition to retained earnings	70,905

MOOSE TOURS, INC. Balance Sheet as of December 31, 2011			
Assets		**Liabilities and Owners' Equity**	
Current assets		Current liabilities	
Cash	$ 24,035	Accounts payable	$ 64,600
Accounts receivable	38,665	Notes payable	16,150
Inventory	82,555	Total	$ 80,750
Total	$145,255	Long-term debt	$150,000
		Owners' equity	
Fixed assets		Common stock and paid-in surplus	$130,000
Net plant and equipment	$392,350	Retained earnings	176,855
		Total	$306,855
Total assets	$537,605	Total liabilities and owners' equity	$537,605

22. **Capacity Usage and Growth**   In the previous problem, suppose the firm was operating at only 80 percent capacity in 2011. What is EFN now?

23. **Calculating EFN**   In Problem 21, suppose the firm wishes to keep its debt–equity ratio constant. What is EFN now?

CHALLENGE (Questions 24–30)

24. **EFN and Internal Growth**   Redo Problem 21 using sales growth rates of 15 and 25 percent in addition to 20 percent. Illustrate graphically the relationship between EFN and the growth rate, and use this graph to determine the relationship between them.

25. **EFN and Sustainable Growth**   Redo Problem 23 using sales growth rates of 30 and 35 percent in addition to 20 percent. Illustrate graphically the relationship between EFN and the growth rate, and use this graph to determine the relationship between them.

26. **Constraints on Growth**   Bulla Recording, Inc., wishes to maintain a growth rate of 12 percent per year and a debt–equity ratio of .40. Profit margin is 5.3 percent, and the

ratio of total assets to sales is constant at .75. Is this growth rate possible? To answer, determine what the dividend payout ratio must be. How do you interpret the result?

27. **EFN** Define the following:

S = Previous year's sales
A = Total assets
E = Total equity
g = Projected growth in sales
PM = Profit margin
b = Retention (plowback) ratio

Assuming that all debt is constant, show that EFN can be written as:

$$EFN = -PM(S)b + [A - PM(S)b] \times g$$

Hint: Asset needs will equal A $\times$ g. The addition to retained earnings will equal PM(S)b $\times$ (1 + g).

28. **Sustainable Growth Rate** Based on the results in Problem 27, show that the internal and sustainable growth rates can be calculated as shown in Equations 3.23 and 3.24. (*Hint:* For the internal growth rate, set EFN equal to zero and solve for g.)

29. **Sustainable Growth Rate** In the chapter, we discussed one calculation of the sustainable growth rate as:

$$\text{Sustainable growth rate} = \frac{\text{ROE} \times b}{1 - \text{ROE} \times b}$$

In practice, probably the most commonly used calculation of the sustainable growth rate is ROE $\times$ b. This equation is identical to the sustainable growth rate equation presented in the chapter if the ROE is calculated using the beginning of period equity. Derive this equation from the equation presented in the chapter.

30. **Sustainable Growth Rate** Use the sustainable growth rate equations from the previous problem to answer the following questions. No Return, Inc., had total assets of $285,000 and equity of $176,000 at the beginning of the year. At the end of the year, the company had total assets of $310,000. During the year the company sold no new equity. Net income for the year was $90,000 and dividends were $43,000. What is the sustainable growth rate for the company? What is the sustainable growth rate if you calculate ROE based on the beginning of period equity?

Excel Master It!

Financial planning can be more complex than the percentage of sales approach indicates. Often, the assumptions behind the percentage of sales approach may be too simple. A more sophisticated model allows important items to vary without being a strict percentage of sales.

Consider a new model in which depreciation is calculated as a percentage of beginning fixed assets, and interest expense depends directly on the amount of debt. Debt is still the plug variable. Note that since depreciation and interest now do not necessarily vary directly with sales, the profit margin is no longer constant. Also, for the same reason, taxes and dividends will no longer be a fixed percentage of sales. The parameter estimates used in the new model are:

Cost percentage = Costs / Sales

Depreciation rate = Depreciation / Beginning fixed assets

Interest rate = Interest paid / Total debt

Tax rate = Taxes / Net income

Payout ratio = Dividends / Net income

Capital intensity ratio = Fixed assets / Sales

Fixed assets ratio = Fixed assets / Total assets

The model parameters can be determined by whatever methods the company deems appropriate. For example, they might be based on average values for the last several years, industry standards, subjective estimates, or even company targets. Alternatively, sophisticated statistical techniques can be used to estimate them.

The Loftis Company is preparing its pro forma financial statements for the next year using this model. The abbreviated financial statements are presented below.

Sales growth	20%
Tax rate	34
Income Statement	
Sales	$780,000
Costs	415,000
Depreciation	135,000
Interest	68,000
Taxable income	$162,000
Taxes	55,080
Net income	$106,920
Dividends	$ 30,000
Additions to retained earnings	76,920

Balance Sheet			
Assets		**Liabilities and Equity**	
Current assets	$ 240,000	Total debt	$ 880,000
Net fixed assets	1,350,000	Owners' equity	710,000
Total assets	$1,590,000	Total debt and equity	$1,590,000

a. Calculate each of the parameters necessary to construct the pro forma balance sheet.

b. Construct the pro forma balance sheet. What is the total debt necessary to balance the pro forma balance sheet?

c. In this financial planning model, show that it is possible to solve algebraically for the amount of new borrowing.

RATIOS AND FINANCIAL PLANNING AT EAST COAST YACHTS

Dan Ervin was recently hired by East Coast Yachts to assist the company with its short-term financial planning and also to evaluate the company's financial performance. Dan graduated from college five years ago with a finance degree, and he has been employed in the treasury department of a *Fortune* 500 company since then.

East Coast Yachts was founded 10 years ago by Larissa Warren. The company's operations are located near Hilton Head Island, South Carolina, and the company is structured as an LLC. The company has manufactured custom midsize, high-performance yachts for clients over this period, and its products have received high reviews for safety and reliability. The company's yachts have also recently received the highest award for customer satisfaction. The yachts are primarily purchased by wealthy individuals for pleasure use. Occasionally, a yacht is manufactured for purchase by a company for business purposes.

The custom yacht industry is fragmented, with a number of manufacturers. As with any industry, there are market leaders, but the diverse nature of the industry ensures that no manufacturer dominates the market. The competition in the market, as well as the product cost, ensures that attention to detail is a necessity. For instance, East Coast Yachts will spend 80 to 100 hours on hand-buffing the stainless steel stem-iron, which is the metal cap on the yacht's bow that conceivably could collide with a dock or another boat.

To get Dan started with his analyses, Larissa has provided the following financial statements. Dan has gathered the industry ratios for the yacht manufacturing industry.

EAST COAST YACHTS
2012 Income Statement

Sales		$234,300,000
Cost of goods sold		165,074,000
Other expenses		27,991,000
Depreciation		7,644,000
Earnings before interest and taxes (EBIT)		$ 33,591,000
Interest		4,212,600
Taxable income		$ 29,378,400
Taxes (40%)		11,751,360
Net income		$ 17,627,040
Dividends	$ 5,288,112	
Add to RE	$12,338,928	

EAST COAST YACHTS
Balance Sheet as of December 31, 2012

Assets		Liabilities & Equity	
Current assets		Current liabilities	
Cash	$ 3,650,700	Accounts payable	$ 7,753,000
Accounts receivable	6,567,600	Notes payable	15,936,300
Inventory	7,363,700		
Total	$ 17,582,000	Total	$ 23,689,300
Fixed assets		Long-term debt	$ 40,480,000
Net plant and equipment	$112,756,900		
		Shareholders' equity	
		Common stock	$ 6,200,000
		Retained earnings	59,969,600
		Total equity	$ 66,169,600
Total assets	$130,338,900	Total liabilities and equity	$130,338,900

Yacht Industry Ratios			
	Lower Quartile	Median	Upper Quartile
Current ratio	0.50	1.43	1.89
Quick ratio	0.21	0.38	0.62
Total asset turnover	0.68	0.85	1.38
Inventory turnover	6.85	9.15	16.13
Receivables turnover	6.27	11.81	21.45
Debt ratio	0.44	0.52	0.61
Debt–equity ratio	0.79	1.08	1.56
Equity multiplier	1.79	2.08	2.56
Interest coverage	5.18	8.06	9.83
Profit margin	4.05%	6.98%	9.87%
Return on assets	6.05%	10.53%	15.83%
Return on equity	9.93%	16.54%	28.14%

1. Calculate all of the ratios listed in the industry table for East Coast Yachts.
2. Compare the performance of East Coast Yachts to the industry as a whole. For each ratio, comment on why it might be viewed as positive or negative relative to the industry. Suppose you create an inventory ratio calculated as inventory divided by current liabilities. How do you interpret this ratio? How does East Coast Yachts compare to the industry average?
3. Calculate the sustainable growth rate of East Coast Yachts. Calculate external funds needed (EFN) and prepare pro forma income statements and balance sheets assuming growth at precisely this rate. Recalculate the ratios in the previous question. What do you observe?
4. As a practical matter, East Coast Yachts is unlikely to be willing to raise external equity capital, in part because the owners don't want to dilute their existing ownership and control positions. However, East Coast Yachts is planning for a growth rate of 20 percent next year. What are your conclusions and recommendations about the feasibility of East Coast's expansion plans?
5. Most assets can be increased as a percentage of sales. For instance, cash can be increased by any amount. However, fixed assets often must be increased in specific amounts because it is impossible, as a practical matter, to buy part of a new plant or machine. In this case a company has a "staircase" or "lumpy" fixed cost structure. Assume that East Coast Yachts is currently producing at 100 percent of capacity. As a result, to expand production, the company must set up an entirely new line at a cost of $30 million. Calculate the new EFN with this assumption. What does this imply about capacity utilization for East Coast Yachts next year?

Valuation and Capital Budgeting

CHAPTER 4

Discounted Cash Flow Valuation

The signing of big-name athletes is often accompanied by great fanfare, but the numbers are often misleading. For example, in late 2010, catcher Victor Martinez reached a deal with the Detroit Tigers, signing a contract with a reported value of $50 million. Not bad, especially for someone who makes a living using the "tools of ignorance" (jock jargon for a catcher's equipment). Another example is the contract signed by Jayson Werth of the Washington Nationals, which had a stated value of $126 million.

It looks like Victor and Jayson did pretty well, but then there was Carl Crawford, who signed to play in front of Boston's Red Sox nation. Carl's contract has a stated value of $142 million, but this amount was actually payable over several years. The contract consisted of a $6 million signing bonus, along with $14 million in the first year plus $122 million in future salary to be paid in the years 2011 through 2017. Victor's and Jayson's payments were similarly spread over time. Because all three contracts called for payments that are made at future dates, we must consider the time value of money, which means none of these players received the quoted amounts. How much did they really get? This chapter gives you the "tools of knowledge" to answer this question.

▲ For updates on the latest happenings in finance, visit www. rwjcorporatefinance. blogspot.com

4.1 Valuation: The One-Period Case

Keith Vaughn is trying to sell a piece of raw land in Alaska. Yesterday he was offered $10,000 for the property. He was about ready to accept the offer when another individual offered him $11,424. However, the second offer was to be paid a year from now. Keith has satisfied himself that both buyers are honest and financially solvent, so he has no fear that the offer he selects will fall through. These two offers are pictured as cash flows in Figure 4.1. Which offer should Keith choose?

Mike Tuttle, Keith's financial adviser, points out that if Keith takes the first offer, he could invest the $10,000 in the bank at an insured rate of 12 percent. At the end of one year, he would have:

$$\underset{\substack{\text{Return of} \\ \text{principal}}}{\$10,000} + \underset{\text{Interest}}{(.12 \times \$10,000)} = \$10,000 \times 1.12 = \$11,200$$

Because this is less than the $11,424 Keith could receive from the second offer, Mike recommends that he take the latter. This analysis uses the concept of **future value (FV)** or **compound value,** which is the value of a sum after investing over one or more periods. The compound or future value of $10,000 at 12 percent is $11,200.

Figure 4.1
Cash Flow for Keith Vaughn's Sale

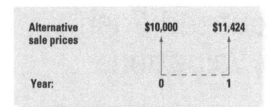

An alternative method employs the concept of **present value (PV).** One can determine present value by asking the following question: How much money must Keith put in the bank today so that he will have $11,424 next year? We can write this algebraically as:

$$PV \times 1.12 = \$11,424$$

We want to solve for PV, the amount of money that yields $11,424 if invested at 12 percent today. Solving for PV, we have:

$$PV = \frac{\$11,424}{1.12} = \$10,200$$

The formula for PV can be written as follows:

Present Value of Investment:

$$PV = \frac{C_1}{1 + r} \tag{4.1}$$

where C_1 is cash flow at date 1 and r is the rate of return that Keith Vaughn requires on his land sale. It is sometimes referred to as the *discount rate.*

Present value analysis tells us that a payment of $11,424 to be received next year has a present value of $10,200 today. In other words, at a 12 percent interest rate, Keith is indifferent between $10,200 today or $11,424 next year. If you gave him $10,200 today, he could put it in the bank and receive $11,424 next year.

Because the second offer has a present value of $10,200, whereas the first offer is for only $10,000, present value analysis also indicates that Keith should take the second offer. In other words, both future value analysis and present value analysis lead to the same decision. As it turns out, present value analysis and future value analysis must always lead to the same decision.

As simple as this example is, it contains the basic principles that we will be working with over the next few chapters. We now use another example to develop the concept of net present value.

EXAMPLE 4.1

Present Value   Diane Badame, a financial analyst at Kaufman & Broad, a leading real estate firm, is thinking about recommending that Kaufman & Broad invest in a piece of land that costs $85,000. She is certain that next year the land will be worth $91,000, a sure $6,000 gain. Given that the interest rate in similar alternative investments is 10 percent, should Kaufman & Broad undertake the investment in land? Diane's choice is described in Figure 4.2 with the cash flow time chart.

A moment's thought should be all it takes to convince her that this is not an attractive business deal. By investing $85,000 in the land, she will have $91,000 available next year. Suppose, instead,

Figure 4.2 **Cash Flows for Land Investment**

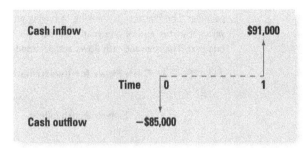

that Kaufman & Broad puts the same $85,000 into similar alternative investments. At the interest rate of 10 percent, this $85,000 would grow to:

$$(1 + .10) \times \$85,000 = \$93,500$$

next year.

It would be foolish to buy the land when investing the same $85,000 in similar alternative investments would produce an extra $2,500 (that is, $93,500 from the bank minus $91,000 from the land investment). This is a future value calculation.

Alternatively, she could calculate the present value of the sale price next year as:

$$\text{Present value} = \frac{\$91,000}{1.10} = \$82,727.27$$

Because the present value of next year's sales price is less than this year's purchase price of $85,000, present value analysis also indicates that she should not recommend purchasing the property.

Frequently, financial analysts want to determine the exact *cost* or *benefit* of a decision. In Example 4.1, the decision to buy this year and sell next year can be evaluated as:

$$-\$2,273 = \underset{\substack{\text{Cost of land} \\ \text{today}}}{-\$85,000} + \underset{\substack{\text{Present value of} \\ \text{next year's sales price}}}{\frac{\$91,000}{1.10}}$$

The formula for NPV can be written as follows:

Net Present Value of Investment:
$$\text{NPV} = -\text{Cost} + \text{PV} \qquad (4.2)$$

Equation 4.2 says that the value of the investment is −$2,273, after stating all the benefits and all the costs as of date 0. We say that −$2,273 is the **net present value** (NPV) of the investment. That is, NPV is the present value of future cash flows minus the present value of the cost of the investment. Because the net present value is negative, Diane Badame should not recommend purchasing the land.

Both the Vaughn and the Badame examples deal with a high degree of certainty. That is, Keith Vaughn knows with a high degree of certainty that he could sell his land for $11,424 next year. Similarly, Diane Badame knows with a high degree of certainty that Kaufman & Broad could receive $91,000 for selling its land. Unfortunately, businesspeople frequently do not know future cash flows. This uncertainty is treated in the next example.

EXAMPLE 4.2

Uncertainty and Valuation Professional Artworks, Inc., is a firm that speculates in modern paintings. The manager is thinking of buying an original Picasso for $400,000 with the intention of selling it at the end of one year. The manager expects that the painting will be worth $480,000 in one year. The relevant cash flows are depicted in Figure 4.3.

Figure 4.3 **Cash Flows for Investment in Painting**

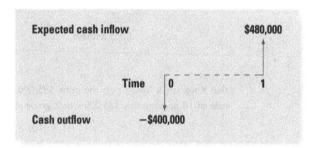

Of course, this is only an expectation—the painting could be worth more or less than $480,000. Suppose the guaranteed interest rate granted by banks is 10 percent. Should the firm purchase the piece of art?

Our first thought might be to discount at the interest rate, yielding:

$$\frac{\$480,000}{1.10} = \$436,364$$

Because $436,364 is greater than $400,000, it looks at first glance as if the painting should be purchased. However, 10 percent is the return one can earn on a low risk investment. Because the painting is quite risky, a higher discount rate is called for. The manager chooses a rate of 25 percent to reflect this risk. In other words, he argues that a 25 percent expected return is fair compensation for an investment as risky as this painting.

The present value of the painting becomes:

$$\frac{\$480,000}{1.25} = \$384,000$$

Thus, the manager believes that the painting is currently overpriced at $400,000 and does not make the purchase.

The preceding analysis is typical of decision making in today's corporations, though real-world examples are, of course, much more complex. Unfortunately, any example with risk poses a problem not faced in a riskless example. Conceptually, the correct discount rate for an expected cash flow is the expected return available in the market on other investments of the same risk. This is the appropriate discount rate to apply because it represents an economic opportunity cost to investors. It is the expected return they will require before committing funding to a project. However, the selection of the discount rate for a risky investment is quite a difficult task. We simply don't know at this point whether the discount rate on the painting in Example 4.2 should be 11 percent, 15 percent, 25 percent, or some other percentage.

Because the choice of a discount rate is so difficult, we merely wanted to broach the subject here. We must wait until the specific material on risk and return is covered in later chapters before a risk-adjusted analysis can be presented.

4.2 The Multiperiod Case

The previous section presented the calculation of future value and present value for one period only. We will now perform the calculations for the multiperiod case.

FUTURE VALUE AND COMPOUNDING

Suppose an individual were to make a loan of $1. At the end of the first year, the borrower would owe the lender the principal amount of $1 plus the interest on the loan at the interest rate of r. For the specific case where the interest rate is, say, 9 percent, the borrower owes the lender:

$$\$1 \times (1 + r) = \$1 \times 1.09 = \$1.09$$

At the end of the year, though, the lender has two choices. She can either take the $1.09—or, more generally, $(1 + r)$—out of the financial market, or she can leave it in and lend it again for a second year. The process of leaving the money in the financial market and lending it for another year is called **compounding.**

Suppose the lender decides to compound her loan for another year. She does this by taking the proceeds from her first one-year loan, $1.09, and lending this amount for the next year. At the end of next year, then, the borrower will owe her:

$$\$1 \times (1 + r) \times (1 + r) = \$1 \times (1 + r)^2 = 1 + 2r + r^2$$
$$\$1 \times (1.09) \times (1.09) = \$1 \times (1.09)^2 = \$1 + \$.18 + \$.0081 = \$1.1881$$

This is the total she will receive two years from now by compounding the loan.

In other words, the capital market enables the investor, by providing a ready opportunity for lending, to transform $1 today into $1.1881 at the end of two years. At the end of three years, the cash will be $1 \times (1.09)^3 = \$1.2950$.

The most important point to notice is that the total amount the lender receives is not just the $1 that she lent plus two years' worth of interest on $1:

$$2 \times r = 2 \times \$.09 = \$.18$$

The lender also gets back an amount r^2, which is the interest in the second year on the interest that was earned in the first year. The term $2 \times r$ represents **simple interest** over the two years, and the term r^2 is referred to as the *interest on interest.* In our example, this latter amount is exactly:

$$r^2 = (\$.09)^2 = \$.0081$$

When cash is invested at **compound interest,** each interest payment is reinvested. With simple interest, the interest is not reinvested. Benjamin Franklin's statement, "Money makes money and the money that money makes makes more money," is a colorful way of explaining compound interest. The difference between compound interest and simple interest is illustrated in Figure 4.4. In this example, the difference does not amount to much because the loan is for $1. If the loan were for $1 million, the lender would receive $1,188,100 in two years' time. Of this amount, $8,100 is interest on interest. The lesson is that those small numbers beyond the decimal point can add up to big dollar amounts when the transactions are for big amounts. In addition, the longer-lasting the loan, the more important interest on interest becomes.

Figure 4.4
Simple and
Compound Interest

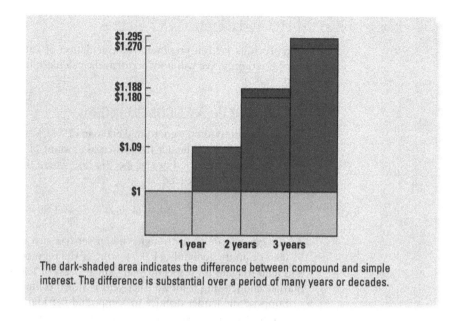

The dark-shaded area indicates the difference between compound and simple interest. The difference is substantial over a period of many years or decades.

The general formula for an investment over many periods can be written as follows:

Future Value of an Investment:

$$\text{FV} = C_0 \times (1 + r)^T \tag{4.3}$$

where C_0 is the cash to be invested at Date 0 (i.e., today), r is the interest rate per period, and T is the number of periods over which the cash is invested.

EXAMPLE 4.3

Interest on Interest   Suh-Pyng Ku has put $500 in a savings account at the First National Bank of Kent. The account earns 7 percent, compounded annually. How much will Ms. Ku have at the end of three years? The answer is:

$$\$500 \times 1.07 \times 1.07 \times 1.07 = \$500 \times (1.07)^3 = \$612.52$$

Figure 4.5 illustrates the growth of Ms. Ku's account.

Figure 4.5   **Suh-Pyng Ku's Savings Account**

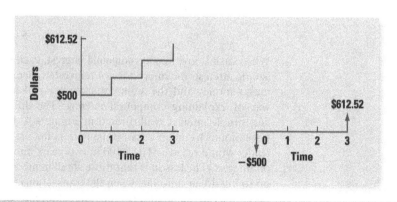

| EXAMPLE 4.4 | **Compound Growth**   Jay Ritter invested $1,000 in the stock of the SDH Company. The company pays a current dividend of $2, which is expected to grow by 20 percent per year for the next two years. What will the dividend of the SDH Company be after two years? A simple calculation gives: |

$$\$2 \times (1.20)^2 = \$2.88$$

Figure 4.6 illustrates the increasing value of SDH's dividends.

Figure 4.6   The Growth of the SDH Dividends

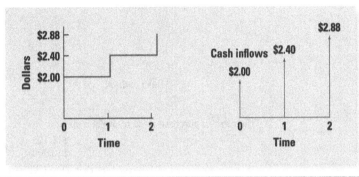

The two previous examples can be calculated in any one of several ways. The computations could be done by hand, by calculator, by spreadsheet, or with the help of a table. We will introduce spreadsheets in a few pages, and we show how to use a calculator in Appendix 4B on the website. The appropriate table is Table A.3, which appears in the back of the text. This table presents *future value of $1 at the end of T periods*. The table is used by locating the appropriate interest rate on the horizontal and the appropriate number of periods on the vertical. For example, Suh-Pyng Ku would look at the following portion of Table A.3:

	Interest Rate		
Period	**6%**	**7%**	**8%**
1	1.0600	1.0700	1.0800
2	1.1236	1.1449	1.1664
3	1.1910	1.2250	1.2597
4	1.2625	1.3108	1.3605

She could calculate the future value of her $500 as:

$$\underset{\substack{\text{Initial} \\ \text{investment}}}{\$500} \times \underset{\substack{\text{Future value} \\ \text{of }\$1}}{1.2250} = \$612.50$$

In the example concerning Suh-Pyng Ku, we gave you both the initial investment and the interest rate and then asked you to calculate the future value. Alternatively, the interest rate could have been unknown, as shown in the following example.

94   **Part II**   Valuation and Capital Budgeting

EXAMPLE 4.5

Finding the Rate   Carl Voigt, who recently won $10,000 in the lottery, wants to buy a car in five years. Carl estimates that the car will cost $16,105 at that time. His cash flows are displayed in Figure 4.7.
   What interest rate must he earn to be able to afford the car?

Figure 4.7   Cash Flows for Purchase of Carl Voigt's Car

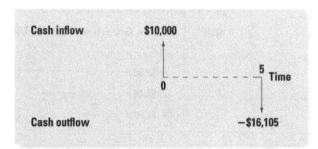

The ratio of purchase price to initial cash is:

$$\frac{\$16,105}{\$10,000} = 1.6105$$

Thus, he must earn an interest rate that allows $1 to become $1.6105 in five years. Table A.3 tells us that an interest rate of 10 percent will allow him to purchase the car.
   We can express the problem algebraically as:

$$\$10,000 \times (1 + r)^5 = \$16,105$$

where r is the interest rate needed to purchase the car. Because $16,105/$10,000 = 1.6105, we have:

$$(1 + r)^5 = 1.6105$$
$$r = 10\%$$

Either the table, a spreadsheet, or a hand calculator lets us solve for r.

THE POWER OF COMPOUNDING: A DIGRESSION

Most people who have had any experience with compounding are impressed with its power over long periods. Take the stock market, for example. Ibbotson and Sinquefield have calculated what the stock market returned as a whole from 1926 through 2010.[1] They find that one dollar placed in large U.S. stocks at the beginning of 1926 would have been worth $2,982.24 at the end of 2010. This is 9.87 percent compounded annually for 85 years—that is, $(1.0987)^{85} = \$2,982.24$, ignoring a small rounding error.

The example illustrates the great difference between compound and simple interest. At 9.87 percent, simple interest on $1 is 9.87 cents a year. Simple interest over 85 years is $8.39 (=85 × $.0987). That is, an individual withdrawing 9.87 cents every year would have withdrawn $8.39 (=85 × $.0987) over 85 years. This is quite a bit below the $2,982.24 that was obtained by reinvestment of all principal and interest.

The results are more impressive over even longer periods. A person with no experience in compounding might think that the value of $1 at the end of 170 years would

---

[1]*Stocks, Bonds, Bills, and Inflation [SBBI]. 2011 Yearbook.* Morningstar, Chicago, 2011.

be twice the value of $1 at the end of 85 years, if the yearly rate of return stayed the same. Actually the value of $1 at the end of 170 years would be the *square* of the value of $1 at the end of 85 years. That is, if the annual rate of return remained the same, a $1 investment in common stocks would be worth $8,893,755.42 (=$1 × 2,982.24 × 2,982.24).

A few years ago, an archaeologist unearthed a relic stating that Julius Caesar lent the Roman equivalent of one penny to someone. Because there was no record of the penny ever being repaid, the archaeologist wondered what the interest and principal would be if a descendant of Caesar tried to collect from a descendant of the borrower in the 20th century. The archaeologist felt that a rate of 6 percent might be appropriate. To his surprise, the principal and interest due after more than 2,000 years was vastly greater than the entire wealth on earth.

The power of compounding can explain why the parents of well-to-do families frequently bequeath wealth to their grandchildren rather than to their children. That is, they skip a generation. The parents would rather make the grandchildren very rich than make the children moderately rich. We have found that in these families the grandchildren have a more positive view of the power of compounding than do the children.

EXAMPLE 4.6

How Much for That Island?   Some people have said that it was the best real estate deal in history. Peter Minuit, director general of New Netherlands, the Dutch West India Company's colony in North America, in 1626 allegedly bought Manhattan Island for 60 guilders' worth of trinkets from native Americans. By 1667, the Dutch were forced by the British to exchange it for Suriname (perhaps the worst real estate deal ever). This sounds cheap; but did the Dutch really get the better end of the deal? It is reported that 60 guilders was worth about $24 at the prevailing exchange rate. If the native Americans had sold the trinkets at a fair market value and invested the $24 at 5 percent (tax free), it would now, about 385 years later, be worth more than $3.45 billion. Today, Manhattan is undoubtedly worth more than $3.45 billion, so at a 5 percent rate of return the native Americans got the worst of the deal. However, if invested at 10 percent, the amount of money they received would be worth about:

$$\$24(1 + r)^T = 24 \times 1.1^{385} \cong \$207 \text{ quadrillion}$$

This is a lot of money. In fact, $207 quadrillion is more than all the real estate in the world is worth today. Note that no one in the history of the world has ever been able to find an investment yielding 10 percent every year for 385 years.

PRESENT VALUE AND DISCOUNTING

We now know that an annual interest rate of 9 percent enables the investor to transform $1 today into $1.1881 two years from now. In addition, we would like to know the following:

> How much would an investor need to lend today so that she could receive $1 two years from today?

Algebraically, we can write this as:

$$PV \times (1.09)^2 = \$1$$

Figure 4.8
Compounding and
Discounting

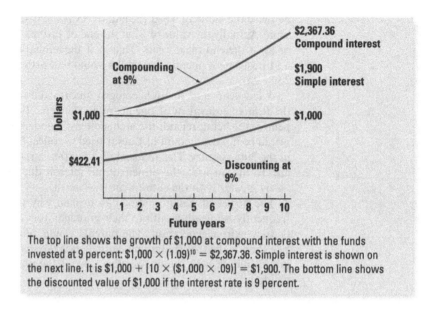

The top line shows the growth of $1,000 at compound interest with the funds invested at 9 percent: $1,000 × (1.09)^{10} = $2,367.36. Simple interest is shown on the next line. It is $1,000 + [10 × ($1,000 × .09)] = $1,900. The bottom line shows the discounted value of $1,000 if the interest rate is 9 percent.

In the preceding equation, PV stands for present value, the amount of money we must lend today to receive $1 in two years' time.

Solving for PV in this equation, we have:

$$PV = \frac{\$1}{1.1881} = \$.84$$

This process of calculating the present value of a future cash flow is called **discounting.** It is the opposite of compounding. The difference between compounding and discounting is illustrated in Figure 4.8.

To be certain that $.84 is in fact the present value of $1 to be received in two years, we must check whether or not, if we lent $.84 today and rolled over the loan for two years, we would get exactly $1 back. If this were the case, the capital markets would be saying that $1 received in two years' time is equivalent to having $.84 today. Checking the exact numbers, we get:

$$\$.84168 \times 1.09 \times 1.09 = \$1$$

In other words, when we have capital markets with a sure interest rate of 9 percent, we are indifferent between receiving $.84 today or $1 in two years. We have no reason to treat these two choices differently from each other because if we had $.84 today and lent it out for two years, it would return $1 to us at the end of that time. The value .84 [$=1/(1.09)^2$] is called the **present value factor.** It is the factor used to calculate the present value of a future cash flow.

In the multiperiod case, the formula for PV can be written as follows:

Present Value of Investment:

$$PV = \frac{C_T}{(1 + r)^T} \tag{4.4}$$

Here, C_T is the cash flow at date T and r is the appropriate discount rate.

EXAMPLE 4.7

Multiperiod Discounting Bernard Dumas will receive $10,000 three years from now. Bernard can earn 8 percent on his investments, so the appropriate discount rate is 8 percent. What is the present value of his future cash flow? The answer is:

$$PV = \$10{,}000 \times \left(\frac{1}{1.08}\right)^3$$
$$= \$10{,}000 \times .7938$$
$$= \$7{,}938$$

Figure 4.9 illustrates the application of the present value factor to Bernard's investment.

Figure 4.9 Discounting Bernard Dumas's Opportunity

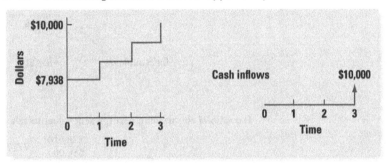

When his investments grow at an 8 percent rate of interest, Bernard Dumas is equally inclined toward receiving $7,938 now and receiving $10,000 in three years' time. After all, he could convert the $7,938 he receives today into $10,000 in three years by lending it at an interest rate of 8 percent.

Bernard Dumas could have reached his present value calculation in one of several ways. The computation could have been done by hand, by calculator, with a spreadsheet, or with the help of Table A.1, which appears in the back of the text. This table presents the *present value of $1 to be received after T periods.* We use the table by locating the appropriate interest rate on the horizontal and the appropriate number of periods on the vertical. For example, Bernard Dumas would look at the following portion of Table A.1:

	Interest Rate		
Period	**7%**	**8%**	**9%**
1	.9346	.9259	.9174
2	.8734	.8573	.8417
3	.8163	.7938	.7722
4	.7629	.7350	.7084

The appropriate present value factor is .7938.

In the preceding example we gave both the interest rate and the future cash flow. Alternatively, the interest rate could have been unknown.

EXAMPLE 4.8

Finding the Rate   A customer of the Chaffkin Corp. wants to buy a tugboat today. Rather than paying immediately, he will pay $50,000 in three years. It will cost the Chaffkin Corp. $38,610 to build the tugboat immediately. The relevant cash flows to Chaffkin Corp. are displayed in Figure 4.10. What interest rate would the Chaffkin Corp. charge to neither gain nor lose on the sale?

Figure 4.10   Cash Flows for Tugboat

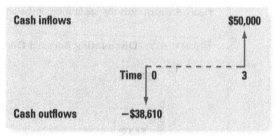

The ratio of construction cost (present value) to sale price (future value) is:

$$\frac{\$38,610}{\$50,000} = .7722$$

We must determine the interest rate that allows $1 to be received in three years to have a present value of $.7722. Table A.1 tells us that 9 percent is that interest rate.

FINDING THE NUMBER OF PERIODS

Suppose we are interested in purchasing an asset that costs $50,000. We currently have $25,000. If we can earn 12 percent on this $25,000, how long until we have the $50,000? Finding the answer involves solving for the last variable in the basic present value equation, the number of periods. You already know how to get an approximate answer to this particular problem. Notice that we need to double our money. From the Rule of 72 (see Problem 74 at the end of the chapter), this will take about $72/12 = 6$ years at 12 percent.

To come up with the exact answer, we can again manipulate the basic present value equation. The present value is $25,000, and the future value is $50,000. With a 12 percent discount rate, the basic equation takes one of the following forms:

$$\$25,000 = \$50,000/1.12^t$$
$$\$50,000/25,000 = 1.12^t = 2$$

We thus have a future value factor of 2 for a 12 percent rate. We now need to solve for t. If you look down the column in Table A.3 that corresponds to 12 percent, you will see that a future value factor of 1.9738 occurs at six periods. It will thus take about six years, as we calculated. To get the exact answer, we have to explicitly solve for t (by using a financial calculator or the spreadsheet on the next page). If you do this, you will see that the answer is 6.1163 years, so our approximation was quite close in this case.

SPREADSHEET APPLICATIONS

Using a Spreadsheet for Time Value of Money Calculations

More and more, businesspeople from many different areas (not just finance and accounting) rely on spreadsheets to do all the different types of calculations that come up in the real world. As a result, in this section, we will show you how to use a spreadsheet to handle the various time value of money problems we present in this chapter. We will use Microsoft Excel™, but the commands are similar for other types of software. We assume you are already familiar with basic spreadsheet operations.

As we have seen, you can solve for any one of the following four potential unknowns: future value, present value, the discount rate, or the number of periods. With a spreadsheet, there is a separate formula for each. In Excel, these are shown in a nearby box.

In these formulas, pv and fv are present and future value, nper is the number of periods, and rate is the discount, or interest, rate.

To Find	Enter This Formula
Future value	= FV (rate,nper,pmt,pv)
Present value	= PV (rate,nper,pmt,fv)
Discount rate	= RATE (nper,pmt,pv,fv)
Number of periods	= NPER (rate,pmt,pv,fv)

Two things are a little tricky here. First, unlike a financial calculator, the spreadsheet requires that the rate be entered as a decimal. Second, as with most financial calculators, you have to put a negative sign on either the present value or the future value to solve for the rate or the number of periods. For the same reason, if you solve for a present value, the answer will have a negative sign unless you input a negative future value. The same is true when you compute a future value.

To illustrate how you might use these formulas, we will go back to an example in the chapter. If you invest $25,000 at 12 percent per year, how long until you have $50,000? You might set up a spreadsheet like this:

	A	B	C	D	E	F	G	H
1								
2		Using a spreadsheet for time value of money calculations						
3								
4	If we invest $25,000 at 12 percent, how long until we have $50,000? We need to solve							
5	for the unknown number of periods, so we use the formula NPER(rate, pmt, pv, fv).							
6								
7	Present value (pv):	$25,000						
8	Future value (fv):	$50,000						
9	Rate (rate):	.12						
10								
11	Periods:	6.1162554						
12								
13	The formula entered in cell B11 is =NPER(B9,0,-B7,B8); notice that pmt is zero and that pv							
14	has a negative sign on it. Also notice that rate is entered as a decimal, not a percentage.							

EXAMPLE 4.9

Waiting for Godot You've been saving up to buy the Godot Company. The total cost will be $10 million. You currently have about $2.3 million. If you can earn 5 percent on your money, how long will you have to wait? At 16 percent, how long must you wait?

At 5 percent, you'll have to wait a long time. From the basic present value equation:

$$\$2.3 \text{ million} = \$10 \text{ million}/1.05^t$$
$$1.05^t = 4.35$$
$$t = 30 \text{ years}$$

At 16 percent, things are a little better. Verify for yourself that it will take about 10 years.

Learn more about using Excel for time value and other calculations at **www.studyfinance. com**.

Frequently, an investor or a business will receive more than one cash flow. The present value of a set of cash flows is simply the sum of the present values of the individual cash flows. This is illustrated in the following two examples.

EXAMPLE 4.10

Cash Flow Valuation   Kyle Mayer has won the Kentucky State Lottery and will receive the following set of cash flows over the next two years:

Year	Cash Flow
1	$20,000
2	50,000

Mr. Mayer can currently earn 6 percent in his money market account, so the appropriate discount rate is 6 percent. The present value of the cash flows is:

Year	Cash Flow × Present Value Factor = Present Value
1	$20,000 \times \dfrac{1}{1.06} = \$20,000 \times \dfrac{1}{1.06} = \$18,867.9$
2	$50,000 \times \left(\dfrac{1}{1.06}\right)^2 = \$50,000 \times \dfrac{1}{(1.06)^2} = \underline{\$44,499.8}$
	Total $63,367.7

In other words, Mr. Mayer is equally inclined toward receiving $63,367.7 today and receiving $20,000 and $50,000 over the next two years.

EXAMPLE 4.11

NPV   Finance.com has an opportunity to invest in a new high-speed computer that costs $50,000. The computer will generate cash flows (from cost savings) of $25,000 one year from now, $20,000 two years from now, and $15,000 three years from now. The computer will be worthless after three years, and no additional cash flows will occur. Finance.com has determined that the appropriate discount rate is 7 percent for this investment. Should Finance.com make this investment in a new high-speed computer? What is the net present value of the investment?

The cash flows and present value factors of the proposed computer are as follows:

	Cash Flows	Present Value Factor
Year 0	−$50,000	$1 = 1$
1	$25,000	$\dfrac{1}{1.07} = .9346$
2	$20,000	$\left(\dfrac{1}{1.07}\right)^2 = .8734$
3	$15,000	$\left(\dfrac{1}{1.07}\right)^3 = .8163$

The present value of the cash flows is:

Cash Flows × Present value factor = Present value

Year 0	−$50,000 × 1	=	−$50,000
1	$25,000 × .9346	=	$23,365
2	$20,000 × .8734	=	$17,468
3	$15,000 × .8163	=	$12,244.5
		Total:	$ 3,077.5

Finance.com should invest in the new high-speed computer because the present value of its future cash flows is greater than its cost. The NPV is $3,077.5.

THE ALGEBRAIC FORMULA

To derive an algebraic formula for the net present value of a cash flow, recall that the PV of receiving a cash flow one year from now is:

$$PV = C_1/(1 + r)$$

and the PV of receiving a cash flow two years from now is:

$$PV = C_2/(1 + r)^2$$

We can write the NPV of a T-period project as:

$$NPV = -C_0 + \frac{C_1}{1 + r} + \frac{C_2}{(1 + r)^2} + \cdots + \frac{C_T}{(1 + r)^T} = -C_0 + \sum_{i=1}^{T} \frac{C_i}{(1 + r)^i} \qquad (4.5)$$

The initial flow, $-C_0$, is assumed to be negative because it represents an investment. The Σ is shorthand for the sum of the series.

We will close this section by answering the question we posed at the beginning of the chapter concerning baseball player Carl Crawford's contract. Recall that the contract called for a $6 million signing bonus and $14 million in 2011. The remaining $122 million was to be paid as $19.5 million in 2012, $20 million in 2013, $20.25 million in 2014, $20.5 million in 2015, $20.75 million in 2016, and $21 million in 2017. If 12 percent is the appropriate interest rate, what kind of deal did the Red Sox outfielder snag?

To answer, we can calculate the present value by discounting each year's salary back to the present as follows (notice we assume that all the payments are made at year-end):

Year 0 (2010): $ 6,000,000 = $ 6,000,000.00
Year 1 (2011): $14,000,000 × 1/1.12^1 = $12,500,000.00
Year 2 (2012): $19,500,000 × 1/1.12^2 = $15,545,280.61
Year 3 (2013): $20,000,000 × 1/1.12^3 = $14,235,604.96

. .   .
. .   .
. .   .

Year 7 (2017): $21,000,000 × 1/1.12^7 = $ 9,499,332.52

If you fill in the missing rows and then add (do it for practice), you will see that Carl's contract had a present value of about $92.8 million, or only about 65 percent of the stated $142 million value (but still pretty good).

4.3 Compounding Periods

So far, we have assumed that compounding and discounting occur yearly. Sometimes, compounding may occur more frequently than just once a year. For example, imagine that a bank pays a 10 percent interest rate "compounded semiannually." This means that a $1,000 deposit in the bank would be worth $1,000 × 1.05 = $1,050 after six months, and $1,050 × 1.05 = $1,102.50 at the end of the year.

The end-of-the-year wealth can be written as:

$$\$1,000 \left(1 + \frac{.10}{2}\right)^2 = \$1,000 \times (1.05)^2 = \$1,102.50$$

Of course, a $1,000 deposit would be worth $1,100 (=$1,000 × 1.10) with yearly compounding. Note that the future value at the end of one year is greater with semiannual compounding than with yearly compounding. With yearly compounding, the original $1,000 remains the investment base for the full year. The original $1,000 is the investment base only for the first six months with semiannual compounding. The base over the second six months is $1,050. Hence one gets *interest on interest* with semiannual compounding.

Because $1,000 × 1.1025 = $1,102.50, 10 percent compounded semiannually is the same as 10.25 percent compounded annually. In other words, a rational investor could not care less whether she is quoted a rate of 10 percent compounded semiannually or a rate of 10.25 percent compounded annually.

Quarterly compounding at 10 percent yields wealth at the end of one year of:

$$\$1,000 \left(1 + \frac{.10}{4}\right)^4 = \$1,103.81$$

More generally, compounding an investment m times a year provides end-of-year wealth of:

$$C_0\left(1 + \frac{r}{m}\right)^m \tag{4.6}$$

where C_0 is the initial investment and r is the **stated annual interest rate.** The stated annual interest rate is the annual interest rate without consideration of compounding. Banks and other financial institutions may use other names for the stated annual interest rate. **Annual percentage rate (APR)** is perhaps the most common synonym.

EXAMPLE 4.12

EARs   What is the end-of-year wealth if Jane Christine receives a stated annual interest rate of 24 percent compounded monthly on a $1 investment?

Using Equation 4.6, her wealth is:

$$\$1\left(1 + \frac{.24}{12}\right)^{12} = \$1 \times (1.02)^{12}$$
$$= \$1.2682$$

The annual rate of return is 26.82 percent. This annual rate of return is called either the **effective annual rate (EAR)** or the **effective annual yield (EAY).** Due to compounding, the effective annual interest rate is greater than the stated annual interest rate of 24 percent. Algebraically, we can rewrite the effective annual interest rate as follows:

Effective Annual Rate:
$$\left(1 + \frac{r}{m}\right)^m - 1 \tag{4.7}$$

Students are often bothered by the subtraction of 1 in Equation 4.7. Note that end-of-year wealth is composed of both the interest earned over the year and the original principal. We remove the original principal by subtracting 1 in Equation 4.7.

EXAMPLE 4.13

Compounding Frequencies   If the stated annual rate of interest, 8 percent, is compounded quarterly, what is the effective annual rate?
Using Equation 4.7, we have:

$$\left(1 + \frac{r}{m}\right)^m - 1 = \left(1 + \frac{.08}{4}\right)^4 - 1 = .0824 = 8.24\%$$

Referring back to our original example where $C_0 =$ \$1,000 and $r =$ 10%, we can generate the following table:

C_0	Compounding Frequency (m)	C_1	Effective Annual Rate = $\left(1 + \frac{r}{m}\right)^m - 1$
\$1,000	Yearly ($m = 1$)	\$1,100.00	.10
1,000	Semiannually ($m = 2$)	1,102.50	.1025
1,000	Quarterly ($m = 4$)	1,103.81	.10381
1,000	Daily ($m = 365$)	1,105.16	.10516

DISTINCTION BETWEEN STATED ANNUAL INTEREST RATE AND EFFECTIVE ANNUAL RATE

The distinction between the stated annual interest rate (SAIR), or APR, and the effective annual rate (EAR) is frequently troubling to students. We can reduce the confusion by noting that the SAIR becomes meaningful only if the compounding interval is given. For example, for an SAIR of 10 percent, the future value at the end of one year with semiannual compounding is $[1 + (.10/2)]^2 = 1.1025$. The future value with quarterly compounding is $[1 + (.10/4)]^4 = 1.1038$. If the SAIR is 10 percent but no compounding interval is given, we cannot calculate future value. In other words, we do not know whether to compound semiannually, quarterly, or over some other interval.

By contrast, the EAR is meaningful *without* a compounding interval. For example, an EAR of 10.25 percent means that a \$1 investment will be worth \$1.1025 in one year. We can think of this as an SAIR of 10 percent with semiannual compounding or an SAIR of 10.25 percent with annual compounding, or some other possibility.

There can be a big difference between an SAIR and an EAR when interest rates are large. For example, consider "payday loans." Payday loans are short-term loans made to consumers, often for less than two weeks. They are offered by companies such as Check Into Cash and AmeriCash Advance. The loans work like this: You write a check today that is postdated. When the check date arrives, you go to the store and pay the cash for the check, or the company cashes the check. For example, in one particular state, Check Into Cash allows you to write a check for \$115 dated 14 days in the future, for which they give you \$100 today. So what are the APR and EAR of this arrangement? First, we need to find the interest rate, which we can find by the FV equation as follows:

$$FV = PV \times (1 + r)^1$$
$$\$115 = \$100 \times (1 + r)^1$$
$$1.15 = (1 + r)$$
$$r = .15 \text{ or } 15\%$$

That doesn't seem too bad until you remember this is the interest rate for *14 days!* The APR of the loan is:

$$APR = .15 \times 365/14$$
$$APR = 3.9107 \text{ or } 391.07\%$$

And the EAR for this loan is:

$$EAR = (1 + \text{Quoted rate}/m)^m - 1$$
$$EAR = (1 + .15)^{365/14} - 1$$
$$EAR = 37.2366 \text{ or } 3{,}723.66\%$$

Now that's an interest rate! Just to see what a difference a small difference in fees can make, AmeriCash Advance will make you write a check for $117.50 for the same amount. Check for yourself that the APR of this arrangement is 456.25 percent and the EAR is 6,598.65 percent. Still not a loan we would like to take out!

By law, lenders are required to report the APR on all loans. In this text, we compute the APR as the interest rate per period multiplied by the number of periods in a year. According to federal law, the APR is a measure of the cost of consumer credit expressed as a yearly rate, and it includes interest and certain noninterest charges and fees. In practice, the APR can be much higher than the interest rate on the loan if the lender charges substantial fees that must be included in the federally mandated APR calculation.

COMPOUNDING OVER MANY YEARS

Equation 4.6 applies for an investment over one year. For an investment over one or more (*T*) years, the formula becomes this:

Future Value with Compounding:

$$FV = C_0\left(1 + \frac{r}{m}\right)^{mT} \tag{4.8}$$

EXAMPLE 4.14

Multiyear Compounding Harry DeAngelo is investing $5,000 at a stated annual interest rate of 12 percent per year, compounded quarterly, for five years. What is his wealth at the end of five years?

Using Equation 4.8, his wealth is:

$$\$5{,}000 \times \left(1 + \frac{.12}{4}\right)^{4\times5} = \$5{,}000 \times (1.03)^{20} = \$5{,}000 \times 1.8061 = \$9{,}030.50$$

CONTINUOUS COMPOUNDING

The previous discussion shows that we can compound much more frequently than once a year. We could compound semiannually, quarterly, monthly, daily, hourly, each minute, or even more often. The limiting case would be to compound every infinitesimal instant, which is commonly called **continuous compounding.** Surprisingly, banks and other financial institutions sometimes quote continuously compounded rates, which is why we study them.

Though the idea of compounding this rapidly may boggle the mind, a simple formula is involved. With continuous compounding, the value at the end of T years is expressed as:

$$C_0 \times e^{rT} \qquad (4.9)$$

where C_0 is the initial investment, r is the stated annual interest rate, and T is the number of years over which the investment runs. The number e is a constant and is approximately equal to 2.718. It is not an unknown like C_0, r, and T.

EXAMPLE 4.15

Continuous Compounding   Linda DeFond invested $1,000 at a continuously compounded rate of 10 percent for one year. What is the value of her wealth at the end of one year?

From Equation 4.9 we have:

$$\$1,000 \times e^{.10} = \$1,000 \times 1.1052 = \$1,105.20$$

This number can easily be read from Table A.5. We merely set r, the value on the horizontal dimension, to 10 percent and T, the value on the vertical dimension, to 1. For this problem the relevant portion of the table is shown here:

Period (T)	Continuously Compounded Rate (r)		
	9%	10%	11%
1	1.0942	1.1052	1.1163
2	1.1972	1.2214	1.2461
3	1.3100	1.3499	1.3910

Note that a continuously compounded rate of 10 percent is equivalent to an annually compounded rate of 10.52 percent. In other words, Linda DeFond would not care whether her bank quoted a continuously compounded rate of 10 percent or a 10.52 percent rate, compounded annually.

EXAMPLE 4.16

Continuous Compounding, Continued   Linda DeFond's brother, Mark, invested $1,000 at a continuously compounded rate of 10 percent for two years.

The appropriate formula here is:

$$\$1,000 \times e^{.10 \times 2} = \$1,000 \times e^{.20} = \$1,221.40$$

Using the portion of the table of continuously compounded rates shown in the previous example, we find the value to be 1.2214.

Figure 4.11 illustrates the relationship among annual, semiannual, and continuous compounding. Semiannual compounding gives rise to both a smoother curve and a higher ending value than does annual compounding. Continuous compounding has both the smoothest curve and the highest ending value of all.

Figure 4.11
Annual, Semiannual, and Continuous Compounding

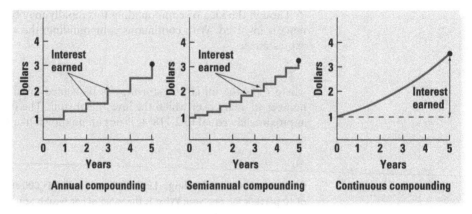

EXAMPLE 4.17

Present Value with Continuous Compounding   The Michigan State Lottery is going to pay you $100,000 at the end of four years. If the annual continuously compounded rate of interest is 8 percent, what is the present value of this payment?

$$\$100,000 \times \frac{1}{e^{.08 \times 4}} = \$100,000 \times \frac{1}{1.3771} = \$72,616.37$$

4.4   Simplifications

The first part of this chapter has examined the concepts of future value and present value. Although these concepts allow us to answer a host of problems concerning the time value of money, the human effort involved can be excessive. For example, consider a bank calculating the present value of a 20-year monthly mortgage. This mortgage has 240 (=20 × 12) payments, so a lot of time is needed to perform a conceptually simple task.

Because many basic finance problems are potentially time-consuming, we search for simplifications in this section. We provide simplifying formulas for four classes of cash flow streams:

• Perpetuity.
• Growing perpetuity.
• Annuity.
• Growing annuity.

PERPETUITY

A **perpetuity** is a constant stream of cash flows without end. If you are thinking that perpetuities have no relevance to reality, it will surprise you that there is a well-known case of an unending cash flow stream: The British bonds called *consols*. An investor purchasing a consol is entitled to receive yearly interest from the British government forever.

How can the price of a consol be determined? Consider a consol that pays a coupon of C dollars each year and will do so forever. Simply applying the PV formula gives us:

$$PV = \frac{C}{1 + r} + \frac{C}{(1 + r)^2} + \frac{C}{(1 + r)^3} + \cdots$$

where the dots at the end of the formula stand for the infinite string of terms that continues the formula. Series like the preceding one are called *geometric series*. It is well known that even though they have an infinite number of terms, the whole series has a finite sum because each term is only a fraction of the preceding term. Before turning to our calculus books, though, it is worth going back to our original principles to see if a bit of financial intuition can help us find the PV.

The present value of the consol is the present value of all of its future coupons. In other words, it is an amount of money that, if an investor had it today, would enable him to achieve the same pattern of expenditures that the consol and its coupons would. Suppose an investor wanted to spend exactly C dollars each year. If he had the consol, he could do this. How much money must he have today to spend the same amount? Clearly, he would need exactly enough so that the interest on the money would be C dollars per year. If he had any more, he could spend more than C dollars each year. If he had any less, he would eventually run out of money spending C dollars per year.

The amount that will give the investor C dollars each year, and therefore the present value of the consol, is simply:

$$PV = \frac{C}{r} \tag{4.10}$$

To confirm that this is the right answer, notice that if we lend the amount C/r, the interest it earns each year will be:

$$\text{Interest} = \frac{C}{r} \times r = C$$

which is exactly the consol payment. We have arrived at this formula for a consol:

Formula for Present Value of Perpetuity:

$$PV = \frac{C}{1 + r} + \frac{C}{(1 + r)^2} + \frac{C}{(1 + r)^3} + \cdots \tag{4.11}$$
$$= \frac{C}{r}$$

It is comforting to know how easily we can use a bit of financial intuition to solve this mathematical problem.

EXAMPLE 4.18

Perpetuities   Consider a perpetuity paying $100 a year. If the relevant interest rate is 8 percent, what is the value of the consol?

Using Equation 4.10 we have:

$$PV = \frac{\$100}{.08} = \$1,250$$

Now suppose that interest rates fall to 6 percent. Using Equation 4.10 the value of the perpetuity is:

$$PV = \frac{\$100}{.06} = \$1,666.67$$

Note that the value of the perpetuity rises with a drop in the interest rate. Conversely, the value of the perpetuity falls with a rise in the interest rate.

GROWING PERPETUITY

Imagine an apartment building where cash flows to the landlord after expenses will be $100,000 next year. These cash flows are expected to rise at 5 percent per year. If one assumes that this rise will continue indefinitely, the cash flow stream is termed a **growing perpetuity.** The relevant interest rate is 11 percent. Therefore, the appropriate discount rate is 11 percent, and the present value of the cash flows can be represented as:

$$\text{PV} = \frac{\$100{,}000}{1.11} + \frac{\$100{,}000(1.05)}{(1.11)^2} + \frac{\$100{,}000(1.05)^2}{(1.11)^3} + \cdots$$
$$+ \frac{\$100{,}000(1.05)^{N-1}}{(1.11)^N} + \cdots$$

Algebraically, we can write the formula as:

$$\text{PV} = \frac{C}{1+r} + \frac{C \times (1+g)}{(1+r)^2} + \frac{C \times (1+g)^2}{(1+r)^3} + \cdots + \frac{C \times (1+g)^{N-1}}{(1+r)^N} + \cdots$$

where C is the cash flow to be received one period hence, g is the rate of growth per period, expressed as a percentage, and r is the appropriate discount rate.

Fortunately, this formula reduces to the following simplification:

Formula for Present Value of Growing Perpetuity:

$$\text{PV} = \frac{C}{r - g} \tag{4.12}$$

From Equation 4.12 the present value of the cash flows from the apartment building is:

$$\frac{\$100{,}000}{.11 - .05} = \$1{,}666{,}667$$

There are three important points concerning the growing perpetuity formula:

1. *The numerator:* The numerator in Equation 4.12 is the cash flow one period hence, not at date 0. Consider the following example.

EXAMPLE 4.19

Paying Dividends   Popovich Corporation is *just about* to pay a dividend of $3.00 per share. Investors anticipate that the annual dividend will rise by 6 percent a year forever. The applicable discount rate is 11 percent. What is the price of the stock today?

The numerator in Equation 4.12 is the cash flow to be received next period. Since the growth rate is 6 percent, the dividend next year is $3.18 (=$3.00 × 1.06). The price of the stock today is:

$$\$66.60 \quad = \quad \$3.00 \quad + \quad \frac{\$3.18}{.11 - .06}$$

| | Imminent dividend | Present value of all dividends beginning a year from now |

The price of $66.60 includes both the dividend to be received immediately and the present value of all dividends beginning a year from now. Equation 4.12 makes it possible to calculate only the present value of all dividends beginning a year from now. Be sure you understand this example; test questions on this subject always seem to trip up a few of our students.

---

2. *The discount rate and the growth rate:* The discount rate r must be greater than the growth rate g for the growing perpetuity formula to work. Consider the case

in which the growth rate approaches the interest rate in magnitude. Then, the denominator in the growing perpetuity formula gets infinitesimally small and the present value grows infinitely large. The present value is in fact undefined when r is less than g.

3. *The timing assumption:* Cash generally flows into and out of real-world firms both randomly and nearly continuously. However, Equation 4.12 assumes that cash flows are received and disbursed at regular and discrete points in time. In the example of the apartment, we assumed that the net cash flows of $100,000 occurred only once a year. In reality, rent checks are commonly received every month. Payments for maintenance and other expenses may occur anytime within the year.

   We can apply the growing perpetuity formula of Equation 4.12 only by assuming a regular and discrete pattern of cash flow. Although this assumption is sensible because the formula saves so much time, the user should never forget that it is an *assumption*. This point will be mentioned again in the chapters ahead.

A few words should be said about terminology. Authors of financial textbooks generally use one of two conventions to refer to time. A minority of financial writers treat cash flows as being received on exact *dates*—for example Date 0, Date 1, and so forth. Under this convention, Date 0 represents the present time. However, because a year is an interval, not a specific moment in time, the great majority of authors refer to cash flows that occur at the end of a year (or alternatively, the end of a *period*). Under this *end-of-the-year* convention, the end of Year 0 is the present, the end of Year 1 occurs one period hence, and so on. (The beginning of Year 0 has already passed and is not generally referred to.)[2]

The interchangeability of the two conventions can be seen from the following chart:

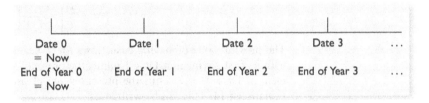

We strongly believe that the *dates convention* reduces ambiguity. However, we use both conventions because you are likely to see the *end-of-year convention* in later courses. In fact, both conventions may appear in the same example for the sake of practice.

ANNUITY

An **annuity** is a level stream of regular payments that lasts for a fixed number of periods. Not surprisingly, annuities are among the most common kinds of financial instruments. The pensions that people receive when they retire are often in the form of an annuity. Leases and mortgages are also often annuities.

To figure out the present value of an annuity we need to evaluate the following equation:

$$\frac{C}{1+r} + \frac{C}{(1+r)^2} + \frac{C}{(1+r)^3} + \cdots + \frac{C}{(1+r)^T}$$

---

[2]Sometimes, financial writers merely speak of a cash flow in Year x. Although this terminology is ambiguous, such writers generally mean the *end of Year x*.

The present value of receiving the coupons for only T periods must be less than the present value of a consol, but how much less? To answer this, we have to look at consols a bit more closely.

Consider the following time chart:

Consol 1 is a normal consol with its first payment at Date 1. The first payment of consol 2 occurs at Date $T + 1$.

The present value of having a cash flow of C at each of T dates is equal to the present value of Consol 1 minus the present value of Consol 2. The present value of Consol 1 is given by:

$$PV = \frac{C}{r} \tag{4.13}$$

Consol 2 is just a consol with its first payment at Date $T + 1$. From the perpetuity formula, this consol will be worth C/r at Date T.[3] However, we do not want the value at Date T. We want the value now, in other words, the present value at Date 0. We must discount C/r back by T periods. Therefore, the present value of Consol 2 is:

$$PV = \frac{C}{r}\left[\frac{1}{(1 + r)^T}\right] \tag{4.14}$$

The present value of having cash flows for T years is the present value of a consol with its first payment at Date 1 minus the present value of a consol with its first payment at Date $T + 1$. Thus the present value of an annuity is Equation 4.13 minus Equation 4.14. This can be written as:

$$\frac{C}{r} - \frac{C}{r}\left[\frac{1}{(1 + r)^T}\right]$$

This simplifies to the following:

Formula for Present Value of Annuity:

$$PV = C\left[\frac{1}{r} - \frac{1}{r(1 + r)^T}\right]$$

This can also be written as:

$$PV = C\left[\frac{1 - \dfrac{1}{(1 + r)^T}}{r}\right] \tag{4.15}$$

---

[3]Students frequently think that C/r is the present value at Date $T + 1$ because the consol's first payment is at Date $T + 1$. However, the formula values the consol as of one period prior to the first payment.

EXAMPLE 4.20

Lottery Valuation Mark Young has just won the state lottery, paying $50,000 a year for 20 years. He is to receive his first payment a year from now. The state advertises this as the Million Dollar Lottery because $1,000,000 = $50,000 × 20. If the interest rate is 8 percent, what is the present value of the lottery?

Equation 4.15 yields:

$$\text{Present value of Million Dollar Lottery} = \$50,000 \times \left[\frac{1 - \frac{1}{(1.08)^{20}}}{.08} \right]$$

$$\underbrace{= \$50,000}_{\text{Periodic payment}} \times \underbrace{9.8181}_{\text{Annuity factor}}$$

$$= \$490,905$$

Rather than being overjoyed at winning, Mr. Young sues the state for misrepresentation and fraud. His legal brief states that he was promised $1 million but received only $490,905.

The term we use to compute the present value of the stream of level payments, C, for T years is called a **present value interest factor for annuities.** The present value interest factor for annuities in the current example is 9.8181. Because the present value interest factor for annuities is used so often in PV calculations, we have included it in Table A.2 in the back of this book. The table gives the values of these factors for a range of interest rates, r, and maturity dates, T.

The present value interest factor for annuities as expressed in the brackets of Equation 4.15 is a complex formula. For simplification, we may from time to time refer to the annuity factor as:

$$\text{PVIA} \, (r, \, T)$$

This expression stands for the present value of $1 a year for T years at an interest rate of r.

We can also provide a formula for the future value of an annuity:

$$\text{FV} = C \left[\frac{(1 + r)^T}{r} - \frac{1}{r} \right] = C \left[\frac{(1 + r)^T - 1}{r} \right] \tag{4.16}$$

As with present value factors for annuities, we have compiled future value factors in Table A.4 in the back of this book.

EXAMPLE 4.21

Retirement Investing Suppose you put $3,000 per year into a Roth IRA. The account pays 6 percent interest per year. How much will you have when you retire in 30 years?

This question asks for the future value of an annuity of $3,000 per year for 30 years at 6 percent, which we can calculate as follows:

$$\text{FV} = C \left[\frac{(1 + r)^T - 1}{r} \right] = \$3,000 \times \left[\frac{1.06^{30} - 1}{.06} \right]$$

$$= \$3,000 \times 79.0582$$

$$= \$237,174.56$$

So, you'll have close to a quarter million dollars in the account.

Our experience is that annuity formulas are not hard, but tricky, for the beginning student. We present four tricks next.

SPREADSHEET APPLICATIONS

Annuity Present Values

Using a spreadsheet to find annuity present values goes like this:

	A	B	C	D	E	F	G
1							
2	Using a spreadsheet to find annuity present values						
3							
4	What is the present value of $500 per year for 3 years if the discount rate is 10 percent?						
5	We need to solve for the unknown present value, so we use the formula PV(rate, nper, pmt, fv).						
6							
7	Payment amount per period:	$500					
8	Number of payments:	3					
9	Discount rate:	0.1					
10							
11	Annuity present value:	$1,243.43					
12							
13	The formula entered in cell B11 is =PV(B9,B8,-B7,0); notice that fv is zero and that						
14	pmt has a negative sign on it. Also notice that rate is entered as a decimal, not a percentage.						
15							
16							
17							

Trick 1: A Delayed Annuity   One of the tricks in working with annuities or perpetuities is getting the timing exactly right. This is particularly true when an annuity or perpetuity begins at a date many periods in the future. We have found that even the brightest beginning student can make errors here. Consider the following example.

EXAMPLE 4.22

Delayed Annuities   Danielle Caravello will receive a four-year annuity of $500 per year, beginning at date 6. If the interest rate is 10 percent, what is the present value of her annuity? This situation can be graphed as follows:

The analysis involves two steps:

1. Calculate the present value of the annuity using Equation 4.15:

Present Value of Annuity at Date 5:

$$\$500 \left[\frac{1 - \frac{1}{(1.10)^4}}{.10} \right] = \$500 \times \text{PVIA}(.10, 4)$$

$$= \$500 \times 3.1699$$

$$= \$1,584.95$$

Note that $1,584.95 represents the present value at *Date 5*.

Students frequently think that $1,584.95 is the present value at Date 6 because the annuity begins at Date 6. However, our formula values the annuity as of one period prior to the first payment. This can be seen in the most typical case where the first payment occurs at Date 1. The formula values the annuity as of Date 0 in that case.

2. Discount the present value of the annuity back to Date 0:

Present Value at Date 0:

$$\frac{\$1,584.95}{(1.10)^5} = \$984.13$$

Again, it is worthwhile mentioning that because the annuity formula brings Danielle's annuity back to Date 5, the second calculation must discount over the remaining five periods. The two-step procedure is graphed in Figure 4.12.

Figure 4.12   Discounting Danielle Caravello's Annuity

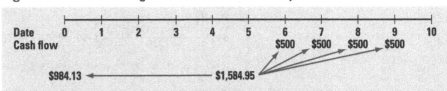

Step one: Discount the four payments back to Date 5 by using the annuity formula.
Step two: Discount the present value at Date 5 ($1,584.95) back to present value at Date 0.

Trick 2: Annuity Due   The annuity formula of Equation 4.15 assumes that the first annuity payment begins a full period hence. This type of annuity is sometimes called an *annuity in arrears* or an *ordinary annuity*. What happens if the annuity begins today—in other words, at Date 0?

EXAMPLE 4.23

Annuity Due   In a previous example, Mark Young received $50,000 a year for 20 years from the state lottery. In that example, he was to receive the first payment a year from the winning date. Let us now assume that the first payment occurs immediately. The total number of payments remains 20.

Under this new assumption, we have a 19-date annuity with the first payment occurring at Date 1—plus an extra payment at Date 0. The present value is:

$$\$50,000 \quad + \quad \$50,000 \times \text{PVIA} \,(.08, 19)$$

$$\text{Payment at date 0} \qquad \text{19-year annuity}$$

$$= \$50,000 + (\$50,000 \times 9.6036)$$

$$= \$530,180$$

$530,180, the present value in this example, is greater than $490,905, the present value in the earlier lottery example. This is to be expected because the annuity of the current example begins earlier. An annuity with an immediate initial payment is called an *annuity in advance* or, more commonly, an *annuity due*. Always remember that Equation 4.15 and Table A.2 in this book refer to an *ordinary annuity*.

114   **Part II**   Valuation and Capital Budgeting

Trick 3: The Infrequent Annuity

The following example treats an annuity with payments occurring less frequently than once a year.

EXAMPLE 4.24

Infrequent Annuities   Ann Chen receives an annuity of $450, payable once every two years. The annuity stretches out over 20 years. The first payment occurs at Date 2—that is, two years from today. The annual interest rate is 6 percent.

The trick is to determine the interest rate over a two-year period. The interest rate over two years is:

$$(1.06 \times 1.06) - 1 = 12.36\%$$

That is, $100 invested over two years will yield $112.36.

What we want is the present value of a $450 annuity over 10 periods, with an interest rate of 12.36 percent per period:

$$\$450 \left[\frac{1 - \dfrac{1}{(1 + .1236)^{10}}}{.1236} \right] = \$450 \times \text{PVIA} \,(.1236, 10) = \$2,505.57$$

Trick 4: Equating Present Value of Two Annuities

The following example equates the present value of inflows with the present value of outflows.

EXAMPLE 4.25

Working with Annuities   Harold and Helen Nash are saving for the college education of their newborn daughter, Susan. The Nashes estimate that college expenses will run $30,000 per year when their daughter reaches college in 18 years. The annual interest rate over the next few decades will be 14 percent. How much money must they deposit in the bank each year so that their daughter will be completely supported through four years of college?

To simplify the calculations, we assume that Susan is born today. Her parents will make the first of her four annual tuition payments on her 18th birthday. They will make equal bank deposits on each of her first 17 birthdays, but no deposit at Date 0. This is illustrated as follows:

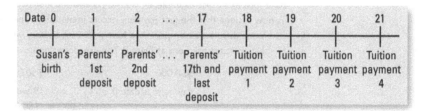

Mr. and Ms. Nash will be making deposits to the bank over the next 17 years. They will be withdrawing $30,000 per year over the following four years. We can be sure they will be able to withdraw fully $30,000 per year if the present value of the deposits is equal to the present value of the four $30,000 withdrawals.

This calculation requires three steps. The first two determine the present value of the withdrawals. The final step determines yearly deposits that will have a present value equal to that of the withdrawals.

1. We calculate the present value of the four years at college using the annuity formula:

$$\$30{,}000 \times \left[\frac{1 - \dfrac{1}{(1.14)^4}}{.14}\right] = \$30{,}000 \times \text{PVIA}\,(.14, 4)$$

$$= \$30{,}000 \times 2.9137 = \$87{,}411$$

We assume that Susan enters college on her 18th birthday. Given our discussion in Trick 1, $87,411 represents the present value at Date 17.

2. We calculate the present value of the college education at Date 0 as:

$$\frac{\$87{,}411}{(1.14)^{17}} = \$9{,}422.91$$

3. Assuming that Harold and Helen Nash make deposits to the bank at the end of each of the 17 years, we calculate the annual deposit that will yield a present value of all deposits of $9,422.91. This is calculated as:

$$C \times \text{PVIA}\,(.14, 17) = \$9{,}422.91$$

Because PVIA (.14, 17) = 6.3729,

$$C = \frac{\$9{,}422.91}{6.3729} = \$1{,}478.59$$

Thus deposits of $1,478.59 made at the end of each of the first 17 years and invested at 14 percent will provide enough money to make tuition payments of $30,000 over the following four years.

An alternative method in Example 4.25 would be to (1) calculate the present value of the tuition payments at Susan's 18th birthday and (2) calculate annual deposits so that the future value of the deposits at her 18th birthday equals the present value of the tuition payments at that date. Although this technique can also provide the right answer, we have found that it is more likely to lead to errors. Therefore, we equate only present values in our presentation.

GROWING ANNUITY

Cash flows in business are likely to grow over time, due either to real growth or to inflation. The growing perpetuity, which assumes an infinite number of cash flows, provides one formula to handle this growth. We now consider a **growing annuity,** which is a *finite* number of growing cash flows. Because perpetuities of any kind are rare, a formula for a growing annuity would be useful indeed. Here is the formula:

Formula for Present Value of Growing Annuity:

$$\text{PV} = C\left[\frac{1}{r - g} - \frac{1}{r - g} \times \left(\frac{1 + g}{1 + r}\right)^T\right] = C\left[\frac{1 - \left(\dfrac{1 + g}{1 + r}\right)^T}{r - g}\right] \tag{4.17}$$

As before, C is the payment to occur at the end of the first period, r is the interest rate, g is the rate of growth per period, expressed as a percentage, and T is the number of periods for the annuity.

EXAMPLE 4.26

Growing Annuities   Stuart Gabriel, a second-year MBA student, has just been offered a job at $80,000 a year. He anticipates his salary increasing by 9 percent a year until his retirement in 40 years. Given an interest rate of 20 percent, what is the present value of his lifetime salary?

We simplify by assuming he will be paid his $80,000 salary exactly one year from now, and that his salary will continue to be paid in annual installments. The appropriate discount rate is 20 percent. From Equation 4.17, the calculation is:

$$\text{Present value of Stuart's lifetime salary} = \$80,000 \times \left[\frac{1 - \left(\frac{1.09}{1.20}\right)^{40}}{.20 - .09} \right] = \$711,730.71$$

Though the growing annuity formula is quite useful, it is more tedious than the other simplifying formulas. Whereas most sophisticated calculators have special programs for perpetuity, growing perpetuity, and annuity, there is no special program for a growing annuity. Hence, we must calculate all the terms in Equation 4.17 directly.

EXAMPLE 4.27

More Growing Annuities   In a previous example, Helen and Harold Nash planned to make 17 identical payments to fund the college education of their daughter, Susan. Alternatively, imagine that they planned to increase their payments at 4 percent per year. What would their first payment be?

The first two steps of the previous Nash family example showed that the present value of the college costs was $9,422.91. These two steps would be the same here. However, the third step must be altered. Now we must ask, How much should their first payment be so that, if payments increase by 4 percent per year, the present value of all payments will be $9,422.91?

We set the growing annuity formula equal to $9,422.91 and solve for C:

$$C \left[\frac{1 - \left(\frac{1 + g}{1 + r}\right)^{T}}{r - g} \right] = C \left[\frac{1 - \left(\frac{1.04}{1.14}\right)^{17}}{.14 - .04} \right] = \$9,422.91$$

Here, C = $1,192.78. Thus, the deposit on their daughter's first birthday is $1,192.78, the deposit on the second birthday is $1,240.49 (=1.04 × $1,192.78), and so on.

4.5   Loan Amortization

Whenever a lender extends a loan, some provision will be made for repayment of the principal (the original loan amount). A loan might be repaid in equal installments, for example, or it might be repaid in a single lump sum. Because the way that the principal and interest are paid is up to the parties involved, there are actually an unlimited number of possibilities.

In this section, we describe amortized loans. Working with these loans is a very straightforward application of the present value principles that we have already developed.

An *amortized loan* may require the borrower to repay parts of the loan amount over time. The process of providing for a loan to be paid off by making regular principal reductions is called *amortizing* the loan.

A simple way of amortizing a loan is to have the borrower pay the interest each period plus some fixed amount. This approach is common with medium-term business loans. For example, suppose a business takes out a $5,000, five-year loan at 9 percent. The loan agreement calls for the borrower to pay the interest on the loan balance each year and to reduce the loan balance each year by $1,000. Because the loan amount declines by $1,000 each year, it is fully paid in five years.

In the case we are considering, notice that the total payment will decline each year. The reason is that the loan balance goes down, resulting in a lower interest charge each year, whereas the $1,000 principal reduction is constant. For example, the interest in the first year will be $5,000 × .09 = $450. The total payment will be $1,000 + 450 = $1,450. In the second year, the loan balance is $4,000, so the interest is $4,000 × .09 = $360, and the total payment is $1,360. We can calculate the total payment in each of the remaining years by preparing a simple *amortization schedule* as follows:

Year	Beginning Balance	Total Payment	Interest Paid	Principal Paid	Ending Balance
1	$5,000	$1,450	$ 450	$1,000	$4,000
2	4,000	1,360	360	1,000	3,000
3	3,000	1,270	270	1,000	2,000
4	2,000	1,180	180	1,000	1,000
5	1,000	1,090	90	1,000	0
Totals		$6,350	$1,350	$5,000	

Notice that in each year, the interest paid is given by the beginning balance multiplied by the interest rate. Also notice that the beginning balance is given by the ending balance from the previous year.

Probably the most common way of amortizing a loan is to have the borrower make a single, fixed payment every period. Almost all consumer loans (such as car loans) and mortgages work this way. For example, suppose our five-year, 9 percent, $5,000 loan was amortized this way. How would the amortization schedule look?

We first need to determine the payment. From our discussion earlier in the chapter, we know that this loan's cash flows are in the form of an ordinary annuity. In this case, we can solve for the payment as follows:

$$\$5,000 = C \times \{[1 - (1/1.09^5)]/.09\}$$
$$= C \times [(1 - .6499)/.09]$$

This gives us:

$$C = \$5,000/3.8897$$
$$= \$1,285.46$$

The borrower will therefore make five equal payments of $1,285.46. Will this pay off the loan? We will check by filling in an amortization schedule.

In our previous example, we knew the principal reduction each year. We then calculated the interest owed to get the total payment. In this example, we know the total payment. We will thus calculate the interest and then subtract it from the total payment to calculate the principal portion in each payment.

In the first year, the interest is $450, as we calculated before. Because the total payment is $1,285.46, the principal paid in the first year must be:

$$\text{Principal paid} = \$1,285.46 - 450 = \$835.46$$

The ending loan balance is thus:

$$\text{Ending balance} = \$5,000 - 835.46 = \$4,164.54$$

The interest in the second year is $4,164.54 \times .09 = \$374.81$, and the loan balance declines by $1,285.46 - 374.81 = \$910.65$. We can summarize all of the relevant calculations in the following schedule:

Year	Beginning Balance	Total Payment	Interest Paid	Principal Paid	Ending Balance
1	$5,000.00	$1,285.46	$ 450.00	$ 835.46	$4,164.54
2	4,164.54	1,285.46	374.81	910.65	3,253.88
3	3,253.88	1,285.46	292.85	992.61	2,261.27
4	2,261.27	1,285.46	203.51	1,081.95	1,179.32
5	1,179.32	1,285.46	106.14	1,179.32	0.00
Totals		$6,427.30	$1,427.31	$5,000.00	

Because the loan balance declines to zero, the five equal payments do pay off the loan. Notice that the interest paid declines each period. This isn't surprising because the loan balance is going down. Given that the total payment is fixed, the principal paid must be rising each period.

If you compare the two loan amortizations in this section, you will see that the total interest is greater for the equal total payment case: $1,427.31 versus $1,350. The reason for this is that the loan is repaid more slowly early on, so the interest is somewhat higher. This doesn't mean that one loan is better than the other; it simply means that one is effectively paid off faster than the other. For example, the principal reduction in the first year is $835.46 in the equal total payment case as compared to $1,000 in the first case.

EXAMPLE 4.28

Partial Amortization, or "Bite the Bullet"   A common arrangement in real estate lending might call for a 5-year loan with, say, a 15-year amortization. What this means is that the borrower makes a payment every month of a fixed amount based on a 15-year amortization. However, after 60 months, the borrower makes a single, much larger payment called a "balloon" or "bullet" to pay off the loan. Because the monthly payments don't fully pay off the loan, the loan is said to be partially amortized.

Suppose we have a $100,000 commercial mortgage with a 12 percent APR and a 20-year (240-month) amortization. Further suppose the mortgage has a five-year balloon. What will the monthly payment be? How big will the balloon payment be?

The monthly payment can be calculated based on an ordinary annuity with a present value of $100,000. There are 240 payments, and the interest rate is 1 percent per month. The payment is:

$$\$100,000 = C \times [1 - (1/1.01^{240})]/.01$$
$$= C \times 90.8194$$
$$C = \$1,101.09$$

Now, there is an easy way and a hard way to determine the balloon payment. The hard way is to actually amortize the loan for 60 months to see what the balance is at that time. The easy way is to recognize that after 60 months, we have a $240 - 60 = 180$-month loan. The payment is still $1,101.09 per month, and the interest rate is still 1 percent per month. The loan balance is thus the present value of the remaining payments:

$$\text{Loan balance} = \$1,101.09 \times [1 - (1/1.01^{180})]/.01$$
$$= \$1,101.09 \times 83.3217$$
$$= \$91,744.69$$

The balloon payment is a substantial $91,744. Why is it so large? To get an idea, consider the first payment on the mortgage. The interest in the first month is $100,000 × .01 = $1,000. Your payment is $1,101.09, so the loan balance declines by only $101.09. Because the loan balance declines so slowly, the cumulative "pay down" over five years is not great.

We will close this section with an example that may be of particular relevance. Federal Stafford loans are an important source of financing for many college students, helping to cover the cost of tuition, books, new cars, condominiums, and many other things. Sometimes students do not seem to fully realize that Stafford loans have a serious drawback: They must be repaid in monthly installments, usually beginning six months after the student leaves school.

Some Stafford loans are subsidized, meaning that the interest does not begin to accrue until repayment begins (this is a good thing). If you are a dependent undergraduate student under this particular option, the total debt you can run up is, at most, $23,000. The maximum interest rate is 8.25 percent, or 8.25/12 = .6875 percent per month. Under

SPREADSHEET APPLICATIONS

Loan Amortization Using a Spreadsheet

Loan amortization is a common spreadsheet application. To illustrate, we will set up the problem that we examined earlier: a five-year, $5,000, 9 percent loan with constant payments. Our spreadsheet looks like this:

	A	B	C	D	E	F	G	H
1								
2				Using a spreadsheet to amortize a loan				
3								
4			Loan amount:	$5,000				
5			Interest rate:	0.09				
6			Loan term:	5				
7			Loan payment:	$1,285.46				
8				Note: Payment is calculated using PMT(rate, nper, -pv, fv).				
9			Amortization table:					
10								
11		Year	Beginning	Total	Interest	Principal	Ending	
12			Balance	Payment	Paid	Paid	Balance	
13		1	$5,000.00	$1,285.46	$450.00	$835.46	$4,164.54	
14		2	4,164.54	1,285.46	374.81	910.65	3,253.88	
15		3	3,253.88	1,285.46	292.85	992.61	2,261.27	
16		4	2,261.27	1,285.46	203.51	1,081.95	1,179.32	
17		5	1,179.32	1,285.46	106.14	1,179.32	0.00	
18		Totals		6,427.31	1,427.31	5,000.00		
19								
20			Formulas in the amortization table:					
21								
22		Year	Beginning	Total	Interest	Principal	Ending	
23			Balance	Payment	Paid	Paid	Balance	
24		1	=+D4	=$D$7	=+$D$5*C13	=+D13-E13	=+C13-F13	
25		2	=+G13	=$D$7	=+$D$5*C14	=+D14-E14	=+C14-F14	
26		3	=+G14	=$D$7	=+$D$5*C15	=+D15-E15	=+C15-F15	
27		4	=+G15	=$D$7	=+$D$5*C16	=+D16-E16	=+C16-F16	
28		5	=+G16	=$D$7	=+$D$5*C17	=+D17-E17	=+C17-F17	
29								
30			Note: Totals in the amortization table are calculated using the SUM formula.					
31								

the "standard repayment plan," the loans are amortized over 10 years (subject to a minimum payment of $50).

Suppose you max out borrowing under this program and also get stuck paying the maximum interest rate. Beginning six months after you graduate (or otherwise depart the ivory tower), what will your monthly payment be? How much will you owe after making payments for four years?

Given our earlier discussions, see if you don't agree that your monthly payment assuming a $23,000 total loan is $282.10 per month. Also, as explained in Example 4.28, after making payments for four years, you still owe the present value of the remaining payments. There are 120 payments in all. After you make 48 of them (the first four years), you have 72 to go. By now, it should be easy for you to verify that the present value of $282.10 per month for 72 months at .6875 percent per month is just under $16,000, so you still have a long way to go.

Of course, it is possible to rack up much larger debts. According to the Association of American Medical Colleges, medical students who borrowed to attend medical school and graduated in 2009 had an average student loan balance of $160,000. Ouch! How long will it take the average student to pay off her medical school loans?

4.6 What Is a Firm Worth?

Suppose you are a business appraiser trying to determine the value of small companies. How can you determine what a firm is worth? One way to think about the question of how much a firm is worth is to calculate the present value of its future cash flows.

Let us consider the example of a firm that is expected to generate net cash flows (cash inflows minus cash outflows) of $5,000 in the first year and $2,000 for each of the next five years. The firm can be sold for $10,000 seven years from now. After considering other investments available in the market with similar risks, the owners of the firm would like to be able to make 10 percent on their investment in the firm.

The value of the firm is found by multiplying the net cash flows by the appropriate present value factor. The value of the firm is simply the sum of the present values of the individual net cash flows.

The present value of the net cash flows is given next.

The Present Value of the Firm

End of Year	Net Cash Flow of the Firm	Present Value Factor (10%)	Present Value of Net Cash Flows
1	$ 5,000	.90909	$ 4,545.45
2	2,000	.82645	1,652.90
3	2,000	.75131	1,502.62
4	2,000	.68301	1,366.02
5	2,000	.62092	1,241.84
6	2,000	.56447	1,128.94
7	10,000	.51316	5,131.58
		Present value of firm	$16,569.35

We can also use the simplifying formula for an annuity:

$$\frac{\$5,000}{1.1} + \frac{(\$2,000 \times \text{PVIA}(.10, 5))}{1.1} + \frac{\$10,000}{(1.1)^7} = \$16,569.35$$

Chapter 4   Discounted Cash Flow Valuation   **121**

Suppose you have the opportunity to acquire the firm for $12,000. Should you acquire the firm? The answer is yes because the NPV is positive:

$$\text{NPV} = \text{PV} - \text{Cost}$$
$$\$4,569.35 = \$16,569.35 - \$12,000$$

The incremental value (NPV) of acquiring the firm is $4,569.35.

EXAMPLE 4.29

Firm Valuation   The Trojan Pizza Company is contemplating investing $1 million in four new outlets in Los Angeles. Andrew Lo, the firm's chief financial officer (CFO), has estimated that the investments will pay out cash flows of $200,000 per year for nine years and nothing thereafter. (The cash flows will occur at the end of each year and there will be no cash flow after year 9.) Mr. Lo has determined that the relevant discount rate for this investment is 15 percent. This is the rate of return that the firm can earn at comparable projects. Should the Trojan Pizza Company make the investments in the new outlets?

The decision can be evaluated as follows:

$$\text{NPV} = -\$1,000,000 + \frac{\$200,000}{1.15} + \frac{\$200,000}{(1.15)^2} + \cdots + \frac{\$200,000}{(1.15)^9}$$
$$= -\$1,000,000 + \$200,000 \times \text{PVIA} (.15, 9)$$
$$= -\$1,000,000 + \$954,316.78$$
$$= -\$45,683.22$$

 ◄ To test your mastery of this material, take a quiz at mhhe. com/rwj

The present value of the four new outlets is only $954,316.78. The outlets are worth less than they cost. The Trojan Pizza Company should not make the investment because the NPV is −$45,683.22. If the Trojan Pizza Company requires a 15 percent rate of return, the new outlets are not a good investment.

SPREADSHEET APPLICATIONS

How to Calculate Present Values with Multiple Future Cash Flows Using a Spreadsheet

We can set up a basic spreadsheet to calculate the present values of the individual cash flows as follows. Notice that we have simply calculated the present values one at a time and added them up:

	A	B	C	D	E
1					
2		Using a spreadsheet to value multiple future cash flows			
3					
4	What is the present value of $200 in one year, $400 the next year, $600 the next year, and				
5	$800 the last year if the discount rate is 12 percent?				
6					
7	Rate:	0.12			
8					
9	Year	Cash flows	Present values	Formula used	
10	1	$200	$178.57	=PV($B$7,A10,0,−B10)	
11	2	$400	$318.88	=PV($B$7,A11,0,−B11)	
12	3	$600	$427.07	=PV($B$7,A12,0,−B12)	
13	4	$800	$508.41	=PV($B$7,A13,0,−B13)	
14					
15		Total PV:	$1,432.93	=SUM(C10:C13)	
16					
17	Notice the negative signs inserted in the PV formulas. These just make the present values have				
18	positive signs. Also, the discount rate in cell B7 is entered as $B$7 (an "absolute" reference)				
19	because it is used over and over. We could have just entered ".12" instead, but our approach is more				
20	flexible.				
21					
22					

Summary and Conclusions

1. Two basic concepts, *future value* and *present value,* were introduced in the beginning of this chapter. With a 10 percent interest rate, an investor with $1 today can generate a future value of $1.10 in a year, $1.21 [=$1 × (1.10)^2] in two years, and so on. Conversely, present value analysis places a current value on a future cash flow. With the same 10 percent interest rate, a dollar to be received in one year has a present value of $.909 (=$1/1.10) in Year 0. A dollar to be received in two years has a present value of $.826 [=$1/(1.10)^2].

2. We commonly express an interest rate as, say, 12 percent per year. However, we can speak of the interest rate as 3 percent per quarter. Although the stated annual interest rate remains 12 percent (=3 percent × 4), the effective annual interest rate is 12.55 percent [=(1.03)^4 − 1]. In other words, the compounding process increases the future value of an investment. The limiting case is continuous compounding, where funds are assumed to be reinvested every infinitesimal instant.

3. A basic quantitative technique for financial decision making is net present value analysis. The net present value formula for an investment that generates cash flows (C_i) in future periods is:

$$\text{NPV} = -C_0 + \frac{C_1}{(1 + r)} + \frac{C_2}{(1 + r)^2} + \cdots + \frac{C_T}{(1 + r)^T} = -C_0 + \sum_{i=1}^{T} \frac{C_i}{(1 + r)^i}$$

The formula assumes that the cash flow at date 0 is the initial investment (a cash outflow). r is the appropriate interest rate reflecting time and risk.

4. Frequently, the actual calculation of present value is long and tedious. The computation of the present value of a long-term mortgage with monthly payments is a good example of this. We presented four simplifying formulas:

$$\text{Perpetuity: } PV = \frac{C}{r}$$

$$\text{Growing perpetuity: } PV = \frac{C}{r - g}$$

$$\text{Annuity: } PV = C\left[\frac{1 - \frac{1}{(1 + r)^T}}{r}\right]$$

$$\text{Growing annuity: } PV = C\left[\frac{1 - \left(\frac{1 + g}{1 + r}\right)^T}{r - g}\right]$$

5. We stressed a few practical considerations in the application of these formulas:
   a. The numerator in each of the formulas, C, is the cash flow to be received *one full period hence.*
   b. Cash flows are generally irregular in practice. To avoid unwieldy problems, assumptions to create more regular cash flows are made both in this textbook and in the real world.
   c. A number of present value problems involve annuities (or perpetuities) beginning a few periods hence. Students should practice combining the annuity (or perpetuity) formula with the discounting formula to solve these problems.
   d. Annuities and perpetuities may have periods of every two or every n years, rather than once a year. The annuity and perpetuity formulas can easily handle such circumstances.
   e. We frequently encounter problems where the present value of one annuity must be equated with the present value of another annuity.

Concept Questions

1. **Compounding and Period** As you increase the length of time involved, what happens to future values? What happens to present values?

2. **Interest Rates** What happens to the future value of an annuity if you increase the rate r? What happens to the present value?

3. **Present Value** Suppose two athletes sign 10-year contracts for $80 million. In one case, we're told that the $80 million will be paid in 10 equal installments. In the other case, we're told that the $80 million will be paid in 10 installments, but the installments will increase by 5 percent per year. Who got the better deal?

4. **APR and EAR** Should lending laws be changed to require lenders to report EARs instead of APRs? Why or why not?

5. **Time Value** On subsidized Stafford loans, a common source of financial aid for college students, interest does not begin to accrue until repayment begins. Who receives a bigger subsidy, a freshman or a senior? Explain.

Use the following information to answer the next five questions:
Toyota Motor Credit Corporation (TMCC), a subsidiary of Toyota Motor Corporation, offered some securities for sale to the public on March 28, 2008. Under the terms of the deal, TMCC promised to repay the owner of one of these securities $100,000 on March 28, 2038, but investors would receive nothing until then. Investors paid TMCC $24,099 for each of these securities; so they gave up $24,099 on March 28, 2008, for the promise of a $100,000 payment 30 years later.

6. **Time Value of Money** Why would TMCC be willing to accept such a small amount today ($24,099) in exchange for a promise to repay about four times that amount ($100,000) in the future?

7. **Call Provisions** TMCC has the right to buy back the securities on the anniversary date at a price established when the securities were issued (this feature is a term of this particular deal). What impact does this feature have on the desirability of this security as an investment?

8. **Time Value of Money** Would you be willing to pay $24,099 today in exchange for $100,000 in 30 years? What would be the key considerations in answering yes or no? Would your answer depend on who is making the promise to repay?

9. **Investment Comparison** Suppose that when TMCC offered the security for $24,099 the U.S. Treasury had offered an essentially identical security. Do you think it would have had a higher or lower price? Why?

10. **Length of Investment** The TMCC security is bought and sold on the New York Stock Exchange. If you looked at the price today, do you think the price would exceed the $24,099 original price? Why? If you looked in the year 2019, do you think the price would be higher or lower than today's price? Why?

Questions and Problems

BASIC
(Questions 1–20)

1. **Simple Interest versus Compound Interest** First City Bank pays 8 percent simple interest on its savings account balances, whereas Second City Bank pays 8 percent interest compounded annually. If you made a $5,000 deposit in each bank, how much more money would you earn from your Second City Bank account at the end of 10 years?

2. **Calculating Future Values** Compute the future value of $1,000 compounded annually for

    a. 10 years at 5 percent.
    b. 10 years at 10 percent.
    c. 20 years at 5 percent.
    d. Why is the interest earned in part (c) not twice the amount earned in part (a)?

3. **Calculating Present Values** For each of the following, compute the present value:

Present Value	Years	Interest Rate	Future Value
	6	7%	$ 13,827
	9	15	43,852
	18	11	725,380
	23	18	590,710

4. **Calculating Interest Rates** Solve for the unknown interest rate in each of the following:

Present Value	Years	Interest Rate	Future Value
$ 242	4		$ 307
410	8		896
51,700	16		162,181
18,750	27		483,500

5. **Calculating the Number of Periods** Solve for the unknown number of years in each of the following:

Present Value	Years	Interest Rate	Future Value
$ 625		9%	$ 1,284
810		11	4,341
18,400		17	402,662
21,500		8	173,439

6. **Calculating the Number of Periods** At 8 percent interest, how long does it take to double your money? To quadruple it?

7. **Calculating Present Values** Imprudential, Inc., has an unfunded pension liability of $630 million that must be paid in 20 years. To assess the value of the firm's stock, financial analysts want to discount this liability back to the present. If the relevant discount rate is 7.1 percent, what is the present value of this liability?

8. **Calculating Rates of Return** Although appealing to more refined tastes, art as a collectible has not always performed so profitably. During 2010, Deutscher-Menzies sold *Arkies under the Shower,* a painting by renowned Australian painter Brett Whiteley, at auction for a price of $1,100,000. Unfortunately for the previous owner, he had purchased it three years earlier at a price of $1,680,000. What was his annual rate of return on this painting?

9. **Perpetuities** An investor purchasing a British consol is entitled to receive annual payments from the British government forever. What is the price of a consol that

Chapter 4   Discounted Cash Flow Valuation   **125**

pays $150 annually if the next payment occurs one year from today? The market interest rate is 4.6 percent.

10. **Continuous Compounding**   Compute the future value of $1,900 continuously compounded for

   a. 7 years at a stated annual interest rate of 12 percent.
   b. 5 years at a stated annual interest rate of 10 percent.
   c. 12 years at a stated annual interest rate of 5 percent.
   d. 10 years at a stated annual interest rate of 7 percent.

11. **Present Value and Multiple Cash Flows**   Conoly Co. has identified an investment project with the following cash flows. If the discount rate is 10 percent, what is the present value of these cash flows? What is the present value at 18 percent? At 24 percent?

Year	Cash Flow
1	$ 960
2	840
3	935
4	1,350

12. **Present Value and Multiple Cash Flows**   Investment X offers to pay you $4,500 per year for nine years, whereas Investment Y offers to pay you $7,000 per year for five years. Which of these cash flow streams has the higher present value if the discount rate is 5 percent? If the discount rate is 22 percent?

13. **Calculating Annuity Present Value**   An investment offers $4,900 per year for 15 years, with the first payment occurring one year from now. If the required return is 8 percent, what is the value of the investment? What would the value be if the payments occurred for 40 years? For 75 years? Forever?

14. **Calculating Perpetuity Values**   The Perpetual Life Insurance Co. is trying to sell you an investment policy that will pay you and your heirs $15,000 per year forever. If the required return on this investment is 5.2 percent, how much will you pay for the policy? Suppose the Perpetual Life Insurance Co. told you the policy costs $320,000. At what interest rate would this be a fair deal?

15. **Calculating EAR**   Find the EAR in each of the following cases:

Stated Rate (APR)	Number of Times Compounded	Effective Rate (EAR)
7%	Quarterly	
16	Monthly	
11	Daily	
12	Infinite	

16. **Calculating APR**   Find the APR, or stated rate, in each of the following cases:

Stated Rate (APR)	Number of Times Compounded	Effective Rate (EAR)
	Semiannually	9.8%
	Monthly	19.6
	Weekly	8.3
	Infinite	14.2

126   **Part II**   Valuation and Capital Budgeting

17. **Calculating EAR** First National Bank charges 11.2 percent compounded monthly on its business loans. First United Bank charges 11.4 percent compounded semiannually. As a potential borrower, to which bank would you go for a new loan?

18. **Interest Rates** Well-known financial writer Andrew Tobias argues that he can earn 177 percent per year buying wine by the case. Specifically, he assumes that he will consume one $10 bottle of fine Bordeaux per week for the next 12 weeks. He can either pay $10 per week or buy a case of 12 bottles today. If he buys the case, he receives a 10 percent discount and, by doing so, earns the 177 percent. Assume he buys the wine and consumes the first bottle today. Do you agree with his analysis? Do you see a problem with his numbers?

19. **Calculating Number of Periods** One of your customers is delinquent on his accounts payable balance. You've mutually agreed to a repayment schedule of $700 per month. You will charge 1.3 percent per month interest on the overdue balance. If the current balance is $21,500, how long will it take for the account to be paid off?

20. **Calculating EAR** Friendly's Quick Loans, Inc., offers you "three for four or I knock on your door." This means you get $3 today and repay $4 when you get your paycheck in one week (or else). What's the effective annual return Friendly's earns on this lending business? If you were brave enough to ask, what APR would Friendly's say you were paying?

INTERMEDIATE (Questions 21–50)

21. **Future Value** What is the future value in six years of $1,000 invested in an account with a stated annual interest rate of 9 percent,
    a. Compounded annually?
    b. Compounded semiannually?
    c. Compounded monthly?
    d. Compounded continuously?
    e. Why does the future value increase as the compounding period shortens?

22. **Simple Interest versus Compound Interest** First Simple Bank pays 5 percent simple interest on its investment accounts. If First Complex Bank pays interest on its accounts compounded annually, what rate should the bank set if it wants to match First Simple Bank over an investment horizon of 10 years?

23. **Calculating Annuities** You are planning to save for retirement over the next 30 years. To do this, you will invest $800 a month in a stock account and $350 a month in a bond account. The return of the stock account is expected to be 11 percent, and the bond account will pay 6 percent. When you retire, you will combine your money into an account with an 8 percent return. How much can you withdraw each month from your account assuming a 25-year withdrawal period?

24. **Calculating Rates of Return** Suppose an investment offers to quadruple your money in 12 months (don't believe it). What rate of return per quarter are you being offered?

25. **Calculating Rates of Return** You're trying to choose between two different investments, both of which have up-front costs of $65,000. Investment G returns $125,000 in six years. Investment H returns $185,000 in 10 years. Which of these investments has the higher return?

26. **Growing Perpetuities** Mark Weinstein has been working on an advanced technology in laser eye surgery. His technology will be available in the near term. He anticipates his first annual cash flow from the technology to be $175,000, received two years from today. Subsequent annual cash flows will grow at 3.5 percent in perpetuity. What is the present value of the technology if the discount rate is 10 percent?

27. **Perpetuities** A prestigious investment bank designed a new security that pays a quarterly dividend of $4.50 in perpetuity. The first dividend occurs one quarter

from today. What is the price of the security if the stated annual interest rate is 6.5 percent, compounded quarterly?

28. **Annuity Present Values**   What is the present value of an annuity of $6,500 per year, with the first cash flow received three years from today and the last one received 25 years from today? Use a discount rate of 7 percent.

29. **Annuity Present Values**   What is the value today of a 15-year annuity that pays $650 a year? The annuity's first payment occurs six years from today. The annual interest rate is 11 percent for Years 1 through 5, and 13 percent thereafter.

30. **Balloon Payments**   Audrey Sanborn has just arranged to purchase a $550,000 vacation home in the Bahamas with a 20 percent down payment. The mortgage has a 6.1 percent stated annual interest rate, compounded monthly, and calls for equal monthly payments over the next 30 years. Her first payment will be due one month from now. However, the mortgage has an eight-year balloon payment, meaning that the balance of the loan must be paid off at the end of Year 8. There were no other transaction costs or finance charges. How much will Audrey's balloon payment be in eight years?

31. **Calculating Interest Expense**   You receive a credit card application from Shady Banks Savings and Loan offering an introductory rate of 2.40 percent per year, compounded monthly for the first six months, increasing thereafter to 18 percent compounded monthly. Assuming you transfer the $7,500 balance from your existing credit card and make no subsequent payments, how much interest will you owe at the end of the first year?

32. **Perpetuities**   Barrett Pharmaceuticals is considering a drug project that costs $2.5 million today and is expected to generate end-of-year annual cash flows of $227,000, forever. At what discount rate would Barrett be indifferent between accepting or rejecting the project?

33. **Growing Annuity**   Southern California Publishing Company is trying to decide whether to revise its popular textbook, *Financial Psychoanalysis Made Simple*. The company has estimated that the revision will cost $75,000. Cash flows from increased sales will be $21,000 the first year. These cash flows will increase by 4 percent per year. The book will go out of print five years from now. Assume that the initial cost is paid now and revenues are received at the end of each year. If the company requires a return of 10 percent for such an investment, should it undertake the revision?

34. **Growing Annuity**   Your job pays you only once a year for all the work you did over the previous 12 months. Today, December 31, you just received your salary of $65,000, and you plan to spend all of it. However, you want to start saving for retirement beginning next year. You have decided that one year from today you will begin depositing 5 percent of your annual salary in an account that will earn 10 percent per year. Your salary will increase at 4 percent per year throughout your career. How much money will you have on the date of your retirement 40 years from today?

35. **Present Value and Interest Rates**   What is the relationship between the value of an annuity and the level of interest rates? Suppose you just bought a 15-year annuity of $6,800 per year at the current interest rate of 10 percent per year. What happens to the value of your investment if interest rates suddenly drop to 5 percent? What if interest rates suddenly rise to 15 percent?

36. **Calculating the Number of Payments**   You're prepared to make monthly payments of $350, beginning at the end of this month, into an account that pays 10 percent interest compounded monthly. How many payments will you have made when your account balance reaches $35,000?

Part II   Valuation and Capital Budgeting

37. **Calculating Annuity Present Values**   You want to borrow $65,000 from your local bank to buy a new sailboat. You can afford to make monthly payments of $1,320, but no more. Assuming monthly compounding, what is the highest APR you can afford on a 60-month loan?

38. **Calculating Loan Payments**   You need a 30-year, fixed-rate mortgage to buy a new home for $250,000. Your mortgage bank will lend you the money at a 5.3 percent APR for this 360-month loan. However, you can only afford monthly payments of $950, so you offer to pay off any remaining loan balance at the end of the loan in the form of a single balloon payment. How large will this balloon payment have to be for you to keep your monthly payments at $950?

39. **Present and Future Values**   The present value of the following cash flow stream is $7,300 when discounted at 8 percent annually. What is the value of the missing cash flow?

Year	Cash Flow
1	$1,500
2	?
3	2,700
4	2,900

40. **Calculating Present Values**   You just won the TVM Lottery. You will receive $1 million today plus another 10 annual payments that increase by $275,000 per year. Thus, in one year you receive $1.275 million. In two years, you get $1.55 million, and so on. If the appropriate interest rate is 9 percent, what is the present value of your winnings?

41. **EAR versus APR**   You have just purchased a new warehouse. To finance the purchase, you've arranged for a 30-year mortgage for 80 percent of the $4,500,000 purchase price. The monthly payment on this loan will be $27,500. What is the APR on this loan? The EAR?

42. **Present Value and Break-Even Interest**   Consider a firm with a contract to sell an asset for $115,000 three years from now. The asset costs $76,000 to produce today. Given a relevant discount rate on this asset of 13 percent per year, will the firm make a profit on this asset? At what rate does the firm just break even?

43. **Present Value and Multiple Cash Flows**   What is the present value of $5,000 per year, at a discount rate of 6 percent, if the first payment is received 6 years from now and the last payment is received 25 years from now?

44. **Variable Interest Rates**   A 15-year annuity pays $1,500 per month, and payments are made at the end of each month. If the interest rate is 12 percent compounded monthly for the first seven years, and 6 percent compounded monthly thereafter, what is the present value of the annuity?

45. **Comparing Cash Flow Streams**   You have your choice of two investment accounts. Investment A is a 15-year annuity that features end-of-month $1,500 payments and has an interest rate of 8.7 percent compounded monthly. Investment B is an 8 percent continuously compounded lump-sum investment, also good for 15 years. How much money would you need to invest in B today for it to be worth as much as Investment A 15 years from now?

46. **Calculating Present Value of a Perpetuity**   Given an interest rate of 6.1 percent per year, what is the value at Date $t = 7$ of a perpetual stream of $2,500 annual payments that begins at Date $t = 15$?

47. **Calculating EAR**   A local finance company quotes a 16 percent interest rate on one-year loans. So, if you borrow $26,000, the interest for the year will be $4,160.

Because you must repay a total of $30,160 in one year, the finance company requires you to pay $30,160/12, or $2,513.33, per month over the next 12 months. Is this a 15 percent loan? What rate would legally have to be quoted? What is the effective annual rate?

48. **Calculating Present Values** A 5-year annuity of ten $5,300 semiannual payments will begin 9 years from now, with the first payment coming 9.5 years from now. If the discount rate is 12 percent compounded monthly, what is the value of this annuity five years from now? What is the value three years from now? What is the current value of the annuity?

49. **Calculating Annuities Due** Suppose you are going to receive $20,000 per year for five years. The appropriate interest rate is 7 percent.
   a. What is the present value of the payments if they are in the form of an ordinary annuity? What is the present value if the payments are an annuity due?
   b. Suppose you plan to invest the payments for five years. What is the future value if the payments are an ordinary annuity? What if the payments are an annuity due?
   c. Which has the highest present value, the ordinary annuity or annuity due? Which has the highest future value? Will this always be true?

50. **Calculating Annuities Due** You want to buy a new sports car from Muscle Motors for $73,000. The contract is in the form of a 60-month annuity due at a 6.45 percent APR. What will your monthly payment be?

CHALLENGE
(Questions 51–75)

51. **Calculating Annuities Due** You want to lease a set of golf clubs from Pings Ltd. The lease contract is in the form of 24 equal monthly payments at a 10.4 percent stated annual interest rate, compounded monthly. Because the clubs cost $2,300 retail, Pings wants the PV of the lease payments to equal $2,300. Suppose that your first payment is due immediately. What will your monthly lease payments be?

52. **Annuities** You are saving for the college education of your two children. They are two years apart in age; one will begin college 15 years from today and the other will begin 17 years from today. You estimate your children's college expenses to be $45,000 per year per child, payable at the beginning of each school year. The annual interest rate is 7.5 percent. How much money must you deposit in an account each year to fund your children's education? Your deposits begin one year from today. You will make your last deposit when your oldest child enters college. Assume four years of college.

53. **Growing Annuities** Tom Adams has received a job offer from a large investment bank as a clerk to an associate banker. His base salary will be $55,000. He will receive his first annual salary payment one year from the day he begins to work. In addition, he will get an immediate $10,000 bonus for joining the company. His salary will grow at 3.5 percent each year. Each year he will receive a bonus equal to 10 percent of his salary. Mr. Adams is expected to work for 25 years. What is the present value of the offer if the discount rate is 9 percent?

54. **Calculating Annuities** You have recently won the super jackpot in the Washington State Lottery. On reading the fine print, you discover that you have the following two options:
   a. You will receive 31 annual payments of $250,000, with the first payment being delivered today. The income will be taxed at a rate of 28 percent. Taxes will be withheld when the checks are issued.
   b. You will receive $530,000 now, and you will not have to pay taxes on this amount. In addition, beginning one year from today, you will receive $200,000 each year for 30 years. The cash flows from this annuity will be taxed at 28 percent.

Using a discount rate of 7 percent, which option should you select?

www.mhhe.com/rwj

55. Calculating Growing Annuities You have 30 years left until retirement and want to retire with $2 million. Your salary is paid annually, and you will receive $70,000 at the end of the current year. Your salary will increase at 3 percent per year, and you can earn a return of 9 percent on the money you invest. If you save a constant percentage of your salary, what percentage of your salary must you save each year?

56. Balloon Payments On September 1, 2009, Susan Chao bought a motorcycle for $30,000. She paid $1,000 down and financed the balance with a five-year loan at a stated annual interest rate of 7.2 percent, compounded monthly. She started the monthly payments exactly one month after the purchase (i.e., October 1, 2009). Two years later, at the end of October 2011, Susan got a new job and decided to pay off the loan. If the bank charges her a 1 percent prepayment penalty based on the loan balance, how much must she pay the bank on November 1, 2011?

57. Calculating Annuity Values Bilbo Baggins wants to save money to meet three objectives. First, he would like to be able to retire 30 years from now with a retirement income of $23,000 per month for 20 years, with the first payment received 30 years and 1 month from now. Second, he would like to purchase a cabin in Rivendell in 10 years at an estimated cost of $320,000. Third, after he passes on at the end of the 20 years of withdrawals, he would like to leave an inheritance of $1,000,000 to his nephew Frodo. He can afford to save $2,100 per month for the next 10 years. If he can earn an 11 percent EAR before he retires and an 8 percent EAR after he retires, how much will he have to save each month in Years 11 through 30?

58. Calculating Annuity Values After deciding to buy a new car, you can either lease the car or purchase it with a three-year loan. The car you wish to buy costs $31,000. The dealer has a special leasing arrangement where you pay $1,500 today and $405 per month for the next three years. If you purchase the car, you will pay it off in monthly payments over the next three years at an APR of 6 percent. You believe that you will be able to sell the car for $20,000 in three years. Should you buy or lease the car? What break-even resale price in three years would make you indifferent between buying and leasing?

59. Calculating Annuity Values An All-Pro defensive lineman is in contract negotiations. The team has offered the following salary structure:

Time	Salary
0	$8,500,000
1	3,900,000
2	4,600,000
3	5,300,000
4	5,800,000
5	6,400,000
6	7,300,000

All salaries are to be paid in a lump sum. The player has asked you as his agent to renegotiate the terms. He wants a $10 million signing bonus payable today and a contract value increase of $1,500,000. He also wants an equal salary paid every three months, with the first paycheck three months from now. If the interest rate is 5 percent compounded daily, what is the amount of his quarterly check? Assume 365 days in a year.

60. Discount Interest Loans This question illustrates what is known as *discount interest*. Imagine you are discussing a loan with a somewhat unscrupulous lender. You want to borrow $20,000 for one year. The interest rate is 15 percent. You and the lender agree that the interest on the loan will be .15 × $20,000 = $3,000. So, the lender deducts this interest amount from the loan up front and gives you $17,000. In this case, we say that the discount is $3,000. What's wrong here?

61. **Calculating Annuity Values**   You are serving on a jury. A plaintiff is suing the city for injuries sustained after a freak street sweeper accident. In the trial, doctors testified that it will be five years before the plaintiff is able to return to work. The jury has already decided in favor of the plaintiff. You are the foreperson of the jury and propose that the jury give the plaintiff an award to cover the following: (1) The present value of two years' back pay. The plaintiff's annual salary for the last two years would have been $37,000 and $39,000, respectively. (2) The present value of five years' future salary. You assume the salary will be $43,000 per year. (3) $150,000 for pain and suffering. (4) $25,000 for court costs. Assume that the salary payments are equal amounts paid at the end of each month. If the interest rate you choose is a 9 percent EAR, what is the size of the settlement? If you were the plaintiff, would you like to see a higher or lower interest rate?

62. **Calculating EAR with Points**   You are looking at a one-year loan of $10,000. The interest rate is quoted as 8 percent plus three points. A *point* on a loan is simply 1 percent (one percentage point) of the loan amount. Quotes similar to this one are very common with home mortgages. The interest rate quotation in this example requires the borrower to pay three points to the lender up front and repay the loan later with 8 percent interest. What rate would you actually be paying here? What is the EAR for a one-year loan with a quoted interest rate of 11 percent plus two points? Is your answer affected by the loan amount?

63. **EAR versus APR**   Two banks in the area offer 30-year, $200,000 mortgages at 5.3 percent and charge a $2,400 loan application fee. However, the application fee charged by Insecurity Bank and Trust is refundable if the loan application is denied, whereas that charged by I. M. Greedy and Sons Mortgage Bank is not. The current disclosure law requires that any fees that will be refunded if the applicant is rejected be included in calculating the APR, but this is not required with nonrefundable fees (presumably because refundable fees are part of the loan rather than a fee). What are the EARs on these two loans? What are the APRs?

64. **Calculating EAR with Add-On Interest**   This problem illustrates a deceptive way of quoting interest rates called *add-on interest*. Imagine that you see an advertisement for Crazy Judy's Stereo City that reads something like this: "$1,000 Instant Credit! 18% Simple Interest! Three Years to Pay! Low, Low Monthly Payments!" You're not exactly sure what all this means and somebody has spilled ink over the APR on the loan contract, so you ask the manager for clarification.

Judy explains that if you borrow $1,000 for three years at 18 percent interest, in three years you will owe:

$$\$1,000 \times 1.18^3 = \$1,000 \times 1.64303 = \$1,643.03$$

Judy recognizes that coming up with $1,643.03 all at once might be a strain, so she lets you make "low, low monthly payments" of $1,643.03/36 = $45.64 per month, even though this is extra bookkeeping work for her.

Is the interest rate on this loan 18 percent? Why or why not? What is the APR on this loan? What is the EAR? Why do you think this is called add-on interest?

65. **Calculating the Number of Periods**   Your Christmas ski vacation was great, but it unfortunately ran a bit over budget. All is not lost: You just received an offer in the mail to transfer your $10,000 balance from your current credit card, which charges an annual rate of 18.6 percent, to a new credit card charging a rate of 8.2 percent. How much faster could you pay the loan off by making your planned monthly payments of $200 with the new card? What if there was a 2 percent fee charged on any balances transferred?

66. **Future Value and Multiple Cash Flows**   An insurance company is offering a new policy to its customers. Typically the policy is bought by a parent or grandparent for a child at the child's birth. The details of the policy are as follows: The purchaser (say, the parent) makes the following six payments to the insurance company:

    First birthday: \$ 500
    Second birthday: \$ 600
    Third birthday: \$ 700
    Fourth birthday: \$ 800
    Fifth birthday: \$ 900
    Sixth birthday: \$1,000

    After the child's sixth birthday, no more payments are made. When the child reaches age 65, he or she receives \$275,000. If the relevant interest rate is 11 percent for the first six years and 7 percent for all subsequent years, is the policy worth buying?

67. **Annuity Present Values and Effective Rates**   You have just won the lottery. You will receive \$2,500,000 today, and then receive 40 payments of \$1,250,000. These payments will start one year from now and will be paid every six months. A representative from Greenleaf Investments has offered to purchase all the payments from you for \$23 million. If the appropriate interest rate is a 9 percent APR compounded daily, should you take the offer? Assume there are 12 months in a year, each with 30 days.

68. **Calculating Interest Rates**   A financial planning service offers a college savings program. The plan calls for you to make six annual payments of \$11,000 each, with the first payment occurring today, your child's 12th birthday. Beginning on your child's 18th birthday, the plan will provide \$25,000 per year for four years. What return is this investment offering?

69. **Break-Even Investment Returns**   Your financial planner offers you two different investment plans. Plan X is a \$15,000 annual perpetuity. Plan Y is a 10-year, \$26,000 annual annuity. Both plans will make their first payment one year from today. At what discount rate would you be indifferent between these two plans?

70. **Perpetual Cash Flows**   What is the value of an investment that pays \$30,000 every *other* year forever, if the first payment occurs one year from today and the discount rate is 13 percent compounded daily? What is the value today if the first payment occurs four years from today? Assume 365 days in a year.

71. **Ordinary Annuities and Annuities Due**   As discussed in the text, an annuity due is identical to an ordinary annuity except that the periodic payments occur at the beginning of each period and not at the end of the period. Show that the relationship between the value of an ordinary annuity and the value of an otherwise equivalent annuity due is:

    $$\text{Annuity due value} = \text{Ordinary annuity value} \times (1 + r)$$

    Show this for both present and future values.

72. **Calculating EAR**   A check-cashing store is in the business of making personal loans to walk-up customers. The store makes only one-week loans at 7 percent interest per week.

    a. What APR must the store report to its customers? What is the EAR that the customers are actually paying?

    b. Now suppose the store makes one-week loans at 7 percent discount interest per week (see Question 60). What's the APR now? The EAR?

    c. The check-cashing store also makes one-month add-on interest loans at 7 percent discount interest per week. Thus, if you borrow \$100 for one month (four weeks), the interest will be (\$100 × 1.07^4) − 100 = \$31.08. Because this is discount interest, your net loan proceeds today will be \$68.92. You must then repay the store

$100 at the end of the month. To help you out, though, the store lets you pay off this $100 in installments of $25 per week. What is the APR of this loan? What is the EAR?

73. **Present Value of a Growing Perpetuity**   What is the equation for the present value of a growing perpetuity with a payment of C one period from today if the payments grow by C each period?

74. **Rule of 72**   A useful rule of thumb for the time it takes an investment to double with discrete compounding is the "Rule of 72." To use the Rule of 72, you simply divide 72 by the interest rate to determine the number of periods it takes for a value today to double. For example, if the interest rate is 6 percent, the Rule of 72 says it will take $72/6 = 12$ years to double. This is approximately equal to the actual answer of 11.90 years. The Rule of 72 can also be applied to determine what interest rate is needed to double money in a specified period. This is a useful approximation for many interest rates and periods. At what rate is the Rule of 72 exact?

75. **Rule of 69.3**   A corollary to the Rule of 72 is the Rule of 69.3. The Rule of 69.3 is exactly correct except for rounding when interest rates are compounded continuously. Prove the Rule of 69.3 for continuously compounded interest.

Excel Master It!

Excel is a great tool for solving problems, but with many time value of money problems, you may still need to draw a time line. For example, consider a classic retirement problem. A friend is celebrating her birthday and wants to start saving for her anticipated retirement. She has the following years to retirement and retirement spending goals:

Years until retirement	30
Amount to withdraw each year	$90,000
Years to withdraw in retirement	20
Interest rate	8%

Because your friend is planning ahead, the first withdrawal will not take place until one year after she retires. She wants to make equal annual deposits into her account for her retirement fund.

a. If she starts making these deposits in one year and makes her last deposit on the day she retires, what amount must she deposit annually to be able to make the desired withdrawals in retirement?

b. Suppose your friend has just inherited a large sum of money. Rather than making equal annual payments, she has decided to make one lump sum deposit today to cover her retirement needs. What amount does she have to deposit today?

c. Suppose your friend's employer will contribute to the account each year as part of the company's profit sharing plan. In addition, your friend expects a distribution from a family trust several years from now. What amount must she deposit annually now to be able to make the desired withdrawals in retirement? The details are:

Employer's annual contribution	$ 1,500
Years until trust fund distribution	20
Amount of trust fund distribution	$25,000

THE MBA DECISION

Ben Bates graduated from college six years ago with a finance undergraduate degree. Although he is satisfied with his current job, his goal is to become an investment banker. He feels that an MBA degree would allow him to achieve this goal. After examining schools, he has narrowed his choice to either Wilton University or Mount Perry College. Although internships are encouraged by both schools, to get class credit for the internship, no salary can be paid. Other than internships, neither school will allow its students to work while enrolled in its MBA program.

Ben currently works at the money management firm of Dewey and Louis. His annual salary at the firm is $65,000 per year, and his salary is expected to increase at 3 percent per year until retirement. He is currently 28 years old and expects to work for 40 more years. His current job includes a fully paid health insurance plan, and his current average tax rate is 26 percent. Ben has a savings account with enough money to cover the entire cost of his MBA program.

The Ritter College of Business at Wilton University is one of the top MBA programs in the country. The MBA degree requires two years of full-time enrollment at the university. The annual tuition is $70,000, payable at the beginning of each school year. Books and other supplies are estimated to cost $3,000 per year. Ben expects that after graduation from Wilton, he will receive a job offer for about $110,000 per year, with a $20,000 signing bonus. The salary at this job will increase at 4 percent per year. Because of the higher salary, his average income tax rate will increase to 31 percent.

The Bradley School of Business at Mount Perry College began its MBA program 16 years ago. The Bradley School is smaller and less well known than the Ritter College. Bradley offers an accelerated, one-year program, with a tuition cost of $85,000 to be paid upon matriculation. Books and other supplies for the program are expected to cost $4,500. Ben thinks that he will receive an offer of $92,000 per year upon graduation, with an $18,000 signing bonus. The salary at this job will increase at 3.5 percent per year. His average tax rate at this level of income will be 29 percent.

Both schools offer a health insurance plan that will cost $3,000 per year, payable at the beginning of the year. Ben also estimates that room and board expenses will cost $2,000 more per year at both schools than his current expenses, payable at the beginning of each year. The appropriate discount rate is 6.5 percent.

1. How does Ben's age affect his decision to get an MBA?
2. What other, perhaps nonquantifiable factors affect Ben's decision to get an MBA?
3. Assuming all salaries are paid at the end of each year, what is the best option for Ben—from a strictly financial standpoint?
4. Ben believes that the appropriate analysis is to calculate the future value of each option. How would you evaluate this statement?
5. What initial salary would Ben need to receive to make him indifferent between attending Wilton University and staying in his current position?
6. Suppose, instead of being able to pay cash for his MBA, Ben must borrow the money. The current borrowing rate is 5.4 percent. How would this affect his decision?

Appendix 4A   Net Present Value: First Principles of Finance

To access the appendix for this chapter, please go to www.mhhe.com/rwj.

Appendix 4B   Using Financial Calculators

To access the appendix for this chapter, please go to www.mhhe.com/rwj.

Appendix 4A   Net Present Value: First Principles of Finance

In this appendix, we show the theoretical underpinnings of the net present value rule. We first show how individuals make intertemporal consumption choices, and then we explain the net present value (NPV) rule. The appendix should appeal to students who like a theoretical model. Those of you who can accept the NPV analysis contained in Chapter 4 can skip to Chapter 5.

4A.1 Making Consumption Choices over Time

Figure 4A.1 illustrates the situation faced by a representative individual in the financial market. This person is assumed to have an income of $50,000 this year and an income of $60,000 next year. The market allows him not only to consume $50,000 worth of goods this year and $60,000 next year, but also to borrow and lend at the equilibrium interest rate.

The line AB in Figure 4A.1 shows all of the consumption possibilities open to the person through borrowing or lending, and the shaded area contains all of the feasible choices. Let's look at this figure more closely to see exactly why points in the shaded area are available.

We will use the letter r to denote the interest rate—the equilibrium rate—in this market. The rate is risk-free because we assume that no default can take place. Look at point A on the vertical axis of Figure 4A.1. Point A is a height of:

$$A = \$60,000 + [\$50,000 \times (1 + r)]$$

For example, if the rate of interest is 10 percent, then point A would be:

$$\begin{aligned} A &= \$60,000 + [\$50,000 \times (1 + 0.1)] \\ &= \$60,000 + \$55,000 \\ &= \$115,000 \end{aligned}$$

Point A is the maximum amount of wealth that this person can spend in the second year. He gets to point A by lending the full income that is available this year, $50,000, and consuming none of it. In the second year, then, he will have the second year's income

Figure 4A.1
Intertemporal Consumption Opportunities

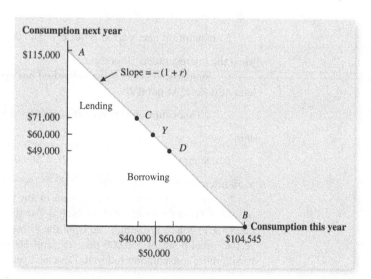

Part II Valuation and Capital Budgeting

of $60,000 plus the proceeds from the loan that he made in the first year, $55,000, for a total of $115,000.

Now let's take a look at point *B*. Point *B* is a distance of:

$$B = \$50,000 + [\$60,000/(1 + r)]$$

along the horizontal axis. If the interest rate is 10 percent, point *B* will be:

$$B = \$50,000 + [\$60,000/(1 + 0.1)]$$
$$= \$50,000 + \$54,545$$
$$= \$104,545$$

(We have rounded off to the nearest dollar.)

Why do we divide next year's income of $60,000 by $(1 + r)$, or 1.1 in the preceding computation? Point *B* represents the maximum amount available for this person to consume this year. To achieve that maximum he would borrow as much as possible and repay the loan from the income, $60,000, that he was going to receive next year. Because $60,000 will be available to repay the loan next year, we are asking how much he could borrow this year at an interest rate of *r* and still be able to repay the loan. The answer is:

$$\$60,000/(1 + r)$$

because if he borrows this amount, he must repay it next year with interest. Thus, next year he must repay:

$$[\$60,000/(1 + r)] \times (1 + r) = \$60,000$$

no matter what the interest rate, *r*, is. In our example we found that he could borrow $54,545 and, sure enough:

$$\$54,545 \times 1.1 = \$60,000$$

(after rounding off to the nearest dollar).

Furthermore, by borrowing and lending different amounts the person can achieve any point on the line *AB*. For example, point *C* is a point where he has chosen to lend $10,000 of today's income. This means that at point *C* he will have:

Consumption this year at point *C* = $50,000 − $10,000 = $40,000

and

Consumption next year at point *C* = $60,000 + [$10,000 × (1 + *r*)] = $71,000

when the interest rate is 10 percent.

Similarly, at point *D* the individual has decided to borrow $10,000 and repay the loan next year. At point *D*:

Consumption this year at point *D* = $50,000 + $10,000 = $60,000

and:

Consumption next year at point *D* = $60,000 − [$10,000 × (1 + *r*)] = $49,000

at an interest rate of 10 percent.

In fact, this person can consume at any point on the line *AB*. This line has a slope of $-(1 + r)$, which means that for each dollar that is added to the *x* coordinate along the line, $(1 + r)$ dollars are subtracted from the *y* coordinate. Moving along the line from point *A,* the initial point of $50,000 this year and $60,000 next year, toward point *B* gives the person more consumption today and less next year. In other words, moving toward point *B*

**Figure 4A.2
The Effect
of Different
Interest Rates
on Consumption
Opportunities**

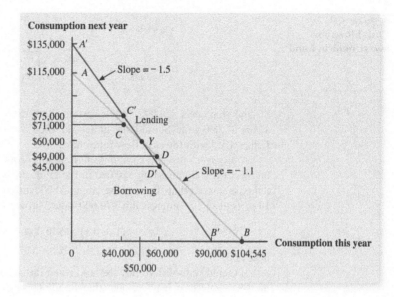

is borrowing. Similarly, moving up toward point *A*, he is consuming less today and more next year and is lending. The line is a straight line because the individual has no effect on the interest rate. This is one of the assumptions of perfectly competitive financial markets.

Where will the person actually be? The answer to that question depends on the individual's tastes and personal situation, just as it did before there was a market. If the person is impatient, he might wish to borrow money at a point such as *D*. If he is patient, he might wish to lend some of this year's income and enjoy more consumption next year at, for example, a point such as *C*.[1]

Notice that whether we think of someone as patient or impatient depends on the interest rate he or she faces in the market. Suppose that our individual was impatient and chose to borrow $10,000 and move to point *D*. Now suppose that we raise the interest rate to 20 percent or even 50 percent. Suddenly our impatient person may become very patient and might prefer to lend some of this year's income to take advantage of the very high interest rate. The general result is depicted in Figure 4A.2. We can see that lending at point *C'* yields much greater future income and consumption possibilities than before.[2]

4A.2 Making Investment Choices

A Lending Example   Consider a person who is concerned only about this year and the next. She has an income of $100,000 this year and expects to make the same amount next year. The interest rate is 10 percent. This individual is thinking about investing in a piece

---

[1]In this section, we are assuming a certain kind of financial market. In the language of economics, individuals who respond to rates and prices by acting as though they have no influence on them are called *price takers*, and this assumption is sometimes called the *price-taking assumption*. It is the condition of **perfectly competitive financial markets** (or, more simply, *perfect markets*). The following conditions are likely to lead to this:

1. Trading is costless. Access to the financial markets is free.
2. Information about borrowing and lending opportunities is available.
3. There are many traders, and no single trader can have a significant impact on market prices.

[2]Those familiar with consumer theory might be aware of the surprising case where raising the interest rate actually makes people borrow more or lowering the rate makes them lend more. The latter case might occur, for example, if the decline in the interest rate made the lenders have so little consumption next year that they have no choice but to lend out even more than they were lending before just to subsist. Nothing we do depends on excluding such cases, but it is much easier to ignore them, and the resulting analysis fits the real markets more closely.

Figure 4A.3
Cash Flows for
Investment in Land

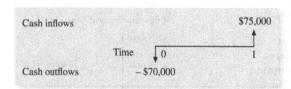

of land that costs $70,000. She is certain that next year the land will be worth $75,000, a sure $5,000 gain. Should she undertake the investment? This situation is described in Figure 4A.3 with the cash flow time chart.

A moment's thought should be all it takes to convince her that this is not an attractive business deal. By investing $70,000 in the land, she will have $75,000 available next year. Suppose instead that she puts the same $70,000 into a loan in the financial market. At the 10 percent rate of interest this $70,000 would grow to:

$$(1 + 0.1) \times \$70,000 = \$77,000$$

next year.

It would be foolish to buy the land when the same $70,000 investment in the financial market would beat it by $2,000 (that is, $77,000 from the loan minus $75,000 from the land investment). Figure 4A.4 illustrates this situation. Notice that the $70,000 loan gives no less income today and $2,000 more next year. This example illustrates some amazing features of the financial markets. It is remarkable to consider all of the information that we did *not* use when arriving at the decision not to invest in the land. We did not need to know how much income the person has this year or next year. We also did not need to know whether the person preferred more income this year or next.

We did not need to know any of these other facts, and more important, the person making the decision did not need to know them either. She needed only to be able to compare the investment with a relevant alternative available in the financial market. When this investment fell short of that standard—by $2,000 in the previous example—regardless of what the individual wanted to do, she knew that she should not buy the land.

A Borrowing Example Let us sweeten the deal a bit. Suppose that instead of being worth $75,000 next year, the land would be worth $80,000. What should our investor do now? This case is a bit more difficult. After all, even if the land seems like a good deal, this

Figure 4A.4
Consumption
Opportunities with
Borrowing and
Lending

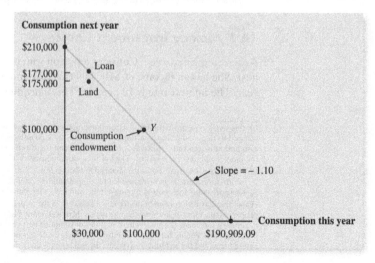

person's income this year is $100,000. Does she really want to make a $70,000 investment this year? Won't that leave only $30,000 for consumption?

The answers to these questions are yes, the individual should buy the land; yes, she does want to make a $70,000 investment this year; and, most surprising of all, even though her income is $100,000, making the $70,000 investment will not leave her with $30,000 to consume this year! Now let us see how finance lets us get around the basic laws of arithmetic.

The financial markets are the key to solving our problem. First, the financial markets can be used as a standard of comparison against which any investment project must be measured. Second, they can be used as a tool to actually help the individual undertake investments. These twin features of the financial markets enable us to make the right investment decision.

Suppose that the person borrows the $70,000 initial investment that is needed to purchase the land. Next year she must repay this loan. Because the interest rate is 10 percent, she will owe the financial market $77,000 next year. This is depicted in Figure 4A.5. Because the land will be worth $80,000 next year, she can sell it, pay off her debt of $77,000, and have $3,000 extra cash.

If she wishes, this person can now consume an extra $3,000 worth of goods and services next year. This possibility is illustrated in Figure 4A.6. In fact, even if she wants to do all of her consuming this year, she is still better off taking the investment. All she must do is take out a loan this year and repay it from the proceeds of the land next year and profit by $3,000.

Furthermore, instead of borrowing just the $70,000 that she needed to purchase the land, she could have borrowed $72,727.27. She could have used $70,000 to buy the land and consumed the remaining $2,727.27.

We will call $2,727.27 the net present value of the transaction. Notice that it is equal to $3,000 × 1/1.1. How did we figure out that this was the exact amount that she could borrow? It was easy: If $72,727.27 is the amount that she borrows, then, because the interest rate is 10 percent, she must repay:

$$\$72,727.27 \times (1 + 0.1) = \$80,000$$

Figure 4A.5
Cash Flows of Borrowing to Purchase the Land

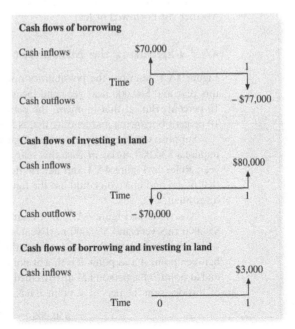

Figure 4A.6
Consumption
Opportunities
with Investment
Opportunity and
Borrowing and
Lending

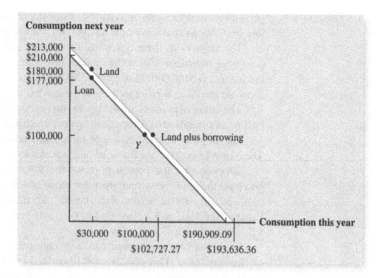

next year, and that is exactly what the land will be worth. The line through the investment position in Figure 4A.6 illustrates this borrowing possibility.

The amazing thing about both of these cases, one where the land is worth $75,000 next year and the other where it is worth $80,000 next year, is that we needed only to compare the investment with the financial markets to decide whether it was worth undertaking. This is one of the more important points in all of finance. It is true regardless of the consumption preferences of the individual. This is one of a number of **separation theorems** in finance. It states that the value of an investment to an individual is not dependent on consumption preferences. In our examples we showed that the person's decision to invest in land was not affected by consumption preferences. However, these preferences dictated whether she borrowed or lent.

4A.3 Illustrating the Investment Decision

Figure 4A.1 describes the possibilities open to a person who has an income of $50,000 this year and $60,000 next year and faces a financial market in which the interest rate is 10 percent. But, at that moment, the person has no investment possibilities beyond the 10 percent borrowing and lending that is available in the financial market.

Suppose we give this person the chance to undertake an investment project that will require a $30,000 outlay of cash this year and that will return $40,000 to the investor next year. Refer to Figure 4A.1 and determine how you could include this new possibility in that figure and how you could use the figure to help you decide whether to undertake the investment.

Now look at Figure 4A.7. In Figure 4A.7 we have labeled the original point with $50,000 this year and $60,000 next year as point A. We have also added a new point B, with $20,000 available for consumption this year and $100,000 next year. The difference between point A and point B is that at point A the person is just where we started him off, and at point B the person has also decided to undertake the investment project. As a result of this decision the person at point B has:

$$\$50,000 - 30,000 = \$20,000$$

Figure 4A.7
Consumption
Choices with
Investment but No
Financial Markets

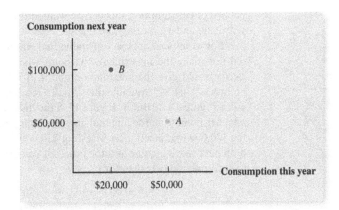

left for consumption this year, and:

$$\$60,000 + 40,000 = \$100,000$$

available next year. These are the coordinates of point B.

We must use our knowledge of the individual's borrowing and lending opportunities to decide whether to accept or reject the investment. This is illustrated in Figure 4A.8. Figure 4A.8 is similar to Figure 4A.7, but in it we have drawn a line through point A that shows the possibilities open to the person if he stays at point A and does not make the investment. This line is exactly the same as the one in Figure 4A.1. We have also drawn a parallel line through point B that shows the new possibilities that are available to the person if he undertakes the investment. The two lines are parallel because the slope of each is determined by the same interest rate, 10 percent. It does not matter whether the person takes the investment and goes to point B or does not and stays at point A: in the financial market, each dollar of lending is a dollar less available for consumption this year and moves him to the left by a dollar along the x-axis. Because the interest rate is 10 percent, the \$1 loan repays \$1.10 and moves him up by \$1.10 along the y-axis.

It is easy to see from Figure 4A.8 that the investment has made the person better off. The line through point B is higher than the line through point A. Thus, no matter what

Figure 4A.8
Consumption
Choices with
Investment
Opportunities and
Financial Markets

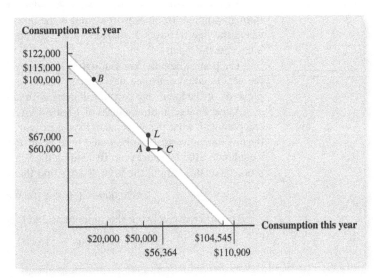

pattern of consumption this person wanted this year and next, he could have more in each year if he undertook the investment.

For example, suppose our individual wanted to consume everything this year. If he did not make the investment, the point where the line through point A intersected the x-axis would give the maximum amount of consumption he could enjoy this year. This point has $104,545 available this year. To recall how we found this figure, review the analysis of Figure 4A.1. But in Figure 4A.8 the line that goes through point B hits the x-axis at a higher point than the line that goes through point A. Along this line the person can have the $20,000 that is left after investing $30,000, plus all that he can borrow and repay with both next year's income and the proceeds from the investment. The total amount available to consume today is therefore:

$$= \$50,000 - 30,000 + (\$60,000 + 40,000)/(1 + 0.1)$$
$$= \$20,000 + (\$100,000/1.1)$$
$$= \$110,909$$

The additional consumption available this year from undertaking the investment and using the financial market is the difference on the x-axis between the points where these two lines intersect:

$$\$110,909 - 104,545 = \$6,364$$

This difference is an important measure of what the investment is worth to the person. It answers a variety of questions. For example, it reveals how much money we would need to give the investor this year to make him just as well off as he is with the investment.

Because the line through point B is parallel to the line through point A but has been moved over by $6,364, we know that if we were to add this amount to the investor's current income this year at point A and take away the investment, he would wind up on the line through point B and with the same possibilities. If we do this, the person will have $56,364 this year and $60,000 next year, which is the situation of the point on the line through point B that lies to the right of point A in Figure 4A.8. This is point C.

We could also ask a different question: How much money would we need to give the investor next year to make him just as well off as he is with the investment?

This is the same as asking how much higher the line through point B is than the line through point A. In other words, what is the difference in Figure 4A.8 between the point where the line through A intercepts the y-axis and the point where the line through B intercepts the y-axis?

The point where the line through A intercepts the y-axis shows the maximum amount the person could consume next year if all of his current income were lent out and the proceeds of the loan were consumed along with next year's income.

As we showed in our analysis of Figure 4A.1, this amount is $115,000. How does this compare with what the person can have next year if he makes the investment? By making the investment we saw that he would be at point B, where he has $20,000 left this year and would have $100,000 next year. By lending the $20,000 that is left this year and adding the proceeds of this loan to the $100,000, we find the line through B intercepts the y-axis at

$$(\$20,000 \times 1.1) + \$100,000 = \$122,000$$

The difference between this amount and $115,000 is

$$\$122,000 - 115,000 = \$7,000$$

Chapter 4 Discounted Cash Flow Valuation   **4A-9**

Figure 4A.9
Cash Flows for the
Investment Project

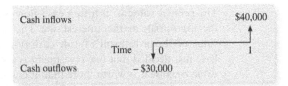

which is the answer to the question of how much we would need to give the person next year to make him as well off as he is with the investment.

There is a simple relationship between these two numbers. If we multiply $6,364 by 1.1 we get $7,000! Consider why this must be so. The $6,364 is the amount of extra cash we must give the person this year to substitute for having the investment. In a financial market with a 10 percent rate of interest, however, $1 this year is worth exactly the same as $1.10 next year. Thus, $6,364 this year is the same as $6,364 × 1.1 next year. In other words, the person does not care whether he has the investment, $6,364, this year or $6,364 × 1.1 next year. But we already showed that the investor is equally willing to have the investment and to have $7,000 next year. This must mean that:

$$\$6,364 \times 1.1 = \$7,000$$

You can also verify this relationship between these two variables by using Figure 4A.8. Because the lines through *A* and *B* each have the same slope of −1.1, the difference of $7,000 between where they intersect on the *x*-axis must be in the ratio of 1.1 to 1.

Now we can show you how to evaluate the investment opportunity on a stand-alone basis. Here are the relevant facts: The individual must give up $30,000 this year to get $40,000 next year. These cash flows are illustrated in Figure 4A.9.

The investment rule that follows from the previous analysis is the net present value (NPV) rule. Here, we convert all consumption values to the present and add them up:

$$\begin{aligned}
\text{Net present value} &= -\$30,000 + \$40,000 \times (1/1.1) \\
&= -\$30,000 + \$36,364 \\
&= \$6,364
\end{aligned}$$

The future amount, $40,000, is called the *future value* (FV).

The net present value of an investment is a simple criterion for deciding whether to undertake an investment. NPV answers the question of how much cash an investor would need to have today as a substitute for making the investment. If the net present value is positive, the investment is worth taking on because doing so is essentially the same as receiving a cash payment equal to the net present value. If the net present value is negative, taking on the investment today is equivalent to giving up some cash today, and the investment should be rejected.

We use the term *net present value* to emphasize that we are already including the current cost of the investment in determining its value and not simply what it will return. For example, if the interest rate is 10 percent and an investment of $30,000 today will produce a total cash return of $40,000 in one year's time, the *present value* of the $40,000 by itself is:

$$\$40,000/1.1 = \$36,364$$

but, the *net present value* of the investment is $36,364 minus the original investment:

$$\text{Net present value} = \$36,364 - \$30,000 = \$6,364$$

4A-10   **Part II**   Valuation and Capital Budgeting

The present value of a future cash flow is the value of that cash flow after considering the appropriate market interest rate. The net present value of an investment is the present value of the investment's future cash flows, minus the initial cost of the investment. We have just decided that our investment is a good opportunity. It has a positive net present value because it is worth more than it costs.

In general, our results can be stated in terms of the net present value rule:

An investment is worth making if it has a positive NPV. If an investment's NPV is negative, it should be rejected.

Appendix 4B Using Financial Calculators

This appendix is intended to help you use your Hewlett-Packard HP-10B or Texas Instruments BA II Plus financial calculator to solve problems encountered in the introductory finance course. It describes the various calculator settings and provides keystroke solutions for nine selected problems from this book. Please see your owner's manual for more complete instructions. For more examples and problem-solving techniques, please see *Financial Analysis with an Electronic Calculator,* Fourth Edition, by Mark A. White (New York: The McGraw-Hill Companies, 2000).

Calculator Settings

Most calculator errors in the introductory finance course are the result of inappropriate settings. Before beginning a calculation, you should ask yourself the following questions:

1. Did I clear the financial registers?
2. Is the compounding frequency set to once per period?
3. Is the calculator in END mode?
4. Did I enter negative numbers using the +/– key?

Clearing the Registers   All calculators have areas of memory, called registers, where variables and intermediate results are stored. There are two sets of financial registers, the time value of money (TVM) registers and the cash flow (CF) registers. These must be cleared before beginning a new calculation. On the Hewlett-Packard HP-10B, pressing ▒ {CLEAR ALL} clears both the TVM and the CF registers.[1] To clear the TVM registers on the BA II Plus, press **2nd** {CLR TVM}. Press **2nd** {CLR Work} from within the cash flow worksheet to clear the CF registers.

Compounding Frequency   Both the HP-10B and the BA II Plus are hardwired to assume monthly compounding, that is, compounding 12 times per period. Because very few problems in the introductory finance course make this assumption, you should change this default setting to once per period. On the HP-10B, press 1 ▒ {P/YR}. To verify that the default has been changed, press the ▒ key, then press and briefly hold the **INPUT** key.[2] The display should read "**1 P_Yr**".

On the BA II Plus, you can specify both payment frequency and compounding frequency, although they should normally be set to the same number. To set both to once per period, press the key sequence **2nd** {P/Y} 1 **ENTER**, then press ↓ 1 **ENTER**. Pressing **2nd** {QUIT} returns you to standard calculator mode.

END Mode and Annuities Due   In most problems, payment is made at the end of a period, and this is the default setting (end mode) for both the HP-10B and the BA II Plus. *Annuities due* assumes payments are made at the *beginning* of each period (begin mode). On the HP-10B, pressing ▒ {BEG/END} toggles between begin and end mode. Press the key sequence **2nd** {BGN} **2nd** {SET} **2nd** {QUIT} to accomplish the same task on the BA II Plus. Both calculators will indicate on the display that your calculator is set for begin mode.

---

[1] The ▒ key is colored orange and serves as a Shift key for the functions in curly brackets.
[2] This is the same keystroke used to clear all registers; pretty handy, eh?

Sign Changes   Sign changes are used to identify the direction of cash inflows and outflows. Generally, cash inflows are entered as positive numbers and cash outflows are entered as negative numbers. To enter a negative number on either the HP-10B or the BA II Plus, first press the appropriate digit keys and then press the change sign key, **+/−**. Do *not* use the minus sign key, **−**, as its effects are quite unpredictable.

Sample Problems

This section provides keystroke solutions for selected problems from the text illustrating the nine basic financial calculator skills.

1. Future Value or Present Value of a Single Sum   Compute the future value of $2,250 at a 17 percent annual rate for 30 years.

HP-10B		BA II PLUS	
−2,250.00 **PV**		−2,250.00 **PV**	
30.00 **N**		30.00 **N**	
17.00 **I/YR**		17.00 **I/Y**	
FV 249,895.46		**CPT FV** 249,895.46	

The future value is $249,895.46.

2. Present Value or Future Value of an Ordinary Annuity   Betty's Bank offers you a $20,000, seven-year term loan at 11 percent annual interest. What will your annual loan payment be?

HP-10B		BA II PLUS	
−20,000.00 **PV**		−20,000.00 **PV**	
7.00 **N**		7.00 **N**	
11.00 **I/YR**		11.00 **I/Y**	
PMT 4,244.31		**CPT PMT** 4,244.31	

Your annual loan payment will be $4,244.31.

3. Finding an Unknown Interest Rate   Assume that the total cost of a college education will be $75,000 when your child enters college in 18 years. You presently have $7,000 to invest. What rate of interest must you earn on your investment to cover the cost of your child's college education?

HP-10B		BA II PLUS	
−7,000.00 **PV**		−7,000.00 **PV**	
18.00 **N**		18.00 **N**	
75,000.00 **FV**		75,000.00 **FV**	
I/YR 14.08		**CPT I/Y** 14.08	

You must earn an annual interest rate of at least 14.08 percent to cover the expected future cost of your child's education.

4. Finding an Unknown Number of Periods   One of your customers is delinquent on his accounts payable balance. You've mutually agreed to a repayment schedule of $374 per month. You will charge 1.4 percent per month interest on the overdue balance. If the current balance is $12,000, how long will it take for the account to be paid off?

HP-10B		BA II PLUS	
-12,000.00	**PV**	-12,000.00	**PV**
1.40	**I/YR**	1.40	**I/Y**
374.00	**PMT**	374.00	**PMT**
N	42.90	**CPT** **N**	42.90

The loan will be paid off in 42.90 months.

5. Simple Bond Pricing   Mullineaux Co. issued 11-year bonds 1 year ago at a coupon rate of 8.25 percent. The bonds make semiannual payments. If the YTM on these bonds is 7.10 percent, what is the current bond price?

HP-10B		BA II PLUS	
41.25	**PMT**	41.25	**PMT**
1,000.00	**FV**	1,000.00	**FV**
20.00	**N**	20.00	**N**
3.55	**I/YR**	3.55	**I/Y**
PV	-1,081.35	**CPT** **PV**	-1,081.35

Because the bonds make semiannual payments, we must halve the coupon payment (8.25 ÷ 2 = 4.125 ==> $41.25) and double the number of periods (10 years remaining × 2 = 20 periods). Then, the current bond price is $1,081.35.

6. Simple Bond Yields to Maturity   Vasicek Co. has 12.5 percent coupon bonds on the market with eight years left to maturity. The bonds make annual payments. If one of these bonds currently sells for $1,145.68, what is its YTM?

HP-10B		BA II PLUS	
-1,145.68	**PV**	-1,145.68	**PV**
125.00	**PMT**	125.00	**PMT**
1,000.00	**FV**	1,000.00	**FV**
8.00	**N**	8.00	**N**
I/YR	9.79	**CPT** **I/Y**	9.79

The bond has a yield to maturity of 9.79 percent.

4B-4

7. Cash Flow Analysis   What are the IRR and NPV of the following set of cash flows? Assume a discount rate of 10 percent.

Year	Cash Flow
0	−$1,300
1	400
2	300
3	1,200

HP-10B		BA II PLUS	
−1,300.00 **CFj**		**CF**	
400.00 **CFj**		**2nd** {CLR Work}	
1.00 ▉ {Nj}		−1,300.00 **ENTER** ↓	
300.00 **CFj**		400.00 **ENTER** ↓	
1.00 ▉ {Nj}		1.00 **ENTER** ↓	
1,200.00 **CFj**		300.00 **ENTER** ↓	
1.00 ▉ {Nj}		1.00 **ENTER** ↓	
▉ {IRR/YR} 17.40		1,200.00 **ENTER** ↓	
10.00 **I/YR**		1.00 **ENTER** ↓	
▉ {NPV} 213.15		**IRR** **CPT** 17.40	
		NPV	
		10.00 **ENTER**	
		↓ **CPT** 213.15	

The project has an IRR of 17.40 percent and an NPV of $213.15.

8. Loan Amortization   Prepare an amortization schedule for a three-year loan of $24,000. The interest rate is 16 percent per year, and the loan calls for equal annual payments. How much interest is paid in the third year? How much total interest is paid over the life of the loan?

To prepare a complete amortization schedule, you must amortize each payment one at a time:

Chapter 4 Discounted Cash Flow Valuation   4B-5

HP-10B					BA II PLUS	
		−24,000.00 **PV**			−24,000.00 **PV**	
		16.00 **I/YR**			16.00 **I/Y**	
		3.00 **N**			3.00 **N**	
		PMT 10,686.19			**CPT** **PMT** 10,686.19	
1.00 **INPUT**		{AMORT} = 3,840.00 <== Interest		**2nd** {AMORT} **2nd** {CLR Work}		
		= 6,846.19 <== Principal	1.00 **ENTER** ↓			
		= −17,153.81 <== Balance	1.00 **ENTER** ↓	−17,153.81 <== Balance		
2.00 **INPUT**		{AMORT} = 2,744.61 <== Interest		↓ 6,846.19 <== Principal		
		= 7,941.58 <== Principal		↓ 3,840.00 <== Interest		
		= −9,212.23 <== Balance	2.00 **ENTER** ↓			
3.00 **INPUT**		{AMORT} = 1,473.96 <== Interest	2.00 **ENTER** ↓	−9,212.23 <== Balance		
		= 9,212.23 <== Principal		↓ 7,941.58 <== Principal		
		= 0.00 <== Balance		↓ 2,744.61 <== Interest		
				↓		
			3.00 **ENTER** ↓			
			3.00 **ENTER** ↓	0.00 <== Balance		
				↓ 9,212.23 <== Principal		
				↓ 1,473.96 <== Interest		

Interest of \$1,473.96 is paid in the third year.

Enter both a beginning and an ending period to compute the total amount of interest or principal paid over a particular period of time.

HP-10B				BA II PLUS	
		−24,000.00 **PV**		−24,000.00 **PV**	
		16.00 **I/YR**		16.00 **I/Y**	
		3.00 **N**		3.00 **N**	
		PMT 10,686.19		**CPT** **PMT** 10,686.19	
	1.00 **INPUT**			**2nd** {AMORT} **2nd** {CLR Work}	
3.00	{AMORT} = 8,058.57 <== Interest		1.00 **ENTER** ↓		
	= 24,000.00 <== Principal		3.00 **ENTER** ↓	0.00 <== Balance	
	= 0.00 <== Balance			↓ 24,000.00 <== Principal	
				↓ 8,058.57 <== Interest	

Total interest of \$8,058.57 is paid over the life of the loan.

9. Interest Rate Conversions Find the effective annual rate, EAR, corresponding to a 7 percent annual percentage rate, APR, compounded quarterly.

4B-6   **Part II**   Valuation and Capital Budgeting

HP-10B		BA II PLUS	
4.00 ☐ {P/YR}		2nd {IConv}	
7.00 ☐ {NOM%}		7.00 **ENTER**	
☐ {EFF%} 7.19		↓ ↓	
		4.00 **ENTER**	
		↑ **CPT** 7.19	

The effective annual rate equals 7.19 percent.

CHAPTER 5

Net Present Value and Other Investment Rules

The semiconductor industry is fast moving, with ever increasing technological advancements. As such, new plants are constantly being built. In 2011, Intel announced it would spend $5 billion to build the most advanced high-volume semiconductor plant in the world in Arizona. The plant, which will employ about 1,000 people, is expected to open in 2013. Soon after, Samsung Electronics announced plans to spend $3.6 billion to build a plant in Texas that would manufacture logic chips for Apple's iPhones and iPads. While these may seem like large investments, at about the same time, South Korean steel manufacturer POSCO announced plans to build a $12 billion steel mill in India. Decisions such as these, with price tags of up to $12 billion, are obviously major undertakings, and the risks and rewards must be carefully weighed. In this chapter, we discuss the basic tools used in making such decisions.

In Chapter 1, we show that increasing the value of a company's stock is the goal of financial management. Thus, what we need to know is how to tell whether a particular investment will achieve that purpose or not. This chapter considers a variety of techniques financial analysts routinely use. More importantly, it shows how many of these techniques can be misleading, and it explains why the net present value approach is the right one.

▲ For updates on the latest happenings in finance, visit www. rwjcorporatefinance. blogspot.com

5.1 Why Use Net Present Value?

ExcelMaster
coverage online

This section introduces the NPV and XNPV functions.

This chapter, as well as the next two, focuses on *capital budgeting*, the decision-making process for accepting or rejecting projects. This chapter develops the basic capital budgeting methods, leaving much of the practical application to subsequent chapters. But we don't have to develop these methods from scratch. In Chapter 4, we pointed out that a dollar received in the future is worth less than a dollar received today. The reason, of course, is that today's dollar can be reinvested, yielding a greater amount in the future. And we showed in Chapter 4 that the exact worth of a dollar to be received in the future is its present value. Furthermore, Section 4.1 suggested calculating the *net present value* of any project. That is, the section suggested calculating the difference between the sum of the present values of the project's future cash flows and the initial cost of the project.

The net present value (NPV) method is the first one to be considered in this chapter. We begin by reviewing the approach with a simple example. Then, we ask why the method leads to good decisions.

Find out more about capital budgeting for small businesses at www. missouribusiness. net.

EXAMPLE 5.1

Net Present Value   The Alpha Corporation is considering investing in a riskless project costing $100. The project receives $107 in one year and has no other cash flows. The riskless discount rate is 6 percent.

The NPV of the project can easily be calculated as:

$$\$.94 = -\$100 + \frac{\$107}{1.06} \tag{5.1}$$

From Chapter 4, we know that the project should be accepted because its NPV is positive. Had the NPV of the project been negative, as would have been the case with an interest rate greater than 7 percent, the project should be rejected.

The basic investment rule can be generalized to:

Accept a project if the NPV is greater than zero.

Reject a project if NPV is less than zero.

We refer to this as the **NPV rule.**

Why does the NPV rule lead to good decisions? Consider the following two strategies available to the managers of Alpha Corporation:

1. Use $100 of corporate cash to invest in the project. The $107 will be paid as a dividend in one year.
2. Forgo the project and pay the $100 of corporate cash as a dividend today.

If Strategy 2 is employed, the stockholder might deposit the dividend in a bank for one year. With an interest rate of 6 percent, Strategy 2 would produce cash of $106 (=$100 × 1.06) at the end of the year. The stockholder would prefer Strategy 1 because Strategy 2 produces less than $107 at the end of the year.

Our basic point is:

Accepting positive NPV projects benefits the stockholders.

How do we interpret the exact NPV of $.94? This is the increase in the value of the firm from the project. For example, imagine that the firm today has productive assets worth $V and has $100 of cash. If the firm forgoes the project, the value of the firm today would simply be:

$$\$V + \$100$$

If the firm accepts the project, the firm will receive $107 in one year but will have no cash today. Thus, the firm's value today would be:

$$\$V + \frac{\$107}{1.06}$$

The difference between these equations is just $.94, the net present value of Equation 5.1. Thus:

The value of the firm rises by the NPV of the project.

Note that the value of the firm is merely the sum of the values of the different projects, divisions, or other entities within the firm. This property, called **value additivity,** is quite important. It implies that the contribution of any project to a firm's value is simply the NPV of the project. As we will see later, alternative methods discussed in this chapter do not generally have this nice property.

The NPV rule uses the correct discount rate.

One detail remains. We assumed that the project was riskless, a rather implausible assumption. Future cash flows of real-world projects are invariably risky. In other words, cash flows can only be estimated, rather than known. Imagine that the managers of Alpha *expect* the cash flow of the project to be $107 next year. That is, the cash flow could be higher, say $117, or lower, say $97. With this slight change, the project is risky. Suppose the project is about as risky as the stock market as a whole, where the expected return this year is perhaps 10 percent. Then 10 percent becomes the discount rate, implying that the NPV of the project would be:

$$-\$2.73 = -\$100 + \frac{\$107}{1.10}$$

Because the NPV is negative, the project should be rejected. This makes sense: A stockholder of Alpha receiving a $100 dividend today could invest it in the stock market, expecting a 10 percent return. Why accept a project with the same risk as the market but with an expected return of only 7 percent?

SPREADSHEET APPLICATIONS

Calculating NPVs with a Spreadsheet

Spreadsheets are commonly used to calculate NPVs. Examining the use of spreadsheets in this context also allows us to issue an important warning. Consider the following:

	A	B	C	D	E	F	G	H
1								
2			Using a spreadsheet to calculate net present values					
3								
4	A project's cost is $10,000. The cash flows are $2,000 per year for the first two years,							
5	$4,000 per year for the next two, and $5,000 in the last year. The discount rate is							
6	10 percent; what's the NPV?							
7								
8		Year	Cash flow					
9		0	-$10,000		Discount rate =	10%		
10		1	2,000					
11		2	2,000		NPV =	$2,102.72	(*wrong* answer)	
12		3	4,000		NPV =	$2,312.99	(*right* answer)	
13		4	4,000					
14		5	5,000					
15								
16	The formula entered in cell F11 is =NPV(F9, C9:C14). However, this gives the wrong answer because the							
17	NPV function actually calculates present values, not *net* present values.							
18								
19	The formula entered in cell F12 is =NPV(F9, C10:C14) + C9. This gives the right answer because the							
20	NPV function is used to calculate the present value of the cash flows and then the initial cost is							
21	subtracted to calculate the answer. Notice that we added cell C9 because it is already negative.							

In our spreadsheet example, notice that we have provided two answers. The first answer is wrong even though we used the spreadsheet's NPV formula. What happened is that the "NPV" function in our spreadsheet is actually a PV function; unfortunately, one of the original spreadsheet programs many years ago got the definition wrong, and subsequent spreadsheets have copied it! Our second answer shows how to use the formula properly.

The example here illustrates the danger of blindly using calculators or computers without understanding what is going on; we shudder to think of how many capital budgeting decisions in the real world are based on incorrect use of this particular function.

Conceptually, the discount rate on a risky project is the return that one can expect to earn on a financial asset of comparable risk. This discount rate is often referred to as an *opportunity cost* because corporate investment in the project takes away the stockholder's option to invest the dividend in other opportunities. Conceptually, we should look for the expected return of investments with similar risks available in the market. The calculation of the discount rate is by no means impossible. We forgo the calculation in this chapter but present it in later chapters of the text.

Having shown that NPV is a sensible approach, how can we tell whether alternative methods are as good as NPV? The key to NPV is its three attributes:

1. *NPV uses cash flows.* Cash flows from a project can be used for other corporate purposes (such as dividend payments, other capital budgeting projects, or payments of corporate interest). By contrast, earnings are an artificial construct. Although earnings are useful to accountants, they should not be used in capital budgeting because they do not represent cash.

2. *NPV uses all the cash flows of the project.* Other approaches ignore cash flows beyond a particular date; beware of these approaches.

3. *NPV discounts the cash flows properly.* Other approaches may ignore the time value of money when handling cash flows. Beware of these approaches as well.

Calculating NPVs by hand can be tedious. A nearby *Spreadsheet Applications* box shows how to do it the easy way and also illustrates an important *caveat calculator*.

5.2 The Payback Period Method

DEFINING THE RULE

One of the most popular alternatives to NPV is **payback.** Here is how payback works: Consider a project with an initial investment of −$50,000. Cash flows are $30,000, $20,000, and $10,000 in the first three years, respectively. These flows are illustrated in Figure 5.1. A useful way of writing down investments like the preceding is with the notation:

$$(-\$50,000, \$30,000, \$20,000, \$10,000)$$

The minus sign in front of the $50,000 reminds us that this is a cash outflow for the investor, and the commas between the different numbers indicate that they are received—or if they are cash outflows, that they are paid out—at different times. In

Figure 5.1
Cash Flows of an Investment Project

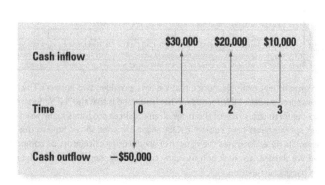

this example we are assuming that the cash flows occur one year apart, with the first one occurring the moment we decide to take on the investment.

The firm receives cash flows of $30,000 and $20,000 in the first two years, which add up to the $50,000 original investment. This means that the firm has recovered its investment within two years. In this case two years is the *payback period* of the investment.

The **payback period rule** for making investment decisions is simple. A particular cutoff date, say two years, is selected. All investment projects that have payback periods of two years or less are accepted, and all of those that pay off in more than two years—if at all—are rejected.

PROBLEMS WITH THE PAYBACK METHOD

There are at least three problems with payback. To illustrate the first two problems, we consider the three projects in Table 5.1. All three projects have the same three-year payback period, so they should all be equally attractive—right?

Actually, they are not equally attractive, as can be seen by a comparison of different *pairs* of projects.

Problem 1: Timing of Cash Flows within the Payback Period Let us compare project *A* with Project *B*. In Years 1 through 3, the cash flows of Project *A* rise from $20 to $50, while the cash flows of Project *B* fall from $50 to $20. Because the large cash flow of $50 comes earlier with Project *B*, its net present value must be higher. Nevertheless, we just saw that the payback periods of the two projects are identical. Thus, a problem with the payback method is that it does not consider the timing of the cash flows within the payback period. This example shows that the payback method is inferior to NPV because, as we pointed out earlier, the NPV method *discounts the cash flows properly.*

Problem 2: Payments after the Payback Period Now consider Projects *B* and *C*, which have identical cash flows within the payback period. However, Project *C* is clearly preferred because it has a cash flow of $60,000 in the fourth year. Thus, another problem with the payback method is that it ignores all cash flows occurring after the payback period. Because of the short-term orientation of the payback method, some valuable long-term projects are likely to be rejected. The NPV method does not have this flaw because, as we pointed out earlier, this method *uses all the cash flows of the project.*

Problem 3: Arbitrary Standard for Payback Period We do not need to refer to Table 5.1 when considering a third problem with the payback method. Capital markets help us estimate the discount rate used in the NPV method. The

Table 5.1
Expected Cash Flows for Projects A through C ($)

Year	A	B	C
0	−$100	−$100	−$100
1	20	50	50
2	30	30	30
3	50	20	20
4	60	60	60,000
Payback period (years)	3	3	3

riskless rate, perhaps proxied by the yield on a Treasury instrument, would be the appropriate rate for a riskless investment. Later chapters of this textbook show how to use historical returns in the capital markets to estimate the discount rate for a risky project. However, there is no comparable guide for choosing the payback cutoff date, so the choice is somewhat arbitrary.

MANAGERIAL PERSPECTIVE

The payback method is often used by large, sophisticated companies when making relatively small decisions. The decision to build a small warehouse, for example, or to pay for a tune-up for a truck is the sort of decision that is often made by lower-level management. Typically, a manager might reason that a tune-up would cost, say, $200, and if it saved $120 each year in reduced fuel costs, it would pay for itself in less than two years. On such a basis the decision would be made.

Although the treasurer of the company might not have made the decision in the same way, the company endorses such decision making. Why would upper management condone or even encourage such retrograde activity in its employees? One answer would be that it is easy to make decisions using payback. Multiply the tune-up decision into 50 such decisions a month, and the appeal of this simple method becomes clearer.

The payback method also has some desirable features for managerial control. Just as important as the investment decision itself is the company's ability to evaluate the manager's decision-making ability. Under the NPV method, a long time may pass before one decides whether a decision was correct. With the payback method we know in two years whether the manager's assessment of the cash flows was correct.

It has also been suggested that firms with good investment opportunities but no available cash may justifiably use payback. For example, the payback method could be used by small, privately held firms with good growth prospects but limited access to the capital markets. Quick cash recovery increases the reinvestment possibilities for such firms.

Finally, practitioners often argue that standard academic criticisms of the payback method overstate any real-world problems with the method. For example, textbooks typically make fun of payback by positing a project with low cash inflows in the early years but a huge cash inflow right after the payback cutoff date. This project is likely to be rejected under the payback method, though its acceptance would, in truth, benefit the firm. Project *C* in our Table 5.1 is an example of such a project. Practitioners point out that the pattern of cash flows in these textbook examples is much too stylized to mirror the real world. In fact, a number of executives have told us that for the overwhelming majority of real-world projects, both payback and NPV lead to the same decision. In addition, these executives indicate that if an investment-like Project *C* were encountered in the real world, decision makers would almost certainly make ad hoc adjustments to the payback rule so that the project would be accepted.

Notwithstanding all of the preceding rationale, it is not surprising to discover that as the decisions grow in importance, which is to say when firms look at bigger projects, NPV becomes the order of the day. When questions of controlling and evaluating the manager become less important than making the right investment decision, payback is used less frequently. For big-ticket decisions, such as whether or not to buy a machine, build a factory, or acquire a company, the payback method is seldom used.

SUMMARY OF PAYBACK

The payback method differs from NPV and is therefore conceptually wrong. With its arbitrary cutoff date and its blindness to cash flows after that date, it can lead to some flagrantly foolish decisions if used too literally. Nevertheless, because of its simplicity, as well as its other mentioned advantages, companies often use it as a screen for making the myriad of minor investment decisions they continually face.

Although this means that you should be wary of trying to change approaches such as the payback method when you encounter them in companies, you should probably be careful not to accept the sloppy financial thinking they represent. After this course, you would do your company a disservice if you used payback instead of NPV when you had a choice.

5.3 The Discounted Payback Period Method

ExcelMaster
coverage online

Aware of the pitfalls of payback, some decision makers use a variant called the **discounted payback period method.** Under this approach, we first discount the cash flows. Then we ask how long it takes for the discounted cash flows to equal the initial investment.

For example, suppose that the discount rate is 10 percent and the cash flows on a project are given by:

$$(-\$100, \$50, \$50, \$20)$$

This investment has a payback period of two years because the investment is paid back in that time.

To compute the project's discounted payback period, we first discount each of the cash flows at the 10 percent rate. These discounted cash flows are:

$$[-\$100, \$50/1.1, \$50/(1.1)^2, \$20/(1.1)^3] = (-\$100, \$45.45, \$41.32, \$15.03)$$

The discounted payback period of the original investment is simply the payback period for these discounted cash flows. The payback period for the discounted cash flows is slightly less than three years because the discounted cash flows over the three years are $101.80 (=$45.45 + 41.32 + 15.03). As long as the cash flows and discount rate are positive, the discounted payback period will never be smaller than the payback period because discounting reduces the value of the cash flows.

At first glance discounted payback may seem like an attractive alternative, but on closer inspection we see that it has some of the same major flaws as payback. Like payback, discounted payback first requires us to choose an arbitrary cutoff period, and then it ignores all cash flows after that date.

If we have already gone to the trouble of discounting the cash flows, we might just as well add up all the discounted cash flows and use NPV to make the decision. Although discounted payback looks a bit like NPV, it is just a poor compromise between the payback method and NPV.

5.4 The Internal Rate of Return

ExcelMaster
coverage online

This section introduces the
IRR and XIRR functions.

Now we come to the most important alternative to the NPV method: The internal rate of return, universally known as the IRR. The IRR is about as close as you can get to the NPV without actually being the NPV. The basic rationale behind the IRR method is that it provides a single number summarizing the merits of a project. That number

Figure 5.2
Cash Flows for a
Simple Project

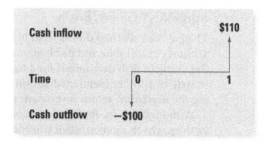

does not depend on the interest rate prevailing in the capital market. That is why it is called the internal rate of return; the number is internal or intrinsic to the project and does not depend on anything except the cash flows of the project.

For example, consider the simple project (−$100, $110) in Figure 5.2. For a given rate, the net present value of this project can be described as:

$$NPV = -\$100 + \frac{\$110}{1 + R}$$

where R is the discount rate. What must the discount rate be to make the NPV of the project equal to zero?

We begin by using an arbitrary discount rate of .08, which yields:

$$\$1.85 = -\$100 + \frac{\$110}{1.08}$$

Because the NPV in this equation is positive, we now try a higher discount rate, such as .12. This yields:

$$-\$1.79 = -\$100 + \frac{\$110}{1.12}$$

Because the NPV in this equation is negative, we try lowering the discount rate to .10. This yields:

$$0 = -\$100 + \frac{\$110}{1.10}$$

This trial-and-error procedure tells us that the NPV of the project is zero when R equals 10 percent.[1] Thus, we say that 10 percent is the project's **internal rate of return** (IRR). In general, the IRR is the rate that causes the NPV of the project to be zero. The implication of this exercise is very simple. The firm should be equally willing to accept or reject the project if the discount rate is 10 percent. The firm should accept the project if the discount rate is below 10 percent. The firm should reject the project if the discount rate is above 10 percent.

The general investment rule is clear:

Accept the project if the IRR is greater than the discount rate. Reject the project if the IRR is less than the discount rate.

---

[1]Of course, we could have directly solved for R in this example after setting NPV equal to zero. However, with a long series of cash flows, one cannot generally solve for R directly. Instead, one is forced to use trial and error (or let a machine use trial and error).

Chapter 5 Net Present Value and Other Investment Rules **143**

Figure 5.3
Cash Flows for a
More Complex
Project

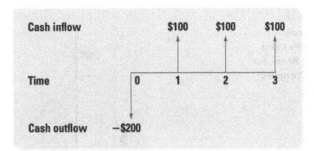

We refer to this as the **basic IRR rule.** Now we can try the more complicated example (−$200, $100, $100, $100) in Figure 5.3.

As we did previously, let's use trial and error to calculate the internal rate of return. We try 20 percent and 30 percent, yielding the following:

Discount Rate	NPV
20%	$10.65
30	−18.39

After much more trial and error, we find that the NPV of the project is zero when the discount rate is 23.37 percent. Thus, the IRR is 23.37 percent. With a 20 percent discount rate, the NPV is positive and we would accept it. However, if the discount rate were 30 percent, we would reject it.

Algebraically, IRR is the unknown in the following equation:[2]

$$0 = -\$200 + \frac{\$100}{1 + IRR} + \frac{\$100}{(1 + IRR)^2} + \frac{\$100}{(1 + IRR)^3}$$

Figure 5.4 illustrates what the IRR of a project means. The figure plots the NPV as a function of the discount rate. The curve crosses the horizontal axis at the IRR of 23.37 percent because this is where the NPV equals zero.

It should also be clear that the NPV is positive for discount rates below the IRR and negative for discount rates above the IRR. If we accept projects like this one when the discount rate is less than the IRR, we will be accepting positive NPV projects. Thus, the IRR rule coincides exactly with the NPV rule.

If this were all there were to it, the IRR rule would always coincide with the NPV rule. But the world of finance is not so kind. Unfortunately, the IRR rule and the NPV rule are consistent with each other only for examples like the one just discussed. Several problems with the IRR approach occur in more complicated situations, a topic to be examined in the next section.

The IRR in the previous example was computed through trial and error. This laborious process can be averted through spreadsheets. A nearby *Spreadsheet Applications* box shows how.

---

[2]One can derive the IRR directly for a problem with an initial cash outflow and up to four subsequent inflows. In the case of two subsequent inflows, for example, the quadratic formula is needed. In general, however, only trial and error will work for an outflow and five or more subsequent inflows.

144   **Part II**   Valuation and Capital Budgeting

Figure 5.4
Net Present
Value (NPV) and
Discount Rates for
a More Complex
Project

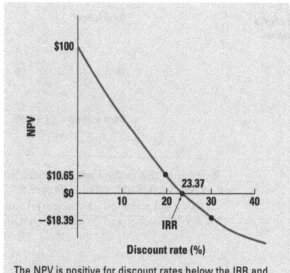

The NPV is positive for discount rates below the IRR and
negative for discount rates above the IRR.

SPREADSHEET APPLICATIONS

Calculating IRRs with a Spreadsheet

Because IRRs are so tedious to calculate by hand, financial calculators and, especially, spreadsheets are generally
used. The procedures used by various financial calculators are too different for us to illustrate here, so we will
focus on using a spreadsheet. As the following example illustrates, using a spreadsheet is very easy.

	A	B	C	D	E	F	G	H
1								
2			Using a spreadsheet to calculate internal rates of return					
3								
4	Suppose we have a four-year project that costs $500. The cash flows over the four-year life will be							
5	$100, $200, $300, and $400. What is the IRR?							
6								
7		Year	Cash flow					
8		0	-$500					
9		1	100		IRR =	27.3%		
10		2	200					
11		3	300					
12		4	400					
13								
14								
15	The formula entered in cell F9 is =IRR(C8:C12). Notice that the Year 0 cash flow has a negative							
16	sign representing the initial cost of the project.							
17								

5.5 Problems with the IRR Approach

ExcelMaster
coverage online

This section introduces the MIRR functions.

DEFINITION OF INDEPENDENT AND MUTUALLY EXCLUSIVE PROJECTS

An **independent project** is one whose acceptance or rejection is independent of the acceptance or rejection of other projects. For example, imagine that McDonald's is considering putting a hamburger outlet on a remote island. Acceptance or rejection of this unit is likely to be unrelated to the acceptance or rejection of any other restaurant in its system. The remoteness of the outlet in question ensures that it will not pull sales away from other outlets.

Now consider the other extreme, **mutually exclusive investments.** What does it mean for two projects, *A* and *B*, to be mutually exclusive? You can accept *A* or you can accept *B* or you can reject both of them, but you cannot accept both of them. For example, *A* might be a decision to build an apartment house on a corner lot that you own, and *B* might be a decision to build a movie theater on the same lot.

We now present two general problems with the IRR approach that affect both independent and mutually exclusive projects. Then we deal with two problems affecting mutually exclusive projects only.

TWO GENERAL PROBLEMS AFFECTING BOTH INDEPENDENT AND MUTUALLY EXCLUSIVE PROJECTS

We begin our discussion with Project *A*, which has the following cash flows:

$$(-\$100, \$130)$$

The IRR for Project *A* is 30 percent. Table 5.2 provides other relevant information about the project. The relationship between NPV and the discount rate is shown for this project in Figure 5.5. As you can see, the NPV declines as the discount rate rises.

Problem 1: Investing or Financing? Now consider project *B*, with cash flows of:

$$(\$100, -\$130)$$

These cash flows are exactly the reverse of the flows for Project *A*. In Project *B*, the firm receives funds first and then pays out funds later. While unusual, projects of this type do exist. For example, consider a corporation conducting a seminar where the participants pay in advance. Because large expenses are frequently incurred at the seminar date, cash inflows precede cash outflows.

Table 5.2 **The Internal Rate of Return and Net Present Value**

Dates:	Project A			Project B			Project C		
	0	1	2	0	1	2	0	1	2
Cash flows	−$100	$130		$100	−$130		−$100	$230	−$132
IRR	30%			30%			10% and 20%		
NPV @10%	$ 18.2			−$ 18.2			0		
Accept if market rate	<30%			>30%			>10% but <20%		
Financing or investing	Investing			Financing			Mixture		

Figure 5.5   Net Present Value and Discount Rates for Projects *A*, *B*, and *C*

Project A has a cash outflow at Date 0 followed by a cash inflow at Date 1. Its NPV is negatively related to the discount rate.
Project B has a cash inflow at Date 0 followed by a cash outflow at Date 1. Its NPV is positively related to the discount rate.
Project C has two changes of sign in its cash flows. It has an outflow at Date 0, an inflow at Date 1, and an outflow at Date 2.
Projects with more than one change of sign can have multiple rates of return.

Consider our trial-and-error method to calculate IRR:

$$-\$4 = +\$100 - \frac{\$130}{1.25}$$

$$\$3.70 = +\$100 - \frac{\$130}{1.35}$$

$$\$0 = +\$100 - \frac{\$130}{1.30}$$

As with Project *A*, the internal rate of return is 30 percent. However, notice that the net present value is *negative* when the discount rate is *below* 30 percent. Conversely, the net present value is positive when the discount rate is above 30 percent. The decision rule is exactly the opposite of our previous result. For this type of project, the following rule applies:

Accept the project when the IRR is less than the discount rate. Reject the project when the IRR is greater than the discount rate.

This unusual decision rule follows from the graph of Project *B* in Figure 5.5. The curve is upward sloping, implying that NPV is *positively* related to the discount rate.

The graph makes intuitive sense. Suppose the firm wants to obtain $100 immediately. It can either (1) accept Project *B* or (2) borrow $100 from a bank. Thus, the project is actually a substitute for borrowing. In fact, because the IRR is 30 percent, taking on Project *B* is equivalent to borrowing at 30 percent. If the firm can borrow from a bank at, say, only 25 percent, it should reject the project. However, if a firm can borrow from a bank only at, say, 35 percent, it should accept the project. Thus Project *B* will be accepted if and only if the discount rate is *above* the IRR.[3]

This should be contrasted with Project *A*. If the firm has $100 cash to invest, it can either (1) accept Project *A* or (2) lend $100 to the bank. The project is actually a substitute for lending. In fact, because the IRR is 30 percent, taking on Project *A* is tantamount to lending at 30 percent. The firm should accept Project *A* if the lending rate is below 30 percent. Conversely, the firm should reject Project *A* if the lending rate is above 30 percent.

---

[3]This paragraph implicitly assumes that the cash flows of the project are risk-free. In this way we can treat the borrowing rate as the discount rate for a firm needing $100. With risky cash flows, another discount rate would be chosen. However, the intuition behind the decision to accept when the IRR is less than the discount rate would still apply.

Because the firm initially pays out money with Project *A* but initially receives money with Project *B*, we refer to Project *A* as an *investing type project* and Project *B* as a *financing type project*. Investing type projects are the norm. Because the IRR rule is reversed for financing type projects, be careful when using it with this type of project.

Problem 2: Multiple Rates of Return   Suppose the cash flows from a project are:

$$(-\$100, \$230, -\$132)$$

Because this project has a negative cash flow, a positive cash flow, and another negative cash flow, we say that the project's cash flows exhibit two changes of sign, or "flip-flops." Although this pattern of cash flows might look a bit strange at first, many projects require outflows of cash after some inflows. An example would be a strip-mining project. The first stage in such a project is the initial investment in excavating the mine. Profits from operating the mine are received in the second stage. The third stage involves a further investment to reclaim the land and satisfy the requirements of environmental protection legislation. Cash flows are negative at this stage.

Projects financed by lease arrangements may produce a similar pattern of cash flows. Leases often provide substantial tax subsidies, generating cash inflows after an initial investment. However, these subsidies decline over time, frequently leading to negative cash flows in later years. (The details of leasing will be discussed in a later chapter.)

It is easy to verify that this project has not one but two IRRs, 10 percent and 20 percent.[4] In a case like this, the IRR does not make any sense. What IRR are we to use—10 percent or 20 percent? Because there is no good reason to use one over the other, IRR simply cannot be used here.

Why does this project have multiple rates of return? Project *C* generates multiple internal rates of return because both an inflow and an outflow occur after the initial investment. In general, these flip-flops or changes in sign produce multiple IRRs. In theory, a cash flow stream with *K* changes in sign can have up to *K* sensible internal rates of return (IRRs above –100 percent). Therefore, because Project *C* has two changes in sign, it can have as many as two IRRs. As we pointed out, projects whose cash flows change sign repeatedly can occur in the real world.

NPV Rule   Of course, we should not be too worried about multiple rates of return. After all, we can always fall back on the NPV rule. Figure 5.5 plots the NPV of Project *C* (–$100, $230, –$132) as a function of the discount rate. As the figure shows, the NPV is zero at both 10 percent and 20 percent and negative outside the range. Thus, the NPV rule tells us to accept the project if the appropriate discount rate is between 10 percent and 20 percent. The project should be rejected if the discount rate lies outside this range.

---

[4]The calculations are:

$$-\$100 + \frac{\$230}{1.1} - \frac{\$132}{(1.1)^2}$$

$$-\$100 + 209.09 - 109.09 = 0$$

and

$$-\$100 + \frac{\$230}{1.2} - \frac{\$132}{(1.2)^2}$$

$$-\$100 + 191.67 - 91.67 = 0$$

Thus, we have multiple rates of return.

Modified IRR As an alternative to NPV, we now introduce the **modified IRR (MIRR)** method, which handles the multiple IRR problem by combining cash flows until only one change in sign remains. To see how it works, consider Project C again. With a discount rate of, say, 14 percent, the value of the last cash flow, $-\$132$, is:

$$-\$132/1.14 = -\$115.79$$

as of Date 1. Because $230 is already received at that time, the "adjusted" cash flow at Date 1 is $114.21 (=$230 − 115.79). Thus, the MIRR approach produces the following two cash flows for the project:

$$(-\$100, \$114.21)$$

Note that by discounting and then combining cash flows, we are left with only one change in sign. The IRR rule can now be applied. The IRR of these two cash flows is 14.21 percent, implying that the project should be accepted given our assumed discount rate of 14 percent.

Of course, Project C is relatively simple to begin with: It has only three cash flows and two changes in sign. However, the same procedure can easily be applied to more complex projects—that is, just keep discounting and combining the later cash flows until only one change of sign remains.

Although this adjustment does correct for multiple IRRs, it appears, at least to us, to violate the "spirit" of the IRR approach. As stated earlier, the basic rationale behind the IRR method is that it provides a single number summarizing the merits of a project. That number does not depend on the discount rate. In fact, that is why it is called the internal rate of return: The number is *internal,* or intrinsic, to the project and does not depend on anything except the project's cash flows. By contrast, MIRR is clearly a function of the discount rate. However, a firm using this adjustment will avoid the multiple IRR problem, just as a firm using the NPV rule will avoid it.[5]

The Guarantee against Multiple IRRs If the first cash flow of a project is negative (because it is the initial investment) and if all of the remaining flows are positive, there can be only a single, unique IRR, no matter how many periods the project lasts. This is easy to understand by using the concept of the time value of money. For example, it is simple to verify that Project A in Table 5.2 has an IRR of 30 percent because using a 30 percent discount rate gives:

$$NPV = -\$100 + \$130/(1.3)$$
$$= \$0$$

---

[5]There is more than one version of modified IRR. In the discussion above, MIRR combines the present values of the later cash flows, leaving a set of cash flows with only one change in sign. Alternatively, investors often combine the future values of the cash flows as of the termination date of the project. In our example, the sum of the future values, as of Date 2, is:

Date of cash flow	1	2	Sum
Future value as of Date 2	$230 (1.14) = $262.20	−$132	$130.02 = 262.20 + (−132)

Under this version, the MIRR of the project becomes:

$$-100 + \frac{130.02}{(1 + MIRR)^2}$$

implying an MIRR of 14.11 percent.

The MIRR here differs from the MIRR of 14.21 percent in the text. However, both MIRRs are above the discount rate of 14 percent, implying acceptance of the project. This consistency should always hold between the two variants of modified IRR. And, as in the version in the text, the multiple IRR problem is avoided.

How do we know that this is the only IRR? Suppose we were to try a discount rate greater than 30 percent. In computing the NPV, changing the discount rate does not change the value of the initial cash flow of −$100 because that cash flow is not discounted. Raising the discount rate can only lower the present value of the future cash flows. In other words, because the NPV is zero at 30 percent, any increase in the rate will push the NPV into the negative range. Similarly, if we try a discount rate of less than 30 percent, the overall NPV of the project will be positive. Though this example has only one positive flow, the above reasoning still implies a single, unique IRR if there are many inflows (but no outflows) after the initial investment.

If the initial cash flow is positive—and if all of the remaining flows are negative—there can only be a single, unique IRR. This result follows from similar reasoning. Both these cases have only one change of sign or flip-flop in the cash flows. Thus, we are safe from multiple IRRs whenever there is only one sign change in the cash flows.

General Rules The following chart summarizes our rules:

Flows	Number of IRRs	IRR Criterion	NPV Criterion
First cash flow is negative and all remaining cash flows are positive.	1	Accept if IRR > R. Reject if IRR < R.	Accept if NPV > 0. Reject if NPV < 0.
First cash flow is positive and all remaining cash flows are negative.	1	Accept if IRR < R. Reject if IRR > R.	Accept if NPV > 0. Reject if NPV < 0.
Some cash flows after first are positive and some cash flows after first are negative.	May be more than 1.	No valid IRR.	Accept if NPV > 0. Reject if NPV < 0.

Note that the NPV criterion is the same for each of the three cases. In other words, NPV analysis is always appropriate. Conversely, the IRR can be used only in certain cases. When it comes to NPV, the preacher's words, "You just can't lose with the stuff I use," clearly apply.

PROBLEMS SPECIFIC TO MUTUALLY EXCLUSIVE PROJECTS

As mentioned earlier, two or more projects are mutually exclusive if the firm can accept only one of them. We now present two problems dealing with the application of the IRR approach to mutually exclusive projects. These two problems are quite similar, though logically distinct.

The Scale Problem A professor we know motivates class discussions of this topic with this statement: "Students, I am prepared to let one of you choose between two mutually exclusive 'business' propositions. Opportunity 1—You give me $1 now and I'll give you $1.50 back at the end of the class period. Opportunity 2—You give me $10 and I'll give you $11 back at the end of the class period. You can choose only one of the two opportunities. And you cannot choose either opportunity more than once. I'll pick the first volunteer."

Which would you choose? The correct answer is Opportunity 2.[6] To see this, look at the following chart:

	Cash Flow at Beginning of Class	Cash Flow at End of Class (90 Minutes Later)	NPV[7]	IRR
Opportunity 1	−$ 1	+$ 1.50	$ .50	50%
Opportunity 2	−10	+11.00	1.00	10

As we have stressed earlier in the text, one should choose the opportunity with the highest NPV. This is Opportunity 2 in the example. Or, as one of the professor's students explained it, "I'm bigger than the professor, so I know I'll get my money back. And I have $10 in my pocket right now so I can choose either opportunity. At the end of the class, I'll be able to buy one song on itunes with Opportunity 2 and still have my original investment, safe and sound. The profit on Opportunity 1 pays for only one half of a song."

This business proposition illustrates a defect with the internal rate of return criterion. The basic IRR rule indicates the selection of Opportunity 1 because the IRR is 50 percent. The IRR is only 10 percent for Opportunity 2.

Where does IRR go wrong? The problem with IRR is that it ignores issues of *scale*. Although Opportunity 1 has a greater IRR, the investment is much smaller. In other words, the high percentage return on Opportunity 1 is more than offset by the ability to earn at least a decent return[8] on a much bigger investment under Opportunity 2.

Because IRR seems to be misguided here, can we adjust or correct it? We illustrate how in the next example.

EXAMPLE 5.2

NPV versus IRR Stanley Jaffe and Sherry Lansing have just purchased the rights to *Corporate Finance: The Motion Picture*. They will produce this major motion picture on either a small budget or a big budget. Here are the estimated cash flows:

	Cash Flow at Date 0	Cash Flow at Date 1	NPV @25%	IRR
Small budget	−$10 million	$40 million	$22 million	300%
Large budget	−25 million	65 million	27 million	160

Because of high risk, a 25 percent discount rate is considered appropriate. Sherry wants to adopt the large budget because the NPV is higher. Stanley wants to adopt the small budget because the IRR is higher. Who is right?

---

[6]The professor uses real money here. Though many students have done poorly on the professor's exams over the years, no student ever chose Opportunity 1. The professor claims that his students are "money players."

[7]We assume a zero rate of interest because his class lasted only 90 minutes. It just seemed like a lot longer.

[8]A 10 percent return is more than decent over a 90-minute interval!

For the reasons espoused in the classroom example, NPV is correct. Hence Sherry is right. However, Stanley is very stubborn where IRR is concerned. How can Sherry justify the large budget to Stanley using the IRR approach?

This is where *incremental IRR* comes in. Sherry calculates the incremental cash flows from choosing the large budget instead of the small budget as follows:

	Cash Flow at Date 0 (in $ millions)	Cash Flow at Date 1 (in $ millions)
Incremental cash flows from choosing large budget instead of small budget	$-\$25 - (-10) = -\$15$	$\$65 - 40 = \$25$

This chart shows that the incremental cash flows are $-\$15$ million at Date 0 and $\$25$ million at Date 1. Sherry calculates incremental IRR as follows:

Formula for Calculating the Incremental IRR:

$$0 = -\$15 \text{ million} + \frac{\$25 \text{ million}}{1 + IRR}$$

IRR equals 66.67 percent in this equation, implying that the **incremental IRR** is 66.67 percent. Incremental IRR is the IRR on the incremental investment from choosing the large project instead of the small project.

In addition, we can calculate the NPV of the incremental cash flows:

NPV of Incremental Cash Flows:

$$-\$15 \text{ million} + \frac{\$25 \text{ million}}{1.25} = \$5 \text{ million}$$

We know the small-budget picture would be acceptable as an independent project because its NPV is positive. We want to know whether it is beneficial to invest an additional $15 million to make the large-budget picture instead of the small-budget picture. In other words, is it beneficial to invest an additional $15 million to receive an additional $25 million next year? First, our calculations show the NPV on the incremental investment to be positive. Second, the incremental IRR of 66.67 percent is higher than the discount rate of 25 percent. For both reasons, the incremental investment can be justified, so the large-budget movie should be made. The second reason is what Stanley needed to hear to be convinced.

In review, we can handle this example (or any mutually exclusive example) in one of three ways:

1. *Compare the NPVs of the two choices.* The NPV of the large-budget picture is greater than the NPV of the small-budget picture. That is, $27 million is greater than $22 million.

2. *Calculate the incremental NPV from making the large-budget picture instead of the small-budget picture.* Because the incremental NPV equals $5 million, we choose the large-budget picture.

3. *Compare the incremental IRR to the discount rate.* Because the incremental IRR is 66.67 percent and the discount rate is 25 percent, we take the large-budget picture.

All three approaches always give the same decision. However, we must *not* compare the IRRs of the two pictures. If we did, we would make the wrong choice. That is, we would accept the small-budget picture.

Although students frequently think that problems of scale are relatively unimportant, the truth is just the opposite. No real-world project comes in one clear-cut size. Rather, the firm has to *determine* the best size for the project. The movie budget of $25 million is not fixed in stone. Perhaps an extra $1 million to hire a bigger star or to film at a better location will increase the movie's gross. Similarly, an industrial firm must decide whether it wants a warehouse of, say, 500,000 square feet or 600,000 square feet. And, earlier in the chapter, we imagined McDonald's opening an outlet on a remote island. If it does this, it must decide how big the outlet should be. For almost any project, someone in the firm has to decide on its size, implying that problems of scale abound in the real world.

One final note here. Students often ask which project should be subtracted from the other in calculating incremental flows. Notice that we are subtracting the smaller project's cash flows from the bigger project's cash flows. This leaves an *outflow* at Date 0. We then use the basic IRR rule on the incremental flows.[9]

The Timing Problem   Next we illustrate another, somewhat similar problem with the IRR approach to evaluating mutually exclusive projects.

EXAMPLE 5.3

Mutually Exclusive Investments   Suppose that the Kaufold Corporation has two alternative uses for a warehouse. It can store toxic waste containers (Investment A) or electronic equipment (Investment B). The cash flows are as follows:

	Cash Flow at Year				NPV			
Year:	**0**	**1**	**2**	**3**	**@ 0%**	**@10%**	**@15%**	**IRR**
Investment A	−$10,000	$10,000	$1,000	$ 1,000	$2,000	$669	$109	16.04%
Investment B	−10,000	1,000	1,000	12,000	4,000	751	−484	12.94

We find that the NPV of Investment B is higher with low discount rates, and the NPV of Investment A is higher with high discount rates. This is not surprising if you look closely at the cash flow patterns. The cash flows of A occur early, whereas the cash flows of B occur later. If we assume a high discount rate, we favor Investment A because we are implicitly assuming that the early cash flow (for example, $10,000 in Year 1) can be reinvested at that rate. Because most of Investment B's cash flows occur in Year 3, B's value is relatively high with low discount rates.

The patterns of cash flow for both projects appear in Figure 5.6. Project *A* has an NPV of $2,000 at a discount rate of zero. This is calculated by simply adding up the cash flows without discounting them. Project *B* has an NPV of $4,000 at the zero rate. However, the NPV of Project *B* declines more rapidly as the discount rate increases than does the NPV of Project *A*. As we mentioned, this occurs because the cash flows of *B* occur later. Both Projects have the same NPV at a discount rate of 10.55 percent.

---

[9]Alternatively, we could have subtracted the larger project's cash flows from the smaller project's cash flows. This would have left an *inflow* at Date 0, making it necessary to use the IRR rule for financing situations. This would work, but we find it more confusing.

Figure 5.6
Net Present Value and the Internal Rate of Return for Mutually Exclusive Projects

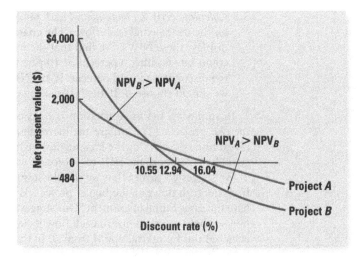

The IRR for a project is the rate at which the NPV equals zero. Because the NPV of *B* declines more rapidly, *B* actually has a lower IRR.

As with the movie example, we can select the better project with one of three different methods:

1. *Compare NPVs of the two projects.* Figure 5.6 aids our decision. If the discount rate is below 10.55 percent, we should choose Project *B* because *B* has a higher NPV. If the rate is above 10.55 percent, we should choose Project *A* because *A* has a higher NPV.

2. *Compare incremental IRR to discount rate.* Method 1 employed NPV. Another way of determining that *B* is a better project is to subtract the cash flows of *A* from the cash flows of *B* and then to calculate the IRR. This is the incremental IRR approach we spoke of earlier.

   Here are the incremental cash flows:

						NPV of Incremental Cash Flows		
Year:	0	1	2	3	Incremental IRR	@ 0%	@10%	@15%
B − A	0	−$9,000	0	$11,000	10.55%	$2,000	$83	−$593

   This chart shows that the incremental IRR is 10.55 percent. In other words, the NPV on the incremental investment is zero when the discount rate is 10.55 percent. Thus, if the relevant discount rate is below 10.55 percent, Project *B* is preferred to Project *A*. If the relevant discount rate is above 10.55 percent, Project *A* is preferred to Project *B*.

   Figure 5.6 shows that the NPVs of the two projects are equal when the discount rate is 10.55 percent. In other words, the *crossover rate* in the figure is 10.55. The incremental cash flows chart shows that the incremental IRR is also 10.55 percent. It is not a coincidence that the crossover rate and the incremental IRR are the same; this equality must *always* hold. The incremental IRR is the rate that causes the incremental cash flows to have zero NPV. The incremental cash flows have zero NPV when the two projects have the same NPV.

3. *Calculate NPV on incremental cash flows.* Finally, we could calculate the NPV on the incremental cash flows. The chart that appears with the previous method displays these NPVs. We find that the incremental NPV is positive when the discount rate is either 0 percent or 10 percent. The incremental NPV is negative if the discount rate is 15 percent. If the NPV is positive on the incremental flows, we should choose *B*. If the NPV is negative, we should choose *A*.

In summary, the same decision is reached whether we (1) compare the NPVs of the two projects, (2) compare the incremental IRR to the relevant discount rate, or (3) examine the NPV of the incremental cash flows. However, as mentioned earlier, we should *not* compare the IRR of Project *A* with the IRR of Project *B*.

We suggested earlier that we should subtract the cash flows of the smaller project from the cash flows of the bigger project. What do we do here when the two projects have the same initial investment? Our suggestion in this case is to perform the subtraction so that the *first* nonzero cash flow is negative. In the Kaufold Corp. example we achieved this by subtracting *A* from *B*. In this way, we can still use the basic IRR rule for evaluating cash flows.

The preceding examples illustrate problems with the IRR approach in evaluating mutually exclusive projects. Both the professor–student example and the motion picture example illustrate the problem that arises when mutually exclusive projects have different initial investments. The Kaufold Corp. example illustrates the problem that arises when mutually exclusive projects have different cash flow timing. When working with mutually exclusive projects, it is not necessary to determine whether it is the scale problem or the timing problem that exists. Very likely both occur in any real-world situation. Instead, the practitioner should simply use either an incremental IRR or an NPV approach.

REDEEMING QUALITIES OF IRR

IRR probably survives because it fills a need that NPV does not. People seem to want a rule that summarizes the information about a project in a single rate of return. This single rate gives people a simple way of discussing projects. For example, one manager in a firm might say to another, "Remodeling the north wing has a 20 percent IRR."

To their credit, however, companies that employ the IRR approach seem to understand its deficiencies. For example, companies frequently restrict managerial projections of cash flows to be negative at the beginning and strictly positive later. Perhaps, then, both the ability of the IRR approach to capture a complex investment project in a single number, and the ease of communicating that number explain the survival of the IRR.

A TEST

To test your knowledge, consider the following two statements:

1. You must know the discount rate to compute the NPV of a project, but you compute the IRR without referring to the discount rate.

2. Hence, the IRR rule is easier to apply than the NPV rule because you don't use the discount rate when applying IRR.

The first statement is true. The discount rate is needed to *compute* NPV. The IRR is *computed* by solving for the rate where the NPV is zero. No mention is made of the discount rate in the mere computation. However, the second statement is false. To *apply* IRR, you must compare the internal rate of return with the discount rate. Thus the discount rate is needed for making a decision under either the NPV or IRR approach.

5.6 The Profitability Index

Another method used to evaluate projects is called the **profitability index.** It is the ratio of the present value of the future expected cash flows *after* initial investment divided by the amount of the initial investment. The profitability index can be represented as:

$$\text{Profitability index (PI)} = \frac{\text{PV of cash flows } subsequent \text{ to initial investment}}{\text{Initial investment}}$$

EXAMPLE 5.4

Profitability Index   Hiram Finnegan Inc. (HFI) applies a 12 percent discount rate to two investment opportunities.

	Cash Flows ($000,000)			PV @ 12% of Cash Flows Subsequent to Initial Investment ($000,000)	Profitability Index	NPV @12% ($000,000)
Project	C_0	C_1	C_2			
1	−$20	$70	$10	$70.5	3.53	$50.5
2	−10	15	40	45.3	4.53	35.3

CALCULATION OF PROFITABILITY INDEX

The profitability index is calculated for Project 1 as follows. The present value of the cash flows *after* the initial investment is:

$$\$70.5 = \frac{\$70}{1.12} + \frac{\$10}{(1.12)^2}$$

The profitability index is obtained by dividing this result by the initial investment of $20. This yields:

$$3.53 = \frac{\$70.5}{\$20}$$

Application of the Profitability Index   How do we use the profitability index? We consider three situations:

1. *Independent projects:* Assume that HFI's two projects are independent. According to the NPV rule, both projects should be accepted because NPV is positive in each case. The profitability index (PI) is greater than 1 whenever the NPV is positive. Thus, the PI *decision rule* is:
   - Accept an independent project if PI > 1.
   - Reject it if PI < 1.

2. *Mutually exclusive projects:* Let us now assume that HFI can only accept one of its two projects. NPV analysis says accept Project 1 because this project has the bigger NPV. Because Project 2 has the higher PI, the profitability index leads to the wrong selection.

For mutually exclusive projects, the profitability index suffers from the scale problem that IRR also suffers from. Project 2 is smaller than Project 1. Because the PI is a ratio, it ignores Project 1's larger investment. Thus, like IRR, PI ignores differences of scale for mutually exclusive projects.

However, like IRR, the flaw with the PI approach can be corrected using incremental analysis. We write the incremental cash flows after subtracting Project 2 from project 1 as follows:

Project	Cash Flows ($000,000)			PV @12% of Cash Flows Subsequent to Initial Investment ($000,000)	Profitability Index	NPV @12% ($000,000)
	C_0	C_1	C_2			
1-2	−$10	$55	−$30	$25.2	2.52	$15.2

Because the profitability index on the incremental cash flows is greater than 1.0, we should choose the bigger project—that is, Project 1. This is the same decision we get with the NPV approach.

3. *Capital rationing:* The first two cases implicitly assumed that HFI could always attract enough capital to make any profitable investments. Now consider the case when the firm does not have enough capital to fund all positive NPV projects. This is the case of **capital rationing.**

Imagine that the firm has a third project, as well as the first two. Project 3 has the following cash flows:

Project	Cash Flows ($000,000)			PV @12% of Cash Flows Subsequent to Initial Investment ($000,000)	Profitability Index	NPV @12% ($000,000)
	C_0	C_1	C_2			
3	−$10	−$5	$60	$43.4	4.34	$33.4

Further, imagine that (1) the projects of Hiram Finnegan Inc. are independent, but (2) the firm has only $20 million to invest. Because Project 1 has an initial investment of $20 million, the firm cannot select both this project and another one. Conversely, because Projects 2 and 3 have initial investments of $10 million each, both these projects can be chosen. In other words, the cash constraint forces the firm to choose either Project 1 or Projects 2 and 3.

What should the firm do? Individually, Projects 2 and 3 have lower NPVs than Project 1 has. However, when the NPVs of Projects 2 and 3 are added together, the sum is higher than the NPV of Project 1. Thus, common sense dictates that Projects 2 and 3 should be accepted.

What does our conclusion have to say about the NPV rule or the PI rule? In the case of limited funds, we cannot rank projects according to their NPVs. Instead we should rank them according to the ratio of present value to initial investment. This is the PI rule. Both Project 2 and Project 3 have higher PI ratios than does Project 1. Thus they should be ranked ahead of Project 1 when capital is rationed.

The usefulness of the profitability index under capital rationing can be explained in military terms. The Pentagon speaks highly of a weapon with a lot of "bang for the buck." In capital budgeting, the profitability index measures the bang (the dollar return) for the buck invested. Hence it is useful for capital rationing.

It should be noted that the profitability index does not work if funds are also limited beyond the initial time period. For example, if heavy cash outflows elsewhere in the firm were to occur at Date 1, Project 3, which also has a cash outflow at Date 1, might need to be rejected. In other words, the profitability index cannot handle capital rationing over multiple time periods.

In addition, what economists term *indivisibilities* may reduce the effectiveness of the PI rule. Imagine that HFI has $30 million available for capital investment, not just $20 million. The firm now has enough cash for Projects 1 and 2. Because the sum of the NPVs of these two projects is greater than the sum of the NPVs of Projects 2 and 3, the firm would be better served by accepting Projects 1 and 2. But because Projects 2 and 3 still have the highest profitability indexes, the PI rule now leads to the wrong decision. Why does the PI rule lead us astray here? The key is that Projects 1 and 2 use up all of the $30 million, whereas Projects 2 and 3 have a combined initial investment of only $20 million (= $10 + 10). If Projects 2 and 3 are accepted, the remaining $10 million must be left in the bank.

This situation points out that care should be exercised when using the profitability index in the real world. Nevertheless, while not perfect, the profitability index goes a long way toward handling capital rationing.

5.7 The Practice of Capital Budgeting

So far this chapter has asked "Which capital budgeting methods should companies be using?" An equally important question is this: Which methods *are* companies using? Table 5.3 helps answer this question. As can be seen from the table, approximately three-quarters of U.S. and Canadian companies use the IRR and NPV methods. This is not surprising, given the theoretical advantages of these approaches. Over half of these companies use the payback method, a rather surprising result given the conceptual problems with this approach. And while discounted payback represents a theoretical improvement over regular payback, the usage here is far less. Perhaps companies are attracted to the user-friendly nature of payback. In addition, the flaws of this approach, as mentioned in the current chapter, may be relatively easy to correct. For example, while the payback method ignores all cash flows after the

Table 5.3

Percentage of CFOs Who Always or Almost Always Use a Given Technique

	% Always or Almost Always
Internal rate of return (IRR)	75.6%
Net present value (NPV)	74.9
Payback method	56.7
Discounted payback	29.5
Profitability index	11.9

SOURCE: Figure 2 from John R. Graham and Campbell R. Harvey, "The Theory and Practice of Corporate Finance: Evidence from the Field," *Journal of Financial Economics* 60 (2001). Based on a survey of 392 CFOs.

158   Part II   Valuation and Capital Budgeting

payback period, an alert manager can make ad hoc adjustments for a project with back-loaded cash flows.

Capital expenditures by individual corporations can add up to enormous sums for the economy as a whole. For example, in 2011, ExxonMobil announced that it expected to make about $34 billion in capital outlays during the year, up 6 percent from the previous year. The company further indicated that it expected to spend $33 billion to $37 billion per year through 2015. About the same time, ChevronTexaco announced that it would increase its capital budget for 2011 to $26 billion, up 21 percent from the previous year, and ConocoPhillips announced a 23 percent increase in capital spending to $13.5 billion for 2011. Other companies with large capital spending budgets in 2011 were Intel, which projected capital spending of about $10.2 billion, and semiconductor company Samsung Electronics, which projected capital spending of about $9 billion.

Large-scale capital spending is often an industrywide occurrence. For example, in 2011, capital spending in the semiconductor industry was expected to reach $60.4 billion. This tidy sum represented a 47 percent increase over industry capital spending in 2010.

According to information released by the United States Census Bureau in 2011, capital investment for the economy as a whole was $1.090 trillion in 2009, $1.374 trillion in 2008, and $1.355 trillion in 2007. The totals for the three years therefore equaled approximately $3.819 trillion! Given the sums at stake, it is not too surprising that successful corporations carefully analyze capital expenditures.

One might expect the capital budgeting methods of large firms to be more sophisticated than the methods of small firms. After all, large firms have the financial resources to hire more sophisticated employees. Table 5.4 provides some support for this idea. Here firms indicate frequency of use of the various capital budgeting methods on a scale of 0 (never) to 4 (always). Both the IRR and NPV methods are used more frequently, and payback less frequently, in large firms than in small firms. Conversely, large and small firms employ the last three approaches about equally.

The use of quantitative techniques in capital budgeting varies with the industry. As one would imagine, firms that are better able to estimate cash flows are more likely to use NPV. For example, estimation of cash flow in certain aspects of the oil business is quite feasible. Because of this, energy-related firms were among the first to use NPV analysis. Conversely, the cash flows in the motion picture business are very hard to project. The grosses of great hits like *Spiderman, Harry Potter,* and *Star Wars* were far, far greater than anyone imagined. The big failures like *Alamo* and *Waterworld* were unexpected as well. Because of this, NPV analysis is frowned upon in the movie business.

Table 5.4
Frequency of Use of Various Capital Budgeting Methods

	Large Firms	Small Firms
Internal rate of return (IRR)	3.41	2.87
Net present value (NPV)	3.42	2.83
Payback method	2.25	2.72
Discounted payback	1.55	1.58
Profitability index	0.75	0.78

Firms indicate frequency of use on a scale from 0 (never) to 4 (always). Numbers in table are averages across respondents.
SOURCE: Table 2 from Graham and Harvey (2001), op. cit.

How does Hollywood perform capital budgeting? The information that a studio uses to accept or reject a movie idea comes from the *pitch*. An independent movie producer schedules an extremely brief meeting with a studio to pitch his or her idea for a movie. Consider the following four paragraphs of quotes concerning the pitch from the thoroughly delightful book *Reel Power*:[10]

> "They [studio executives] don't want to know too much," says Ron Simpson. "They want to know concept. . . . They want to know what the three-liner is, because they want it to suggest the ad campaign. They want a title. . . . They don't want to hear any esoterica. And if the meeting lasts more than five minutes, they're probably not going to do the project."

> "A guy comes in and says this is my idea: '*Jaws* on a spaceship,'" says writer Clay Frohman (*Under Fire*). "And they say, 'Brilliant, fantastic.' Becomes *Alien*. That is *Jaws* on a spaceship, ultimately. . . . And that's it. That's all they want to hear. Their attitude is 'Don't confuse us with the details of the story.'"

> ". . . Some high-concept stories are more appealing to the studios than others. The ideas liked best are sufficiently original that the audience will not feel it has already seen the movie, yet similar enough to past hits to reassure executives wary of anything too far-out. Thus, the frequently used shorthand: It's *Flashdance* in the country (*Footloose*) or *High Noon* in outer space (*Outland*)."

> ". . . One gambit not to use during a pitch," says executive Barbara Boyle, "is to talk about big box-office grosses your story is sure to make. Executives know as well as anyone that it's impossible to predict how much money a movie will make, and declarations to the contrary are considered pure malarkey."

 ◄ To test your mastery of this material, take a quiz at mhhe. com/rwj

---

[10]Mark Litwak, *Reel Power: The Struggle for Influence and Success in the New Hollywood* (New York: William Morrow and Company, Inc., 1986), pp. 73, 74, and 77.

Summary and Conclusions

1. In this chapter, we covered different investment decision rules. We evaluated the most popular alternatives to the NPV: The payback period, the discounted payback period, the internal rate of return, and the profitability index. In doing so we learned more about the NPV.

2. While we found that the alternatives have some redeeming qualities, when all is said and done, they are not the NPV rule; for those of us in finance, that makes them decidedly second-rate.

3. Of the competitors to NPV, IRR must be ranked above payback. In fact, IRR always reaches the same decision as NPV in the normal case where the initial outflows of an independent investment project are followed only by a series of inflows.

4. We classified the flaws of IRR into two types. First, we considered the general case applying to both independent and mutually exclusive projects. There appeared to be two problems here:
   a. Some projects have cash inflows followed by one or more outflows. The IRR rule is inverted here: One should accept when the IRR is *below* the discount rate.
   b. Some projects have a number of changes of sign in their cash flows. Here, there are likely to be multiple internal rates of return. The practitioner must use either NPV or modified internal rate of return here.

5. Next, we considered the specific problems with the NPV for mutually exclusive projects. We showed that, due to differences in either size or timing, the project with the highest IRR need not have the highest NPV. Hence, the IRR rule should not be applied. (Of course, NPV can still be applied.)

   However, we then calculated incremental cash flows. For ease of calculation, we suggested subtracting the cash flows of the smaller project from the cash flows of the larger project. In that way the incremental initial cash flow is negative. One can always reach a correct decision by accepting the larger project if the incremental IRR is greater than the discount rate.

6. We described capital rationing as the case where funds are limited to a fixed dollar amount. With capital rationing the profitability index is a useful method of adjusting the NPV.

Concept Questions

1. **Payback Period and Net Present Value** If a project with conventional cash flows has a payback period less than the project's life, can you definitively state the algebraic sign of the NPV? Why or why not? If you know that the discounted payback period is less than the project's life, what can you say about the NPV? Explain.

2. **Net Present Value** Suppose a project has conventional cash flows and a positive NPV. What do you know about its payback? Its discounted payback? Its profitability index? Its IRR? Explain.

3. **Comparing Investment Criteria** Define each of the following investment rules and discuss any potential shortcomings of each. In your definition, state the criterion for accepting or rejecting independent projects under each rule.
   a. Payback period.
   b. Internal rate of return.
   c. Profitability index.
   d. Net present value.

4. **Payback and Internal Rate of Return** A project has perpetual cash flows of C per period, a cost of I, and a required return of R. What is the relationship between the project's payback and its IRR? What implications does your answer have for long-lived projects with relatively constant cash flows?

5. **International Investment Projects** In October 2010, BMW announced plans to spend $1 billion to expand production at its plant in South Carolina. The plant produced the second generation BMW X3 as well as the company's X5 and X6 models. BMW apparently felt it would be better able to compete and create value with a U.S.–based facility. In fact, BMW actually expected to export 70 percent of the X3s produced in South Carolina. About the same time, Samsung Electronics announced plans to build a $3.6 billion plant in Texas, and Novartis announced plans to open a $1 billion-plus plant in North Carolina. What are some of the reasons that foreign manufacturers of products as diverse as automobiles, electronics, and pharmaceuticals might arrive at the same conclusion to build plants in the U.S.?

6. **Capital Budgeting Problems** What are some of the difficulties that might come up in actual applications of the various criteria we discussed in this chapter? Which one would be the easiest to implement in actual applications? The most difficult?

7. **Capital Budgeting in Not-for-Profit Entities** Are the capital budgeting criteria we discussed applicable to not-for-profit corporations? How should such entities make capital budgeting decisions? What about the U.S. government? Should it evaluate spending proposals using these techniques?

8. **Net Present Value** The investment in Project *A* is $1 million, and the investment in Project *B* is $2 million. Both projects have a unique internal rate of return of 20 percent. Is the following statement true or false?

    For any discount rate from 0 percent to 20 percent, Project *B* has an NPV twice as great as that of Project *A*.

    Explain your answer.

9. **Net Present Value versus Profitability Index** Consider the following two mutually exclusive projects available to Global Investments, Inc.:

	C_0	C_1	C_2	Profitability Index	NPV
A	−$1,000	$1,000	$500	1.32	$322
B	−500	500	400	1.57	285

    The appropriate discount rate for the projects is 10 percent. Global Investments chose to undertake Project *A*. At a luncheon for shareholders, the manager of a pension fund that owns a substantial amount of the firm's stock asks you why the firm chose Project *A* instead of Project *B* when Project *B* has a higher profitability index.

    How would you, the CFO, justify your firm's action? Are there any circumstances under which Global Investments should choose Project *B*?

10. **Internal Rate of Return** Projects *A* and *B* have the following cash flows:

Year	Project A	Project B
0	−$1,000	−$2,000
1	C1A	C1B
2	C2A	C2B
3	C3A	C3B

    a. If the cash flows from the projects are identical, which of the two projects would have a higher IRR? Why?

    b. If C1B = 2C1A, C2B = 2C2A, and C3B = 2C3A, then is $IRR_A = IRR_B$?

11. **Net Present Value** You are evaluating Project *A* and Project *B*. Project *A* has a short period of future cash flows, while Project *B* has relatively long future cash flows. Which project will be more sensitive to changes in the required return? Why?

12. **Modified Internal Rate of Return** One of the less flattering interpretations of the acronym MIRR is "meaningless internal rate of return." Why do you think this term is applied to MIRR?

13. **Net Present Value** It is sometimes stated that "the net present value approach assumes reinvestment of the intermediate cash flows at the required return." Is this claim correct? To answer, suppose you calculate the NPV of a project in the usual way. Next, suppose you do the following:

    a. Calculate the future value (as of the end of the project) of all the cash flows other than the initial outlay assuming they are reinvested at the required return, producing a single future value figure for the project.

    b. Calculate the NPV of the project using the single future value calculated in the previous step and the initial outlay. It is easy to verify that you will get the same NPV as in your original calculation only if you use the required return as the reinvestment rate in the previous step.

14. **Internal Rate of Return** It is sometimes stated that "the internal rate of return approach assumes reinvestment of the intermediate cash flows at the internal rate of return." Is this claim correct? To answer, suppose you calculate the IRR of a project in the usual way. Next, suppose you do the following:

a. Calculate the future value (as of the end of the project) of all the cash flows other than the initial outlay assuming they are reinvested at the IRR, producing a single future value figure for the project.

b. Calculate the IRR of the project using the single future value calculated in the previous step and the initial outlay. It is easy to verify that you will get the same IRR as in your original calculation only if you use the IRR as the reinvestment rate in the previous step.

Questions and Problems

BASIC
(Questions 1–8)

1. **Calculating Payback Period and NPV** Fuji Software, Inc., has the following mutually exclusive projects.

Year	Project A	Project B
0	−$15,000	−$18,000
1	9,500	10,500
2	6,000	7,000
3	2,400	6,000

a. Suppose Fuji's payback period cutoff is two years. Which of these two projects should be chosen?

b. Suppose Fuji uses the NPV rule to rank these two projects. Which project should be chosen if the appropriate discount rate is 15 percent?

2. **Calculating Payback** An investment project provides cash inflows of $840 per year for eight years. What is the project payback period if the initial cost is $3,200? What if the initial cost is $4,800? What if it is $7,300?

3. **Calculating Discounted Payback** An investment project has annual cash inflows of $5,000, $5,500, $6,000, and $7,000, and a discount rate of 14 percent. What is the discounted payback period for these cash flows if the initial cost is $8,000? What if the initial cost is $12,000? What if it is $16,000?

4. **Calculating Discounted Payback** An investment project costs $15,000 and has annual cash flows of $3,800 for six years. What is the discounted payback period if the discount rate is 0 percent? What if the discount rate is 10 percent? If it is 15 percent?

5. **Calculating IRR** Stone Sour, Inc., has a project with the following cash flows:

Year	Cash Flows ($)
0	−$20,000
1	8,500
2	10,200
3	6,200

Chapter 5   Net Present Value and Other Investment Rules   **163**

The company evaluates all projects by applying the IRR rule. If the appropriate interest rate is 9 percent, should the company accept the project?

6. **Calculating IRR**   Compute the internal rate of return for the cash flows of the following two projects:

	Cash Flows ($)	
Year	Project A	Project B
0	−$5,300	−$2,900
1	2,000	1,100
2	2,800	1,800
3	1,600	1,200

7. **Calculating Profitability Index**   Bill plans to open a self-serve grooming center in a storefront. The grooming equipment will cost $385,000, to be paid immediately. Bill expects aftertax cash inflows of $84,000 annually for seven years, after which he plans to scrap the equipment and retire to the beaches of Nevis. The first cash inflow occurs at the end of the first year. Assume the required return is 13 percent. What is the project's PI? Should it be accepted?

8. **Calculating Profitability Index**   Suppose the following two independent investment opportunities are available to Greenplain, Inc. The appropriate discount rate is 10 percent.

Year	Project Alpha	Project Beta
0	−$2,300	−$3,900
1	1,200	800
2	1,100	2,300
3	900	2,900

a. Compute the profitability index for each of the two projects.
b. Which project(s) should Greenplain accept based on the profitability index rule?

INTERMEDIATE
(Questions 9–19)

9. **Cash Flow Intuition**   A project has an initial cost of I, has a required return of R, and pays C annually for N years.

a. Find C in terms of I and N such that the project has a payback period just equal to its life.
b. Find C in terms of I, N, and R such that this is a profitable project according to the NPV decision rule.
c. Find C in terms of I, N, and R such that the project has a benefit–cost ratio of 2.

10. **Problems with IRR**   Suppose you are offered $7,000 today but must make the following payments:

Year	Cash Flows ($)
0	$7,000
1	−3,700
2	−2,400
3	−1,500
4	−1,200

a. What is the IRR of this offer?

b. If the appropriate discount rate is 10 percent, should you accept this offer?

c. If the appropriate discount rate is 20 percent, should you accept this offer?

d. What is the NPV of the offer if the appropriate discount rate is 10 percent? 20 percent?

e. Are the decisions under the NPV rule in part (d) consistent with those of the IRR rule?

 11. NPV versus IRR   Consider the following cash flows on two mutually exclusive projects for the Bahamas Recreation Corporation (BRC). Both projects require an annual return of 14 percent.

Year	Deepwater Fishing	New Submarine Ride
0	−$950,000	−$1,850,000
1	370,000	900,000
2	510,000	800,000
3	420,000	750,000

As a financial analyst for BRC, you are asked the following questions:

a. If your decision rule is to accept the project with the greater IRR, which project should you choose?

b. Because you are fully aware of the IRR rule's scale problem, you calculate the incremental IRR for the cash flows. Based on your computation, which project should you choose?

c. To be prudent, you compute the NPV for both projects. Which project should you choose? Is it consistent with the incremental IRR rule?

12. Problems with Profitability Index   The Robb Computer Corporation is trying to choose between the following two mutually exclusive design projects:

Year	Cash Flow (I)	Cash Flow (II)
0	−$30,000	−$12,000
1	18,000	7,500
2	18,000	7,500
3	18,000	7,500

a. If the required return is 10 percent and Robb Computer applies the profitability index decision rule, which project should the firm accept?

b. If the company applies the NPV decision rule, which project should it take?

c. Explain why your answers in (a) and (b) are different.

13. Problems with IRR   Cutler Petroleum, Inc., is trying to evaluate a generation project with the following cash flows:

Year	Cash Flow
0	−$ 85,000,000
1	125,000,000
2	−15,000,000

Chapter 5   Net Present Value and Other Investment Rules **165**

a. If the company requires a 10 percent return on its investments, should it accept this project? Why?

b. Compute the IRR for this project. How many IRRs are there? If you apply the IRR decision rule, should you accept the project or not? What's going on here?

 14. **Comparing Investment Criteria**   Mario Brothers, a game manufacturer, has a new idea for an adventure game. It can market the game either as a traditional board game or as an interactive DVD, but not both. Consider the following cash flows of the two mutually exclusive projects for Mario Brothers. Assume the discount rate for Mario Brothers is 10 percent.

Year	Board Game	DVD
0	−$750	−$1,800
1	600	1,300
2	450	850
3	120	350

a. Based on the payback period rule, which project should be chosen?
b. Based on the NPV, which project should be chosen?
c. Based on the IRR, which project should be chosen?
d. Based on the incremental IRR, which project should be chosen?

15. **Profitability Index versus NPV**   Hanmi Group, a consumer electronics conglomerate, is reviewing its annual budget in wireless technology. It is considering investments in three different technologies to develop wireless communication devices. Consider the following cash flows of the three independent projects for Hanmi. Assume the discount rate for Hanmi is 10 percent. Further, Hanmi Group has only $20 million to invest in new projects this year.

	Cash Flows (in $ millions)		
Year	CDMA	G4	Wi-Fi
0	−$ 8	−$12	−$20
1	11	10	18
2	7.5	25	32
3	2.5	20	20

a. Based on the profitability index decision rule, rank these investments.
b. Based on the NPV, rank these investments.
c. Based on your findings in (a) and (b), what would you recommend to the CEO of Hanmi Group and why?

16. **Comparing Investment Criteria**   Consider the following cash flows of two mutually exclusive projects for AZ-Motorcars. Assume the discount rate for AZ-Motorcars is 10 percent.

Year	AZM Mini-SUV	AZF Full-SUV
0	−$450,000	−$800,000
1	320,000	350,000
2	180,000	420,000
3	150,000	290,000

a. Based on the payback period, which project should be accepted?
b. Based on the NPV, which project should be accepted?
c. Based on the IRR, which project should be accepted?
d. Based on this analysis, is incremental IRR analysis necessary? If yes, please conduct the analysis.

17. **Comparing Investment Criteria** The treasurer of Amaro Canned Fruits, Inc., has projected the cash flows of projects A, B, and C as follows:

Year	Project A	Project B	Project C
0	−$150,000	−$300,000	−$150,000
1	110,000	200,000	120,000
2	110,000	200,000	90,000

Suppose the relevant discount rate is 12 percent a year.

a. Compute the profitability index for each of the three projects.
b. Compute the NPV for each of the three projects.
c. Suppose these three projects are independent. Which project(s) should Amaro accept based on the profitability index rule?
d. Suppose these three projects are mutually exclusive. Which project(s) should Amaro accept based on the profitability index rule?
e. Suppose Amaro's budget for these projects is $450,000. The projects are not divisible. Which project(s) should Amaro accept?

18. **Comparing Investment Criteria** Consider the following cash flows of two mutually exclusive projects for Tokyo Rubber Company. Assume the discount rate for Tokyo Rubber Company is 10 percent.

Year	Dry Prepreg	Solvent Prepreg
0	−$1,700,000	−$750,000
1	1,100,000	375,000
2	900,000	600,000
3	750,000	390,000

a. Based on the payback period, which project should be taken?
b. Based on the NPV, which project should be taken?
c. Based on the IRR, which project should be taken?
d. Based on this analysis, is incremental IRR analysis necessary? If yes, please conduct the analysis.

19. **Comparing Investment Criteria** Consider two mutually exclusive new product launch projects that Nagano Golf is considering. Assume the discount rate for Nagano Golf is 15 percent.

Project A: Nagano NP-30.

     Professional clubs that will take an initial investment of $550,000 at time 0.

     Next five years (Years 1–5) of sales will generate a consistent cash flow of $185,000 per year.

     Introduction of new product at Year 6 will terminate further cash flows from this project.

Chapter 5 Net Present Value and Other Investment Rules **167**

Project *B:* Nagano NX-20.

High-end amateur clubs that will take an initial investment of $350,000 at Time 0.

Cash flow at Year 1 is $100,000. In each subsequent year cash flow will grow at 10 percent per year.

Introduction of new product at Year 6 will terminate further cash flows from this project.

Year	NP-30	NX-20
0	−$550,000	−$350,000
1	185,000	100,000
2	185,000	110,000
3	185,000	121,000
4	185,000	133,100
5	185,000	146,410

Please fill in the following table:

	NP-30	NX-20	Implications
Payback			
IRR			
PI			
NPV			

CHALLENGE
(Questions 20–28)

20. **NPV and Multiple IRRs** You are evaluating a project that costs $75,000 today. The project has an inflow of $155,000 in one year and an outflow of $65,000 in two years. What are the IRRs for the project? What discount rate results in the maximum NPV for this project? How can you determine that this is the maximum NPV?

21. **Payback and NPV** An investment under consideration has a payback of six years and a cost of $434,000. If the required return is 12 percent, what is the worst-case NPV? The best-case NPV? Explain. Assume the cash flows are conventional.

22. **Multiple IRRs** This problem is useful for testing the ability of financial calculators and computer software. Consider the following cash flows. How many different IRRs are there? (*Hint:* Search between 20 percent and 70 percent.) When should we take this project?

Year	Cash Flow
0	−$ 1,008
1	5,724
2	−12,140
3	11,400
4	−4,000

23. **NPV Valuation** The Yurdone Corporation wants to set up a private cemetery business. According to the CFO, Barry M. Deep, business is "looking up." As a result, the cemetery project will provide a net cash inflow of $290,000 for the firm

during the first year, and the cash flows are projected to grow at a rate of 5 percent per year forever. The project requires an initial investment of $3,900,000.

a. If Yurdone requires a return of 11 percent on such undertakings, should the cemetery business be started?

b. The company is somewhat unsure about the assumption of a growth rate of 5 percent in its cash flows. At what constant growth rate would the company just break even if it still required a return of 11 percent on investment?

24. Calculating IRR The Utah Mining Corporation is set to open a gold mine near Provo, Utah. According to the treasurer, Monty Goldstein, "This is a golden opportunity." The mine will cost $2,400,000 to open and will have an economic life of 11 years. It will generate a cash inflow of $345,000 at the end of the first year, and the cash inflows are projected to grow at 8 percent per year for the next 10 years. After 11 years, the mine will be abandoned. Abandonment costs will be $400,000 at the end of year 11.

a. What is the IRR for the gold mine?

b. The Utah Mining Corporation requires a return of 10 percent on such undertakings. Should the mine be opened?

25. NPV and IRR Butler International Limited is evaluating a project in Erewhon. The project will create the following cash flows:

Year	Cash Flow
0	−$950,000
1	285,000
2	345,000
3	415,000
4	255,000

All cash flows will occur in Erewhon and are expressed in dollars. In an attempt to improve its economy, the Erewhonian government has declared that all cash flows created by a foreign company are "blocked" and must be reinvested with the government for one year. The reinvestment rate for these funds is 4 percent. If Butler uses a required return of 11 percent on this project, what are the NPV and IRR of the project? Is the IRR you calculated the MIRR of the project? Why or why not?

26. Calculating IRR Consider two streams of cash flows, A and B. Stream A's first cash flow is $8,900 and is received three years from today. Future cash flows in Stream A grow by 4 percent in perpetuity. Stream B's first cash flow is −$10,000, is received two years from today, and will continue in perpetuity. Assume that the appropriate discount rate is 12 percent.

a. What is the present value of each stream?

b. Suppose that the two streams are combined into one project, called C. What is the IRR of Project C?

c. What is the correct IRR rule for Project C?

27. Calculating Incremental Cash Flows Darin Clay, the CFO of MakeMoney.com, has to decide between the following two projects:

Year	Project Million	Project Billion
0	−$1,200	−$$I_o$
1	$I_o + 160$	$I_o + 400$
2	960	1,200
3	1,200	1,600

The expected rate of return for either of the two projects is 12 percent. What is the range of initial investment (I_o) for which Project Billion is more financially attractive than Project Million?

28. **Problems with IRR** McKeekin Corp. has a project with the following cash flows:

Year	Cash Flow
0	$20,000
1	−26,000
2	13,000

What is the IRR of the project? What is happening here?

Excel Master It!

As you have already seen, Excel does not have a function to calculate the payback period. We have shown three ways to calculate the payback period, but there are numerous other methods as well. The cash flows for a project are shown below. You need to calculate the payback period using two different methods:

a. Calculate the payback period in a table. The first three columns of the table will be the year, the cash flow for that year, and the cumulative cash flow. The fourth column will show the whole year for the payback. In other words, if the payback period is 3 plus years, this column will have a 3, otherwise it will be a zero. The next column will calculate the fractional part of the payback period, or else it will display zero. The last column will add the previous two columns and display the final payback period calculation. You should also have a cell that displays the final payback period by itself, and a cell that returns the correct accept or reject decision based on the payback criteria.

b. Write a nested IF statement that calculates the payback period using only the project cash flow column. The IF statement should return a value of "Never" if the project has no payback period. In contrast to the example we showed previously, the nested IF function should test for the payback period starting with shorter payback periods and working towards longer payback periods. Another cell should display the correct accept or reject decision based on the payback criteria.

Year	Cash Flow
0	−$250,000
1	41,000
2	48,000
3	63,000
4	79,000
5	88,000
6	64,000
7	41,000
Required payback:	5

www.mhhe.com/rwj

BULLOCK GOLD MINING

Seth Bullock, the owner of Bullock Gold Mining, is evaluating a new gold mine in South Dakota. Dan Dority, the company's geologist, has just finished his analysis of the mine site. He has estimated that the mine would be productive for eight years, after which the gold would be completely mined. Dan has taken an estimate of the gold deposits to Alma Garrett, the company's financial officer. Alma has been asked by Seth to perform an analysis of the new mine and present her recommendation on whether the company should open the new mine.

Alma has used the estimates provided by Dan to determine the revenues that could be expected from the mine. She has also projected the expense of opening the mine and the annual operating expenses. If the company opens the mine, it will cost $750 million today, and it will have a cash outflow of $75 million nine years from today in costs associated with closing the mine and reclaiming the area surrounding it. The expected cash flows each year from the mine are shown in the following table. Bullock Mining has a 12 percent required return on all of its gold mines.

Year	Cash Flow
0	−$750,000,000
1	130,000,000
2	180,000,000
3	190,000,000
4	245,000,000
5	205,000,000
6	155,000,000
7	135,000,000
8	95,000,000
9	−75,000,000

1. Construct a spreadsheet to calculate the payback period, internal rate of return, modified internal rate of return, and net present value of the proposed mine.
2. Based on your analysis, should the company open the mine?
3. Bonus question: Most spreadsheets do not have a built-in formula to calculate the payback period. Write a VBA script that calculates the payback period for a project.

CHAPTER 6

Making Capital Investment Decisions

Is there green in green? General Electric (GE) thinks so. Through its "Ecomagination" program, the company planned to double research and development spending on green products. In fact, GE originally invested over $5 billion in its Ecomagination program, and it announced plans to invest another $10 billion from 2011 to 2015. With products such as a hybrid railroad locomotive (described as a 200-ton, 6,000-horsepower "Prius on rails"), GE's green initiative seems to be paying off. Revenue from green products was $19 billion in 2009, with a target of $20 billion in 2010. Even further, revenues from Ecomagination products were growing at twice the rate of the rest of the company's revenues. The company's internal commitment to reduced energy consumption through green "Treasure Hunts" saved it more than $100 million, and by 2010 the company reduced its water consumption by 30 percent from its 2006 baseline, another considerable cost savings.

▲ For updates on the latest happenings in finance, visit www. rwjcorporatefinance. blogspot.com

As you no doubt recognize from your study of the previous chapter, GE's decision to develop and market green technology represents a capital budgeting decision. In this chapter, we further investigate such decisions—how they are made and how to look at them objectively. We have two main tasks. First, recall that in the last chapter, we saw that cash flow estimates are the critical input into a net present value analysis, but we didn't say much about where these cash flows come from. We will now examine this question in some detail. Our second goal is to learn how to critically examine NPV estimates, and, in particular, how to evaluate the sensitivity of NPV estimates to assumptions made about the uncertain future.

The previous chapter discussed the basic principles behind capital budgeting approaches such as net present value, internal rate of return, and payback. We pointed out there that these three approaches all use cash flows. We did not, however, indicate how cash flows are to be estimated in the real world. Chapter 6 addresses this task. We begin with the idea that one should estimate *incremental* cash flows.

6.1 Incremental Cash Flows: The Key to Capital Budgeting

CASH FLOWS—NOT ACCOUNTING INCOME

You may not have thought about it, but there is a big difference between corporate finance courses and financial accounting courses. Techniques in corporate finance generally use cash flows, whereas financial accounting generally stresses income or earnings numbers. Certainly our text follows this tradition: Our net present value techniques discount cash flows, not earnings. When considering a single project, we discount the cash flows that the firm receives from the project. When valuing the firm as a whole, we discount dividends—not earnings—because dividends are the cash flows that an investor receives.

EXAMPLE 6.1

Relevant Cash Flows   The Weber-Decker Co. just paid $1 million in cash for a building as part of a new capital budgeting project. This entire $1 million is an immediate cash outflow. However, assuming straight-line depreciation over 20 years, only $50,000 (=$1 million/20) is considered an accounting expense in the current year. Current earnings are thereby reduced by only $50,000. The remaining $950,000 is expensed over the following 19 years. For capital budgeting purposes, the relevant cash outflow at Date 0 is the full $1 million, not the reduction in earnings of only $50,000.

Always discount cash flows, not earnings, when performing a capital budgeting calculation. Earnings do not represent real money. You can't spend out of earnings, you can't eat out of earnings, and you can't pay dividends out of earnings. You can do these things only out of cash flows.

In addition, it's not enough to use cash flows. In calculating the NPV of a project, only cash flows that are *incremental* to the project should be used. These cash flows are the changes in the firm's cash flows that occur as a direct consequence of accepting the project. That is, we are interested in the difference between the cash flows of the firm with the project and the cash flows of the firm without the project.

The use of incremental cash flows sounds easy enough, but pitfalls abound in the real world. We describe how to avoid some of the pitfalls of determining incremental cash flows.

SUNK COSTS

A **sunk cost** is a cost that has already occurred. Because sunk costs are in the past, they cannot be changed by the decision to accept or reject the project. Just as we "let bygones be bygones," we should ignore such costs. Sunk costs are not incremental cash outflows.

EXAMPLE 6.2

Sunk Costs   The General Milk Company (GMC) is currently evaluating the NPV of establishing a line of chocolate milk. As part of the evaluation, the company paid a consulting firm $100,000 last year for a test marketing analysis. Is this cost relevant for the capital budgeting decision now confronting GMC's management?

The answer is no. The $100,000 is not recoverable, so the $100,000 expenditure is a sunk cost, or spilled milk. In other words, one must ask, "What is the difference between the cash flows of the entire firm with the chocolate milk project and the cash flows of the entire firm without the project?" Since the $100,000 was already spent, acceptance of the project does not affect this cash flow. Therefore, the cash flow should be ignored for capital budgeting purposes.

Of course, the decision to spend $100,000 for a marketing analysis was a capital budgeting decision itself and was perfectly relevant *before* it was sunk. Our point is that once the company incurred the expense, the cost became irrelevant for any future decision.

OPPORTUNITY COSTS

Your firm may have an asset that it is considering selling, leasing, or employing elsewhere in the business. If the asset is used in a new project, potential revenues from alternative uses are lost. These lost revenues can meaningfully be viewed as costs.

They are called **opportunity costs** because, by taking the project, the firm forgoes other opportunities for using the assets.

EXAMPLE 6.3

Opportunity Costs Suppose the Weinstein Trading Company has an empty warehouse in Philadelphia that can be used to store a new line of electronic pinball machines. The company hopes to sell these machines to affluent northeastern consumers. Should the warehouse be considered a cost in the decision to sell the machines?

The answer is yes. The company could sell the warehouse if the firm decides not to market the pinball machines. Thus, the sales price of the warehouse is an opportunity cost in the pinball machine decision.

SIDE EFFECTS

Another difficulty in determining incremental cash flows comes from the side effects of the proposed project on other parts of the firm. A side effect is classified as either **erosion** or **synergy**. Erosion occurs when a new product reduces the sales and, hence, the cash flows of existing products. For example, one of Walt Disney Company's concerns when it built Euro Disney was that the new park would drain visitors from the Florida park, a popular vacation destination for Europeans. Synergy occurs when a new project increases the cash flows of existing projects. For example, while a shaving-supplies firm may appear to lose money on its new razor, the increase in sales of its new razor blades may make the razor an overall winner for the firm.

EXAMPLE 6.4

Erosion Suppose the Innovative Motors Corporation (IMC) is determining the NPV of a new convertible sports car. Some of the would-be purchasers are owners of IMC's compact sedans. Are all sales and profits from the new convertible sports car incremental?

The answer is no because some of the cash flow represents transfers from other elements of IMC's product line. This is erosion, which must be included in the NPV calculation. Without taking erosion into account, IMC might erroneously calculate the NPV of the sports car to be, say, $100 million. If half the customers are transfers from the sedan and lost sedan sales have an NPV of −$150 million, the true NPV is −$50 million (=$100 million − $150 million).

Synergy IMC is also contemplating the formation of a racing team. The team is forecast to lose money for the foreseeable future, with perhaps the best projection showing an NPV of −$35 million for the operation. However, IMC's managers are aware that the team will likely generate great publicity for all of IMC's products. A consultant estimates that the increase in cash flows elsewhere in the firm has a present value of $65 million. Assuming that the consultant's estimates of synergy are trustworthy, the net present value of the team is $30 million (=$65 million − $35 million). The managers should form the team.

ALLOCATED COSTS

Frequently a particular expenditure benefits a number of projects. Accountants allocate this cost across the different projects when determining income. However, for capital budgeting purposes, this **allocated cost** should be viewed as a cash outflow of a project only if it is an incremental cost of the project.

EXAMPLE 6.5

Allocated Costs   The Voetmann Consulting Corp. devotes one wing of its suite of offices to a library requiring a cash outflow of $100,000 a year in upkeep. A proposed capital budgeting project is expected to generate revenue equal to 5 percent of the overall firm's sales. An executive at the firm, David Pedersen, argues that $5,000 (=5 percent × $100,000) should be viewed as the proposed project's share of the library's costs. Is this appropriate for capital budgeting?

The answer is no. One must ask what the difference is between the cash flows of the entire firm with the project and the cash flows of the entire firm without the project. The firm will spend $100,000 on library upkeep whether or not the proposed project is accepted. Because acceptance of the proposed project does not affect this cash flow, the cash flow should be ignored when calculating the NPV of the project.

6.2 The Baldwin Company: An Example

ExcelMaster
coverage online

This section introduces the VDB function.

We next consider the example of a proposed investment in machinery and related items. Our example involves the Baldwin Company and colored bowling balls.

The Baldwin Company, originally established 16 years ago to make footballs, is now a leading producer of tennis balls, baseballs, footballs, and golf balls. Nine years ago, the company introduced "High Flite," its first line of high-performance golf balls. Baldwin management has sought opportunities in whatever businesses seem to have some potential for cash flow. Recently W. C. Meadows, vice president of the Baldwin Company, identified another segment of the sports ball market that looked promising and that he felt was not adequately served by larger manufacturers. That market was for brightly colored bowling balls, and he believed many bowlers valued appearance and style above performance. He also believed that it would be difficult for competitors to take advantage of the opportunity because of both Baldwin's cost advantages and its highly developed marketing skills.

As a result, the Baldwin Company investigated the marketing potential of brightly colored bowling balls. Baldwin sent a questionnaire to consumers in three markets: Philadelphia, Los Angeles, and New Haven. The results of the three questionnaires were much better than expected and supported the conclusion that the brightly colored bowling balls could achieve a 10 to 15 percent share of the market. Of course, some people at Baldwin complained about the cost of the test marketing, which was $250,000. (As we shall see later, this is a sunk cost and should not be included in project evaluation.)

In any case, the Baldwin Company is now considering investing in a machine to produce bowling balls. The bowling balls would be manufactured in a building owned by the firm and located near Los Angeles. This building, which is vacant, and the land can be sold for $150,000 after taxes.

Working with his staff, Meadows is preparing an analysis of the proposed new product. He summarizes his assumptions as follows: The cost of the bowling ball machine is $100,000 and it is expected to last five years. At the end of five years, the machine will be sold at a price estimated to be $30,000. Production by year during the five-year life of the machine is expected to be as follows: 5,000 units, 8,000 units, 12,000 units, 10,000 units, and 6,000 units. The price of bowling balls in the first year will be $20. The bowling ball market is highly competitive, so Meadows believes that the price of bowling balls will increase at only 2 percent per year, as compared to the anticipated general inflation rate of 5 percent. Conversely, the plastic used to produce bowling balls is rapidly becoming more expensive. Because of this, production cash outflows are expected to grow at 10 percent per year. First-year production costs will be $10 per unit. Meadows has determined, based on Baldwin's taxable income, that the appropriate incremental corporate tax rate in the bowling ball project is 34 percent.

Net working capital is defined as the difference between current assets and current liabilities. Like any other manufacturing firm, Baldwin finds that it must maintain an investment in working capital. It will purchase raw materials before production and sale, giving rise to an investment in inventory. It will maintain cash as a buffer against unforeseen expenditures. And, its credit sales will not generate cash until payment is made at a later date. Management determines that an initial investment (at Year 0) in net working capital of $10,000 is required. Subsequently, net working capital at the end of each year will be equal to 10 percent of sales for that year. In the final year of the project, net working capital will decline to zero as the project is wound down. In other words, the investment in working capital is to be completely recovered by the end of the project's life.

Projections based on these assumptions and Meadows's analysis appear in Tables 6.1 through 6.4. In these tables all cash flows are assumed to occur at the *end* of the year. Because of the large amount of information in these tables, it is important to see how the tables are related. Table 6.1 shows the basic data for both investment and income. Supplementary schedules on operations and depreciation, as presented in Tables 6.2 and 6.3, help explain the numbers in Table 6.1. Our goal is to obtain

Table 6.1 **Worksheet for Cash Flows of the Baldwin Company ($ in thousands) (All cash flows occur at the *end* of the year.)**

	Year 0	Year 1	Year 2	Year 3	Year 4	Year 5
Investments:						
(1) Bowling ball machine	−$100.00					$ 21.76*
(2) Accumulated depreciation		$ 20.00	$ 52.00	$ 71.20	$ 82.72	94.24
(3) Adjusted basis of machine after depreciation (end of year)		80.00	48.00	28.80	17.28	5.76
(4) Opportunity cost (warehouse)	−150.00					150.00
(5) Net working capital (end of year)	10.00	10.00	16.32	24.97	21.22	
(6) Change in net working capital	−10.00		−6.32	−8.65	3.75	21.22
(7) Total cash flow of investment [(1) + (4) + (6)]	−260.00		−6.32	−8.65	3.75	192.98
Income:						
(8) Sales revenues		$100.00	$163.20	$249.70	$212.24	$129.89
(9) Operating costs		−50.00	−88.00	−145.20	−133.10	−87.85
(10) Depreciation		−20.00	−32.00	−19.20	−11.52	−11.52
(11) Income before taxes [(8) + (9) + (10)]		$ 30.00	$ 43.20	$ 85.30	$ 67.62	$ 30.53
(12) Tax at 34 percent		−10.20	−14.69	−29.00	−22.99	−10.38
(13) Net income		$ 19.80	$ 28.51	$ 56.30	$ 44.63	$ 20.15

*We assume that the sale price of the bowling ball machine at year 5 will be $30 (in thousands). The machine will have been depreciated to $5.76 at that time. Therefore, the taxable gain from the sale will be $24.24 (=$30 − $5.76). The aftertax salvage value will be $30 − [.34 × ($30 − $5.76)] = $21.76.

Table 6.2

Operating Revenues and Costs of the Baldwin Company

(1) Year	(2) Quantity Sold	(3) Price	(4) Sales Revenues	(5) Cost per Unit	(6) Operating Costs
1	5,000	$20.00	$100,000	$10.00	$ 50,000
2	8,000	20.40	163,200	11.00	88,000
3	12,000	20.81	249,696	12.10	145,200
4	10,000	21.22	212,242	13.31	133,100
5	6,000	21.65	129,892	14.64	87,846

Price rises at 2% per year. Unit cost rises at 10% per year. Reported prices and costs (columns 3 and 5) are rounded to two digits after the decimal. Sales revenues and operating costs (columns 4 and 6) are calculated using exact, i.e., nonrounded, prices and costs.

Table 6.3

Depreciation under Modified Accelerated Cost Recovery System (MACRS)

	Recovery Period Class					
Year	3 Years	5 Years	7 Years	10 Years	15 Years	20 Years
1	.3333	.2000	.1429	.1000	.0500	.03750
2	.4445	.3200	.2449	.1800	.0950	.07219
3	.1481	.1920	.1749	.1440	.0855	.06677
4	.0741	.1152	.1249	.1152	.0770	.06177
5		.1152	.0893	.0922	.0693	.05713
6		.0576	.0892	.0737	.0623	.05285
7			.0893	.0655	.0590	.04888
8			.0446	.0655	.0590	.04522
9				.0656	.0591	.04462
10				.0655	.0590	.04461
11				.0328	.0591	.04462
12					.0590	.04461
13					.0591	.04462
14					.0590	.04461
15					.0591	.04462
16					.0295	.04461
17						.04462
18						.04461
19						.04462
20						.04461
21						.02231

Depreciation is expressed as a percentage of the asset's initial cost. These schedules are based on the IRS Publication 946, entitled *How to Depreciate Property*. Details of depreciation are presented later in the chapter. Three-year depreciation actually carries over four years because the IRS assumes the purchase is made in midyear.

projections of cash flow. The data in Table 6.1 are all that are needed to calculate the relevant cash flows, as shown in Table 6.4.

AN ANALYSIS OF THE PROJECT

For most projects, cash flows follow a common pattern. First, firms invest at the beginning of the project, generating cash outflows. Second, product sales provide cash

Table 6.4   Incremental Cash Flows for the Baldwin Company ($ in thousands)

	Year 0	Year 1	Year 2	Year 3	Year 4	Year 5
(1) Sales revenue [Line 8, Table 6.1]		$100.00	$163.20	$249.70	$212.24	$129.89
(2) Operating costs [Line 9, Table 6.1]		−50.00	−88.00	−145.20	−133.10	−87.85
(3) Taxes [Line 12, Table 6.1]		−10.20	−14.69	−29.00	−22.99	−10.38
(4) Cash flow from operations [(1) + (2) + (3)]		39.80	60.51	$ 75.50	$ 56.15	$ 31.67
(5) Total cash flow of investment [Line 7, Table 6.1]	−$260.00		−6.32	−8.65	3.75	192.98
(6) Total cash flow of project [(4) + (5)]	−260.00	39.80	54.19	66.85	$ 59.90	$224.65

NPV @		
	4%	$123.64
	10%	$ 51.59
	15%	$ 5.47
	15.68%	$ 0.00
	20%	($ 31.35)

inflows over the life of the project. Third, plant and equipment are sold off at the end of the project, generating more cash inflow. We now discuss Baldwin's cash flows for each of these three steps.

Investments   The investment outlays for the project are summarized in the top segment of Table 6.1. They consist of three parts:

1. *The bowling ball machine:* The purchase requires an immediate (Year 0) cash outflow of $100,000. The firm realizes a cash inflow when the machine is sold in Year 5. These cash flows are shown in Line 1 of Table 6.1. As indicated in the footnote to the table, taxes are incurred when the asset is sold.

2. *The opportunity cost of not selling the warehouse:* If Baldwin accepts the bowling ball project, it will use a warehouse and land that could otherwise be sold. The estimated aftertax sales price of the warehouse and land is therefore included as an *opportunity cost* in Year 0, as presented in Line 4. Opportunity costs are treated as cash outflows for purposes of capital budgeting. However, note that if the project is accepted, management assumes that the warehouse will be sold for $150,000 (after taxes) in Year 5.

   The test marketing cost of $250,000 is not included. As stated earlier, the tests occurred in the past and should be viewed as a *sunk cost*.

3. *The investment in working capital:* Required working capital appears in Line 5. Working capital rises over the early years of the project as expansion occurs. However, all working capital is assumed to be recovered at the end, a common assumption in capital budgeting. In other words, all inventory is sold by the end, the cash balance maintained as a buffer is liquidated, and all accounts receivable are collected.

   Increases in working capital in the early years must be funded by cash generated elsewhere in the firm. Hence, these increases are viewed as cash *outflows*. To reiterate, it is the *increase* in working capital over a year that leads to a cash outflow in that year. Even if working capital is at a high level, there will be no cash outflow over a year if working capital stays constant over that year.

Conversely, decreases in working capital in the later years are viewed as cash inflows. All of these cash flows are presented in Line 6 of Table 6.1. A more complete discussion of working capital is provided later in this section.

To recap, there are three investments in this example: the bowling ball machine (Line 1 in Table 6.1), the opportunity cost of the warehouse (Line 4), and the changes in working capital (Line 6). The total cash flow from these three investments is shown in Line 7.

Income and Taxes Next the determination of income is presented in the bottom segment of Table 6.1. While we are ultimately interested in cash flow—not income—we need the income calculation to determine taxes. Lines 8 and 9 of Table 6.1 show sales revenues and operating costs, respectively. The projections in these lines are based on the sales revenues and operating costs computed in Columns 4 and 6 of Table 6.2. The estimates of revenues and costs follow from assumptions made by the corporate planning staff at Baldwin. In other words, the estimates depend on the forecast that product prices will increase at 2 percent per year and costs per unit will increase at 10 percent per year.

Depreciation of the $100,000 capital investment is shown in Line 10 of Table 6.1. Where do these numbers come from? Depreciation for tax purposes for U.S. companies is based on the Modified Accelerated Cost Recovery System (MACRS). Each asset is assigned a useful life under MACRS, with an accompanying depreciation schedule as shown in Table 6.3. The IRS ruled that Baldwin is to depreciate its capital investment over five years, so the second column of the table applies in this case. Because depreciation in the table is expressed as a percentage of the asset's cost, multiply the percentages in this column by $100,000 to arrive at depreciation in dollars. Notice that the percentages in each column of Table 6.3 sum to 100 percent, implying that the IRS allows the asset to be depreciated to zero.

Income before taxes is calculated in Line 11 of Table 6.1. Taxes are provided in Line 12 of this table, and net income is shown in Line 13.

Salvage Value When selling an asset, one must pay taxes on the difference between the asset's sales price and its book value. We stated earlier that Baldwin plans to sell the bowling ball machine at the end of Year 5, estimating the sales price at $30,000.

At the end of the fifth year, the book value of the machine would be $5,760, as shown in Line 3 of Table 6.1. If the company sold the machine for $30,000, it would pay taxes on the difference between this sales price and the book value of $5,760. With a 34 percent tax rate, the tax liability would be $.34 \times (\$30,000 - \$5,760) = \$8,242$. The aftertax salvage value of the equipment, a cash inflow to the company, would be $\$30,000 - \$8,242 = \$21,758$, as indicated in Line 1 of Table 6.1.

Alternatively, if the book value exceeds the market value, the difference is treated as a loss for tax purposes. For example, if Baldwin sold the machine for $4,000, the book value would exceed the market value by $1,760. In this case, taxes of $.34 \times \$1,760 = \$598$ would be saved.

Cash Flow Cash flow is finally determined in Table 6.4. We begin by reproducing Lines 8, 9, and 12 in Table 6.1 as Lines 1, 2, and 3 in Table 6.4. Cash flow from operations, which is sales minus both operating costs and taxes, is provided in Line 4 of Table 6.4. Total investment cash flow, taken from Line 7 of Table 6.1, appears as

Line 5 of Table 6.4. Cash flow from operations plus total cash flow of the investment equals total cash flow of the project, which is displayed as Line 6 of Table 6.4.[1]

Net Present Value The NPV of the Baldwin bowling ball project can be calculated from the cash flows in Line 6. As can be seen at the bottom of Table 6.4, the NPV is $51,590 if 10 percent is the appropriate discount rate and −$31,350 if 20 percent is the appropriate discount rate. If the discount rate is 15.68 percent, the project will have a zero NPV. In other words, the project's internal rate of return is 15.68 percent. If the discount rate of the Baldwin bowling ball project is above 15.68 percent, it should not be accepted because its NPV would be negative.

WHICH SET OF BOOKS?

Corporations must provide a computation of profit or loss to both their own stockholders and tax authorities. While you might think that the numbers going to both parties would be the same, this is not the case. In actual fact, U.S. firms keep two sets of books, one for the Internal Revenue Service (IRS), called *tax books,* and another for their annual reports (called *stockholders' books*), with the numbers differing across the two sets.

How can this be? The two sets of books differ because their rules were developed by two separate bodies. The tax books follow the rules of the IRS and the stockholders' books follow the rules of the *Financial Accounting Standards Board* (FASB), the governing body in accounting. For example, interest on municipal bonds is ignored for tax purposes while the FASB treats the interest as income. As another example, companies typically use accelerated depreciation for their taxes and straight-line depreciation for their stockholders' books.

The differences almost always benefit the firm; the rules permit income on the stockholders' books to be higher than income on the tax books. Thus, management can look profitable to its stockholders without having to pay taxes on all of that reported profit. In fact, plenty of large companies consistently report positive earnings to their stockholders while reporting losses to the IRS. A cynical interpretation is that members of Congress, who collectively make tax policy, develop favorable rules to help their constituents. Whether or not this interpretation is true, one thing is clear: Companies are following the law, not breaking the law, by creating two sets of books.

Which set of books is relevant for the present chapter? The numbers in the tax books are the relevant ones, since you can only calculate cash flows after subtracting out taxes. While the stockholders' books are relevant for accounting and financial analysis, they are not used for capital budgeting.

Finally, while U.S. firms are allowed two sets of books, this is not the case in all, or perhaps even a majority, of other countries. Knowledge of local rules is needed before estimating international cash flows.

A NOTE ABOUT NET WORKING CAPITAL

Net working capital is the difference between current assets and current liabilities. Investment in net working capital is an important part of any capital budgeting analysis because it affects cash flows. While we considered net working capital in Lines 5 and 6 of Table 6.1, students may be wondering where the numbers in these

---

[1]The total cash flow of the project is frequently referred to as "free cash flow." Free cash flow is the amount of cash that can be distributed to all investors (both debt and equity investors) after all necessary investments have been made.

lines came from. An investment in net working capital arises whenever (1) inventory is purchased, (2) cash is kept in the project as a buffer against unexpected expenditures, and (3) sales are made on credit, generating accounts receivable rather than cash. (The investment in net working capital is reduced by credit purchases, which generate accounts payable.) This investment in net working capital represents a cash *outflow* because cash generated elsewhere in the firm is tied up in the project.

To see how the investment in net working capital is built from its component parts, we focus on Year 1. We see in Table 6.1 that Baldwin's managers predict sales in Year 1 to be $100,000 and operating costs to be $50,000. If both the sales and costs were cash transactions, the firm would receive $50,000 (=$100,000 − $50,000). As stated earlier, this cash flow would occur at the *end* of Year 1.

Now let's give you more information. The managers:

1. Forecast that $9,000 of the sales will be on credit, implying that cash receipts at the end of Year 1 will be only $91,000 (=$100,000 − $9,000). The accounts receivable of $9,000 will be collected at the end of Year 2.

2. Believe that they can defer payment on $3,000 of the $50,000 of costs, implying that cash disbursements at the end of Year 1 will be only $47,000 (=$50,000 − $3,000). Baldwin will pay off the $3,000 of accounts payable at the end of Year 2.

3. Decide that inventory of $2,500 should be left on hand at the end of Year 1 to avoid *stockouts* (that is, running out of inventory).

4. Decide that cash of $1,500 should be earmarked for the project at the end of Year 1 to avoid running out of cash.

Thus, net working capital at the end of Year 1 is:

$9,000	−	$3,000	+	$2,500	+	$1,500	=	$10,000
Accounts receivable		Accounts payable		Inventory		Cash		Net working capital

Because $10,000 of cash generated elsewhere in the firm must be used to offset this requirement for net working capital, Baldwin's managers correctly view the investment in net working capital as a cash outflow of the project. As the project grows over time, needs for net working capital increase. *Changes* in net working capital from year to year represent further cash flows, as indicated by the negative numbers for the first few years on Line 6 of Table 6.1. However, in the declining years of the project, net working capital is reduced—ultimately to zero. That is, accounts receivable are finally collected, the project's cash buffer is returned to the rest of the corporation, and all remaining inventory is sold off. This frees up cash in the later years, as indicated by positive numbers in Years 4 and 5 on Line 6.

Typically, corporate worksheets (such as Table 6.1) treat net working capital as a whole. The individual components of working capital (receivables, inventory, and the like) do not generally appear in the worksheets. However, the reader should remember that the working capital numbers in the worksheets are not pulled out of thin air. Rather, they result from a meticulous forecast of the components, just as we illustrated for Year 1.

A NOTE ABOUT DEPRECIATION

The Baldwin case made some assumptions about depreciation. Where did these assumptions come from? Depreciation rules are set forth in IRS Publication 946, entitled *How to Depreciate Property*. This publication sorts different property types into classes, thereby determining their depreciable lives for tax purposes. For example:

- The 3-year class includes certain specialized short-lived property. Tractor units and racehorses over two years old are among the few items fitting into this class.
- The 5-year class includes cars, trucks, computers and peripheral equipment, office machinery, as well as property used in research.
- The 7-year class includes office furniture and fixtures, as well as agricultural machinery and equipment.
- The 10-year class includes vessels, barges, and tugs, as well as some agricultural and horticultural structures.
- The 15-year class includes improvements to land, such as shrubbery, fences, roads, sidewalks, and bridges, as well as certain restaurant property.
- The 20-year class includes farm buildings, as well as land improvements for electric utility plants.
- Real property is separated into two classes: residential and nonresidential. The cost of residential property is recovered over 27½ years and nonresidential property over 39 years.

Items in the 3-, 5-, 7-, 10-, 15-, and 20-year classes are depreciated according to the schedules in Table 6.3. All real estate is depreciated on a straight-line basis.

Calculations of depreciation include a half-year convention, which treats all property as if it were placed in service at midyear. To be consistent, the IRS allows half a year of depreciation for the year in which property is disposed of or retired. The effect of this is to spread the deductions for property over one year more than the name of its class—for example, six tax years for five-year property.

INTEREST EXPENSE

It may have bothered you that interest expense was ignored in the Baldwin example. After all, many projects are at least partially financed with debt, particularly a bowling ball machine that is likely to increase the debt capacity of the firm. As it turns out, our approach of assuming no debt financing is rather standard in the real world. Firms typically calculate a project's cash flows under the assumption that the project is financed only with equity. In this analysis, we want to determine the NPV of the project independent of financing decisions. Any adjustments for debt financing are reflected in the discount rate, not the cash flows. The treatment of debt in capital budgeting will be covered in depth in Chapter 13.

6.3 Inflation and Capital Budgeting

ExcelMaster
coverage online

This section introduces the
SLN function.

Inflation is an important fact of economic life, and it must be considered in capital budgeting. We begin our examination of inflation by considering the relationship between interest rates and inflation.

INTEREST RATES AND INFLATION

Suppose a bank offers a one-year interest rate of 10 percent. This means that an individual who deposits $1,000 will receive $1,100 (=$1,000 × 1.10) in one year. Although 10 percent may seem like a handsome return, one can put it in perspective only after examining the rate of inflation.

Figure 6.1
Calculation of Real Rate of Interest

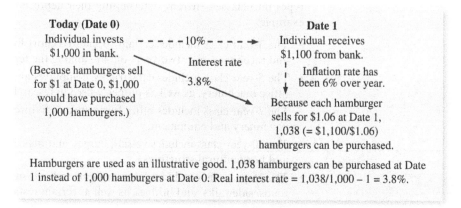

Hamburgers are used as an illustrative good. 1,038 hamburgers can be purchased at Date 1 instead of 1,000 hamburgers at Date 0. Real interest rate = 1,038/1,000 − 1 = 3.8%.

Imagine that the rate of inflation is 6 percent over the year and it affects all goods equally. For example, a fast-food restaurant charging $1.00 for a hamburger today will charge $1.06 for the same hamburger at the end of the year. You can use your $1,000 to buy 1,000 hamburgers today (Date 0). Alternatively, if you put your money in the bank, you can buy 1,038 (=$1,100/$1.06) hamburgers at Date 1. Thus, lending increases your hamburger consumption by only 3.8 percent.

Because the prices of all goods rise at this 6 percent rate, lending lets you increase your consumption of any single good or any combination of goods by 3.8 percent. Thus, 3.8 percent is what you are *really* earning through your savings account, after adjusting for inflation. Economists refer to the 3.8 percent number as the *real interest rate*. Economists refer to the 10 percent rate as the *nominal interest rate* or simply the *interest rate*. This discussion is illustrated in Figure 6.1.

We have used an example with a specific nominal interest rate and a specific inflation rate. In general, the formula between real and nominal interest rates can be written as follows:

$$1 + \text{Nominal interest rate} = (1 + \text{Real interest rate}) \times (1 + \text{Inflation rate})$$

Rearranging terms, we have:

$$\text{Real interest rate} = \frac{1 + \text{Nominal interest rate}}{1 + \text{Inflation rate}} - 1 \qquad (6.1)$$

The formula indicates that the real interest rate in our example is 3.8 percent (=1.10/1.06 − 1).

Equation 6.1 determines the real interest rate precisely. The following formula is an approximation:

$$\text{Real interest rate} \cong \text{Nominal interest rate} - \text{Inflation rate} \qquad (6.2)$$

The symbol $\cong$ indicates that the equation is approximately true. This latter formula calculates the real rate in our example as:

$$4\% = 10\% - 6\%$$

You should be aware that, although Equation 6.2 may seem more intuitive than Equation 6.1, 6.2 is only an approximation. This approximation is reasonably accurate for low rates of interest and inflation. In our example the difference between the approximate calculation and the exact one is only .2 percent (=4 percent − 3.8 percent). Unfortunately, the approximation becomes poor when rates are higher.

EXAMPLE 6.6

Real and Nominal Rates The little-known monarchy of Gerberovia recently had a nominal interest rate of 300 percent and an inflation rate of 280 percent. According to Equation 6.2, the real interest rate is:

$$300\% - 280\% = 20\% \text{ (Approximate formula)}$$

However, according to Equation 6.1, this rate is:

$$\frac{1 + 300\%}{1 + 280\%} - 1 = 5.26\% \quad \text{(Exact formula)}$$

How do we know that the second formula is indeed the exact one? Let's think in terms of hamburgers again. Had you deposited $1,000 in a Gerberovian bank a year ago, the account would be worth $4,000 [=$1,000 × (1 + 300%)] today. However, while a hamburger cost $1 a year ago, it costs $3.80 (=1 + 280%) today. Therefore, you would now be able to buy 1,052.6 (=$4,000/3.80) hamburgers, implying a real interest rate of 5.26 percent.

CASH FLOW AND INFLATION

The previous analysis defines two types of interest rates, nominal rates and real rates, and relates them through Equation 6.1. Capital budgeting requires data on cash flows as well as on interest rates. Like interest rates, cash flows can be expressed in either nominal or real terms.

A **nominal cash flow** refers to the actual dollars to be received (or paid out). A **real cash flow** refers to the cash flow's purchasing power. These definitions are best explained by examples.

EXAMPLE 6.7

Nominal versus Real Cash Flow Burrows Publishing has just purchased the rights to the next book of famed romantic novelist Barbara Musk. Still unwritten, the book should be available to the public in four years. Currently, romantic novels sell for $10.00 in softcover. The publishers believe that inflation will be 6 percent a year over the next four years. Because romantic novels are so popular, the publishers anticipate that their prices will rise about 2 percent per year more than the inflation rate over the next four years. Burrows Publishing plans to sell the novel at $13.60 [=(1.08)⁴ × $10.00] four years from now, anticipating sales of 100,000 copies.

The expected cash flow in the fourth year of $1.36 million (=$13.60 × 100,000) is a *nominal cash flow*. That is, the firm expects to receive $1.36 million at that time. In other words, a nominal cash flow refers to the actual dollars to be received in the future.

The purchasing power of $1.36 million in four years is:

$$\$1.08 \text{ million} = \frac{\$1.36 \text{ million}}{(1.06)^4}$$

The figure of $1.08 million is a *real cash flow* because it is expressed in terms of purchasing power. Extending our hamburger example, the $1.36 million to be received in four years will only buy 1.08 million hamburgers because the price of a hamburger will rise from $1 to $1.26 [=$1 × (1.06)⁴] over the period.

EXAMPLE 6.8

Depreciation EOBII Publishers, a competitor of Burrows, recently bought a printing press for $2,000,000 to be depreciated to zero by the straight-line method over five years. This implies yearly depreciation of $400,000 (=$2,000,000/5). Is this $400,000 figure a real or a nominal quantity?

Depreciation is a *nominal* quantity because $400,000 is the actual tax deduction over each of the next five years. Depreciation becomes a real quantity if it is adjusted for purchasing power. Assuming an annual inflation rate of 6 percent, depreciation in the fourth year, expressed as a real quantity is $316,837 [=$400,000/(1.06)^4].

DISCOUNTING: NOMINAL OR REAL?

Our previous discussion showed that interest rates can be expressed in either nominal or real terms. Similarly, cash flows can be expressed in either nominal or real terms. Given these choices, how should one express interest rates and cash flows when performing capital budgeting?

Financial practitioners correctly stress the need to maintain *consistency* between cash flows and discount rates. That is:

Nominal cash flows must be discounted at the *nominal* rate.

Real cash flows must be discounted at the *real* rate.

As long as one is consistent, either approach is correct. To minimize computational error, it is generally advisable in practice to choose the approach that is easiest. This idea is illustrated in the following two examples.

EXAMPLE 6.9

Real and Nominal Discounting Shields Electric forecasts the following nominal cash flows on a particular project:

Cash Flow	0	1	2
	−$1,000	$600	$650

The nominal discount rate is 14 percent, and the inflation rate is forecast to be 5 percent. What is the value of the project?

Using Nominal Quantities The NPV can be calculated as:

$$\$26.47 = -\$1,000 + \frac{\$600}{1.14} + \frac{\$650}{(1.14)^2}$$

The project should be accepted.

Using Real Quantities The real cash flows are these:

Cash Flow	0	1	2
	−$1,000	$571.43	$589.57
		$=\left(\frac{\$600}{1.05}\right)$	$=\left(\frac{\$650}{(1.05)^2}\right)$

According to Equation 6.1, the real discount rate is 8.57143 percent (=1.14/1.05 − 1). The NPV can be calculated as:

$$\$26.47 = -\$1,000 + \frac{\$571.43}{1.0857143} + \frac{\$589.57}{(1.0857143)^2}$$

The NPV is the same whether cash flows are expressed in nominal or in real quantities. It must always be the case that the NPV is the same under the two different approaches.

Because both approaches always yield the same result, which one should be used? Use the approach that is simpler because the simpler approach generally leads to fewer computational errors. The Shields Electric example begins with nominal cash flows, so nominal quantities produce a simpler calculation here.

EXAMPLE 6.10

Real and Nominal NPV Altshuler, Inc. generated the following forecast for a capital budgeting project:

	Year 0	Year 1	Year 2
Capital expenditure	$1,210		
Revenues (in real terms)		$1,900	$2,000
Cash expenses (in real terms)		950	1000
Depreciation (straight-line)		605	605

The CEO, David Altshuler, estimates inflation to be 10 percent per year over the next two years. In addition, he believes that the cash flows of the project should be discounted at the nominal rate of 15.5 percent. His firm's tax rate is 40 percent.

Mr. Altshuler forecasts all cash flows in *nominal* terms, leading to the following table and NPV calculation:

	Year 0	Year 1	Year 2
Capital expenditure	−$1,210		
Revenues		$2,090 (=1,900 × 1.10)	$2,420 [=2,000 × (1.10)^2]
−Expenses		−1,045 (=950 × 1.10)	−1,210 [=1,000 × (1.10)^2]
−Depreciation		−605 (=1210/2)	−605
Taxable income		440	605
−Taxes (40%)		−176	−242
Income after taxes		264	363
+Depreciation		605	605
Cash flow		869	968

$$\text{NPV} = -\$1,210 + \frac{\$869}{1.155} + \frac{\$968}{(1.155)^2} = \$268$$

(continued)

The firm's CFO, Stuart Weiss, prefers working in real terms. He first calculates the real rate to be 5 percent ($=1.155/1.10 - 1$). Next, he generates the following table in *real* quantities:

	Year 0	Year 1	Year 2
Capital expenditure	−$1,210		
Revenues		$1,900	$2,000
−Expenses		−950	−1,000
−Depreciation		−550 (=605/1.10)	−500 [=605/(1.10)²]
Taxable income		400	500
−Taxes (40%)		−160	−200
Income after taxes		240	300
+Depreciation		550	500
Cash flow		790	800

Mr. Weiss calculates the value of the project as:

$$NPV = -\$1,210 + \frac{\$790}{1.05} + \frac{\$800}{(1.05)^2} = \$268$$

In explaining his calculations to Mr. Altshuler, Mr. Weiss points out these facts:

1. The capital expenditure occurs at Date 0 (today), so its nominal value and its real value are equal.

2. Because yearly depreciation of $605 is a nominal quantity, one converts it to a real quantity by discounting at the inflation rate of 10 percent.

It is no coincidence that both Mr. Altshuler and Mr. Weiss arrive at the same NPV number. Both methods must always generate the same NPV.

6.4 Alternative Definitions of Operating Cash Flow

As can be seen in the examples of this chapter, proper calculation of cash flow is essential to capital budgeting. A number of different definitions of operating cash flow are in common usage, a fact frequently bedeviling corporate finance students. However, the good news is that these definitions are consistent with each other. That is, if used correctly, they will all lead to the same answer for a given problem. We now consider some of the common definitions, showing in the process that they are identical with each other.[2]

In the discussion that follows, keep in mind that when we speak of cash flow, we literally mean dollars in less dollars out. This is all we are concerned with.

---

[2]For simplicity, working capital is ignored in this discussion.

For a particular project and year under consideration, suppose we have the following estimates:

$$Sales = \$1,500$$
$$Cash\ costs^3 = \$700$$
$$Depreciation = \$600$$

With these estimates, earnings before taxes (EBT) is:

$$EBT = Sales - Cash\ costs - Depreciation$$
$$= \$1,500 - 700 - 600 \tag{6.3}$$
$$= \$200$$

As is customary in capital budgeting, we assume that no interest is paid, so the tax bill is:

$$Taxes = (Sales - Cash\ costs - Depreciation) \times t_c = EBT \times t_c$$
$$(\$1,500 - 700 - 600) \times .34 = \$200 \times .34 = \$68, \tag{6.4}$$

where t_c, the corporate tax rate, is 34 percent.

Now that we have calculated earnings before taxes in Equation 6.3 and taxes in Equation 6.4, how do we determine operating cash flow (OCF)? Below we show three different approaches, all of them consistent with each other. The first is perhaps the most commonsensical because it simply asks, "What cash goes into the owner's pockets and what cash goes out of his pockets?"

THE TOP-DOWN APPROACH

Let's follow the cash. The owner receives sales of $1,500, pays cash costs of $700 and pays taxes of $68. Thus, operating cash flow must equal:

$$OCF = Sales - Cash\ costs - Taxes$$
$$= \$1,500 - 700 - 68 \tag{6.5}$$
$$= \$732$$

We call this the *top-down* approach because we start at the top of the income statement and work our way down to cash flow by subtracting costs, taxes, and other expenses.

Along the way, we left out depreciation. Why? Because depreciation is not a cash outflow. That is, the owner is not writing a $600 check to any Mr. Depreciation! While depreciation is an accounting concept, it is not a cash flow. Nevertheless, does depreciation play a part in the cash flow calculation? Yes, but only indirectly. Under current tax rules, depreciation is a deduction, lowering taxable income. A lower income number leads to lower taxes, which in turn leads to higher cash flow.

THE BOTTOM-UP APPROACH

This is the approach you would have had in an accounting class. First, income is calculated as:

$$Project\ net\ income = EBT - Taxes$$
$$= \$200 - 68$$
$$= \$132$$

---

³Cash costs ignore depreciation.

Next, depreciation is added back, giving us:

$$\begin{aligned} \text{OCF} &= \text{Net income} + \text{Depreciation} \\ &= \$132 + 600 \\ &= \$732 \end{aligned} \tag{6.6}$$

Expressing net income in terms of its components, we could write OCF more completely as:

$$\begin{aligned} \text{OCF} &= (\text{Sales} - \text{Cash costs} - \text{Depreciation})\,(1 - t_c) + \text{Depreciation} \\ &= (\$1,500 - 700 - 600)(1 - .34) + 600 = \$732 \end{aligned} \tag{6.6$'$}$$

This is the *bottom-up* approach, whether written as Equation 6.6 or Equation 6.6′. Here we start with the accountant's bottom line (net income) and add back any non-cash deductions such as depreciation. It is crucial to remember that this definition of operating cash flow as net income plus depreciation is correct only if there is no interest expense subtracted in the calculation of net income.

A typical man or woman off the street would generally find the top-down approach easier to understand, and that is why we presented it first. The top-down approach simply asks what cash flows come in and what cash flows go out. However, anyone with accounting training may find the bottom-up approach easier because accountants use this latter approach all the time. In fact, a student with an accounting course under her belt knows from force of habit that depreciation is to be added back to get cash flow.

Can we explain intuitively why one should add back depreciation as was done here? Accounting texts devote a lot of space explaining the intuition behind the bottom-up approach, and we don't want to duplicate their efforts in a finance text. However, let's give a two-sentence explanation a try. As mentioned above, while depreciation reduces income, depreciation is *not* a cash outflow. Thus, one must add depreciation back when going from income to cash flow.

THE TAX SHIELD APPROACH

The tax shield approach is just a variant of the top-down approach, as presented in Equation 6.5. One of the terms comprising OCF in Equation 6.5 is taxes, which is defined in Equation 6.4. If we plug the formula for taxes provided in 6.4 into Equation 6.5, we get:

$$\text{OCF} = \text{Sales} - \text{Cash costs} - (\text{Sales} - \text{Cash costs} - \text{Depreciation}) \times t_c$$

which simplifies to:

$$\text{OCF} = (\text{Sales} - \text{Cash costs}) \times (1 - t_c) + \text{Depreciation} \times t_c \tag{6.7}$$

where t_c is again the corporate tax rate. Assuming that $t_c = 34$ percent, OCF works out to be:

$$\begin{aligned} \text{OCF} &= (\$1,500 - 700) \times .66 + 600 \times .34 \\ &= \$528 + 204 \\ &= \$732 \end{aligned}$$

This is just what we had before.

This approach views OCF as having two components. The first part is what the project's cash flow would be if there were no depreciation expense. In our example, this would-have-been cash flow is $528.

The second part of OCF in this approach is the depreciation deduction multiplied by the tax rate. This is called the **depreciation tax shield.** We know that depreciation is a noncash expense. The only cash flow effect of deducting depreciation is to reduce our taxes, a benefit to us. At the current 34 percent corporate tax rate, every dollar in depreciation expense saves us 34 cents in taxes. So, in our example, the $600 depreciation deduction saves us $600 × .34 = $204 in taxes.

Students often think that the tax shield approach contradicts the bottom-up approach because depreciation is added back in Equation 6.6, but only the tax shield on depreciation is added back in Equation 6.7. However, the two formulae are perfectly consistent with each other, an idea most easily seen by comparing Equation 6.6′ to Equation 6.7. Depreciation is subtracted out in the first term on the right-hand side of 6.6′. No comparable subtraction occurs on the right-hand side of 6.7. We add the full amount of depreciation at the end of Equation 6.6′ (and at the end of its equivalent, Equation 6.6) because we subtracted out depreciation earlier in the equation.

CONCLUSION

Now that we've seen that all of these approaches are the same, you're probably wondering why everybody doesn't just agree on one of them. One reason is that different approaches are useful in different circumstances. The best one to use is whichever happens to be the most convenient for the problem at hand.

6.5 Some Special Cases of Discounted Cash Flow Analysis

ExcelMaster
coverage online

This section introduces the SOLVER function.

To finish our chapter, we look at three common cases involving discounted cash flow analysis. The first case considers cost-cutting investments. The second case considers competitive bidding. The third case compares equipment with different lives.

There are many other special cases, but these three are particularly common. Also, they illustrate some diverse applications of cash flow analysis and DCF valuation.

EVALUATING COST-CUTTING PROPOSALS

Firms must frequently decide whether to make existing facilities cost-effective. The issue is whether the cost savings are large enough to justify the necessary capital expenditure.

For example, suppose we are considering automating some part of an existing production process. The necessary equipment costs $80,000 to buy and install. The automation will save $22,000 per year (before taxes) by reducing labor and material costs. For simplicity, assume that the equipment has a five-year life and is depreciated to zero on a straight-line basis over that period. It will actually be worth $20,000 in five years. Should we automate? The tax rate is 34 percent, and the discount rate is 10 percent.

Let's begin by identifying the relevant cash flows. Determining the relevant capital spending is easy enough. The initial cost is $80,000. The aftertax salvage value is $20,000 × (1 − .34) = $13,200 because the book value will be zero in five years. There are no working capital consequences here, so we don't need to worry about changes in net working capital.

Operating cash flows must also be considered. Buying the new equipment affects our operating cash flows in three ways. First, we save $22,000 before taxes every year.

In other words, the firm's operating income increases by $22,000, so this is the relevant incremental project operating income.

Second (and it's easy to overlook this), we have an additional depreciation deduction. In this case, the depreciation is $80,000/5 = $16,000 per year.

Because the project has an operating income of $22,000 (the annual pretax cost savings) and a depreciation deduction of $16,000, the project will increase the firm's earnings before interest and taxes (EBIT) by $22,000 − 16,000 = $6,000. In other words, $6,000 is the project's EBIT.

Third, because EBIT is rising for the firm, taxes will increase. This increase in taxes will be $6,000 × .34 = $2,040. With this information, we can compute operating cash flow in the usual way:

EBIT	$ 6,000
+Depreciation	16,000
−Taxes	2,040
Operating cash flow	$19,960

So, our aftertax operating cash flow is $19,960.

We can also calculate operating cash flow using a different approach. What is actually going on here is very simple. First, the cost savings increase our pretax income by $22,000. We have to pay taxes on this amount, so our tax bill increases by .34 × $22,000 = $7,480. In other words, the $22,000 pretax saving amounts to $22,000 × (1 − .34) = $14,520 after taxes.

Second, while the extra $16,000 in depreciation isn't a cash outflow, it does reduce our taxes by $16,000 × .34 = $5,440. The sum of these two components is $14,520 + 5,440 = $19,960, just as we had before. Notice that the $5,440 is the depreciation tax shield we discussed earlier, and we have effectively used the tax shield approach here.

We can now finish our analysis. Based on our discussion, here are the relevant cash flows:

	Year					
	0	1	2	3	4	5
Operating cash flow		$19,960	$19,960	$19,960	$19,960	$19,960
Capital spending	−$80,000					13,200
Total cash flow	−$80,000	$19,960	$19,960	$19,960	$19,960	$33,160

At 10 percent, it's straightforward to verify that the NPV here is $3,860, so we should go ahead and automate.

EXAMPLE 6.11

To Buy or Not to Buy   We are considering the purchase of a $200,000 computer-based inventory management system. It will be depreciated straight-line to zero over its four-year life. It will be worth $30,000 at the end of that time. The system will save us $60,000 before taxes in inventory-related costs. The relevant tax rate is 39 percent. Because the new setup is more efficient than our existing one, we can carry less total inventory, thereby freeing up $45,000 in net working capital. What is the NPV at 16 percent? What is the IRR on this investment?

Let's first calculate the operating cash flow. The aftertax cost savings are $60,000 \times (1 - .39) =$ $36,600 per year. The depreciation is $200,000/4 = $50,000 per year, so the depreciation tax shield is $50,000 \times .39 = $19,500. Operating cash flow is thus $36,600 + 19,500 = $56,100 per year.

The system involves a $200,000 up front cost to buy the system. The aftertax salvage is $30,000 \times (1 - .39) = $18,300. Finally, and this is somewhat tricky, the initial investment in net working capital (NWC) is a $45,000 *inflow* because the system frees up working capital. Furthermore, we will have to put this back in at the end of the project's life. What this really means is simple: While the system is in operation, we have $45,000 to use elsewhere.

To finish our analysis, we can compute the total cash flows:

		Year			
	0	**1**	**2**	**3**	**4**
Operating cash flow		$56,100	$56,100	$56,100	$56,100
Change in NWC	$ 45,000				−45,000
Capital spending	−200,000				18,300
Total cash flow	−$155,000	$56,100	$56,100	$56,100	$29,400

At 16 percent, the NPV is −$12,768, so the investment is not attractive. After some trial and error, we find that the NPV is zero when the discount rate is 11.48 percent, implying an IRR of about 11.5 percent.

SETTING THE BID PRICE

One generally uses the NPV approach to evaluate a new project. The NPV approach can also be used when submitting a competitive bid to win a job. Under such circumstances, the winner is whoever submits the lowest bid.

There is an old joke concerning this process: The low bidder is whoever makes the biggest mistake. This is called the winner's curse. In other words, if you win, there is a good chance you underbid. In this section, we look at how to go about setting the bid price to avoid the winner's curse. The procedure we describe is useful anytime we have to set a price on a product or service.

As with any other capital budgeting project, we must be careful to account for all relevant cash flows. For example, industry analysts estimated that the materials in Microsoft's Xbox 360 cost $470 before assembly. Other items such as the power supply, cables, and controllers increased the materials cost by another $55. At a retail price of $399, Microsoft obviously loses a significant amount on each Xbox 360 it sells. Why would a manufacturer sell at a price well below breakeven? A Microsoft spokesperson stated that the company believed that sales of its game software would make the Xbox 360 a profitable project.

To illustrate how to go about setting a bid price, imagine we are in the business of buying stripped-down truck platforms and then modifying them to customer specifications for resale. A local distributor has requested bids for 5 specially modified trucks each year for the next four years, for a total of 20 trucks in all.

We need to decide what price to bid per truck. The goal of our analysis is to determine the lowest price we can profitably charge. This maximizes our chances of being awarded the contract while guarding against the winner's curse.

Suppose we can buy the truck platforms for $10,000 each. The facilities we need can be leased for $24,000 per year. The labor and material for the modification cost about $4,000 per truck. Total cost per year will thus be $24,000 + 5 × (10,000 + 4,000) = $94,000.

We will need to invest $60,000 in new equipment. This equipment will be depreciated straight-line to a zero salvage value over the four years. It will be worth about $5,000 at the end of that time. We will also need to invest $40,000 in raw materials inventory and other working capital items. The relevant tax rate is 39 percent. What price per truck should we bid if we require a 20 percent return on our investment?

We start by looking at the capital spending and net working capital investment. We have to spend $60,000 today for new equipment. The aftertax salvage value is $5,000 × (1 − .39) = $3,050. Furthermore, we have to invest $40,000 today in working capital. We will get this back in four years.

We can't determine the operating cash flow (OCF) just yet because we don't know the sales price. Thus, if we draw a time line, here is what we have so far:

	Year				
	0	**1**	**2**	**3**	**4**
Operating cash flow		+OCF	+OCF	+OCF	+OCF
Change in NWC	−$ 40,000				$40,000
Capital spending	− 60,000				3,050
Total cash flow	−$100,000	+OCF	+OCF	+OCF	+OCF + $43,050

With this in mind, note that the key observation is the following: The lowest possible price we can profitably charge will result in a zero NPV at 20 percent. At that price, we earn exactly 20 percent on our investment.

Given this observation, we first need to determine what the operating cash flow must be for the NPV to equal zero. To do this, we calculate the present value of the $43,050 nonoperating cash flow from the last year and subtract it from the $100,000 initial investment:

$$\$100,000 - 43,050/1.20^4 = \$100,000 - 20,761 = \$79,239$$

Once we have done this, our time line is:

	Year				
	0	**1**	**2**	**3**	**4**
Total cash flow	−$79,239	+OCF	+OCF	+OCF	+OCF

As the time line suggests, the operating cash flow is now an unknown ordinary annuity amount. The four-year annuity factor for 20 percent, PVIA (.20, 4), is 2.58873, so we have:

$$NPV = 0 = -\$79,239 + OCF \times 2.58873$$

This implies that:

$$OCF = \$79,239/2.58873 = \$30,609$$

So the operating cash flow needs to be $30,609 each year.

We're not quite finished. The final problem is to find out what sales price results in an operating cash flow of $30,609. The easiest way to do this is to recall that operating cash flow can be written as net income plus depreciation (the bottom-up definition).

The depreciation here is $60,000/4 = $15,000$. Given this, we can determine what net income must be:

$$\text{Operating cash flow} = \text{Net income} + \text{Depreciation}$$
$$\$30,609 = \text{Net income} + \$15,000$$
$$\text{Net income} = \$15,609$$

From here, we work our way backward up the income statement. If net income is $15,609, then our income statement is as follows:

Sales	?
Costs	$94,000
Depreciation	15,000
Taxes (39%)	?
Net income	$15,609

We can solve for sales by noting that:

$$\text{Net income} = (\text{Sales} - \text{Costs} - \text{Depreciation}) \times (1 - T)$$
$$\$15,609 = (\text{Sales} - \$94,000 - \$15,000) \times (1 - .39)$$
$$\text{Sales} = \$15,609/.61 + 94,000 + 15,000$$
$$= \$134,589$$

Sales per year must be $134,589. Because the contract calls for five trucks per year, the sales price has to be $134,589/5 = $26,918$. If we round this up a bit, it looks as though we need to bid about $27,000 per truck. At this price, were we to get the contract, our return would be just over 20 percent.

INVESTMENTS OF UNEQUAL LIVES: THE EQUIVALENT ANNUAL COST METHOD

Suppose a firm must choose between two machines of unequal lives. Both machines can do the same job, but they have different operating costs and will last for different time periods. A simple application of the NPV rule suggests taking the machine whose costs have the lower present value. This choice might be a mistake, however, because the lower-cost machine may need to be replaced before the other one.

Let's consider an example. The Downtown Athletic Club must choose between two mechanical tennis ball throwers. Machine *A* costs less than Machine *B* but will not last as long. The cash *outflows* from the two machines are shown here:

			Date		
Machine	0	1	2	3	4
A	$500	$120	$120	$120	
B	$600	$100	$100	$100	$100

Machine *A* costs $500 and lasts three years. There will be maintenance expenses of $120 to be paid at the end of each of the three years. Machine *B* costs $600 and lasts four years. There will be maintenance expenses of $100 to be paid at the end of each of the four years. We express all costs in real terms, an assumption greatly simplifying the analysis. Revenues per year are assumed to be the same, regardless of machine, so they are not considered in the analysis. Note that all numbers in the chart are *outflows*. For simplicity, we ignore taxes.

To get a handle on the decision, let's take the present value of the costs of each of the two machines. Assuming a discount rate of 10 percent, we have:

$$\text{Machine } A: \$798.42 = \$500 + \frac{\$120}{1.1} + \frac{\$120}{(1.1)^2} + \frac{\$120}{(1.1)^3}$$

$$\text{Machine } B: \$916.99 = \$600 + \frac{\$100}{1.1} + \frac{\$100}{(1.1)^2} + \frac{\$100}{(1.1)^3} + \frac{\$100}{(1.1)^4}$$

Machine B has a higher present value of outflows. A naive approach would be to select Machine A because of its lower present value. However, Machine B has a longer life, so perhaps its cost per year is actually lower.

How might one properly adjust for the difference in useful life when comparing the two machines? Perhaps the easiest approach involves calculating something called the *equivalent annual cost* of each machine. This approach puts costs on a per-year basis.

The previous equation for Machine A showed that payments of ($500, $120, $120, $120) are equivalent to a single payment of $798.42 at Date 0. We now wish to equate the single payment of $798.42 at Date 0 with a three-year annuity. Using techniques of previous chapters, we have:

$$\$798.42 = C \times \text{PVIA } (.10, 3)$$

PVIA (.10, 3) is an annuity of $1 a year for three years, discounted at 10 percent. C is the unknown—the annuity payment per year such that the present value of all payments equals $798.42. Because PVIA (.10, 3) equals 2.4869, C equals $321.05 (=$798.42/2.4869). Thus, a payment stream of ($500, $120, $120, $120) is equivalent to annuity payments of $321.05 made at the *end* of each year for three years. We refer to $321.05 as the *equivalent annual cost* of Machine A.

This idea is summarized in the following chart:

	Date			
	0	**1**	**2**	**3**
Cash outflows of Machine A	$500	$120	$120	$120
Equivalent annual cost of Machine A		321.05	321.05	321.05

The Downtown Athletic Club should be indifferent between cash outflows of ($500, $120, $120, $120) and cash outflows of ($0, $321.05, $321.05, $321.05). Alternatively, one can say that the purchase of the machine is financially equivalent to a rental agreement calling for annual lease payments of $321.05.

Now let's turn to Machine B. We calculate its equivalent annual cost from:

$$\$916.99 = C \times \text{PVIA } (.10, 4)$$

Because PVIA (.10, 4) equals 3.1699, C equals $916.99/3.1699, or $289.28.

As we did for Machine A, we can create the following chart for Machine B:

	Date				
	0	**1**	**2**	**3**	**4**
Cash outflows of Machine B	$600	$100	$100	$100	$100
Equivalent annual cost of Machine B		289.28	289.28	289.28	289.28

The decision is easy once the charts of the two machines are compared. Would you rather make annual lease payments of $321.05 or $289.28? Put this way, the problem becomes a no-brainer: A rational person would rather pay the lower amount. Thus, Machine *B* is the preferred choice.

Two final remarks are in order. First, it is no accident that we specified the costs of the tennis ball machines in real terms. Although *B* would still have been the preferred machine had the costs been stated in nominal terms, the actual solution would have been much more difficult. As a general rule, always convert cash flows to real terms when working through problems of this type.

Second, such analysis applies only if one anticipates that both machines can be replaced. The analysis would differ if no replacement were possible. For example, imagine that the only company that manufactured tennis ball throwers just went out of business and no new producers are expected to enter the field. In this case, Machine *B* would generate revenues in the fourth year whereas Machine *A* would not. Here, simple net present value analysis for mutually exclusive projects including both revenues and costs would be appropriate.

 ◄ To test your mastery of this material, take a quiz at mhhe. com/rwj

Summary and Conclusions

This chapter discussed a number of practical applications of capital budgeting.

1. Capital budgeting must be placed on an incremental basis. This means that sunk costs must be ignored, whereas both opportunity costs and side effects must be considered.

2. In the Baldwin case we computed NPV using the following two steps:
   a. Calculate the net cash flow from all sources for each period.
   b. Calculate the NPV using these cash flows.

3. Inflation must be handled consistently. One approach is to express both cash flows and the discount rate in nominal terms. The other approach is to express both cash flows and the discount rate in real terms. Because both approaches yield the same NPV calculation, the simpler method should be used. The simpler method will generally depend on the type of capital budgeting problem.

4. Operating cash flows (OCF) can be computed in a number of different ways. We presented three different methods for calculating OCF: The top-down approach, the bottom-up approach, and the tax shield approach. The three approaches are consistent with each other.

5. The discounted cash flow approach can be applied to many areas of capital budgeting. The last section of this chapter applied the approach to cost-cutting investments, competitive bidding, and choices between equipment of different lives.

Concept Questions

1. **Opportunity Cost**   In the context of capital budgeting, what is an opportunity cost?

2. **Incremental Cash Flows**   Which of the following should be treated as an incremental cash flow when computing the NPV of an investment?

   a. A reduction in the sales of a company's other products caused by the investment.
   b. An expenditure on plant and equipment that has not yet been made and will be made only if the project is accepted.

     c. Costs of research and development undertaken in connection with the product during the past three years.

     d. Annual depreciation expense from the investment.

     e. Dividend payments by the firm.

     f. The resale value of plant and equipment at the end of the project's life.

     g. Salary and medical costs for production personnel who will be employed only if the project is accepted.

3.   **Incremental Cash Flows**   Your company currently produces and sells steel shaft golf clubs. The board of directors wants you to consider the introduction of a new line of titanium bubble woods with graphite shafts. Which of the following costs are *not* relevant?

     a. Land you already own that will be used for the project, but otherwise will be sold for $700,000, its market value.

     b. A $300,000 drop in your sales of steel shaft clubs if the titanium woods with graphite shafts are introduced.

     c. $200,000 spent on research and development last year on graphite shafts.

4.   **Depreciation**   Given the choice, would a firm prefer to use MACRS depreciation or straight-line depreciation? Why?

5.   **Net Working Capital**   In our capital budgeting examples, we assumed that a firm would recover all of the working capital it invested in a project. Is this a reasonable assumption? When might it not be valid?

6.   **Stand-Alone Principle**   Suppose a financial manager is quoted as saying, "Our firm uses the stand-alone principle. Because we treat projects like minifirms in our evaluation process, we include financing costs because they are relevant at the firm level." Critically evaluate this statement.

7.   **Equivalent Annual Cost**   When is EAC analysis appropriate for comparing two or more projects? Why is this method used? Are there any implicit assumptions required by this method that you find troubling? Explain.

8.   **Cash Flow and Depreciation**   "When evaluating projects, we're only concerned with the relevant incremental aftertax cash flows. Therefore, because depreciation is a noncash expense, we should ignore its effects when evaluating projects." Critically evaluate this statement.

9.   **Capital Budgeting Considerations**   A major college textbook publisher has an existing finance textbook. The publisher is debating whether to produce an "essentialized" version, meaning a shorter (and lower-priced) book. What are some of the considerations that should come into play?

     To answer the next three questions, refer to the following example. In 2003, Porsche unveiled its new sports utility vehicle (SUV), the Cayenne. With a price tag of over $40,000, the Cayenne goes from zero to 62 mph in 8.5 seconds. Porsche's decision to enter the SUV market was in response to the runaway success of other high-priced SUVs such as the Mercedes-Benz M class. Vehicles in this class had generated years of very high profits. The Cayenne certainly spiced up the market, and, in 2006, Porsche introduced the Cayenne Turbo S, which goes from zero to 60 mph in 4.8 seconds and has a top speed of 168 mph. The base price for the Cayenne Turbo S in 2011? Almost $105,000!

     Some analysts questioned Porsche's entry into the luxury SUV market. The analysts were concerned because not only was Porsche a late entry into the market, but also the introduction of the Cayenne might damage Porsche's reputation as a maker of high-performance automobiles.

10.   **Erosion**   In evaluating the Cayenne, would you consider the possible damage to Porsche's reputation as erosion?

11. **Capital Budgeting** Porsche was one of the last manufacturers to enter the sports utility vehicle market. Why would one company decide to proceed with a product when other companies, at least initially, decide not to enter the market?

12. **Capital Budgeting** In evaluating the Cayenne, what do you think Porsche needs to assume regarding the substantial profit margins that exist in this market? Is it likely that they will be maintained as the market becomes more competitive, or will Porsche be able to maintain the profit margin because of its image and the performance of the Cayenne?

Questions and Problems

BASIC
(Questions 1–10)

1. **Calculating Project NPV** Raphael Restaurant is considering the purchase of a $9,000 soufflé maker. The soufflé maker has an economic life of five years and will be fully depreciated by the straight-line method. The machine will produce 1,500 soufflés per year, with each costing $2.30 to make and priced at $4.75. Assume that the discount rate is 14 percent and the tax rate is 34 percent. Should Raphael make the purchase?

2. **Calculating Project NPV** The Best Manufacturing Company is considering a new investment. Financial projections for the investment are tabulated here. The corporate tax rate is 34 percent. Assume all sales revenue is received in cash, all operating costs and income taxes are paid in cash, and all cash flows occur at the end of the year. All net working capital is recovered at the end of the project.

	Year 0	Year 1	Year 2	Year 3	Year 4
Investment	$24,000				
Sales revenue		$12,500	$13,000	$13,500	$10,500
Operating costs		2,700	2,800	2,900	2,100
Depreciation		6,000	6,000	6,000	6,000
Net working capital spending	300	350	400	300	?

a. Compute the incremental net income of the investment for each year.
b. Compute the incremental cash flows of the investment for each year.
c. Suppose the appropriate discount rate is 12 percent. What is the NPV of the project?

3. **Calculating Project NPV** Down Under Boomerang, Inc., is considering a new three-year expansion project that requires an initial fixed asset investment of $1.4 million. The fixed asset will be depreciated straight-line to zero over its three-year tax life, after which it will be worthless. The project is estimated to generate $1,120,000 in annual sales, with costs of $480,000. The tax rate is 35 percent and the required return is 12 percent. What is the project's NPV?

4. **Calculating Project Cash Flow from Assets** In the previous problem, suppose the project requires an initial investment in net working capital of $285,000 and the fixed asset will have a market value of $225,000 at the end of the project. What is the project's Year 0 net cash flow? Year 1? Year 2? Year 3? What is the new NPV?

5. **NPV and Modified ACRS**   In the previous problem, suppose the fixed asset actually falls into the three-year MACRS class. All the other facts are the same. What is the project's Year 1 net cash flow now? Year 2? Year 3? What is the new NPV?

6. **Project Evaluation**   Your firm is contemplating the purchase of a new $670,000 computer-based order entry system. The system will be depreciated straight-line to zero over its five-year life. It will be worth $50,000 at the end of that time. You will save $240,000 before taxes per year in order processing costs, and you will be able to reduce working capital by $85,000 (this is a one-time reduction). If the tax rate is 35 percent, what is the IRR for this project?

7. **Project Evaluation**   Dog Up! Franks is looking at a new sausage system with an installed cost of $375,000. This cost will be depreciated straight-line to zero over the project's five-year life, at the end of which the sausage system can be scrapped for $40,000. The sausage system will save the firm $105,000 per year in pretax operating costs, and the system requires an initial investment in net working capital of $28,000. If the tax rate is 34 percent and the discount rate is 10 percent, what is the NPV of this project?

8. **Calculating Salvage Value**   An asset used in a four-year project falls in the five-year MACRS class for tax purposes. The asset has an acquisition cost of $7,100,000 and will be sold for $1,400,000 at the end of the project. If the tax rate is 35 percent, what is the aftertax salvage value of the asset?

9. **Calculating NPV**   Howell Petroleum is considering a new project that complements its existing business. The machine required for the project costs $3.8 million. The marketing department predicts that sales related to the project will be $2.5 million per year for the next four years, after which the market will cease to exist. The machine will be depreciated down to zero over its four-year economic life using the straight-line method. Cost of goods sold and operating expenses related to the project are predicted to be 25 percent of sales. Howell also needs to add net working capital of $150,000 immediately. The additional net working capital will be recovered in full at the end of the project's life. The corporate tax rate is 35 percent. The required rate of return for Howell is 16 percent. Should Howell proceed with the project?

 10. **Calculating EAC**   You are evaluating two different silicon wafer milling machines. The Techron I costs $215,000, has a three-year life, and has pretax operating costs of $35,000 per year. The Techron II costs $270,000, has a five-year life, and has pretax operating costs of $44,000 per year. For both milling machines, use straight-line depreciation to zero over the project's life and assume a salvage value of $20,000. If your tax rate is 35 percent and your discount rate is 12 percent, compute the EAC for both machines. Which do you prefer? Why?

INTERMEDIATE
(Questions 11–27)

11. **Cost-Cutting Proposals**   Massey Machine Shop is considering a four-year project to improve its production efficiency. Buying a new machine press for $640,000 is estimated to result in $270,000 in annual pretax cost savings. The press falls in the MACRS five-year class, and it will have a salvage value at the end of the project of $70,000. The press also requires an initial investment in spare parts inventory of $20,000, along with an additional $3,500 in inventory for each succeeding year of the project. If the shop's tax rate is 35 percent and its discount rate is 14 percent, should Massey buy and install the machine press?

12. **Comparing Mutually Exclusive Projects**   Hagar Industrial Systems Company (HISC) is trying to decide between two different conveyor belt systems. System A costs $290,000, has a four-year life, and requires $85,000 in pretax annual operating costs. System B costs $405,000, has a six-year life, and requires $75,000 in pretax annual operating costs. Both systems are to be depreciated straight-line to zero over their lives and will have zero salvage value. Whichever system is chosen, it will *not* be replaced when it wears out. If the tax rate is 34 percent and the discount rate is 11 percent, which system should the firm choose?

Chapter 6   Making Capital Investment Decisions **199**

13. **Comparing Mutually Exclusive Projects**   Suppose in the previous problem that HISC always needs a conveyor belt system; when one wears out, it must be replaced. Which system should the firm choose now?

14. **Comparing Mutually Exclusive Projects**   Vandalay Industries is considering the purchase of a new machine for the production of latex. Machine A costs $2,900,000 and will last for six years. Variable costs are 35 percent of sales, and fixed costs are $195,000 per year. Machine B costs $5,700,000 and will last for nine years. Variable costs for this machine are 30 percent and fixed costs are $165,000 per year. The sales for each machine will be $12 million per year. The required return is 10 percent and the tax rate is 35 percent. Both machines will be depreciated on a straight-line basis. If the company plans to replace the machine when it wears out on a perpetual basis, which machine should you choose?

 15. **Capital Budgeting with Inflation**   Consider the following cash flows on two mutually exclusive projects:

Year	Project A	Project B
0	−$50,000	−$65,000
1	30,000	29,000
2	25,000	38,000
3	20,000	41,000

The cash flows of project A are expressed in real terms, whereas those of project B are expressed in nominal terms. The appropriate nominal discount rate is 13 percent and the inflation rate is 4 percent. Which project should you choose?

16. **Inflation and Company Value**   Sparkling Water, Inc., expects to sell 2.8 million bottles of drinking water each year in perpetuity. This year each bottle will sell for $1.25 in real terms and will cost $.90 in real terms. Sales income and costs occur at year-end. Revenues will rise at a real rate of 6 percent annually, while real costs will rise at a real rate of 5 percent annually. The real discount rate is 10 percent. The corporate tax rate is 34 percent. What is Sparkling worth today?

 17. **Calculating Nominal Cash Flow**   Etonic Inc. is considering an investment of $365,000 in an asset with an economic life of five years. The firm estimates that the nominal annual cash revenues and expenses at the end of the first year will be $245,000 and $70,000, respectively. Both revenues and expenses will grow thereafter at the annual inflation rate of 3 percent. Etonic will use the straight-line method to depreciate its asset to zero over five years. The salvage value of the asset is estimated to be $45,000 in nominal terms at that time. The one-time net working capital investment of $10,000 is required immediately and will be recovered at the end of the project. All corporate cash flows are subject to a 34 percent tax rate. What is the project's total nominal cash flow from assets for each year?

18. **Cash Flow Valuation**   Phillips Industries runs a small manufacturing operation. For this fiscal year, it expects real net cash flows of $190,000. Phillips is an ongoing operation, but it expects competitive pressures to erode its real net cash flows at 4 percent per year in perpetuity. The appropriate real discount rate for Phillips is 11 percent. All net cash flows are received at year-end. What is the present value of the net cash flows from Phillips's operations?

19. **Equivalent Annual Cost**   Bridgton Golf Academy is evaluating different golf practice equipment. The "Dimple-Max" equipment costs $94,000, has a three-year life, and costs $8,600 per year to operate. The relevant discount rate is 12 percent. Assume that the straight-line depreciation method is used and that the equipment is fully depreciated to zero. Furthermore, assume the equipment has a salvage value of $18,000

at the end of the project's life. The relevant tax rate is 34 percent. All cash flows occur at the end of the year. What is the equivalent annual cost (EAC) of this equipment?

20. **Calculating Project NPV** Scott Investors, Inc., is considering the purchase of a $360,000 computer with an economic life of five years. The computer will be fully depreciated over five years using the straight-line method. The market value of the computer will be $60,000 in five years. The computer will replace five office employees whose combined annual salaries are $105,000. The machine will also immediately lower the firm's required net working capital by $80,000. This amount of net working capital will need to be replaced once the machine is sold. The corporate tax rate is 34 percent. Is it worthwhile to buy the computer if the appropriate discount rate is 12 percent?

21. **Calculating NPV and IRR for a Replacement** A firm is considering an investment in a new machine with a price of $18 million to replace its existing machine. The current machine has a book value of $6 million and a market value of $4.5 million. The new machine is expected to have a four-year life, and the old machine has four years left in which it can be used. If the firm replaces the old machine with the new machine, it expects to save $6.7 million in operating costs each year over the next four years. Both machines will have no salvage value in four years. If the firm purchases the new machine, it will also need an investment of $250,000 in net working capital. The required return on the investment is 10 percent, and the tax rate is 39 percent. What are the NPV and IRR of the decision to replace the old machine?

22. **Project Analysis and Inflation** Sanders Enterprises, Inc., has been considering the purchase of a new manufacturing facility for $270,000. The facility is to be fully depreciated on a straight-line basis over seven years. It is expected to have no resale value after the seven years. Operating revenues from the facility are expected to be $105,000, in nominal terms, at the end of the first year. The revenues are expected to increase at the inflation rate of 5 percent. Production costs at the end of the first year will be $30,000, in nominal terms, and they are expected to increase at 6 percent per year. The real discount rate is 8 percent. The corporate tax rate is 34 percent. Sanders has other ongoing profitable operations. Should the company accept the project?

23. **Calculating Project NPV** With the growing popularity of casual surf print clothing, two recent MBA graduates decided to broaden this casual surf concept to encompass a "surf lifestyle for the home." With limited capital, they decided to focus on surf print table and floor lamps to accent people's homes. They projected unit sales of these lamps to be 7,000 in the first year, with growth of 8 percent each year for the next five years. Production of these lamps will require $35,000 in net working capital to start. Total fixed costs are $95,000 per year, variable production costs are $20 per unit, and the units are priced at $48 each. The equipment needed to begin production will cost $175,000. The equipment will be depreciated using the straight-line method over a five-year life and is not expected to have a salvage value. The effective tax rate is 34 percent, and the required rate of return is 25 percent. What is the NPV of this project?

24. **Calculating Project NPV** You have been hired as a consultant for Pristine Urban-Tech Zither, Inc. (PUTZ), manufacturers of fine zithers. The market for zithers is growing quickly. The company bought some land three years ago for $1 million in anticipation of using it as a toxic waste dump site but has recently hired another company to handle all toxic materials. Based on a recent appraisal, the company believes it could sell the land for $900,000 on an aftertax basis. In four years, the land could be sold for $1,200,000 after taxes. The company also hired a marketing firm to analyze the zither market, at a cost of $125,000. An excerpt of the marketing report is as follows:

The zither industry will have a rapid expansion in the next four years. With the brand name recognition that PUTZ brings to bear, we feel that the company will be able to sell 6,700, 7,500, 9,100, and 6,200 units each year for the next four years, respectively. Again, capitalizing on the name recognition of PUTZ, we feel that a premium price of $275 can be charged for each zither. Because zithers appear to be a fad, we feel at the end of the four-year period, sales should be discontinued.

PUTZ feels that fixed costs for the project will be $350,000 per year, and variable costs are 15 percent of sales. The equipment necessary for production will cost $3.1 million and will be depreciated according to a three-year MACRS schedule. At the end of the project, the equipment can be scrapped for $300,000. Net working capital of $120,000 will be required immediately. PUTZ has a 38 percent tax rate, and the required return on the project is 13 percent. What is the NPV of the project? Assume the company has other profitable projects.

25. **Calculating Project NPV** Pilot Plus Pens is deciding when to replace its old machine. The machine's current salvage value is $2.2 million. Its current book value is $1.4 million. If not sold, the old machine will require maintenance costs of $845,000 at the end of the year for the next five years. Depreciation on the old machine is $280,000 per year. At the end of five years, it will have a salvage value of $120,000 and a book value of $0. A replacement machine costs $4.3 million now and requires maintenance costs of $330,000 at the end of each year during its economic life of five years. At the end of the five years, the new machine will have a salvage value of $800,000. It will be fully depreciated by the straight-line method. In five years a replacement machine will cost $3,200,000. Pilot will need to purchase this machine regardless of what choice it makes today. The corporate tax rate is 40 percent and the appropriate discount rate is 8 percent. The company is assumed to earn sufficient revenues to generate tax shields from depreciation. Should Pilot Plus Pens replace the old machine now or at the end of five years?

26. **EAC and Inflation** Office Automation, Inc., must choose between two copiers, the XX40 or the RH45. The XX40 costs $900 and will last for three years. The copier will require a real aftertax cost of $120 per year after all relevant expenses. The RH45 costs $1,400 and will last five years. The real aftertax cost for the RH45 will be $95 per year. All cash flows occur at the end of the year. The inflation rate is expected to be 5 percent per year, and the nominal discount rate is 14 percent. Which copier should the company choose?

27. **Project Analysis and Inflation** Dickinson Brothers, Inc., is considering investing in a machine to produce computer keyboards. The price of the machine will be $975,000, and its economic life is five years. The machine will be fully depreciated by the straight-line method. The machine will produce 20,000 keyboards each year. The price of each keyboard will be $40 in the first year and will increase by 5 percent per year. The production cost per keyboard will be $15 in the first year and will increase by 6 percent per year. The project will have an annual fixed cost of $195,000 and require an immediate investment of $25,000 in net working capital. The corporate tax rate for the company is 34 percent. If the appropriate discount rate is 11 percent, what is the NPV of the investment?

CHALLENGE
(Questions 28–38)

28. **Project Evaluation** Aguilera Acoustics, Inc. (AAI), projects unit sales for a new seven-octave voice emulation implant as follows:

Year	Unit Sales
1	83,000
2	92,000
3	104,000
4	98,000
5	84,000

Production of the implants will require $1,500,000 in net working capital to start and additional net working capital investments each year equal to 15 percent of the projected sales increase for the following year. Total fixed costs are $2,400,000 per year, variable production costs are $190 per unit, and the units are priced at $345 each. The equipment needed to begin production has an installed cost of $23,000,000. Because the implants are intended for professional singers, this equipment is considered industrial machinery and thus qualifies as seven-year MACRS property. In five years, this equipment can be sold for about 20 percent of its acquisition cost. AAI is in the 35 percent marginal tax bracket and has a required return on all its projects of 18 percent. Based on these preliminary project estimates, what is the NPV of the project? What is the IRR?

29. **Calculating Required Savings**   A proposed cost-saving device has an installed cost of $640,000. The device will be used in a five-year project but is classified as three-year MACRS property for tax purposes. The required initial net working capital investment is $55,000, the marginal tax rate is 35 percent, and the project discount rate is 12 percent. The device has an estimated Year 5 salvage value of $60,000. What level of pretax cost savings do we require for this project to be profitable?

30. **Calculating a Bid Price**   Another utilization of cash flow analysis is setting the bid price on a project. To calculate the bid price, we set the project NPV equal to zero and find the required price. Thus the bid price represents a financial break-even level for the project. Guthrie Enterprises needs someone to supply it with 140,000 cartons of machine screws per year to support its manufacturing needs over the next five years, and you've decided to bid on the contract. It will cost you $1,800,000 to install the equipment necessary to start production; you'll depreciate this cost straight-line to zero over the project's life. You estimate that in five years this equipment can be salvaged for $150,000. Your fixed production costs will be $265,000 per year, and your variable production costs should be $8.50 per carton. You also need an initial investment in net working capital of $130,000. If your tax rate is 35 percent and you require a 14 percent return on your investment, what bid price should you submit?

31. **Financial Break-Even Analysis**   The technique for calculating a bid price can be extended to many other types of problems. Answer the following questions using the same technique as setting a bid price; that is, set the project NPV to zero and solve for the variable in question.

    a. In the previous problem, assume that the price per carton is $16 and find the project NPV. What does your answer tell you about your bid price? What do you know about the number of cartons you can sell and still break even? How about your level of costs?

    b. Solve the previous problem again with the price still at $16—but find the quantity of cartons per year that you can supply and still break even. (*Hint:* It's less than 140,000.)

    c. Repeat (b) with a price of $16 and a quantity of 140,000 cartons per year, and find the highest level of fixed costs you could afford and still break even. (*Hint:* It's more than $265,000.)

32. **Calculating a Bid Price**   Your company has been approached to bid on a contract to sell 15,000 voice recognition (VR) computer keyboards a year for four years. Due to technological improvements, beyond that time they will be outdated and no sales will be possible. The equipment necessary for the production will cost $3.4 million and will be depreciated on a straight-line basis to a zero salvage value. Production will require an investment in net working capital of $75,000 to be returned at the end of the project, and the equipment can be sold for $200,000 at the end of production. Fixed costs are $700,000 per year, and variable costs are $105 per unit. In addition to the contract, you feel your company can sell 4,000, 12,000, 14,000, and 7,000 additional units to companies in other countries over the next four years,

respectively, at a price of $205. This price is fixed. The tax rate is 40 percent, and the required return is 13 percent. Additionally, the president of the company will undertake the project only if it has an NPV of $100,000. What bid price should you set for the contract?

33.   Replacement Decisions   Suppose we are thinking about replacing an old computer with a new one. The old one cost us $450,000; the new one will cost $580,000. The new machine will be depreciated straight-line to zero over its five-year life. It will probably be worth about $130,000 after five years.

The old computer is being depreciated at a rate of $90,000 per year. It will be completely written off in three years. If we don't replace it now, we will have to replace it in two years. We can sell it now for $230,000; in two years it will probably be worth $60,000. The new machine will save us $85,000 per year in operating costs. The tax rate is 38 percent, and the discount rate is 14 percent.

a. Suppose we recognize that if we don't replace the computer now, we will be replacing it in two years. Should we replace now or should we wait? (*Hint:* What we effectively have here is a decision either to "invest" in the old computer—by not selling it—or to invest in the new one. Notice that the two investments have unequal lives.)

b. Suppose we consider only whether we should replace the old computer now without worrying about what's going to happen in two years. What are the relevant cash flows? Should we replace it or not? (*Hint:* Consider the net change in the firm's aftertax cash flows if we do the replacement.)

34.   Project Analysis   Benson Enterprises is evaluating alternative uses for a three-story manufacturing and warehousing building that it has purchased for $1,450,000. The company can continue to rent the building to the present occupants for $61,000 per year. The present occupants have indicated an interest in staying in the building for at least another 15 years. Alternatively, the company could modify the existing structure to use for its own manufacturing and warehousing needs. Benson's production engineer feels the building could be adapted to handle one of two new product lines. The cost and revenue data for the two product alternatives are as follows:

	Product A	Product B
Initial cash outlay for building modifications	$ 95,000	$125,000
Initial cash outlay for equipment	195,000	230,000
Annual pretax cash revenues (generated for 15 years)	180,000	215,000
Annual pretax expenditures (generated for 15 years)	70,000	90,000

The building will be used for only 15 years for either Product A or Product B. After 15 years the building will be too small for efficient production of either product line. At that time, Benson plans to rent the building to firms similar to the current occupants. To rent the building again, Benson will need to restore the building to its present layout. The estimated cash cost of restoring the building if Product A has been undertaken is $55,000. If Product B has been manufactured, the cash cost will be $80,000. These cash costs can be deducted for tax purposes in the year the expenditures occur.

Benson will depreciate the original building shell (purchased for $1,450,000) over a 30-year life to zero, regardless of which alternative it chooses. The building modifications and equipment purchases for either product are estimated to have a 15-year life. They will be depreciated by the straight-line method. The firm's tax rate is 34 percent, and its required rate of return on such investments is 12 percent.

For simplicity, assume all cash flows occur at the end of the year. The initial outlays for modifications and equipment will occur today (Year 0), and the restoration outlays will occur at the end of Year 15. Benson has other profitable ongoing operations that are sufficient to cover any losses. Which use of the building would you recommend to management?

35. **Project Analysis and Inflation** The Biological Insect Control Corporation (BICC) has hired you as a consultant to evaluate the NPV of its proposed toad ranch. BICC plans to breed toads and sell them as ecologically desirable insect control mechanisms. They anticipate that the business will continue into perpetuity. Following the negligible start-up costs, BICC expects the following nominal cash flows at the end of the year:

Revenues	$265,000
Labor costs	185,000
Other costs	55,000

The company will lease machinery for $90,000 per year. The lease payments start at the end of Year 1 and are expressed in nominal terms. Revenues will increase by 4 percent per year in real terms. Labor costs will increase by 3 percent per year in real terms. Other costs will increase by 1 percent per year in real terms. The rate of inflation is expected to be 6 percent per year. BICC's required rate of return is 10 percent in real terms. The company has a 34 percent tax rate. All cash flows occur at year-end. What is the NPV of BICC's proposed toad ranch today?

36. **Project Analysis and Inflation** Sony International has an investment opportunity to produce a new HDTV. The required investment on January 1 of this year is $165 million. The firm will depreciate the investment to zero using the straight-line method over four years. The investment has no resale value after completion of the project. The firm is in the 34 percent tax bracket. The price of the product will be $495 per unit, in real terms, and will not change over the life of the project. Labor costs for Year 1 will be $15.75 per hour, in real terms, and will increase at 2 percent per year in real terms. Energy costs for Year 1 will be $3.80 per physical unit, in real terms, and will increase at 3 percent per year in real terms. The inflation rate is 5 percent per year. Revenues are received and costs are paid at year-end. Refer to the following table for the production schedule:

	Year 1	Year 2	Year 3	Year 4
Physical production, in units	140,000	150,000	170,000	160,000
Labor input, in hours	1,120,000	1,200,000	1,360,000	1,280,000
Energy input, physical units	210,000	225,000	255,000	240,000

The real discount rate for Sony is 4 percent. Calculate the NPV of this project.

37. **Project Analysis and Inflation** After extensive medical and marketing research, Pill, Inc., believes it can penetrate the pain reliever market. It is considering two alternative products. The first is a medication for headache pain. The second is a pill for headache and arthritis pain. Both products would be introduced at a price of $8.35 per package in real terms. The headache-only medication is projected to sell 3 million packages a year, whereas the headache and arthritis remedy would sell 4.5 million packages a year. Cash costs of production in the first year

are expected to be $4.10 per package in real terms for the headache-only brand. Production costs are expected to be $4.65 in real terms for the headache and arthritis pill. All prices and costs are expected to rise at the general inflation rate of 3 percent.

Either product requires further investment. The headache-only pill could be produced using equipment costing $23 million. That equipment would last three years and have no resale value. The machinery required to produce the broader remedy would cost $32 million and last three years. The firm expects that equipment to have a $1 million resale value (in real terms) at the end of Year 3.

Pill, Inc., uses straight-line depreciation. The firm faces a corporate tax rate of 34 percent and believes that the appropriate real discount rate is 7 percent. Which pain reliever should the firm produce?

38. **Calculating Project NPV** J. Smythe, Inc., manufactures fine furniture. The company is deciding whether to introduce a new mahogany dining room table set. The set will sell for $6,100, including a set of eight chairs. The company feels that sales will be 1,800, 1,950, 2,500, 2,350, and 2,100 sets per year for the next five years, respectively. Variable costs will amount to 45 percent of sales, and fixed costs are $1.9 million per year. The new tables will require inventory amounting to 10 percent of sales, produced and stockpiled in the year prior to sales. It is believed that the addition of the new table will cause a loss of 250 tables per year of the oak tables the company produces. These tables sell for $4,500 and have variable costs of 40 percent of sales. The inventory for this oak table is also 10 percent of sales. J. Smythe currently has excess production capacity. If the company buys the necessary equipment today, it will cost $18 million. However, the excess production capacity means the company can produce the new table without buying the new equipment. The company controller has said that the current excess capacity will end in two years with current production. This means that if the company uses the current excess capacity for the new table, it will be forced to spend the $18 million in two years to accommodate the increased sales of its current products. In five years, the new equipment will have a market value of $3.1 million if purchased today, and $7.4 million if purchased in two years. The equipment is depreciated on a seven-year MACRS schedule. The company has a tax rate of 40 percent, and the required return for the project is 11 percent.

a. Should J. Smythe undertake the new project?

b. Can you perform an IRR analysis on this project? How many IRRs would you expect to find?

c. How would you interpret the profitability index?

Excel Master It!

For this Master It! assignment, refer to the Goodweek Tires, Inc., case at the end of this chapter. For your convenience, we have entered the relevant values such as the price and variable costs in the case on the next page. For this project, answer the following questions:

a. What is the profitability index of the project?

b. What is the IRR of the project?

c. At what OEM price would Goodweek Tires be indifferent to accepting the project? Assume the replacement market price is constant.

d. At what level of variable costs per unit would Goodweek Tires be indifferent to accepting the project?

BETHESDA MINING COMPANY

Bethesda Mining is a midsized coal mining company with 20 mines located in Ohio, Pennsylvania, West Virginia, and Kentucky. The company operates deep mines as well as strip mines. Most of the coal mined is sold under contract, with excess production sold on the spot market.

The coal mining industry, especially high-sulfur coal operations such as Bethesda, has been hard-hit by environmental regulations. Recently, however, a combination of increased demand for coal and new pollution reduction technologies has led to an improved market demand for high-sulfur coal. Bethesda has just been approached by Mid-Ohio Electric Company with a request to supply coal for its electric generators for the next four years. Bethesda Mining does not have enough excess capacity at its existing mines to guarantee the contract. The company is considering opening a strip mine in Ohio on 5,000 acres of land purchased 10 years ago for $5 million. Based on a recent appraisal, the company feels it could receive $5.5 million on an aftertax basis if it sold the land today.

Strip mining is a process where the layers of topsoil above a coal vein are removed and the exposed coal is removed. Some time ago, the company would simply remove the coal and leave the land in an unusable condition. Changes in mining regulations now force a company to reclaim the land; that is, when the mining is completed, the land must be restored to near its original condition. The land can then be used for other purposes. Because it is currently operating at full capacity, Bethesda will need to purchase additional necessary equipment, which will cost $85 million. The equipment will be depreciated on a seven-year MACRS schedule. The contract runs for only four years. At that time the coal from the site will be entirely mined. The company feels that the equipment can be sold for 60 percent of its initial purchase price in four years. However, Bethesda plans to open another strip mine at that time and will use the equipment at the new mine.

The contract calls for the delivery of 500,000 tons of coal per year at a price of $82 per ton. Bethesda Mining feels that coal production will be 620,000 tons, 680,000 tons, 730,000 tons, and 590,000 tons, respectively, over the next four years. The excess production will be sold in the spot market at an average of $76 per ton. Variable costs amount to $31 per ton, and fixed costs are $4,100,000 per year. The mine will require a net working capital investment of 5 percent of sales. The NWC will be built up in the year prior to the sales.

Bethesda will be responsible for reclaiming the land at termination of the mining. This will occur in Year 5. The company uses an outside company for reclamation of all the company's strip mines. It is estimated the cost of reclamation will be $2.7 million. In order to get the necessary permits for the strip mine, the company agreed to donate the land after reclamation to the state for use as a public park and recreation area. This will occur in Year 6 and result in a charitable expense deduction of $6 million. Bethesda faces a 38 percent tax rate and has a 12 percent required return on new strip mine projects. Assume that a loss in any year will result in a tax credit.

You have been approached by the president of the company with a request to analyze the project. Calculate the payback period, profitability index, net present value, and internal rate of return for the new strip mine. Should Bethesda Mining take the contract and open the mine?

GOODWEEK TIRES, INC.

After extensive research and development, Goodweek Tires, Inc., has recently developed a new tire, the SuperTread, and must decide whether to make the investment necessary to produce and market it. The tire would be ideal for drivers doing a large amount of wet weather and off-road driving in addition to normal freeway usage. The research and development costs so far have totaled about $10 million. The SuperTread would be put on the market beginning this year, and Goodweek expects it to stay on the market for a total of four years. Test marketing costing $5 million has shown that there is a significant market for a SuperTread-type tire.

As a financial analyst at Goodweek Tires, you have been asked by your CFO, Adam Smith, to evaluate the SuperTread project and provide a recommendation on whether to go ahead with the investment. Except for the initial investment that will occur immediately, assume all cash flows will occur at year-end.

Goodweek must initially invest $160 million in production equipment to make the SuperTread. This equipment can be sold for $65 million at the end of four years. Goodweek intends to sell the SuperTread to two distinct markets:

1. *The original equipment manufacturer (OEM) market:* The OEM market consists primarily of the large automobile companies (like General Motors) that buy tires for new cars. In the OEM market, the SuperTread is expected to sell for $41 per tire. The variable cost to produce each tire is $29.

2. *The replacement market:* The replacement market consists of all tires purchased after the automobile has left the factory. This market allows higher margins; Goodweek expects to sell the SuperTread for $62 per tire there. Variable costs are the same as in the OEM market.

Goodweek Tires intends to raise prices at 1 percent above the inflation rate; variable costs will also increase at 1 percent above the inflation rate. In addition, the SuperTread project will incur $43 million in marketing and general administration costs the first year. This cost is expected to increase at the inflation rate in the subsequent years.

Goodweek's corporate tax rate is 40 percent. Annual inflation is expected to remain constant at 3.25 percent. The company uses a 13.4 percent discount rate to evaluate new product decisions. Automotive industry analysts expect automobile manufacturers to produce 6.2 million new cars this year and production to grow at 2.5 percent per year thereafter. Each new car needs four tires (the spare tires are undersized and are in a different category). Goodweek Tires expects the SuperTread to capture 11 percent of the OEM market.

Industry analysts estimate that the replacement tire market size will be 32 million tires this year and that it will grow at 2 percent annually. Goodweek expects the SuperTread to capture an 8 percent market share.

The appropriate depreciation schedule for the equipment is the seven-year MACRS depreciation schedule. The immediate initial working capital requirement is $9 million. Thereafter, the net working capital requirements will be 15 percent of sales. What are the NPV, payback period, discounted payback period, IRR, and PI on this project?

CHAPTER 7

Risk Analysis, Real Options, and Capital Budgeting

▲ For updates on the latest happenings in finance, visit www. rwicorporatefinance. blogspot.com

In the summer of 2008, the movie *Speed Racer*, starring Emile Hirsch and Christina Ricci, spun its wheels at the box office. The *Speed Racer* slogan was "Go Speed Racer, Go!" but critics said, "Don't go (see) *Speed Racer*, Don't go!" One critic said, "The races felt like a drag." Others were even more harsh, saying the movie "was like spending two hours caroming through a pinball machine" and "a long, dreary, migraine-inducing slog."

Looking at the numbers, Warner Brothers spent close to $150 million making the movie, plus millions more for marketing and distribution. Unfortunately for Warner Brothers, *Speed Racer* crashed and burned at the box office, pulling in only $90 million worldwide. In fact, about 4 of 10 movies lose money in theaters, though DVD sales often help the final tally. Of course, there are movies that do quite well. Also in 2008, the Paramount movie *Indiana Jones and the Kingdom of the Crystal Skull* raked in about $780 million worldwide at a production cost of $185 million.

Obviously, Warner Brothers didn't *plan* to lose $60 million or so on *Speed Racer*, but it happened. As the box office spinout of *Speed Racer* shows, projects don't always go as companies think they will. This chapter explores how this can happen, and what companies can do to analyze and possibly avoid these situations.

7.1 Sensitivity Analysis, Scenario Analysis, and Break-Even Analysis

ExcelMaster
coverage online

This section introduces naming cells, one-way data tables, and the Scenario Manager and Goal Seeker functions.

One main point of this book is that NPV analysis is a superior capital budgeting technique. In fact, because the NPV approach uses cash flows rather than profits, uses all the cash flows, and discounts the cash flows properly, it is hard to find any theoretical fault with it. However, in our conversations with practical businesspeople, we hear the phrase "a false sense of security" frequently. These people point out that the documentation for capital budgeting proposals is often quite impressive. Cash flows are projected down to the last thousand dollars (or even the last dollar) for each year (or even each month). Opportunity costs and side effects are handled quite properly. Sunk costs are ignored—also quite properly. When a high net present value appears at the bottom, one's temptation is to say yes immediately. Nevertheless, the projected cash flow often goes unmet in practice, and the firm ends up with a money loser.

SENSITIVITY ANALYSIS AND SCENARIO ANALYSIS

How can the firm get the net present value technique to live up to its potential? One approach is **sensitivity analysis,** which examines how sensitive a particular NPV calculation is to changes in underlying assumptions. Sensitivity analysis is also known as *what-if* analysis and *bop* (best, optimistic, and pessimistic) analysis.

Table 7.1
Cash Flow Forecasts for Solar Electronics Corporation's Jet Engine: Base Case (millions)*

	Year 1	Years 2–6
Revenues		$6,000
Variable costs		3,000
Fixed costs		1,791
Depreciation		300
Pretax profit		$ 909
Tax ($t_c = .34$)		309
Net profit		$ 600
Cash flow		$ 900
Initial investment costs	$1,500	

*Assumptions: (1) Investment is depreciated in Years 2 through 6 using the straight-line method; (2) tax rate is 34 percent; (3) the company receives no tax benefits for initial development costs.

Consider the following example. Solar Electronics Corporation (SEC) has recently developed a solar-powered jet engine and wants to go ahead with full-scale production. The initial (Year 1)[1] investment is $1,500 million, followed by production and sales over the next five years. The preliminary cash flow projection appears in Table 7.1. Should SEC go ahead with investment in and production of the jet engine, the NPV at a discount rate of 15 percent is (in millions):

$$NPV = -\$1,500 + \sum_{t=1}^{5} \frac{\$900}{(1.15)^t}$$
$$= -\$1,500 + \$900 \times PVIA\ (.15, 5)$$
$$= \$1,517$$

Because the NPV is positive, basic financial theory implies that SEC should accept the project. However, is this all there is to say about the venture? Before actual funding, we ought to check out the project's underlying assumptions about revenues and costs.

Revenues Let's assume that the marketing department has projected annual sales to be:

$$\begin{array}{ccc} \text{Number of jet engines} & = & \text{Market share} \times \begin{array}{c}\text{Size of jet engine}\\\text{market per year}\end{array} \\ \text{sold per year} & & \\ 3,000 & = & .30 \times 10,000 \end{array}$$

$$\begin{array}{ccc} \begin{array}{c}\text{Annual sales}\\\text{revenues}\end{array} & = & \begin{array}{c}\text{Number of jet}\\\text{engines sold}\end{array} \times \begin{array}{c}\text{Price per}\\\text{engine}\end{array} \\ \$6,000\ \text{million} & = & 3,000 \times \$2\ \text{million} \end{array}$$

Thus, it turns out that the revenue estimates depend on three assumptions:

1. Market share.
2. Size of jet engine market.
3. Price per engine.

---

[1] Financial custom generally designates Year 0 as "today." However, we use Year 1 as today in this example because later in this chapter we will consider another decision made a year earlier. That decision will have occurred at Year 0.

Costs Financial analysts frequently divide costs into two types: Variable costs and fixed costs. **Variable costs** change as the output changes, and they are zero when production is zero. Costs of direct labor and raw materials are usually variable. It is common to assume that a variable cost is constant per unit of output, implying that total variable costs are proportional to the level of production. For example, if direct labor is variable and one unit of final output requires $10 of direct labor, then 100 units of final output should require $1,000 of direct labor.

Fixed costs are not dependent on the amount of goods or services produced during the period. Fixed costs are usually measured as costs per unit of time, such as rent per month or salaries per year. Naturally, fixed costs are not fixed forever. They are fixed only over a predetermined time period.

The engineering department has estimated variable costs to be $1 million per engine. Fixed costs are $1,791 million per year. The cost breakdowns are:

$$\begin{array}{ccccc} \text{Variable} & = & \text{Variable cost} & \times & \text{Number of jet engines} \\ \text{cost per year} & & \text{per unit} & & \text{sold per year} \\ \$3{,}000 \text{ million} & = & \$1 \text{ million} & \times & 3{,}000 \end{array}$$

$$\begin{array}{ccccc} \text{Total cost before} & = & \text{Variable cost} & + & \text{Fixed cost per year} \\ \text{taxes per year} & & \text{per year} & & \\ \$4{,}791 \text{ million} & = & \$3{,}000 \text{ million} & + & \$1{,}791 \text{ million} \end{array}$$

These estimates for market size, market share, price, variable cost, and fixed cost, as well as the estimate of initial investment, are presented in the middle column of Table 7.2. These figures represent the firm's expectations or best estimates of the different parameters. For comparison, the firm's analysts also prepared both optimistic and pessimistic forecasts for each of the different variables. These forecasts are provided in the table as well.

Standard sensitivity analysis calls for an NPV calculation for all three possibilities of a single variable, along with the expected forecast for all other variables. This procedure is illustrated in Table 7.3. For example, consider the NPV calculation of $8,154 million provided in the upper right corner of this table. This NPV occurs when the optimistic forecast of 20,000 units per year is used for market size while all other variables are set at their expected forecasts from Table 7.2. Note that each row of the middle column of Table 7.3 shows a value of $1,517 million. This occurs because the expected forecast is used for the variable that was singled out, as well as for all other variables.

Table 7.3 can be used for a number of purposes. First, taken as a whole, the table can indicate whether NPV analysis should be trusted. In other words, it reduces the false sense of security we spoke of earlier. Suppose that NPV is positive when the expected forecast for each variable is used. However, further suppose that every number in the pessimistic column is highly negative and every number in the optimistic column is highly positive.

Table 7.2
Different Estimates for Solar Electronics' Solar Plane Engine

Variable	Pessimistic	Expected or Best	Optimistic
Market size (per year)	5,000	10,000	20,000
Market share	20%	30%	50%
Price	$1.9 million	$2 million	$2.2 million
Variable cost (per plane)	$1.2 million	$1 million	$.8 million
Fixed cost (per year)	$1,891 million	$1,791 million	$1,741 million
Investment	$1,900 million	$1,500 million	$1,000 million

Table 7.3
NPV Calculations ($ in millions) for the Solar Plane Engine Using Sensitivity Analysis

	Pessimistic	Expected or Best	Optimistic
Market size	−$1,802*	$1,517	$8,154
Market share	−696*	1,517	5,942
Price	853	1,517	2,844
Variable cost	189	1,517	2,844
Fixed cost	1,295	1,517	1,628
Investment	1,208	1,517	1,903

Under sensitivity analysis, one input is varied while all other inputs are assumed to meet their expectation. For example, an NPV of −$1,802 occurs when the pessimistic forecast of 5,000 is used for market size, while all other variables are set at their expected forecasts from Table 7.2.

*We assume that the other divisions of the firm are profitable, implying that a loss on this project can offset income elsewhere in the firm, thereby reducing the overall taxes of the firm.

A change in a single forecast greatly alters the NPV estimate, making one leery of the net present value approach. A conservative manager might well scrap the entire NPV analysis in this situation. Fortunately, the solar plane engine does not exhibit this wide dispersion because all but two of the numbers in Table 7.3 are positive. Managers viewing the table will likely consider NPV analysis to be useful for the solar-powered jet engine.

Second, sensitivity analysis shows where more information is needed. For example, an error in the estimate of investment appears to be relatively unimportant because, even under the pessimistic scenario, the NPV of $1,208 million is still highly positive. By contrast, the pessimistic forecast for market share leads to a negative NPV of −$696 million, and a pessimistic forecast for market size leads to a substantially negative NPV of −$1,802 million. Because the effect of incorrect estimates on revenues is so much greater than the effect of incorrect estimates on costs, more information about the factors determining revenues might be needed.

Because of these advantages, sensitivity analysis is widely used in practice. Graham and Harvey[2] report that slightly over 50 percent of the 392 firms in their sample subject their capital budgeting calculations to sensitivity analysis. This number is particularly large when one considers that only about 75 percent of the firms in their sample use NPV analysis.

Unfortunately, sensitivity analysis also suffers from some drawbacks. For example, sensitivity analysis may unwittingly *increase* the false sense of security among managers. Suppose all pessimistic forecasts yield positive NPVs. A manager might feel that there is no way the project can lose money. Of course, the forecasters may simply have an optimistic view of a pessimistic forecast. To combat this, some companies do not treat optimistic and pessimistic forecasts subjectively. Rather, their pessimistic forecasts are always, say, 20 percent less than expected. Unfortunately, the cure in this case may be worse than the disease: A deviation of a fixed percentage ignores the fact that some variables are easier to forecast than others.

In addition, sensitivity analysis treats each variable in isolation when, in reality, the different variables are likely to be related. For example, if ineffective management allows costs to get out of control, it is likely that variable costs, fixed costs, and investment will all rise above expectation at the same time. If the market is not receptive to a solar plane engine, both market share and price should decline together.

[2]See Figure 2 of John Graham and Campbell Harvey, "The Theory and Practice of Corporate Finance: Evidence from the Field," *Journal of Financial Economics* (May/June 2001).

Table 7.4
Cash Flow Forecast ($ in millions) under the Scenario of a Plane Crash*

	Year 1	Years 2–5
Revenues		$2,800
Variable costs		1,400
Fixed costs		1,791
Depreciation		300
Pretax profit		−691
Tax ($t_c = .34$)[†]		235
Net profit		$ −456
Cash flow		$ −156
Initial investment cost	−$1,500	

*Assumptions are:

    Market size   7,000 (70 percent of expectation)

    Market share   20% (2/3 of expectation)

Forecasts for all other variables are the expected forecasts as given in Table 7.2.

[†]Tax loss offsets income elsewhere in firm.

Managers frequently perform **scenario analysis,** a variant of sensitivity analysis, to minimize this problem. Simply put, this approach examines a number of different likely scenarios, where each scenario involves a confluence of factors. As a simple example, consider the effect of a few airline crashes. These crashes are likely to reduce flying in total, thereby limiting the demand for any new engines. Furthermore, even if the crashes do not involve solar-powered aircraft, the public could become more averse to any innovative and controversial technologies. Hence, SEC's market share might fall as well. Perhaps the cash flow calculations would look like those in Table 7.4 under the scenario of a plane crash. Given the calculations in the table, the NPV (in millions) would be:

$$-\$2,023 = -\$1,500 - \$156 \times \text{PVIA} (.15, 5)$$

A series of scenarios like this might illuminate issues concerning the project better than the standard application of sensitivity analysis would.

BREAK-EVEN ANALYSIS

Our discussion of sensitivity analysis and scenario analysis suggests that there are many ways to examine variability in forecasts. We now present another approach, **break-even analysis.** As its name implies, this approach determines the sales needed to break even. The approach is a useful complement to sensitivity analysis because it also sheds light on the severity of incorrect forecasts. We calculate the break-even point in terms of both accounting profit and present value.

Accounting Profit   Annual net profits under four different sales forecasts are as follows:

Annual Unit Sales	Net Profit ($ in millions)
0	−$1,380
1,000	−720
3,000	600
10,000	5,220

Table 7.5 **Revenues and Costs of Project under Different Sales Assumptions ($ in millions, except unit sales)**

Year 1									Years 2–6
Initial Invest- ment	Annual Unit Sales	Revenues	Variable Costs	Fixed Costs	Depreci- ation	Taxes* ($t_c = .34$)	Net Profit	Operating Cash Flows	NPV (evaluated Date 1)
$1,500	0	$ 0	$ 0	−$1,791	−$300	$ 711	−$1,380	−$1,080	−$ 5,120
1,500	1,000	2,000	−1,000	−1,791	−300	371	−720	−420	−2,908
1,500	3,000	6,000	−3,000	−1,791	−300	−309	600	900	1,517
1,500	10,000	20,000	−10,000	−1,791	−300	−2,689	5,220	5,520	17,004

*Loss is incurred in the first two rows. For tax purposes, this loss offsets income elsewhere in the firm.

Figure 7.1
Break-Even Point Using Accounting Numbers

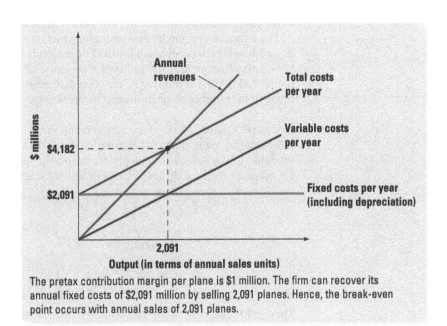

The pretax contribution margin per plane is $1 million. The firm can recover its annual fixed costs of $2,091 million by selling 2,091 planes. Hence, the break-even point occurs with annual sales of 2,091 planes.

A more complete presentation of costs and revenues appears in Table 7.5.

We plot the revenues, costs, and profits under the different assumptions about sales in Figure 7.1. The revenue and cost curves cross at 2,091 jet engines. This is the break-even point—that is, the point where the project generates no profits or losses. As long as annual sales are above 2,091 jet engines, the project will make a profit.

This break-even point can be calculated very easily. Because the sales price is $2 million per engine and the variable cost is $1 million per engine,[3] the difference between sales price and variable cost per engine is:

$$\text{Sales price} - \text{Variable cost} = \$2 \text{ million} - \$1 \text{ million}$$
$$= \$1 \text{ million}$$

---

[3]Though the previous section considered both optimistic and pessimistic forecasts for sales price and variable cost, break-even analysis uses just the expected or best estimates of these variables.

This difference is called the pretax **contribution margin** because each additional engine contributes this amount to pretax profit. (Contribution margin can also be expressed on an aftertax basis.)

Fixed costs are $1,791 million and depreciation is $300 million, implying that the sum of these costs is:

$$\text{Fixed costs} + \text{Depreciation} = \$1,791 \text{ million} + \$300 \text{ million}$$
$$= \$2,091 \text{ million}$$

That is, the firm incurs costs of $2,091 million per year, regardless of the number of sales. Because each engine contributes $1 million, annual sales must reach the following level to offset the costs:

Accounting Profit Break-Even Point:

$$\frac{\text{Fixed costs} + \text{Depreciation}}{\text{Sales price} - \text{Variable costs}} = \frac{\$2,091 \text{ million}}{\$1 \text{ million}} = 2,091$$

Thus, 2,091 engines is the break-even point required for an accounting profit.

The astute reader might be wondering why taxes have been ignored in the calculation of break-even accounting profit. The reason is that a firm with a pretax profit of $0 will also have an aftertax profit of $0 because no taxes are paid if no pretax profit is reported. Thus, the number of units needed to break even on a pretax basis must be equal to the number of units needed to break even on an aftertax basis.

Present Value   As we have stated many times, we are more interested in present value than we are in profit. Therefore, we should calculate breakeven in terms of present value. Given a discount rate of 15 percent, the solar plane engine has the following net present values for different levels of annual sales:

Annual Unit Sales	NPV ($ millions)
0	−5,120
1,000	−2,908
3,000	1,517
10,000	17,004

These NPV calculations are reproduced from the last column of Table 7.5.

Figure 7.2 relates the net present value of both the revenues and the costs to output. There are at least two differences between Figure 7.2 and Figure 7.1, one of which is quite important and the other is much less so. First the less important point: The dollar amounts on the vertical dimension of Figure 7.2 are greater than those on the vertical dimension of Figure 7.1 because the net present values are calculated over five years. More important, accounting breakeven occurs when 2,091 units are sold annually, whereas NPV breakeven occurs when 2,315 units are sold annually.

Of course, the NPV break-even point can be calculated directly. The firm originally invested $1,500 million. This initial investment can be expressed as a five-year equivalent annual cost (EAC), determined by dividing the initial investment by the appropriate five-year annuity factor:

$$\text{EAC} = \frac{\text{Initial investment}}{\text{5-year annuity factor at 15\%}} = \frac{\text{Initial investment}}{\text{PVIA (.15, 5)}}$$
$$= \frac{\$1,500 \text{ million}}{3.3522} = \$447.5 \text{ million}$$

Figure 7.2
Break-Even Point
Using Net Present
Value*

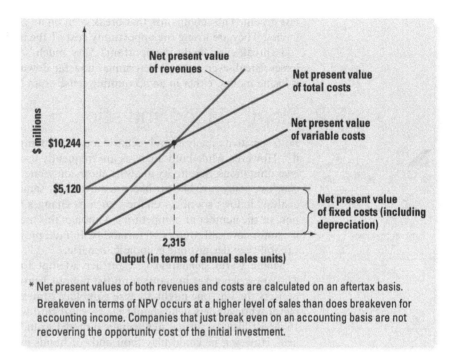

* Net present values of both revenues and costs are calculated on an aftertax basis.
Breakeven in terms of NPV occurs at a higher level of sales than does breakeven for
accounting income. Companies that just break even on an accounting basis are not
recovering the opportunity cost of the initial investment.

Note that the EAC of $447.5 million is greater than the yearly depreciation of
$300 million. This must occur because the calculation of EAC implicitly assumes that
the $1,500 million investment could have been invested at 15 percent.

Aftertax costs, regardless of output, can be viewed like this:

$$\underset{\text{million}}{\$1,528} = \underset{\text{million}}{\$447.5} + \underset{\text{million}}{\$1,791} \times .66 - \$300 \text{ million} \times .34$$

$$= \text{EAC} + \text{Fixed costs} \times (1 - t_c) - \text{Depreciation} \times t_c$$

That is, in addition to the initial investment's equivalent annual cost of $447.5 million,
the firm pays fixed costs each year and receives a depreciation tax shield each year.
The depreciation tax shield is written as a negative number because it offsets the costs
in the equation. Each plane contributes $.66 million to aftertax profit, so it will take
the following sales to offset the costs:

Present Value Break-Even Point:

$$\frac{\text{EAC} + \text{Fixed costs} \times (1 - t_c) - \text{Depreciation} \times t_c}{(\text{Sales price} - \text{Variable costs}) \times (1 - t_c)} = \frac{\$1,528 \text{ million}}{\$.66 \text{ million}} = 2,315$$

Thus, 2,315 planes is the break-even point from the perspective of present value.

Why is the accounting break-even point different from the financial break-even
point? When we use accounting profit as the basis for the break-even calculation, we
subtract depreciation. Depreciation for the solar jet engines project is $300 million per
year. If 2,091 solar jet engines are sold per year, SEC will generate sufficient revenues
to cover the $300 million depreciation expense plus other costs. Unfortunately, at this
level of sales SEC will not cover the economic opportunity costs of the $1,500 million
laid out for the investment. If we take into account that the $1,500 million could have
been invested at 15 percent, the true annual cost of the investment is $447.5 million,
not $300 million. Depreciation understates the true costs of recovering the initial

investment. Thus companies that break even on an accounting basis are really losing money. They are losing the opportunity cost of the initial investment.

Is break-even analysis important? Very much so: All corporate executives fear losses. Break-even analysis determines how far down sales can fall before the project is losing money, either in an accounting sense or an NPV sense.

7.2 Monte Carlo Simulation

ExcelMaster
coverage online

This section introduces RAND, Frequency Distribution, and Frequency Distribution Charts.

Both sensitivity analysis and scenario analysis attempt to answer the question "What if?" However, while both analyses are frequently used in the real world, each has its own limitations. Sensitivity analysis allows only one variable to change at a time. By contrast, many variables are likely to move at the same time in the real world. Scenario analysis follows specific scenarios, such as changes in inflation, government regulation, or the number of competitors. Although this methodology is often quite helpful, it cannot cover all sources of variability. In fact, projects are likely to exhibit a lot of variability under just one economic scenario.

Monte Carlo simulation is a further attempt to model real-world uncertainty. This approach takes its name from the famous European casino because it analyzes projects the way one might analyze gambling strategies. Imagine a serious blackjack player who wonders if he should take a third card whenever his first two cards total 16. Most likely, a formal mathematical model would be too complex to be practical here. However, he could play thousands of hands in a casino, sometimes drawing a third card when his first two cards add to 16 and sometimes not drawing that third card. He could compare his winnings (or losings) under the two strategies to determine which were better. He would probably lose a lot of money performing this test in a real casino, so simulating the results from the two strategies on a computer might be cheaper. Monte Carlo simulation of capital budgeting projects is in this spirit.

Imagine that Backyard Barbeques, Inc. (BBI), a manufacturer of both charcoal and gas grills, has a blueprint for a new grill that cooks with compressed hydrogen. The CFO, Edward H. Comiskey, dissatisfied with simpler capital budgeting techniques, wants a Monte Carlo simulation for this new grill. A consultant specializing in the Monte Carlo approach, Lester Mauney, takes him through the five basic steps of the method.

STEP 1: SPECIFY THE BASIC MODEL

Les Mauney breaks up cash flow into three components: annual revenue, annual costs, and initial investment. The revenue in any year is viewed as:

$$\text{Number of grills sold by entire industry} \times \text{Market share of BBI's hydrogen grill (in percent)} \times \text{Price per hydrogen grill} \qquad (7.1)$$

The cost in any year is viewed as:

$$\text{Fixed manufacturing costs} + \text{Variable manufacturing costs} + \text{Marketing costs} + \text{Selling costs}$$

Initial investment is viewed as:

$$\text{Cost of patent} + \text{Test marketing costs} + \text{Cost of production facility}$$

STEP 2: SPECIFY A DISTRIBUTION FOR EACH VARIABLE IN THE MODEL

Here comes the hard part. Let's start with revenue, which has three components in Equation 7.1. The consultant first models overall market size—that is, the number of

Figure 7.3
Probability
Distributions for
Industrywide Unit
Sales, Market Share
of BBI's Hydrogen
Grill, and Price of
Hydrogen Grill

For each of the three variables, a drawing is generated by computer simulation. In addition, price per grill is dependent on industrywide unit sales.

grills sold by the entire industry. The trade publication *Outdoor Food (OF)* reported that 10 million grills of all types were sold in the continental United States last year, and it forecasts sales of 10.5 million next year. Mr. Mauney, using *OF*'s forecast and his own intuition, creates the following distribution for next year's sales of grills by the entire industry:

Probability	20%	60%	20%
Next Year's Industrywide Unit Sales	10 million	10.5 million	11 million

The tight distribution here reflects the slow but steady historical growth in the grill market. This probability distribution is graphed in Panel A of Figure 7.3.

Lester Mauney realizes that estimating the market share of BBI's hydrogen grill is more difficult. Nevertheless, after a great deal of analysis, he determines the distribution of next year's market share:

Probability	10%	20%	30%	25%	10%	5%
Market Share of BBI's Hydrogen Grill Next Year	1%	2%	3%	4%	5%	8%

Whereas the consultant assumed a symmetrical distribution for industrywide unit sales, he believes a skewed distribution makes more sense for the project's market share. In his mind there is always the small possibility that sales of the hydrogen grill will really take off. This probability distribution is graphed in Panel B of Figure 7.3.

These forecasts assume that unit sales for the overall industry are unrelated to the project's market share. In other words, the two variables are *independent* of each other. Mr. Mauney reasons that although an economic boom might increase industrywide grill sales and a recession might decrease them, the project's market share is unlikely to be related to economic conditions.

Mr. Mauney must determine the distribution of price per grill. Mr. Comiskey, the CFO, informs him that the price will be in the area of $200 per grill, given what other competitors are charging. However, the consultant believes that the price per hydrogen grill will almost certainly depend on the size of the overall market for grills. As in any business, you can usually charge more if demand is high.

After rejecting a number of complex models for price, Mr. Mauney settles on the following specification:

$$\text{Next year's price} \atop \text{per hydrogen grill} = \$190 + \$1 \times \text{Industrywide unit sales} \atop \text{(in millions)} +/- \$3 \qquad (7.2)$$

The grill price in Equation 7.2 depends on the unit sales of the industry. In addition, random variation is modeled via the term "+/−$3," where a drawing of +$3 and a drawing of −$3 each occur 50 percent of the time. For example, if industrywide unit sales are 11 million, the price per share would be either of the following:

$$\$190 + \$11 + \$3 = \$204 \quad (50\% \text{ probability})$$
$$\$190 + \$11 - \$3 = \$198 \quad (50\% \text{ probability})$$

The relationship between the price of a hydrogen grill and industrywide unit sales is graphed in Panel C of Figure 7.3.

The consultant now has distributions for each of the three components of next year's revenue. However, he needs distributions for future years as well. Using forecasts from *Outdoor Food* and other publications, Mr. Mauney forecasts the distribution of growth rates for the entire industry over the second year:

Probability	20%	60%	20%
Growth Rate of Industrywide Unit Sales in Second Year	1%	3%	5%

Given both the distribution of next year's industrywide unit sales and the distribution of growth rates for this variable over the second year, we can generate the distribution of industrywide unit sales for the second year. A similar extension should give Mr. Mauney a distribution for later years as well, though we won't go into the details here. And just as the consultant extended the first component of revenue (industry-wide unit sales) to later years, he would want to do the same thing for market share and unit price.

The preceding discussion shows how the three components of revenue can be modeled. Step 2 would be complete once the components of cost and investment are modeled in a similar way. Special attention must be paid to the interactions between variables here because ineffective management will likely allow the different cost components to rise together. However, you are probably getting the idea now, so we will skip the rest of this step.

STEP 3: THE COMPUTER DRAWS ONE OUTCOME

As we said, next year's revenue in our model is the product of three components. Imagine that the computer randomly picks industrywide unit sales of 10 million, a market share for BBI's hydrogen grill of 2 percent, and a +$3 random price variation. Given these drawings, next year's price per hydrogen grill will be:

$$\$190 + \$10 + \$3 = \$203$$

and next year's revenue for BBI's hydrogen grill will be:

$$10 \text{ million} \times .02 \times \$203 = \$40.6 \text{ million}$$

Of course, we are not done with the entire *outcome* yet. We would have to perform drawings for revenue in each future year. In addition, we would perform drawings for costs in each future year. Finally, a drawing for initial investment would have to be made as well. In this way, a single outcome, made up of a drawing for each variable in the model, would generate a cash flow from the project in each future year.

How likely is it that the specific outcome discussed would be drawn? We can answer this because we know the probability of each component. Because industry sales of $10 million has a 20 percent probability, a market share of 2 percent also has a 20 percent probability, and a random price variation of +$3 has a 50 percent probability, the probability of these three drawings together in the same outcome is:

$$.02 = .20 \times .20 \times .50 \tag{7.3}$$

Of course the probability would get even smaller once drawings for future revenues, future costs, and the initial investment are included in the outcome.

This step generates the cash flow for each year from a single outcome. What we are ultimately interested in is the *distribution* of cash flow each year across many outcomes. We ask the computer to randomly draw over and over again to give us this distribution, which is just what is done in the next step.

STEP 4: REPEAT THE PROCEDURE

The first three steps generate one outcome, but the essence of Monte Carlo simulation is repeated outcomes. Depending on the situation, the computer may be called on to generate thousands or even millions of outcomes. The result of all these drawings is a distribution of cash flow for each future year. This distribution is the basic output of Monte Carlo simulation.

Consider Figure 7.4. Here, repeated drawings have produced the simulated distribution of the third year's cash flow. There would be, of course, a distribution like the one in this figure for each future year. This leaves us with just one more step.

Figure 7.4
Simulated
Distribution of the
Third Year's Cash
Flow for BBI's New
Hydrogen Grill

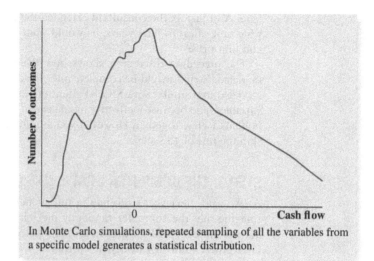

In Monte Carlo simulations, repeated sampling of all the variables from a specific model generates a statistical distribution.

STEP 5: CALCULATE NPV

Given the distribution of cash flow for the third year in Figure 7.4, one can determine the expected cash flow for this year. In a similar manner, one can also determine the expected cash flow for each future year and then calculate the net present value of the project by discounting these expected cash flows at an appropriate rate.

Monte Carlo simulation is often viewed as a step beyond either sensitivity analysis or scenario analysis. Interactions between the variables are explicitly specified in Monte Carlo; so (at least in theory) this methodology provides a more complete analysis. And, as a by-product, having to build a precise model deepens the forecaster's understanding of the project.

Because Monte Carlo simulations have been around for at least 35 years, you might think that most firms would be performing them by now. Surprisingly, this does not seem to be the case. In our experience, executives are frequently skeptical of the complexity. It is difficult to model either the distributions of each variable or the interactions between variables. In addition, the computer output is often devoid of economic intuition. Thus, while Monte Carlo simulations are used in certain real-world situations,[4] the approach is not likely to be "the wave of the future." In fact, Graham and Harvey[5] report that only about 15 percent of the firms in their sample use capital budgeting simulations.

7.3   Real Options

In Chapter 5, we stressed the superiority of net present value (NPV) analysis over other approaches when valuing capital budgeting projects. However, both scholars and practitioners have pointed out problems with NPV. The basic idea here is that NPV analysis, as well as all the other approaches in Chapter 5, ignores the adjustments that a firm can make after a project is accepted. These adjustments are called

---

[4]More than perhaps any other, the pharmaceutical industry has pioneered applications of this methodology. For example, see Nancy A. Nichols, "Scientific Management at Merck: An Interview with CFO Judy Lewent," *Harvard Business Review* (January/February 1994).

[5]See Figure 2 of Graham and Harvey, op. cit.

real options. In this respect NPV underestimates the true value of a project. NPV's conservatism is best explained through a series of examples.

THE OPTION TO EXPAND

Conrad Willig, an entrepreneur, recently learned of a chemical treatment causing water to freeze at 100 degrees Fahrenheit rather than 32 degrees. Of all the many practical applications for this treatment, Mr. Willig liked the idea of hotels made of ice more than anything else. Conrad estimated the annual cash flows from a single ice hotel to be $2 million, based on an initial investment of $12 million. He felt that 20 percent was an appropriate discount rate, given the risk of this new venture. Believing that the cash flows would be perpetual, Mr. Willig determined the NPV of the project to be:

$$-\$12,000,000 + \$2,000,000/.20 = -\$2 \text{ million}$$

Most entrepreneurs would have rejected this venture, given its negative NPV. But Conrad was not your typical entrepreneur. He reasoned that NPV analysis missed a hidden source of value. While he was pretty sure that the initial investment would cost $12 million, there was some uncertainty concerning annual cash flows. His cash flow estimate of $2 million per year actually reflected his belief that there was a 50 percent probability that annual cash flows will be $3 million and a 50 percent probability that annual cash flows will be $1 million.

The NPV calculations for the two forecasts are given here:

Optimistic forecast: $-\$12$ million $+ \$3$ million$/.20 = \$3$ million
Pessimistic forecast: $-\$12$ million $+ \$1$ million$/.20 = -\$7$ million

On the surface, this new calculation doesn't seem to help Mr. Willig much. An average of the two forecasts yields an NPV for the project of:

$$50\% \times \$3 \text{ million} + 50\% \times (-\$7 \text{ million}) = -\$2 \text{ million}$$

which is just the value he calculated in the first place.

However, if the optimistic forecast turns out to be correct, Mr. Willig would want to *expand*. If he believes that there are, say, 10 locations in the country that can support an ice hotel, the true NPV of the venture would be:

$$50\% \times 10 \times \$3 \text{ million} + 50\% \times (-\$7 \text{ million}) = \$11.5 \text{ million}$$

Figure 7.5, which represents Mr. Willig's decision, is often called a decision tree. The idea expressed in the figure is both basic and universal. The entrepreneur has the option to expand if the pilot location is successful. For example, think of all the people who start restaurants, most of them ultimately failing. These individuals are not

Figure 7.5
Decision Tree for Ice Hotel

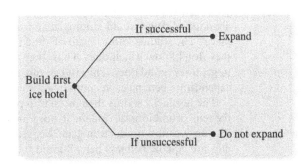

necessarily overly optimistic. They may realize the likelihood of failure but go ahead anyway because of the small chance of starting the next McDonald's or Burger King.

THE OPTION TO ABANDON

Managers also have the option to abandon existing projects. Abandonment may seem cowardly, but it can often save companies a great deal of money. Because of this, the option to abandon increases the value of any potential project.

The example of ice hotels, which illustrated the option to expand, can also illustrate the option to abandon. To see this, imagine that Mr. Willig now believes that there is a 50 percent probability that annual cash flows will be $6 million and a 50 percent probability that annual cash flows will be −$2 million. The NPV calculations under the two forecasts become:

Optimistic forecast: −$12 million + $6 million/.2 = $18 million
Pessimistic forecast: −$12 million − $2 million/.2 = −$22 million

yielding an NPV for the project of:

$$50\% \times \$18 \text{ million} + 50\% \times (-\$22 \text{ million}) = -\$2 \text{ million} \tag{7.4}$$

Furthermore, now imagine that Mr. Willig wants to own, at most, just one ice hotel, implying that there is no option to expand. Because the NPV in Equation 7.4 is negative, it looks as if he will not build the hotel.

But things change when we consider the abandonment option. As of Date 1, the entrepreneur will know which forecast has come true. If cash flows equal those under the optimistic forecast, Conrad will keep the project alive. If, however, cash flows equal those under the pessimistic forecast, he will abandon the hotel. If Mr. Willig knows these possibilities ahead of time, the NPV of the project becomes:

$$50\% \times \$18 \text{ million} + 50\% \times (-\$12 \text{ million} - \$2 \text{ million}/1.20) = \$2.17 \text{ million}$$

Because Mr. Willig abandons after experiencing the cash flow of −$2 million at Date 1, he does not have to endure this outflow in any of the later years. The NPV is now positive, so Conrad will accept the project.

The example here is clearly a stylized one. Whereas many years may pass before a project is abandoned in the real world, our ice hotel was abandoned after just one year. And, while salvage values generally accompany abandonment, we assumed no salvage value for the ice hotel. Nevertheless, abandonment options are pervasive in the real world.

For example, consider the moviemaking industry. As shown in Figure 7.6, movies begin with either the purchase or development of a script. A completed script might cost a movie studio a few million dollars and potentially lead to actual production. However, the great majority of scripts (perhaps well in excess of 80 percent) are abandoned. Why would studios abandon scripts that they commissioned in the first place? The studios know ahead of time that only a few scripts will be promising, and they don't know which ones. Thus, they cast a wide net, commissioning many scripts to get a few good ones. The studios must be ruthless with the bad scripts because the expenditure here pales in comparison to the huge losses from producing a bad movie.

The few lucky scripts then move into production, where costs might be budgeted in the tens of millions of dollars, if not much more. At this stage, the dreaded phrase is that on-location production gets "bogged down," creating cost overruns. But the studios are equally ruthless here. Should these overruns become excessive, production is

Figure 7.6
The Abandonment Option in the Movie Industry

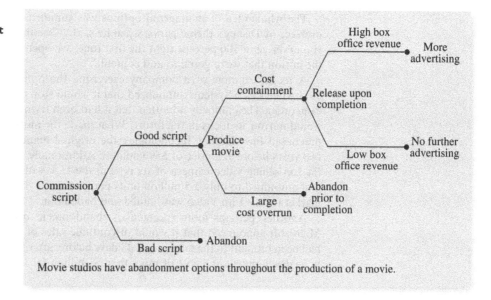

Movie studios have abandonment options throughout the production of a movie.

likely to be abandoned midstream. Interestingly, abandonment almost always occurs due to high costs, not due to the fear that the movie won't be able to find an audience. Little information on that score will be obtained until the movie is actually released.

Release of the movie is accompanied by significant advertising expenditures, perhaps in the range of $10 to $20 million. Advertising will continue following strong ticket sales, but it will likely be abandoned after a few weeks of poor box office performance.

Moviemaking is one of the riskiest businesses around, with studios receiving hundreds of millions of dollars in a matter of weeks from a blockbuster while receiving practically nothing during this period from a flop. The abandonment options contain costs that might otherwise bankrupt the industry.

To illustrate some of these ideas, consider the case of Euro Disney. The deal to open Euro Disney occurred in 1987, and the park opened its doors outside Paris in 1992. Disney's management thought Europeans would go goofy over the new park, but trouble soon began. The number of visitors never met expectations, in part because the company priced tickets too high. Disney also decided not to serve alcohol in a country that was accustomed to wine with meals. French labor inspectors fought Disney's strict dress codes, and so on.

After several years of operations, the park began serving wine in its restaurants, lowered ticket prices, and made other adjustments. In other words, management exercised its option to reformulate the product. The park began to make a small profit. Then the company exercised the option to expand by adding a "second gate," which was another theme park next to Euro Disney named Walt Disney Studios. The second gate was intended to encourage visitors to extend their stays. But the new park flopped. The reasons ranged from high ticket prices, attractions geared toward Hollywood rather than European filmmaking, labor strikes in Paris, and a summer heat wave.

By the summer of 2003, Euro Disney was close to bankruptcy again. Executives discussed a range of options. These options ranged from letting the company go broke (the option to abandon) to pulling the Disney name from the park. In 2005, the company finally agreed to a restructuring with the help of the French government.

The whole idea of managerial options was summed up aptly by Jay Rasulo, the overseer of Disney's theme parks, when he said, "One thing we know for sure is that you never get it 100 percent right the first time. We open every one of our parks with the notion that we're going to add content."

A recent example of a company exercising the option to abandon occurred in 2011 when Cisco Systems announced that it would stop manufacturing its Flip Video camcorder. The company admitted that it had been trying to do too many things and would narrow its focus in the future. What made the move unusual is that Cisco had purchased Pure Digital Technologies, the original manufacturer of the Flip Video, two years before at a price of $590 million. Additionally, although the Flip Video was the top-selling video camera of its type in the U.S. with a 26 percent market share, that amounted to only 2.5 million units per year. So, Cisco concluded that the future market for the Flip Video was limited and bailed out.

Another, perhaps more spectacular, abandonment occurred in June 2010 when Microsoft announced that it would discontinue sales of its Kin cell phone. The Kin had been brought to the market just 48 days before, after Microsoft spent several years in its development at a cost of more than $1 billion.

TIMING OPTIONS

One often finds urban land that has been vacant for many years. Yet this land is bought and sold from time to time. Why would anyone pay a positive price for land that has no source of revenue? Certainly, one could not arrive at a positive price through NPV analysis. However, the paradox can easily be explained in terms of real options.

Suppose that the land's highest and best use is as an office building. Total construction costs for the building are estimated to be $1 million. Currently, net rents (after all costs) are estimated to be $90,000 per year in perpetuity, and the discount rate is 10 percent. The NPV of this proposed building would be:

$$-\$1 \text{ million} + \$90,000/.10 = -\$100,000$$

Because this NPV is negative, one would not currently want to build. However, suppose that the federal government is planning various urban revitalization programs for the city. Office rents will likely increase if the programs succeed. In this case, the property's owner might want to erect the office building after all. Conversely, office rents will remain the same, or even fall, if the programs fail. The owner will not build in this case.

We say that the property owner has a *timing option*. Although she does not currently want to build, she will want to build in the future should rents in the area rise substantially. This timing option explains why vacant land often has value. There are costs, such as taxes, from holding raw land, but the value of an office building after a substantial rise in rents may more than offset these holding costs. Of course the exact value of the vacant land depends on both the probability of success in the revitalization program and the extent of the rent increase. Figure 7.7 illustrates this timing option.

Mining operations almost always provide timing options as well. Suppose you own a copper mine where the cost of mining each ton of copper exceeds the sales revenue. It's a no-brainer to say that you would not want to mine the copper currently. And because there are costs of ownership such as property taxes, insurance, and security, you might actually want to pay someone to take the mine off your hands. However, we would caution you not to do so hastily. Copper prices in the future might increase enough so that production is profitable. Given that possibility, you could likely find someone who would pay a positive price for the property today.

Figure 7.7
Decision Tree for Vacant Land

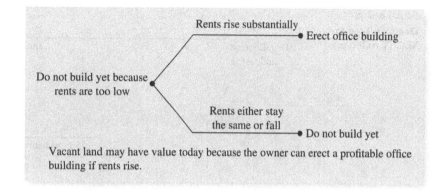

Vacant land may have value today because the owner can erect a profitable office building if rents rise.

7.4 Decision Trees

ExcelMaster
coverage online

This section introduces shapes and lines.

As shown in the previous section, managers adjust their decisions on the basis of new information. For example, a project may be expanded if early experience is promising, whereas the same project might be abandoned in the wake of bad results. As we said earlier, the choices available to managers are called *real options* and an individual project can often be viewed as a series of real options, leading to valuation approaches beyond the basic present value methodology of earlier chapters.

Earlier in this chapter, we considered Solar Electronics Corporation's (SEC's) solar-powered jet engine project, with cash flows as shown in Table 7.1. In that example, SEC planned to invest $1,500 million at Year 1 and expected to receive $900 million per year in each of the next five years. Our calculations showed an NPV of $1,517 million, so the firm would presumably want to go ahead with the project.

To illustrate decision trees in more detail, let's move back one year to Year 0, when SEC's decision was more complicated. At that time, the engineering group had developed the technology for a solar-powered plane engine, but test marketing had not begun. The marketing department proposed that SEC develop some prototypes and conduct test marketing of the engine. A corporate planning group, including representatives from production, marketing, and engineering, estimated that this preliminary phase would take a year and cost $100 million. Furthermore, the group believed there was a 75 percent chance that the marketing test would prove successful. After completion of the marketing tests, SEC would decide whether to engage in full-scale production, necessitating the investment of $1,500 million.

The marketing tests add a layer of complexity to the analysis. Our previous work on the example assumed that the marketing tests had already proved successful. How do we analyze whether we want to go ahead with the marketing tests in the first place? This is where decision trees come in.

To recap, SEC faces two decisions, both of which are represented in Figure 7.8. First the firm must decide whether to go ahead with the marketing tests. And if the tests are performed, the firm must decide whether the results of the tests warrant full-scale production. The important point here, as we will see, is that decision trees answer the two questions in *reverse* order. So let's work backward, first considering what to do with the results of the tests, which can be either successful or unsuccessful.

Figure 7.8
Decision Tree for
SEC ($ millions)

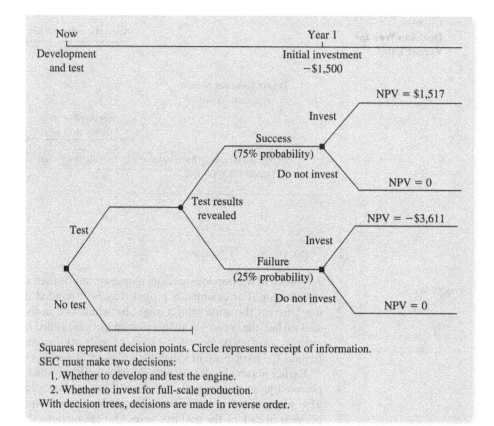

Squares represent decision points. Circle represents receipt of information.
SEC must make two decisions:
1. Whether to develop and test the engine.
2. Whether to invest for full-scale production.
With decision trees, decisions are made in reverse order.

Assume tests have been successful (75 percent probability). Table 7.1 tells us that full-scale production will cost $1,500 million and will generate an annual cash flow of $900 million for five years, yielding an NPV of:

$$= -\$1,500 + \sum_{t=1}^{5} \frac{\$900}{(1.15)^t}$$

$$= -\$1,500 + \$900 \times \text{PVIA}\,(.15, 5)$$

$$= \$1,517$$

Because the NPV is positive, successful marketing tests should lead to full-scale production. (Note that the NPV is calculated as of Year 1, the time at which the investment of $1,500 million is made. Later we will discount this number back to Year 0, when the decision on test marketing is to be made.)

Assume tests have not been successful (25 percent probability). Here, SEC's $1,500 million investment would produce an NPV of −$3,611 million, calculated as of Year 1. (To save space, we will not provide the raw numbers leading to this calculation.) Because the NPV here is negative, SEC will not want full-scale production if the marketing tests are unsuccessful.

Decision on marketing tests. Now we know what to do with the results of the marketing tests. Let's use these results to move back one year. That is, we now want to figure out whether SEC should invest $100 million for the test marketing costs in the first place.

The expected payoff evaluated at Date 1 (in millions) is:

$$
\begin{aligned}
\text{Expected} \atop \text{payoff} &= \left(\begin{array}{ccc} \text{Probability} \\ \text{of} & \times & \text{Payoff} \\ \text{success} & & \text{if success-} \\ & & \text{ful} \end{array} \right) + \left(\begin{array}{ccc} \text{Probability} \\ \text{of} & \times & \text{Payoff} \\ \text{failure} & & \text{if} \\ & & \text{failure} \end{array} \right) \\
&= (.75 \quad \times \quad \$1{,}517) \ + \ (.25 \quad \times \quad \$0) \\
&= \$1{,}138
\end{aligned}
$$

The NPV of testing computed at Date 0 (in millions) is:

$$
\begin{aligned}
\text{NPV} &= -\$100 + \frac{\$1{,}138}{1.15} \\
&= \$890
\end{aligned}
$$

Because the NPV is positive, the firm should test the market for solar-powered jet engines.

Warning We have used a discount rate of 15 percent for both the testing and the investment decisions. Perhaps a higher discount rate should have been used for the initial test marketing decision, which is likely to be riskier than the investment decision.

Recap As mentioned above, the analysis is graphed in Figure 7.8. As can be seen from the figure, SEC must make the following two decisions:

1. Whether to develop and test the solar-powered jet engine.
2. Whether to invest for full-scale production following the results of the test.

Using a decision tree, we answered the second question before we answered the first one.

Decision trees represent the best approach to solving SEC's problem, given the information presented so far in the text. However, we will examine a more sophisticated approach to valuing options in a later chapter. Though this approach was first used to value financial options traded on organized option exchanges, it can be used to value real options as well.

◄ To test your mastery of this material, take a quiz at mhhe. com/rwj

Summary and Conclusions

This chapter discussed a number of practical applications of capital budgeting.

1. Though NPV is the best capital budgeting approach conceptually, it has been criticized in practice for giving managers a false sense of security. Sensitivity analysis shows NPV under varying assumptions, giving managers a better feel for the project's risks. Unfortunately, sensitivity analysis modifies only one variable at a time, but many variables are likely to vary together in the real world. Scenario analysis examines a project's performance under different scenarios (such as war breaking out or oil prices skyrocketing). Finally, managers want to know how bad forecasts must be before a project loses money. Break-even analysis calculates the sales figure at which the project breaks even. Though break-even analysis is frequently performed on an accounting profit basis, we suggest that a net present value basis is more appropriate.

2. Monte Carlo simulation begins with a model of the firm's cash flows, based on both the interactions between different variables and the movement of each individual variable over time. Random sampling generates a distribution of these cash flows for each period, leading to a net present value calculation.

3. We analyzed the hidden options in capital budgeting, such as the option to expand, the option to abandon, and timing options.

4. Decision trees represent an approach for valuing projects with these hidden, or real, options.

www.mhhe.com/rwj

Concept Questions

1. **Forecasting Risk** What is forecasting risk? In general, would the degree of forecasting risk be greater for a new product or a cost-cutting proposal? Why?

2. **Sensitivity Analysis and Scenario Analysis** What is the essential difference between sensitivity analysis and scenario analysis?

3. **Marginal Cash Flows** A coworker claims that looking at all this marginal this and incremental that is just a bunch of nonsense, and states, "Listen, if our average revenue doesn't exceed our average cost, then we will have a negative cash flow, and we will go broke!" How do you respond?

4. **Break-Even Point** As a shareholder of a firm that is contemplating a new project, would you be more concerned with the accounting break-even point, the cash break-even point (the point at which operating cash flow is zero), or the financial break-even point? Why?

5. **Break-Even Point** Assume a firm is considering a new project that requires an initial investment and has equal sales and costs over its life. Will the project reach the accounting, cash, or financial break-even point first? Which will it reach next? Last? Will this order always apply?

6. **Real Options** Why does traditional NPV analysis tend to underestimate the true value of a capital budgeting project?

7. **Real Options** The Mango Republic has just liberalized its markets and is now permitting foreign investors. Tesla Manufacturing has analyzed starting a project in the country and has determined that the project has a negative NPV. Why might the company go ahead with the project? What type of option is most likely to add value to this project?

8. **Sensitivity and Break-even Analysis** How does sensitivity analysis interact with break-even analysis?

9. **Option to Wait** An option can often have more than one source of value. Consider a logging company. The company can log the timber today or wait another year (or more) to log the timber. What advantages would waiting one year potentially have?

10. **Project Analysis** You are discussing a project analysis with a coworker. The project involves real options, such as expanding the project if successful, or abandoning the project if it fails. Your coworker makes the following statement: "This analysis is ridiculous. We looked at expanding or abandoning the project in two years, but there are many other options we should consider. For example, we could expand in one year, and expand further in two years. Or we could expand in one year, and abandon the project in two years. There are too many options for us to examine. Because of this, anything this analysis would give us is worthless." How would you evaluate this statement? Considering that with any capital budgeting project there are an infinite number of real options, when do you stop the option analysis on an individual project?

Questions and Problems

BASIC
(Questions 1–10)

1. **Sensitivity Analysis and Break-Even Point** We are evaluating a project that costs $644,000, has an eight-year life, and has no salvage value. Assume that depreciation is straight-line to zero over the life of the project. Sales are projected at 70,000 units per year. Price per unit is $37, variable cost per unit is $21, and fixed costs are $725,000 per year. The tax rate is 35 percent, and we require a 15 percent return on this project.

Chapter 7   Risk Analysis, Real Options, and Capital Budgeting   **229**

    a. Calculate the accounting break-even point.

    b. Calculate the base-case cash flow and NPV. What is the sensitivity of NPV to changes in the sales figure? Explain what your answer tells you about a 500-unit decrease in projected sales.

    c. What is the sensitivity of OCF to changes in the variable cost figure? Explain what your answer tells you about a $1 decrease in estimated variable costs.

2. **Scenario Analysis**   In the previous problem, suppose the projections given for price, quantity, variable costs, and fixed costs are all accurate to within ±10 percent. Calculate the best-case and worst-case NPV figures.

3. **Calculating Break-even**   In each of the following cases, find the unknown variable. Ignore taxes.

Accounting Break-even	Unit Price	Unit Variable Cost	Fixed Costs	Depreciation
95,300	$41	$30	$820,000	?
143,806	?	56	2,750,000	$1,150,000
7,835	97	?	160,000	105,000

4. **Financial Break-even**   L.J.'s Toys Inc. just purchased a $390,000 machine to produce toy cars. The machine will be fully depreciated by the straight-line method over its five-year economic life. Each toy sells for $25. The variable cost per toy is $11, and the firm incurs fixed costs of $280,000 each year. The corporate tax rate for the company is 34 percent. The appropriate discount rate is 12 percent. What is the financial break-even point for the project?

5. **Option to Wait**   Your company is deciding whether to invest in a new machine. The new machine will increase cash flow by $475,000 per year. You believe the technology used in the machine has a 10-year life; in other words, no matter when you purchase the machine, it will be obsolete 10 years from today. The machine is currently priced at $2,900,000. The cost of the machine will decline by $210,000 per year until it reaches $2,270,000, where it will remain. If your required return is 9 percent, should you purchase the machine? If so, when should you purchase it?

6. **Decision Trees**   Ang Electronics, Inc., has developed a new DVDR. If the DVDR is successful, the present value of the payoff (when the product is brought to market) is $34 million. If the DVDR fails, the present value of the payoff is $12 million. If the product goes directly to market, there is a 50 percent chance of success. Alternatively, Ang can delay the launch by one year and spend $1.3 million to test market the DVDR. Test marketing would allow the firm to improve the product and increase the probability of success to 80 percent. The appropriate discount rate is 11 percent. Should the firm conduct test marketing?

7. **Decision Trees**   The manager for a growing firm is considering the launch of a new product. If the product goes directly to market, there is a 50 percent chance of success. For $175,000 the manager can conduct a focus group that will increase the product's chance of success to 65 percent. Alternatively, the manager has the option to pay a consulting firm $390,000 to research the market and refine the product. The consulting firm successfully launches new products 80 percent of the time. If the firm successfully launches the product, the payoff will be $1.9 million. If the product is a failure, the NPV is zero. Which action will result in the highest expected payoff to the firm?

8. **Decision Trees**   B&B has a new baby powder ready to market. If the firm goes directly to the market with the product, there is only a 55 percent chance of success. However, the firm can conduct customer segment research, which will take a year and cost $1.2 million. By going through research, B&B will be able to better target potential customers and will increase the probability of success to 70 percent.

If successful, the baby powder will bring a present value profit (at time of initial selling) of $19 million. If unsuccessful, the present value payoff is only $6 million. Should the firm conduct customer segment research or go directly to market? The appropriate discount rate is 15 percent.

9. **Financial Break-even Analysis** You are considering investing in a company that cultivates abalone for sale to local restaurants. Use the following information:

Sales price per abalone	= $35
Variable costs per abalone	= $6.10
Fixed costs per year	= $375,000
Depreciation per year	= $120,000
Tax rate	= 35%

The discount rate for the company is 15 percent, the initial investment in equipment is $840,000, and the project's economic life is seven years. Assume the equipment is depreciated on a straight-line basis over the project's life.

a. What is the accounting break-even level for the project?
b. What is the financial break-even level for the project?

10. **Financial Break-even** Niko has purchased a brand new machine to produce its High Flight line of shoes. The machine has an economic life of five years. The depreciation schedule for the machine is straight-line with no salvage value. The machine costs $575,000. The sales price per pair of shoes is $60, while the variable cost is $14. $165,000 of fixed costs per year are attributed to the machine. Assume that the corporate tax rate is 34 percent and the appropriate discount rate is 8 percent. What is the financial break-even point?

INTERMEDIATE
(Questions 11–25)

11. **Break-even Intuition** Consider a project with a required return of R percent that costs I and will last for N years. The project uses straight-line depreciation to zero over the N-year life; there are neither salvage value nor net working capital requirements.

a. At the accounting break-even level of output, what is the IRR of this project? The payback period? The NPV?
b. At the cash break-even level of output, what is the IRR of this project? The payback period? The NPV?
c. At the financial break-even level of output, what is the IRR of this project? The payback period? The NPV?

12. **Sensitivity Analysis** Consider a four-year project with the following information: Initial fixed asset investment = $480,000; straight-line depreciation to zero over the four-year life; zero salvage value; price = $37; variable costs = $23; fixed costs = $195,000; quantity sold = 90,000 units; tax rate = 34 percent. How sensitive is OCF to changes in quantity sold?

13. **Project Analysis** You are considering a new product launch. The project will cost $820,000, have a four-year life, and have no salvage value; depreciation is straight-line to zero. Sales are projected at 450 units per year; price per unit will be $18,000; variable cost per unit will be $15,400; and fixed costs will be $610,000 per year. The required return on the project is 15 percent, and the relevant tax rate is 35 percent.

a. Based on your experience, you think the unit sales, variable cost, and fixed cost projections given here are probably accurate to within ±10 percent. What are the upper and lower bounds for these projections? What is the base-case NPV? What are the best-case and worst-case scenarios?

Chapter 7   Risk Analysis, Real Options, and Capital Budgeting   **231**

   b. Evaluate the sensitivity of your base-case NPV to changes in fixed costs.

   c. What is the accounting break-even level of output for this project?

14. **Project Analysis**   McGilla Golf has decided to sell a new line of golf clubs. The clubs will sell for $875 per set and have a variable cost of $430 per set. The company has spent $150,000 for a marketing study that determined the company will sell 60,000 sets per year for seven years. The marketing study also determined that the company will lose sales of 12,000 sets of its high-priced clubs. The high-priced clubs sell at $1,100 and have variable costs of $620. The company will also increase sales of its cheap clubs by 15,000 sets. The cheap clubs sell for $400 and have variable costs of $210 per set. The fixed costs each year will be $9,300,000. The company has also spent $1,000,000 on research and development for the new clubs. The plant and equipment required will cost $29,400,000 and will be depreciated on a straight-line basis. The new clubs will also require an increase in net working capital of $1,400,000 that will be returned at the end of the project. The tax rate is 40 percent, and the cost of capital is 14 percent. Calculate the payback period, the NPV, and the IRR.

15. **Scenario Analysis**   In the previous problem, you feel that the values are accurate to within only ± 10 percent. What are the best-case and worst-case NPVs? (*Hint:* The price and variable costs for the two existing sets of clubs are known with certainty; only the sales gained or lost are uncertain.)

16. **Sensitivity Analysis**   McGilla Golf would like to know the sensitivity of NPV to changes in the price of the new clubs and the quantity of new clubs sold. What is the sensitivity of the NPV to each of these variables?

17. **Abandonment Value**   We are examining a new project. We expect to sell 9,000 units per year at $35 net cash flow apiece for the next 10 years. In other words, the annual operating cash flow is projected to be $35 × 9,000 = $315,000. The relevant discount rate is 16 percent, and the initial investment required is $1,350,000.

   a. What is the base-case NPV?

   b. After the first year, the project can be dismantled and sold for $950,000. If expected sales are revised based on the first year's performance, when would it make sense to abandon the investment? In other words, at what level of expected sales would it make sense to abandon the project?

   c. Explain how the $950,000 abandonment value can be viewed as the opportunity cost of keeping the project in one year.

18. **Abandonment**   In the previous problem, suppose you think it is likely that expected sales will be revised upward to 11,000 units if the first year is a success and revised downward to 4,000 units if the first year is not a success.

   a. If success and failure are equally likely, what is the NPV of the project? Consider the possibility of abandonment in answering.

   b. What is the value of the option to abandon?

19. **Abandonment and Expansion**   In the previous problem, suppose the scale of the project can be doubled in one year in the sense that twice as many units can be produced and sold. Naturally, expansion would be desirable only if the project were a success. This implies that if the project is a success, projected sales after expansion will be 22,000. Again assuming that success and failure are equally likely, what is the NPV of the project? Note that abandonment is still an option if the project is a failure. What is the value of the option to expand?

20. **Break-even Analysis**   Your buddy comes to you with a sure-fire way to make some quick money and help pay off your student loans. His idea is to sell T-shirts with the words "I get" on them. "You get it?" He says, "You see all those bumper stickers and T-shirts that say 'got milk' or 'got surf.' So this says, 'I get.' It's funny! All we have to do is buy a used silk screen press for $5,600 and we are in business!" Assume there are no fixed costs, and you depreciate the $5,600 in the first period. Taxes are 30 percent.

a. What is the accounting break-even point if each shirt costs $4.50 to make and you can sell them for $10 apiece?

Now assume one year has passed and you have sold 5,000 shirts! You find out that the Dairy Farmers of America have copyrighted the "got milk" slogan and are requiring you to pay $15,000 to continue operations. You expect this craze will last for another three years and that your discount rate is 12 percent.

b. What is the financial break-even point for your enterprise now?

21. **Decision Trees**   Young screenwriter Carl Draper has just finished his first script. It has action, drama, and humor, and he thinks it will be a blockbuster. He takes the script to every motion picture studio in town and tries to sell it but to no avail. Finally, ACME studios offers to buy the script for either (a) $10,000 or (b) 1 percent of the movie's profits. There are two decisions the studio will have to make. First is to decide if the script is good or bad, and second if the movie is good or bad. First, there is a 90 percent chance that the script is bad. If it is bad, the studio does nothing more and throws the script out. If the script is good, they will shoot the movie. After the movie is shot, the studio will review it, and there is a 60 percent chance that the movie is bad. If the movie is bad, the movie will not be promoted and will not turn a profit. If the movie is good, the studio will promote heavily; the average profit for this type of movie is $15 million. Carl rejects the $10,000 and says he wants the 1 percent of profits. Was this a good decision by Carl?

22. **Option to Wait**   Hickock Mining is evaluating when to open a gold mine. The mine has 48,000 ounces of gold left that can be mined, and mining operations will produce 6,000 ounces per year. The required return on the gold mine is 12 percent, and it will cost $34 million to open the mine. When the mine is opened, the company will sign a contract that will guarantee the price of gold for the remaining life of the mine. If the mine is opened today, each ounce of gold will generate an aftertax cash flow of $1,400 per ounce. If the company waits one year, there is a 60 percent probability that the contract price will generate an aftertax cash flow of $1,600 per ounce and a 40 percent probability that the aftertax cash flow will be $1,300 per ounce. What is the value of the option to wait?

23. **Abandonment Decisions**   Allied Products, Inc., is considering a new product launch. The firm expects to have an annual operating cash flow of $10.5 million for the next 10 years. Allied Products uses a discount rate of 13 percent for new product launches. The initial investment is $51 million. Assume that the project has no salvage value at the end of its economic life.

a. What is the NPV of the new product?
b. After the first year, the project can be dismantled and sold for $31 million. If the estimates of remaining cash flows are revised based on the first year's experience, at what level of expected cash flows does it make sense to abandon the project?

24. **Expansion Decisions**   Applied Nanotech is thinking about introducing a new surface cleaning machine. The marketing department has come up with the estimate that Applied Nanotech can sell 15 units per year at $305,000 net cash flow per unit for the next five years. The engineering department has come up with the estimate that developing the machine will take a $15 million initial investment. The finance department has estimated that a 16 percent discount rate should be used.

a. What is the base-case NPV?

b. If unsuccessful, after the first year the project can be dismantled and will have an aftertax salvage value of $11 million. Also, after the first year, expected cash flows will be revised up to 20 units per year or to 0 units, with equal probability. What is the revised NPV?

25. **Scenario Analysis** You are the financial analyst for a tennis racket manufacturer. The company is considering using a graphitelike material in its tennis rackets. The company has estimated the information in the following table about the market for a racket with the new material. The company expects to sell the racket for six years. The equipment required for the project has no salvage value. The required return for projects of this type is 13 percent, and the company has a 40 percent tax rate. Should you recommend the project?

	Pessimistic	Expected	Optimistic
Market size	105,000	120,000	145,000
Market share	20%	23%	25%
Selling price	$ 150	$ 155	$ 161
Variable costs per unit	$ 104	$ 99	$ 98
Fixed costs per year	$ 965,000	$ 920,000	$ 890,000
Initial investment	$1,900,000	$1,800,000	$1,700,000

CHALLENGE
(Questions 26–30)

26. **Scenario Analysis** Consider a project to supply Detroit with 35,000 tons of machine screws annually for automobile production. You will need an initial $2,900,000 investment in threading equipment to get the project started; the project will last for five years. The accounting department estimates that annual fixed costs will be $495,000 and that variable costs should be $285 per ton; accounting will depreciate the initial fixed asset investment straight-line to zero over the five-year project life. It also estimates a salvage value of $300,000 after dismantling costs. The marketing department estimates that the automakers will let the contract at a selling price of $345 per ton. The engineering department estimates you will need an initial net working capital investment of $450,000. You require a 13 percent return and face a marginal tax rate of 38 percent on this project.

a. What is the estimated OCF for this project? The NPV? Should you pursue this project?

b. Suppose you believe that the accounting department's initial cost and salvage value projections are accurate only to within ±15 percent; the marketing department's price estimate is accurate only to within ±10 percent; and the engineering department's net working capital estimate is accurate only to within ±5 percent. What is your worst-case scenario for this project? Your best-case scenario? Do you still want to pursue the project?

27. **Sensitivity Analysis** In Problem 26, suppose you're confident about your own projections, but you're a little unsure about Detroit's actual machine screw requirements. What is the sensitivity of the project OCF to changes in the quantity supplied? What about the sensitivity of NPV to changes in quantity supplied? Given the sensitivity number you calculated, is there some minimum level of output below which you wouldn't want to operate? Why?

28. **Abandonment Decisions** Consider the following project for Hand Clapper, Inc. The company is considering a four-year project to manufacture clap-command garage door openers. This project requires an initial investment of $8 million that will be depreciated straight-line to zero over the project's life. An initial investment in net

www.mhhe.com/rwj

working capital of $950,000 is required to support spare parts inventory; this cost is fully recoverable whenever the project ends. The company believes it can generate $6.85 million in pretax revenues with $2.8 million in total pretax operating costs. The tax rate is 38 percent, and the discount rate is 16 percent. The market value of the equipment over the life of the project is as follows:

Year	Market Value ($ millions)
1	$5.1
2	3.8
3	3.2
4	0.0

a. Assuming Hand Clapper operates this project for four years, what is the NPV?

b. Now compute the project NPVs assuming the project is abandoned after only one year, after two years, and after three years. What economic life for this project maximizes its value to the firm? What does this problem tell you about not considering abandonment possibilities when evaluating projects?

29. **Abandonment Decisions**   M.V.P. Games, Inc., has hired you to perform a feasibility study of a new video game that requires a $7 million initial investment. M.V.P. expects a total annual operating cash flow of $1.3 million for the next 10 years. The relevant discount rate is 10 percent. Cash flows occur at year-end.

a. What is the NPV of the new video game?

b. After one year, the estimate of remaining annual cash flows will be revised either upward to $2.2 million or downward to $285,000. Each revision has an equal probability of occurring. At that time, the video game project can be sold for $2.6 million. What is the revised NPV given that the firm can abandon the project after one year?

30. **Financial Break-even**   The Cornchopper Company is considering the purchase of a new harvester. Cornchopper has hired you to determine the break-even purchase price in terms of present value of the harvester. This break-even purchase price is the price at which the project's NPV is zero. Base your analysis on the following facts:

• The new harvester is not expected to affect revenues, but pretax operating expenses will be reduced by $13,000 per year for 10 years.
• The old harvester is now 5 years old, with 10 years of its scheduled life remaining. It was originally purchased for $65,000 and has been depreciated by the straight-line method.
• The old harvester can be sold for $21,000 today.
• The new harvester will be depreciated by the straight-line method over its 10-year life.
• The corporate tax rate is 34 percent.
• The firm's required rate of return is 15 percent.
• The initial investment, the proceeds from selling the old harvester, and any resulting tax effects occur immediately.
• All other cash flows occur at year-end.
• The market value of each harvester at the end of its economic life is zero.

Excel Master It!

Dahlia Simmons, CFO of Ulrich Enterprises, is analyzing a new project to sell solar powered batteries for cell phones. Dahlia has estimated the following probability distributions for the variables in the project:

Probability	10%	30%	40%	20%		
Industry demand	80,000,000	95,000,000	108,000,000	124,000,000		
Probability	5%	20%	20%	25%	20%	10%
Ulrich market share	1%	2%	3%	4%	5%	6%
Probability	20%	70%	10%			
Initial cost	$60,000,000	$65,000,000	$72,000,000			
Probability	20%	65%	15%			
VC per unit	$24	$26	$29			
Probability	15%	25%	40%	20%		
Fixed costs	$20,000,000	$24,000,000	$27,000,000	$31,000,000		

The unit price depends on the industry demand since a greater demand will result in a higher price. Dahlia determines that the price per unit will be given by the equation:

$$\text{Price} = \text{Industry demand} / 2{,}000{,}000 +/- \$2$$

The random "+/−$2" term represents an increase or decrease in price according to the following distribution:

Probability	45%	55%
Price randomness	−$2	$2

The length of the project, tax rate, and required return are:

Project length (years)	6
Tax rate	34%
Required return	14%

a. Create a Monte Carlo simulation for the project with at least 500 runs. Calculate the IRR for each run. Note that the IRR function in Excel will return an error if the IRR of the project is too low. For example, what is the IRR if both the initial cash flow and the operating cash flows are negative? The IRR is less than −100 percent. This is not a problem when you are calculating the IRR one time since you can see the IRR is too low, but when you are running 500 or more iterations it can create a problem trying to summarize the results. Because of this issue, you should create an IF statement that tests if the operating cash flow divided by the absolute value of the initial investment is less than .1. If this is the case, the cell will return an IRR of −99.99 percent, or else the cell will calculate the IRR.

b. Create a graph of the distribution of the IRRs from the Monte Carlo simulation for different ranges of IRR.

c. Create a graph for the cumulative probability function for the IRR distribution.

BUNYAN LUMBER, LLC

Bunyan Lumber, LLC, harvests timber and delivers logs to timber mills for sale. The company was founded 70 years ago by Pete Bunyan. The current CEO is Paula Bunyan, the granddaughter of the founder. The company is currently evaluating a 5,000-acre forest it owns in Oregon. Paula has asked Steve Boles, the company's finance officer, to evaluate the project. Paula's concern is when the company should harvest the timber.

Lumber is sold by the company for its "pond value." Pond value is the amount a mill will pay for a log delivered to the mill location. The price paid for logs delivered to a mill is quoted in dollars per thousands of board feet (MBF), and the price depends on the grade of the logs. The forest Bunyan Lumber is evaluating was planted by the company 20 years ago and is made up entirely of Douglas fir trees. The table here shows the current price per MBF for the three grades of timber the company feels will come from the stand:

Timber Grade	Price per MBF
1P	$620
2P	605
3P	595

Steve believes that the pond value of lumber will increase at the inflation rate. The company is planning to thin the forest today, and it expects to realize a positive cash flow of $1,000 per acre from thinning. The thinning is done to increase the growth rate of the remaining trees, and it is always done 20 years following a planting.

The major decision the company faces is when to log the forest. When the company logs the forest, it will immediately replant saplings, which will allow for a future harvest. The longer the forest is allowed to grow, the larger the harvest becomes per acre. Additionally, an older forest has a higher grade of timber. Steve has compiled the following table with the expected harvest per acre in thousands of board feet, along with the breakdown of the timber grades:

Years from Today to Begin Harvest	Harvest (MBF) per Acre	Timber Grade		
		1P	2P	3P
20	14.1	16%	36%	48%
25	16.4	20	40	40
30	17.3	22	43	35
35	18.1	24	45	31

The company expects to lose 5 percent of the timber it cuts due to defects and breakage.

The forest will be clear-cut when the company harvests the timber. This method of harvesting allows for faster growth of replanted trees. All of the harvesting, processing, replanting, and transportation are to be handled by subcontractors hired by Bunyan Lumber. The cost of the logging is expected to be $140 per MBF. A road system has to be constructed and is expected to cost $50 per MBF on average. Sales preparation and administrative costs, excluding office overhead costs, are expected to be $18 per MBF.

As soon as the harvesting is complete, the company will reforest the land. Reforesting costs include the following:

	Cost per Acre
Excavator piling	$150
Broadcast burning	300
Site preparation	145
Planting costs	225

All costs are expected to increase at the inflation rate.

Assume all cash flows occur at the year of harvest. For example, if the company begins harvesting the timber 20 years from today, the cash flow from the harvest will be received 20 years from today. When the company logs the land, it will immediately replant the land with new saplings. The harvest period chosen will be repeated for the foreseeable future. The company's nominal required return is 10 percent, and the inflation rate is expected to be 3.7 percent per year. Bunyan Lumber has a 35 percent tax rate.

Clear-cutting is a controversial method of forest management. To obtain the necessary permits, Bunyan Lumber has agreed to contribute to a conservation fund every time it harvests the lumber. If the company harvested the forest today, the required contribution would be $250,000. The company has agreed that the required contribution will grow by 3.2 percent per year. When should the company harvest the forest?

www.mhhe.com/rwj

CHAPTER 8

Interest Rates and Bond Valuation

▲ For updates on the latest happenings in finance, visit www. rwjcorporatefinance. blogspot.com

When states, cities, or other local governments need to raise money, they turn to the municipal bond market. With about $2.8 trillion in total municipal bonds outstanding as of mid-2011, it seems that they reach out to this market quite a lot! Normally considered a relatively quiet financial market, the municipal bond market became much more exciting in 2010 and early 2011 because of the potential of municipal bond defaults. According to Standard & Poor's, 110 municipal bonds entered into default during 2010, representing $2.65 billion. What concerned investors even more was the potential for large defaults in the future. States such as California and Illinois were experiencing large deficits, and municipal bond defaults seemed possible. Congressional leaders furthered the belief that municipal bond defaults could explode when they proposed changing legislation to allow municipalities to declare bankruptcy more easily.

Of course, no municipal bond default to date has exceeded the infamous "Whoops" bonds. These were issued by the Washington Public Power Supply System (WPPSS) to fund the construction of five nuclear power plants. WPPSS defaulted on $2.25 billion worth of the bonds in 1983, the largest municipal bond default in U.S. history. Whoops, indeed! In the end, investors received only 10 to 40 percent of their original investment.

This chapter introduces you to bonds. We first use the techniques shown in Chapter 4 to value bonds. We then discuss bond features and how bonds are bought and sold. One important point is that bond values depend, in large part, on interest rates. We therefore cover the behavior of interest rates in the last section of the chapter.

8.1 Bonds and Bond Valuation

ExcelMaster
coverage online

This section introduces the PRICE, YIELD, DURATION, and MDURATION functions.

Corporations (and governments) frequently borrow money by issuing or selling debt securities called bonds. In this section, we describe the various features of corporate bonds. We then discuss the cash flows associated with a bond and how bonds can be valued using our discounted cash flow procedure.

BOND FEATURES AND PRICES

A bond is normally an interest-only loan, meaning that the borrower will pay the interest every period, but none of the principal will be repaid until the end of the loan. For example, suppose the Beck Corporation wants to borrow $1,000 for 30 years. The interest rate on similar debt issued by similar corporations is 12 percent. Beck will thus pay .12 × $1,000 = $120 in interest every year for 30 years. At the end of 30 years, Beck will repay the $1,000. As this example suggests, a bond is a fairly simple financing arrangement. There is, however, a rich jargon associated with bonds.

In our example, the $120 regular interest payments are called the bond's **coupons.** Because the coupon is constant and paid every year, this type of bond is sometimes called a *level coupon bond*. The amount repaid at the end of the loan is called the bond's **face value,** or **par value.** As in our example, this par value is usually $1,000 for corporate bonds, and a bond that sells for its par value is called a *par value bond*. Government bonds frequently have much larger face, or par, values. Finally, the annual coupon divided by the face value is called the **coupon rate** on the bond. Since $120/1,000 = 12$ percent, the Beck bond has a 12 percent coupon rate.

The number of years until the face value is paid is called the bond's time to **maturity.** A corporate bond will frequently have a maturity of 30 years when it is originally issued, but this varies. Once the bond has been issued, the number of years to maturity declines as time goes by.

BOND VALUES AND YIELDS

As time passes, interest rates change in the marketplace. Because the cash flows from a bond stay the same, the value of the bond fluctuates. When interest rates rise, the present value of the bond's remaining cash flows declines, and the bond is worth less. When interest rates fall, the bond is worth more.

To determine the value of a bond at a particular point in time, we need to know the number of periods remaining until maturity, the face value, the coupon, and the market interest rate for bonds with similar features. This interest rate required in the market on a bond is called the bond's **yield to maturity (YTM).** This rate is sometimes called the bond's *yield* for short. Given all this information, we can calculate the present value of the cash flows as an estimate of the bond's current market value.

For example, suppose the Xanth (pronounced "zanth") Co. were to issue a bond with 10 years to maturity. The Xanth bond has an annual coupon of $80, implying the bond will pay $80 per year for the next 10 years in coupon interest. In addition, Xanth will pay $1,000 to the bondholder in 10 years. The cash flows from the bond are shown in Figure 8.1. As illustrated in the figure, the cash flows have an annuity component (the coupons) and a lump sum (the face value paid at maturity).

Assuming similar bonds have a yield of 8 percent, what will this bond sell for? We estimate the market value of the bond by calculating the present value of the two

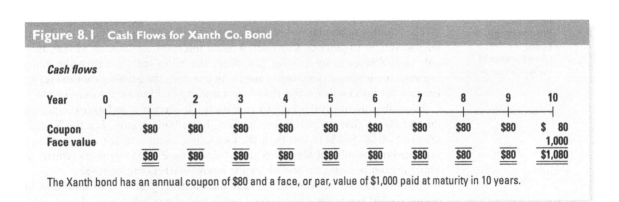

Figure 8.1   **Cash Flows for Xanth Co. Bond**

The Xanth bond has an annual coupon of $80 and a face, or par, value of $1,000 paid at maturity in 10 years.

components separately and adding the results together. First, at the going rate of 8 percent, the present value of the $1,000 paid in 10 years is:

$$\text{Present value} = \$1{,}000/1.08^{10} = \$1{,}000/2.1589 = \$463.19$$

Second, the bond offers $80 per year for 10 years; the present value of this annuity stream is:

$$
\begin{aligned}
\text{Annuity present value} &= \$80 \times (1 - 1/1.08^{10})/.08 \\
&= \$80 \times (1 - 1/2.1589)/.08 \\
&= \$80 \times 6.7101 \\
&= \$536.81
\end{aligned}
$$

We add the values for the two parts together to get the bond's value:

$$\text{Total bond value} = \$463.19 + 536.81 = \$1{,}000$$

This bond sells for exactly its face value. This is not a coincidence. The going interest rate in the market is 8 percent. Considered as an interest-only loan, what interest rate does this bond have? With an $80 coupon, this bond pays exactly 8 percent interest only when it sells for $1,000.

To illustrate what happens as interest rates change, suppose that a year has gone by. The Xanth bond now has nine years to maturity. If the interest rate in the market has risen to 10 percent, what will the bond be worth? To find out, we repeat the present value calculations with 9 years instead of 10, and a 10 percent yield instead of an 8 percent yield. First, the present value of the $1,000 paid in nine years at 10 percent is:

$$\text{Present value} = \$1{,}000/1.10^{9} = \$1{,}000/2.3579 = \$424.10$$

Second, the bond now offers $80 per year for nine years; the present value of this annuity stream at 10 percent is:

$$
\begin{aligned}
\text{Annuity present value} &= \$80 \times (1 - 1/1.10^{9})/.10 \\
&= \$80 \times (1 - 1/2.3579)/.10 \\
&= \$80 \times 5.7590 \\
&= \$460.72
\end{aligned}
$$

We add the values for the two parts together to get the bond's value:

$$\text{Total bond value} = \$424.10 + 460.72 = \$884.82$$

A good bond site to visit is **finance.yahoo.com/bonds,** which has loads of useful information.

Therefore, the bond should sell for about $885. In the vernacular, we say that this bond, with its 8 percent coupon, is priced to yield 10 percent at $885.

The Xanth Co. bond now sells for less than its $1,000 face value. Why? The market interest rate is 10 percent. Considered as an interest-only loan of $1,000, this bond only pays 8 percent, its coupon rate. Since the bond pays less than the going rate, investors are willing to lend only something less than the $1,000 promised repayment. Because the bond sells for less than face value, it is said to be a *discount bond*.

The only way to get the interest rate up to 10 percent is to lower the price to less than $1,000 so that the purchaser, in effect, has a built-in gain. For the Xanth bond, the price of $885 is $115 less than the face value, so an investor who purchased and kept the bond would get $80 per year and would have a $115 gain at maturity as well. This gain compensates the lender for the below-market coupon rate.

Another way to see why the bond is discounted by $115 is to note that the $80 coupon is $20 below the coupon on a newly issued par value bond, based on current market conditions. The bond would be worth $1,000 only if it had a coupon of $100 per year. In a sense, an investor who buys and keeps the bond gives up $20 per year for nine years. At 10 percent, this annuity stream is worth:

$$\text{Annuity present value} = \$20 \times (1 - 1/1.10^9)/.10$$
$$= \$20 \times 5.7590$$
$$= \$115.18$$

This is just the amount of the discount.

What would the Xanth bond sell for if interest rates had dropped by 2 percent instead of rising by 2 percent? As you might guess, the bond would sell for more than $1,000. Such a bond is said to sell at a *premium* and is called a *premium bond.*

This case is just the opposite of a discount bond. The Xanth bond now has a coupon rate of 8 percent when the market rate is only 6 percent. Investors are willing to pay a premium to get this extra coupon amount. In this case, the relevant discount rate is 6 percent, and there are nine years remaining. The present value of the $1,000 face amount is:

$$\text{Present value} = \$1,000/1.06^9 = \$1,000/1.6895 = \$591.89$$

The present value of the coupon stream is:

$$\text{Annuity present value} = \$80 \times (1 - 1/1.06^9)/.06$$
$$= \$80 \times (1 - 1/1.6895)/.06$$
$$= \$80 \times 6.8017$$
$$= \$544.14$$

We add the values for the two parts together to get the bond's value:

$$\text{Total bond value} = \$591.89 + 544.14 = \$1,136.03$$

Total bond value is therefore about $136 in excess of par value. Once again, we can verify this amount by noting that the coupon is now $20 too high, based on current market conditions. The present value of $20 per year for nine years at 6 percent is:

$$\text{Annuity present value} = \$20 \times (1 - 1/1.06^9)/.06$$
$$= \$20 \times 6.8017$$
$$= \$136.03$$

This is just as we calculated.

Based on our examples, we can now write the general expression for the value of a bond. If a bond has (1) a face value of F paid at maturity, (2) a coupon of C paid per period, (3) T periods to maturity, and (4) a yield of r per period, its value is:

$$\text{Bond value} = C \times [1 - 1/(1 + r)^T]/r + F/(1 + r)^T$$

$$\text{Bond value} = \frac{\text{Present value of the}}{\text{coupons}} + \frac{\text{Present value of}}{\text{the face amount}} \qquad (8.1)$$

Online bond calculators are available at **personal.fidelity.com**; interest rate information is available at **money.cnn.com/data/bonds** and **www.bankrate.com**.

EXAMPLE 8.1

Semiannual Coupons   In practice, bonds issued in the United States usually make coupon payments twice a year. So, if an ordinary bond has a coupon rate of 14 percent, the owner will receive a total of $140 per year, but this $140 will come in two payments of $70 each.

Suppose the yield to maturity on our bond is quoted at 16 percent. Bond yields are quoted like annual percentage rates (APRs); the quoted rate is equal to the actual rate per period multiplied

(continued)

by the number of periods. With a 16 percent quoted yield and semiannual payments, the true yield is 8 percent per six months. If our bond matures in seven years, what is the bond's price? What is the effective annual yield on this bond?

Based on our discussion, we know the bond will sell at a discount because it has a coupon rate of 7 percent every six months when the market requires 8 percent every six months. So, if our answer exceeds $1,000, we know that we have made a mistake.

To get the exact price, we first calculate the present value of the bond's face value of $1,000 paid in seven years. This seven-year period has 14 periods of six months each. At 8 percent per period, the value is:

$$\text{Present value} = \$1,000/1.08^{14} = \$1,000/2.9372 = \$340.46$$

The coupons can be viewed as a 14-period annuity of $70 per period. At an 8 percent discount rate, the present value of such an annuity is:

$$
\begin{aligned}
\text{Annuity present value} &= \$70 \times (1 - 1/1.08^{14})/.08 \\
&= \$70 \times (1 - .3405)/.08 \\
&= \$70 \times 8.2442 \\
&= \$577.10
\end{aligned}
$$

The total present value is the bond's price:

$$\text{Total present value} = \$340.46 + 577.10 = \$917.56$$

To calculate the effective yield on this bond, note that 8 percent every six months is equivalent to:

$$\text{Effective annual rate} = (1 + .08)^2 - 1 = 16.64\%$$

The effective yield, therefore, is 16.64 percent.

Learn more about bonds at **investorguide.com**.

As we have illustrated in this section, bond prices and interest rates always move in opposite directions. When interest rates rise, a bond's value, like any other present value, declines. Similarly, when interest rates fall, bond values rise. Even if the borrower is certain to make all payments, there is still risk in owning a bond. We discuss this next.

INTEREST RATE RISK

The risk that arises for bond owners from fluctuating interest rates is called *interest rate risk*. How much interest rate risk a bond has depends on how sensitive its price is to interest rate changes. This sensitivity directly depends on two things: the time to maturity and the coupon rate. As we will see momentarily, you should keep the following in mind when looking at a bond:

1. All other things being equal, the longer the time to maturity, the greater the interest rate risk.
2. All other things being equal, the lower the coupon rate, the greater the interest rate risk.

We illustrate the first of these two points in Figure 8.2. As shown, we compute and plot prices under different interest rate scenarios for 10 percent coupon bonds with maturities of 1 year and 30 years. Notice how the slope of the line connecting the prices is much steeper for the 30-year maturity than it is for the 1-year maturity. This

Figure 8.2
Interest Rate Risk and Time to Maturity

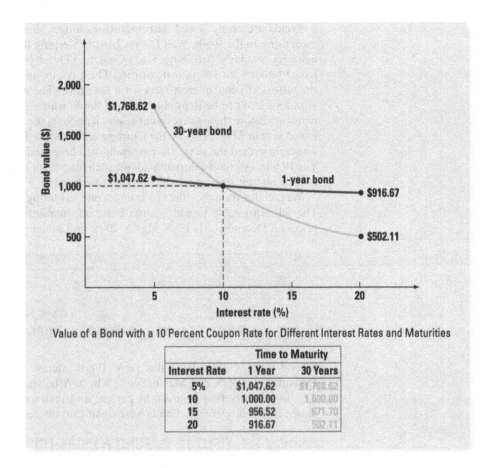

Value of a Bond with a 10 Percent Coupon Rate for Different Interest Rates and Maturities

| | Time to Maturity | |
Interest Rate	1 Year	30 Years
5%	$1,047.62	$1,768.62
10	1,000.00	1,000.00
15	956.52	671.70
20	916.67	502.11

steepness tells us that a relatively small change in interest rates will lead to a substantial change in the bond's value. In comparison, the one-year bond's price is relatively insensitive to interest rate changes.

Intuitively, shorter-term bonds have less interest rate sensitivity because the $1,000 face amount is received so quickly. For example, the present value of this amount isn't greatly affected by a small change in interest rates if the amount is received in, say, one year. However, even a small change in the interest rate, once compounded for, say, 30 years, can have a significant effect on present value. As a result, the present value of the face amount will be much more volatile with a longer-term bond.

The other thing to know about interest rate risk is that, like many things in finance and economics, it increases at a decreasing rate. For example, a 10-year bond has much greater interest rate risk than a 1-year bond has. However, a 30-year bond has only slightly greater interest rate risk than a 10-year bond.

The reason that bonds with lower coupons have greater interest rate risk is essentially the same. As we discussed earlier, the value of a bond depends on the present value of both its coupons and its face amount. If two bonds with different coupon rates have the same maturity, the value of the lower-coupon bond is proportionately more dependent on the face amount to be received at maturity. As a result, its value will fluctuate more as interest rates change. Put another way, the bond with the higher coupon has a larger cash flow early in its life, so its value is less sensitive to changes in the discount rate.

Bonds are rarely issued with maturities longer than 30 years, though there are exceptions. In the 1990s, Walt Disney issued "Sleeping Beauty" bonds with a 100-year maturity. Similarly, BellSouth, Coca-Cola, and Dutch banking giant ABN AMRO all issued bonds with 100-year maturities. These companies evidently wanted to lock in the historically low interest rates for a *long* time. The current record holder for corporations looks to be Republic National Bank, which sold bonds with 1,000 years to maturity. Before these fairly recent issues, it appears the last time 100-year bonds were issued was in May 1954, by the Chicago and Eastern Railroad. Just in case you are wondering when the next 100-year bond will be issued, you might have a long wait. The IRS has warned companies about such long-term issues and threatened to disallow the interest payment deduction on these bonds.

We can illustrate the effect of interest rate risk using the 100-year BellSouth issue. The following table provides some basic information on this issue, along with its prices on December 31, 1995, May 6, 2008, and January 24, 2011.

Maturity	Coupon Rate	Price on 12/31/95	Price on 5/6/08	Percentage Change in Price 1995–2008	Price on 1/24/11	Percentage Change in Price 2008–2011
2095	7.00%	$1,000	$1,008.40	+0.84%	$702.95	−30.3%

Several things emerge from this table. First, interest rates apparently fell between December 31, 1995, and May 6, 2008 (Why?). After that, however, they rose (Why?). The bond's price first gained 0.84 percent and then lost 30.3 percent. These swings illustrate that longer-term bonds have significant interest rate risk.

FINDING THE YIELD TO MATURITY: MORE TRIAL AND ERROR

Frequently, we will know a bond's price, coupon rate, and maturity date, but not its yield to maturity. For example, suppose we are interested in a six-year, 8 percent coupon bond. A broker quotes a price of $955.14. What is the yield on this bond?

We've seen that the price of a bond can be written as the sum of its annuity and lump-sum components. Knowing that there is an $80 coupon for six years and a $1,000 face value, we can say that the price is:

$$\$955.14 = \$80 \times [1 - 1/(1 + r)^6]/r + 1,000/(1 + r)^6$$

where r is the unknown discount rate, or yield to maturity. We have one equation here and one unknown, but we cannot solve for r directly without using a financial calculator or a spreadsheet application. Instead, we must use trial and error.

This problem is essentially identical to the one we examined in Chapter 4 when we tried to find the unknown interest rate on an annuity. However, finding the rate (or yield) on a bond is even more complicated because of the $1,000 face amount.

We can speed up the trial-and-error process by using what we know about bond prices and yields. In this case, the bond has an $80 coupon and is selling at a discount. We thus know that the yield is greater than 8 percent. If we compute the price at 10 percent:

$$\text{Bond value} = \$80 \times (1 - 1/1.10^6)/.10 + 1,000/1.10^6$$
$$= \$80 \times 4.3553 + 1,000/1.7716$$
$$= \$912.89$$

Table 8.1
Summary of Bond Valuation

I. Finding the Value of a Bond

Bond value = $C \times [1 - 1/(1 + r)^T]/r + F/(1 + r)^T$
where
C = Coupon paid each period
r = Discount rate per period
T = Number of periods
F = Bond's face value

II. Finding the Yield on a Bond

Given a bond value, coupon, time to maturity, and face value, one can find the implicit discount rate, or yield to maturity, only by trial and error. To do this, try different discount rates until the calculated bond value equals the given value (or let a spreadsheet do it for you). Remember that increasing the rate *decreases* the bond value.

Current market rates are available at **www.bankrate.com**.

At 10 percent, the value is lower than the actual price, so 10 percent is too high. The true yield must be somewhere between 8 and 10 percent. At this point, it's "plug and chug" to find the answer. You would probably want to try 9 percent next. If you did, you would see that this is in fact the bond's yield to maturity.

A bond's yield to maturity should not be confused with its **current yield,** which is simply a bond's annual coupon divided by its price. In the present example, the bond's annual coupon is $80, and its price is $955.14. Given these numbers, we see that the current yield is $80/955.14 = 8.38 percent, which is less than the yield to maturity of 9 percent. The reason the current yield is too low is that it only considers the coupon portion of your return; it doesn't consider the built-in gain from the price discount. For a premium bond, the reverse is true, meaning the current yield would be higher because it ignores the built-in loss.

Our discussion of bond valuation is summarized in Table 8.1. A nearby *Spreadsheet Applications* box shows how to find prices and yields the easy way.

EXAMPLE 8.2

Current Events A bond has a quoted price of $1,080.42. It has a face value of $1,000, a semi-annual coupon of $30, and a maturity of five years. What is its current yield? What is its yield to maturity? Which is bigger? Why?

Notice that this bond makes semiannual payments of $30, so the annual payment is $60. The current yield is thus $60/1,080.42 = 5.55 percent. To calculate the yield to maturity, refer back to Example 8.1. Now, in this case, the bond pays $30 every six months and it has 10 six-month periods until maturity. So, we need to find r as follows:

$$\$1,080.42 = \$30 \times [1 - 1/(1 + r)^{10}]/r + 1,000/(1 + r)^{10}$$

After some trial and error, we find that r is equal to 2.1 percent. But, the tricky part is that this 2.1 percent is the yield *per six months*. We have to double it to get the yield to maturity, so the yield to maturity is 4.2 percent, which is less than the current yield. The reason is that the current yield ignores the built-in loss of the premium between now and maturity.

EXAMPLE 8.3

Bond Yields   You're looking at two bonds identical in every way except for their coupons and, of course, their prices. Both have 12 years to maturity. The first bond has a 10 percent coupon rate and sells for $935.08. The second has a 12 percent coupon rate. What do you think it would sell for?

Because the two bonds are very similar, we assume they will be priced to yield about the same rate. We first need to calculate the yield on the 10 percent coupon bond. Proceeding as before, we know that the yield must be greater than 10 percent because the bond is selling at a discount. The bond has a fairly long maturity of 12 years. We've seen that long-term bond prices are relatively sensitive to interest rate changes, so the yield is probably close to 10 percent. A little trial and error reveals that the yield is actually 11 percent:

$$\text{Bond value} = \$100 \times (1 - 1/1.11^{12})/.11 + 1{,}000/1.11^{12}$$
$$= \$100 \times 6.4924 + 1{,}000/3.4985$$
$$= \$649.24 + 285.84$$
$$= \$935.08$$

With an 11 percent yield, the second bond will sell at a premium because of its $120 coupon. Its value is:

$$\text{Bond value} = \$120 \times (1 - 1/1.11^{12})/.11 + 1{,}000/1.11^{12}$$
$$= \$120 \times 6.4924 + 1{,}000/3.4985$$
$$= \$779.08 + 285.84$$
$$= \$1{,}064.92$$

ZERO COUPON BONDS

A bond that pays no coupons at all must be offered at a price much lower than its face value. Such bonds are called **zero coupon bonds,** or just zeroes.[1]

EXAMPLE 8.4

Yield to Maturity on a Zero under Annual Compounding   Suppose that the Geneva Electronics Co. issues a $1,000 face value, eight-year zero coupon bond. What is the yield to maturity on the bond if the bond is offered at $627? Assume annual compounding.

The yield to maturity, y, can be calculated from the equation:

$$\frac{\$1{,}000}{(1 + y)^8} = \$627$$

Solving the equation, we find that y equals 6 percent. Thus, the yield to maturity is 6 percent.

The example expresses the yield as an effective annual yield. However, even though no interest payments are made on the bond, zero coupon bond calculations use semi-annual periods in practice, to be consistent with the calculations for coupon bonds. We illustrate this practice in the next example.

---

[1]A bond issued with a very low coupon rate (as opposed to a zero coupon rate) is an original-issue discount (OID) bond.

SPREADSHEET APPLICATIONS

How to Calculate Bond Prices and Yields Using a Spreadsheet

Most spreadsheets have fairly elaborate routines available for calculating bond values and yields; many of these routines involve details that we have not discussed. However, setting up a simple spreadsheet to calculate prices or yields is straightforward, as our next two spreadsheets show:

	A	B	C	D	E	F	G	H
1								
2		Using a spreadsheet to calculate bond values						
3								
4	Suppose we have a bond with 22 years to maturity, a coupon rate of 8 percent, and a yield to							
5	maturity of 9 percent. If the bond makes semiannual payments, what is its price today?							
6								
7	Settlement date:	1/1/00						
8	Maturity date:	1/1/22						
9	Annual coupon rate:	.08						
10	Yield to maturity:	.09						
11	Face value (% of par):	100						
12	Coupons per year:	2						
13	Bond price (% of par):	**90.49**						
14								
15	The formula entered in cell B13 is =PRICE(B7,B8,B9,B10,B11,B12); notice that face value and bond							
16	price are given as a percentage of face value.							

	A	B	C	D	E	F	G	H
1								
2		Using a spreadsheet to calculate bond yields						
3								
4	Suppose we have a bond with 22 years to maturity, a coupon rate of 8 percent, and a price of							
5	$960.17. If the bond makes semiannual payments, what is its yield to maturity?							
6								
7	Settlement date:	1/1/00						
8	Maturity date:	1/1/22						
9	Annual coupon rate:	.08						
10	Bond price (% of par):	96.017						
11	Face value (% of par):	100						
12	Coupons per year:	2						
13	Yield to maturity:	**.084**						
14								
15	The formula entered in cell B13 is =YIELD(B7,B8,B9,B10,B11,B12); notice that face value and bond							
16	price are entered as a percentage of face value.							
17								

In our spreadsheets, notice that we had to enter two dates, a settlement date and a maturity date. The settlement date is just the date you actually pay for the bond, and the maturity date is the day the bond actually matures. In most of our problems, we don't explicitly have these dates, so we have to make them up. For example, since our bond has 22 years to maturity, we just picked 1/1/2000 (January 1, 2000) as the settlement date and 1/1/2022 (January 1, 2022) as the maturity date. Any two dates would do as long as they are exactly 22 years apart, but these are particularly easy to work with. Finally, notice that we had to enter the coupon rate and yield to maturity in annual terms and then explicitly provide the number of coupon payments per year.

EXAMPLE 8.5

Yield on a Zero under Real-World Convention of Semiannual Compounding   Suppose the Eight-Inch Nails (EIN) Company issues a $1,000 face value, five-year zero coupon bond. The initial price is set at $508.35. What is the yield to maturity using semiannual compounding?

The yield can be expressed as:

$$\frac{\$1{,}000}{(1 + y)^{10}} = \$508.35$$

The exponent in the denominator is 10, because five years contains 10 semiannual periods. The yield, y, equals 7 percent. Since y is expressed as a return per *six-month* interval, the yield to maturity, expressed as an annual percentage rate, is 14 percent.

8.2 Government and Corporate Bonds

The previous section investigated the basic principles of bond valuation without much discussion of the differences between government and corporate bonds. In this section, we discuss the differences.

GOVERNMENT BONDS

If you're nervous about the level of debt piled up by the U.S. government, *don't go to* **www.publicdebt. treas.gov**, or to **www.brillig.com/ debt_clock**! Learn all about government bonds at **www.newyorkfed. org**.

The biggest borrower in the world—by a wide margin—is everybody's favorite family member, Uncle Sam. In 2011, the total debt of the U.S. government was about $14.4 *trillion,* or over $46,200 per citizen (and growing!). When the government wishes to borrow money for more than one year, it sells what are known as Treasury notes and bonds to the public (in fact, it does so every month). Currently, outstanding Treasury notes and bonds have original maturities ranging from 2 to 30 years.

While most U.S. Treasury issues are just ordinary coupon bonds, there are two important things to keep in mind. First, U.S. Treasury issues, unlike essentially all other bonds, have no default risk because (we hope) the Treasury can always come up with the money to make the payments. Second, Treasury issues are exempt from state income taxes (though not federal income taxes). In other words, the coupons you receive on a Treasury note or bond are only taxed at the federal level.

State and local governments also borrow money by selling notes and bonds. Such issues are called *municipal* notes and bonds, or just "munis." Unlike Treasury issues, munis have varying degrees of default risk. The most intriguing thing about munis is that their coupons are exempt from federal income taxes (though not necessarily state income taxes), which makes them very attractive to high-income, high–tax bracket investors. Because of this enormous tax break, the yields on municipal bonds are much lower than the yields on taxable bonds.

EXAMPLE 8.6

Another good bond market site is **money.cnn.com**.

Aftertax Yield Comparison   Imagine that a long-term municipal bond selling at par is yielding 4.21 percent while a long-term Treasury bond selling at par yields 6.07 percent.[2] Further suppose an investor is in the 30 percent tax bracket. Ignoring any difference in default risk, would the investor prefer the Treasury bond or the muni?

To answer, we need to compare the *aftertax* yields on the two bonds. Ignoring state and local taxes, the muni pays 4.21 percent on both a pretax and an aftertax basis. The Treasury issue pays 6.07 percent before taxes, but it pays $.0607 \times (1 - .30) = .0425$, or 4.25 percent, once we account for the 30 percent tax bite. Given this, the Treasury bond still has a slightly better yield.

---

[2] Capital gains on municipal bonds are taxed, complicating the analysis somewhat. We avoid capital gains by assuming both bonds are priced at par.

EXAMPLE 8.7

Taxable versus Municipal Bonds Suppose taxable bonds are currently yielding 8 percent, while at the same time, munis of comparable risk and maturity are yielding 6 percent. Which is more attractive to an investor in a 40 percent tax bracket? What is the break-even tax rate? How do you interpret this rate?

For an investor in a 40 percent tax bracket, a taxable bond yields $8 \times (1 - .40) = 4.8$ percent after taxes, so the muni is much more attractive. The break-even tax rate is the tax rate at which an investor would be indifferent between a taxable and a nontaxable issue. If we let t^* stand for the break-even tax rate, we can solve for this tax rate as follows:

$$.08 \times (1 - t^*) = .06$$
$$1 - t^* = .06/.08 = .75$$
$$t^* = .25$$

Thus, an investor in a 25 percent tax bracket would make 6 percent after taxes from either bond.

CORPORATE BONDS

We pointed out that, while U.S. Treasury issues are default-free, municipal bonds face the possibility of default. Corporate bonds also face the possibility of default. This possibility generates a wedge between the *promised yield* and the *expected return* on a bond.

To understand these two terms, imagine a one-year corporate bond with a par value of $1,000 and an annual coupon of $80. Further assume that fixed-income analysts believe that this bond has a 10 percent chance of default and, in the event of default, each bondholder will receive $800. (Bondholders will likely receive something following default because the proceeds from any liquidation or reorganization go to the bondholders first. The stockholders typically receive a payoff only after the bondholders get paid in full.) Since there is a 90 percent probability that the bond will pay off in full and a 10 percent probability that the bond will default, the expected payoff from the bond at maturity is:

$$.90 \times \$1,080 + .10 \times \$800 = \$1,052$$

Assuming that the discount rate on risky bonds such as this one is 9 percent, the bond's value becomes:

$$\frac{\$1,052}{1.09} = \$965.14$$

What is the expected return on the bond? The expected return is clearly 9 percent, because 9 percent is the discount rate in the previous equation. In other words, an investment of $965.14 today provides an expected payoff at maturity of $1,052, implying a 9 percent expected return.

What is the promised yield? The corporation is promising $1,080 in one year, since the coupon is $80. Because the price of the bond is $965.14, the promised yield can be calculated from the following equation:

$$\$965.14 = \frac{\$1,080}{1 + y} \tag{8.2}$$

In this equation, y, which is the promised yield, is 11.9 percent. Why is the promised yield above the expected return? The promised yield calculation assumes that the bondholder *will* receive the full $1,080. In other words, the promised yield calculation ignores the probability of default. By contrast, the expected return calculation specifically takes the probability of default into account. What about in a risk-free security? The promised yield and the expected return are equal here, since the probability of default is zero, by definition, in a risk-free bond.

Now the promised yield on a corporate bond, as calculated in Equation 8.2, is simply the yield to maturity of the previous section. The promised yield can be calculated for any bond, be it corporate or government. All we need is the coupon rate, par value, and maturity. We do not need to know anything about the probability of default. Calculating the promised yield on a corporate bond is just as easy as calculating the yield to maturity on a government bond. In fact, the two calculations are the *same*. However, the promised yield, or equivalently, the yield to maturity, on a corporate bond is somewhat misleading. Our promised yield of 11.9 percent implies only that the bondholder will receive a return of 11.9 percent if the bond does not default. The promised yield does not tell us what the bondholder *expects* to receive.

For example, the Vanguard Intermediate-Term Treasury Bond Fund (TB Fund), a mutual fund composed of intermediate-term government bonds, had a yield of 3.86 percent in June 2011. The Vanguard High Yield Corporate Bond Fund (HY Fund), a mutual fund composed of intermediate-term corporate bonds with high default probabilities, had a yield of 7.16 percent on the same day. The yield on the HY Fund was 1.85 (=7.16/3.86) times as great as the yield on the TB Fund. Does that mean that an investor in the HY Fund expects a return about 2 times the return an investor in the TB Fund expects? Absolutely not. The yields quoted above are promised yields. They do not take into account any chance of default.

A professional analyst might very well find that, because of the high probability of default, the expected return on the HY Fund is actually below that expected on the TB Fund. However, we simply don't know this, one way or the other. Calculation of the expected return on a corporate bond is quite difficult, since one must assess the probability of default. However this number, if it can be calculated, would be very meaningful. As its name implies, it tells us what rate of return the bondholder actually expects to receive.

EXAMPLE 8.8

Yields on Government and Corporate Bonds   Both a default-free two-year government bond and a two-year corporate bond pay a 7 percent coupon. However, the government bond sells at par (or $1,000) and the corporate bond sells at $982.16. What are the yields on these two bonds? Why is there a difference in yields? Are these yields promised yields? Assume annual coupon payments.

Both bonds pay a coupon of $70 per year. The yield on the government bond can be calculated from the following equation:

$$\$1{,}000 = \frac{\$70}{1+y} + \frac{\$1{,}070}{(1+y)^2}$$

The yield on the government bond, y, is 7 percent.

The yield on the corporate bond can be calculated from the following equation:

$$\$982.16 = \frac{\$70}{1+y} + \frac{\$1{,}070}{(1+y)^2}$$

The yield on the corporate bond, y, is 8 percent.

The yield on the government bond is below that on the corporate bond because the corporate bond has default risk, while the government bond does not.

For both bonds, the yields we calculated are promised yields, because the coupons are promised coupons. These coupons will not be paid in full if there is a default. The promised yield is equal to the expected return on the government bond, since there is no chance of default. However, the promised yield is greater than the expected return on the corporate bond because default is a possibility.

While our previous discussion on corporate bonds depended heavily on the concept of default probability, estimation of default probabilities is well beyond the scope of this chapter. However, there is an easy way to obtain a qualitative appreciation of a bond's default risk.

BOND RATINGS

Firms frequently pay to have their debt rated. The two leading bond-rating firms are Moody's and Standard & Poor's (S&P). The debt ratings are an assessment of the creditworthiness of the corporate issuer. The definitions of creditworthiness used by Moody's and S&P are based on how likely the firm is to default and the protection creditors have in the event of a default.

It is important to recognize that bond ratings are concerned *only* with the possibility of default. Earlier, we discussed interest rate risk, which we defined as the risk of a change in the value of a bond resulting from a change in interest rates. Bond ratings do not address this issue. As a result, the price of a highly rated bond can still be quite volatile.

Bond ratings are constructed from information supplied by the corporation and other sources. The rating classes and some information concerning them are shown in the following table:

		Investment-Quality Bond Ratings				Low-Quality, Speculative, and/or "Junk" Bond Ratings					
		High Grade		Medium Grade		Low Grade		Very Low Grade			
Standard & Poor's		AAA	AA	A	BBB	BB	B	CCC	CC	C	D
Moody's		Aaa	Aa	A	Baa	Ba	B	Caa	Ca	C	

Moody's	S&P	
Aaa	AAA	Debt rated Aaa and AAA has the highest rating. Capacity to pay interest and principal is extremely strong.
Aa	AA	Debt rated Aa and AA has a very strong capacity to pay interest and repay principal. Together with the highest rating, this group comprises the high-grade bond class.
A	A	Debt rated A has a strong capacity to pay interest and repay principal, although it is somewhat more susceptible to the adverse effects of changes in circumstances and economic conditions than debt in higher-rated categories.
Baa	BBB	Debt rated Baa and BBB is regarded as having an adequate capacity to pay interest and repay principal. Whereas it normally exhibits adequate protection parameters, adverse economic conditions or changing circumstances are more likely to lead to a weakened capacity to pay interest and repay principal for debt in this category than in higher-rated categories. These bonds are medium-grade obligations.
Ba; B Caa Ca C	BB; B CCC CC C	Debt rated in these categories is regarded, on balance, as predominantly speculative with respect to capacity to pay interest and repay principal in accordance with the terms of the obligation. BB and Ba indicate the lowest degree of speculation, and Ca, CC, and C the highest degree of speculation. Although such debt is likely to have some quality and protective characteristics, these are outweighed by large uncertainties or major risk exposures to adverse conditions. Issues rated C by Moody's are typically in default.
	D	Debt rated D is in default, and payment of interest and/or repayment of principal is in arrears.

NOTE: At times, both Moody's and S&P use adjustments (called notches) to these ratings. S&P uses plus and minus signs: A+ is the strongest A rating and A− the weakest. Moody's uses a 1, 2, or 3 designation, with 1 being the highest. Moody's has no D rating.

Want to know
what criteria are
commonly used to
rate corporate and
municipal bonds?
Go to
**www.
standardandpoors.
com**, **www.
moodys.com**,
or
**www.fitchratings.
com**.

The highest rating a firm's debt can have is AAA or Aaa. Such debt is judged to be the best quality and to have the lowest degree of risk. For example, the 100-year BellSouth issue we discussed earlier was rated AAA. This rating is not awarded very often; AA or Aa ratings indicate very good quality debt and are much more common.

A large part of corporate borrowing takes the form of low-grade, or "junk," bonds. If these low-grade corporate bonds are rated at all, they are rated below investment grade by the major rating agencies. Investment-grade bonds are bonds rated at least BBB by S&P or Baa by Moody's.

Rating agencies don't always agree. Some bonds are known as "crossover" or "5B" bonds. The reason is that they are rated triple-B (or Baa) by one rating agency and double-B (or Ba) by another, implying a "split rating." For example, in May 2011, electric company Duquesne Light issued $350 million worth of 10.5-year notes that were recently rated Ba1 by Moody's and BBB by S&P.

A bond's credit rating can change as the issuer's financial strength improves or deteriorates. Of course downgrades can happen to country, or "sovereign," debt as well as corporate debt. For example, in 2010, S&P, Moody's, and Fitch (another major rating agency), all downgraded debt issued by Greece. For example, Moody's downgraded Greek debt from A3 to Ba1. The major reasons for the downgrades were the relatively large amount of Greek government debt and the country's weakening growth prospects. This combination led the rating agencies to conclude that the government's policy options were becoming more limited.

Credit ratings are important because defaults really do occur, and, when they do, investors can lose heavily. For example, in 2000, AmeriServe Food Distribution, Inc., which supplied restaurants such as Burger King with everything from burgers to giveaway toys, defaulted on $200 million in junk bonds. After the default, the bonds traded at just 18 cents on the dollar, leaving investors with a loss of more than $160 million.

Even worse in AmeriServe's case, the bonds had been issued only four months earlier, thereby making AmeriServe an NCAA champion. While that might be a good thing for a college basketball team, NCAA means "No Coupon At All" in the bond market, not a good thing for investors.

8.3 Bond Markets

ExcelMaster
coverage online

This section introduces the
COUPDAYSNC and ACCRINT
functions.

Bonds are bought and sold in enormous quantities every day. You may be surprised to learn that the trading volume in bonds on a typical day is many, many times larger than the trading volume in stocks (by trading volume, we simply mean the amount of money that changes hands). Here is a finance trivia question: What is the largest securities market in the world? Most people would guess the New York Stock Exchange. In fact, the largest securities market in the world in terms of trading volume is the U.S. Treasury market.

HOW BONDS ARE BOUGHT AND SOLD

Most trading in bonds takes place over the counter, or OTC, which means that there is no particular place where buying and selling occur. Instead, dealers around the country (and around the world) stand ready to buy and sell. The various dealers are connected electronically.

One reason the bond markets are so big is that the number of bond issues far exceeds the number of stock issues. There are two reasons for this. First, a corporation would typically have only one common stock issue outstanding, though there are exceptions. However, a single large corporation could easily have a dozen or more note and bond issues outstanding. Beyond this, federal, state, and local borrowing is simply enormous. For example, even a small city would usually have a wide variety of notes and bonds outstanding, representing money borrowed to pay for items like roads, sewers, and schools. When you think about how many small cities there are in the United States, you begin to get the picture!

Because the bond market is almost entirely OTC, it has historically had little or no *transparency*. A financial market is transparent if its prices and trading volume are easily observed. On the New York Stock Exchange, for example, one can see the price and quantity for every single transaction. In contrast, it is often not possible to observe either in the bond market. Transactions are privately negotiated between parties, and there is little or no centralized reporting of transactions.

Although the total volume of trading in bonds far exceeds that in stocks, only a very small fraction of the total outstanding bond issues actually trades on a given day. This fact, combined with the lack of transparency in the bond market, means that getting up-to-date prices on individual bonds can be difficult or impossible, particularly for smaller corporate or municipal issues. Instead, a variety of sources are commonly used for estimated prices.

BOND PRICE REPORTING

In 2002, transparency in the corporate bond market began to improve dramatically. Under new regulations, corporate bond dealers are now required to report trade information through what is known as the Trade Reporting and Compliance Engine (TRACE).

To learn more about TRACE, visit **www.finra.org**.

TRACE bond quotes are available at cxa.marketwatch.com/finra/marketdata. We went to the site and entered "Deere & Co" for the well-known manufacturer of green tractors. We found a total of 10 bond issues outstanding. Below you can see the information we found for seven of these.

Include in Watchlist	Bond Symbol	Issuer Name	Coupon	Maturity	Callable	Ratings Moody's	S&P	Fitch	Last Sale Price	Yield
☐	DE.IO	DEERE & CO	6.95	04/25/2014	No	A2	A	-	116.127	1.267
☐	DE.LY	DEERE & CO	4.38	10/16/2019	No	A2	A	-	107.179	3.382
☐	DE.GB	DEERE & CO	8.50	01/09/2022	No	A2	A	-	133.375	-
☐	DE.GC	DEERE & CO	6.55	10/01/2028	No	A2	A	-	117.519	5.023
☐	DE.LZ	DEERE & CO	5.38	10/16/2029	No	A2	A	-	109.480	4.604
☐	DE.GF	DEERE & CO	8.10	05/15/2030	No	A2	A	-	138.259	-
☐	DE.GG	DEERE & CO	7.13	03/03/2031	No	A2	A	-	128.373	-

If you go to the website and click on a particular bond, you will get a lot of information about the bond, including the credit rating, original issue information, and trade information. For example, when we checked, the first bond listed had not traded for two weeks.

Figure 8.3
Sample TRACE
Bond Quotations

SOURCE: FINRA reported
TRACE prices.

Issuer Name	Symbol	Coupon	Maturity	Rating Moody s/S&P/Fitch	High	Low	Last	Change	Yield%
HSBC USA INC	HBC.HCI	3.125%	Dec 2011	Aaa /AAA /AAA	101.603	101.596	101.602	-0.007	0.165
AT&T WIRELESS SVCS INC	T.KY	8.125%	May 2012	A2 /A- /A	106.792	106.765	106.780	0.011	0.670
CITIGROUP INC FDIC GTD TLGP	C.CR	2.875%	Dec 2011	Aaa /AAA /AAA	101.426	101.000	101.253	-0.132	0.457
WELLS FARGO & CO NEW	WFC.GDT	5.625%	Dec 2017	A1 /AA- /AA-	113.094	111.500	112.793	0.293	3.421
JPMORGAN CHASE & CO	JPM.LVL	4.650%	Jun 2014	Aa3 /A+ /AA-	108.837	107.874	108.040	-0.161	1.879
BANK OF AMERICA FDIC GTD TLGP	BAC.HGP	3.125%	Jun 2012	Aaa /AAA /AAA	103.034	102.642	102.938	-0.014	0.283
BB&T CORPORATION	BBT.GZ	3.850%	Jul 2012	A2 /A /A+	103.681	103.487	103.641	0.131	0.673
BANK AMER CORP	BAC.ACQ	5.000%	May 2021	A2 /A /	102.063	99.525	102.009	1.550	4.744
LLOYDS TSB BK PLC	LYG.HS	6.375%	Jan 2021	Aa3 /A- /	107.902	105.390	107.831	2.310	5.324
JPMORGAN CHASE & CO	JPM.NAN	4.400%	Jul 2020	Aa3 /A+ /AA-	101.805	98.223	100.928	1.306	4.276

Most Active Investment Grade Bonds

The Federal Reserve
Bank of St. Louis
maintains dozens of
online files containing
macroeconomic data
as well as rates on
U.S. Treasury issues.
Go to
**research.stlouisfed.
org/fred2**.

As shown in Figure 8.3, the Financial Industry Regulatory Authority (FINRA) provides a daily snapshot of the data from TRACE by reporting the most active issues. The information in the figure is largely self-explanatory. Notice that the price of the JP Morgan Chase & Co bond increased by 1.306 on this day. What do you think happened to the yield to maturity for this bond? Figure 8.3 focuses on the most active bonds with investment grade ratings, but the most active high-yield and convertible bonds are also available on the website.

As we mentioned before, the U.S. Treasury market is the largest securities market in the world. As with bond markets in general, it is an OTC market, so there is limited transparency. However, unlike the situation with bond markets in general, trading in Treasury issues, particularly recently issued ones, is very heavy. Each day, representative prices for outstanding Treasury issues are reported.

Figure 8.4 shows a portion of the daily Treasury bond listings from the website wsj .com. Examine the entry that begins "2021 Nov 15." Reading from left to right, the 2021 Nov 15 tells us that the bond's maturity is November of 2021. The 8.000 is the bond's coupon rate.

The next two pieces of information are the **bid** and **asked prices.** In general, in any OTC or dealer market, the bid price represents what a dealer is willing to pay for a security, and the asked price (or just "ask" price) is what a dealer is willing to take for it. The difference between the two prices is called the **bid-ask spread** (or just "spread"), and it represents the dealer's profit.

For historical reasons, Treasury prices are quoted in 32nds. Thus, the bid price on the 8.000 Nov 2021 bond, 143:27, actually translates into 143 $27/_{32}$, or 143.844 percent of face value. With a $1,000 face value, this represents $1,438.44. Because prices are quoted in 32nds, the smallest possible price change is $1/_{32}$. This is called the "tick" size.

The next number is the ask price, which is 143:29 or 143 $29/_{32}$ percent of par. The next number is the change in the asked price from the previous day, measured in ticks (i.e., in 32nds), so this issue's asked price fell by $6/_{32}$ of 1 percent, or .1875 percent,

Figure 8.4

Sample *Wall Street Journal* U.S. Treasury Bond Prices

SOURCE: Reprinted by permission of *The Wall Street Journal,* via Copyright Clearance Center © 2011 Dow Jones and Company, Inc., May 27, 2011. All Rights Reserved Worldwide.

Treasury Notes & Bonds

Maturity	Coupon	Bid	Asked	Chg	Asked yield
2013 May 31	3.500	106:03	106:04	unch.	0.4214
2015 Apr 30	2.500	104:30	104:31	+1	1.1992
2016 Mar 31	2.250	102:27	102:28	unch.	1.6305
2018 May 15	9.125	144:10	144:13	−2	2.2053
2018 May 31	2.375	99:28	99:28	+2	2.3945
2018 Nov 15	3.750	108:23	108:24	+1	2.4595
2019 Feb 15	8.875	145:03	145:06	−2	2.4162
2019 May 15	3.125	103:19	103:20	−1	2.6172
2019 Aug 15	8.125	140:29	141:00	−4	2.5561
2019 Nov 15	3.375	104:23	104:24	−1	2.7417
2020 Feb 15	3.625	106:10	106:11	−2	2.7998
2020 Nov 15	2.625	96:25	96:25	−3	3.0187
2021 Feb 15	3.625	104:31	104:31	−3	3.0292
2021 Aug 15	8.125	144:19	144:22	−6	3.0096
2021 Nov 15	8.000	143:27	143:29	−6	3.0612
2022 Aug 15	7.250	137:27	137:29	−6	3.1987
2022 Nov 15	7.625	141:24	141:26	−6	3.2294
2023 Feb 15	7.125	136:31	137:01	−6	3.2898
2023 Aug 15	6.250	128:14	128:16	−7	3.3810
2024 Nov 15	7.500	142:25	142:27	−9	3.4842
2025 Feb 15	7.625	144:14	144:16	−9	3.5078
2025 Aug 15	6.875	136:12	136:13	−8	3.5827
2026 Feb 15	6.000	126:10	126:12	−9	3.6640
2027 Feb 15	6.625	134:16	134:17	−8	3.7062
2028 Aug 15	5.500	120:29	120:30	−8	3.8274
2028 Nov 15	5.250	117:18	117:20	−9	3.8546
2029 Feb 15	5.250	117:19	117:20	−8	3.8658
2029 Aug 15	6.125	129:14	129:16	−10	3.8549
2030 May 15	6.250	131:16	131:18	−11	3.8823
2031 Feb 15	5.375	119:17	119:18	−9	3.9382
2036 Feb 15	4.500	105:16	105:18	−10	4.1390
2037 Feb 15	4.750	109:11	109:13	−11	4.1519
2037 May 15	5.000	113:15	113:17	−12	4.1440
2038 Feb 15	4.375	102:29	102:31	−11	4.1889
2038 May 15	4.500	104:30	105:00	−11	4.1886
2039 Feb 15	3.500	87:31	88:01	−10	4.2389
2039 May 15	4.250	100:12	100:14	−11	4.2240
2039 Nov 15	4.375	102:11	102:12	−11	4.2306
2040 Feb 15	4.625	106:20	106:22	−12	4.2215
2040 Nov 15	4.250	100:01	100:02	−12	4.2462
2041 Feb 15	4.750	108:24	108:25	−12	4.2287
2041 May 15	4.375	102:08	102:09	−12	4.2406

of face value from the previous day. Finally, the last number reported is the yield to maturity, based on the asked price. Notice that this is a premium bond because it sells for more than its face value. Not surprisingly, its yield to maturity (3.0612 percent) is less than its coupon rate (8 percent).

The last bond listed, the 2041 May 15, is often called the "bellwether" bond. This bond's yield is the one that is usually reported in the evening news. So, for example, when you hear that long-term interest rates rose, what is really being said is that the yield on this bond went up (and its price went down). Beginning in 2001, the Treasury announced that it would no longer sell 30-year bonds, leaving the 10-year note as the longest maturity issue sold. However, in 2006, the 30-year bond was resurrected and once again assumed bellwether status.

If you examine the yields on the various issues in Figure 8.4, you will clearly see that they vary by maturity. Why this occurs and what it might mean is one of the issues we discuss in our next section.

Current and historical Treasury yield information is available at **www.treasurydirect. gov**.

EXAMPLE 8.9

Treasury Quotes Locate the Treasury bond in Figure 8.4 maturing in May 2019. What is its coupon rate? What is its bid price? What was the *previous day's* asked price?

Its coupon rate is 3.125, or 3.125 percent of face value. The bid price is 103:19 or 103.59375 percent of face value. The ask price is 103:20, which is down by one tick from the previous day. This means that the ask price on the previous day was equal to $103\frac{20}{32} + \frac{1}{32} = 103\frac{21}{32} = 103.21$.

A NOTE ON BOND PRICE QUOTES

If you buy a bond between coupon payment dates, the price you pay is usually more than the price you are quoted. The reason is that standard convention in the bond market is to quote prices net of "accrued interest," meaning that accrued interest is deducted to arrive at the quoted price. This quoted price is called the **clean price.** The price you actually pay, however, includes the accrued interest. This price is the **dirty price,** also known as the "full" or "invoice" price.

An example is the easiest way to understand these issues. Suppose you buy a bond with a 12 percent annual coupon, payable semiannually. You actually pay $1,080 for this bond, so $1,080 is the dirty, or invoice, price. Further, on the day you buy it, the next coupon is due in four months, so you are between coupon dates. Notice that the next coupon will be $60.

The accrued interest on a bond is calculated by taking the fraction of the coupon period that has passed, in this case two months out of six, and multiplying this fraction by the next coupon, $60. So, the accrued interest in this example is 2/6 × $60 = $20. The bond's quoted price (i.e., its clean price) would be $1,080 – $20 = $1,060.[3]

---

[3]The calculation of accrued interest differs slightly between Treasury bonds and corporate bonds. The difference involves the calculation of the fractional coupon period. In our example above, we implicitly treated the months as having exactly the same length (i.e., 30 days each, 360 days in a year), which is consistent with the way corporate bonds are quoted. In contrast, actual day counts are used for Treasury bonds.

8.4 Inflation and Interest Rates

So far in this chapter, we have not considered the impact of inflation on interest rates. However, we did cover this relation in Section 6.3. We briefly review our previous discussion before considering additional ideas on the topic.

REAL VERSUS NOMINAL RATES

Suppose the one-year interest rate is 15.5 percent, so that anyone depositing $100 in a bank today will end up with $115.50 next year. Further imagine a pizza costs $5 today, implying that $100 can buy 20 pizzas. Finally, assume that the inflation rate is 5 percent, leading to the price of pizza being $5.25 next year. How many pizzas can you buy next year if you deposit $100 today? Clearly, you can buy $115.50/$5.25 = 22 pizzas. This is up from 20 pizzas, implying a 10 percent increase in purchasing power. Economists say that, while the *nominal* rate of interest is 15.5 percent, the *real* rate of interest is only 10 percent.

The difference between nominal and real rates is important and bears repeating:

The nominal rate on an investment is the percentage change in the number of dollars you have. The real rate on an investment is the percentage change in how much you can buy with your dollars. In other words, the real rate is the percentage change in your buying power.

We can generalize the relation between nominal rates, real rates, and inflation as:

$$1 + R = (1 + r) \times (1 + h)$$

where R is the nominal rate, r is the real rate, and h is the inflation rate.

In the preceding example, the nominal rate was 15.50 percent and the inflation rate was 5 percent. What was the real rate? We can determine it by plugging in these numbers:

$$1 + .1550 = (1 + r) \times (1 + .05)$$
$$1 + r = (1.1550/1.05) = 1.10$$
$$r = 10\%$$

This real rate is the same as we had before.

We can rearrange things a little as follows:

$$1 + R = (1 + r) \times (1 + h) \tag{8.3}$$
$$R = r + h + r \times h$$

What this tells us is that the nominal rate has three components. First, there is the real rate on the investment, r. Next, there is the compensation for the decrease in the value of the money originally invested because of inflation, h. The third component represents compensation for the fact that the dollars earned on the investment are also worth less because of inflation.

This third component is usually small, so it is often dropped. The nominal rate is then approximately equal to the real rate plus the inflation rate:

$$R \approx r + h$$

EXAMPLE 8.10

Nominal vs. Real Rates   If investors require a 10 percent real rate of return, and the inflation rate is 8 percent, what must be the approximate nominal rate? The exact nominal rate?

First of all, the nominal rate is approximately equal to the sum of the real rate and the inflation rate: 10 percent + 8 percent = 18 percent. From Equation 8.3, we have:

$$1 + R = (1 + r) \times (1 + h)$$
$$= 1.10 \times 1.08$$
$$= 1.1880$$

Therefore, the nominal rate will actually be closer to 19 percent.

It is important to note that financial rates, such as interest rates, discount rates, and rates of return, are almost always quoted in nominal terms. To remind you of this, we will henceforth use the symbol R instead of r in most of our discussions about such rates.

INFLATION RISK AND INFLATION-LINKED BONDS

Consider a 20-year Treasury bond with an 8 percent coupon. If the par value or the principal amount is $1,000, the holder will receive $80 a year for each of the next 20 years and, in addition, receive $1,000 in 20 years. Since the U.S. government has never defaulted, the bondholder is essentially guaranteed to receive these promised payments. Therefore, one can make the case that this is a riskless bond.

But is the bond really riskless after all? That depends on how you define risk. Suppose there is no chance of inflation, meaning that pizzas will always cost $5. We can be sure that the $1,080 ($1,000 of principal and $80 of interest) at maturity will allow us to buy $1,080/$5 = 216 pizzas. Alternatively, suppose that, over the next 20 years, there is a 50 percent probability of no inflation and a 50 percent probability of an annual inflation rate of 10 percent. With a 10 percent inflation rate, a pizza will cost $5 \times (1.10)^{20} = \$33.64$ in 20 years. The $1,080 payment will now allow the holder to buy only $1,080/$33.64 = 32.1 pizzas, not the 216 pizzas we calculated for a world of no inflation. Given the uncertain inflation rate, the investor faces **inflation risk;** while he knows that he will receive $1,080 at maturity, he doesn't know whether he can afford 216 or 32.1 pizzas.

Let's now speak in terms of nominal and real quantities. The *nominal value* of the payment at maturity is simply $1,080, because this is the actual cash the investor will receive. Assuming an inflation rate of 10 percent, the *real value* of this payment is only $1,080/(1.10)^{20} = \$160.54$. The real value measures the purchasing power of the payment. Since bondholders care about the purchasing power of their bond payments, they are ultimately concerned with real values, not nominal values. Inflation can erode the real value of the payments, implying that inflation risk is a serious concern, particularly in a time of high and variable inflation.

Do any bonds avoid inflation risk? As a matter of fact, yes. The U.S. government issues Treasury inflation-protected securities (TIPS), with promised payments specified in real terms, not nominal terms. A number of other countries also issue inflation-linked bonds. Imagine that a particular inflation-linked bond matures in two years, has a par value of $1,000, and pays a 2 percent coupon, where both the par value and the coupon are specified in real terms. Assuming annual payments, the bondholder will receive the following *real* payments:

End of Year 1	End of Year 2
$20	$1,020

Thus, the issuer is promising payments in real terms.

What amounts will the bondholder receive, expressed in nominal terms? Suppose the inflation rate over the first year is 3 percent and the inflation rate over the second year is 5 percent. The bondholder will receive the following *nominal* payments:[4]

End of Year 1	End of Year 2
$20 × 1.03 = $20.60	$1,020 × 1.03 × 1.05 = $1,103.13

While the bondholder knows the size of the payments in real terms when he buys the bond, he doesn't know the size of the payments in nominal terms until the inflation numbers are announced each period. Since TIPS and other inflation-linked bonds guarantee payments in real terms, we say that these bonds eliminate inflation risk.

Index-linked bonds are quoted in real yields. For example, suppose the bond trades at $971.50. The yield, y, would be solved by the following equation:

$$971.50 = \frac{20}{1 + y} + \frac{1,020}{(1 + y)^2}$$

In this example, y turns out to be 3.5 percent. Thus, we say that the real yield of the bond is 3.5 percent.

Are the yields on regular Treasury bonds related to the yields on TIPS? As of May 2012, the real yield on a 20-year TIPS was about 0 percent and the (nominal) yield on a 20-year Treasury bond was about 2.6 percent. As a first approximation, one could argue that the differential of 2.6 percent implies that the market expects an annual rate of inflation of 2.6 percent over the next 20 years.[5]

THE FISHER EFFECT

Imagine a world where, initially, there is no inflation and the nominal interest rate is 2 percent. Suppose that something, an action by the Federal Reserve or a change in the foreign exchange rate, unexpectedly triggers an inflation rate of 5 percent. What do you think will happen to the nominal interest rate? Your first thought might be that the interest rate will rise, because if the rate stays at 2 percent, the real rate would become negative. That is, a bank deposit of $100 today will still turn into $102 at the end of the year. However, if a hamburger priced at $1 today costs $1.05 next year, the $102 will only buy about 97 (=102/1.05) hamburgers next year. Since the initial $100 allows one to buy 100 hamburgers today, there is a reduction in purchasing power.

---

[4] This example is simplified. Actual payment calculations are often complex and differ across countries. For example, TIPS have semiannual payments with a lag in the inflation adjustment.

[5] As mentioned earlier, regular Treasury bonds are subject to inflation risk while TIPS are not subject to this risk. Since the risks of the two bonds are not equivalent, this approach should be viewed only as a first-pass estimate of anticipated inflation.

260   **Part II**   Valuation and Capital Budgeting

How much should the interest rate rise? A well-known economist, Irving Fisher, conjectured many decades ago that the nominal interest rate should rise just enough to keep the real interest rate at 2 percent. We can use Equation 8.3 to determine that the new nominal rate will be:

$$2\% + 5\% + 2\% \times 5\% = 7.1\%$$

Fisher's thinking is that investors are not foolish. They know that inflation reduces purchasing power and, therefore, they will demand an increase in the nominal rate before lending money. Fisher's hypothesis, typically called the **Fisher effect,** can be stated as:

A rise in the rate of inflation causes the nominal rate to rise just enough so that the real rate of interest is unaffected. In other words, the real rate is invariant to the rate of inflation.

While Fisher's reasoning makes sense, it's important to point out that the claim that the nominal rate will rise to 7.1 percent is only a hypothesis. It may be true and it may be false in any real-world situation; it does not *have* to be true. For example, if investors are foolish after all, the nominal rate could stay at 2 percent, even in the presence of inflation. Alternatively, even if investors understand the impact of inflation, the nominal rate may not rise all the way to 7.1 percent. That is, there may be some unknown force preventing a full rise.

How can one test the Fisher effect empirically? While a precise empirical test is beyond the scope of this chapter, Figure 8.5 gives at least a hint of the evidence. The

Figure 8.5
The Relation between One-Year Treasury Bond Yields and Inflation

SOURCE: *2011 Ibbotson SBBI® Classic Yearbook.*

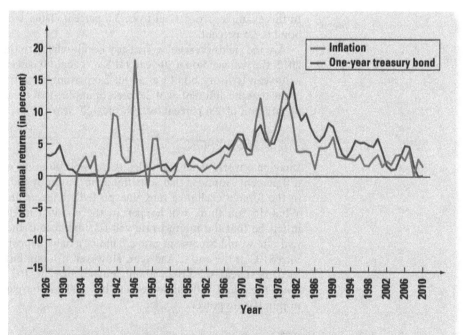

The figure plots both one-year Treasury bond yields and inflation rates in the United States. The two series appear to move together, implying that the inflation rate is an important determinant of the short-term interest rate.

figure plots two curves, one showing yields on one-year Treasury bonds over the last 85 years and the other showing inflation rates over the same period. It is apparent that the two curves move together. Both interest rates and inflation rates rose from the 1950s to the early 1980s while falling in the decades after. Thus, while statistical work is needed to establish a precise relationship, the figure suggests that inflation is an important determinant of the nominal interest rate.

8.5 Determinants of Bond Yields

ExcelMaster
coverage online

This section introduces
scrollbars and HLOOKUP.

We are now in a position to discuss the determinants of a bond's yield. As we will see, the yield on any particular bond is a reflection of a variety of factors.

THE TERM STRUCTURE OF INTEREST RATES

At any point in time, short-term and long-term interest rates will generally be different. Sometimes short-term rates are higher, sometimes lower. Figure 8.6 gives us a long-range perspective on this by showing about two centuries of short- and long-term interest rates. As shown, the difference between short- and long-term rates has ranged from essentially zero to several percentage points, both positive and negative.

The relationship between short- and long-term interest rates is known as the **term structure of interest rates.** To be a little more precise, the term structure of interest

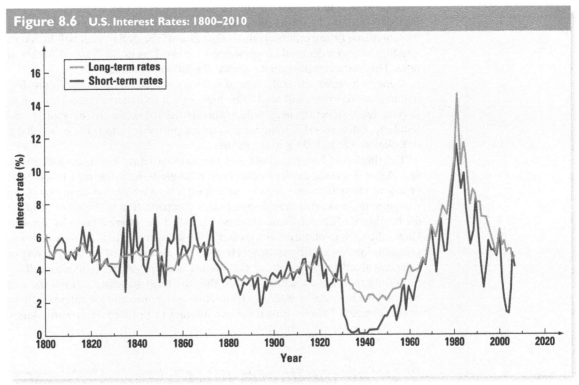

Figure 8.6 U.S. Interest Rates: 1800–2010

SOURCE: Jeremy J. Siegel, *Stocks for the Long Run,* 4th ed., © McGraw-Hill, 2008, updated by the authors.

rates tells us the *nominal* interest rates on *default-free, pure discount* bonds of all maturities. These rates are, in essence, "pure" interest rates because they contain no risk of default and involve just a single, lump-sum future payment. In other words, the term structure tells us the pure time value of money for different lengths of time.

When long-term rates are higher than short-term rates, we say that the term structure is upward sloping, and, when short-term rates are higher, we say it is downward sloping. The term structure can also be "humped." When this occurs, it is usually because rates increase at first, but then decline at longer-term maturities. The most common shape of the term structure, particularly in modern times, is upward sloping, but the degree of steepness has varied quite a bit.

What determines the shape of the term structure? There are three basic components. The first two are the ones we discussed in our previous section, the real rate of interest and the rate of inflation. The real rate of interest is the compensation investors demand for forgoing the use of their money. You can think of it as the pure time value of money after adjusting for the effects of inflation.

The real rate of interest is a function of many factors. For example, consider expected economic growth. High expected growth is likely to raise the real rate, and low expected growth is likely to lower it. The real rate of interest may differ across maturities, due to varying growth expectations among other factors. For example, the real rate may be low for short-term bonds and high for long-term ones because the market expects lower economic growth in the short term than the long term. However, the real rate of interest appears to have only a minor impact on the shape of the term structure.

In contrast, the prospect of future inflation very strongly influences the shape of the term structure. Investors thinking about loaning money for various lengths of time recognize that future inflation erodes the value of the dollars that will be returned. As a result, investors demand compensation for this loss in the form of higher nominal rates. This extra compensation is called the **inflation premium.**

If investors believe that the rate of inflation will be higher in the future, long-term nominal interest rates will tend to be higher than short-term rates. Thus, an upward-sloping term structure may reflect anticipated increases in the rate of inflation. Similarly, a downward-sloping term structure probably reflects the belief that the rate of inflation will be falling in the future.

The third, and last, component of the term structure has to do with interest rate risk. As we discussed earlier in the chapter, longer-term bonds have much greater risk of loss resulting from increases in interest rates than do shorter-term bonds. Investors recognize this risk, and they demand extra compensation in the form of higher rates for bearing it. This extra compensation is called the **interest rate risk premium.** The longer the term to maturity, the greater is the interest rate risk, so the interest rate risk premium increases with maturity. However, as we discussed earlier, interest rate risk increases at a decreasing rate, so the interest rate risk premium does as well.[6]

Putting the pieces together, we see that the term structure reflects the combined effect of the real rate of interest, the inflation premium, and the interest rate risk premium. Figure 8.7 shows how these can interact to produce an upward-sloping term

---

[6]In days of old, the interest rate risk premium was called a "liquidity" premium. Today, the term *liquidity premium* has an altogether different meaning, which we explore in our next section. Also, the interest rate risk premium is sometimes called a maturity risk premium. Our terminology is consistent with the modern view of the term structure.

Figure 8.7
The Term Structure
of Interest Rates

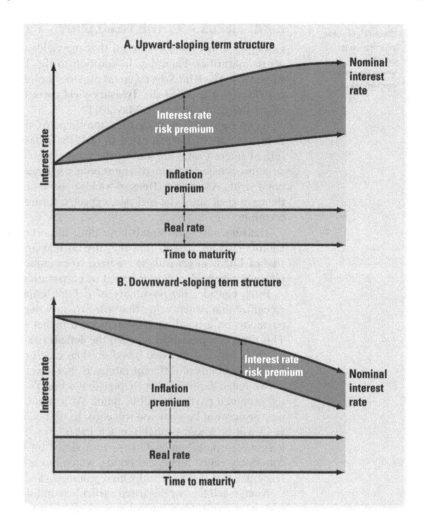

structure (in the top part of Figure 8.7) or a downward-sloping term structure (in the bottom part).

In the top part of Figure 8.7, notice how the rate of inflation is expected to rise gradually. At the same time, the interest rate risk premium increases at a decreasing rate, so the combined effect is to produce a pronounced upward-sloping term structure. In the bottom part of Figure 8.7, the rate of inflation is expected to fall in the future, and the expected decline is enough to offset the interest rate risk premium and produce a downward-sloping term structure. Notice that if the rate of inflation was expected to decline by only a small amount, we could still get an upward-sloping term structure because of the interest rate risk premium.

We assumed in drawing Figure 8.7 that the real rate would remain the same. However, as stated earlier, expected future real rates could be larger or smaller than the current real rate. Also, for simplicity, we used straight lines to show expected future inflation rates as rising or declining, but they do not necessarily have to look like this. They could, for example, rise and then fall, leading to a humped yield curve.

264   **Part II**   Valuation and Capital Budgeting

Online yield curve
information is
available at
**www.bloomberg.
com/markets**.

BOND YIELDS AND THE YIELD CURVE: PUTTING IT ALL TOGETHER

Going back to Figure 8.4, recall that the yields on Treasury notes and bonds differ across maturities. Each day, in addition to the Treasury prices and yields shown in Figure 8.4, *The Wall Street Journal* provides a plot of Treasury yields relative to maturity. This plot is called the **Treasury yield curve** (or just the yield curve). Figure 8.8 shows the yield curve as of May 2011.

As you probably now suspect, the shape of the yield curve is a reflection of the term structure of interest rates. In fact, the Treasury yield curve and the term structure of interest rates are almost the same thing. The only difference is that the term structure is based on pure discount bonds, whereas the yield curve is based on coupon bond yields. As a result, Treasury yields depend on the three components that underlie the term structure—the real rate, expected future inflation, and the interest rate risk premium.

Treasury notes and bonds have three important features that we need to remind you of: They are default-free, they are taxable, and they are highly liquid. This is not true of bonds in general, so we need to examine what additional factors come into play when we look at bonds issued by corporations or municipalities.

First, consider the possibility of default, commonly called credit risk. Investors recognize that issuers other than the Treasury may or may not make all the promised payments on a bond, so they demand a higher yield as compensation for this risk. This extra compensation is called the **default risk premium.** Earlier in the chapter, we saw how bonds were rated based on their credit risk. What you will find if you start looking at bonds of different ratings is that lower-rated bonds have higher yields.

We stated earlier in this chapter that a bond's yield is calculated assuming that all the promised payments will be made. As a result, it is really a promised yield, and it may or may not be what you will earn. In particular, if the issuer defaults, your actual yield will be lower, probably much lower. This fact is particularly important when it comes to junk bonds. Thanks to a clever bit of marketing, such bonds are now commonly called high-yield bonds, which has a much nicer ring to it; but now you recognize that these are really high *promised* yield bonds.

Next, recall that we discussed earlier how municipal bonds are free from most taxes and, as a result, have much lower yields than taxable bonds. Investors demand the

Figure 8.8
**The Treasury Yield
Curve: May 2011**

SOURCE: Reprinted by
permission of *The Wall
Street Journal,* via Copyright
Clearance Center © 2011
by Dow Jones & Company,
Inc. All Rights Reserved
Worldwide.

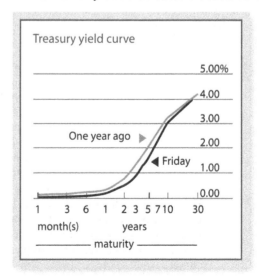

extra yield on a taxable bond as compensation for the unfavorable tax treatment. This extra compensation is the **taxability premium.**

Finally, bonds have varying degrees of liquidity. As we discussed earlier, there are an enormous number of bond issues, most of which do not trade on a regular basis. As a result, if you wanted to sell quickly, you would probably not get as good a price as you could otherwise. Investors prefer liquid assets to illiquid ones, so they demand a **liquidity premium** on top of all the other premiums we have discussed. As a result, all else being the same, less liquid bonds will have higher yields than more liquid bonds.

CONCLUSION

 ◄ To test your mastery of this material, take a quiz at mhhe. com/rwj

If we combine everything we have discussed, we find that bond yields represent the combined effect of no fewer than six factors. The first is the real rate of interest. On top of the real rate are five premiums representing compensation for (1) expected future inflation, (2) interest rate risk, (3) default risk, (4) taxability, and (5) lack of liquidity. As a result, determining the appropriate yield on a bond requires careful analysis of each of these factors.

Summary and Conclusions

This chapter has explored bonds, bond yields, and interest rates. We saw that:

1. Determining bond prices and yields is an application of basic discounted cash flow principles.

2. Bond values move in the direction opposite that of interest rates, leading to potential gains or losses for bond investors.

3. Bonds are rated based on their default risk. Some bonds, such as Treasury bonds, have no risk of default, whereas so-called junk bonds have substantial default risk.

4. Almost all bond trading is OTC, with little or no market transparency in many cases. As a result, bond price and volume information can be difficult to find for some types of bonds.

5. Bond yields and interest rates reflect six different factors: the real interest rate and five premiums that investors demand as compensation for inflation, interest rate risk, default risk, taxability, and lack of liquidity.

In closing, we note that bonds are a vital source of financing to governments and corporations of all types. Bond prices and yields are a rich subject, and our one chapter, necessarily, touches on only the most important concepts and ideas. There is a great deal more we could say, but, instead, we will move on to stocks in our next chapter.

Concept Questions

1. **Treasury Bonds** Is it true that a U.S. Treasury security is risk-free?

2. **Interest Rate Risk** Which has greater interest rate risk, a 30-year Treasury bond or a 30-year BB corporate bond?

3. **Treasury Pricing** With regard to bid and ask prices on a Treasury bond, is it possible for the bid price to be higher? Why or why not?

4. **Yield to Maturity** Treasury bid and ask quotes are sometimes given in terms of yields, so there would be a bid yield and an ask yield. Which do you think would be larger? Explain.

5. **Coupon Rate** How does a bond issuer decide on the appropriate coupon rate to set on its bonds? Explain the difference between the coupon rate and the required return on a bond.

6. **Real and Nominal Returns** Are there any circumstances under which an investor might be more concerned about the nominal return on an investment than the real return?

7. **Bond Ratings** Companies pay rating agencies such as Moody's and S&P to rate their bonds, and the costs can be substantial. However, companies are not required to have their bonds rated in the first place; doing so is strictly voluntary. Why do you think they do it?

8. **Bond Ratings** U.S. Treasury bonds are not rated. Why? Often, junk bonds are not rated. Why?

9. **Term Structure** What is the difference between the term structure of interest rates and the yield curve?

10. **Crossover Bonds** Looking back at the crossover bonds we discussed in the chapter, why do you think split ratings such as these occur?

11. **Municipal Bonds** Why is it that municipal bonds are not taxed at the federal level, but are taxable across state lines? Why is it that U.S. Treasury bonds are not taxable at the state level? (You may need to dust off the history books for this one.)

12. **Bond Market** What are the implications for bond investors of the lack of transparency in the bond market?

13. **Treasury Market** Take a look back at Figure 8.4. Notice the wide range of coupon rates. Why are they so different?

14. **Rating Agencies** A controversy erupted regarding bond-rating agencies when some agencies began to provide unsolicited bond ratings. Why do you think this is controversial?

15. **Bonds as Equity** The 100-year bonds we discussed in the chapter have something in common with junk bonds. Critics charge that, in both cases, the issuers are really selling equity in disguise. What are the issues here? Why would a company want to sell "equity in disguise"?

16. **Bond Prices versus Yields**

    a. What is the relationship between the price of a bond and its YTM?
    b. Explain why some bonds sell at a premium over par value while other bonds sell at a discount. What do you know about the relationship between the coupon rate and the YTM for premium bonds? What about for discount bonds? For bonds selling at par value?
    c. What is the relationship between the current yield and YTM for premium bonds? For discount bonds? For bonds selling at par value?

17. **Interest Rate Risk** All else being the same, which has more interest rate risk, a long-term bond or a short-term bond? What about a low coupon bond compared to a high coupon bond? What about a long-term, high coupon bond compared to a short-term, low coupon bond?

Questions and Problems

1. **Valuing Bonds**   What is the price of a 15-year, zero coupon bond paying $1,000 at maturity if the YTM is:
   a. 5 percent?
   b. 10 percent?
   c. 15 percent?

2. **Valuing Bonds**   Microhard has issued a bond with the following characteristics:
   Par: $1,000
   Time to maturity: 15 years
   Coupon rate: 7 percent
   Semiannual payments

   Calculate the price of this bond if the YTM is:
   a. 7 percent
   b. 9 percent
   c. 5 percent

3. **Bond Yields**   Watters Umbrella Corp. issued 15-year bonds 2 years ago at a coupon rate of 6.4 percent. The bonds make semiannual payments. If these bonds currently sell for 105 percent of par value, what is the YTM?

4. **Coupon Rates**   Rhiannon Corporation has bonds on the market with 11.5 years to maturity, a YTM of 7.6 percent, and a current price of $1,060. The bonds make semiannual payments. What must the coupon rate be on these bonds?

5. **Valuing Bonds**   Even though most corporate bonds in the United States make coupon payments semiannually, bonds issued elsewhere often have annual coupon payments. Suppose a German company issues a bond with a par value of €1,000, 19 years to maturity, and a coupon rate of 4.5 percent paid annually. If the yield to maturity is 3.9 percent, what is the current price of the bond?

6. **Bond Yields**   A Japanese company has a bond outstanding that sells for 92 percent of its ¥100,000 par value. The bond has a coupon rate of 2.8 percent paid annually and matures in 21 years. What is the yield to maturity of this bond?

7. **Calculating Real Rates of Return**   If Treasury bills are currently paying 4.5 percent and the inflation rate is 2.1 percent, what is the approximate real rate of interest? The exact real rate?

8. **Inflation and Nominal Returns**   Suppose the real rate is 2.4 percent and the inflation rate is 3.1 percent. What rate would you expect to see on a Treasury bill?

9. **Nominal and Real Returns**   An investment offers a 14 percent total return over the coming year. Alan Wingspan thinks the total real return on this investment will be only 10 percent. What does Alan believe the inflation rate will be over the next year?

10. **Nominal versus Real Returns**   Say you own an asset that had a total return last year of 12.5 percent. If the inflation rate last year was 5.3 percent, what was your real return?

11. **Using Treasury Quotes**   Locate the Treasury bond in Figure 8.4 maturing in February 2037. What is its coupon rate? What is its bid price? What was the *previous day's* asked price?

12. **Using Treasury Quotes**   Locate the Treasury bond in Figure 8.4 maturing in November 2039. Is this a premium or a discount bond? What is its current yield? What is its yield to maturity? What is the bid-ask spread?

268   **Part II**   Valuation and Capital Budgeting

13. **Zero Coupon Bonds**   You buy a zero coupon bond at the beginning of the year that has a face value of $1,000, a YTM of 7 percent, and 25 years to maturity. If you hold the bond for the entire year, how much in interest income will you have to declare on your tax return?

INTERMEDIATE
(Questions 14–25)

14. **Bond Price Movements**   Miller Corporation has a premium bond making semiannual payments. The bond pays a coupon of 8 percent, has a YTM of 6 percent, and has 13 years to maturity. The Modigliani Company has a discount bond making semiannual payments. This bond pays a coupon of 6 percent, has a YTM of 8 percent, and also has 13 years to maturity. If interest rates remain unchanged, what do you expect the price of these bonds to be 1 year from now? In 3 years? In 8 years? In 12 years? In 13 years? What's going on here? Illustrate your answers by graphing bond prices versus time to maturity.

15. **Interest Rate Risk**   Laurel, Inc., and Hardy Corp. both have 7 percent coupon bonds outstanding, with semiannual interest payments, and both are priced at par value. The Laurel, Inc., bond has 2 years to maturity, whereas the Hardy Corp. bond has 15 years to maturity. If interest rates suddenly rise by 2 percent, what is the percentage change in the price of these bonds? If interest rates were to suddenly fall by 2 percent instead, what would the percentage change in the price of these bonds be then? Illustrate your answers by graphing bond prices versus YTM. What does this problem tell you about the interest rate risk of longer-term bonds?

16. **Interest Rate Risk**   The Faulk Corp. has a 6 percent coupon bond outstanding. The Gonas Company has a 14 percent bond outstanding. Both bonds have 12 years to maturity, make semiannual payments, and have a YTM of 10 percent. If interest rates suddenly rise by 2 percent, what is the percentage change in the price of these bonds? What if interest rates suddenly fall by 2 percent instead? What does this problem tell you about the interest rate risk of lower coupon bonds?

17. **Bond Yields**   Hacker Software has 6.2 percent coupon bonds on the market with 9 years to maturity. The bonds make semiannual payments and currently sell for 105 percent of par. What is the current yield on the bonds? The YTM? The effective annual yield?

18. **Bond Yields**   Pembroke Co. wants to issue new 20-year bonds for some much-needed expansion projects. The company currently has 7 percent coupon bonds on the market that sell for $1,063, make semiannual payments, and mature in 20 years. What coupon rate should the company set on its new bonds if it wants them to sell at par?

19. **Accrued Interest**   You purchase a bond with an invoice price of $950. The bond has a coupon rate of 6.8 percent, and there are 2 months to the next semiannual coupon date. What is the clean price of the bond?

20. **Accrued Interest**   You purchase a bond with a coupon rate of 5.9 percent and a clean price of $1,053. If the next semiannual coupon payment is due in four months, what is the invoice price?

21. **Finding the Bond Maturity**   Argos Corp. has 9 percent coupon bonds making annual payments with a YTM of 7.81 percent. The current yield on these bonds is 8.42 percent. How many years do these bonds have left until they mature?

22. **Using Bond Quotes**   Suppose the following bond quote for IOU Corporation appears in the financial page of today's newspaper. Assume the bond has a face value of $1,000 and the current date is April 15, 2012. What is the yield to maturity of the bond? What is the current yield?

Company (Ticker)	Coupon	Maturity	Last Price	Last Yield	EST Vol (000s)
IOU (IOU)	7.240	Apr 15, 2021	105.312	??	1,827

23. **Finding the Maturity**   You've just found a 10 percent coupon bond on the market that sells for par value. What is the maturity on this bond?

24. **Interest on Zeroes**   Tesla Corporation needs to raise funds to finance a plant expansion, and it has decided to issue 25-year zero coupon bonds to raise the money. The required return on the bonds will be 7 percent.

    a. What will these bonds sell for at issuance?
    b. Using the IRS amortization rule, what interest deduction can the company take on these bonds in the first year? In the last year?
    c. Repeat part (b) using the straight-line method for the interest deduction.
    d. Based on your answers in (b) and (c), which interest deduction method would Tesla Corporation prefer? Why?

25. **Zero Coupon Bonds**   Suppose your company needs to raise $45 million and you want to issue 30-year bonds for this purpose. Assume the required return on your bond issue will be 6 percent, and you're evaluating two issue alternatives: A semiannual coupon bond with a 6 percent coupon rate and a zero coupon bond. Your company's tax rate is 35 percent.

    a. How many of the coupon bonds would you need to issue to raise the $45 million? How many of the zeroes would you need to issue?
    b. In 30 years, what will your company's repayment be if you issue the coupon bonds? What if you issue the zeroes?
    c. Based on your answers in (a) and (b), why would you ever want to issue the zeroes? To answer, calculate the firm's aftertax cash outflows for the first year under the two different scenarios. Assume the IRS amortization rules apply for the zero coupon bonds.

CHALLENGE
(Questions 26–32)

26. **Components of Bond Returns**   Bond P is a premium bond with a 9 percent coupon. Bond D is a 5 percent coupon bond currently selling at a discount. Both bonds make annual payments, have a YTM of 7 percent, and have 10 years to maturity. What is the current yield for Bond P? For Bond D? If interest rates remain unchanged, what is the expected capital gains yield over the next year for Bond P? For Bond D? Explain your answers and the interrelationship among the various types of yields.

27. **Holding Period Yield**   The YTM on a bond is the interest rate you earn on your investment if interest rates don't change. If you actually sell the bond before it matures, your realized return is known as the holding period yield (HPY).

    a. Suppose that today you buy a 5.6 percent annual coupon bond for $930. The bond has 10 years to maturity. What rate of return do you expect to earn on your investment?
    b. Two years from now, the YTM on your bond has declined by 1 percent, and you decide to sell. What price will your bond sell for? What is the HPY on your investment? Compare this yield to the YTM when you first bought the bond. Why are they different?

28. **Valuing Bonds**   The Morgan Corporation has two different bonds currently outstanding. Bond M has a face value of $30,000 and matures in 20 years. The bond makes no payments for the first six years, then pays $800 every six months over the subsequent eight years, and finally pays $1,000 every six months over the last six years. Bond N also has a face value of $30,000 and a maturity of 20 years; it makes no coupon payments over the life of the bond. If the required return on both these bonds is 8 percent compounded semiannually, what is the current price of Bond M? Of Bond N?

29. **Treasury Bonds**   The following Treasury bond quote appeared in *The Wall Street Journal* on May 11, 2004:

9.125	May 09	100:03	100:04	—	−2.15

Why would anyone buy this Treasury bond with a negative yield to maturity? How is this possible?

30. **Real Cash Flows** When Marilyn Monroe died, ex-husband Joe DiMaggio vowed to place fresh flowers on her grave every Sunday as long as he lived. The week after she died in 1962, a bunch of fresh flowers that the former baseball player thought appropriate for the star cost about $8. Based on actuarial tables, "Joltin' Joe" could expect to live for 30 years after the actress died. Assume that the EAR is 6.9 percent. Also, assume that the price of the flowers will increase at 3.2 percent per year, when expressed as an EAR. Assuming that each year has exactly 52 weeks, what is the present value of this commitment? Joe began purchasing flowers the week after Marilyn died.

31. **Real Cash Flows** You are planning to save for retirement over the next 30 years. To save for retirement, you will invest $900 a month in a stock account in real dollars and $300 a month in a bond account in real dollars. The effective annual return of the stock account is expected to be 12 percent, and the bond account will earn 7 percent. When you retire, you will combine your money into an account with an 8 percent effective return. The inflation rate over this period is expected to be 4 percent. How much can you withdraw each month from your account in real terms assuming a 25-year withdrawal period? What is the nominal dollar amount of your last withdrawal?

32. **Real Cash Flows** Paul Adams owns a health club in downtown Los Angeles. He charges his customers an annual fee of $500 and has an existing customer base of 600. Paul plans to raise the annual fee by 6 percent every year and expects the club membership to grow at a constant rate of 3 percent for the next five years. The overall expenses of running the health club are $125,000 a year and are expected to grow at the inflation rate of 2 percent annually. After five years, Paul plans to buy a luxury boat for $500,000, close the health club, and travel the world in his boat for the rest of his life. What is the annual amount that Paul can spend while on his world tour if he will have no money left in the bank when he dies? Assume Paul has a remaining life of 25 years and earns 9 percent on his savings.

Excel Master It!

Companies often buy bonds to meet a future liability or cash outlay. Such an investment is called a dedicated portfolio since the proceeds of the portfolio are dedicated to the future liability. In such a case, the portfolio is subject to reinvestment risk. Reinvestment risk occurs because the company will be reinvesting the coupon payments it receives. If the YTM on similar bonds falls, these coupon payments will be reinvested at a lower interest rate, which will result in a portfolio value that is lower than desired at maturity. Of course, if interest rates increase, the portfolio value at maturity will be higher than needed.

Suppose Ice Cubes, Inc., has the following liability due in five years. The company is going to buy five-year bonds today in order to meet the future obligation. The liability and current YTM are below:

Amount of liability	$100,000,000
Current YTM	8%

a. At the current YTM, what is the face value of the bonds the company has to purchase today in order to meet its future obligation? Assume that the bonds in the relevant range will have the same coupon rate as the current YTM and these bonds make semiannual coupon payments.

b. Assume that the interest rates remain constant for the next five years. Thus, when the company reinvests the coupon payments, it will reinvest at the current YTM. What will be the value of the portfolio in five years?

c. Assume that immediately after the company purchases the bonds, interest rates either rise or fall by 1 percent. What will be the value of the portfolio in five years under these circumstances?

One way to eliminate reinvestment risk is called immunization. Rather than buying bonds with the same maturity as the liability, the company instead buys bonds with the same duration as the liability. If you think about the dedicated portfolio, if the interest rate falls, the future value of the reinvested coupon payments decreases. However, as interest rates fall, the price of the bond increases. These effects offset each other in an immunized portfolio.

Another advantage of using duration to immunize a portfolio is that the duration of a portfolio is simply the weighted average of the duration of the assets in the portfolio. In other words, to find the duration of a portfolio, you simply take the weight of each asset multiplied by its duration and then sum the results.

d. What is the duration of the liability for Ice Cubes, Inc.?

e. Suppose the two bonds shown below are the only bonds available to immunize the liability. What face amount of each bond will the company need to purchase to immunize the portfolio?

	Bond A	Bond B
Settlement	1/1/2000	1/1/2000
Maturity	1/1/2003	1/1/2008
Coupon rate	7.00%	8.00%
YTM	7.50%	9.00%
Coupons per year	2	2

Mini Case

FINANCING EAST COAST YACHTS'S EXPANSION PLANS WITH A BOND ISSUE

After Dan's EFN analysis for East Coast Yachts (see the Mini Case in Chapter 3), Larissa has decided to expand the company's operations. She has asked Dan to enlist an underwriter to help sell $50 million in new 20-year bonds to finance new construction. Dan has entered into discussions with Kim McKenzie, an underwriter from the firm of Crowe & Mallard, about which bond features East Coast Yachts should consider and also what coupon rate the issue will likely have. Although Dan is aware of bond features, he is uncertain as to the costs and benefits of some of them, so he isn't clear on how each feature would affect the coupon rate of the bond issue.

1. You are Kim's assistant, and she has asked you to prepare a memo to Dan describing the effect of each of the following bond features on the coupon rate of the bond. She would also like you to list any advantages or disadvantages of each feature.

   a. The security of the bond, that is, whether or not the bond has collateral.
   b. The seniority of the bond.
   c. The presence of a sinking fund.
   d. A call provision with specified call dates and call prices.

272   **Part II**   Valuation and Capital Budgeting

e. A deferred call accompanying the above call provision.

f. A make-whole call provision.

g. Any positive covenants. Also, discuss several possible positive covenants East Coast Yachts might consider.

h. Any negative covenants. Also, discuss several possible negative covenants East Coast Yachts might consider.

i. A conversion feature (note that East Coast Yachts is not a publicly traded company).

j. A floating rate coupon.

Dan is also considering whether to issue coupon bearing bonds or zero coupon bonds. The YTM on either bond issue will be 7.5 percent. The coupon bond would have a 6.5 percent coupon rate. The company's tax rate is 35 percent.

2. How many of the coupon bonds must East Coast Yachts issue to raise the $50 million? How many of the zeroes must it issue?

3. In 20 years, what will be the principal repayment due if East Coast Yachts issues the coupon bonds? What if it issues the zeroes?

4. What are the company's considerations in issuing a coupon bond compared to a zero coupon bond?

5. Suppose East Coast Yachts issues the coupon bonds with a make-whole call provision. The make-whole call rate is the Treasury rate plus .40 percent. If East Coast calls the bonds in seven years when the Treasury rate is 4.8 percent, what is the call price of the bond? What if it is 8.2 percent?

6. Are investors really made whole with a make-whole call provision?

7. After considering all the relevant factors, would you recommend a zero coupon issue or a regular coupon issue? Why? Would you recommend an ordinary call feature or a make-whole call feature? Why?

CHAPTER 9

Stock Valuation

When the stock market closed on October 18, 2011, the common stock of McGraw-Hill, publisher of high-quality college textbooks, was selling for $44.24 per share. On that same day, DIRECTV, the satellite television company, closed at $46.68 per share, while AmeriGas Partners, which distributes propane gas, closed at $45.10. Since the stock prices of these three companies were so similar, you might expect they would be offering similar dividends to their stockholders, but you would be wrong. In fact, AmeriGas Partner's annual dividend was $2.60 per share; McGraw-Hill's was $1 per share; and DIRECTV was paying no dividend at all!

▲ For updates on the latest happenings in finance, visit www. rwjcorporatefinance. blogspot.com

As we will see in this chapter, the current dividend is one of the primary factors in valuing common stocks. However, it is obvious from looking at DIRECTV that current dividends are not the end of the story. This chapter explores dividends, stock values, and the connection between the two.

In our previous chapter, we introduced you to bonds and bond valuation. In this chapter, we turn to the other major source of external financing for corporations, common stock. We first describe the cash flows associated with a share of stock and then develop a famous result, the dividend growth model. Next, we examine growth opportunities. We point out that stocks are frequently priced using comparables as well. We also show that the discounted cash flow approach introduced in Chapters 5 and 6 works for entire firms and shares of stock as well as for projects. We close out the chapter with a discussion of how shares of stock are traded and how stock prices and other important information are reported in the financial press.

9.1 The Present Value of Common Stocks

ExcelMaster
coverage online

DIVIDENDS VERSUS CAPITAL GAINS

Our goal in this section is to value common stocks. We learned in previous chapters that an asset's value is determined by the present value of its future cash flows. A stock provides two kinds of cash flows. First, many stocks pay dividends on a regular basis. Second, the stockholder receives the sale price when she sells the stock. Thus, in order to value common stocks, we need to answer an important question: Is the price of a share of stock equal to:

1. The discounted present value of the sum of next period's dividend plus next period's stock price, or
2. The discounted present value of all future dividends?

This is the kind of question that students would love to see on a multiple-choice exam, because both (1) and (2) are right.

To see that (1) and (2) are the same, let's start with an individual who will buy the stock and hold it for one year. In other words, she has a one-year *holding period*. In addition, she is willing to pay P_0 for the stock today. That is, she calculates:

$$P_0 = \frac{\text{Div}_1}{1 + R} + \frac{P_1}{1 + R} \qquad (9.1)$$

Div_1 is the expected dividend paid at year's end and P_1 is the expected price at year's end. P_0 is the present value of the common stock investment. The term in the denominator, R, is the appropriate discount rate for the stock and represents the expected return that investors require in order to commit funds to the stock (or simply, the required return).

That seems easy enough, but where does P_1 come from? P_1 is not pulled out of thin air. Rather, there must be a buyer at the end of Year 1 who is willing to purchase the stock for P_1. This buyer determines the price by:

$$P_1 = \frac{\text{Div}_2}{1 + R} + \frac{P_2}{1 + R} \qquad (9.2)$$

Substituting the value of P_1 from Equation 9.2 into Equation 9.1 yields:

$$\begin{aligned} P_0 &= \frac{1}{1 + R}\left[\text{Div}_1 + \left(\frac{\text{Div}_2 + P_2}{1 + R}\right)\right] \\ &= \frac{\text{Div}_1}{1 + R} + \frac{\text{Div}_2}{(1 + R)^2} + \frac{P_2}{(1 + R)^2} \end{aligned} \qquad (9.3)$$

We can ask a similar question for Formula 9.3: Where does P_2 come from? An investor at the end of Year 2 is willing to pay P_2 because of the dividend and stock price at Year 3. This process can be repeated *ad nauseam*.[1] At the end, we are left with

$$P_0 = \frac{\text{Div}_1}{1 + R} + \frac{\text{Div}_2}{(1 + R)^2} + \frac{\text{Div}_3}{(1 + R)^3} + \cdots = \sum_{t=1}^{\infty} \frac{\text{Div}_t}{(1 + R)^t} \qquad (9.4)$$

Thus the price of a share of common stock to the investor is equal to the present value of all of the expected future dividends.

This is a very useful result. A common objection to applying present value analysis to stocks is that investors are too shortsighted to care about the long-run stream of dividends. These critics argue that an investor will generally not look past his or her time horizon. Thus, prices in a market dominated by short-term investors will reflect only near-term dividends. However, our discussion shows that a long-run dividend discount model holds even when investors have short-term time horizons. Although an investor may want to cash out early, she must find another investor who is willing to buy. The price this second investor pays is dependent on dividends *after* his date of purchase.

VALUATION OF DIFFERENT TYPES OF STOCKS

The above discussion shows that the price of a share of stock is the present value of its future dividends. How do we apply this idea in practice? Equation 9.4 represents a general model that is applicable whether dividends are expected to grow, decline, or

---

[1] This procedure reminds us of the physicist lecturing on the origins of the universe. He was approached by an elderly gentleman in the audience who disagreed with the lecture. The attendee said that the universe rests on the back of a huge turtle. When the physicist asked what the turtle rested on, the gentleman said another turtle. Anticipating the physicist's objections, the attendee said, "Don't tire yourself out, young fellow. It's turtles all the way down."

Figure 9.1
Zero Growth,
Constant Growth,
and Differential
Growth Patterns

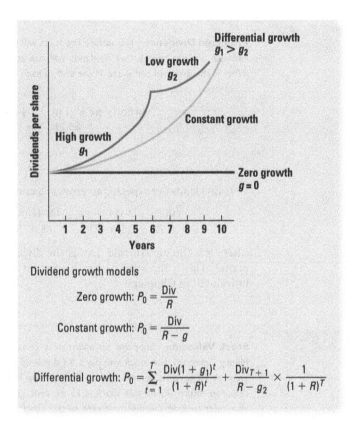

Dividend growth models

Zero growth: $P_0 = \dfrac{Div}{R}$

Constant growth: $P_0 = \dfrac{Div}{R - g}$

Differential growth: $P_0 = \displaystyle\sum_{t=1}^{T} \dfrac{Div(1 + g_1)^t}{(1 + R)^t} + \dfrac{Div_{T+1}}{R - g_2} \times \dfrac{1}{(1 + R)^T}$

stay the same. The general model can be simplified if dividends are expected to follow some basic patterns: (1) zero growth, (2) constant growth, and (3) differential growth. These cases are illustrated in Figure 9.1.

Case 1 (Zero Growth)   The price of a share of stock with a constant dividend is given by:

$$P_0 = \frac{Div_1}{1 + R} + \frac{Div_2}{(1 + R)^2} + \cdots = \frac{Div}{R}$$

Here it is assumed that $Div_1 = Div_2 = \cdots = Div$. This is just an application of the perpetuity formula from Chapter 4.

Case 2 (Constant Growth)   Dividends are expected to grow at rate g, as follows:

End of Year	1	2	3	4	...
Dividend	Div	Div(1 + g)	Div(1 + g)²	Div(1 + g)³	...

Note that Div is the dividend at the end of the *first* period.

EXAMPLE 9.1

Projected Dividends   Hampshire Products will pay a dividend of $4 per share a year from now. Financial analysts believe that dividends will rise at 6 percent per year for the foreseeable future. What is the dividend per share at the end of each of the first five years?

End of Year	1	2	3	4	5
Dividend	$4.00	$4 × (1.06) = $4.24	$4 × (1.06)^2 = $4.4944	$4 × (1.06)^3 = $4.7641	$4 × (1.06)^4 = $5.0499

If dividends are expected to grow at a constant rate the price of a share of stock is:

$$P_0 = \frac{\text{Div}}{1 + R} + \frac{\text{Div}(1 + g)}{(1 + R)^2} + \frac{\text{Div}(1 + g)^2}{(1 + R)^3} + \frac{\text{Div}(1 + g)^3}{(1 + R)^4} + \cdots = \frac{\text{Div}}{R - g}$$

where g is the growth rate. Div is the dividend on the stock at the end of the first period. This is the formula for the present value of a growing perpetuity, which we introduced in Chapter 4.

EXAMPLE 9.2

Stock Valuation   Suppose an investor is considering the purchase of a share of the Utah Mining Company. The stock will pay a $3 dividend a year from today. This dividend is expected to grow at 10 percent per year ($g = 10\%$) for the foreseeable future. The investor thinks that the required return (R) on this stock is 15 percent, given her assessment of Utah Mining's risk. (We also refer to R as the discount rate of the stock.) What is the price of a share of Utah Mining Company's stock?

Using the constant growth formula of Case 2, we assess the price to be $60:

$$\$60 = \frac{\$3}{.15 - .10}$$

P_0 is quite dependent on the value of g. If g had been estimated to be 12½ percent, the value of the share would have been:

$$\$120 = \frac{\$3}{.15 - .125}$$

The stock price doubles (from $60 to $120) when g only increases 25 percent (from 10 percent to 12.5 percent). Because of P_0's dependency on g, one should maintain a healthy sense of skepticism when using this constant growth of dividends model.

Furthermore, note that P_0 is equal to infinity when the growth rate, g, equals the discount rate, R. Because stock prices are never infinite, an estimate of g equal to or greater than R implies an error in estimation. More will be said of this point later.

The assumption of steady dividend growth might strike you as peculiar. Why would the dividend grow at a constant rate? The reason is that, for many companies, steady growth in dividends is an explicit goal. For example, in 2011, Procter & Gamble, the Cincinnati-based maker of personal care and household products, increased its dividend by 8.9 percent to $1.97 per share; this increase was notable because it was the 55th in a row. The subject of dividend growth falls under the general heading of dividend policy, so we will defer further discussion of it to a later chapter.[2]

Case 3 (Differential Growth) In this case, an algebraic formula would be too unwieldy. Instead, we present examples.

EXAMPLE 9.3

Differential Growth Consider Elixir Drug Company, which is expected to enjoy rapid growth from the introduction of its new back-rub ointment. The dividend for a share of Elixir's stock a year from today is expected to be $1.15. During the next four years, the dividend is expected to grow at 15 percent per year ($g_1 = 15\%$). After that, growth (g_2) will be equal to 10 percent per year. Calculate the present value of a share of stock if the required return (R) is 15 percent.

Figure 9.2 Growth in Dividends for Elixir Drug Company

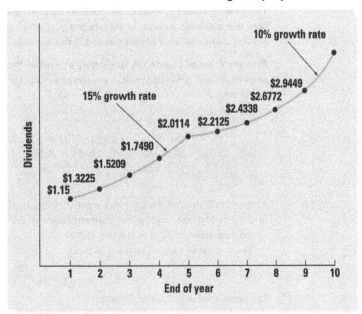

Figure 9.2 displays the growth in the dividends. We need to apply a two-step process to discount these dividends. We first calculate the present value of the dividends growing at 15 percent per annum. That is, we first calculate the present value of the dividends at the end of each of the first five years. Second, we calculate the present value of the dividends beginning at the end of Year 6.

(continued)

---

[2]So far we have assumed that dividends are the only cash payouts of the firm to its shareholders. Actually, firms frequently pay cash to shareholders by buying back shares of stock outstanding. Share repurchase payouts can be thought of as substitutes for cash dividend payouts. Much more will be said about the pros and cons of dividends versus share repurchase payouts in Chapter 19.

To see how share repurchase payouts might work in the constant growth version of the dividend discount model, suppose Trojan Industries has 100 million shares outstanding and expects net income at the end of the year of $400 million. Trojan plans to pay out 60 percent of its net income, paying 30 percent in dividends and 30 percent to repurchase shares. Trojan expects net income to increase by 5 percent per year in perpetuity. If Trojan's required return is 10 percent, what is its share price?

Solution:

$$\text{Total PV} = \frac{\$240 \text{ million}}{.10 - .05} = \$4.8 \text{ billion}$$

$$\text{Price per share} = \frac{\$4.8 \text{ billion}}{100 \text{ million shares}} = \$48 \text{ per share}$$

Present Value of First Five Dividends   The present value of dividend payments in Years 1 through 5 is calculated as follows:

Future Year	Growth Rate (g_1)	Expected Dividend	Present Value
1	.15	$1.15	$1
2	.15	1.3225	1
3	.15	1.5209	1
4	.15	1.7490	1
5	.15	2.0114	1
Years 1–5		The present value of dividends = $5	

The growing annuity formula of the previous chapter could normally be used in this step. However, note that dividends grow at 15 percent per year, which is also the discount rate. Since $g = R$, the growing annuity formula cannot be used in this example.

Present Value of Dividends Beginning at End of Year 6   We use the procedure for deferred perpetuities and deferred annuities presented in Chapter 4. The dividends beginning at the end of Year 6 are:

End of Year	6	7	8	9	$\cdots$
Dividend	$Div_5 \times (1 + g_2)$	$Div_5 \times (1 + g_2)^2$	$Div_5 \times (1 + g_2)^3$	$Div_5 \times (1 + g_2)^4$	$\cdots$
	2.0114×1.10	$2.0114 \times (1.10)^2$	$2.0114 \times (1.10)^3$	$2.0114 \times (1.10)^4$	$\cdots$
	$= \$2.2125$	$= \$2.4338$	$= \$2.6772$	$= \$2.9449$	

As stated in Chapter 4, the growing perpetuity formula calculates present value as of one year prior to the first payment. Because the payment begins at the end of Year 6, the present value formula calculates present value as of the end of Year 5.

The price at the end of Year 5 is given by:

$$P_5 = \frac{Div_6}{R - g_2} = \frac{\$2.2125}{.15 - .10} = \$44.25$$

The present value of P_5 as of today is:

$$\frac{P_5}{(1 + R)^5} = \frac{\$44.25}{(1.15)^5} = \$22$$

The present value of *all* dividends as of today is $27 ($22 + $5).

9.2 Estimates of Parameters in the Dividend Discount Model

The value of the firm is a function of its growth rate, g, and its discount rate, R. How does one estimate these variables?

WHERE DOES g COME FROM?

The previous discussion assumed that dividends grow at the rate g. We now want to estimate this rate of growth. Consider a business whose earnings next year are expected to be the same as earnings this year unless a *net investment* is made. This situation is quite plausible because net investment is equal to gross, or total, investment less depreciation. A net investment of zero occurs when *total investment* equals depreciation. If total investment is equal to depreciation, the firm's physical plant is just maintained, consistent with no growth in earnings.

Net investment will be positive only if some earnings are not paid out as dividends, that is, only if some earnings are retained.[3] This leads to the following equation:

$$
\underset{\text{Increase in earnings}}{\underbrace{\begin{array}{c}\text{Earnings}\\\text{next}\\\text{year}\end{array}}}=\begin{array}{c}\text{Earnings}\\\text{this}\\\text{year}\end{array}+\begin{array}{c}\text{Retained}\\\text{earnings}\\\text{this year}\end{array}\times\begin{array}{c}\text{Return on}\\\text{retained}\\\text{earnings}\end{array} \tag{9.5}
$$

The increase in earnings is a function of both the *retained earnings* and the *return on the retained earnings*.

We now divide both sides of Equation 9.5 by earnings this year, yielding

$$
\frac{\text{Earnings next year}}{\text{Earnings this year}}=\frac{\text{Earnings this year}}{\text{Earnings this year}}+\left(\frac{\text{Retained earnings this year}}{\text{Earnings this year}}\right) \tag{9.6}
$$
$$
\times\text{ Return on retained earnings}
$$

The left-hand side of Equation 9.6 is simply one plus the growth rate in earnings, which we write as $1 + g$. The ratio of retained earnings to earnings is called the **retention ratio.** Thus, we can write

$$
1 + g = 1 + \text{Retention ratio} \times \text{Return on retained earnings} \tag{9.7}
$$

It is difficult for a financial analyst to determine the return expected on currently retained earnings, because the details on forthcoming projects are not generally public information. However, it is frequently assumed that projects selected in the current year have an anticipated return equal to returns from past projects. Here, we can estimate the anticipated return on current retained earnings by the historical **return on equity** or ROE. After all, ROE is simply the return on the firm's entire equity, which is the return on the cumulation of all the firm's past projects.

From Equation 9.7, we have a simple way to estimate growth in earnings:

Formula for Firm's Growth Rate:
$$
g = \text{Retention ratio} \times \text{Return on retained earnings (ROE)} \tag{9.8}
$$

The estimate for the growth rate in earnings, g, is also the estimate for the growth rate in dividends under the common assumption that the ratio of dividends to earnings is held constant.[4]

EXAMPLE 9.4

Earnings Growth Pagemaster Enterprises just reported earnings of $2 million. The firm plans to retain 40 percent of its earnings in all years going forward. In other words, the retention ratio is 40 percent. We could also say that 60 percent of earnings will be paid out as dividends. The ratio of dividends to earnings is often called the **payout ratio,** so the payout ratio for Pagemaster is

(continued)

---

[3]We ignore the issuance of new shares or the buyback of existing shares of stock. These possibilities are considered in later chapters.

[4]In Chapter 3, we also discussed methods for *g*'s calculation.

60 percent. The historical return on equity (ROE) has been .16, a figure expected to continue into the future. How much will earnings grow over the coming year?

We first perform the calculation without reference to Equation 9.8. Then we use (9.8) as a check.

Calculation without Reference to Equation 9.8   The firm will retain $800,000 (40% × $2 million). Assuming that historical ROE is an appropriate estimate for future returns, the anticipated increase in earnings is:

$$\$800,000 \times .16 = \$128,000$$

The percentage growth in earnings is:

$$\frac{\text{Change in earnings}}{\text{Total earnings}} = \frac{\$128,000}{\$2 \text{ million}} = .064$$

This implies that earnings in one year will be $2,128,000 (=$2,000,000 × 1.064).

Check Using Equation 9.8   We use g = Retention ratio × ROE. We have:

$$g = .4 \times .16 = .064$$

Since Pagemaster's ratio of dividends to earnings, that is, its payout ratio, is constant going forward, .064 is the growth rate of *both* earnings and dividends.

WHERE DOES R COME FROM?

Thus far, we have taken the required return or discount rate, R, as given. Conceptually, the required return is the return on assets with the same risk as the firm's shares. We show how to estimate R in Chapter 13. For now, we want to examine the implications of the dividend growth model for this required return. Earlier, we calculated P_0 as:

$$P_0 = \text{Div}/(R - g)$$

Rearranging the equation to solve for R, we get:

$$R - g = \text{Div}/P_0$$
$$R = \text{Div}/P_0 + g \tag{9.9}$$

Equation 9.9 tells us that the required return, R, has two components. The first of these, Div/P_0, is called the **dividend yield.** Because this is calculated as the expected cash dividend divided by the current price, it is conceptually similar to the current yield on a bond.

The second part of the total return is the expected growth rate, g. As we will verify shortly, the dividend growth rate is also the stock price's growth rate. Thus, this growth rate can be interpreted as the **capital gains yield,** that is, the rate at which the value of the investment grows.

To illustrate the components of the required return, suppose we observe a stock selling for $20 per share. The next dividend is expected to be $1 per share. You think that the dividend will grow by 10 percent per year more or less indefinitely. What expected return does this stock offer you?

The dividend growth model calculates total return as:

$$R = \text{Dividend yield} + \text{Capital gains yield}$$
$$R = \quad \text{Div}/P_0 \quad + \qquad g$$

In this case, total return works out to be:

$$R = \$1/20 + 10\%$$
$$= 5\% + 10\%$$
$$= 15\%$$

This stock, therefore, has an expected return of 15 percent.

We can verify this answer by calculating the price in one year, P_1, using 15 percent as the required expected return. Since the dividend expected to be received in one year is $1 and the expected growth rate of dividends is 10 percent, the dividend expected to be received in two years, Div_2, is $1.10. Based on the dividend growth model, the stock price in one year will be:

$$P_1 = \text{Div}_2/(R - g)$$
$$= \$1.10/(.15 - .10)$$
$$= \$1.10/.05$$
$$= \$22$$

Notice that this $22 is $20 × 1.1, so the stock price has grown by 10 percent as it should. That is, the capital gains yield is 10 percent, which equals the growth rate in dividends.

What is the investor's total expected return? If you pay $20 for the stock today, you will get a $1 dividend at the end of the year, and you will have a $22 − 20 = $2 gain. Your dividend yield is thus $1/20 = 5 percent. Your capital gains yield is $2/20 = 10 percent, so your total expected return would be 5 percent + 10 percent = 15 percent, just as we calculated above.

To get a feel for actual numbers in this context, consider that, according to the 2011 *Value Line Investment Survey,* Procter & Gamble's dividends were expected to grow by 5.2 percent over the next 5 or so years, compared to a historical growth rate of 11.5 percent over the preceding 5 years and 11 percent over the preceding 10 years. In 2011, the projected dividend for the coming year was given as $2.10. The stock price at that time was $60.93 per share. What is the expected return investors require on P&G? Here, the dividend yield is 3.4 (2.10/60.93) percent and the capital gains yield is 5.2 percent, giving a total required return of 8.6 percent on P&G stock.

EXAMPLE 9.5

Calculating the Required Return Pagemaster Enterprises, the company examined in the previous example, has 1,000,000 shares of stock outstanding. The stock is selling at $10. What is the required return on the stock?

Because the retention ratio is 40 percent, the payout ratio is 60 percent (1 − Retention ratio). The payout ratio is the ratio of dividends/earnings. Because earnings a year from now will be $2,128,000 ($2,000,000 × 1.064), dividends will be $1,276,800 (.60 × $2,128,000). Dividends per share will be $1.28 ($1,276,800/1,000,000). Given our previous result that $g = .064$, we calculate R from (9.9) as follows:

$$.192 = \frac{\$1.28}{\$10.00} + .064$$

A HEALTHY SENSE OF SKEPTICISM

It is important to emphasize that our approach merely *estimates* g; our approach does not *determine* g precisely. We mentioned earlier that our estimate of g is based on a number of assumptions. For example, we assume that the return on reinvestment of future retained earnings is equal to the firm's past ROE. We assume that the future retention ratio is equal to the past retention ratio. Our estimate for g will be off if these assumptions prove to be wrong.

Unfortunately, the determination of R is highly dependent on g. For example, if g for Pagemaster is estimated to be 0, R equals 12.8 percent ($1.28/$10.00). If g is estimated to be 12 percent, R equals 24.8 percent ($1.28/$10.00 + 12%). Thus, one should view estimates of R with a healthy sense of skepticism.

Because of the preceding, some financial economists generally argue that the estimation error for R for a single security is too large to be practical. Therefore, they suggest calculating the average R for an entire industry. This R would then be used to discount the dividends of a particular stock in the same industry.

One should be particularly skeptical of two polar cases when estimating R for individual securities. First, consider a firm not currently paying a dividend. If the firm initiates a dividend at some point, its dividend growth rate over the interval becomes *infinite*. Thus, Equation 9.9 must be used with extreme caution here, if at all—a point we emphasize later in this chapter.

Second, we mentioned earlier that share price is infinite when g is equal to R. Because stock prices are never infinite in the real world, an analyst whose estimate of g for a particular firm is equal to or above R must have made a mistake. Most likely, the analyst's high estimate for g is correct for the next few years. However, firms simply cannot maintain an abnormally high growth rate *forever*. The analyst's error was to use a short-run estimate of g in a model requiring a perpetual growth rate.

DIVIDENDS OR EARNINGS: WHICH TO DISCOUNT?

As mentioned earlier, this chapter applied the growing perpetuity formula to the valuation of stocks. In our application, we discounted dividends, not earnings. This is sensible since investors select a stock for the cash they can get out of it. They only get two things out of a stock: Dividends and the ultimate sales price, which is determined by what future investors expect to receive in dividends.

The calculated stock price would usually be too high were earnings to be discounted instead of dividends. As we saw in our estimation of a firm's growth rate, only a portion of earnings goes to the stockholders as dividends. The remainder is retained to generate future dividends. In our model, retained earnings are equal to the firm's investment. To discount earnings instead of dividends would be to ignore the investment that a firm must make today in order to generate future earnings and dividends.

THE NO-DIVIDEND FIRM

Students frequently ask the following question: If the dividend discount model is correct, why aren't no-dividend stocks selling at zero? This is a good question and gets at the goals of the firm. A firm with many growth opportunities is faced with a dilemma. The firm can pay out dividends now, or it can forgo dividends now so that it can make investments that will generate even greater dividends in the future.[5] This is often a painful choice, because a strategy of dividend deferment may be optimal yet unpopular among certain stockholders.

Many firms choose to pay no dividends—and these firms sell at positive prices. For example, most Internet firms, such as Amazon.com, Google, and eBay, pay no

---

[5]A third alternative is to issue stock so that the firm has enough cash both to pay dividends and to invest. This possibility is explored in a later chapter.

dividends. Rational shareholders believe that they will either receive dividends at some point or they will receive something just as good. That is, the firm will be acquired in a merger, with the stockholders receiving either cash or shares of stock at that time.

Of course, actual application of the dividend discount model is difficult for no-dividend firms. Clearly, the model for constant growth of dividends does not apply. Though the differential growth model can work in theory, the difficulties of estimating the date of the first dividend, the growth rate of dividends after that date, and the ultimate merger price make application of the model quite difficult in reality.

Empirical evidence suggests that firms with high growth rates are likely to pay lower dividends, a result consistent with the above analysis. For example, consider Microsoft Corporation. The company started in 1975 and grew rapidly for many years. It paid its first dividend in 2003, though it was a billion-dollar company (in both sales and market value of stockholders' equity) prior to that date. Why did it wait so long to pay a dividend? It waited because it had so many positive growth opportunities, such as new software products, to fund. (Also, it may have purposely held excessive levels of cash and short-term securities.)

9.3 Growth Opportunities

ExcelMaster
coverage online

This section introduces the
ROUND function.

We previously spoke of the expected growth rate of dividends. We now want to address the related concept of growth opportunities. Imagine a company with a level stream of earnings per share in perpetuity. The company pays all of these earnings out to stockholders as dividends. Hence,

$$EPS = Div$$

where EPS is *earnings per share* and Div is dividends per share. A company of this type is frequently called a *cash cow*.

From the perpetuity formula of the previous chapter, the value of a share of stock is:

Value of a Share of Stock When Firm Acts as a Cash Cow:

$$\frac{EPS}{R} = \frac{Div}{R}$$

where R is the discount rate on the firm's stock.

This policy of paying out all earnings as dividends may not be the optimal one. Many firms have *growth* opportunities, that is, opportunities to invest in profitable projects. Because these projects can represent a significant fraction of the firm's value, it would be foolish to forgo them in order to pay out all earnings as dividends.

Although firms frequently think in terms of a *set* of growth opportunities, let's focus on the opportunity to invest in a single project. Suppose the firm retains the entire dividend at Date 1 in order to invest in a particular capital budgeting project. The net present value *per share* of the project as of Date 0 is *NPVGO*, which stands for the *net present value (per share) of the growth opportunity*.

What is the price of a share of stock at Date 0 if the firm decides to take on the project at Date 1? Because the per share value of the project is added to the original stock price, the stock price must now be:

Stock Price after Firm Commits to New Project:

$$\frac{EPS}{R} + NPVGO \tag{9.10}$$

Thus, Equation 9.10 indicates that the price of a share of stock can be viewed as the sum of two different items. The first term (EPS/R) is the value of the firm if it rested on its laurels, that is, if it simply distributed all earnings to the stockholders. The second term is the *additional* value if the firm retains earnings in order to fund new projects.

EXAMPLE 9.6

Growth Opportunities   Sarro Shipping, Inc., expects to earn $1 million per year in perpetuity if it undertakes no new investment opportunities. There are 100,000 shares of stock outstanding, so earnings per share equal $10 ($1,000,000/100,000). The firm will have an opportunity at Date 1 to spend $1,000,000 on a new marketing campaign. The new campaign will increase earnings in every subsequent period by $210,000 (or $2.10 per share). This is a 21 percent return per year on the project. The firm's discount rate is 10 percent. What is the value per share before and after deciding to accept the marketing campaign?

The value of a share of Sarro Shipping before the campaign is:

Value of a Share of Sarro When Firm Acts as a Cash Cow:

$$\frac{EPS}{R} = \frac{\$10}{.1} = \$100$$

The value of the marketing campaign as of Date 1 is:

Value of Marketing Campaign at Date 1:

$$-\$1,000,000 + \frac{\$210,000}{.1} = \$1,100,000 \tag{9.11}$$

Because the investment is made at Date 1 and the first cash inflow occurs at Date 2, Equation 9.11 represents the value of the marketing campaign as of Date 1. We determine the value at Date 0 by discounting back one period as follows:

Value of Marketing Campaign at Date 0:

$$\frac{\$1,100,000}{1.1} = \$1,000,000$$

Thus, NPVGO per share is $10 ($1,000,000/100,000).

The price per share is:

$$EPS/R + NPVGO = \$100 + \$10 = \$110$$

The calculation can also be made on a straight net present value basis. Because all the earnings at Date 1 are spent on the marketing effort, no dividends are paid to stockholders at that date. Dividends in all subsequent periods are $1,210,000 ($1,000,000 + 210,000). In this case, $1,000,000 is the annual dividend when Sarro is a cash cow. The additional contribution to the dividend from the marketing effort is $210,000. Dividends per share are $12.10 ($1,210,000/100,000). Because these dividends start at Date 2, the price per share at Date 1 is $121 ($12.10/.1). The price per share at Date 0 is $110 ($121/1.1).

Note that value is created in Example 9.6 because the project earned a 21 percent rate of return when the discount rate was only 10 percent. No value would have been created had the project earned a 10 percent rate of return. In other words, the

NPVGO would have been zero. The NPVGO would have been negative had the project earned a percentage return below 10 percent.

Two conditions must be met in order to increase value:

1. Earnings must be retained so that projects can be funded.[6]
2. The projects must have positive net present value.

Surprisingly, a number of companies seem to invest in projects known to have *negative* net present values. For example, in the late 1970s, oil companies and tobacco companies were flush with cash. Due to declining markets in both industries, high dividends and low investment would have been the rational action. Unfortunately, a number of companies in both industries reinvested heavily in what were widely perceived to be negative NPVGO projects.

Given that NPV analysis (such as that presented in Chapters 5 and 6) is common knowledge in business, why would managers choose projects with negative NPVs? One conjecture is that some managers enjoy controlling a large company. Because paying dividends in lieu of reinvesting earnings reduces the size of the firm, some managers find it emotionally difficult to pay high dividends.

NPVGOS OF REAL-WORLD COMPANIES

The Sarro Shipping Company in Example 9.6 had one new project. In reality, companies have a whole series of projects, some to be developed in the near term and others to be developed in the long term. The stock price of any real-world company should reflect the market's perception of the net present values of all of these future projects. In other words, the stock price should reflect the market's estimate of the firm's NPVGO.

Can one estimate NPVGOs for real companies? Yes, while Equation 9.10 may seem conceptual in nature, the equation can easily be used to estimate NPVGOs in the real world. For example, consider Home Depot (HD). A recent issue of *Value Line* forecasted earnings per share for HD to be $2.25 in 2011. With a discount rate of .073,[7] the price of one share of HD, assuming that projected nominal earnings are constant over time and are fully paid out as dividends, would be:

$$\frac{\$2.25}{.073} = \$30.82$$

In other words, a share of HD's stock would be worth $30.82 if no earnings were ever to be retained for investment.

Was HD selling for $30.82 when the *Value Line* issue came out? No, HD was selling for $36.29. Why the difference? The difference between HD's market price and its per share value as a cash cow is $5.47 (=36.29 − 30.82), which can be viewed as HD's NPVGO. That is, the market expects HD's investment strategy to increase value by

---

[6]Later in the text, we speak of issuing stock or debt in order to fund projects.

[7]Recall that discount rates represent expected returns that investors require to invest in a stock. We use the methodology of chapter 13 to determine HD's discount rate. Specifically, we employ the capital asset pricing model under the assumption that the risk-free rate is 1 percent, the expected risk premium of the market portfolio above the risk-free rate is 7 percent, and HD's beta is .9, generating a discount rate for HD's stock of:

$$1\% + .9 \times 7\% = 7.3\%$$

$5.47 above the firm's worth as a cash cow. HD's NPVGO, as calculated above, represents 15.1 percent (=5.47/36.29) of HD's price per share.

We calculated the ratio of NPVGO to share price for each of the companies listed below, all of which are on the Dow-Jones 30 Industrials Index.

Company Name	Ratio of NPVGO to Share Price
Alcoa	.553
American Express	.230
Bank of America	.461
Caterpillar	.443
Disney (Walt)	.216
DuPont	.252
Home Depot	.151

The firms represent a number of industries, indicating that growth opportunities come from many different market sectors.

GROWTH IN EARNINGS AND DIVIDENDS VERSUS GROWTH OPPORTUNITIES

As mentioned earlier, a firm's value increases when it invests in growth opportunities with positive NPVGOs. A firm's value falls when it selects opportunities with negative NPVGOs. However, earnings and dividends grow whether projects with positive NPVs or negative NPVs are selected. This surprising result can be explained by the following example.

EXAMPLE 9.7

NPV versus Dividends   Lane Supermarkets, a new firm, will earn $100,000 a year in perpetuity if it pays out all its earnings as dividends. However, the firm plans to invest 20 percent of its earnings in projects that are expected to earn 10 percent per year. The expected return that investors require to compensate for the risks of the new firm, for example, the discount rate, is 18 percent.

Does the firm's investment policy lead to an increase or decrease in the value of the firm? The policy reduces value because the expected return on future projects of 10 percent is less than the discount rate of 18 percent. In other words, the firm will be investing in negative NPV projects, implying that the firm would have had a higher value at Date 0 if it simply paid all of its earnings out as dividends.

Is the firm growing? Yes, the firm will grow over time, both in terms of earnings and in terms of dividends. Equation 9.8 tells us that the annual growth rate of earnings is:

$$g = \text{Retention ratio} \times \text{Return on retained earnings} = .2 \times .10 = 2\%.$$

Since earnings in the first year will be $100,000, earnings in the second year will be $100,000 × 1.02 = $102,000, earnings in the third year will be $100,000 × (1.02)² = $104,040, and so on.

> Because dividends are a constant proportion of earnings, dividends must grow at 2 percent per year as well. Since Lane's retention ratio is 20 percent, dividends are (1 − 20%) = 80% of earnings. In the first year of the new policy, dividends will be $80,000 [=(1 − .2) × $100,000]. Dividends next year will be $81,600 (=$80,000 × 1.02). Dividends the following year will be $83,232 [=$80,000 × (1.02)²] and so on.
>
> In conclusion, Lane's policy of investing in negative NPV projects produces two outcomes. First, the policy reduces the value of the firm. Second, the policy creates growth in both earnings and dividends. In other words, Lane Supermarkets' policy of growth actually *destroys* firm value.
>
> Under what conditions would Lane's earnings and dividends actually *fall* over time? Earnings and dividends would fall over time only if the firm invested in projects with negative rates of return.

The previous example leads to two conclusions:

1. Negative NPV projects lower the value of the firm. In other words, projects with rates of return below the discount rate lower firm value.

2. Both the earnings and dividends of a firm will grow as long as its projects have positive rates of return.

Thus, as with Lane Supermarkets above, any firm selecting projects with rates of return below the discount rate will grow in terms of earnings and dividends but will destroy firm value.

9.4 Comparables

So far in this chapter, we have valued stocks by discounting either dividends or by determining the NPVGO. In addition to these two approaches, practitioners commonly value by comparables as well. The comparables approach is similar to valuation in real estate. If your neighbor's home just sold for $200,000 and it has similar size and amenities to your home, your home is probably worth around $200,000 also. In the stock market, comparable firms are assumed to have similar *multiples*. To see how the comparables approach works, let's look at perhaps the most common multiple, the price-to-earnings (PE) multiple, or PE ratio.

PRICE-TO-EARNINGS RATIO

A stock's price-to-earnings ratio is, as the name suggests, the ratio of the stock's price to its earnings per share. For example, if the stock of Sun Aerodynamic Systems (SAS) is selling at $27.00 per share and its earnings per share over the last year was $4.50, SAS's PE ratio would be 6 (=27/4.50).

It is generally assumed that similar firms have similar PE ratios. For example, imagine the average price-to-earnings (PE) ratio across all publicly traded companies in the specialty retail industry is 12 and a particular company in the industry has earnings of $10 million. If this company is judged to be similar to the rest of the industry, one might estimate that company's value to be $120 million (=12 × $10 million).

Valuation via PE certainly looks easier than valuation via discounted cash flow (DCF), since the DCF approach calls for estimates of yearly cash flows. But is the PE approach better? That depends on the similarity across comparables.

On a particular day in May 2011, Google's stock price was $535.30 and its EPS was $26.69, implying a PE ratio slightly above 20.[8] On the same day in 2011, Hewlett Packard's PE was 10, Microsoft's was 10, and Dell's was 12. Why would stocks in the same industry trade at different PE ratios? Do the differences imply that Google was overpriced and Dell was underpriced, or are there rational reasons for the differences?

Both the dividend discount model (in 9.1) and the NPVGO model (in 9.10) imply that the PE ratio is related to growth opportunities. As an example, consider two firms, each having just reported earnings per share of $1. However, one firm has many valuable growth opportunities, while the other firm has no growth opportunities at all. The firm with growth opportunities should sell at a higher price, because an investor is buying both current income of $1 and growth opportunities. Suppose that the firm with growth opportunities sells for $16 and the other firm sells for $8. The $1 earnings per share number appears in the denominator of the PE ratio for both firms. Thus, the PE ratio is 16 for the firm with growth opportunities, but only 8 for the firm without the opportunities.

This explanation seems to hold fairly well in the real world. Electronics and other high-tech stocks generally sell at high PE ratios because they are perceived to have high growth rates. In fact, some technology stocks sell at high prices even though the companies have never earned a profit. The PE ratios of these companies are infinite. Conversely, railroads, utilities, and steel companies sell at lower multiples because of the prospects of lower growth. Table 9.1 contains PE ratios in 2011 for some well-known companies and the S&P 500 Index. Notice the variations across industries.

There are at least two additional factors explaining the PE ratio. The first is the discount rate, R. Since R appears in the denominator of the dividend discount model (in 9.1) and the NPVGO model (in 9.10), the formula implies that the PE ratio is *negatively* related to the firm's discount rate. We have already suggested that the discount rate is positively related to the stock's risk or variability. Thus, the PE ratio is negatively related to the stock's risk. To see that this is a sensible result, consider two firms, A and B, behaving as cash cows. The stock market *expects* both firms to have annual earnings of $1 per share forever. However, the earnings of Firm A are known

Table 9.1
Selected PE Ratios, 2011

Company	Industry	PE Ratio
Adobe Systems	Application software	20
Charles Schwab	Financial Services	32
Chubb	Insurance	9
Coca-Cola	Beverages	13
Pfizer	Pharmaceuticals	20
Whirlpool	Home Appliances	11
S&P 500 average	n/a	16.84

---

[8]We just calculated PE as the ratio of current price to last year's EPS. Alternatively, PE can be computed as the ratio of current price to projected EPS over the next year.

with certainty while the earnings of Firm *B* are quite variable. A rational stockholder is likely to pay more for a share of Firm *A* because of the absence of risk. If a share of Firm *A* sells at a higher price and both firms have the same EPS, the PE ratio of Firm *A* must be higher.

The second additional factor concerns the firm's choice of accounting methods. Under current accounting rules, companies are given a fair amount of leeway. For example, consider inventory accounting where either FIFO or LIFO may be used. In an inflationary environment, *FIFO* (*first in–first out*) accounting understates the true cost of inventory and hence inflates reported earnings. Inventory is valued according to more recent costs under *LIFO* (*last in–first out*), implying that reported earnings are lower here than they would be under FIFO. Thus, LIFO inventory accounting is a more *conservative* method than FIFO. Similar accounting leeway exists for construction costs (*completed contracts* versus *percentage-of-completion methods*) and depreciation (*accelerated depreciation* versus *straight-line depreciation*).

As an example, consider two identical firms, *C* and *D*. Firm *C* uses LIFO and reports earnings of $2 per share. Firm *D* uses the less conservative accounting assumptions of FIFO and reports earnings of $3 per share. The market knows that both firms are identical and prices both at $18 per share. The price–earnings ratio is 9 ($18/$2) for firm *C* and 6 ($18/$3) for Firm *D*. Thus, the firm with the more conservative principles has the higher PE ratio.

In conclusion, we have argued that a stock's PE ratio is likely a function of three factors:

1. *Growth opportunities.* Companies with significant growth opportunities are likely to have high PE ratios.
2. *Risk.* Low-risk stocks are likely to have high PE ratios.
3. *Accounting practices.* Firms following conservative accounting practices will likely have high PE ratios.

Which of these factors is most important in the real world? The consensus among finance professionals is that growth opportunities typically have the biggest impact on PE ratios. For example, high-tech companies generally have higher PE ratios than, say, utilities, because utilities have fewer opportunities for growth, even though utilities typically have lower risk. And, within industries, differences in growth opportunities also generate the biggest differences in PE ratios. In our example at the beginning of this section, Google's high PE is almost certainly due to its growth opportunities, not its low risk or its accounting conservatism. In fact, due to its youth, the risk of Google is likely higher than the risk of many of its competitors. Microsoft's PE is lower than Google's PE because Microsoft's growth opportunities are a small fraction of its existing business lines. However, Microsoft had a much higher PE decades ago, when it had huge growth opportunities but little in the way of existing business.

Thus, while multiples such as the PE ratio can be used to price stocks, care must be taken. Firms in the same industry are likely to have different multiples if they have different growth rates, risk levels and accounting treatments. Average multiples should not be calculated across all firms in any industry. Rather, an average multiple should be calculated only across those firms in an industry with similar characteristics.

ENTERPRISE VALUE RATIOS

The PE ratio is an equity ratio. That is, the numerator is the price per share of *stock* and the denominator is the earnings per share of *stock*. In addition, practitioners often use ratios involving both equity and debt. Perhaps the most common is the enterprise value EV to EBITDA ratio. Enterprise value is equal to the market value of the firm's equity plus the market value of the firm's debt minus cash. Recall, EBITDA stands for earnings before interest, taxes, depreciation, and amortization.

For example, imagine that Illinois Food Products Co. (IFPC) has equity worth $800 million, debt worth $300 million, and cash of $100 million. The enterprise value here is $1 billion (=800 + 300 − 100). Further imagine the firm has the following income statement:

Revenue	$700 million
−Cost of goods sold	−500 million
Earnings before interest, taxes, depreciation, and amortization (EBITDA)	$200 million
−Depreciation and amortization	−100 million
−Interest	−24 million
Pre-tax income	76 million
−Taxes (@ 30%)	−22.8 million
Profit after taxes	$53.2 million

The EV to EBITDA ratio is 5 (=1 billion/200 million). Note that all the items in the income statement below EBITDA are ignored when calculating this ratio.

As with PE ratios, it is generally assumed that similar firms have similar EV/EBITDA ratios. For example, imagine that the average EV/EBITDA ratio in an industry is 6. If QRT Corporation, a firm in the industry with EBITDA of $50 million, is judged to be similar to the rest of the industry, its enterprise value might be estimated at $300 million (=6 × 50). Now imagine that QRT has $75 million of debt and $25 million of cash. Given our estimate of QRT's enterprise value, QRT's stock would be worth $250 million (=300 − 75 + 25).

A number of questions arise with value ratios:

1. Is there any advantage to the EV/EBITDA ratio over the PE ratio? Yes. Companies in the same industry may differ by leverage, i.e., the ratio of debt to equity. As you will learn in Chapter 16, leverage increases the risk of equity, impacting the discount rate, R. Thus, while firms in the same industry may be otherwise comparable, they are likely to have different PE ratios if they have different degrees of leverage. Since enterprise value includes debt and equity, the impact of leverage on the EV/EBITDA ratio is less.[9]

2. Why is EBITDA used in the denominator? The numerator and denominator of a ratio should be consistent. Since the numerator of the PE ratio is the price of a share of *stock,* it makes sense that the denominator is the earnings per share (EPS) of *stock.* That is, interest is specifically subtracted before EPS is calculated. By contrast, since EV involves the sum of debt and equity, it is sensible that the denominator is unaffected by interest payments. This is the case with EBITDA since, as its name implies, earnings are calculated before interest is taken out.

[9]However, leverage does impact the ratio of EV to EBITDA to some extent. As we discuss in Chapter 16, leverage creates a tax shield, increasing EV. Since leverage should not impact EBITDA, the ratio should increase with leverage.

3. Why does the denominator ignore depreciation and amortization? Many practitioners argue that, since depreciation and amortization are not cash flows, earnings should be calculated before taking out depreciation and amortization. In other words, depreciation and amortization merely reflect the sunk cost of a previous purchase. However, this view is by no means universal. Others point out that depreciable assets will eventually be replaced in an ongoing business. Since depreciation charges reflect the cost of future replacement, it can be argued that these charges should be considered in a calculation of income.

4. What other denominators are used in value ratios? Among others, practitioners may use EBIT (earnings before interest and taxes), EBITA (earnings before interest, taxes, and amortization), and free cash flow.

5. Why is cash subtracted out? Many firms seem to hold amounts of cash well in excess of what is needed. For example, Microsoft held tens of billions of dollars of cash and short-term investments throughout the last decade, far more than many analysts believed was optimal. Since an enterprise value ratio should reflect the ability of *productive* assets to create earnings or cash flow, cash should be subtracted out when calculating the ratio. However, the viewpoint that all cash should be ignored can be criticized. Some cash holdings are necessary to run a business, and this amount of cash should be included in EV.

9.5 Valuing the Entire Firm

In Chapters 5 and 6, we valued corporate projects by discounting the projects' cash flows. Cash flows were determined by a top-down approach beginning with estimates of revenues and expenses. So far in this chapter, we have discounted dividends to price a single share of stock. As an alternative, one can value entire firms by discounting their cash flows in a manner analogous to the project valuation of Chapters 5 and 6.

As an example, consider Global Harmonic Control Systems (GHCS). Revenues, which are forecasted to be $500 million in one year, are expected to grow at 10 percent per year for the two years after that, 8 percent per year for the next two years, and 6 percent per year after that. Expenses including depreciation are 60 percent of revenues. Net investment, including net working capital and capital spending less depreciation, is 10 percent of revenues. Because all costs are proportional to revenues, net cash flow (sometimes referred to as free cash flow) grows at the same rate as do revenues. GHCS is an all-equity firm with 12 million shares outstanding. A discount rate of 16 percent is appropriate for a firm of GHCS's risk.

The relevant numbers for the first five years, rounded to two decimals, are:

Year (000,000)	1	2	3	4	5
Revenues	500.0	550.0	605.0	653.4	705.67
−Expenses	300.0	330.0	363.0	392.04	423.40
Earnings before taxes	200.0	220.0	242.0	261.36	282.27
−Taxes (@ 0.40)	80.0	88.0	96.8	104.54	112.91
Earnings after taxes	120.0	132.0	145.2	156.82	169.36
−Net investment	50.0	55.0	60.5	65.34	70.57
Net cash flow	70.0	77.0	84.7	91.48	98.79

Since net cash flow grows at 6 percent per year after Year 5, net cash flow in Year 6 is forecasted to be $104.72 ($=98.79 \times 1.06$). Using the growing perpetuity formula, we can calculate the present value as of Year 5 of all future cash flows to be $1047.22 million ($=\$104.72/(0.16 - 0.06)$).

The present value as of today of that terminal value is

$$\$1047.22 \times \frac{1}{(1.16)^5} = \$498.59 \text{ million}$$

The present value of the net cash flows during the first five years is:

$$\frac{\$70}{1.16} + \frac{\$77}{(1.16)^2} + \frac{\$84.7}{(1.16)^3} + \frac{\$91.48}{(1.16)^4} + \frac{\$98.79}{(1.16)^5} = \$269.39 \text{ million}$$

Adding in the terminal value, today's value of the firm is $767.98 million ($=269.39 + 498.59$). Given the number of shares outstanding, the price per share is $64.00 ($=\$767.98/12$).

The above calculation assumes a growing perpetuity after Year 5. However, we pointed out in the previous section that stocks are often valued by multiples. An investor might estimate the terminal value of GHCS via a multiple, rather than the growing perpetuity formula. For example, suppose that the price–earnings ratio for comparable firms in GHCS's industry is 7.

Since earnings after tax in Year 5, are $169.36, using the PE multiple of 7, the value of the firm at Year 5 would be estimated as $1185.52 million ($=169.36 \times 7$).

The firm's value today is:

$$\frac{\$70}{1.16} + \frac{\$77}{(1.16)^2} + \frac{\$84.7}{(1.16)^3} + \frac{\$91.48}{(1.16)^4} + \frac{\$98.79}{(1.16)^5} + \frac{\$1185.52}{(1.16)^5} = \$833.83$$

With 12 million shares outstanding, the price per share of GHCS would be $69.49 ($=\$833.83/12$).

Now we have two estimates of the value of a share of equity in GHCS. The different estimates reflect the different ways of calculating terminal value. Using the constant growth discounted cash flow method for terminal value our estimate of the equity value per share of GHCS is $64 and using the PE comparable method our estimate is $69.49. There is no best method. If the comparable firms were all identical to GHCS, perhaps the PE method would be best. Unfortunately, firms are not identical. On the other hand, if we were very sure of the terminal date and the growth in subsequent cash flows, perhaps the constant growth method would be best. In practice, both methods are used.

Conceptually, the dividend discount model, the NPVGO model, and the firm cash flow model are mutually consistent and can be used to determine the value of a share of stock. In practice, the dividend discount model is especially useful for firms paying very steady dividends and the NPVGO model is useful for firms with attractive growth opportunities. The firm cash flow model is helpful for non-dividend paying firms with external financing needs.

9.6 The Stock Markets

ExcelMaster
coverage online

This section introduces Web Query and Stock Chart functions.

The stock market consists of a **primary market** and a **secondary market.** In the primary, or new-issue market, shares of stock are first brought to the market and sold to investors. In the secondary market, existing shares are traded among investors. In the primary market, companies sell securities to raise money. We will discuss this process in detail in a later chapter. We therefore focus mainly on secondary-market activity in this section. We conclude with a discussion of how stock prices are quoted in the financial press.

DEALERS AND BROKERS

Because most securities transactions involve dealers and brokers, it is important to understand exactly what is meant by the terms *dealer* and *broker*. A **dealer** maintains an inventory and stands ready to buy and sell at any time. In contrast, **a broker** brings buyers and sellers together but does not maintain an inventory. For example, when we speak of used car dealers and real estate brokers, we recognize that the used car dealer maintains an inventory, whereas the real estate broker does not.

In the securities markets, a dealer stands ready to buy securities from investors wishing to sell them and sell securities to investors wishing to buy them. The price the dealer is willing to pay is called the *bid price*. The price at which the dealer will sell is called the *ask price* (sometimes called the *asked, offered,* or *offering price*). The difference between the bid and ask prices is called the *spread,* and it is the basic source of dealer profits.

How big is the bid-ask spread on your favorite stock? Check out the latest quotes at **www.bloomberg.com**.

Dealers exist in all areas of the economy, not just the stock markets. For example, your local college bookstore is probably both a primary and a secondary market textbook dealer. If you buy a new book, this is a primary market transaction. If you buy a used book, this is a secondary market transaction, and you pay the store's ask price. If you sell the book back, you receive the store's bid price, often half of the ask price. The bookstore's spread is the difference between the two prices.

In contrast, a securities broker arranges transactions between investors, matching those wishing to buy securities with those wishing to sell securities. The distinctive characteristic of security brokers is that they do not buy or sell securities for their own accounts. Facilitating trades by others is their business.

ORGANIZATION OF THE NYSE

The New York Stock Exchange, or NYSE, popularly known as the Big Board, recently celebrated its bicentennial. It has occupied its current location on Wall Street since the turn of the twentieth century. Measured in terms of dollar volume of activity and the total value of shares listed, it is the largest stock market in the world.

Members Historically, the NYSE had 1,366 exchange **members.** Prior to 2006, the exchange members were said to own "seats" on the exchange, and, collectively, the members of the exchange were also the owners. For this and other reasons, seats were valuable and were bought and sold fairly regularly. Seat prices reached a record $4 million in 2005.

In 2006, all of this changed when the NYSE became a publicly owned corporation called NYSE Group, Inc. Naturally, its stock is listed on the NYSE. Now, instead of purchasing seats, exchange members must purchase trading licenses, the number of which is limited to 1,500. In 2009, a license cost $44,000 per year. Having a license entitles you to buy and sell securities on the floor of the exchange.

In April 2007, the NYSE completed a merger with Euronext to form the NYSE Euronext. NYSE Euronext operates a number of markets (including four stock markets in the United States alone), but the NYSE is the biggest and best-known. As we briefly describe how the NYSE operates, keep in mind that other markets owned by

NYSE Euronext may function differently. What makes the NYSE somewhat unique is that it is a *hybrid market*. In a hybrid market, trading takes place both electronically and face-to-face.

With electronic trading, orders to buy and orders to sell are submitted to the exchange. Orders are compared by a computer and whenever there is a match, the orders are executed with no human intervention. Most trades on the NYSE occur this way. For orders that are not handled electronically, the NYSE relies on its license holders. There are three different types of license holders, **designated market makers (DMMs), floor brokers,** and **supplemental liquidity providers (SLPs).**

The DMMs, formerly known as "specialists," act as dealers in particular stocks. Typically, each stock on the NYSE is assigned to a single DMM. As a dealer, a DMM maintains a two-sided market, meaning that the DMM continually posts and updates bid and ask prices. By doing so, the DMM ensures that there is always a buyer or seller available, thereby promoting market liquidity.

Floor brokers execute trades for customers, trying to get the best price possible. Floor brokers are generally employees of large brokerage firms such as Merrill Lynch, the wealth management division of Bank of America. The interaction between floor brokers and DMMs is the key to non-electronic trading on the NYSE. We discuss this interaction in detail in just a moment.

The SLPs are essentially investment firms who agree to be active participants in stocks assigned to them. Their job is to regularly make a one-sided market (i.e., offering to either buy or sell). They trade purely for their own accounts (using their own money), so they do not represent customers. They are given a small rebate on their buys and sells, thereby encouraging them to be more aggressive. The NYSE's goal is to generate as much liquidity as possible, which makes it easier for ordinary investors to quickly buy and sell at prevailing prices. Unlike DMMs and floor brokers, SLPs do not operate on the floor of the stock exchange.

Operations   Now that we have a basic idea of how the NYSE is organized and who the major players are, we turn to the question of how trading actually takes place. Fundamentally, the business of the NYSE is to attract and process **order flow.** The term *order flow* means the flow of customer orders to buy and sell stocks. The customers of the NYSE are the millions of individual investors and tens of thousands of institutional investors who place their orders to buy and sell shares in NYSE-listed companies. The NYSE has been quite successful in attracting order flow. Currently, it is common for more than one billion shares to change hands in a single day.

Floor Activity   It is quite likely that you have seen footage of the NYSE trading floor on television, or you may have visited the NYSE and viewed exchange floor activity from the visitors' gallery (it's worth the trip). Either way, you would have seen a big room, about the size of a basketball gym. This big room is called, technically, "the Big Room." There are a couple of other, smaller rooms that you normally don't see, one of which is called "the Garage" because that is literally what it was before it was taken over for trading.

On the floor of the exchange are a number of stations. These stations have multiple counters with numerous terminal screens above and on the sides. People operate behind and in front of the counters in relatively stationary positions.

Other people move around on the exchange floor, frequently returning to the many work stations positioned along the exchange walls. In all, you may be reminded of worker ants moving around an ant colony. It is natural to wonder: "What are all those people doing down there (and why are so many wearing funny-looking coats)?"

As an overview of exchange floor activity, here is a quick look at what goes on. Each of the stations is a **DMM's post.** DMMs normally operate in front of their posts to monitor and manage trading in the stocks assigned to them. Clerical employees working for the DMMs operate behind the counter. Moving around the exchange floor are swarms of floor brokers, receiving customer orders, walking out to DMMs' posts where the orders can be executed, and returning to confirm order executions and receive new customer orders.

To better understand activity on the NYSE trading floor, imagine yourself as a floor broker. Your clerk has just handed you an order to sell 2,000 shares of Walmart for a customer of the brokerage company that employs you. The customer wants to sell the stock at the best possible price as soon as possible. You immediately walk (running violates exchange rules) to the DMM's post where Walmart stock is traded.

As you approach the DMM's post where Walmart is traded, you check the terminal screen for information on the current market price. The screen reveals that the last executed trade was at $25.63, and that the DMM is bidding $25.50 per share. You could immediately sell to the DMM at $25.50, but that would be too easy.

Instead, as the customer's representative, you are obligated to get the best possible price. It is your job to "work" the order, and your job depends on providing satisfactory order execution service. So, you look around for another broker who represents a customer who wants to buy Walmart stock. Luckily, you quickly find another broker at the DMM's post with an order to buy 2,000 shares. Noticing that the dealer is asking $25.76 per share, you both agree to execute your orders with each other at a price of $25.63. This price is about halfway between the DMM's bid and ask prices, and it saves each of your customers $.13 × 2,000 = $260 as compared to dealing at the posted prices.

For a very actively traded stock, there may be many buyers and sellers around the DMM's post, and most of the trading will be done directly between brokers. This is called trading in the "crowd." In such cases, the DMM's responsibility is to maintain order and to make sure that all buyers and sellers receive a fair price. In other words, the DMM essentially functions as a referee.

More often, however, there will be no crowd at the DMM's post. Going back to our Walmart example, suppose you are unable to quickly find another broker with an order to buy 2,000 shares. Because you have an order to sell immediately, you may have no choice but to sell to the DMM at the bid price of $25.50. In this case, the need to execute an order quickly takes priority, and the DMM provides the liquidity necessary to allow immediate order execution.

Finally, note that colored coats are worn by many of the people on the floor of the exchange. The color of the coat indicates the person's job or position. Clerks, runners, visitors, exchange officials, and so on wear particular colors to identify themselves. Also, things can get a little hectic on a busy day, with the result that good clothing doesn't last long; the cheap coats offer some protection.

NASDAQ OPERATIONS

In terms of the number of companies listed and, on many days, the number of shares traded, the NASDAQ is even bigger than the NYSE. The somewhat odd name is derived from the acronym *NASDAQ*, which originally stood for National

Association of Securities Dealers Automated Quotations system, but now is a name in its own right.

Introduced in 1971, the NASDAQ market is a computer network of securities dealers who disseminate timely security price quotes to NASDAQ subscribers. These dealers act as market makers for securities listed on the NASDAQ. As market makers, NASDAQ dealers post bid and asked prices at which they accept sell and buy orders, respectively. With each price quote, they also post the number of stock shares that they obligate themselves to trade at their quoted prices.

Not to be outdone by the NYSE, the NASDAQ in May 2007 acquired the OMX, which controlled seven Nordic and Baltic stock exchanges. Since the merger, the NASDAQ is officially the NASDAQ OMX Group, although it is still often referred to as simply NASDAQ.

Unlike the NYSE DMM system, NASDAQ relies on multiple market makers for actively traded stocks. Thus, there are two key differences between the NYSE and NASDAQ: (1) NASDAQ is a computer network and has no physical location where trading takes place and (2) NASDAQ has a multiple market maker system rather than a DMM system. Notice that there is no direct trading in the crowd as there may be on the NYSE.

About 3,200 companies are listed on the NASDAQ system, with an average of about a dozen market makers for each security. Traditionally, shares of stock in smaller companies were listed on the NASDAQ, and there was a tendency for companies to move from the NASDAQ to the NYSE once they became large enough. Today, however, giant companies such as Amazon, Microsoft, and Intel have chosen to remain on the NASDAQ.

The NASDAQ network operates with three levels of information access. Level 1 is designed to provide a timely, accurate source of price quotations. These prices are freely available over the Internet. Level 2 allows users to view price quotes from all NASDAQ market makers. In particular, this level allows access to **inside quotes.** Inside quotes are the highest bid quotes and the lowest asked quotes for a NASDAQ-listed security. Level 2 is now available on the Web, usually for a small fee. Level 3 is for the use of market makers only. This access level allows NASDAQ dealers to enter or change their price quote information.

The NASDAQ is actually made up of three separate markets: the NASDAQ Global Select Market, the NASDAQ Global Market, and the NASDAQ Capital Market. As the market for NASDAQ's larger and more actively traded securities, the Global Select Market lists about 1,200 companies (as of early 2009), including some of the best-known companies in the world, such as Microsoft and Intel. The Global Market companies are somewhat smaller in size, and NASDAQ lists about 1,450 of these companies. Finally, the smallest companies listed on NASDAQ are in the NASDAQ Capital Market; about 550 are currently listed. Of course, as Capital Market companies become more established, they may move up to the Global Market or Global Select Market.

ECNs   In a very important development in the late 1990s, the NASDAQ system was opened to so-called **electronic communications networks (ECNs).** ECNs are basically websites that allow investors to trade directly with one another. Investor buy and sell orders placed on ECNs are transmitted to the NASDAQ and displayed along with market maker bid and ask prices. The ECNs open up the NASDAQ by essentially allowing individual investors, not just market makers, to enter orders. As a result, the ECNs act to increase liquidity and competition.

Chapter 9   Stock Valuation   **297**

STOCK MARKET REPORTING

You can get real-time stock quotes on the Web. See **finance.yahoo.com** for details.

In recent years, stock price quotes and related information have increasingly moved from traditional print media, such as *The Wall Street Journal,* to various websites. Yahoo! Finance (finance.yahoo.com) is a good example. We went there and requested a stock quote on wholesale club Costco, which is listed on the NASDAQ. Here is a portion of what we found:

Costco Wholesale Corporation (NasdaqGS: COST)

REAL-TIME 72.07 ↓ 0.55 (0.76%) 1:21PM EST

Last Trade	**72.05**	Day's Range	71.86 - 72.61
Trade Time	1:07PM EST	52wk Range	53.41 - 73.45
Change	↓ 0.57 (0.78%)	Volume	1,360,720
Prev Close	72.62	Avg Vol (3m)	3,049,930
Open	72.51	Market Cap	31.45B
Bid	72.05 x 800	P/E (ttm)	23.78
Ask	72.06 x 2800	EPS (ttm)	3.03
1y Target Est	73.25	Div & Yield	0.82 (1.10%)

Most of this information is self-explanatory. Two prices are reported, one in real time ($72.07) and one with a 15-minute delay ($72.05). Availability of real-time prices for free is a relatively new development. The reported change is from the previous day's closing price. The opening price is the first trade of the day. We see the bid and ask prices of $72.05 and $72.06, respectively, along with the market "depth," which is the number of shares sought at the bid price and offered at the ask price. The "1y Target Est" is the average estimated stock price one year ahead based on estimates from security analysts who follow the stock.

Moving to the second column, we have the range of prices for this day, followed by the range over the previous 52 weeks. Volume is the number of shares traded today, followed by average daily volume over the last three months. Market cap is number of shares outstanding (from the most recent quarterly financial statements) multiplied by the current price per share. P/E is the PE ratio we discussed in Section 9.4. The earnings per share (EPS) used in the calculation is "ttm," meaning "trailing twelve months." Finally, we have the dividend on the stock, which is actually the most recent quarterly dividend multiplied by 4, and the dividend yield. Notice that the yield is just the reported dividend divided by the stock price: $.82/$72.05 = .011 = 1.1%.

◄ To test your mastery of this material, take a quiz at mhhe. com/rwj

Summary and Conclusions

This chapter has covered the basics of stocks and stock valuations. The key points include:

1. A stock can be valued by discounting its dividends. We mention three types of situations:
   a. The case of zero growth of dividends.
   b. The case of constant growth of dividends.
   c. The case of differential growth.

2. An estimate of the growth rate of dividends is needed for the dividend discount model. A useful estimate of the growth rate is:

$$g = \text{Retention ratio} \times \text{Return on retained earnings (ROE)}$$

www.mhhe.com/rwj

As long as the firm holds its ratio of dividends to earnings constant, g represents the growth rate of both dividends and earnings.

3. The price of a share of stock can be viewed as the sum of its price under the assumption that the firm is a "cash cow" plus the per-share value of the firm's growth opportunities. A company is termed a cash cow if it pays out all of its earnings as dividends.

   We write the value of a share as:

$$\frac{EPS}{R} + NPVGO$$

4. Negative NPV projects lower the value of the firm. That is, projects with rates of return below the discount rate lower firm value. Nevertheless, both the earnings and dividends of a firm will grow as long as the firm's projects have positive rates of return.

5. From accounting, we know that earnings are divided into two parts: dividends and retained earnings. Most firms continually retain earnings in order to create future dividends. One should not discount earnings to obtain price per share since part of earnings must be reinvested. Only dividends reach the stockholders and only they should be discounted to obtain share price.

6. Some analysts value stock via multiples, such as the price-earnings ratio. However, we caution that one must apply the same multiple only to similar companies.

7. We suggest that a firm's price–earnings ratio is a function of three factors:
   a. The per-share amount of the firm's valuable growth opportunities.
   b. The risk of the stock.
   c. The type of accounting method used by the firm.

8. The two biggest stock markets in the United States are the NYSE and the NASDAQ. We discussed the organization and operation of these two markets, and we saw how stock price information is reported.

Concept Questions

1. **Stock Valuation** Why does the value of a share of stock depend on dividends?

2. **Stock Valuation** A substantial percentage of the companies listed on the NYSE and the NASDAQ don't pay dividends, but investors are nonetheless willing to buy shares in them. How is this possible given your answer to the previous question?

3. **Dividend Policy** Referring to the previous questions, under what circumstances might a company choose not to pay dividends?

4. **Dividend Growth Model** Under what two assumptions can we use the dividend growth model presented in the chapter to determine the value of a share of stock? Comment on the reasonableness of these assumptions.

5. **Common versus Preferred Stock** Suppose a company has a preferred stock issue and a common stock issue. Both have just paid a $2 dividend. Which do you think will have a higher price, a share of the preferred or a share of the common?

6. **Dividend Growth Model** Based on the dividend growth model, what are the two components of the total return on a share of stock? Which do you think is typically larger?

7. **Growth Rate** In the context of the dividend growth model, is it true that the growth rate in dividends and the growth rate in the price of the stock are identical?

8. **Price–Earnings Ratio** What are the three factors that determine a company's price–earnings ratio?

Chapter 9   Stock Valuation   **299**

9.   **Corporate Ethics**   Is it unfair or unethical for corporations to create classes of stock with unequal voting rights?

10.   **Stock Valuation**   Evaluate the following statement: Managers should not focus on the current stock value because doing so will lead to an overemphasis on short-term profits at the expense of long-term profits.

Questions and Problems

BASIC (Questions 1–10)

1.   **Stock Values**   The Starr Co. just paid a dividend of $2.15 per share on its stock. The dividends are expected to grow at a constant rate of 5 percent per year, indefinitely. If investors require a return of 11 percent on the stock, what is the current price? What will the price be in three years? In 15 years?

2.   **Stock Values**   The next dividend payment by ECY, Inc., will be $3.20 per share. The dividends are anticipated to maintain a growth rate of 6 percent, forever. If ECY stock currently sells for $63.50 per share, what is the required return?

3.   **Stock Values**   For the company in the previous problem, what is the dividend yield? What is the expected capital gains yield?

4.   **Stock Values**   White Wedding Corporation will pay a $2.65 per share dividend next year. The company pledges to increase its dividend by 4.75 percent per year, indefinitely. If you require a return of 11 percent on your investment, how much will you pay for the company's stock today?

5.   **Stock Valuation**   Siblings, Inc., is expected to maintain a constant 6.4 percent growth rate in its dividends, indefinitely. If the company has a dividend yield of 4.3 percent, what is the required return on the company's stock?

6.   **Stock Valuation**   Suppose you know that a company's stock currently sells for $72 per share and the required return on the stock is 11.5 percent. You also know that the total return on the stock is evenly divided between a capital gains yield and a dividend yield. If it's the company's policy to always maintain a constant growth rate in its dividends, what is the current dividend per share?

7.   **Stock Valuation**   Gruber Corp. pays a constant $9 dividend on its stock. The company will maintain this dividend for the next 12 years and will then cease paying dividends forever. If the required return on this stock is 10 percent, what is the current share price?

8.   **Valuing Preferred Stock**   Ayden, Inc., has an issue of preferred stock outstanding that pays a $5.90 dividend every year, in perpetuity. If this issue currently sells for $87 per share, what is the required return?

9.   **Growth Rate**   The newspaper reported last week that Bennington Enterprises earned $34 million this year. The report also stated that the firm's return on equity is 16 percent. Bennington retains 80 percent of its earnings. What is the firm's earnings growth rate? What will next year's earnings be?

10.   **Stock Valuation and PE**   The Germinating Flower Co. has earnings of $1.75 per share. The benchmark PE for the company is 18. What stock price would you consider appropriate? What if the benchmark PE were 21?

INTERMEDIATE
(Questions 11–32)

11.   **Stock Valuation**   Universal Laser, Inc., just paid a dividend of $3.10 on its stock. The growth rate in dividends is expected to be a constant 6 percent per year, indefinitely. Investors require a 15 percent return on the stock for the first three years, a 13 percent return for the next three years, and then an 11 percent return thereafter. What is the current share price for the stock?

12. **Nonconstant Growth** Metallica Bearings, Inc., is a young start-up company. No dividends will be paid on the stock over the next nine years, because the firm needs to plow back its earnings to fuel growth. The company will pay a $15 per share dividend in 10 years and will increase the dividend by 5.5 percent per year thereafter. If the required return on this stock is 13 percent, what is the current share price?

13. **Nonconstant Dividends** Bucksnort, Inc., has an odd dividend policy. The company has just paid a dividend of $12 per share and has announced that it will increase the dividend by $3 per share for each of the next five years, and then never pay another dividend. If you require a return of 12 percent on the company's stock, how much will you pay for a share today?

14. **Nonconstant Dividends** Lohn Corporation is expected to pay the following dividends over the next four years: $10, $7, $6, and $2.75. Afterwards, the company pledges to maintain a constant 5 percent growth rate in dividends forever. If the required return on the stock is 13 percent, what is the current share price?

15. **Differential Growth** Hughes Co. is growing quickly. Dividends are expected to grow at a rate of 20 percent for the next three years, with the growth rate falling off to a constant 5 percent thereafter. If the required return is 12 percent and the company just paid a $2.80 dividend, what is the current share price?

16. **Differential Growth** Janicek Corp. is experiencing rapid growth. Dividends are expected to grow at 30 percent per year during the next three years, 18 percent over the following year, and then 8 percent per year indefinitely. The required return on this stock is 11 percent, and the stock currently sells for $65 per share. What is the projected dividend for the coming year?

17. **Negative Growth** Antiques R Us is a mature manufacturing firm. The company just paid a dividend of $9, but management expects to reduce the payout by 4 percent per year, indefinitely. If you require an 11 percent return on this stock, what will you pay for a share today?

18. **Finding the Dividend** Mau Corporation stock currently sells for $58.32 per share. The market requires a return of 11.5 percent on the firm's stock. If the company maintains a constant 5 percent growth rate in dividends, what was the most recent dividend per share paid on the stock?

19. **Valuing Preferred Stock** Fifth National Bank just issued some new preferred stock. The issue will pay an annual dividend of $8 in perpetuity, beginning five years from now. If the market requires a return of 5.6 percent on this investment, how much does a share of preferred stock cost today?

20. **Using Stock Quotes** You have found the following stock quote for RJW Enterprises, Inc., in the financial pages of today's newspaper. What is the annual dividend? What was the closing price for this stock that appeared in *yesterday's* paper? If the company currently has 25 million shares of stock outstanding, what was net income for the most recent four quarters?

YTD %Chg	Stock	SYM	YLD	PE	Last	Net Chg
−1.1	RJW Enterp.	RJW	1.9	23	26.18	−.13

21. **Taxes and Stock Price** You own $100,000 worth of Smart Money stock. One year from now, you will receive a dividend of $2.25 per share. You will receive a $2.40 dividend two years from now. You will sell the stock for $65 per share three years from now. Dividends are taxed at the rate of 28 percent. Assume there is no capital gains tax. The aftertax required rate of return is 15 percent. How many shares of stock do you own?

Chapter 9   Stock Valuation **301**

22. **Nonconstant Growth and Quarterly Dividends**   Pasqually Mineral Water, Inc., will pay a quarterly dividend per share of $.80 at the end of each of the next 12 quarters. Thereafter, the dividend will grow at a quarterly rate of 1 percent, forever. The appropriate rate of return on the stock is 10 percent, compounded quarterly. What is the current stock price?

23. **Finding the Dividend**   Briley, Inc., is expected to pay equal dividends at the end of each of the next two years. Thereafter, the dividend will grow at a constant annual rate of 4 percent, forever. The current stock price is $45. What is next year's dividend payment if the required rate of return is 11 percent?

24. **Finding the Required Return**   Juggernaut Satellite Corporation earned $18 million for the fiscal year ending yesterday. The firm also paid out 30 percent of its earnings as dividends yesterday. The firm will continue to pay out 30 percent of its earnings as annual, end-of-year dividends. The remaining 70 percent of earnings is retained by the company for use in projects. The company has 2 million shares of common stock outstanding. The current stock price is $93. The historical return on equity (ROE) of 13 percent is expected to continue in the future. What is the required rate of return on the stock?

25. **Dividend Growth**   Four years ago, Bling Diamond, Inc., paid a dividend of $1.35 per share. Bling paid a dividend of $1.77 per share yesterday. Dividends will grow over the next five years at the same rate they grew over the last four years. Thereafter, dividends will grow at 5 percent per year. What will Bling Diamond's cash dividend be in seven years?

26. **Price–Earnings Ratio**   Consider Pacific Energy Company and U.S. Bluechips, Inc., both of which reported earnings of $950,000. Without new projects, both firms will continue to generate earnings of $950,000 in perpetuity. Assume that all earnings are paid as dividends and that both firms require a return of 12 percent.

   a. What is the current PE ratio for each company?
   b. Pacific Energy Company has a new project that will generate additional earnings of $100,000 each year in perpetuity. Calculate the new PE ratio of the company.
   c. U.S. Bluechips has a new project that will increase earnings by $200,000 in perpetuity. Calculate the new PE ratio of the firm.

27. **Growth Opportunities**   The Stambaugh Corporation currently has earnings per share of $9.40. The company has no growth and pays out all earnings as dividends. It has a new project that will require an investment of $1.95 per share in one year. The project is only a two-year project, and it will increase earnings in the two years following the investment by $2.75 and $3.05, respectively. Investors require a return of 12 percent on Stambaugh stock.

   a. What is the value per share of the company's stock assuming the firm does not undertake the investment opportunity?
   b. If the company does undertake the investment, what is the value per share now?
   c. Again, assume the company undertakes the investment. What will the price per share be four years from today?

28. **Growth Opportunities**   Rite Bite Enterprises sells toothpicks. Gross revenues last year were $7.5 million, and total costs were $3.4 million. Rite Bite has 1 million shares of common stock outstanding. Gross revenues and costs are expected to grow at 5 percent per year. Rite Bite pays no income taxes. All earnings are paid out as dividends.

   a. If the appropriate discount rate is 13 percent and all cash flows are received at year's end, what is the price per share of Rite Bite stock?
   b. Rite Bite has decided to produce toothbrushes. The project requires an immediate outlay of $17 million. In one year, another outlay of $6 million will be needed. The year after that, earnings will increase by $4.2 million. That profit level will

be maintained in perpetuity. What effect will undertaking this project have on the price per share of the stock?

29. **Growth Opportunities** California Real Estate, Inc., expects to earn $71 million per year in perpetuity if it does not undertake any new projects. The firm has an opportunity to invest $16 million today and $5 million in one year in real estate. The new investment will generate annual earnings of $11 million in perpetuity, beginning two years from today. The firm has 15 million shares of common stock outstanding, and the required rate of return on the stock is 12 percent. Land investments are not depreciable. Ignore taxes.

   a. What is the price of a share of stock if the firm does not undertake the new investment?

   b. What is the value of the investment?

   c. What is the per-share stock price if the firm undertakes the investment?

30. **Stock Valuation and PE** Ramsay Corp. currently has an EPS of $2.35, and the benchmark PE for the company is 21. Earnings are expected to grow at 7 percent per year.

   a. What is your estimate of the current stock price?

   b. What is the target stock price in one year?

   c. Assuming the company pays no dividends, what is the implied return on the company's stock over the next year? What does this tell you about the implicit stock return using PE valuation?

31. **Stock Valuation and EV** FFDP Corp. has yearly sales of $28 million and costs of $12 million. The company's balance sheet shows debt of $54 million and cash of $18 million. There are 950,000 shares outstanding and the industry EV/EBITDA multiple is 7.5. What is the company's enterprise value? What is the stock price per share?

32. **Stock Valuation and Cash Flows** Eberhart Manufacturing has projected sales of $145 million next year. Costs are expected to be $81 million and net investment is expected to be $15 million. Each of these values is expected to grow at 14 percent the following year, with the growth rate declining by 2 percent per year until the growth rate reaches 6 percent, where it is expected to remain indefinitely. There are 5.5 million shares of stock outstanding and investors require a return of 13 percent return on the company's stock. The corporate tax rate is 40 percent.

   a. What is your estimate of the current stock price?

   b. Suppose instead that you estimate the terminal value of the company using a PE multiple. The industry PE multiple is 11. What is your new estimate of the company's stock price?

CHALLENGE
(Questions 33–38)

33. **Capital Gains versus Income** Consider four different stocks, all of which have a required return of 17 percent and a most recent dividend of $3.50 per share. Stocks W, X, and Y are expected to maintain constant growth rates in dividends for the foreseeable future of 8.5 percent, 0 percent, and −5 percent per year, respectively. Stock Z is a growth stock that will increase its dividend by 30 percent for the next two years and then maintain a constant 8 percent growth rate thereafter. What is the dividend yield for each of these four stocks? What is the expected capital gains yield? Discuss the relationship among the various returns that you find for each of these stocks.

34. **Stock Valuation** Most corporations pay quarterly dividends on their common stock rather than annual dividends. Barring any unusual circumstances during the year, the board raises, lowers, or maintains the current dividend once a year and then pays this dividend out in equal quarterly installments to its shareholders.

   a. Suppose a company currently pays a $3.20 annual dividend on its common stock in a single annual installment, and management plans on raising this dividend by

5 percent per year indefinitely. If the required return on this stock is 11 percent, what is the current share price?

b. Now suppose that the company in (a) actually pays its annual dividend in equal quarterly installments; thus, this company has just paid a dividend of $.80 per share, as it has for the previous three quarters. What is your value for the current share price now? (*Hint:* Find the equivalent annual end-of-year dividend for each year.) Comment on whether or not you think that this model of stock valuation is appropriate.

35. Growth Opportunities   Lewin Skis, Inc., today expects to earn $8.50 per share for each of the future operating periods (beginning at Time 1), today if the firm makes no new investments and returns the earnings as dividends to the shareholders. However, Clint Williams, president and CEO, has discovered an opportunity to retain and invest 20 percent of the earnings beginning three years from today. This opportunity to invest will continue for each period indefinitely. He expects to earn 10 percent on this new equity investment, the return beginning one year after each investment is made. The firm's equity discount rate is 12 percent.

a. What is the price per share of Lewin Skis, Inc., stock without making the new investment?

b. If the new investment is expected to be made, per the preceding information, what would the price of the stock be now?

c. Suppose the company could increase the investment in the project by whatever amount it chose. What would the retention ratio need to be to make this project attractive?

36. Nonconstant Growth   Storico Co. just paid a dividend of $3.85 per share. The company will increase its dividend by 20 percent next year and will then reduce its dividend growth rate by 5 percentage points per year until it reaches the industry average of 5 percent dividend growth, after which the company will keep a constant growth rate forever. If the required return on Storico stock is 13 percent, what will a share of stock sell for today?

37. Nonconstant Growth   This one's a little harder. Suppose the current share price for the firm in the previous problem is $78.43 and all the dividend information remains the same. What required return must investors be demanding on Storico stock? (*Hint:* Set up the valuation formula with all the relevant cash flows, and use trial and error to find the unknown rate of return.)

38. Growth Opportunities   Burklin, Inc., has earnings of $18 million and is projected to grow at a constant rate of 5 percent forever because of the benefits gained from the learning curve. Currently, all earnings are paid out as dividends. The company plans to launch a new project two years from now that would be completely internally funded and require 30 percent of the earnings that year. The project would start generating revenues one year after the launch of the project and the earnings from the new project in any year are estimated to be constant at $6.5 million. The company has 7.5 million shares of stock outstanding. Estimate the value of the stock. The discount rate is 10 percent.

Excel Master It!

In practice, the use of the dividend discount model is refined from the method we presented in the textbook. Many analysts will estimate the dividend for the next five years and then estimate a perpetual growth rate at some point in the future, typically 10 years. Rather than have the dividend growth fall dramatically from the fast growth period to the perpetual growth period, linear interpolation is applied. That is, the dividend growth is projected to fall by an equal amount each year. For example, if the high-growth period is 15 percent for the next five years and the dividends are expected to fall to a 5 percent perpetual growth rate five years later, the dividend growth rate would decline by 2 percent each year.

The *Value Line Investment Survey* provides information for investors. Below, you will find information for IBM found in the 2012 edition of *Value Line:*

2011 dividend	$2.90
5-year dividend growth rate	9.5%

a. Assume that the perpetual growth rate of 5 percent begins 11 years from now and use linear interpolation between the high growth rate and perpetual growth rate. Construct a table that shows the dividend growth rate and dividend each year. What is the stock price at Year 10? What is the stock price today?

b. How sensitive is the current stock price to changes in the perpetual growth rate? Graph the current stock price against the perpetual growth rate in 11 years to find out.

Instead of applying the constant dividend growth model to find the stock price in the future, analysts will often combine the dividend discount method with price ratio valuation, often with the PE ratio. Remember that the PE ratio is the price per share divided by the earnings per share. So, if we know what the PE ratio is, we can solve for the stock price. Suppose we also have the following information about Boeing:

Payout ratio	30%
PE ratio at constant growth rate	15

c. Use the PE ratio to calculate the stock price when Boeing reaches a perpetual growth rate in dividends. Now find the value of the stock today finding the present value of the dividends during the supernormal growth rate and the price you calculated using the PE ratio.

d. How sensitive is the current stock price to changes in PE ratio when the stock reaches the perpetual growth rate? Graph the current stock price against the PE ratio in 11 years to find out.

STOCK VALUATION AT RAGAN ENGINES

Larissa has been talking with the company's directors about the future of East Coast Yachts. To this point, the company has used outside suppliers for various key components of the company's yachts, including engines. Larissa has decided that East Coast Yachts should consider the purchase of an engine manufacturer to allow East Coast Yachts to better integrate its supply chain and get more control over engine features. After investigating several possible companies, Larissa feels that the purchase of Ragan Engines, Inc., is a possibility. She has asked Dan Ervin to analyze Ragan's value.

Ragan Engines, Inc., was founded nine years ago by a brother and sister—Carrington and Genevieve Ragan—and has remained a privately owned company. The company manufactures marine engines for a variety of applications. Ragan has experienced rapid growth because of a proprietary technology that increases the fuel efficiency of its engines with very little sacrifice in performance. The company is equally owned by Carrington and Genevieve. The original agreement between the siblings gave each 150,000 shares of stock.

Mini Case

Larissa has asked Dan to determine a value per share of Ragan stock. To accomplish this, Dan has gathered the following information about some of Ragan's competitors that are publicly traded:

	EPS	DPS	Stock Price	ROE	R
Blue Ribband Motors Corp.	$1.09	$.19	$16.32	10.00%	12.00%
Bon Voyage Marine, Inc.	1.26	.55	13.94	12.00	17.00
Nautilus Marine Engines	(.27)	.57	23.97	N/A	16.00
Industry average	$ .73	$.44	$18.08	11.00%	15.00%

Nautilus Marine Engines's negative earnings per share (EPS) were the result of an accounting write-off last year. Without the write-off, EPS for the company would have been $2.07. Last year, Ragan had an EPS of $5.35 and paid a dividend to Carrington and Genevieve of $320,000 each. The company also had a return on equity of 21 percent. Larissa tells Dan that a required return for Ragan of 18 percent is appropriate.

1. Assuming the company continues its current growth rate, what is the value per share of the company's stock?
2. Dan has examined the company's financial statements, as well as examining those of its competitors. Although Ragan currently has a technological advantage, Dan's research indicates that Ragan's competitors are investigating other methods to improve efficiency. Given this, Dan believes that Ragan's technological advantage will last only for the next five years. After that period, the company's growth will likely slow to the industry average. Additionally, Dan believes that the required return the company uses is too high. He believes the industry average required return is more appropriate. Under Dan's assumptions, what is the estimated stock price?
3. What is the industry average price–earnings ratio? What is Ragan's price–earnings ratio? Comment on any differences and explain why they may exist.
4. Assume the company's growth rate declines to the industry average after five years. What percentage of the stock's value is attributable to growth opportunities?
5. Assume the company's growth rate slows to the industry average in five years. What future return on equity does this imply?
6. Carrington and Genevieve are not sure if they should sell the company. If they do not sell the company outright to East Coast Yachts, they would like to try and increase the value of the company's stock. In this case, they want to retain control of the company and do not want to sell stock to outside investors. They also feel that the company's debt is at a manageable level and do not want to borrow more money. What steps can they take to try and increase the price of the stock? Are there any conditions under which this strategy would *not* increase the stock price?

www.mhhe.com/rwj

Risk

PART III: RISK

CHAPTER 10

Risk and Return

LESSONS FROM MARKET HISTORY

▲ For updates on the latest happenings in finance, visit www. rwjcorporatefinance. blogspot.com

With the S&P 500 Index returning about 2 percent and the NASDAQ Composite Index down about 1 percent in 2011, stock market performance overall was not very good. However, investors in software company eGain Communications had to be happy about the 412 percent gain in that stock, and investors in semiconductor company Silicon Motion Technology had to feel pretty good following that company's 382 percent gain. Of course, not all stocks increased in value during the year. Stock in First Solar fell 74 percent during the year, and stock in Alpha Natural Resources dropped 66 percent.

These examples show that there were tremendous potential profits to be made during 2011, but there was also the risk of losing money—and lots of it. So what should you, as a stock market investor, expect when you invest your own money? In this chapter, we study more than eight decades of market history to find out.

10.1 Returns

DOLLAR RETURNS

ExcelMaster coverage online

How did the market do today? Find out at **finance.yahoo.com**.

Suppose the Video Concept Company has several thousand shares of stock outstanding and you are a shareholder. Further suppose that you purchased some of the shares of stock in the company at the beginning of the year; it is now year-end and you want to figure out how well you have done on your investment. The return you get on an investment in stocks, like that in bonds or any other investment, comes in two forms.

As the owner of stock in the Video Concept Company, you are a part owner of the company. If the company is profitable, it generally could distribute some of its profits to the shareholders. Therefore, as the owner of shares of stock, you could receive some cash, called a *dividend,* during the year. This cash is the *income component* of your return. In addition to the dividends, the other part of your return is the *capital gain*—or, if it is negative, the *capital loss* (negative capital gain)—on the investment.

For example, suppose we are considering the cash flows of the investment in Figure 10.1, showing that you purchased 100 shares of stock at the beginning of the year at a price of $37 per share. Your total investment, then, was:

$$C_0 = \$37 \times 100 = \$3,700$$

Suppose that over the year the stock paid a dividend of $1.85 per share. During the year, then, you received income of:

$$\text{Div} = \$1.85 \times 100 = \$185$$

Figure 10.1
Dollar Returns

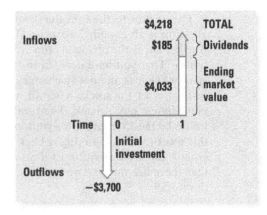

Suppose, finally, that at the end of the year the market price of the stock is $40.33 per share. Because the stock increased in price, you had a capital gain of:

$$\text{Gain} = (\$40.33 - \$37) \times 100 = \$333$$

The capital gain, like the dividend, is part of the return that shareholders require to maintain their investment in the Video Concept Company. Of course, if the price of Video Concept stock had dropped in value to, say, $34.78, you would have recorded this capital loss:

$$\text{Loss} = (\$34.78 - \$37) \times 100 = -\$222$$

The *total dollar return* on your investment is the sum of the dividend income and the capital gain or loss on the investment:

$$\text{Total dollar return} = \text{Dividend income} + \text{Capital gain (or loss)}$$

(From now on we will refer to *capital losses* as *negative capital gains* and not distinguish them.) In our first example, the total dollar return is given by:

$$\text{Total dollar return} = \$185 + \$333 = \$518$$

Notice that if you sold the stock at the end of the year, your total amount of cash would be the initial investment plus the total dollar return. In the preceding example you would have:

$$\begin{aligned}\text{Total cash if stock is sold} &= \text{Initial investment} + \text{Total dollar return} \\ &= \$3,700 + \$518 \\ &= \$4,218\end{aligned}$$

As a check, notice that this is the same as the proceeds from the sale of stock plus the dividends:

$$\begin{aligned}\text{Proceeds from stock sale} &+ \text{Dividends} \\ &= \$40.33 \times 100 + \$185 \\ &= \$4,033 + \$185 \\ &= \$4,218\end{aligned}$$

Suppose, however, that you hold your Video Concept stock and don't sell it at year-end. Should you still consider the capital gain as part of your return? Does this violate our previous present value rule that only cash matters?

The answer to the first question is a strong yes, and the answer to the second question is an equally strong no. The capital gain is every bit as much a part of your return as the dividend, and you should certainly count it as part of your total return. That you have decided to hold onto the stock and not sell, or *realize* the gain or the loss, in no way changes the fact that, if you wanted, you could get the cash value of the stock. After all, you could always sell the stock at year-end and immediately buy it back. The total amount of cash you would have at year-end would be the $518 gain plus your initial investment of $3,700. You would not lose this return when you bought back 100 shares of stock. In fact, you would be in exactly the same position as if you had not sold the stock (assuming, of course, that there are no tax consequences and no brokerage commissions from selling the stock).

PERCENTAGE RETURNS

It is more convenient to summarize the information about returns in percentage terms than in dollars because the percentages apply to any amount invested. The question we want to answer is this: How much return do we get for each dollar invested? To find this out, let t stand for the year we are looking at, let P_t be the price of the stock at the beginning of the year, and let Div_{t+1} be the dividend paid on the stock during the year. Consider the cash flows in Figure 10.2.

In our example, the price at the beginning of the year was $37 per share and the dividend paid during the year on each share was $1.85. Hence, the percentage income return, sometimes called the *dividend yield,* is:

$$
\begin{aligned}
\text{Dividend yield} &= Div_{t+1}/P_t \\
&= \$1.85/\$37 \\
&= .05 \\
&= 5\%
\end{aligned}
$$

Go to
**www.smartmoney.
com/marketmap**
for a Java applet that
shows today's returns
by market sector.

Figure 10.2
Percentage Returns

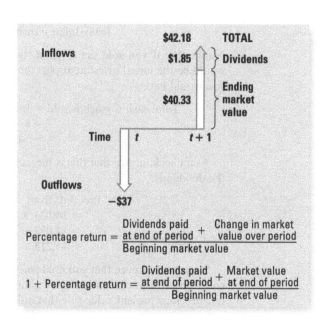

The **capital gain** (or loss) is the change in the price of the stock divided by the initial price. Letting P_{t+1} be the price of the stock at year-end, we can compute the capital gain as follows:

$$\text{Capital gain} = (P_{t+1} - P_t)/P_t$$
$$= (\$40.33 - \$37)/\$37$$
$$= \$3.33/\$37$$
$$= .09$$
$$= 9\%$$

Combining these two results, we find that the *total return* on the investment in Video Concept stock over the year, which we will label R_{t+1}, was:

$$R_{t+1} = \frac{\text{Div}_{t+1}}{P_t} + \frac{(P_{t+1} - P_t)}{P_t}$$
$$= 5\% + 9\%$$
$$= 14\%$$

From now on, we will refer to returns in percentage terms.

To give a more concrete example, stock in McDonald's, the famous hamburger chain, began 2011 at $76.34 per share. McDonald's paid dividends of $2.53 during 2011, and the stock price at the end of the year was $100.33. What was the return on McDonald's for the year? For practice, see if you agree that the answer is 34.74 percent. Of course, negative returns occur as well. For example, again in 2011, JP Morgan's stock price at the beginning of the year was $42.42 per share, and dividends of $.80 were paid. The stock ended the year at $33.25 per share. Verify that the loss was 19.73 percent for the year.

EXAMPLE 10.1

Calculating Returns Suppose a stock begins the year with a price of $25 per share and ends with a price of $35 per share. During the year, it paid a $2 dividend per share. What are its dividend yield, its capital gains yield, and its total return for the year? We can imagine the cash flows in Figure 10.3.

$$R_1 = \frac{\text{Div}_1}{P_0} + \frac{P_1 - P_0}{P_0}$$
$$= \frac{\$2}{\$25} + \frac{\$35 - 25}{\$25} = \frac{\$12}{\$25}$$
$$= 8\% \quad + 40\% \qquad = 48\%$$

Figure 10.3 **Cash Flow—An Investment Example**

(continued)

Thus, the stock's dividend yield, its capital gains yield, and its total return are 8 percent, 40 percent, and 48 percent, respectively.

Suppose you had $5,000 invested. The total dollar return you would have received on an investment in the stock is $5,000 × .48 = $2,400. If you know the total dollar return on the stock, you do not need to know how many shares you would have had to purchase to figure out how much money you would have made on the $5,000 investment. You just use the total dollar return.

10.2 Holding Period Returns

ExcelMaster
coverage online

This section covers Column Charts, COUNTIF, Sorting Data, Filtering Data, and Rank and percentile.

A famous set of studies dealing with rates of return on common stocks, bonds, and Treasury bills is found in *Ibbotson SBBI 2012 Classic Yearbook*.[1] It presents year-by-year historical rates of return for the following five important types of financial instruments in the United States:

1. *Large-company common stocks:* This common stock portfolio is based on the Standard & Poor's (S&P) Composite Index. At present the S&P Composite includes 500 of the largest (in terms of market value) stocks in the United States.

2. *Small-company common stocks:* This is a portfolio corresponding to the bottom fifth of stocks traded on the New York Stock Exchange in which stocks are ranked by market value (that is, the price of the stock multiplied by the number of shares outstanding).

3. *Long-term corporate bonds:* This is a portfolio of high-quality corporate bonds with 20-year maturities.

4. *Long-term U.S. government bonds:* This is based on U.S. government bonds with maturities of 20 years.

5. *U.S. Treasury bills:* This is based on Treasury bills with a one-month maturity.

None of the returns are adjusted for taxes or transaction costs. In addition to the year-by-year returns on financial instruments, the year-to-year change in the consumer price index is computed. This is a basic measure of inflation. We can calculate year-by-year real returns by subtracting annual inflation.

Before looking closely at the different portfolio returns, we graphically present the returns and risks available from U.S. capital markets in the 86-year period from 1926 to 2011. Figure 10.4 shows the growth of $1 invested at the beginning of 1926. Notice that the vertical axis is logarithmic, so that equal distances measure the same percentage change. The figure shows that if $1 was invested in large-company common stocks and all dividends were reinvested, the dollar would have grown to $3,045.22 by the end of 2011. The biggest growth was in the small stock portfolio. If $1 was invested in small stocks in 1926, the investment would have grown to $15,532.07. However, when you look carefully at Figure 10.4, you can see great variability in the returns on small stocks, especially in the earlier part of the period. A dollar in long-term government bonds was very stable as compared with a dollar in common stocks. Figures 10.5 to 10.8 plot each year-to-year percentage return as a vertical bar drawn from the horizontal axis for large-company common stocks, small-company stocks, long-term bonds and Treasury bills, and inflation, respectively.

Figure 10.4 gives the growth of a dollar investment in the stock market from 1926 through 2011. In other words, it shows what the value of the investment would have

---

[1]*Ibbotson SBBI 2012 Classic Yearbook* (Chicago: Morningstar).

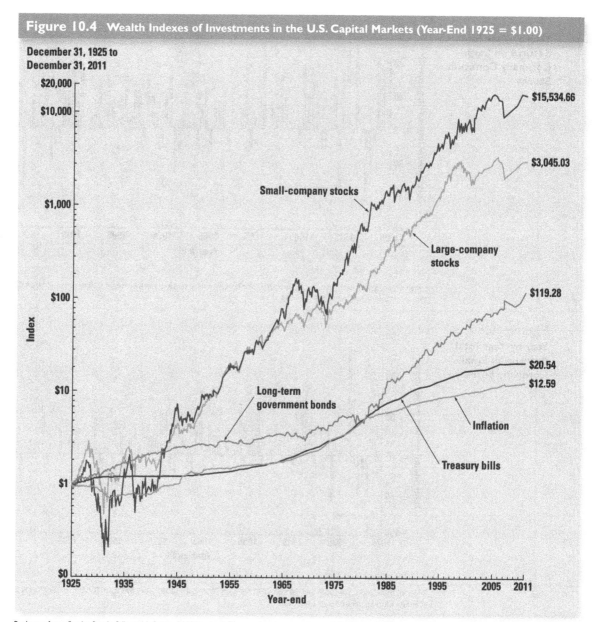

Figure 10.4 Wealth Indexes of Investments in the U.S. Capital Markets (Year-End 1925 = $1.00)

December 31, 1925 to
December 31, 2011

been if the dollar had been left in the stock market and if each year the dividends from the previous year had been reinvested in more stock. If R_t is the return in year t (expressed in decimals), the value you would have at the end of year T is the product of 1 plus the return in each of the years:

$$\text{Value} = (1 + R_1) \times (1 + R_2) \times \cdots \times (1 + R_t) \times \cdots \times (1 + R_T)$$

Figure 10.5
Year-by-Year Total Returns on Large-Company Common Stocks

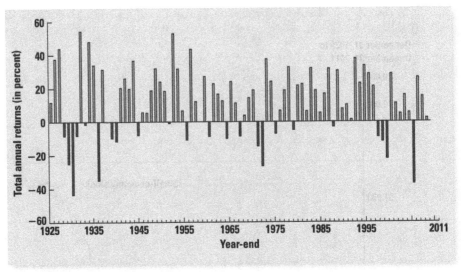

Figure 10.6
Year-by-Year Total Returns on Small-Company Stocks

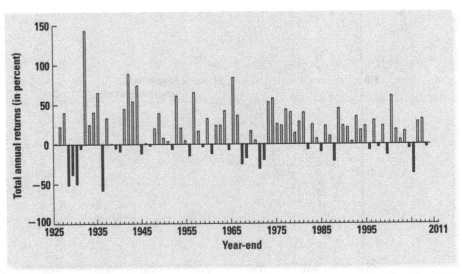

For example, if the returns were 11 percent, −5 percent, and 9 percent in a three-year period, an investment of $1 at the beginning of the period would be worth:

$$(1 + R_1) \times (1 + R_2) \times (1 + R_3) = (\$1 + .11) \times (\$1 - .05) \times (\$1 + .09)$$
$$= \$1.11 \times \$.95 \times \$1.09$$
$$= \$1.15$$

Go to
**bigcharts.
marketwatch.com**
to see both intraday
and long-term charts.

at the end of the three years. Notice that .15 or 15 percent is the total return. This includes the return from reinvesting the first-year dividends in the stock market for two more years and reinvesting the second-year dividends for the final year. The

Figure 10.7
Year-by-Year Total Returns on Bonds and U.S. Treasury Bills

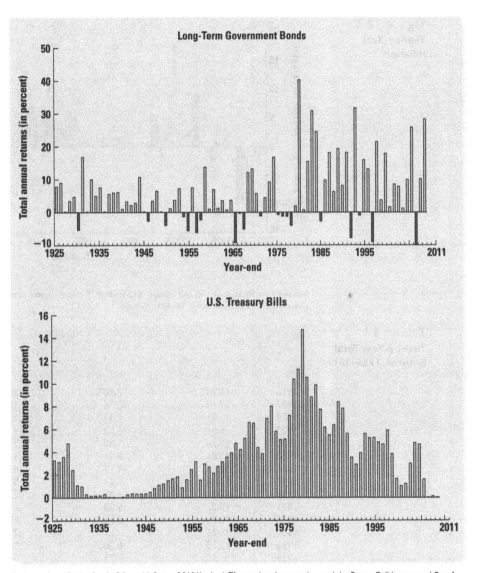

15 percent is called a three-year **holding period return.** Table 10.1 gives the annual returns each year for selected investments from 1926 to 2011. From this table, you can determine holding period returns for any combination of years.

10.3 Return Statistics

ExcelMaster
coverage online

This section covers
AVERAGE and sorting data
functions.

The history of capital market returns is too complicated to be handled in its undigested form. To use the history, we must first find some manageable ways of describing it, dramatically condensing the detailed data into a few simple statements.

This is where two important numbers summarizing the history come in. The first and most natural number is some single measure that best describes the past annual

314   **Part III**   Risk

Figure 10.8
Year-by-Year
Inflation

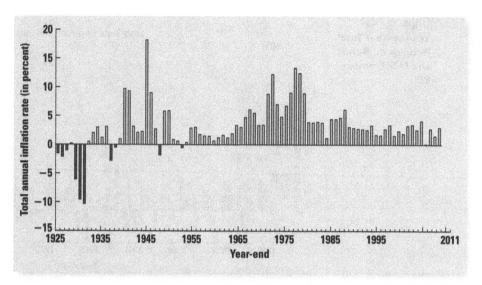

Table 10.1
Year-by-Year Total
Returns, 1926–2011

Year	Large-Company Stocks	Long-Term Government Bonds	U.S. Treasury Bills	Consumer Price Index
1926	11.14%	7.90%	3.30%	−1.12%
1927	37.13	10.36	3.15	−2.26
1928	43.31	−1.37	4.05	−1.16
1929	−8.91	5.23	4.47	.58
1930	−25.26	5.80	2.27	−6.40
1931	−43.86	−8.04	1.15	−9.32
1932	−8.85	14.11	.88	−10.27
1933	52.88	.31	.52	.76
1934	−2.34	12.98	.27	1.52
1935	47.22	5.88	.17	2.99
1936	32.80	8.22	.17	1.45
1937	−35.26	−.13	.27	2.86
1938	33.20	6.26	.06	−2.78
1939	−.91	5.71	.04	.00
1940	−10.08	10.34	.04	.71
1941	−11.77	−8.66	.14	9.93
1942	21.07	2.67	.34	9.03
1943	25.76	2.50	.38	2.96
1944	19.69	2.88	.38	2.30
1945	36.46	5.17	.38	2.25
1946	−8.18	4.07	.38	18.13
1947	5.24	−1.15	.62	8.84
1948	5.10	2.10	1.06	2.99
1949	18.06	7.02	1.12	−2.07
1950	30.58	−1.44	1.22	5.93
1951	24.55	−3.53	1.56	6.00
1952	18.50	1.82	1.75	.75
1953	−1.10	−.88	1.87	.75
1954	52.40	7.89	.93	−.74
1955	31.43	−1.03	1.80	.37
1956	6.63	−3.14	2.66	2.99

Chapter 10   Risk and Return

Table 10.1
Year-by-Year Total Returns, 1926–2011
(concluded)

Year	Large-Company Stocks	Long-Term Government Bonds	U.S. Treasury Bills	Consumer Price Index
1957	−10.85%	5.25%	3.28%	2.90%
1958	43.34	−6.70	1.71	1.76
1959	11.90	−1.35	3.48	1.73
1960	.48	7.74	2.81	1.36
1961	26.81	3.02	2.40	.67
1962	−8.78	4.63	2.82	1.33
1963	22.69	1.37	3.23	1.64
1964	16.36	4.43	3.62	.97
1965	12.36	1.40	4.06	1.92
1966	−10.10	−1.61	4.94	3.46
1967	23.94	−6.38	4.39	3.04
1968	11.00	5.33	5.49	4.72
1969	−8.47	−7.45	6.90	6.20
1970	3.94	12.24	6.50	5.57
1971	14.30	12.67	4.36	3.27
1972	18.99	9.15	4.23	3.41
1973	−14.69	−12.66	7.29	8.71
1974	−26.47	−3.28	7.99	12.34
1975	37.23	4.67	5.87	6.94
1976	23.93	18.34	5.07	4.86
1977	−7.16	2.31	5.45	6.70
1978	6.57	−2.07	7.64	9.02
1979	18.61	−2.76	10.56	13.29
1980	32.50	−5.91	12.10	12.52
1981	−4.92	−.16	14.60	8.92
1982	21.55	49.99	10.94	3.83
1983	22.56	−2.11	8.99	3.79
1984	6.27	16.53	9.90	3.95
1985	31.73	39.03	7.71	3.80
1986	18.67	32.51	6.09	1.10
1987	5.25	−8.09	5.88	4.43
1988	16.61	8.71	6.94	4.42
1989	31.69	22.15	8.44	4.65
1990	−3.10	5.44	7.69	6.11
1991	30.46	20.04	5.43	3.06
1992	7.62	8.09	3.48	2.90
1993	10.08	22.32	3.03	2.75
1994	1.32	−11.46	4.39	2.67
1995	37.58	37.28	5.61	2.54
1996	22.96	−2.59	5.14	3.32
1997	33.36	17.70	5.19	1.70
1998	28.58	19.22	4.86	1.61
1999	21.04	−12.76	4.80	2.68
2000	−9.10	22.16	5.98	3.39
2001	−11.89	5.30	3.33	1.55
2002	−22.10	14.08	1.61	2.38
2003	28.68	1.62	1.03	1.88
2004	10.88	10.34	1.43	3.26
2005	4.91	10.35	3.30	3.42
2006	15.79	.28	4.97	2.54
2007	5.49	10.85	4.52	4.08
2008	−37.00	19.24	1.24	.09
2009	26.46	−25.61	0.15	2.72
2010	15.06	7.73	0.14	1.50
2011	2.11	35.75	0.06	2.96

SOURCE: Global Financial Data (www.globalfindata.com) copyright 2012.

returns on the stock market. In other words, what is our best estimate of the return that an investor could have realized in a particular year over the 1926 to 2011 period? This is the *average return*.

Figure 10.9 plots the histogram of the yearly stock market returns given in Table 10.1. This plot is the **frequency distribution** of the numbers. The height of the graph gives the number of sample observations in the range on the horizontal axis.

Given a frequency distribution like that in Figure 10.9, we can calculate the **average** or **mean** of the distribution. To compute the average of the distribution, we add up

Figure 10.9   Histogram of Returns on Common Stocks, 1926–2011

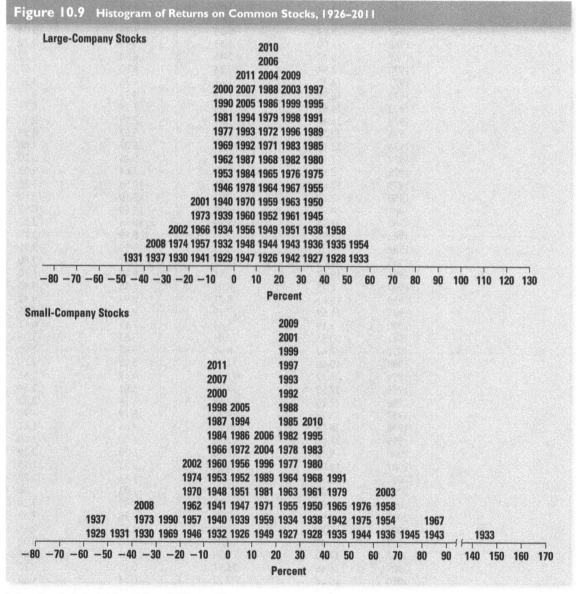

all of the values and divide by the total (T) number (86 in our case because we have 86 years of data). The bar over the R is used to represent the mean, and the formula is the ordinary formula for calculating an average:

$$\text{Mean} = \overline{R} = \frac{(R_1 + \cdots + R_T)}{T}$$

The mean of the 86 annual large-company stock returns from 1926 to 2011 is 11.8 percent.

EXAMPLE 10.2

Calculating Average Returns   Suppose the returns on common stock from 1926 to 1929 are .1370, .3580, .4514, and −.0888, respectively. The average, or mean return over these four years is:

$$\overline{R} = \frac{.1370 + .3580 + .4514 - .0888}{4} = .2144 \text{ or } 21.44\%$$

10.4 Average Stock Returns and Risk-Free Returns

Now that we have computed the average return on the stock market, it seems sensible to compare it with the returns on other securities. The most obvious comparison is with the low-variability returns in the government bond market. These are free of most of the volatility we see in the stock market.

An interesting comparison, then, is between the virtually risk-free return on T-bills and the very risky return on common stocks. This difference between risky returns and risk-free returns is often called the *excess return on the risky asset*. Of course, in any particular year the excess return might be positive or negative.

Table 10.2 shows the average stock return, bond return, T-bill return, and inflation rate for the period from 1926 through 2011. From this we can derive average excess returns. The average excess return from large-company common stocks relative to T-bills for the entire period was 8.2 percent (11.8 percent − 3.6 percent). The average excess return on common stocks is called the historical *equity risk premium* because it is the additional return from bearing risk.

One of the most significant observations of stock market data is this long-term excess of the stock return over the risk-free return. An investor for this period was rewarded for investment in the stock market with an extra, or excess, return over what would have been achieved by simply investing in T-bills.

Why was there such a reward? Does it mean that it never pays to invest in T-bills, and that someone who invested in them instead of in the stock market needs a course in finance? A complete answer to these questions lies at the heart of modern finance. However, part of the answer can be found in the variability of the various types of investments. There are many years when an investment in T-bills achieves higher returns than an investment in large common stocks. Also, we note that the returns from an investment in common stocks are frequently negative, whereas an investment in T-bills never produces a negative return. So, we now turn our attention to measuring the variability of returns and an introductory discussion of risk.

10.5 Risk Statistics

The second number that we use to characterize the distribution of returns is a measure of the risk in returns. There is no universally agreed-upon definition of risk. One way to think about the risk of returns on common stock is in terms of how spread out the

Table 10.2 Total Annual Returns, 1926–2011

Series	Arithmetic Mean (%)	Standard Deviation (%)	Distribution (%)
Small-company stocks*	16.5	32.5	
Large-company stocks	11.8	20.3	
Long-term corporate bonds	6.4	8.4	
Long-term government bonds	6.1	9.8	
Intermediate-term government bonds	5.5	5.7	
U.S. Treasury bills	3.6	3.1	
Inflation	3.1	4.2	

*The 1933 small-company stock total return was 142.9 percent.

SOURCE: Modified from *Stocks, Bonds, Bills and Inflation: 2012 Yearbook,*™ annual updates to the work by Roger G. Ibbotson and Rex A. Sinquefield (Chicago: Morningstar). All rights reserved.

ExcelMaster
coverage online

This section covers
Frequency distribution,
Frequency Distribution
charts, VAR, STDEV, VARP,
STDEVP, NORMDIST,
NORMINV, and Descriptive
Statistics.

frequency distribution in Figure 10.9 is. The spread, or dispersion, of a distribution is a measure of how much a particular return can deviate from the mean return. If the distribution is very spread out, the returns that will occur are very uncertain. By contrast, a distribution whose returns are all within a few percentage points of each other is tight, and the returns are less uncertain. The measures of risk we will discuss are variance and standard deviation.

VARIANCE

The **variance** and its square root, the **standard deviation,** are the most common measures of variability, or dispersion. We will use Var and σ^2 to denote the variance and SD and σ to represent the standard deviation. σ is, of course, the Greek letter sigma.

EXAMPLE 10.3

Volatility   Suppose the returns on common stocks are (in decimals) .1370, .3580, .4514, and −.0888, respectively. The variance of this sample is computed as follows:

$$\text{Var} = \frac{1}{T-1}[(R_1 - \bar{R})^2 + (R_2 - \bar{R})^2 + (R_3 - \bar{R})^2 + (R_4 - \bar{R})^2]$$

$$.0582 = \frac{1}{3}[(.1370 - .2144)^2 + (.3580 - .2144)^2$$

$$+ (.4514 - .2144)^2 + (-.0888 - .2144)^2]$$

$$\text{SD} = \sqrt{.0582} = .2412 \text{ or } 24.12\%$$

This formula in Example 10.3 tells us just what to do: Take the T individual returns $(R_1, R_2, \ldots)$ and subtract the average return $\bar{R}$, square the result, and add them up. Finally, this total must be divided by the number of returns less one $(T - 1)$. The standard deviation is always just the square root of the variance.

Using the stock returns for the 86-year period from 1926 through 2011 in this formula, the resulting standard deviation of large-company stock returns is 20.3 percent. The standard deviation is the standard statistical measure of the spread of a sample, and it will be the measure we use most of the time. Its interpretation is facilitated by a discussion of the normal distribution.

Standard deviations are widely reported for mutual funds. For example, the Fidelity Magellan Fund is one of the largest mutual funds in the United States. How volatile is it? To find out, we went to www.morningstar.com, entered the ticker symbol FMAGX, and hit the "Ratings Risk" link. Here is what we found:

MPT Statistics FMAGX

3-Year	5-Year	10-Year	15-Year

3-Year Trailing	Index	R-Squared	Beta	Alpha	Treynor Ratio	Currency
vs. Best-Fit Index						
FMAGX	Russell Mid Cap Growth TR USD	97.09	1.04	-8.90	--	USD
vs. Standard Index						
FMAGX	S&P 500 TR	91.64	1.22	-5.48	-2.25	USD
Category: LG	S&P 500 TR	91.70	1.00	-0.11	2.78	USD

06/30/2011

Volatility Measures FMAGX

3-Year	5-Year	10-Year	15-Year

3-Year Trailing	Standard Deviation	Mean	Sharpe Ratio	Sortino Ratio	Bear Market Percentile Rank
FMAGX	27.11	-2.47	0.04	0.05	--
S&P 500 TR	21.21	3.34	0.25	0.34	--
Category: LG	22.20	3.02	0.23	0.32	--

Over the last three years, the standard deviation of the returns on the Fidelity Magellan Fund was 27.11 percent. When you consider the average stock has a standard deviation of about 50 percent, this seems like a low number. But the Magellan Fund is a relatively well-diversified portfolio, so this is an illustration of the power of diversification, a subject we will discuss in detail later. The mean is the average return; so over the last three years, investors in the Magellan Fund earned a −2.47 percent return per year. Also under the Volatility Measurements section, you will see the **Sharpe ratio.** The Sharpe ratio is calculated as the risk premium of the asset divided by the standard deviation. As such, it is a measure of return to the level of risk taken (as measured by standard deviation). The "beta" for the Fidelity Magellan Fund is 1.22. We will have more to say about this number—lots more—in the next chapter.

EXAMPLE 10.4

Sharpe Ratio   The Sharpe ratio is the average equity risk premium over a period of time divided by the standard deviation. From 1926 to 2011 the average risk premium (relative to Treasury bills) for large-company stocks was 8.2 percent while the standard deviation was 20.3 percent. The Sharpe ratio of this sample is computed as:

$$\text{Sharpe ratio} = 8.2\%/20.3\% = .404$$

The Sharpe ratio is sometimes referred to as the reward-to-risk ratio where the reward is the average excess return and the risk is the standard deviation.

NORMAL DISTRIBUTION AND ITS IMPLICATIONS FOR STANDARD DEVIATION

A large enough sample drawn from a **normal distribution** looks like the bell-shaped curve drawn in Figure 10.10. As you can see, this distribution is *symmetric* about its mean, not *skewed,* and has a much cleaner shape than the actual distribution of yearly returns drawn in Figure 10.9. Of course, if we had been able to observe stock market returns for 1,000 years, we might have filled in a lot of the jumps and jerks in Figure 10.9 and had a smoother curve.

In classical statistics, the normal distribution plays a central role, and the standard deviation is the usual way to represent the spread of a normal distribution. For the normal distribution, the probability of having a return that is above or below the mean by a certain amount depends only on the standard deviation. For example, the probability of having a return that is within one standard deviation of the mean of the distribution is approximately .68, or 2/3, and the probability of having a return that is within two standard deviations of the mean is approximately .95.

The 20.3 percent standard deviation we found for stock returns from 1926 through 2011 can now be interpreted in the following way: If stock returns are roughly normally distributed, the probability that a yearly return will fall within 20.3 percent of the mean of 11.8 percent will be approximately 2/3. That is, about 2/3 of the yearly returns will be between −8.5 percent and 32.1 percent. (Note that −8.5 = 11.8 − 20.3 and 32.1 = 11.8 + 20.3.) The probability that the return in any year will fall within two standard deviations is about .95. That is, about 95 percent of yearly returns will be between −28.8 percent and 52.4 percent.

Figure 10.10
The Normal
Distribution

In the case of a normal distribution, there is a 68.26 percent probability that a return will be within one standard deviation of the mean. In this example, there is a 68.26 percent probability that a yearly return will be between −8.5 percent and 32.1 percent.

There is a 95.44 percent probability that a return will be within two standard deviations of the mean. In this example, there is a 95.44 percent probability that a yearly return will be between −28.8 percent and 52.4 percent.

Finally, there is a 99.74 percent probability that a return will be within three standard deviations of the mean. In this example, there is a 99.74 percent probability that a yearly return will be between −49.1 percent and 72.7 percent.

10.6 More on Average Returns

ExcelMaster
coverage online

This section introduces the
GEOMEAN function.

Thus far in this chapter we have looked closely at simple average returns. But there is another way of computing an average return. The fact that average returns are calculated two different ways leads to some confusion, so our goal in this section is to explain the two approaches and also the circumstances under which each is appropriate.

ARITHMETIC VERSUS GEOMETRIC AVERAGES

Let's start with a simple example. Suppose you buy a particular stock for $100. Unfortunately, the first year you own it, it falls to $50. The second year you own it, it rises back to $100, leaving you where you started (no dividends were paid).

What was your average return on this investment? Common sense seems to say that your average return must be exactly zero because you started with $100 and ended with $100. But if we calculate the returns year-by-year, we see that you lost 50 percent the first year (you lost half of your money). The second year, you made 100 percent (you doubled your money). Your average return over the two years was thus (−50 percent + 100 percent)/2 = 25 percent!

So which is correct, 0 percent or 25 percent? The answer is that both are correct; they just answer different questions. The 0 percent is called the **geometric average return.** The 25 percent is called the **arithmetic average return.** The geometric average return answers the question, *"What was your average compound return per year over a particular period?"* The arithmetic average return answers the question, *"What was your return in an average year over a particular period?"*

Notice that in previous sections, the average returns we calculated were all arithmetic averages, so we already know how to calculate them. What we need to do now is (1) learn how to calculate geometric averages and (2) learn the circumstances under which average is more meaningful than the other.

CALCULATING GEOMETRIC AVERAGE RETURNS

First, to illustrate how we calculate a geometric average return, suppose a particular investment had annual returns of 10 percent, 12 percent, 3 percent, and −9 percent over the last four years. The geometric average return over this four-year period is calculated as $(1.10 \times 1.12 \times 1.03 \times .91)^{1/4} - 1 = 3.66$ percent. In contrast, the average arithmetic return we have been calculating is $(.10 + .12 + .03 - .09)/4 = 4.0$ percent.

In general, if we have T years of returns, the geometric average return over these T years is calculated using this formula:

$$\text{Geometric average return} = [(1 + R_1) \times (1 + R_2) \times \cdots \times (1 + R_T)]^{1/T} - 1 \quad (10.1)$$

This formula tells us that four steps are required:

1. Take each of the T annual returns $R_1, R_2, \ldots, R_T$ and add 1 to each (after converting them to decimals).
2. Multiply all the numbers from step 1 together.
3. Take the result from step 2 and raise it to the power of $1/T$.
4. Finally, subtract 1 from the result of step 3. The result is the geometric average return.

EXAMPLE 10.5

Calculating the Geometric Average Return   Calculate the geometric average return for S&P 500 large-cap stocks for a five-year period using the numbers given here.

First convert percentages to decimal returns, add 1, and then calculate their product:

S&P 500 Returns	Product
13.75%	1.1375
35.70	× 1.3570
45.08	× 1.4508
−8.80	× .9120
−25.13	× .7487
	1.5291

Notice that the number 1.5291 is what our investment is worth after five years if we started with a $1 investment. The geometric average return is then calculated as:

$$\text{Geometric average return} = 1.5291^{1/5} - 1 = .0887, \text{ or } 8.87\%$$

Thus, the geometric average return is about 8.87 percent in this example. Here is a tip: If you are using a financial calculator, you can put $1 in as the present value, $1.5291 as the future value, and 5 as the number of periods. Then solve for the unknown rate. You should get the same answer we did.

You may have noticed in our examples thus far that the geometric average returns seem to be smaller. It turns out that this will always be true (as long as the returns are not all identical, in which case the two "averages" would be the same). To illustrate, Table 10.3 shows the arithmetic averages and standard deviations from Table 10.2, along with the geometric average returns.

Table 10.3
Geometric versus Arithmetic Average Returns: 1926–2011

Series	Geometric Mean	Arithmetic Mean	Standard Deviation
Small-company stocks	11.9%	16.5%	32.5%
Large-company stocks	9.8	11.8	20.3
Long-term corporate bonds	6.1	6.4	8.4
Long-term government bonds	5.7	6.1	9.8
Intermediate-term government bonds	5.4	5.5	5.7
U.S. Treasury bills	3.6	3.6	3.1
Inflation	3.0	3.1	4.2

SOURCE: *Ibbotson SBBI 2012 Classic Yearbook.*

As shown in Table 10.3, the geometric averages are all smaller, but the magnitude of the difference varies quite a bit. The reason is that the difference is greater for more volatile investments. In fact, there is a useful approximation. Assuming all the numbers are expressed in decimals (as opposed to percentages), the geometric average return is approximately equal to the arithmetic average return minus half the variance. For example, looking at the large-company stocks, the arithmetic average is 11.8 and the standard deviation is .203, implying that the variance is .041. The approximate geometric average is thus $.118 - \frac{.041}{2} = .097$ ($=9.7\%$), which is very close to the actual value.

EXAMPLE 10.6

More Geometric Averages Take a look back at Figure 10.4. There we showed the value of a $1 investment after 86 years. Use the value for the large-company stock investment to check the geometric average in Table 10.3.

In Figure 10.4, the large-company investment grew to $3045.22 over 86 years. The geometric average return is thus:

$$\text{Geometric average return} = \$3045.22^{1/86} - 1 = .098, \text{ or } 9.8\%$$

This 9.8 percent is the value shown in Table 10.3. For practice, check some of the other numbers in Table 10.3 the same way.

ARITHMETIC AVERAGE RETURN OR GEOMETRIC AVERAGE RETURN?

When we look at historical returns, the difference between the geometric and arithmetic average returns isn't too hard to understand. To put it slightly differently, the geometric average tells you what you actually earned per year on average, compounded annually. The arithmetic average tells you what you earned in a typical year and is an unbiased estimate of the true mean of the distribution. The geometric average is very useful in describing the actual historical investment experience. The arithmetic average is useful in making estimates of the future.[2]

---

[2]Another way of thinking about estimating an investment's return over a particular future horizon is to recall from your statistics class that the arithmetic average is a "sample" mean. As such, it provides an unbiased estimate of the underlying true mean. To use the arithmetic average to estimate the future returns, we must make sure the historical returns are measured using the same interval as the future forecasting period. For example, we could use yearly (annual) returns to estimate next year's return. The arithmetic average would be a good basis for forecasting the next two-year returns if two-year holding period returns were used. We also must be confident that the past distribution of returns is the same as that of the future.

10.7 The U.S. Equity Risk Premium: Historical and International Perspectives

So far, in this chapter, we have studied the United States in the period from 1926 to 2011. As we have discussed, the historical U.S. stock market risk premium has been substantial. Of course, anytime we use the past to predict the future, there is a danger that the past period isn't representative of what the future will hold. Perhaps U.S. investors got lucky over this period and earned particularly large returns. Data from earlier years for the United States is available, though it is not of the same quality. With that caveat in mind, researchers have tracked returns back to 1802, and the U.S. equity risk premium in the pre-1926 era was smaller. Using the U.S. return data from 1802, the historical equity risk premium was 5.4 percent.[3]

Also, we have not looked at other major countries. Actually, more than half of the value of tradable stock is not in the United States. From Table 10.4, we can see that while the total world stock market capitalization was $22.3 trillion in 2011, only about 53 percent was in the United States. Thanks to Dimson, Marsh, and Staunton, data from earlier periods and other countries are now available to help us take a closer look at equity risk premiums. Table 10.5 and Figure 10.11 show the historical stock market risk premiums for 17 countries around the world in the period from 1900 to 2010. Looking at the numbers, the U.S. historical equity risk premium is the 7th highest at 7.2 percent (which differs from our earlier estimate because of the different time periods examined). The overall world average risk premium is 6.9 percent. It seems clear that U.S. investors did well, but not exceptionally so relative to many other countries. The top-performing countries according to the Sharpe ratio were the United States, Australia, South Africa, and France, while the worst performers were

Table 10.4
World Stock Market Capitalization, 2011

Country	$ in Trillions	Percent
United States	$11.9	53%
Europe (excluding U.K.)	3.8	17
Japan	2.2	10
United Kingdom	2.0	9
Pacific (excluding Japan)	1.3	6
Canada	1.1	5
	$22.3	100%

SOURCE: *Ibbotson SBBI 2012 Classic Yearbook*, Morningstar, p. 216.

---

[3]Jeremy J. Siegel has estimated the U.S. equity risk premium with data from 1802. As can be seen in the following table, from 1802 to 2011 the historical equity risk premium was 5.4 percent.

	Average Returns 1802–2011 (%)
Common stock	9.6
Treasury bills	4.2
Equity risk premium	5.4

Adopted and updated from J. Siegel, *Stocks for the Long Run*, 4th ed. (New York: McGraw-Hill, 2008).

Table 10.5
Annualized Equity Risk Premiums and Sharpe Ratios for 17 Countries, 1900–2010

Country	Historical Equity Risk Premiums (%) (1)	Standard Deviation (%) (2)	The Sharpe Ratio (1)/(2)
Australia	8.3%	17.6%	0.47
Belgium	5.5	24.7	0.22
Canada	5.6	17.2	0.33
Denmark	4.6	20.5	0.22
France	8.7	24.5	0.36
Germany*	9.8	31.8	0.31
Ireland	5.3	21.5	0.25
Italy	9.8	32.0	0.31
Japan	9.0	27.7	0.32
Netherlands	6.5	22.8	0.29
Norway	5.9	26.5	0.22
South Africa	8.3	22.1	0.37
Spain	5.4	21.9	0.25
Sweden	6.6	22.1	0.30
Switzerland	5.1	18.9	0.27
United Kingdom	6.0	19.9	0.30
United States	7.2	19.8	0.36
Average	**6.9**	**23.0**	**0.30**

*Germany omits 1922–1923.

SOURCE: Elroy Dimson, Paul Marsh, and Michael Staunton, Credit Suisse Global Investment Returns Sourcebook, 2011, published by Credit Suisse Research Institute 2011. The Dimson-Marsh-Staunton data set is distributed by Morningstar, Inc.

Belgium, Norway, and Denmark. Germany, Japan, and Italy might make an interesting case study because they have the highest stock returns over this period (despite World Wars I and II), but also the highest risk.

So what is a good estimate of the U.S. equity risk premium going forward? Unfortunately, nobody can know for sure what investors expect in the future. If history is a guide, the expected U.S. equity risk premium could be 7.2 percent based upon estimates from 1900–2010. We should also be mindful that the average world equity risk premium was 6.9 percent over this same period. On the other hand, the more recent periods (1926–2011) suggest higher estimates of the U.S. equity risk premium, and earlier periods going back to 1802 suggest lower estimates.

The standard error (SE) helps with the issue of how much confidence we can have in our historical average of 7.2 percent. The SE is the standard deviation of the historical risk premium and is given by the following formula:

$$SE = SD(\overline{R}) = \frac{SD(R)}{\sqrt{\text{The number of observations}}}$$

If we assume that the distribution of returns is normal and that each year's return is independent of all the others, we know there is a 95.4 percent probability that the true mean return is within two standard errors of the historical average.

Figure 10.11
Stock Market Risk Premiums for 17 Countries: 1900–2010

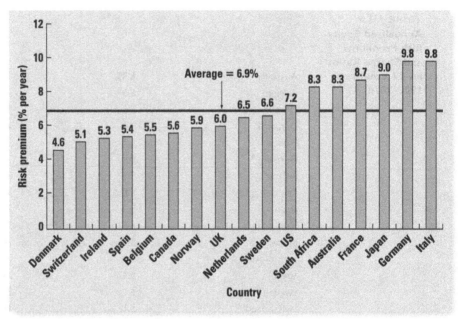

SOURCE: Elroy Dimson, Paul Marsh, and Michael Staunton, "The Worldwide Equity Premium: A Smaller Puzzle," in *Handbook of the Equity Risk Premium*, Rajnish Mehra, ed. (Elsevier, 2007). Updates by the authors.

More specifically, the 95.4 percent confidence interval for the true equity risk premium is the historical average return ± (2 × standard error). As we have seen from 1900 to 2010, the historical equity risk premium of U.S. stocks was 7.2 percent and the standard deviation was 19.8 percent. Therefore 95.4 percent of the time the true equity risk premium should be within 3.43 and 10.97 percent:

$$7.2 \pm 2\left(\frac{19.8}{\sqrt{111}}\right) = 7.2 \pm 2\left(\frac{19.8}{10.5}\right) = 7.2 \pm 3.77$$

In other words, we can be 95.4 percent confident that our estimate of the U.S. equity risk premium from historical data is in the range from 3.43 percent to 10.97 percent.

Taking a slightly different approach, Ivo Welch asked the opinions of 226 financial economists regarding the future U.S. equity risk premium, and the median response was 7 percent.[4]

We are comfortable with an estimate based on the historical U.S. equity risk premium of about 7 percent, but estimates of the future U.S. equity risk premium that are somewhat higher or lower could be reasonable if we have good reason to believe the past is not representative of the future.[5] The bottom line is that any estimate of

---

[4]For example, see I. Welch, "Views of Financial Economists on the Equity Risk Premium and Other Issues," *Journal of Business,* 73 (2000), pp. 501–537. Shannon P. Pratt and Roger J. Grabowski ("Cost of Capital: Applications and Examples," John Wiley, 2010) conclude, after reviewing a variety of evidence, that the equity risk premium is in the 3.5 to 6 percent range.

[5]In Elroy Dimson, Paul Marsh, and Mike Staunton, "The Worldwide Equity Premium: A Smaller Puzzle," from *Handbook of the Equity Risk Premium,* R. Mehra, ed., the authors argue that a good estimate of the world equity risk premium going forward should be about 5 percent, largely because of nonrecurring factors that positively affected worldwide historical returns. However, it could be argued that the global financial crisis of 2008–2009 was a negative shock to the stock market that has increased the equity risk premium from its historical levels.

the future equity risk premium will involve assumptions about the future risk environment as well as the amount of risk aversion of future investors.

10.8 2008: A Year of Financial Crisis

2008 entered the record books as one of the worst years for stock market investors in U.S. history. How bad was it? The widely followed S&P 500 Index, which tracks the total market value of 500 of the largest U.S. corporations, decreased 37 percent for the year. Of the 500 stocks in the index, 485 were down for the year.

Over the period 1926–2008, only the year 1931 had a lower return than 2008 (−43 percent versus −37 percent). Making matters worse, the downdraft continued with a further decline of 8.43 percent in January 2009. In all, from November 2007 (when the decline began) through January 2009, the S&P 500 lost 45 percent of its value.

Figure 10.12 shows the month-by-month performance of the S&P 500 decline during 2008. As indicated, returns were negative in eight of the twelve months. Most of the decline occurred in the fall, with investors losing almost 17 percent in October alone. Small stocks fared no better. They also fell 37 percent for the year (with a 21 percent drop in October), their worst performance since losing 58 percent in 1937.

As Figure 10.12 suggests, stock prices were highly volatile at the end the year—more than has been generally true historically. Oddly, the S&P had 126 up days and 126 down days (remember the markets are closed weekends and holidays). Of course, the down days were much worse on average.

The drop in stock prices was a global phenomenon, and many of the world's major markets declined by much more than the S&P. China, India, and Russia, for example, all experienced declines of more than 50 percent. Tiny Iceland saw share prices drop by more than 90 percent for the year. Trading on the Icelandic exchange was temporarily suspended on October 9. In what has to be a modern record for a single day, stocks fell by 76 percent when trading resumed on October 14.

Did any types of securities perform well in 2008? The answer is yes, because, as stock values declined, bond values increased, particularly U.S. Treasury bonds. In fact, long-term Treasury bonds *gained* 20 percent, while shorter-term Treasury bonds were up 13 percent. Higher quality long-term corporate bonds did less well, but still managed

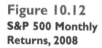

Figure 10.12
S&P 500 Monthly Returns, 2008

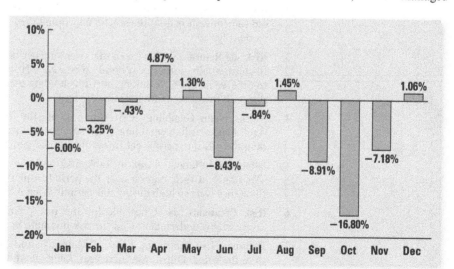

to achieve a positive return of about 9 percent. These returns were especially impressive considering that the rate of inflation, as measured by the CPI, was very close to zero.

Of course, stock prices can be volatile in both directions. From March 2009 through February 2011, a period of about 700 days, the S&P 500 doubled in value. This climb was the fastest doubling since 1936 when the S&P did it in just 500 days. So, what lessons should investors take away from this recent, and very turbulent, bit of capital market history? First, and most obviously, stocks have significant risk! But there is a second, equally important lesson. Depending on the mix, a diversified portfolio of stocks and bonds might have suffered in 2008, but the losses would have been much smaller than those experienced by an all-stock portfolio. In other words, diversification matters, a point we will examine in detail in our next chapter.

 ◀ To test your mastery of this material, take a quiz at mhhe. com/rwj

Summary and Conclusions

1. This chapter presented returns for a number of different asset classes. The general conclusion is that stocks have outperformed bonds over most of the 20th century, though stocks have also exhibited more risk.

2. The statistical measures in this chapter are necessary building blocks for the material of the next three chapters. In particular, standard deviation and variance measure the variability of the return on an individual security and on portfolios of securities. In the next chapter, we will argue that standard deviation and variance are appropriate measures of the risk of an individual security if an investor's portfolio is composed of that security only.

Concept Questions

1. **Investment Selection**   Given that eGain Communications was up by almost 412 percent for 2011, why didn't all investors hold eGain Communications?

2. **Investment Selection**   Given that First Solar was down by 74 percent for 2011, why did some investors hold the stock? Why didn't they sell out before the price declined so sharply?

3. **Risk and Return**   We have seen that over long periods stock investments have tended to substantially outperform bond investments. However, it is not at all uncommon to observe investors with long horizons holding their investments entirely in bonds. Are such investors irrational?

4. **Stocks versus Gambling**   Critically evaluate the following statement: Playing the stock market is like gambling. Such speculative investing has no social value, other than the pleasure people get from this form of gambling.

5. **Effects of Inflation**   Look at Table 10.1 and Figure 10.7 in the text. When were T-bill rates at their highest over the period from 1926 through 2011? Why do you think they were so high during this period? What relationship underlies your answer?

6. **Risk Premiums**   Is it possible for the risk premium to be negative before an investment is undertaken? Can the risk premium be negative after the fact? Explain.

7. **Returns**   Two years ago, General Materials' and Standard Fixtures' stock prices were the same. During the first year, General Materials' stock price increased by 10 percent while Standard Fixtures' stock price decreased by 10 percent. During the

Chapter 10 Risk and Return **329**

second year, General Materials' stock price decreased by 10 percent and Standard Fixtures' stock price increased by 10 percent. Do these two stocks have the same price today? Explain.

8. **Returns** Two years ago, the Lake Minerals and Small Town Furniture stock prices were the same. The average annual return for both stocks over the past two years was 10 percent. Lake Minerals' stock price increased 10 percent each year. Small Town Furniture's stock price increased 25 percent in the first year and lost 5 percent last year. Do these two stocks have the same price today?

9. **Arithmetic versus Geometric Returns** What is the difference between arithmetic and geometric returns? Suppose you have invested in a stock for the last 10 years. Which number is more important to you, the arithmetic or geometric return?

10. **Historical Returns** The historical asset class returns presented in the chapter are not adjusted for inflation. What would happen to the estimated risk premium if we did account for inflation? The returns are also not adjusted for taxes. What would happen to the returns if we accounted for taxes? What would happen to the volatility?

Questions and Problems

BASIC
(Questions 1–18)

1. **Calculating Returns** Suppose a stock had an initial price of $75 per share, paid a dividend of $1.20 per share during the year, and had an ending share price of $86. Compute the percentage total return.

2. **Calculating Yields** In Problem 1, what was the dividend yield? The capital gains yield?

3. **Calculating Returns** Rework Problems 1 and 2 assuming the ending share price is $67.

4. **Calculating Returns** Suppose you bought a 6 percent coupon bond one year ago for $1,040. The bond sells for $1,063 today.

   a. Assuming a $1,000 face value, what was your total dollar return on this investment over the past year?
   b. What was your total nominal rate of return on this investment over the past year?
   c. If the inflation rate last year was 3 percent, what was your total real rate of return on this investment?

5. **Nominal versus Real Returns** What was the arithmetic average annual return on large-company stocks from 1926 through 2011?

   a. In nominal terms?
   b. In real terms?

6. **Bond Returns** What is the historical real return on long-term government bonds? On long-term corporate bonds?

7. **Calculating Returns and Variability** Using the following returns, calculate the average returns, the variances, and the standard deviations for X and Y:

Year	Returns	
	X	Y
1	8%	12%
2	21	27
3	−27	−32
4	11	18
5	18	24

8. **Risk Premiums** Refer to Table 10.1 in the text and look at the period from 1973 through 1978.

   a. Calculate the arithmetic average returns for large-company stocks and T-bills over this period.

   b. Calculate the standard deviation of the returns for large-company stocks and T-bills over this period.

   c. Calculate the observed risk premium in each year for the large-company stocks versus the T-bills. What was the arithmetic average risk premium over this period? What was the standard deviation of the risk premium over this period?

9. **Calculating Returns and Variability** You've observed the following returns on Mary Ann Data Corporation's stock over the past five years: 27 percent, 13 percent, 18 percent, −14 percent, and 9 percent.

   a. What was the arithmetic average return on Mary Ann's stock over this five-year period?

   b. What was the variance of Mary Ann's returns over this period? The standard deviation?

10. **Calculating Real Returns and Risk Premiums** In Problem 9, suppose the average inflation rate over this period was 4.2 percent, and the average T-bill rate over the period was 5.1 percent.

    a. What was the average real return on Mary Ann's stock?

    b. What was the average nominal risk premium on Mary Ann's stock?

11. **Calculating Real Rates** Given the information in Problem 10, what was the average real risk-free rate over this time period? What was the average real risk premium?

12. **Holding Period Return** A stock has had returns of 16.12 percent, 12.11 percent, 5.83 percent, 26.14 percent, and −13.19 percent over the past five years, respectively. What was the holding period return for the stock?

13. **Calculating Returns** You purchased a zero coupon bond one year ago for $109.83. The market interest rate is now 9 percent. If the bond had 25 years to maturity when you originally purchased it, what was your total return for the past year?

14. **Calculating Returns** You bought a share of 4 percent preferred stock for $94.89 last year. The market price for your stock is now $96.12. What was your total return for last year?

15. **Calculating Returns** You bought a stock three months ago for $43.18 per share. The stock paid no dividends. The current share price is $46.21. What is the APR of your investment? The EAR?

16. **Calculating Real Returns** Refer to Table 10.1. What was the average real return for Treasury bills from 1926 through 1932?

17. **Return Distributions** Refer back to Table 10.2. What range of returns would you expect to see 68 percent of the time for long-term corporate bonds? What about 95 percent of the time?

18. **Return Distributions** Refer back to Table 10.2. What range of returns would you expect to see 68 percent of the time for large-company stocks? What about 95 percent of the time?

INTERMEDIATE
(Questions 19–26)

19. **Calculating Returns and Variability** You find a certain stock that had returns of 12 percent, −21 percent, 9 percent, and 32 percent for four of the last five years. If the average return of the stock over this period was 11 percent, what was the

stock's return for the missing year? What is the standard deviation of the stock's returns?

20. **Arithmetic and Geometric Returns**   A stock has had returns of 27 percent, 12 percent, 32 percent, −12 percent, 19 percent, and −31 percent over the last six years. What are the arithmetic and geometric returns for the stock?

21. **Arithmetic and Geometric Returns**   A stock has had the following year-end prices and dividends:

Year	Price	Dividend
1	$61.18	—
2	64.83	$ .72
3	72.18	.78
4	63.12	.86
5	69.27	.95
6	76.93	1.08

What are the arithmetic and geometric returns for the stock?

22. **Calculating Returns**   Refer to Table 10.1 in the text and look at the period from 1973 through 1980.

   a. Calculate the average return for Treasury bills and the average annual inflation rate (consumer price index) for this period.
   b. Calculate the standard deviation of Treasury bill returns and inflation over this period.
   c. Calculate the real return for each year. What is the average real return for Treasury bills?
   d. Many people consider Treasury bills to be risk-free. What do these calculations tell you about the potential risks of Treasury bills?

23. **Calculating Investment Returns**   You bought one of Bergen Manufacturing Co.'s 7 percent coupon bonds one year ago for $1,080.50. These bonds make annual payments and mature six years from now. Suppose you decide to sell your bonds today when the required return on the bonds is 5.5 percent. If the inflation rate was 3.2 percent over the past year, what would be your total real return on the investment?

24. **Using Return Distributions**   Suppose the returns on long-term government bonds are normally distributed. Based on the historical record, what is the approximate probability that your return on these bonds will be less than −3.7 percent in a given year? What range of returns would you expect to see 95 percent of the time? What range would you expect to see 99 percent of the time?

25. **Using Return Distributions**   Assuming that the returns from holding small-company stocks are normally distributed, what is the approximate probability that your money will double in value in a single year? Triple in value?

26. **Distributions**   In the previous problem, what is the probability that the return is less than −100 percent? (Think.) What are the implications for the distribution of returns?

CHALLENGE
(Questions 27–28)

27. **Using Probability Distributions**   Suppose the returns on large-company stocks are normally distributed. Based on the historical record, use the NORMDIST function in Excel® to determine the probability that in any given year you will lose money by investing in common stock.

28. **Using Probability Distributions** Suppose the returns on long-term corporate bonds and T-bills are normally distributed. Based on the historical record, use the NORMDIST function in Excel® to answer the following questions:

   a. What is the probability that in any given year, the return on long-term corporate bonds will be greater than 10 percent? Less than 0 percent?

   b. What is the probability that in any given year, the return on T-bills will be greater than 10 percent? Less than 0 percent?

   c. In 1979, the return on long-term corporate bonds was −4.18 percent. How likely is it that this low of a return will recur at some point in the future? T-bills had a return of 10.56 percent in this same year. How likely is it that this high of a return on T-bills will recur at some point in the future?

Excel Master It!

As we have seen, over the 1926–2011 period, small company stocks had the highest return and the highest risk, while U.S. Treasury bills had the lowest return and the lowest risk. While we certainly hope you have an 86-year holding period, it is likely your investment horizon will be somewhat shorter. One way risk and return are examined over a shorter investment period is by using rolling returns and standard deviations. Suppose you have a series of annual returns and you want to calculate a 3-year rolling average return. You would calculate the first rolling average at Year 3 using the returns for the first three years. The next rolling average would be calculated using the returns from Years 2, 3, and 4, and so on.

   a. Using the annual returns for large company stocks and Treasury bills, calculate both the 5- and 10-year rolling average return and standard deviation.

   b. Over how many 5-year periods did Treasury bills outperform large company stocks? How many 10-year periods?

   c. Over how many 5-year periods did Treasury bills have a larger standard deviation than large company stocks? Over how many 10-year periods?

   d. Graph the rolling 5-year and 10-year average returns for large company stocks and Treasury bills.

   e. What conclusions do you draw from the above results?

A JOB AT EAST COAST YACHTS

You recently graduated from college, and your job search led you to East Coast Yachts. Because you felt the company's business was seaworthy, you accepted a job offer. The first day on the job, while you are finishing your employment paperwork, Dan Ervin, who works in Finance, stops by to inform you about the company's 401(k) plan.

A 401(k) plan is a retirement plan offered by many companies. Such plans are tax-deferred savings vehicles, meaning that any deposits you make into the plan are deducted from your current pretax income, so no current taxes are paid on the money. For example, assume your salary will be $50,000 per year. If you contribute $3,000 to the 401(k) plan, you will pay taxes on only $47,000 in income. There are also no taxes paid on any capital gains or income while you are invested in the plan, but you do pay taxes when you withdraw money at retirement. As is fairly common, the company also has a 5 percent match.

This means that the company will match your contribution up to 5 percent of your salary, but you must contribute to get the match.

The 401(k) plan has several options for investments, most of which are mutual funds. A mutual fund is a portfolio of assets. When you purchase shares in a mutual fund, you are actually purchasing partial ownership of the fund's assets. The return of the fund is the weighted average of the return of the assets owned by the fund, minus any expenses. The largest expense is typically the management fee, paid to the fund manager. The management fee is compensation for the manager, who makes all of the investment decisions for the fund.

East Coast Yachts uses Bledsoe Financial Services as its 401(k) plan administrator. Here are the investment options offered for employees:

Company Stock One option in the 401(k) plan is stock in East Coast Yachts. The company is currently privately held. However, when you interviewed with the owner, Larissa Warren, she informed you the company was expected to go public in the next three to four years. Until then, a company stock price is simply set each year by the board of directors.

Bledsoe S&P 500 Index Fund This mutual fund tracks the S&P 500. Stocks in the fund are weighted exactly the same as the S&P 500. This means the fund return is approximately the return on the S&P 500, minus expenses. Because an index fund purchases assets based on the composition of the index it is following, the fund manager is not required to research stocks and make investment decisions. The result is that the fund expenses are usually low. The Bledsoe S&P 500 Index Fund charges expenses of .15 percent of assets per year.

Bledsoe Small-Cap Fund This fund primarily invests in small-capitalization stocks. As such, the returns of the fund are more volatile. The fund can also invest 10 percent of its assets in companies based outside the United States. This fund charges 1.70 percent in expenses.

Bledsoe Large-Company Stock Fund This fund invests primarily in large-capitalization stocks of companies based in the United States. The fund is managed by Evan Bledsoe and has outperformed the market in six of the last eight years. The fund charges 1.50 percent in expenses.

Bledsoe Bond Fund This fund invests in long-term corporate bonds issued by U.S.–domiciled companies. The fund is restricted to investments in bonds with an investment-grade credit rating. This fund charges 1.40 percent in expenses.

Bledsoe Money Market Fund This fund invests in short-term, high–credit quality debt instruments, which include Treasury bills. As such, the return on the money market fund is only slightly higher than the return on Treasury bills. Because of the credit quality and short-term nature of the investments, there is only a very slight risk of negative return. The fund charges .60 percent in expenses.

1. What advantages do the mutual funds offer compared to the company stock?

2. Assume that you invest 5 percent of your salary and receive the full 5 percent match from East Coast Yachts. What EAR do you earn from the match? What conclusions do you draw about matching plans?

3. Assume you decide you should invest at least part of your money in large-capitalization stocks of companies based in the United States. What are the advantages and disadvantages of choosing the Bledsoe Large-Company Stock Fund compared to the Bledsoe S&P 500 Index Fund?

4. The returns on the Bledsoe Small-Cap Fund are the most volatile of all the mutual funds offered in the 401(k) plan. Why would you ever want to invest in this fund? When you examine the expenses of the mutual funds, you will notice that this fund also has the highest expenses. Does this affect your decision to invest in this fund?

5. A measure of risk-adjusted performance that is often used is the Sharpe ratio. The Sharpe ratio is calculated as the risk premium of an asset divided by its standard

deviation. The standard deviations and returns of the funds over the past 10 years are listed here. Calculate the Sharpe ratio for each of these funds. Assume that the expected return and standard deviation of the company stock will be 16 percent and 65 percent, respectively. Calculate the Sharpe ratio for the company stock. How appropriate is the Sharpe ratio for these assets? When would you use the Sharpe ratio? Assume a 3.2 percent risk-free rate.

	10-Year Annual Return	Standard Deviation
Bledsoe S&P 500 Index Fund	9.18%	20.43%
Bledsoe Small-Cap Fund	14.12	25.13
Bledsoe Large-Company Stock Fund	8.58	23.82
Bledsoe Bond Fund	6.45	9.85

6. What portfolio allocation would you choose? Why? Explain your thinking carefully.

CHAPTER 11

Return and Risk

THE CAPITAL ASSET PRICING MODEL (CAPM)

Expected returns on common stocks can vary quite a bit. One important determinant is the industry in which a company operates. For example, according to recent estimates from Morningstar, the median expected return for department stores, which includes companies such as Sears and Kohl's, is 14.47 percent, whereas air transportation companies such as Delta and Southwest have a median expected return of 10.99 percent. Computer software companies such as Microsoft and Oracle have a median expected return of 11.61 percent.

▲ For updates on the latest happenings in finance, visit www. rwjcorporatefinance. blogspot.com

These estimates raise some obvious questions. First, why do these industry expected returns differ so much, and how are these specific numbers calculated? Also, does the higher return offered by department store stocks mean that investors should prefer these to, say, air transportation companies? As we will see in this chapter, the Nobel prize–winning answers to these questions form the basis of our modern understanding of risk and return.

11.1 Individual Securities

In the first part of Chapter 11, we will examine the characteristics of individual securities. In particular, we will discuss:

1. *Expected return:* This is the return that an individual expects a stock to earn over the next period. Of course, because this is only an expectation, the actual return may be either higher or lower. An individual's expectation may simply be the average return per period a security has earned in the past. Alternatively, the expectation may be based on a detailed analysis of a firm's prospects, on some computer-based model, or on special (or inside) information.

2. *Variance and standard deviation:* There are many ways to assess the volatility of a security's return. One of the most common is variance, which is a measure of the squared deviations of a security's return from its expected return. Standard deviation is the square root of the variance.

3. *Covariance and correlation*: Returns on individual securities are related to one another. Covariance is a statistic measuring the interrelationship between two securities. Alternatively, this relationship can be restated in terms of the correlation between the two securities. Covariance and correlation are building blocks to an understanding of the beta coefficient.

11.2 Expected Return, Variance, and Covariance

EXPECTED RETURN AND VARIANCE

ExcelMaster
coverage online

This section introduces the
SORT, COVAR, and CORREL
functions.

Suppose financial analysts believe that there are four equally likely states of the economy: Depression, recession, normal, and boom. The returns on the Supertech Company are expected to follow the economy closely, while the returns on the Slowpoke Company are not. The return predictions are as follows:

	Supertech Returns R_{At}	Slowpoke Returns R_{Bt}
Depression	−20%	5%
Recession	10	20
Normal	30	−12
Boom	50	9

Variance can be calculated in four steps. An additional step is needed to calculate standard deviation. (The calculations are presented in Table 11.1.) The steps are:

1. Calculate the expected return:

Supertech
$$\frac{-.20 + .10 + .30 + .50}{4} = .175 = 17.5\% = \overline{R}_A$$

Slowpoke
$$\frac{.05 + .20 - .12 + .09}{4} = .055 = 5.5\% = \overline{R}_B$$

2. For each company, calculate the deviation of each possible return from the company's expected return given previously. This is presented in the third column of Table 11.1.

3. The deviations we have calculated are indications of the dispersion of returns. However, because some are positive and some are negative, it is difficult to work with them in this form. For example, if we were simply to add up all the deviations for a single company, we would get zero as the sum.

    To make the deviations more meaningful, we multiply each one by itself. Now all the numbers are positive, implying that their sum must be positive as well. The squared deviations are presented in the last column of Table 11.1.

4. For each company, calculate the average squared deviation, which is the variance:[1]

Supertech
$$\frac{.140625 + .005625 + .015625 + .105625}{4} = .066875$$

---

[1]In this example, the four states give rise to four equally likely possible outcomes. The expected return is calculated by taking a probability weighted average of the possible outcomes. For Supertech,

$$.25 \times (-.20) + .25 \times .10 + .25 \times .30 + .25 \times .50 = .175$$

Because the four possible outcomes are equally likely, we can simplify by adding up the possible outcomes and dividing by 4. If outcomes are not equally likely, this simplification does not work.

The same type of calculation is required for variance. We take a probability weighted average of the squared deviations. For Supertech,

$$.25 \times .140625 + .25 \times .005625 + .25 \times .015625 + .25 \times .105625 = .066875$$

This is the same as adding up the possible squared deviations and dividing by 4.

If we use past data (as in Chapter 10), the divisor is always the number of historical observations less 1.

Table 11.1
Calculating Variance and Standard Deviation

(1) State of Economy	(2) Rate of Return	(3) Deviation from Expected Return	(4) Squared Value of Deviation
	Supertech	(Expected return = .175)	
	R_{At}	$(R_{At} - \bar{R}_A)$	$(R_{At} - \bar{R}_A)^2$
Depression	−.20	−.375 (= −.20 − .175)	.140625 [= (−.375)²]
Recession	.10	−.075	.005625
Normal	.30	.125	.015625
Boom	.50	.325	.105625
	Slowpoke	(Expected return = .055)	
	R_{Bt}	$(R_{Bt} - \bar{R}_B)$	$(R_{Bt} - \bar{R}_B)^2$
Depression	.05	−.005 (= .05 − .055)	.000025 [= (−.005)²]
Recession	.20	.145	.021025
Normal	−.12	−.175	.030625
Boom	.09	.035	.001225

Slowpoke

$$\frac{.000025 + .021025 + .030625 + .001225}{4} = .013225$$

Thus, the variance of Supertech is .066875, and the variance of Slowpoke is: .013225.

5. Calculate standard deviation by taking the square root of the variance:

Supertech

$$\sqrt{.066875} = .2586 = 25.86\%$$

Slowpoke

$$\sqrt{.013225} = .1150 = 11.50\%$$

Algebraically, the formula for variance can be expressed as:

$$\text{Var}(R) = \text{Expected value of } (R - \bar{R})^2$$

where $\bar{R}$ is the security's expected return and R is the actual return.

A look at the four-step calculation for variance makes it clear why it is a measure of the spread of the sample of returns. For each observation we square the difference between the actual return and the expected return. We then take an average of these squared differences. Squaring the differences makes them all positive. If we used the differences between each return and the expected return and then averaged these differences, we would get zero because the returns that were above the mean would cancel the ones below.

However, because the variance is still expressed in squared terms, it is difficult to interpret. Standard deviation has a much simpler interpretation, which was provided in Section 10.5. Standard deviation is simply the square root of the variance. The general formula for the standard deviation is:

$$SD(R) = \sqrt{\mathrm{Var}(R)}$$

COVARIANCE AND CORRELATION

Variance and standard deviation measure the variability of individual stocks. We now wish to measure the relationship between the return on one stock and the return on another. Enter **covariance** and **correlation.**

Covariance and correlation measure how two random variables are related. We explain these terms by extending the Supertech and Slowpoke example.

EXAMPLE 11.1

Calculating Covariance and Correlation We have already determined the expected returns and standard deviations for both Supertech and Slowpoke. (The expected returns are .175 and .055 for Supertech and Slowpoke, respectively. The standard deviations are .2586 and .1150, respectively.) In addition, we calculated the deviation of each possible return from the expected return for each firm. Using these data, we can calculate covariance in two steps. An extra step is needed to calculate correlation.

1. For each state of the economy, multiply Supertech's deviation from its expected return and Slowpoke's deviation from its expected return together. For example, Supertech's rate of return in a depression is −.20, which is −.375 (=−.20 − .175) from its expected return. Slowpoke's rate of return in a depression is .05, which is −.005 (=.05 − .055) from its expected return. Multiplying the two deviations together yields .001875 [=(−.375) × (−.005)]. The actual calculations are given in the last column of Table 11.2. This procedure can be written algebraically as:

$$(R_{At} - \overline{R}_A) \times (R_{Bt} - \overline{R}_B) \tag{11.1}$$

where R_{At} and R_{Bt} are the returns on Supertech and Slowpoke in state t. $\overline{R}_A$ and $\overline{R}_B$ are the expected returns on the two securities.

2. Calculate the average value of the four states in the last column. This average is the covariance. That is:[2]

$$\sigma_{AB} = \mathrm{Cov}(R_A, R_B) = \frac{-.0195}{4} = -.004875$$

Note that we represent the covariance between Supertech and Slowpoke as either $\mathrm{Cov}(R_A, R_B)$ or σ_{AB}. Equation 11.1 illustrates the intuition of covariance. Suppose Supertech's return is generally

---

[2]As with variance, we divided by N (4 in this example) because the four states give rise to four equally likely *possible* outcomes.

Table 11.2 **Calculating Covariance and Correlation**

State of Economy	Rate of Return of Supertech R_{At}	Deviation from Expected Return $(R_{At} - \bar{R}_A)$	Rate of Return of Slowpoke R_{Bt}	Deviation from Expected Return $(R_{Bt} - \bar{R}_B)$	Product of Deviations $(R_{At} - \bar{R}_A) \times (R_{Bt} - \bar{R}_B)$
	(Expected return = .175)		(Expected return = .055)		
Depression	−.20	−.375 (= −.20 − .175)	.05	−.005 (= .05 − .055)	.001875 (= −.375 × −.005)
Recession	.10	−.075	.20	.145	−.010875 (= −.075 × .145)
Normal	.30	.125	−.12	−.175	−.021875 (= .125 × −.175)
Boom	.50	.325	.09	.035	.011375 (= .325 × .035)
					−.0195

$$\sigma_{AB} = \text{Cov}(R_A, R_B) = \frac{-.0195}{4} = -.004875$$

$$\rho_{AB} = \text{Corr}(R_A, R_B) = \frac{\text{Cov}(R_A, R_B)}{\text{SD}(R_A) \times \text{SD}(R_B)} = \frac{-.004875}{.2586 \times .1150} = -.1639$$

above its average when Slowpoke's return is above its average, and Supertech's return is generally below its average when Slowpoke's return is below its average. This shows a positive dependency or a positive relationship between the two returns. Note that the term in Equation 11.1 will be *positive* in any state where both returns are *above* their averages. In addition, Equation 11.1 will still be *positive* in any state where both terms are *below* their averages. Thus a positive relationship between the two returns will give rise to a positive value for covariance.

Conversely, suppose Supertech's return is generally above its average when Slowpoke's return is below its average, and Supertech's return is generally below its average when Slowpoke's return is above its average. This demonstrates a negative dependency or a negative relationship between the two returns. Note that the term in Equation 11.1 will be *negative* in any state where one return is above its average and the other return is below its average. Thus a negative relationship between the two returns will give rise to a negative value for covariance.

Finally, suppose there is no relationship between the two returns. In this case, knowing whether the return on Supertech is above or below its expected return tells us nothing about the return on Slowpoke. In the covariance formula, then, there will be no tendency for the deviations to be positive or negative together. On average, they will tend to offset each other and cancel out, making the covariance zero.

Of course, even if the two returns are unrelated to each other, the covariance formula will not equal zero exactly in any actual history. This is due to sampling error; randomness alone will make the calculation positive or negative. But for a historical sample that is long enough, if the two returns are not related to each other, we should expect the covariance to come close to zero.

The covariance formula seems to capture what we are looking for. If the two returns are positively related to each other, they will have a positive covariance, and if they are negatively related to each other, the covariance will be negative. Last, and very important, if they are unrelated, the covariance should be zero.

(continued)

The formula for covariance can be written algebraically as:

$$\sigma_{AB} = \text{Cov}(R_A, R_B) = \text{Expected value of } [(R_A - \overline{R}_A) \times (R_B - \overline{R}_B)]$$

where $\overline{R}_A$ and $\overline{R}_B$ are the expected returns on the two securities and R_A and R_B are the actual returns. The ordering of the two variables is unimportant. That is, the covariance of A with B is equal to the covariance of B with A. This can be stated more formally as $\text{Cov}(R_A, R_B) = \text{Cov}(R_B, R_A)$ or $\sigma_{AB} = \sigma_{BA}$.

The covariance we calculated is $-.004875$. A negative number like this implies that the return on one stock is likely to be above its average when the return on the other stock is below its average, and vice versa. However, the size of the number is difficult to interpret. Like the variance figure, the covariance is in squared deviation units. Until we can put it in perspective, we don't know what to make of it.

We solve the problem by computing the correlation.

3. To calculate the correlation, divide the covariance by the standard deviations of both of the two securities. For our example, we have:

$$\rho_{AB} = \text{Corr}(R_A, R_B) = \frac{\text{Cov}(R_A, R_B)}{\sigma_A \times \sigma_B} = \frac{-.004875}{.2586 \times .1150} = -.1639 \qquad (11.2)$$

where σ_A and σ_B are the standard deviations of Supertech and Slowpoke, respectively. Note that we represent the correlation between Supertech and Slowpoke either as $\text{Corr}(R_A, R_B)$ or ρ_{AB}. As with covariance, the ordering of the two variables is unimportant. That is, the correlation of A with B is equal to the correlation of B with A. More formally, $\text{Corr}(R_A, R_B) = \text{Corr}(R_B, R_A)$ or $\rho_{AB} = \rho_{BA}$.

Figure 11.1   Examples of Different Correlation Coefficients—Graphs Plotting the Separate Returns on Two Securities through Time

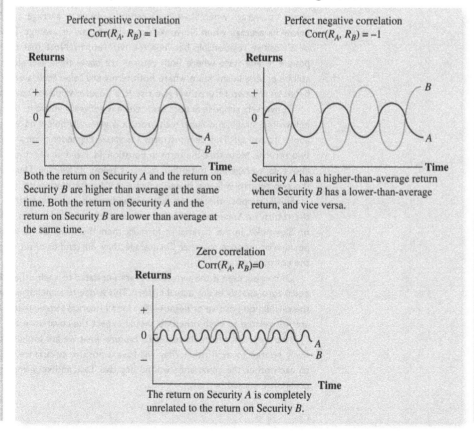

Perfect positive correlation
$\text{Corr}(R_A, R_B) = 1$

Both the return on Security A and the return on Security B are higher than average at the same time. Both the return on Security A and the return on Security B are lower than average at the same time.

Perfect negative correlation
$\text{Corr}(R_A, R_B) = -1$

Security A has a higher-than-average return when Security B has a lower-than-average return, and vice versa.

Zero correlation
$\text{Corr}(R_A, R_B) = 0$

The return on Security A is completely unrelated to the return on Security B.

Because the standard deviation is always positive, the sign of the correlation between two variables must be the same as that of the covariance between the two variables. If the correlation is positive, we say that the variables are *positively correlated*; if it is negative, we say that they are *negatively correlated*; and if it is zero, we say that they are *uncorrelated*. Furthermore, it can be proved that the correlation is always between $+1$ and -1. This is due to the standardizing procedure of dividing by the two standard deviations.

We can also compare the correlation between different *pairs* of securities. For example, it turns out that the correlation between General Motors and Ford is much higher than the correlation between General Motors and IBM. Hence, we can state that the first pair of securities is more interrelated than the second pair.

Figure 11.1 shows the three benchmark cases for two assets, *A* and *B*. The figure shows two assets with return correlations of $+1$, -1, and 0. This implies perfect positive correlation, perfect negative correlation, and no correlation, respectively. The graphs in the figure plot the separate returns on the two securities through time.

11.3   The Return and Risk for Portfolios

ExcelMaster
coverage online

Suppose an investor has estimates of the expected returns and standard deviations on individual securities and the correlations between securities. How does the investor choose the best combination or **portfolio** of securities to hold? Obviously, the investor would like a portfolio with a high expected return and a low standard deviation of return. It is therefore worthwhile to consider:

1.   The relationship between the expected returns on individual securities and the expected return on a portfolio made up of these securities.

2.   The relationship between the standard deviations of individual securities, the correlations between these securities, and the standard deviation of a portfolio made up of these securities.

To analyze these two relationships, we will use the same example of Supertech and Slowpoke. The relevant calculations follow.

THE EXPECTED RETURN ON A PORTFOLIO

The formula for expected return on a portfolio is very simple:

The expected return on a portfolio is a weighted average of the expected returns on the individual securities.

Relevant Data from Example of Supertech and Slowpoke		
Item	**Symbol**	**Value**
Expected return on Supertech	$\overline{R}_{Super}$	.175 = 17.5%
Expected return on Slowpoke	$\overline{R}_{Slow}$	.055 = 5.5%
Variance of Supertech	σ^2_{Super}	.066875
Variance of Slowpoke	σ^2_{Slow}	.013225
Standard deviation of Supertech	σ_{Super}	.2586 = 25.86%
Standard deviation of Slowpoke	σ_{Slow}	.1150 = 11.50%
Covariance between Supertech and Slowpoke	$\sigma_{Super,Slow}$	−.004875
Correlation between Supertech and Slowpoke	$\rho_{Super,Slow}$	−.1639

EXAMPLE 11.2

Portfolio Expected Returns   Consider Supertech and Slowpoke. From our earlier calculations, we find that the expected returns on these two securities are 17.5 percent and 5.5 percent, respectively.

The expected return on a portfolio of these two securities alone can be written as:

$$\text{Expected return on portfolio} = X_{\text{Super}}(17.5\%) + X_{\text{Slow}}(5.5\%) = \bar{R}_P$$

where X_{Super} is the percentage of the portfolio in Supertech and X_{Slow} is the percentage of the portfolio in Slowpoke. If the investor with \$100 invests \$60 in Supertech and \$40 in Slowpoke, the expected return on the portfolio can be written as:

$$\text{Expected return on portfolio} = .6 \times 17.5\% + .4 \times 5.5\% = 12.7\%$$

Algebraically, we can write:

$$\text{Expected return on portfolio} = X_A\bar{R}_A + X_B\bar{R}_B = \bar{R}_P \qquad (11.3)$$

where X_A and X_B are the proportions of the total portfolio in the assets A and B, respectively. (Because our investor can invest in only two securities, $X_A + X_B$ must equal 1 or 100 percent.) $\bar{R}_A$ and $\bar{R}_B$ are the expected returns on the two securities.

Now consider two stocks, each with an expected return of 10 percent. The expected return on a portfolio composed of these two stocks must be 10 percent, regardless of the proportions of the two stocks held. This result may seem obvious at this point, but it will become important later. The result implies that you do not reduce or *dissipate* your expected return by investing in a number of securities. Rather, the expected return on your portfolio is simply a weighted average of the expected returns on the individual assets in the portfolio.

VARIANCE AND STANDARD DEVIATION OF A PORTFOLIO

The Variance   The formula for the variance of a portfolio composed of two securities, A and B, is:

The Variance of the Portfolio

$$\text{Var(portfolio)} = X_A^2\sigma_A^2 + 2X_AX_B\sigma_{A,B} + X_B^2\sigma_B^2$$

Note that there are three terms on the right side of the equation. The first term involves the variance of Security A (σ_A^2), the second term involves the covariance between the two securities ($\sigma_{A,B}$), and the third term involves the variance of Security B (σ_B^2). (Remember, $\sigma_{A,B} = \sigma_{B,A}$. That is, the ordering of the variables is not relevant when we are expressing the covariance between two securities.)

The formula indicates an important point. The variance of a portfolio depends on both the variances of the individual securities and the covariance between the two securities. The variance of a security measures the variability of an individual security's return. Covariance measures the relationship between the two securities. For given variances of the individual securities, a positive relationship or covariance between the two securities increases the variance of the entire portfolio. A negative relationship or covariance between the two securities decreases the variance of the entire portfolio. This important result seems to square with common sense. If one of your securities tends to go up when the other goes down, or vice versa, your two securities are offsetting each other. You are achieving what we call a *hedge* in finance, and the risk of your entire portfolio will be low. However, if both your securities rise and fall together, you are not hedging at all. Hence, the risk of your entire portfolio will be higher.

The variance formula for our two securities, Super and Slow, is:

$$\text{Var(portfolio)} = X^2_{\text{Super}}\sigma^2_{\text{Super}} + 2X_{\text{Super}}X_{\text{Slow}}\sigma_{\text{Super, Slow}} + X^2_{\text{Slow}}\sigma^2_{\text{Slow}} \tag{11.4}$$

Given our earlier assumption that an individual with \$100 invests \$60 in Supertech and \$40 in Slowpoke, $X_{\text{Super}} = .6$ and $X_{\text{Slow}} = .4$. Using this assumption and the relevant data from our previous calculations, the variance of the portfolio is:

$$.023851 = .36 \times .066875 + 2 \times [.6 \times .4 \times (-.004875)] + .16 \times .013225 \tag{11.4'}$$

The Matrix Approach   Alternatively, Equation 11.4 can be expressed in the following matrix format:

	Supertech	**Slowpoke**
Supertech	$X^2_{\text{Super}}\sigma^2_{\text{Super}}$ $.024075 = .36 \times .066875$	$X_{\text{Super}}X_{\text{Slow}}\sigma_{\text{Super, Slow}}$ $-.00117 = .6 \times .4 \times (-.004875)$
Slowpoke	$X_{\text{Super}}X_{\text{Slow}}\sigma_{\text{Super, Slow}}$ $-.00117 = .6 \times .4 \times (-.004875)$	$X^2_{\text{Slow}}\sigma^2_{\text{Slow}}$ $.002116 = .16 \times .013225$

There are four boxes in the matrix. We can add the terms in the boxes to obtain Equation 11.4, the variance of a portfolio composed of the two securities. The term in the upper left corner involves the variance of Supertech. The term in the lower right corner involves the variance of Slowpoke. The other two boxes contain the term involving the covariance. These two boxes are identical, indicating why the covariance term is multiplied by two in Equation 11.4.

At this point, students often find the box approach to be more confusing than Equation 11.4. However, the box approach is easily generalized to more than two securities, a task we perform later in this chapter.

Standard Deviation of a Portfolio   Given Equation 11.4', we can now determine the standard deviation of the portfolio's return. This is:

$$\sigma_P = \text{SD(portfolio)} = \sqrt{\text{Var(portfolio)}} = \sqrt{.023851}$$
$$= .1544 = 15.44\% \tag{11.5}$$

The interpretation of the standard deviation of the portfolio is the same as the interpretation of the standard deviation of an individual security. The expected return on our portfolio is 12.7 percent. A return of −2.74 percent (=12.7% − 15.44%) is one standard deviation below the mean, and a return of 28.14 percent (=12.7% + 15.44%) is one standard deviation above the mean. If the return on the portfolio is normally distributed, a return between −2.74 percent and +28.14 percent occurs about 68 percent of the time.[3]

---

[3]There are only four equally probable returns for Supertech and Slowpoke, so neither security possesses a normal distribution. Thus, probabilities would be slightly different in our example.

344   **Part III**   Risk

The Diversification Effect   It is instructive to compare the standard deviation of the portfolio with the standard deviation of the individual securities. The weighted average of the standard deviations of the individual securities is:

$$\text{Weighted average of standard deviations} = X_{\text{Super}}\sigma_{\text{Super}} + X_{\text{Slow}}\sigma_{\text{Slow}} \tag{11.6}$$
$$.2012 = .6 \times .2586 + .4 \times .115$$

One of the most important results in this chapter concerns the difference between Equations 11.5 and 11.6. In our example, the standard deviation of the portfolio is *less* than a weighted average of the standard deviations of the individual securities.

We pointed out earlier that the expected return on the portfolio is a weighted average of the expected returns on the individual securities. Thus, we get a different type of result for the standard deviation of a portfolio than we do for the expected return on a portfolio.

Our result for the standard deviation of a portfolio is due to diversification. For example, Supertech and Slowpoke are slightly negatively correlated ($\rho = -.1639$). Supertech's return is likely to be a little below average if Slowpoke's return is above average. Similarly, Supertech's return is likely to be a little above average if Slowpoke's return is below average. Thus, the standard deviation of a portfolio composed of the two securities is less than a weighted average of the standard deviations of the two securities.

Our example has negative correlation. Clearly, there will be less benefit from diversification if the two securities exhibit positive correlation. How high must the positive correlation be before all diversification benefits vanish?

To answer this question, let us rewrite Equation 11.4 in terms of correlation rather than covariance. The covariance can be rewritten as:[4]

$$\sigma_{\text{Super,Slow}} = \rho_{\text{Super,Slow}}\sigma_{\text{Super}}\sigma_{\text{Slow}} \tag{11.7}$$

This formula states that the covariance between any two securities is simply the correlation between the two securities multiplied by the standard deviations of each. In other words, covariance incorporates both (1) the correlation between the two assets and (2) the variability of each of the two securities as measured by standard deviation.

From our calculations earlier in this chapter we know that the correlation between the two securities is $-.1639$. Given the variances used in Equation 11.4′, the standard deviations are .2586 and .115 for Supertech and Slowpoke, respectively. Thus, the variance of a portfolio can be expressed as follows:

Variance of the Portfolio's Return

$$= X^2_{\text{Super}}\sigma^2_{\text{Super}} + 2X_{\text{Super}}X_{\text{Slow}}\rho_{\text{Super, Slow}}\sigma_{\text{Super}}\sigma_{\text{Slow}} + X^2_{\text{Slow}}\sigma^2_{\text{Slow}}$$
$$.023851 = .36 \times .066875 + 2 \times (.6 \times .4 \times (-.1639) \tag{11.8}$$
$$\times .2586 \times .115) + .16 \times .013225$$

The middle term on the right side is now written in terms of correlation, ρ, not covariance.

Suppose $\rho_{\text{Super,Slow}} = 1$, the highest possible value for correlation. Assume all the other parameters in the example are the same. The variance of the portfolio is:

$$\begin{aligned}\text{Variance of the} \\ \text{portfolio's return}\end{aligned} = .040466 = .36 \times .066875 + 2 \times (.6 \times .4 \times 1 \times .2586 \\ \times .115) + .16 \times .013225$$

---

[4]As with covariance, the ordering of the two securities is not relevant when we express the correlation between the two securities. That is, $\rho_{\text{Super,Slow}} = \rho_{\text{Slow,Super}}$

Chapter 11   Return and Risk   345

Table 11.3

Standard Deviations for Standard & Poor's 500 Index and for Selected Stocks in the Index, 2007–2011

Asset	Standard Deviation
S&P 500 Index	20.64%
General Mills	14.57
McDonald's	15.55
Microsoft	26.38
Google	36.51
Yahoo!	41.02
General Electronic Co.	41.20
Sprint Nextel	62.88
Bank of America	71.75

As long as the correlations between pairs of securities are less than 1, the standard deviation of an index is less than the weighted average of the standard deviations of the individual securities within the index.

The standard deviation is:

$$\text{Standard deviation of portfolio's return} = \sqrt{.040466} = .2012 = 20.12\% \quad (11.9)$$

Note that Equations 11.9 and 11.6 are equal. That is, the standard deviation of a portfolio's return is equal to the weighted average of the standard deviations of the individual returns when $\rho = 1$. Inspection of Equation 11.8 indicates that the variance and hence the standard deviation of the portfolio must fall as the correlation drops below 1. This leads to the following result:

As long as $\rho < 1$, the standard deviation of a portfolio of two securities is *less* than the weighted average of the standard deviations of the individual securities.

In other words, the diversification effect applies as long as there is less than perfect correlation (as long as $\rho < 1$). Thus, our Supertech–Slowpoke example is a case of overkill. We illustrated diversification by an example with negative correlation. We could have illustrated diversification by an example with positive correlation—as long as it was not *perfect* positive correlation.

An Extension to Many Assets   The preceding insight can be extended to the case of many assets. That is, as long as correlations between pairs of securities are less than 1, the standard deviation of a portfolio of many assets is less than the weighted average of the standard deviations of the individual securities.

Now consider Table 11.3, which shows the standard deviation of the Standard & Poor's 500 Index and the standard deviations of some of the individual securities listed in the index over a recent 10-year period. Note that all of the individual securities in the table have higher standard deviations than that of the index. In general, the standard deviations of most of the individual securities in an index will be above the standard deviation of the index itself, though a few of the securities could have lower standard deviations than that of the index.

11.4 The Efficient Set for Two Assets

Our results for expected returns and standard deviations are graphed in Figure 11.2. The figure shows a dot labeled Slowpoke and a dot labeled Supertech. Each dot represents both the expected return and the standard deviation for an individual security.

Figure 11.2
Expected Returns and Standard Deviations for Supertech, Slowpoke, and a Portfolio Composed of 60 Percent in Supertech and 40 Percent in Slowpoke

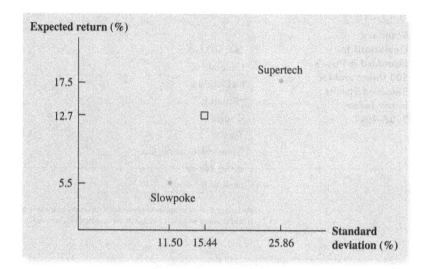

As can be seen, Supertech has both a higher expected return and a higher standard deviation.

The box or "□" in the graph represents a portfolio with 60 percent invested in Supertech and 40 percent invested in Slowpoke. You will recall that we previously calculated both the expected return and the standard deviation for this portfolio.

The choice of 60 percent in Supertech and 40 percent in Slowpoke is just one of an infinite number of portfolios that can be created. The set of portfolios is sketched by the curved line in Figure 11.3.

Consider Portfolio *1*. This is a portfolio composed of 90 percent Slowpoke and 10 percent Supertech. Because the portfolio is weighted so heavily toward Slowpoke, it appears close to the Slowpoke point on the graph. Portfolio *2* is higher on the curve because it is composed of 50 percent Slowpoke and 50 percent Supertech. Portfolio *3* is close to the Supertech point on the graph because it is composed of 90 percent Supertech and 10 percent Slowpoke.

There are a few important points concerning this graph:

1. We previously argued that the diversification effect occurs whenever the correlation between two securities is below 1. The correlation between Supertech and Slowpoke is $-.1639$. The straight line in the graph represents points that would have been generated had the correlation coefficient between the two securities been 1. Note that the curved line is always to the left of the straight line. Consider Point *1′*. This point represents a portfolio composed of 90 percent in Slowpoke and 10 percent in Supertech *if* the correlation between the two were exactly 1. There is no diversification effect if $\rho = 1$. However, the diversification effect applies to the curved line because Point *1* has the same expected return as Point *1′* but has a lower standard deviation. (Points *2′* and *3′* are omitted to reduce the clutter of Figure 11.3.)

   Though the straight line and the curved line are both represented in Figure 11.3, they do not simultaneously exist in the same world. *Either* $\rho = -.1639$ and the curve exists *or* $\rho = 1$ and the straight line exists. In other words, though an investor can choose between different points on the curve if $\rho = -.1639$, she cannot choose between points on the curve and points on the straight line.

2. Point MV represents the minimum variance portfolio. This is the portfolio with the lowest possible variance. By definition, this portfolio must also have

Figure 11.3
Set of Portfolios Composed of Holdings in Supertech and Slowpoke (correlation between the two securities is –.1639)

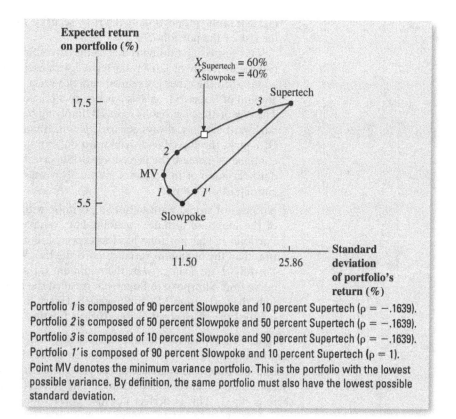

Portfolio *1* is composed of 90 percent Slowpoke and 10 percent Supertech (ρ = –.1639).
Portfolio *2* is composed of 50 percent Slowpoke and 50 percent Supertech (ρ = –.1639).
Portfolio *3* is composed of 10 percent Slowpoke and 90 percent Supertech (ρ = –.1639).
Portfolio *1'* is composed of 90 percent Slowpoke and 10 percent Supertech (ρ = 1).
Point MV denotes the minimum variance portfolio. This is the portfolio with the lowest possible variance. By definition, the same portfolio must also have the lowest possible standard deviation.

the lowest possible standard deviation. (The term *minimum variance portfolio* is standard, and we will use that term. Perhaps minimum standard deviation would actually be better because standard deviation, not variance, is measured on the horizontal axis of Figure 11.3.)

3. An individual contemplating an investment in a portfolio of Slowpoke and Supertech faces an **opportunity set** or **feasible set** represented by the curved line in Figure 11.3. That is, he can achieve any point on the curve by selecting the appropriate mix between the two securities. He cannot achieve any point above the curve because he cannot increase the return on the individual securities, decrease the standard deviations of the securities, or decrease the correlation between the two securities. Neither can he achieve points below the curve because he cannot lower the returns on the individual securities, increase the standard deviations of the securities, or increase the correlation. (Of course, he would not want to achieve points below the curve, even if he were able to do so.)

    Were he relatively tolerant of risk, he might choose Portfolio *3*. (In fact, he could even choose the end point by investing all his money in Supertech.) An investor with less tolerance for risk might choose Portfolio *2*. An investor wanting as little risk as possible would choose MV, the portfolio with minimum variance or minimum standard deviation.

4. Note that the curve is backward bending between the Slowpoke point and MV. This indicates that, for a portion of the feasible set, standard deviation actually decreases as we increase expected return. Students frequently ask, "How can an

increase in the proportion of the risky security, Supertech, lead to a reduction in the risk of the portfolio?"

This surprising finding is due to the diversification effect. The returns on the two securities are negatively correlated with each other. One security tends to go up when the other goes down and vice versa. Thus, an addition of a small amount of Supertech acts as a hedge to a portfolio composed only of Slowpoke. The risk of the portfolio is reduced, implying backward bending. Actually, backward bending always occurs if $\rho \leq 0$. It may or may not occur when $\rho > 0$. Of course, the curve bends backward only for a portion of its length. As we continue to increase the percentage of Supertech in the portfolio, the high standard deviation of this security eventually causes the standard deviation of the entire portfolio to rise.

5. No investor would want to hold a portfolio with an expected return below that of the minimum variance portfolio. For example, no investor would choose Portfolio *1*. This portfolio has less expected return but more standard deviation than the minimum variance portfolio has. We say that portfolios such as Portfolio *1* are *dominated* by the minimum variance portfolio. Though the entire curve from Slowpoke to Supertech is called the *feasible set,* investors consider only the curve from MV to Supertech. Hence the curve from MV to Supertech is called the **efficient set** or the **efficient frontier.**

Figure 11.3 represents the opportunity set where $\rho = -.1639$. It is worthwhile to examine Figure 11.4, which shows different curves for different correlations. As can be seen, the lower the correlation, the more the curve bends. This indicates that the diversification effect rises as ρ declines. The greatest bend occurs in the limiting case where $\rho = -1$. This is perfect negative correlation. While this extreme case where $\rho = -1$ seems to fascinate students, it has little practical importance. Most pairs of

Figure 11.4
Opportunity Sets Composed of Holdings in Supertech and Slowpoke

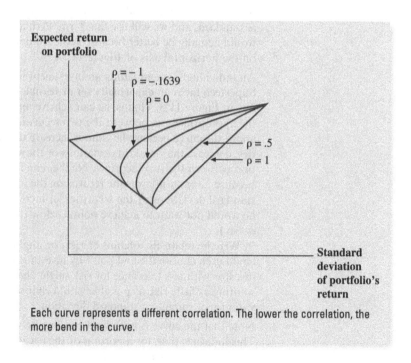

Each curve represents a different correlation. The lower the correlation, the more bend in the curve.

securities exhibit positive correlation. Strong negative correlations, let alone perfect negative correlation, are unlikely occurrences indeed.[5]

Note that there is only one correlation between a pair of securities. We stated earlier that the correlation between Slowpoke and Supertech is −.1639. Thus, the curve in Figure 11.4 representing this correlation is the correct one, and the other curves should be viewed as merely hypothetical.

The graphs we examined are not mere intellectual curiosities. Rather, efficient sets can easily be calculated in the real world. As mentioned earlier, data on returns, standard deviations, and correlations are generally taken from past observations, though subjective notions can be used to determine the values of these parameters as well. Once the parameters have been determined, any one of a whole host of software packages can be purchased to generate the efficient set. However, the choice of the preferred portfolio within the efficient set is up to you. As with other important decisions like what job to choose, what house or car to buy, and how much time to allocate to this course, there is no computer program to choose the preferred portfolio.

An efficient set can be generated where the two individual assets are portfolios themselves. For example, the two assets in Figure 11.5 are a diversified portfolio of American stocks and a diversified portfolio of foreign stocks. Expected returns, standard deviations, and the correlation coefficient were calculated over the recent past. No subjectivity entered the analysis. The U.S. stock portfolio with a standard deviation of about .151 is less risky than the foreign stock portfolio, which has a standard deviation of about .166. However, combining a small percentage of the

Figure 11.5
Return/Risk Trade-off for World Stocks: Portfolio of U.S. and Foreign Stocks

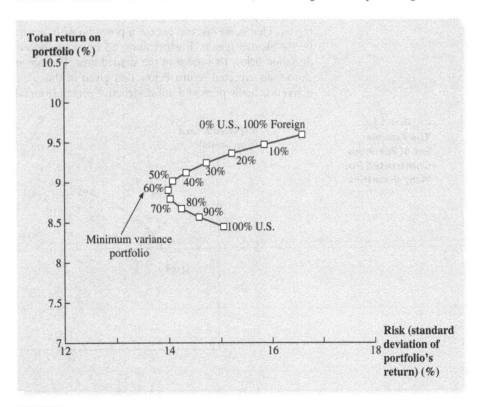

---

[5]A major exception occurs with derivative securities. For example, the correlation between a stock and a put on the stock is generally strongly negative. Puts will be treated later in the text.

350   Part III   Risk

foreign stock portfolio with the U.S. portfolio actually reduces risk, as can be seen by the backward-bending nature of the curve. In other words, the diversification benefits from combining two different portfolios more than offset the introduction of a riskier set of stocks into our holdings. The minimum variance portfolio occurs with about 60 percent of our funds in American stocks and about 40 percent in foreign stocks. Addition of foreign securities beyond this point increases the risk of the entire portfolio. The backward-bending curve in Figure 11.5 is important information that has not bypassed American institutional investors. In recent years, pension funds and other institutions in the United States have sought investment opportunities overseas.

11.5   The Efficient Set for Many Securities

The previous discussion concerned two securities. We found that a simple curve sketched out all the possible portfolios. Because investors generally hold more than two securities, we should look at the same graph when more than two securities are held. The shaded area in Figure 11.6 represents the opportunity set or feasible set when many securities are considered. The shaded area represents all the possible combinations of expected return and standard deviation for a portfolio. For example, in a universe of 100 securities, Point 1 might represent a portfolio of, say, 40 securities. Point 2 might represent a portfolio of 80 securities. Point 3 might represent a different set of 80 securities, or the same 80 securities held in different proportions, or something else. Obviously, the combinations are virtually endless. However, note that all possible combinations fit into a confined region. No security or combination of securities can fall outside the shaded region. That is, no one can choose a portfolio with an expected return above that given by the shaded region. Furthermore, no one can choose a portfolio with a standard deviation below that given in the shaded area. Perhaps more surprisingly, no one can choose an expected return below that given in this area. In other words, the capital markets actually prevent a self-destructive person from taking on a guaranteed loss.[6]

Figure 11.6
The Feasible Set of Portfolios Constructed from Many Securities

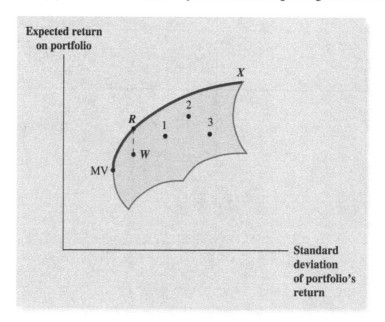

___

[6]Of course, someone dead set on parting with his money can do so. For example, he can trade frequently without purpose, so that commissions more than offset the positive expected returns on the portfolio.

So far, Figure 11.6 is different from the earlier graphs. When only two securities are involved, all the combinations lie on a single curve. Conversely, with many securities the combinations cover an entire area. However, notice that an individual will want to be somewhere on the upper edge between MV and X. The upper edge, which we indicate in Figure 11.6 by a thick curve, is called the *efficient set*. Any point below the efficient set would receive less expected return and the same standard deviation as a point on the efficient set. For example, consider R on the efficient set and W directly below it. If W contains the risk level you desire, you should choose R instead to receive a higher expected return.

In the final analysis, Figure 11.6 is quite similar to Figure 11.3. The efficient set in Figure 11.3 runs from MV to Supertech. It contains various combinations of the securities Supertech and Slowpoke. The efficient set in Figure 11.6 runs from MV to X. It contains various combinations of many securities. The fact that a whole shaded area appears in Figure 11.6 but not in Figure 11.3 is just not an important difference; no investor would choose any point below the efficient set in Figure 11.6 anyway.

We mentioned before that an efficient set for two securities can be traced out easily in the real world. The task becomes more difficult when additional securities are included because the number of observations grows. For example, using analysis to estimate expected returns and standard deviations for, say, 100 or 500 securities may very well become overwhelming, and the difficulties with correlations may be greater still. There are almost 5,000 correlations between pairs of securities from a universe of 100 securities.

Though much of the mathematics of efficient set computation had been derived in the 1950s,[7] the high cost of computer time restricted application of the principles. In recent years this cost has been drastically reduced. A number of software packages allow the calculation of an efficient set for portfolios of moderate size. By all accounts these packages sell quite briskly, implying that our discussion is important in practice.

VARIANCE AND STANDARD DEVIATION IN A PORTFOLIO OF MANY ASSETS

We earlier calculated the formulas for variance and standard deviation in the two-asset case. Because we considered a portfolio of many assets in Figure 11.6, it is worthwhile to calculate the formulas for variance and standard deviation in the many-asset case. The formula for the variance of a portfolio of many assets can be viewed as an extension of the formula for the variance of two assets.

To develop the formula, we employ the same type of matrix that we used in the two-asset case. This matrix is displayed in Table 11.4. Assuming that there are N assets, we write the numbers 1 through N on the horizontal axis and 1 through N on the vertical axis. This creates a matrix of $N \times N = N^2$ boxes. The variance of the portfolio is the sum of the terms in all the boxes.

Consider, for example, the box in the second row and the third column. The term in the box is $X_2 X_3 \, \text{Cov}(R_2, R_3)$. X_2 and X_3 are the percentages of the entire portfolio that are invested in the second asset and the third asset, respectively. For example, if an individual with a portfolio of \$1,000 invests \$100 in the second asset, $X_2 = 10\%$ $(=\$100/\$1,000)$. $\text{Cov}(R_2, R_3)$ is the covariance between the returns on the second asset and the returns on the third asset. Next, note the box in the third row and the second column. The term in this box is $X_3 X_2 \, \text{Cov}(R_3, R_2)$. Because $\text{Cov}(R_3, R_2) = \text{Cov}(R_2, R_3)$,

---

[7]The classic treatise is Harry Markowitz, *Portfolio Selection* (New York: John Wiley & Sons, 1959). Markowitz won the Nobel Prize in Economics in 1990 for his work on modern portfolio theory.

Table 11.4

Matrix Used to Calculate the Variance of a Portfolio

Stock	1	2	3	... N
1	$X_1^2\sigma_1^2$	$X_1X_2\text{Cov}(R_1,R_2)$	$X_1X_3\text{Cov}(R_1,R_3)$	$X_1X_N\text{Cov}(R_1,R_N)$
2	$X_2X_1\text{Cov}(R_2,R_1)$	$X_2^2\sigma_2^2$	$X_2X_3\text{Cov}(R_2,R_3)$	$X_2X_N\text{Cov}(R_2,R_N)$
3	$X_3X_1\text{Cov}(R_3,R_1)$	$X_3X_2\text{Cov}(R_3,R_2)$	$X_3^2\sigma_3^2$	$X_3X_N\text{Cov}(R_3,R_N)$
.				
.				
.				
N	$X_NX_1\text{Cov}(R_N,R_1)$	$X_NX_2\text{Cov}(R_N,R_2)$	$X_NX_3\text{Cov}(R_N,R_3)$	$X_N^2\sigma_N^2$

The variance of the portfolio is the sum of the terms in all the boxes.

σ_i is the standard deviation of Stock i.

$\text{Cov}(R_i, R_j)$ is the covariance between Stock i and Stock j.

Terms involving the standard deviation of a single security appear on the diagonal. Terms involving covariance between two securities appear off the diagonal.

Table 11.5

Number of Variance and Covariance Terms as a Function of the Number of Stocks in the Portfolio

Number of Stocks in Portfolio	Total Number of Terms	Number of Variance Terms (number of terms on diagonal)	Number of Covariance Terms (number of terms off diagonal)
1	1	1	0
2	4	2	2
3	9	3	6
10	100	10	90
100	10,000	100	9,900
.	.	.	.
.	.	.	.
.	.	.	.
N	N^2	N	$N^2 - N$

In a large portfolio, the number of terms involving covariance between two securities is much greater than the number of terms involving variance of a single security.

both boxes have the same value. The second security and the third security make up one pair of stocks. In fact, every pair of stocks appears twice in the table: once in the lower left side and once in the upper right side.

Now consider boxes on the diagonal. For example, the term in the first box on the diagonal is $X_1^2\sigma_1^2$. Here, σ_1^2 is the variance of the return on the first security.

Thus, the diagonal terms in the matrix contain the variances of the different stocks. The off-diagonal terms contain the covariances. Table 11.5 relates the numbers of diagonal and off-diagonal elements to the size of the matrix. The number of diagonal terms (number of variance terms) is always the same as the number of stocks in the portfolio. The number of off-diagonal terms (number of covariance terms) rises much faster than the number of diagonal terms. For example, a portfolio of 100 stocks has 9,900 covariance terms. Because the variance of a portfolio's return is the sum of all the boxes, we have the following:

The variance of the return on a portfolio with many securities is more dependent on the covariances between the individual securities than on the variances of the individual securities.

11.6 Diversification

So far, in this chapter we have examined how the risks and returns of individual assets impact the risk and return of the portfolio. We also touched on one aspect of this impact, diversification. To give a recent example, the Dow Jones Industrial Average (DJIA), which contains 30 large, well-known U.S. stocks, rose about 5.5 percent in 2011, an increase somewhat below historical standards. The biggest individual gainers in that year were McDonald's (up 31 percent), IBM (up 25 percent), and Pfizer (up 24 percent), while the biggest losers were Bank of America (down 58 percent), Alcoa (down 44 percent), and Hewlett-Packard (down 39 percent). As can be seen, variation among these individual stocks was reduced through diversification. While this example shows that diversification is good we now want to examine *why* it is good. And just how good is it?

THE ANTICIPATED AND UNANTICIPATED COMPONENTS OF NEWS

We begin the discussion of diversification by focusing on the stock of one company, which we will call Flyers. What will determine this stock's return in, say, the coming month?

The return on any stock consists of two parts. First, the *normal* or *expected return* from the stock is the part of the return that shareholders in the market predict or expect. It depends on all of the information shareholders have that bears on the stock, and it uses all of our understanding of what will influence the stock in the next month.

The second part is the *uncertain* or *risky return* on the stock. This is the portion that comes from information that will be revealed within the month. The list of such information is endless, but here are some examples:

- News about Flyers' research.
- Government figures released for the gross national product (GNP).
- Results of the latest arms control talks.
- Discovery that a rival's product has been tampered with.
- News that Flyers' sales figures are higher than expected.
- A sudden drop in interest rates.
- The unexpected retirement of Flyers' founder and president.

A way to write the return on Flyers' stock in the coming month, then, is:

$$R = \overline{R} + U$$

where R is the actual total return in the month, $\overline{R}$ is the expected part of the return, and U stands for the unexpected part of the return.

RISK: SYSTEMATIC AND UNSYSTEMATIC

The unanticipated part of the return—that portion resulting from surprises—is the true risk of any investment. After all, if we got what we had expected, there would be no risk and no uncertainty.

There are important differences, though, among various sources of risk. Look at our previous list of news stories. Some of these stories are directed specifically at Flyers, and some are more general. Which of the news items are of specific importance to Flyers?

Announcements about interest rates or GNP are clearly important for nearly all companies, whereas the news about Flyers' president, its research, its sales, or the affairs of a rival company are of specific interest to Flyers. We will divide these two types of announcements and the resulting risk, then, into two components: a systematic portion, called *systematic risk,* and the remainder, which we call *specific* or *unsystematic risk*. The following definitions describe the difference:

- A *systematic risk* is any risk that affects a large number of assets, each to a greater or lesser degree.
- An *unsystematic risk* is a risk that specifically affects a single asset or a small group of assets.

Uncertainty about general economic conditions, such as GNP, interest rates, or inflation, is an example of systematic risk. These conditions affect nearly all stocks to some degree. An unanticipated or surprise increase in inflation affects wages and the costs of the supplies that companies buy, the value of the assets that companies own, and the prices at which companies sell their products. These forces to which all companies are susceptible are the essence of systematic risk.

In contrast, the announcement of a small oil strike by a company may affect that company alone or a few other companies. Certainly, it is unlikely to have an effect on the world oil market. To stress that such information is unsystematic and affects only some specific companies, we sometimes call it an *idiosyncratic risk*.

The distinction between a systematic risk and an unsystematic risk is never as exact as we make it out to be. Even the most narrow and peculiar bit of news about a company ripples through the economy. It reminds us of the tale of the war that was lost because one horse lost a shoe; even a minor event may have an impact on the world. But this degree of hairsplitting should not trouble us much. To paraphrase a Supreme Court justice's comment when speaking of pornography, we may not be able to define a systematic risk and an unsystematic risk exactly, but we know them when we see them.

This permits us to break down the risk of Flyers' stock into its two components: the systematic and the unsystematic. As is traditional, we will use the Greek epsilon, ϵ, to represent the unsystematic risk and write:

$$\begin{aligned} R &= \overline{R} + U \\ &= \overline{R} + m + \epsilon \end{aligned} \tag{11.10}$$

where we have used the letter m to stand for the systematic risk. Sometimes systematic risk is referred to as *market risk*. This emphasizes the fact that m influences all assets in the market to some extent.

The important point about the way we have broken the total risk, U, into its two components, m and ϵ, is that ϵ, because it is specific to the company, is unrelated to the specific risk of most other companies. For example, the unsystematic risk on Flyers' stock, ϵ_F, is unrelated to the unsystematic risk of, say, General Electric's stock, ϵ_{GE}. The risk that Flyers' stock will go up or down because of a discovery by its research team—or its failure to discover something—probably is unrelated to any of the specific uncertainties that affect General Electric's stock. This means that the unsystematic risks of Flyers' stock and General Electric's stock are unrelated to each other, or uncorrelated.

THE ESSENCE OF DIVERSIFICATION

Now what happens when we combine Flyers' stock with another stock in a portfolio? Because the unsystematic risks or epsilons of the two stocks are uncorrelated, the epsilon may be positive for one stock when the epsilon of the other is negative. Since the epsilons can offset each other, the unsystematic risk of the portfolio will be lower than the unsystematic risk of either of the two securities. In other words, we see the

Chapter 11 Return and Risk 355

beginnings of diversification. And, if we add a third security to our portfolio, the unsystematic risk of the portfolio will be lower than the unsystematic risk of the two-security portfolio. The effect continues when we add a fourth, a fifth, or a sixth security. In fact, if we were able, hypothetically, to combine an infinite number of securities, the unsystematic risk of the portfolio would disappear.

Now let's consider what happens to the portfolio's systematic risk when we add a second security. If the return on the second security is also modeled by Equation 11.10, the systematic risk of the portfolio will not be reduced. For example, suppose inflation turns out to be higher than previously anticipated, or GNP turns out to be lower than anticipated. Both stocks will likely decline, implying a decline in the portfolio. And we would get the same result with three securities, four securities, or more. In fact, suppose the portfolio had an infinite number of securities. Bad news for the economy would impact all of these securities negatively, implying a negative impact for the portfolio. Unlike unsystematic risk, systematic risk cannot be diversified away.

This insight can be illustrated in Figure 11.7. The graph, relating the standard deviation of a portfolio to the number of securities in the portfolio, shows a high standard deviation for one security. We often speak of standard deviation as the total risk, or simply the risk, of the portfolio. Addition of a second security reduces standard deviation, or risk, as does the addition of a third security, and so on. The total risk of the portfolio steadily falls with diversification.

But note that diversification does not allow total risk to go to zero. There is a limit to the benefit of diversification, because only unsystematic risk is getting diversified away. Systematic risk is left untouched. Thus, while diversification is good, it is not as good as we might have hoped. Systematic risk just doesn't decrease through diversification.

The previous discussion implicitly assumed that all securities have the same level of systematic risk. While essentially all securities have some systematic risk, certain

Figure 11.7

Relationship between the Standard Deviation of a Portfolio's Return and the Number of Securities in the Portfolio

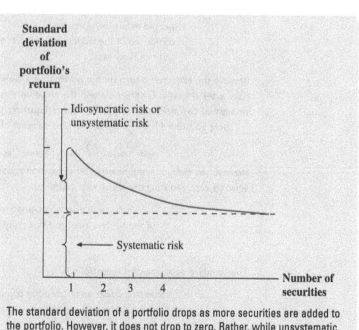

The standard deviation of a portfolio drops as more securities are added to the portfolio. However, it does not drop to zero. Rather, while unsystematic risk can be eliminated through diversification, systematic risk cannot be.

securities have more of this risk than others. The amount of systematic risk is measured by something called *beta,* a concept that will be explained in Section 11.8. But first we must consider the impact of riskless borrowing and lending.

11.7   Riskless Borrowing and Lending

Figure 11.6 assumes that all the securities in the efficient set are risky. Alternatively, an investor could combine a risky investment with an investment in a riskless or *risk-free* security, such as U.S. Treasury bills. This is illustrated in the following example.

EXAMPLE 11.3

Riskless Lending and Portfolio Risk   Ms. Bagwell is considering investing in the common stock of Merville Enterprises. In addition, Ms. Bagwell will either borrow or lend at the risk-free rate. The relevant parameters are these:

	Common Stock of Merville	Risk-Free Asset
Expected return	14%	10%
Standard deviation	.20	0

Suppose Ms. Bagwell chooses to invest a total of $1,000, $350 of which is to be invested in Merville Enterprises and $650 placed in the risk-free asset. The expected return on her total investment is simply a weighted average of the two returns:

$$\text{Expected return on portfolio composed of the riskless asset and one risky asset} = .114 = (.35 \times .14) + (.65 \times .10) \quad (11.11)$$

Because the expected return on the portfolio is a weighted average of the expected return on the risky asset (Merville Enterprises) and the risk-free return, the calculation is analogous to the way we treated two risky assets. In other words, Equation 11.3 applies here.

Using Equation 11.4, the formula for the variance of the portfolio can be written as:

$$X^2_{\text{Merville}} \sigma^2_{\text{Merville}} + 2X_{\text{Merville}} X_{\text{Risk-free}} \sigma_{\text{Merville, Risk-free}} + X^2_{\text{Risk-free}} \sigma^2_{\text{Risk-free}}$$

However, by definition, the risk-free asset has no variability. Thus both $\sigma_{\text{Merville, Risk-free}}$ and $\sigma^2_{\text{Risk-free}}$ are equal to zero, reducing the above expression to:

$$\begin{aligned}\text{Variance of portfolio composed of the riskless asset and one risky asset} &= X^2_{\text{Merville}} \sigma^2_{\text{Merville}} \\ &= (.35)^2 \times (.20)^2 \\ &= .0049\end{aligned} \quad (11.12)$$

The standard deviation of the portfolio is:

$$\begin{aligned}\text{Standard deviation of portfolio composed of the riskless asset and one risky asset} &= X_{\text{Merville}} \sigma_{\text{Merville}} \\ &= .35 \times .20 \\ &= .07\end{aligned} \quad (11.13)$$

Figure 11.8   **Relationship between Expected Return and Risk for Portfolios Composed of the Riskless Asset and One Risky Asset**

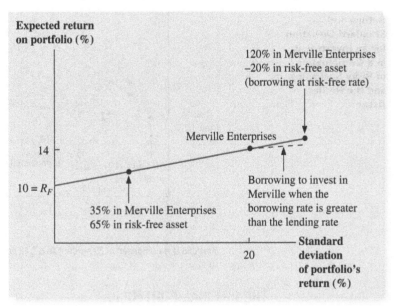

The relationship between risk and expected return for portfolios composed of one risky asset and the riskless asset can be seen in Figure 11.8. Ms. Bagwell's split of 35–65 percent between the two assets is represented on a *straight* line between the risk-free rate and a pure investment in Merville Enterprises. Note that, unlike the case of two risky assets, the opportunity set is straight, not curved.

Suppose that, alternatively, Ms. Bagwell borrows $200 at the risk-free rate. Combining this with her original sum of $1,000, she invests a total of $1,200 in Merville. Her expected return would be:

$$\text{Expected return on portfolio formed by borrowing to invest in risky asset} = 14.8\% = 1.20 \times .14 + (-.2 \times .10)$$

Here, she invests 120 percent of her original investment of $1,000 by borrowing 20 percent of her original investment. Note that the return of 14.8 percent is greater than the 14 percent expected return on Merville Enterprises. This occurs because she is borrowing at 10 percent to invest in a security with an expected return greater than 10 percent.

The standard deviation is:

$$\text{Standard deviation of portfolio formed by borrowing to invest in risky asset} = .24 = 1.20 \times .2$$

The standard deviation of .24 is greater than .20, the standard deviation of the Merville investment, because borrowing increases the variability of the investment. This investment also appears in Figure 11.8.

So far, we have assumed that Ms. Bagwell is able to borrow at the same rate at which she can lend.[8] Now let us consider the case where the borrowing rate is above the lending rate. The dotted line in Figure 11.8 illustrates the opportunity set for borrowing opportunities in this case. The dotted line is below the solid line because a higher borrowing rate lowers the expected return on the investment.

---

[8]Surprisingly, this appears to be a decent approximation because many investors can borrow from a stockbroker (called *going on margin*) when purchasing stocks. The borrowing rate here is very near the riskless rate of interest, particularly for large investors. More will be said about this in a later chapter.

Figure 11.9
**Relationship
between Expected
Return and
Standard Deviation
for an Investment
in a Combination
of Risky Securities
and the Riskless
Asset**

Portfolio Q is composed of 30 percent AT&T, 45 percent GM, and 25 percent IBM.

THE OPTIMAL PORTFOLIO

The previous section concerned a portfolio formed between the riskless asset and one risky asset. In reality, an investor is likely to combine an investment in the riskless asset with a *portfolio* of risky assets. This is illustrated in Figure 11.9.

Consider Point Q, representing a portfolio of securities. Point Q is in the interior of the feasible set of risky securities. Let us assume the point represents a portfolio of 30 percent in AT&T, 45 percent in General Motors (GM), and 25 percent in IBM. Individuals combining investments in Q with investments in the riskless asset would achieve points along the straight line from R_F to Q. We refer to this as Line I. For example, Point I on the line represents a portfolio of 70 percent in the riskless asset and 30 percent in stocks represented by Q. An investor with $100 choosing Point I as his portfolio would put $70 in the risk-free asset and $30 in Q. This can be restated as $70 in the riskless asset, $9 ($=.3 \times$ 30) in AT&T, $13.50 ($=.45 \times$ 30) in GM, and $7.50 ($=.25 \times$ 30) in IBM. Point 2 also represents a portfolio of the risk-free asset and Q, with more (65%) being invested in Q.

Point 3 is obtained by borrowing to invest in Q. For example, an investor with $100 of her own would borrow $40 from the bank or broker to invest $140 in Q. This can be stated as borrowing $40 and contributing $100 of her money to invest $42 ($=.3 \times$ 140) in AT&T, $63 ($=.45 \times$ 140) in GM, and $35 ($=.25 \times$ 140) in IBM.

These investments can be summarized as follows:

	Point Q	Point I (Lending $70)	Point 3 (Borrowing $40)
AT&T	$ 30	$ 9.00	$ 42
GM	45	13.50	63
IBM	25	7.50	35
Risk-free	0	70.00	−40
Total investment	$100	$100	$100

Though any investor can obtain any point on Line I, no point on the line is optimal. To see this, consider Line II, a line running from R_F through A. Point A represents a portfolio of risky securities. Line II represents portfolios formed by combinations of the risk-free asset and the securities in A. Points between R_F and A are portfolios in which some money is invested in the riskless asset and the rest is placed in A. Points past A are achieved by borrowing at the riskless rate to buy more of A than we could with our original funds alone.

As drawn, Line II is tangent to the efficient set of risky securities. Whatever point an individual can obtain on Line I, he can obtain a point with the same standard deviation and a higher expected return on Line II. In fact, because Line II is tangent to the efficient set of risky assets, it provides the investor with the best possible opportunities. In other words, Line II can be viewed as the efficient set of *all* assets, both risky and riskless. An investor with a fair degree of risk aversion might choose a point between R_F and A, perhaps Point 4. An individual with less risk aversion might choose a point closer to A or even beyond A. For example, Point 5 corresponds to an individual borrowing money to increase investment in A.

The graph illustrates an important point. With riskless borrowing and lending, the portfolio of *risky* assets held by any investor would always be Point A. Regardless of the investor's tolerance for risk, she would never choose any other point on the efficient set of risky assets (represented by Curve XAY) nor any point in the interior of the feasible region. Rather, she would combine the securities of A with the riskless asset if she had high aversion to risk. She would borrow the riskless asset to invest more funds in A if she had low aversion to risk.

This result establishes what financial economists call the **separation principle.** That is, the investor's investment decision consists of two separate steps:

1. After estimating (a) the expected returns and variances of individual securities, and (b) the covariances between pairs of securities, the investor calculates the efficient set of risky assets, represented by Curve XAY in Figure 11.9. He then determines Point A, the tangency between the risk-free rate and the efficient set of risky assets (Curve XAY). Point A represents the portfolio of risky assets that the investor will hold. This point is determined solely from his estimates of returns, variances, and covariances. No personal characteristics, such as degree of risk aversion, are needed in this step.

2. The investor must now determine how he will combine Point A, his portfolio of risky assets, with the riskless asset. He might invest some of his funds in the riskless asset and some in Portfolio A. He would end up at a point on the line between R_F and A in this case. Alternatively, he might borrow at the risk-free rate and contribute some of his own funds as well, investing the sum in Portfolio A. He would end up at a point on Line II beyond A. His position in the riskless asset—that is, his choice of where on the line he wants to be—is determined by his internal characteristics, such as his ability to tolerate risk.

11.8 Market Equilibrium

DEFINITION OF THE MARKET EQUILIBRIUM PORTFOLIO

ExcelMaster
coverage online

This section introduces trendlines, regression estimates, and SLOPE and INTERCEPT functions.

The preceding analysis concerns one investor. His estimates of the expected returns and variances for individual securities and the covariances between pairs of securities are his and his alone. Other investors would obviously have different estimates of these variables. However, the estimates might not vary much because all investors would be forming expectations from the same data about past price movements and other publicly available information.

360   Part III   Risk

Financial economists often imagine a world where all investors possess the *same* estimates of expected returns, variances, and covariances. Though this is never literally true, it is a useful simplifying assumption in a world where investors have access to similar sources of information. This assumption is called **homogeneous expectations.**[9]

If all investors had homogeneous expectations, Figure 11.9 would be the same for all individuals. That is, all investors would sketch out the same efficient set of risky assets because they would be working with the same inputs. This efficient set of risky assets is represented by the Curve *XAY*. Because the same risk-free rate would apply to everyone, all investors would view Point *A* as the portfolio of risky assets to be held.

This Point *A* takes on great importance because all investors would purchase the risky securities that it represents. Investors with a high degree of risk aversion might combine *A* with an investment in the riskless asset, achieving Point *4*, for example. Others with low aversion to risk might borrow to achieve, say, Point *5*. Because this is a very important conclusion, we restate it:

In a world with homogeneous expectations, all investors would hold the portfolio of risky assets represented by Point *A*.

If all investors choose the same portfolio of risky assets, one can determine what that portfolio is. Common sense tells us that it is a market value weighted portfolio of all existing securities. It is the **market portfolio.**

In practice, economists use a broad-based index such as the Standard & Poor's (S&P) 500 as a proxy for the market portfolio. Of course all investors do not hold the same portfolio in practice. However, we know that many investors hold diversified portfolios, particularly when mutual funds or pension funds are included. A broad-based index is a good proxy for the highly diversified portfolios of many investors.

DEFINITION OF RISK WHEN INVESTORS HOLD THE MARKET PORTFOLIO

Earlier in this chapter we pointed out that the risk or standard deviation of a stock could be broken down into systematic and unsystematic risk. Unsystematic risk can be diversified away in a large portfolio but systematic risk cannot. Thus, a diversified investor must worry about the systematic risk, but not the unsystematic risk, of every security in a portfolio. Is there a way to measure the systematic risk of a security? Yes, it is best measured by *beta*, which we illustrate in an example. It turns out that beta is the best measure of the risk of an individual security from the point of view of a diversified investor.

EXAMPLE 11.4

Beta   Consider the following possible returns both on the stock of Jelco, Inc., and on the market:

State	Type of Economy	Return on Market (percent)	Return on Jelco, Inc. (percent)
I	Bull	15	25
II	Bull	15	15
III	Bear	−5	−5
IV	Bear	−5	−15

---

[9]The assumption of homogeneous expectations states that all investors have the same beliefs concerning returns, variances, and covariances. It does not say that all investors have the same aversion to risk.

Though the return on the market has only two possible outcomes (15% and −5%), the return on Jelco has four possible outcomes. It is helpful to consider the expected return on a security for a given return on the market. Assuming each state is equally likely, we have:

Type of Economy	Return on Market (percent)	Expected Return on Jelco, Inc. (percent)
Bull	15%	$20\% = 25\% \times \frac{1}{2} + 15\% \times \frac{1}{2}$
Bear	−5%	$-10\% = -5\% \times \frac{1}{2} + (-15\%) \times \frac{1}{2}$

Jelco, Inc., responds to market movements because its expected return is greater in bullish states than in bearish states. We now calculate exactly how responsive the security is to market movements. The market's return in a bullish economy is 20 percent [=15% − (−5%)] greater than the market's return in a bearish economy. However, the expected return on Jelco in a bullish economy is 30 percent [=20% − (−10%)] greater than its expected return in a bearish state. Thus Jelco, Inc., has a responsiveness coefficient of 1.5 (=30%/20%).

Figure 11.10   **Performance of Jelco, Inc., and the Market Portfolio**

The two points marked X represent the expected return on Jelco for each possible outcome of the market portfolio. The expected return on Jelco is positively related to the return on the market. Because the slope is 1.5, we say that Jelco's beta is 1.5. Beta measures the responsiveness of the security's return to movement in the market.

*(15%, 20%) refers to the point where the return on the market is 15 percent and the return on the security is 20 percent.

This relationship appears in Figure 11.10. The returns for both Jelco and the market in each state are plotted as four points. In addition, we plot the expected return on the security for each of the two possible returns on the market. These two points, each of which we designate by an X, are joined by a line called the **characteristic line** of the security. The slope of the line is 1.5, the number calculated in the previous paragraph. This responsiveness coefficient of 1.5 is the **beta** of Jelco.

The interpretation of beta from Figure 11.10 is intuitive. The graph tells us that the returns of Jelco are magnified 1.5 times over those of the market. When the market does well, Jelco's stock

(continued)

is expected to do even better. When the market does poorly, Jelco's stock is expected to do even worse. Now imagine an individual with a portfolio near that of the market who is considering the addition of Jelco to her portfolio. Because of Jelco's *magnification factor* of 1.5, she will view this stock as contributing much to the risk of the portfolio. (We will show shortly that the beta of the average security in the market is 1.) Jelco contributes more to the risk of a large, diversified portfolio than does an average security because Jelco is more responsive to movements in the market.

Further insight can be gleaned by examining securities with negative betas. One should view these securities as either hedges or insurance policies. The security is expected to do well when the market does poorly and vice versa. Because of this, adding a negative-beta security to a large, diversified portfolio actually reduces the risk of the portfolio.[10]

Table 11.6 presents empirical estimates of betas for individual securities. As can be seen, some securities are more responsive to the market than others. For example, Ford has a beta of 2.35. This means that for every 1 percent movement in the market,[11] Ford is expected to move 2.35 percent in the same direction. Conversely, 3M has a beta of only .83. This means that for every 1 percent movement in the market, 3M is expected to move .83 percent in the same direction.

We can summarize our discussion of beta by saying:

Beta measures the responsiveness of a security to movements in the market portfolio.

THE FORMULA FOR BETA

Our discussion so far has stressed the intuition behind beta. The actual definition of beta is:

$$\beta_i = \frac{\text{Cov}(R_i, R_M)}{\sigma^2(R_M)} \qquad (11.14)$$

where $\text{Cov}(R_i, R_M)$ is the covariance between the return on Asset i and the return on the market portfolio and $\sigma^2(R_M)$ is the variance of the market.

Table 11.6
Estimates of Beta for Selected Individual Stocks

Stock	Beta
CVS Caremark	.79
3M	.83
Amazon.com	.90
Tyson Foods	1.14
McGraw-Hill	1.23
Dell	1.42
Ford	2.35
Louisiana Pacific	2.82

The beta is defined as $\text{Cov}(R_i, R_M)/\text{Var}(R_M)$, where $\text{Cov}(R_i, R_M)$ is the covariance of the return on an individual stock, R_i, and the return on the market, R_M. $\text{Var}(R_M)$ is the variance of the return on the market, R_M.

---

[10]Unfortunately, empirical evidence shows that few, if any, stocks have negative betas.
[11]In Table 11.6, we use the Standard & Poor's 500 Index as a proxy for the market portfolio.

One useful property is that the average beta across all securities, when weighted by the proportion of each security's market value to that of the market portfolio, is 1. That is:

$$\sum_{i=1}^{N} X_i \beta_i = 1 \tag{11.15}$$

where X_i is the proportion of Security i's market value to that of the entire market and N is the number of securities in the market.

Equation 11.15 is intuitive, once you think about it. If you weight all securities by their market values, the resulting portfolio is the market. By definition, the beta of the market portfolio is 1. That is, for every 1 percent movement in the market, the market must move 1 percent—*by definition.*

A TEST

We have put these questions on past corporate finance examinations:

1. What sort of investor rationally views the variance (or standard deviation) of an individual security's return as the security's proper measure of risk?

2. What sort of investor rationally views the beta of a security as the security's proper measure of risk?

A good response answering both questions might be something like the following:

> A rational, risk-averse investor views the variance (or standard deviation) of her portfolio's return as the proper measure of the portfolio's risk. If for some reason the investor can hold only one security, the variance of that security's return becomes the variance of the portfolio's return. Hence, the variance of the security's return is the security's proper measure of risk.
>
> If an individual holds a diversified portfolio, she still views the variance (or standard deviation) of her portfolio's return as the proper measure of the risk of her portfolio. However, she is no longer interested in the variance of each individual security's return. Rather, she is interested in the contribution of an individual security to the variance of the portfolio. The contribution of a security to the variance of a diversified portfolio is best measured by beta. Therefore, beta is the proper measure of the risk of an individual security for a diversified investor.
>
> Beta measures the systematic risk of a security. Thus, diversified investors pay attention to the systematic risk of each security. However, they ignore the unsystematic risks of individual securities, since unsystematic risks are diversified away in a large portfolio.

11.9 Relationship between Risk and Expected Return (CAPM)

It is commonplace to argue that the expected return on an asset should be positively related to its risk. That is, individuals will hold a risky asset only if its expected return compensates for its risk. In this section, we first estimate the expected return on the stock market as a whole. Next, we estimate expected returns on individual securities.

EXPECTED RETURN ON MARKET

Economists frequently argue that the expected return on the market can be represented as:

$$\overline{R}_M = R_F + \text{Risk premium}$$

In words, the expected return on the market is the sum of the risk-free rate plus some compensation for the risk inherent in the market portfolio. Note that the equation refers to the *expected* return on the market, not the actual return in a particular month or year. Because stocks have risk, the actual return on the market over a particular period can, of course, be below R_F or can even be negative.

Because investors want compensation for risk, the risk premium is presumably positive. But exactly how positive is it? It is generally argued that the place to start looking for the risk premium in the future is the average risk premium in the past. As reported in Chapter 10, Dimson, Marsh, and Staunton found the average excess annual return of U.S. common stocks over the risk-free rate (i.e., one-year Treasury bills) was 7.2 percent over 1900–2010. We referred to 7.2 percent as the historical U.S. equity risk premium. The average historical worldwide equity premium was 6.9 percent. Taking into account a number of factors, we find 7 percent to be a reasonable estimate of the future U.S. equity risk premium.

For example, if the risk-free rate, estimated by the current yield on a one-year Treasury bill, is 1 percent, the expected return on the market is:

$$8\% = 1\% + 7\%$$

Of course, the future equity risk premium could be higher or lower than the historical equity risk premium. This could be true if future risk is higher or lower than past risk or if individual risk aversions are higher or lower than those of the past.

EXPECTED RETURN ON INDIVIDUAL SECURITY

Now that we have estimated the expected return on the market as a whole, what is the expected return on an individual security? We have argued that the beta of a security is the appropriate measure of its risk in a large, diversified portfolio. Because most investors are diversified, the expected return on a security should be positively related to its beta. This idea is illustrated in Figure 11.11.

Actually, economists can be more precise about the relationship between expected return and beta. They posit that under plausible conditions the

Figure 11.11
Relationship between Expected Return on an Individual Security and Beta of the Security

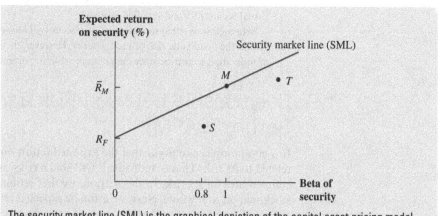

The security market line (SML) is the graphical depiction of the capital asset pricing model (CAPM).
The expected return on a stock with a beta of 0 is equal to the risk-free rate.
The expected return on a stock with a beta of 1 is equal to the expected return on the market.

relationship between expected return and beta can be represented by the following equation:[12]

Capital Asset Pricing Model

$$\overline{R} \quad = \quad R_F \quad + \quad \beta \quad \times \quad (\overline{R}_M - R_F)$$

| Expected return on a security | = | Risk-free rate | + | Beta of the security | × | Difference between expected return on market and risk-free rate | (11.16) |

This formula, which is called the **capital asset pricing model** (or CAPM for short), implies that the expected return on a security is linearly related to its beta. Because the average return on the market has been higher than the average risk-free rate over long periods of time, $\overline{R}_M - R_F$ is presumably positive. Thus, the formula implies that the expected return on a security is *positively* related to its beta. The formula can be illustrated by assuming a few special cases:

- *Assume that* $\beta = 0$. Here $\overline{R} = R_F$—that is, the expected return on the security is equal to the risk-free rate. Because a security with zero beta has no relevant risk, its expected return should equal the risk-free rate.
- *Assume that* $\beta = 1$. Equation 11.16 reduces to $\overline{R} = \overline{R}_M$. That is, the expected return on the security is equal to the expected return on the market. This makes sense because the beta of the market portfolio is also 1.

Equation 11.16 can be represented graphically by the upward-sloping line in Figure 11.11. Note that the line begins at R_F and rises to $\overline{R}_M$ when beta is 1. This line is frequently called the **security market line** (SML).

As with any line, the SML has both a slope and an intercept. R_F, the risk-free rate, is the intercept. Because the beta of a security is the horizontal axis, $\overline{R}_M - R_F$ is the slope. The line will be upward-sloping as long as the expected return on the market is greater than the risk-free rate. Because the market portfolio is a risky asset, theory suggests that its expected return is above the risk-free rate, a result consistent with the empirical evidence of the previous chapter.

EXAMPLE 11.5

The stock of Aardvark Enterprises has a beta of 1.5 and that of Zebra Enterprises has a beta of .7. The risk-free rate is assumed to be 3 percent, and the difference between the expected return on the market and the risk-free rate is assumed to be 8.0 percent. The expected returns on the two securities are:

Expected Return for Aardvark

$$15.0\% = 3\% + 1.5 \times 8.0\% \tag{11.17}$$

Expected Return for Zebra

$$8.6\% = 3\% + .7 \times 8.0\%$$

---

[12]This relationship was first proposed independently by John Lintner and William F. Sharpe.

Three additional points concerning the CAPM should be mentioned:

1. *Linearity:* The intuition behind an upwardly sloping curve is clear. Because beta is the appropriate measure of risk, high-beta securities should have an expected return above that of low-beta securities. However, both Figure 11.11 and Equation 11.16 show something more than an upwardly sloping curve: The relationship between expected return and beta corresponds to a *straight* line.

   It is easy to show that the line of Figure 11.11 is straight. To see this, consider Security S with, say, a beta of .8. This security is represented by a point below the security market line in the figure. Any investor could duplicate the beta of Security S by buying a portfolio with 20 percent in the risk-free asset and 80 percent in a security with a beta of 1. However, the homemade portfolio would itself lie on the SML. In other words, the portfolio dominates Security S because the portfolio has a higher expected return and the same beta.

   Now consider Security T with, say, a beta greater than 1. This security is also below the SML in Figure 11.11. Any investor could duplicate the beta of Security T by borrowing to invest in a security with a beta of 1. This portfolio must also lie on the SML, thereby dominating Security T.

   Because no one would hold either S or T, their stock prices would drop. This price adjustment would raise the expected returns on the two securities. The price adjustment would continue until the two securities lay on the security market line. The preceding example considered two overpriced stocks and a straight SML. Securities lying above the SML are *underpriced.* Their prices must rise until their expected returns lie on the line. If the SML is itself curved, many stocks would be mispriced. In equilibrium, all securities would be held only when prices changed so that the SML became straight. In other words, linearity would be achieved.

2. *Portfolios as well as securities:* Our discussion of the CAPM considered individual securities. Does the relationship in Figure 11.11 and Equation 11.16 hold for portfolios as well?

   Yes. To see this, consider a portfolio formed by investing equally in our two securities from Example 11.5, Aardvark and Zebra. The expected return on the portfolio is:

Expected Return on Portfolio

$$11.8\% = .5 \times 15.0\% + .5 \times 8.6\% \tag{11.18}$$

The beta of the portfolio is simply a weighted average of the betas of the two securities. Thus, we have:

Beta of Portfolio

$$1.1 = .5 \times 1.5 + .5 \times .7$$

Under the CAPM, the expected return on the portfolio is:

$$11.8\% = 3\% + 1.1 \times 8.0\% \tag{11.19}$$

Because the expected return in Equation 11.18 is the same as the expected return in Equation 11.19, the example shows that the CAPM holds for portfolios as well as for individual securities.

3. *A potential confusion:* Students often confuse the SML in Figure 11.11 with Line *II* in Figure 11.9. Actually, the lines are quite different. Line *II* traces the

efficient set of portfolios formed from both risky assets and the riskless asset. Each point on the line represents an entire portfolio. Point *A* is a portfolio composed entirely of risky assets. Every other point on the line represents a portfolio of the securities in *A* combined with the riskless asset. The axes on Figure 11.9 are the expected return on a *portfolio* and the standard deviation of a *portfolio*. Individual securities do not lie along Line *II*.

The SML in Figure 11.11 relates expected return to beta. Figure 11.11 differs from Figure 11.9 in at least two ways. First, beta appears in the horizontal axis of Figure 11.11, but standard deviation appears in the horizontal axis of Figure 11.9. Second, the SML in Figure 11.11 holds both for all individual securities and for all possible portfolios, whereas Line *II* in Figure 11.9 holds only for efficient portfolios.

◄ To test your mastery of this material, take a quiz at mhhe. com/rwj

We stated earlier that, under homogeneous expectations, Point *A* in Figure 11.9 becomes the market portfolio. In this situation, Line *II* is referred to as the **capital market line** (CML).

Summary and Conclusions

This chapter set forth the fundamentals of modern portfolio theory. Our basic points are these:

1. This chapter showed us how to calculate the expected return and variance for individual securities, and the covariance and correlation for pairs of securities. Given these statistics, the expected return and variance for a portfolio of two securities *A* and *B* can be written as:

$$\text{Expected return on portfolio} = X_A \overline{R}_A + X_B \overline{R}_B$$
$$\text{Var(portfolio)} = X_A^2 \sigma_A^2 + 2 X_A X_B \sigma_{AB} + X_B^2 \sigma_B^2$$

2. In our notation, *X* stands for the proportion of a security in a portfolio. By varying *X* we can trace out the efficient set of portfolios. We graphed the efficient set for the two-asset case as a curve, pointing out that the degree of curvature or bend in the graph reflects the diversification effect: The lower the correlation between the two securities, the greater the bend. The same general shape of the efficient set holds in a world of many assets.

3. Just as the formula for variance in the two-asset case is computed from a 2×2 matrix, the variance formula is computed from an *N×N* matrix in the *N*-asset case. We showed that with a large number of assets, there are many more covariance terms than variance terms in the matrix. In fact the variance terms are effectively diversified away in a large portfolio, but the covariance terms are not. Thus, a diversified portfolio can eliminate some, but not all, of the risk of the individual securities.

4. The efficient set of risky assets can be combined with riskless borrowing and lending. In this case a rational investor will always choose to hold the portfolio of risky securities represented by Point *A* in Figure 11.9. Then he can either borrow or lend at the riskless rate to achieve any desired point on Line *II* in the figure.

5. The contribution of a security to the risk of a large, well-diversified portfolio is proportional to the covariance of the security's return with the market's return. This contribution, when standardized, is called the beta. The beta of a security can also be interpreted as the responsiveness of a security's return to that of the market.

www.mhhe.com/rwj

6. The CAPM states that:

$$\overline{R} = R_F + \beta(\overline{R}_M - R_F)$$

In other words, the expected return on a security is positively (and linearly) related to the security's beta.

Concept Questions

1. **Diversifiable and Nondiversifiable Risks** In broad terms, why is some risk diversifiable? Why are some risks nondiversifiable? Does it follow that an investor can control the level of unsystematic risk in a portfolio, but not the level of systematic risk?

2. **Systematic versus Unsystematic Risk** Classify the following events as mostly systematic or mostly unsystematic. Is the distinction clear in every case?
   a. Short-term interest rates increase unexpectedly.
   b. The interest rate a company pays on its short-term debt borrowing is increased by its bank.
   c. Oil prices unexpectedly decline.
   d. An oil tanker ruptures, creating a large oil spill.
   e. A manufacturer loses a multimillion-dollar product liability suit.
   f. A Supreme Court decision substantially broadens producer liability for injuries suffered by product users.

3. **Expected Portfolio Returns** If a portfolio has a positive investment in every asset, can the expected return on the portfolio be greater than that on every asset in the portfolio? Can it be less than that on every asset in the portfolio? If you answer yes to one or both of these questions, give an example to support your answer.

4. **Diversification** True or false: The most important characteristic in determining the expected return of a well-diversified portfolio is the variances of the individual assets in the portfolio. Explain.

5. **Portfolio Risk** If a portfolio has a positive investment in every asset, can the standard deviation on the portfolio be less than that on every asset in the portfolio? What about the portfolio beta?

6. **Beta and CAPM** Is it possible that a risky asset could have a beta of zero? Explain. Based on the CAPM, what is the expected return on such an asset? Is it possible that a risky asset could have a negative beta? What does the CAPM predict about the expected return on such an asset? Can you give an explanation for your answer?

7. **Covariance** Briefly explain why the covariance of a security with the rest of a well-diversified portfolio is a more appropriate measure of the risk of the security than the security's variance.

8. **Beta** Consider the following quotation from a leading investment manager: "The shares of Southern Co. have traded close to $12 for most of the past three years. Since Southern's stock has demonstrated very little price movement, the stock has a low beta. Texas Instruments, on the other hand, has traded as high as $150 and as low as its current $75. Since TI's stock has demonstrated a large amount of price movement, the stock has a very high beta." Do you agree with this analysis? Explain.

9. **Risk** A broker has advised you not to invest in oil industry stocks because they have high standard deviations. Is the broker's advice sound for a risk-averse investor like yourself? Why or why not?

10. **Security Selection** Is the following statement true or false? A risky security cannot have an expected return that is less than the risk-free rate because no risk-averse investor would be willing to hold this asset in equilibrium. Explain.

Questions and Problems

BASIC
(Questions 1–19)

1. **Determining Portfolio Weights**   What are the portfolio weights for a portfolio that has 135 shares of Stock *A* that sell for $47 per share and 105 shares of Stock *B* that sell for $41 per share?

2. **Portfolio Expected Return**   You own a portfolio that has $2,100 invested in Stock *A* and $3,200 invested in Stock *B*. If the expected returns on these stocks are 11 percent and 14 percent, respectively, what is the expected return on the portfolio?

3. **Portfolio Expected Return**   You own a portfolio that is 25 percent invested in Stock *X*, 40 percent in Stock *Y*, and 35 percent in Stock *Z*. The expected returns on these three stocks are 11 percent, 17 percent, and 14 percent, respectively. What is the expected return on the portfolio?

4. **Portfolio Expected Return**   You have $10,000 to invest in a stock portfolio. Your choices are Stock *X* with an expected return of 14 percent and Stock *Y* with an expected return of 9 percent. If your goal is to create a portfolio with an expected return of 12.9 percent, how much money will you invest in Stock *X*? In Stock *Y*?

5. **Calculating Returns and Standard Deviations**   Based on the following information, calculate the expected return and standard deviation for the two stocks:

State of Economy	Probability of State of Economy	Rate of Return if State Occurs	
		Stock A	Stock B
Recession	.20	.06	−.20
Normal	.55	.07	.13
Boom	.25	.11	.33

6. **Calculating Returns and Standard Deviations**   Based on the following information, calculate the expected return and standard deviation:

State of Economy	Probability of State of Economy	Rate of Return if State Occurs
Depression	.10	−.105
Recession	.25	.059
Normal	.45	.130
Boom	.20	.211

7. **Calculating Expected Returns**   A portfolio is invested 10 percent in Stock *G*, 65 percent in Stock *J*, and 25 percent in Stock *K*. The expected returns on these stocks are 9 percent, 11 percent, and 14 percent, respectively. What is the portfolio's expected return? How do you interpret your answer?

8. **Returns and Standard Deviations**   Consider the following information:

State of Economy	Probability of State of Economy	Rate of Return if State Occurs		
		Stock A	Stock B	Stock C
Boom	.65	.07	.15	.33
Bust	.35	.13	.03	−.06

   a. What is the expected return on an equally weighted portfolio of these three stocks?

   b. What is the variance of a portfolio invested 20 percent each in *A* and *B*, and 60 percent in *C*?

9.   **Returns and Standard Deviations**   Consider the following information:

State of Economy	Probability of State of Economy	Rate of Return if State Occurs		
		Stock A	Stock B	Stock C
Boom	.20	.24	.45	.33
Good	.35	.09	.10	.15
Poor	.30	.03	−.10	−.05
Bust	.15	−.05	−.25	−.09

   a. Your portfolio is invested 30 percent each in *A* and *C*, and 40 percent in *B*. What is the expected return of the portfolio?

   b. What is the variance of this portfolio? The standard deviation?

10.   **Calculating Portfolio Betas**   You own a stock portfolio invested 10 percent in Stock *Q*, 35 percent in Stock *R*, 20 percent in Stock *S*, and 35 percent in Stock *T*. The betas for these four stocks are .75, 1.90, 1.38, and 1.16, respectively. What is the portfolio beta?

11.   **Calculating Portfolio Betas**   You own a portfolio equally invested in a risk-free asset and two stocks. If one of the stocks has a beta of 1.65 and the total portfolio is equally as risky as the market, what must the beta be for the other stock in your portfolio?

12.   **Using CAPM**   A stock has a beta of 1.15, the expected return on the market is 11 percent, and the risk-free rate is 5 percent. What must the expected return on this stock be?

13.   **Using CAPM**   A stock has an expected return of 10.2 percent, the risk-free rate is 4 percent, and the market risk premium is 7 percent. What must the beta of this stock be?

14.   **Using CAPM**   A stock has an expected return of 13.4 percent, its beta is 1.60, and the risk-free rate is 5.5 percent. What must the expected return on the market be?

15.   **Using CAPM**   A stock has an expected return of 13.1 percent, a beta of 1.28, and the expected return on the market is 11 percent. What must the risk-free rate be?

16.   **Using CAPM**   A stock has a beta of 1.13 and an expected return of 12.1 percent. A risk-free asset currently earns 5 percent.

   a. What is the expected return on a portfolio that is equally invested in the two assets?

   b. If a portfolio of the two assets has a beta of .50, what are the portfolio weights?

   c. If a portfolio of the two assets has an expected return of 10 percent, what is its beta?

   d. If a portfolio of the two assets has a beta of 2.26, what are the portfolio weights? How do you interpret the weights for the two assets in this case? Explain.

17.   **Using the SML**   Asset *W* has an expected return of 12.3 percent and a beta of 1.3. If the risk-free rate is 4 percent, complete the following table for portfolios of Asset *W* and a risk-free asset. Illustrate the relationship between portfolio expected return and portfolio beta by plotting the expected returns against the betas. What is the slope of the line that results?

www.mhhe.com/rwj

Percentage of Portfolio in Asset W	Portfolio Expected Return	Portfolio Beta
0%		
25		
50		
75		
100		
125		
150		

18. **Reward-to-Risk Ratios** Stock Y has a beta of 1.35 and an expected return of 14 percent. Stock Z has a beta of .80 and an expected return of 11.5 percent. If the risk-free rate is 4.5 percent and the market risk premium is 7.3 percent, are these stocks correctly priced?

19. **Reward-to-Risk Ratios** In the previous problem, what would the risk-free rate have to be for the two stocks to be correctly priced?

INTERMEDIATE
(Questions 20–32)

20. **Portfolio Returns** Using information from the previous chapter about capital market history, determine the return on a portfolio that is equally invested in large-company stocks and long-term government bonds. What is the return on a portfolio that is equally invested in small-company stocks and Treasury bills?

21. **CAPM** Using the CAPM, show that the ratio of the risk premiums on two assets is equal to the ratio of their betas.

22. **Portfolio Returns and Deviations** Consider the following information about three stocks:

State of Economy	Probability of State of Economy	Rate of Return if State Occurs		
		Stock A	Stock B	Stock C
Boom	.30	.20	.25	.60
Normal	.45	.15	.11	.05
Bust	.25	.01	−.15	−.50

   a. If your portfolio is invested 40 percent each in A and B and 20 percent in C, what is the portfolio expected return? The variance? The standard deviation?

   b. If the expected T-bill rate is 3.80 percent, what is the expected risk premium on the portfolio?

   c. If the expected inflation rate is 3.50 percent, what are the approximate and exact expected real returns on the portfolio? What are the approximate and exact expected real risk premiums on the portfolio?

23. **Analyzing a Portfolio** You want to create a portfolio equally as risky as the market, and you have $1,000,000 to invest. Given this information, fill in the rest of the following table:

Asset	Investment	Beta
Stock A	$180,000	.85
Stock B	$290,000	1.40
Stock C		1.45
Risk-free asset		

www.mhhe.com/rwj

24. **Analyzing a Portfolio**   You have $100,000 to invest in a portfolio containing Stock X, Stock Y, and a risk-free asset. You must invest all of your money. Your goal is to create a portfolio that has an expected return of 11.22 percent and that has only 96 percent of the risk of the overall market. If X has an expected return of 15.35 percent and a beta of 1.55, Y has an expected return of 9.4 percent and a beta of .7, and the risk-free rate is 4.5 percent, how much money will you invest in Stock X? How do you interpret your answer?

25. **Covariance and Correlation**   Based on the following information, calculate the expected return and standard deviation of each of the following stocks. Assume each state of the economy is equally likely to happen. What are the covariance and correlation between the returns of the two stocks?

State of Economy	Return on Stock A	Return on Stock B
Bear	.102	−.045
Normal	.115	.148
Bull	.073	.233

26. **Covariance and Correlation**   Based on the following information, calculate the expected return and standard deviation for each of the following stocks. What are the covariance and correlation between the returns of the two stocks?

State of Economy	Probability of State of Economy	Return on Stock J	Return on Stock K
Bear	.25	−.020	.034
Normal	.60	.138	.062
Bull	.15	.218	.092

27. **Portfolio Standard Deviation**   Security F has an expected return of 10 percent and a standard deviation of 43 percent per year. Security G has an expected return of 15 percent and a standard deviation of 62 percent per year.

   a. What is the expected return on a portfolio composed of 30 percent of Security F and 70 percent of Security G?

   b. If the correlation between the returns of Security F and Security G is .25, what is the standard deviation of the portfolio described in part (a)?

28. **Portfolio Standard Deviation**   Suppose the expected returns and standard deviations of Stocks A and B are $E(R_A) = .09$, $E(R_B) = .15$, $\sigma_A = .36$, and $\sigma_B = .62$.

   a. Calculate the expected return and standard deviation of a portfolio that is composed of 35 percent A and 65 percent B when the correlation between the returns on A and B is .5.

   b. Calculate the standard deviation of a portfolio with the same portfolio weights as in part (a) when the correlation coefficient between the returns on A and B is −.5.

   c. How does the correlation between the returns on A and B affect the standard deviation of the portfolio?

Chapter 11   Return and Risk   373

29.   **Correlation and Beta**   You have been provided the following data about the securities of three firms, the market portfolio, and the risk-free asset:

Security	Expected Return	Standard Deviation	Correlation*	Beta
Firm A	.10	.31	(i)	.85
Firm B	.14	(ii)	.50	1.40
Firm C	.16	.65	.35	(iii)
The market portfolio	.12	.20	(iv)	(v)
The risk-free asset	.05	(vi)	(vii)	(viii)

*With the market portfolio.

a.   Fill in the missing values in the table.
b.   Is the stock of Firm A correctly priced according to the capital asset pricing model (CAPM)? What about the stock of Firm B? Firm C? If these securities are not correctly priced, what is your investment recommendation for someone with a well-diversified portfolio?

30.   **CML**   The market portfolio has an expected return of 12 percent and a standard deviation of 22 percent. The risk-free rate is 5 percent.

a.   What is the expected return on a well-diversified portfolio with a standard deviation of 9 percent?
b.   What is the standard deviation of a well-diversified portfolio with an expected return of 20 percent?

31.   **Beta and CAPM**   A portfolio that combines the risk-free asset and the market portfolio has an expected return of 7 percent and a standard deviation of 10 percent. The risk-free rate is 4 percent, and the expected return on the market portfolio is 12 percent. Assume the capital asset pricing model holds. What expected rate of return would a security earn if it had a .45 correlation with the market portfolio and a standard deviation of 55 percent?

32.   **Beta and CAPM**   Suppose the risk-free rate is 4.2 percent and the market portfolio has an expected return of 10.9 percent. The market portfolio has a variance of .0382. Portfolio Z has a correlation coefficient with the market of .28 and a variance of .3285. According to the capital asset pricing model, what is the expected return on Portfolio Z?

CHALLENGE
(Questions 33–38)

33.   **Systematic versus Unsystematic Risk**   Consider the following information about Stocks *I* and *II*:

State of Economy	Probability of State of Economy	Rate of Return if State Occurs	
		Stock *I*	Stock *II*
Recession	.15	.11	−.25
Normal	.55	.18	.11
Irrational exuberance	.30	.08	.31

The market risk premium is 7.5 percent, and the risk-free rate is 4 percent. Which stock has the most systematic risk? Which one has the most unsystematic risk? Which stock is "riskier"? Explain.

34.   SML   Suppose you observe the following situation:

Security	Beta	Expected Return
Pete Corp.	1.35	12.28%
Repete Co.	.80	8.54

Assume these securities are correctly priced. Based on the CAPM, what is the expected return on the market? What is the risk-free rate?

35.   Covariance and Portfolio Standard Deviation   There are three securities in the market. The following chart shows their possible payoffs:

State	Probability of Outcome	Return on Security 1	Return on Security 2	Return on Security 3
1	.15	.20	.20	.05
2	.35	.15	.10	.10
3	.35	.10	.15	.15
4	.15	.05	.05	.20

   a. What are the expected return and standard deviation of each security?
   b. What are the covariances and correlations between the pairs of securities?
   c. What are the expected return and standard deviation of a portfolio with half of its funds invested in Security 1 and half in Security 2?
   d. What are the expected return and standard deviation of a portfolio with half of its funds invested in Security 1 and half in Security 3?
   e. What are the expected return and standard deviation of a portfolio with half of its funds invested in Security 2 and half in Security 3?
   f. What do your answers in Parts (a), (c), (d), and (e) imply about diversification?

36.   SML   Suppose you observe the following situation:

State of Economy	Probability of State	Return if State Occurs Stock A	Stock B
Bust	.15	−.10	−.08
Normal	.60	.09	.08
Boom	.25	.32	.26

   a. Calculate the expected return on each stock.
   b. Assuming the capital asset pricing model holds and Stock A's beta is greater than Stock B's beta by .25, what is the expected market risk premium?

37.   Standard Deviation and Beta   There are two stocks in the market, Stock A and Stock B. The price of Stock A today is $75. The price of Stock A next year will be $64 if the economy is in a recession, $87 if the economy is normal, and $97 if the economy is expanding. The probabilities of recession, normal times, and expansion are .2, .6, and .2, respectively. Stock A pays no dividends and has a correlation of .7 with the market portfolio. Stock B has an expected return of 14 percent, a standard deviation of 34 percent, a correlation with the market portfolio of .24, and a correlation with Stock A of .36. The market portfolio has a standard deviation of 18 percent. Assume the CAPM holds.

   a. If you are a typical, risk-averse investor with a well-diversified portfolio, which stock would you prefer? Why?

    b. What are the expected return and standard deviation of a portfolio consisting of 70 percent of Stock *A* and 30 percent of Stock *B*?

    c. What is the beta of the portfolio in part (b)?

38. **Minimum Variance Portfolio** Assume Stocks *A* and *B* have the following characteristics:

Stock	Expected Return (%)	Standard Deviation (%)
A	9	33
B	15	62

The covariance between the returns on the two stocks is .001.

    a. Suppose an investor holds a portfolio consisting of only Stock *A* and Stock *B*. Find the portfolio weights, X_A and X_B, such that the variance of her portfolio is minimized. (*Hint:* Remember that the sum of the two weights must equal 1.)

    b. What is the expected return on the minimum variance portfolio?

    c. If the covariance between the returns on the two stocks is −.05, what are the minimum variance weights?

    d. What is the variance of the portfolio in part (c)?

Excel Master It!

The CAPM is one of the most thoroughly researched models in financial economics. When beta is estimated in practice, a variation of CAPM called the market model is often used. To derive the market model, we start with the CAPM:

$$E(R_i) = R_f + \beta[E(R_M) - R_f]$$

Since CAPM is an equation, we can subtract the risk–free rate from both sides, which gives us:

$$E(R_i) - R_f = \beta[E(R_M) - R_f]$$

This equation is deterministic, that is, exact. In a regression, we realize that there is some indeterminate error. We need to formally recognize this in the equation by adding epsilon, which represents this error:

$$E(R_i) - R_f = \beta[E(R_M) - R_f] + \varepsilon$$

Finally, think of the above equation in a regression. Since there is no intercept in the equation, the intercept is zero. However, when we estimate the regression equation, we can add an intercept term, which we will call alpha:

$$E(R_i) - R_f = \alpha_i + \beta[E(R_M) - R_f] + \varepsilon$$

This equation, known as the market model, is generally the model used for estimating beta. The intercept term is known as Jensen's alpha, and it represents the excess return. If CAPM holds exactly, this intercept should be zero. If you think of alpha in terms of the SML, if the alpha is positive, the stock plots above the SML and if alpha is negative, the stock plots below the SML.

    a. You want to estimate the market model for an individual stock and a mutual fund. First, go to finance.yahoo.com and download the adjusted prices for the last 61 months for an individual stock, a mutual fund, and the S&P 500. Next, go to the St. Louis

Federal Reserve website at www.stlouisfed.org. You should find the FRED® database there. Look for the 1-Month Treasury Constant Maturity Rate and download this data. This series will be the proxy for the risk-free rate. When using this rate, you should be aware that this interest rate is the annualized interest rate, so while we are using monthly stock returns, you will need to adjust the 1-month T-bill rate. For the stock and mutual fund you select, estimate the beta and alpha using the market model. When you estimate the regression model, find the box that says "Residuals" and check this box when you do each regression. Because you are saving the residuals, you may want to save the regression output in a new worksheet.

1. Are the alpha and beta for each regression statistically different from zero?

2. How do you interpret the alpha and beta for the stock and the mutual fund?

3. Which of the two regression estimates has the highest R-squared? Is this what you would have expected? Why?

b. In part a, you asked Excel to return the residuals of the regression, which is the epsilon in the regression equation. If you remember back to basic statistics, the residuals are the linear distance from each observation to the regression line. In this context, the residuals are the part of the monthly return that is not explained by the market model estimate. The residuals can be used to calculate the appraisal ratio, which is the alpha divided by the standard deviation of the residuals.

1. What do you think the appraisal ratio is intended to measure?

2. Calculate the appraisal ratios for the stock and the mutual fund. Which has a better appraisal ratio?

3. Often, the appraisal ratio is used to evaluate the performance of mutual fund managers. Why do you think the appraisal ratio is used more often for mutual funds, which are portfolios, than for individual stocks?

Mini Case

A JOB AT EAST COAST YACHTS, PART 2

You are discussing your 401(k) with Dan Ervin when he mentions that Sarah Brown, a representative from Bledsoe Financial Services, is visiting East Coast Yachts today. You decide that you should meet with Sarah, so Dan sets up an appointment for you later in the day.

When you sit down with Sarah, she discusses the various investment options available in the company's 401(k) account. You mention to Sarah that you researched East Coast Yachts before you accepted your new job. You are confident in management's ability to lead the company. Analysis of the company has led to your belief that the company is growing and will achieve a greater market share in the future. You also feel you should support your employer. Given these considerations, along with the fact that you are a conservative investor, you are leaning toward investing 100 percent of your 401(k) account in East Coast Yachts.

Assume the risk-free rate is 3.2 percent. The correlation between the Bledsoe bond fund and large-cap stock fund is .15. Note that the spreadsheet graphing and "solver" functions may assist you in answering the following questions.

1. Considering the effects of diversification, how should Sarah respond to the suggestion that you invest 100 percent of your 401(k) account in East Coast Yachts stock?

2. Sarah's response to investing your 401(k) account entirely in East Coast Yachts stock has convinced you that this may not be the best alternative. Because you are a conservative investor, you tell Sarah that a 100 percent investment in the bond fund may be the best alternative. Is it?

3. Using the returns for the Bledsoe Large-Cap Stock Fund and the Bledsoe Bond Fund, graph the opportunity set of feasible portfolios.

4. After examining the opportunity set, you notice that you can invest in a portfolio consisting of the bond fund and the large-cap stock fund that will have exactly the same standard deviation as the bond fund. This portfolio will also have a greater expected return. What are the portfolio weights and expected return of this portfolio?

5. Examining the opportunity set, notice there is a portfolio that has the lowest standard deviation. This is the minimum variance portfolio. What are the portfolio weights, expected return, and standard deviation of this portfolio? Why is the minimum variance portfolio important?

6. A measure of risk-adjusted performance that is often used is the Sharpe ratio. The Sharpe ratio is calculated as the risk premium of an asset divided by its standard deviation. The portfolio with the highest possible Sharpe ratio on the opportunity set is called the Sharpe optimal portfolio. What are the portfolio weights, expected return, and standard deviation of the Sharpe optimal portfolio? How does the Sharpe ratio of this portfolio compare to the Sharpe ratios of the bond fund and the large-cap stock fund? Do you see a connection between the Sharpe optimal portfolio and the CAPM? What is the connection?

Appendix 11A Is Beta Dead?

To access Appendix 11A, please go to www.mhhe.com/rwj.

Appendix 11A   Is Beta Dead?

The capital asset pricing model represents one of the most important advances in financial economics. It is clearly useful for investment purposes because it shows how the expected return on an asset is related to its beta. In addition, we will show in Chapter 13 that it is useful in corporate finance because the discount rate on a project is a function of the project's beta. However, never forget that, as with any other model, the CAPM is not revealed truth but, rather, a construct to be empirically tested.

The first empirical tests of the CAPM occurred over 20 years ago and were quite supportive. Using data from the 1930s to the 1960s, researchers showed that the average return on a portfolio of stocks was positively related to the beta of the portfolio,[1] a finding consistent with the CAPM. Though some evidence in these studies was less consistent with the CAPM,[2] financial economists were quick to embrace the CAPM following these empirical papers.

Although a large body of empirical work developed in the following decades, often with varying results, the CAPM was not seriously called into question until the 1990s. Two papers by Fama and French[3] (yes, the same Fama whose joint paper in 1973 with James MacBeth supported the CAPM) present evidence inconsistent with the model. Their work has received a great deal of attention, both in academic circles and in the popular press, with newspaper articles displaying headlines such as "Beta Is Dead!" These papers make two related points. First, they conclude that the relationship between average return and beta is weak over the period from 1941 to 1990 and virtually nonexistent from 1963 to 1990. Second, they argue that the average return on a security is negatively related to both the firm's price-earnings (P/E) ratio and the firm's market-to-book (M/B) ratio. These contentions, if confirmed by other research, would be quite damaging to the CAPM. After all, the CAPM states that the expected returns on stocks should be related only to beta, and not to other factors such as P/E and M/B.

However, a number of researchers have criticized the Fama–French papers. We avoid an in-depth discussion of the fine points of the debate, but we mention a few issues. First, although Fama and French cannot reject the hypothesis that average returns are unrelated to beta, we can also not reject the hypothesis that average returns are related to beta exactly as specified by the CAPM. In other words, although 50 years of data seem like a lot, they may simply not be enough to test the CAPM properly. Second, the result with P/E and M/B may be due to a statistical fallacy called a hindsight bias.[4] Third, P/E and M/B are merely two of an infinite number of possible factors. Thus, the relationship between average return and both P/E and M/B may be spurious, being nothing more than the result of data mining.

---

[1]Perhaps the two most well-known papers were Fischer Black, Michael C. Jensen, and Myron S. Scholes, "The Capital Asset Pricing Model: Some Empirical Tests," in M. Jensen, ed., *Studies in the Theory of Capital Markets* (New York: Praeger, 1972), and Eugene F. Fama and James MacBeth, "Risk, Return and Equilibrium: Some Empirical Tests," *Journal of Political Economy* 8 (1973), pp. 607–36

[2]For example, the studies suggest that the average return on a zero-beta portfolio is above the risk-free rate, a finding inconsistent with the CAPM.

[3]Eugene F. Fama and Kenneth R. French, "The Cross-Section of Expected Stock Returns," *Journal of Finance* 47 (1992), pp. 427–66, and E. F. Fama and K. R. French, "Common Risk Factors in the Returns on Stocks and Bonds," *Journal of Financial Economics* 17 (1993), pp. 3–56.

[4]For example, see William J. Breen and Robert A. Koraczyk, "On Selection Biases in Book-to-Market Based Tests of Asset Pricing Models," unpublished paper. Northwestern University, November 1993; and S. P. Kothari, Jay Shanken, and Richard G. Sloan, "Another Look at the Cross-Section of Expected Stock Returns," *Journal of Finance* (March 1995).

11A-2

Part III   Risk

Fourth, average returns are positively related to beta over the period from 1927 to the present. There appears to be no compelling reason for emphasizing a shorter period than this one. Fifth, average returns are actually positively related to beta over shorter periods when annual data, rather than monthly data, are used to estimate beta.[5] There appears to be no compelling reason for preferring either monthly data over annual data or vice versa. Thus we believe that although the results of Fama and French are quite intriguing, they cannot be viewed as the final word.

---

[5]Points 4 and 5 are addressed in the Kothari, Shanken, and Sloan paper

CHAPTER 12

An Alternative View of Risk and Return

THE ARBITRAGE PRICING THEORY

▲ For updates on the latest happenings in finance, visit www.rwjcorporatefinance.blogspot.com

In February 2011, Home Depot, Campbell Soup Co., and car rental company, Avis Budget Group, joined a host of other companies in announcing their earnings. Home Depot announced that its fourth quarter profit had increased 72 percent from the previous year. The company's EPS was 36 cents per share, easily beating analysts' estimates of 31 cents. For Campbell Soup, EPS was 71 cents, exactly as predicated by market analysts. In Avis Budget's case, analysts had estimated a loss of 7 cents per share, but the company actually lost 36 cents per share. You would expect that these three cases represent good news, no news, and bad news, and usually you would be right. Even so, Home Depot's stock price dropped just over 1 percent, Campbell Soup's stock price dropped by about 3.9 percent, and Avis Budget's stock price increased by just under 1 percent.

For these companies, good news seemed to be bad news (and vice versa). So when is good news really good news? The answer is fundamental to understanding risk and return, and—the good news is—this chapter explores it in some detail.

12.1 Introduction

We learned in the previous chapter that the risk of a stock could be broken down into systematic and unsystematic risk. Unsystematic risk can be eliminated with diversification in portfolios but systematic risk cannot. As a consequence, in portfolios, only the systematic risk of an individual stock matters. We also learned that systematic risk can be best measured by beta. Finally, we learned the capital asset pricing model (CAPM) implies the expected return on a security is linearly related to its beta.

In this chapter, we take a closer look at where betas come from and the important role of arbitrage in asset pricing.

12.2 Systematic Risk and Betas

As we have learned, the return of any stock can be written as:

$$R = \overline{R} + U$$

where R is the actual return, $\overline{R}$ is the expected return, and U stands for the unexpected part of the return. The U is the surprise and constitutes the risk.

We also know that the risk of any stock can be further broken down into two components: The systematic and the unsystematic. So, we can write:

$$R = \overline{R} + m + \epsilon$$

where we have used the letter m to represent systematic risk and the Greek letter epsilon, ϵ, to represent unsystematic risk.

The fact that the unsystematic parts of the returns on two companies are unrelated to each other does not mean that the systematic portions are unrelated. On the contrary, because both companies are influenced by the same systematic risks, individual companies' systematic risks, and therefore their total returns, will be related.

For example, a surprise about inflation will influence almost all companies to some extent. How sensitive is a particular stock return to unanticipated changes in inflation? If the stock tends to go up on news that inflation is exceeding expectations, we would say that it is positively related to inflation. If the stock goes down when inflation exceeds expectations and up when inflation falls short of expectations, it is negatively related. In the unusual case where a stock's return is uncorrelated with inflation surprises, inflation has no effect on it.

We capture the influence of a systematic risk like inflation on a stock by using the **beta coefficient.** The beta coefficient, β, tells us the response of the stock's return to a systematic risk. In the previous chapter, beta measured the responsiveness of a security's return to a specific risk factor, the return on the market portfolio. We used this type of responsiveness to develop the capital asset pricing model. Because we now consider many types of systematic risks, our current work can be viewed as a generalization of our work in the previous chapter.

If a company's stock is positively related to the risk of inflation, that stock has a positive inflation beta. If it is negatively related to inflation, its inflation beta is negative; and if it is uncorrelated with inflation, its inflation beta is zero.

It's not hard to imagine some stocks with positive inflation betas and other stocks with negative inflation betas. The stock of a company owning gold mines will probably have a positive inflation beta because an unanticipated rise in inflation is usually associated with an increase in gold prices. On the other hand, an automobile company facing stiff foreign competition might find that an increase in inflation means that the wages it pays are higher, but that it cannot raise its prices to cover the increase. This profit squeeze, as the company's expenses rise faster than its revenues, would give its stock a negative inflation beta.

Some companies that have few assets and that act as brokers—buying items in competitive markets and reselling them in other markets—might be relatively unaffected by inflation because their costs and their revenues would rise and fall together. Their stock would have an inflation beta of zero.

Some structure is useful at this point. Suppose we have identified three systematic risks on which we want to focus. We may believe that these three are sufficient to describe the systematic risks that influence stock returns. Three likely candidates are inflation, GNP, and interest rates. Thus, every stock will have a beta associated with each of these systematic risks: An inflation beta, a GNP beta, and an interest rate beta. We can write the return on the stock, then, in the following form:

$$
\begin{aligned}
R &= \overline{R} + U \\
&= \overline{R} + m + \epsilon \\
&= \overline{R} + \beta_I F_I + \beta_{GNP} F_{GNP} + \beta_r F_r + \epsilon
\end{aligned}
$$

where we have used the symbol β_I to denote the stock's inflation beta, β_{GNP} for its GNP beta, and β_r to stand for its interest rate beta. In the equation, F stands for a surprise, whether it be in inflation, GNP, or interest rates.

Let us go through an example to see how the surprises and the expected return add up to produce the total return, R, on a given stock. To make it more familiar, suppose that the return is over a horizon of a year and not just a month. Suppose that at the beginning of the year, inflation is forecast to be 5 percent for the year, GNP is forecast to increase by 2 percent, and interest rates are expected not to change. Suppose the stock we are looking at has the following betas:

$$\beta_I = 2$$
$$\beta_{GNP} = 1$$
$$\beta_r = -1.8$$

The magnitude of the beta describes how great an impact a systematic risk has on a stock's return. A beta of $+1$ indicates that the stock's return rises and falls one for one with the systematic factor. This means, in our example, that because the stock has a GNP beta of 1, it experiences a 1 percent increase in return for every 1 percent surprise increase in GNP. If its GNP beta were -2, it would fall by 2 percent when there was an unanticipated increase of 1 percent in GNP, and it would rise by 2 percent if GNP experienced a surprise 1 percent decline.

Let us suppose that during the year the following events occur: Inflation rises by 7 percent, GNP rises by only 1 percent, and interest rates fall by 2 percent. Suppose we learn some good news about the company, perhaps that it is succeeding quickly with some new business strategy, and that this unanticipated development contributes 5 percent to its return. In other words:

$$\epsilon = 5\%$$

Let us assemble all of this information to find what return the stock had during the year.

First, we must determine what news or surprises took place in the systematic factors. From our information we know that:

$$\text{Expected inflation} = 5\%$$
$$\text{Expected GNP change} = 2\%$$

and:

$$\text{Expected change in interest rates} = 0\%$$

This means that the market had discounted these changes, and the surprises will be the difference between what actually takes place and these expectations:

$$
\begin{aligned}
F_I &= \text{Surprise in inflation} \\
&= \text{Actual inflation} - \text{Expected inflation} \\
&= 7\% - 5\% \\
&= 2\%
\end{aligned}
$$

Similarly:

$$
\begin{aligned}
F_{GNP} &= \text{Surprise in GNP} \\
&= \text{Actual GNP} - \text{Expected GNP} \\
&= 1\% - 2\% \\
&= -1\%
\end{aligned}
$$

and:

$$
\begin{aligned}
F_r &= \text{Surprise in change in interest rates} \\
&= \text{Actual change} - \text{Expected change} \\
&= -2\% - 0\% \\
&= -2\%
\end{aligned}
$$

The total effect of the systematic risks on the stock return, then, is:

$$m = \text{Systematic risk portion of return}$$
$$= \beta_I F_I + \beta_{GNP} F_{GNP} + \beta_r F_r$$
$$= [2 \times 2\%] + [1 \times (-1\%)] + [(-1.8) \times (-2\%)]$$
$$= 6.6\%$$

Combining this with the unsystematic risk portion, the total risky portion of the return on the stock is:

$$m + \epsilon = 6.6\% + 5\% = 11.6\%$$

Last, if the expected return on the stock for the year was, say, 4 percent, the total return from all three components will be:

$$R = \overline{R} + m + \epsilon$$
$$= 4\% + 6.6\% + 5\%$$
$$= 15.6\%$$

The model we have been looking at is called a **factor model,** and the systematic sources of risk, designated F, are called the *factors.* To be perfectly formal, a *k-factor model* is a model where each stock's return is generated by:

$$R = \overline{R} + \beta_1 F_1 + \beta_2 F_2 + \cdots + \beta_k F_k + \epsilon$$

where ϵ is specific to a particular stock and uncorrelated with the ϵ term for other stocks. In our preceding example we had a three-factor model. We used inflation, GNP, and the change in interest rates as examples of systematic sources of risk, or factors. Researchers have not settled on what is the correct set of factors. Like so many other questions, this might be one of those matters that is never laid to rest.

In practice, researchers frequently use a one-factor model for returns. They do not use all of the sorts of economic factors we used previously as examples; instead they use an index of stock market returns—like the S&P 500, or even a more broadly based index with more stocks in it—as the single factor. Using the single-factor model we can write returns like this:

$$R = \overline{R} + \beta(R_{S\&P500} - \overline{R}_{S\&P500}) + \epsilon$$

When there is only one factor (the returns on the S&P 500 portfolio index), we do not need to put a subscript on the beta. In this form (with minor modifications) the factor model is called a **market model.** This term is employed because the index that is used for the factor is an index of returns on the whole (stock) market. The market model is written as:

$$R = \overline{R} + \beta(R_M - \overline{R}_M) + \epsilon$$

where R_M is the return on the market portfolio.[1] The single β is called the *beta coefficient.*

12.3 Portfolios and Factor Models

Now let us see what happens to portfolios of stocks when each of the stocks follows a one-factor model. For purposes of discussion, we will take the coming one-month period and examine returns. We could have used a day or a year or any other period.

---

[1]Alternatively, the market model could be written as:

$$R = \alpha + \beta R_M + \epsilon$$

Here, alpha (α) is an intercept term equal to $\overline{R} - \beta \overline{R}_M$

If the period represents the time between decisions, however, we would rather it be short than long, and a month is a reasonable time frame to use.

We will create portfolios from a list of N stocks, and we will use a one-factor model to capture the systematic risk. The ith stock in the list will therefore have returns:

$$R_i = \overline{R}_i + \beta_i F + \epsilon_i \qquad (12.1)$$

where we have subscripted the variables to indicate that they relate to the ith stock. Notice that the factor F is not subscripted. The factor that represents systematic risk could be a surprise in GNP, or we could use the market model and let the difference between the S&P 500 return and what we expect that return to be, $R_{S\&P500} - \overline{R}_{S\&P500}$, be the factor. In either case, the factor applies to all of the stocks.

The β_i is subscripted because it represents the unique way the factor influences the ith stock. To recapitulate our discussion of factor models, if β_i is zero, the returns on the ith stock are:

$$R_i = \overline{R}_i + \epsilon_i$$

In other words, the ith stock's returns are unaffected by the factor, F, if β_i is zero. If β_i is positive, positive changes in the factor raise the ith stock's returns, and negative changes lower them. Conversely, if β_i is negative, its returns and the factor move in opposite directions.

Figure 12.1 illustrates the relationship between a stock's excess returns, $R_i - \overline{R}_i$, and the factor F for different betas, where $\beta_i > 0$. The lines in Figure 12.1 plot Equation 12.1 on the assumption that there has been no unsystematic risk. That is, $\epsilon_i = 0$. Because we are assuming positive betas, the lines slope upward, indicating that the return on the stock rises with F. Notice that if the factor is zero ($F = 0$), the line passes through zero on the y-axis.

Figure 12.1
The One-Factor Model

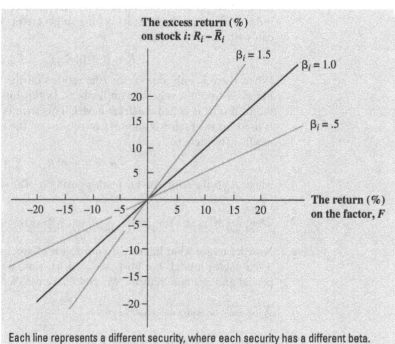

Each line represents a different security, where each security has a different beta.

Now let us see what happens when we create stock portfolios where each stock follows a one-factor model. Let X_i be the proportion of Security i in the portfolio. That is, if an individual with a portfolio of \$100 wants \$20 in General Motors, we say $X_{GM} = 20\%$. Because the Xs represent the proportions of wealth we are investing in each of the stocks, we know that they must add up to 100 percent or 1:

$$X_1 + X_2 + X_3 + \cdots + X_N = 1$$

We know that the portfolio return is the weighted average of the returns on the individual assets in the portfolio. Algebraically, this can be written as follows:

$$R_P = X_1 R_1 + X_2 R_2 + X_3 R_3 + \cdots + X_N R_N \tag{12.2}$$

We saw from Equation 12.1 that each asset, in turn, is determined by both the factor F, and the unsystematic risk of ϵ_i. Thus, by substituting Equation 12.1 for each R_i in Equation 12.2, we have:

$$
\begin{array}{ll}
R_P = X_1(\overline{R}_1 + \beta_1 F + \epsilon_1) & + X_2(\overline{R}_2 + \beta_2 F + \epsilon_2) \\
\text{(Return on Stock 1)} & \text{(Return on Stock 2)} \\
+ X_3(\overline{R}_3 + \beta_3 F + \epsilon_3) + \cdots + X_N(\overline{R}_N + \beta_N F + \epsilon_N) \\
\text{(Return on Stock 3)} & \text{(Return on Stock } N)
\end{array}
\tag{12.3}
$$

Equation 12.3 shows us that the return on a portfolio is determined by three sets of parameters:

1. The expected return on each individual security, $\overline{R}_i$.
2. The beta of each security multiplied by the factor, F.
3. The unsystematic risk of each individual security, ϵ_i.

We express Equation 12.3 in terms of these three sets of parameters like this:

$$
\begin{array}{c}
\textbf{Weighted Average of Expected Returns} \\
R_P = X_1\overline{R}_1 + X_2\overline{R}_2 + X_3\overline{R}_3 + \cdots + X_N\overline{R}_N \\
\textbf{Weighted Average of Betas} \times F \\
+ (X_1\beta_1 + X_2\beta_2 + X_3\beta_3 + \cdots + X_N\beta_N)F \\
\textbf{Weighted Average of Unsystematic Risks} \\
+ X_1\epsilon_1 + X_2\epsilon_2 + X_3\epsilon_3 + \cdots + X_N\epsilon_N
\end{array}
\tag{12.4}
$$

This rather imposing equation is actually straightforward. The first row is the weighted average of each security's expected return. The items in the parentheses of the second row represent the weighted average of each security's beta. This weighted average is, in turn, multiplied by the factor, F. The third row represents a weighted average of the unsystematic risks of the individual securities.

Where does uncertainty appear in Equation 12.4? There is no uncertainty in the first row because only the expected value of each security's return appears there. Uncertainty in the second row is reflected by only one item, F. That is, while we know that the expected value of F is zero, we do not know what its value will be over a particular period. Uncertainty in the third row is reflected by each unsystematic risk, ϵ_i.

PORTFOLIOS AND DIVERSIFICATION

In the previous sections of this chapter, we expressed the return on a single security in terms of our factor model. Portfolios were treated next. Because investors generally hold diversified portfolios, we now want to know what Equation 12.4 looks like in a *large* or diversified portfolio.[2]

As it turns out, something unusual occurs to Equation 12.4: The third row actually *disappears* in a large portfolio. To see this, consider a gambler who divides $1,000 by betting on red over many spins of the roulette wheel. For example, he may participate in 1,000 spins, betting $1 at a time. Though we do not know ahead of time whether a particular spin will yield red or black, we can be confident that red will win about 50 percent of the time. Ignoring the house take, the investor can be expected to end up with just about his original $1,000.

Though we are concerned with stocks, not roulette wheels, the same principle applies. Each security has its own unsystematic risk, where the surprise for one stock is unrelated to the surprise of another stock. By investing a small amount in each security, we bring the weighted average of the unsystematic risks close to zero in a large portfolio.[3]

Although the third row completely vanishes in a large portfolio, nothing unusual occurs in either Row 1 or Row 2. Row 1 remains a weighted average of the expected returns on the individual securities as securities are added to the portfolio. Because there is no uncertainty at all in the first row, there is no way for diversification to cause this row to vanish. The terms inside the parentheses of the second row remain a weighted average of the betas. They do not vanish, either, when securities are added. Because the factor, F, is unaffected when securities are added to the portfolios, the second row does not vanish.

Why does the third row vanish while the second row does not, though both rows reflect uncertainty? The key is that there are many unsystematic risks in Row 3. Because these risks are independent of each other, the effect of diversification becomes stronger as we add more assets to the portfolio. The resulting portfolio becomes less and less risky, and the return becomes more certain. However, the systematic risk, F, affects all securities because it is outside the parentheses in Row 2. Because we cannot avoid this factor by investing in many securities, diversification does not occur in this row.

EXAMPLE 12.1

Diversification and Unsystematic Risk The preceding material can be further explained by the following example. We keep our one-factor model here but make three specific assumptions:

1. All securities have the same expected return of 10 percent. This assumption implies that the first row of Equation 12.4 must also equal 10 percent because this row is a weighted average of the expected returns of the individual securities.

2. All securities have a beta of 1. The sum of the terms inside the parentheses in the second row of Equation 12.4 must equal 1 because these terms are a weighted average of the individual betas. Because the terms inside the parentheses are multiplied by F, the value of the second row is $1 \times F = F$.

---

[2]Technically, we can think of a large portfolio as one where an investor keeps increasing the number of securities without limit. In practice, *effective* diversification would occur if at least a few dozen securities were held.

[3]More precisely, we say that the weighted average of the unsystematic risk approaches zero as the number of equally weighted securities in a portfolio approaches infinity.

3. In this example, we focus on the behavior of one individual, Walter V. Bagehot. Mr. Bagehot decides to hold an equally weighted portfolio. That is, the proportion of each security in his portfolio is $1/N$.

We can express the return on Mr. Bagehot's portfolio as follows:

Return on Walter V. Bagehot's Portfolio

$$R_P = \underset{\substack{\text{From} \\ \text{Row 1 of} \\ \text{Equation 12.4}}}{10\%} + \underset{\substack{\text{From} \\ \text{Row 2 of} \\ \text{Equation 12.4}}}{F} + \underset{\substack{\text{From Row 3 of} \\ \text{Equation 12.4}}}{\left(\frac{1}{N}\epsilon_1 + \frac{1}{N}\epsilon_2 + \frac{1}{N}\epsilon_3 + \cdots + \frac{1}{N}\epsilon_N\right)} \tag{12.4'}$$

We mentioned before that as N increases without limit, Row 3 of Equation 12.4 becomes equal to zero.[4] Thus, the return on Walter Bagehot's portfolio when the number of securities is very large is:

$$R_P = 10\% + F \tag{12.4''}$$

The key to diversification is exhibited in Equation 12.4″. The unsystematic risk of Row 3 vanishes while the systematic risk of Row 2 remains.

This is illustrated in Figure 12.2. Systematic risk, captured by variation in the factor, F, is not reduced through diversification. Conversely, unsystematic risk diminishes as securities are added, vanishing as the number of securities becomes infinite. Our result is analogous to the diversification example of the previous chapter. In that chapter, we said that undiversifiable or systematic risk arises from positive covariances between securities. In this chapter, we say that systematic risk arises from a common factor, F. Because a common factor causes positive covariances, the arguments of the two chapters are parallel.

Figure 12.2   **Diversification and the Portfolio Risk for an Equally Weighted Portfolio**

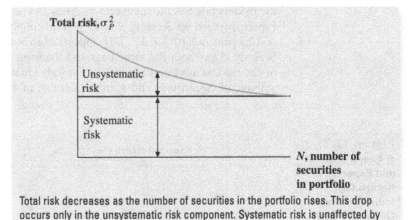

Total risk decreases as the number of securities in the portfolio rises. This drop occurs only in the unsystematic risk component. Systematic risk is unaffected by diversification.

---

[4]Our presentation on this point has not been rigorous. The student interested in more rigor should note that the variance of Row 3 is:

$$\frac{1}{N^2}\sigma_\epsilon^2 + \frac{1}{N^2}\sigma_\epsilon^2 + \frac{1}{N^2}\sigma_\epsilon^2 + \cdots + \frac{1}{N^2}\sigma_\epsilon^2 = \frac{1}{N^2}N\sigma_\epsilon^2$$

where σ_ϵ^2 is the variance of each ϵ. This can be rewritten as σ_ϵ^2/N, which tends to 0 as N goes to infinity.

12.4   Betas, Arbitrage, and Expected Returns

THE LINEAR RELATIONSHIP

We have argued many times that the expected return on a security compensates for its risk. In the previous chapter, we showed that market beta (the standardized covariance of the security's returns with those of the market) was the appropriate measure of risk under the assumptions of homogeneous expectations and riskless borrowing and lending. The capital asset pricing model, which posited these assumptions, implied that the expected return on a security was positively (and linearly) related to its beta. We will find a similar relationship between risk and return in the one-factor model of this chapter.

We begin by noting that the relevant risk in large and well-diversified portfolios is all systematic because unsystematic risk is diversified away. An implication is that when a well-diversified shareholder considers changing her holdings of a particular stock, she can ignore the security's unsystematic risk.

Notice that we are not claiming that stocks, like portfolios, have no unsystematic risk. Nor are we saying that the unsystematic risk of a stock will not affect its returns. Stocks do have unsystematic risk, and their actual returns do depend on the unsystematic risk. Because this risk washes out in a well-diversified portfolio, however, shareholders can ignore this unsystematic risk when they consider whether to add a stock to their portfolio. Therefore, if shareholders are ignoring the unsystematic risk, only the systematic risk of a stock can be related to its *expected* return.

This relationship is illustrated in the security market line of Figure 12.3. Points P, C, A, and L all lie on the line emanating from the risk-free rate of 10 percent. The points representing each of these four assets can be created by combinations of the risk-free rate and any of the other three assets. For example, because A has a beta of 2.0 and P has a beta of 1.0, a portfolio of 50 percent in Asset A and 50 percent in the riskless rate has the same beta as Asset P. The risk-free rate is 10 percent and the expected return on Security A is 35 percent, implying that the combination's return of 22.5 percent $[(10\% + 35\%)/2]$ is identical to Security P's expected return. Because Security P has both the same beta and the same expected return as a combination of the riskless asset and Security A, an individual is equally inclined to add a small amount of Security P and a small amount of this combination to her portfolio.

Figure 12.3
A Graph of Beta and Expected Return for Individual Stocks Under the One-Factor Model

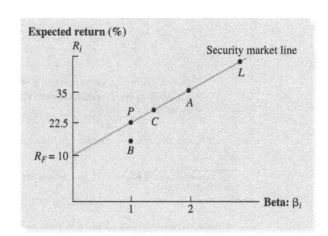

However, the unsystematic risk of Security P need not be equal to the unsystematic risk of the combination of Security A and the risk-free rate because unsystematic risk is diversified away in a large portfolio.

Of course, the potential combinations of points on the security market line are endless. We can duplicate P by combinations of the risk-free rate and either C or L (or both of them). We can duplicate C (or A or L) by borrowing at the risk-free rate to invest in P. The infinite number of points on the security market line that are not labeled can be used as well.

Now consider Security B. Because its expected return is below the line, no investor would hold it. Instead, the investor would prefer Security P, a combination of Security A and the riskless asset, or some other combination. Thus, Security B's price is too high. Its price will fall in a competitive market, forcing its expected return back up to the line in equilibrium. Investors who try to spot situations where securities of the same risk have different expected returns are called arbitrageurs. The arbitrage trade here is to sell short Security B and buy Security P. The profit would be the difference in the market prices of Security B and Security P. The idea of arbitrage, and its significance in asset pricing, is referred to as the arbitrage pricing theory.

The preceding discussion allows us to provide an equation for the security market line of Figure 12.3. We know that a line can be described algebraically from two points. It is perhaps easiest to focus on the risk-free rate and Asset P because the risk-free rate has a beta of 0 and P has a beta of 1.

Because we know that the return on any zero-beta asset is R_F and the expected return on asset P is $\overline{R}_P$, it can easily be shown that:

$$\overline{R} = R_F + \beta(\overline{R}_P - R_F) \tag{12.5}$$

In Equation 12.5, $\overline{R}$ can be thought of as the expected return on any security or portfolio lying on the security market line. β is the beta of that security or portfolio.

THE MARKET PORTFOLIO AND THE SINGLE FACTOR

In the CAPM, the beta of a security measures the security's responsiveness to movements in the market portfolio. In the one-factor model of the arbitrage pricing theory (APT), the beta of a security measures its responsiveness to the factor. We now relate the market portfolio to the single factor.

A large, diversified portfolio has no unsystematic risk because the unsystematic risks of the individual securities are diversified away. Assuming enough securities so that the market portfolio is fully diversified and assuming that no security has a disproportionate market share, this portfolio is fully diversified and contains no unsystematic risk.[5] In other words, the market portfolio is perfectly correlated with the single factor, implying that the market portfolio is really a scaled-up or scaled-down version of the factor. After scaling properly, we can treat the market portfolio as the factor itself.

The market portfolio, like every security or portfolio, lies on the security market line. When the market portfolio is the factor, the beta of the market portfolio is 1 by definition. This is shown in Figure 12.4. (We deleted the securities and the specific expected returns from Figure 12.3 for clarity: The two graphs are otherwise identical.) With the market portfolio as the factor, Equation 12.5 becomes:

$$\overline{R} = R_F + \beta(\overline{R}_M - R_F)$$

[5]This assumption is plausible in the real world. For example, even the market value of General Electric is only 1 percent to 2 percent of the market value of the S&P 500 Index.

Figure 12.4
A Graph of Beta and Expected Return for Market Portfolio under the One-Factor Model

Expected return (%)

Security market line

$\overline{R}_M$

R_F

Beta

1

The factor is scaled so that it is identical to the market portfolio. The beta of the market portfolio is 1.

where $\overline{R}_M$ is the expected return on the market. This equation shows that the expected return on any asset, $\overline{R}$, is linearly related to the security's beta. The equation is identical to that of the CAPM, which we developed in the previous chapter.

12.5 The Capital Asset Pricing Model and the Arbitrage Pricing Theory

The CAPM and the APT are alternative models of risk and return. It is worthwhile to consider the differences between the two models, both in terms of pedagogy and in terms of application.

DIFFERENCES IN PEDAGOGY

We feel that the CAPM has at least one strong advantage from the student's point of view. The derivation of the CAPM necessarily brings the reader through a discussion of efficient sets. This treatment—beginning with the case of two risky assets, moving to the case of many risky assets, and finishing when a riskless asset is added to the many risky ones—is of great intuitive value. This sort of presentation is not as easily accomplished with the APT.

However, the APT has some offsetting advantages. The model adds factors until the unsystematic risk of any security is uncorrelated with the unsystematic risk of every other security. Under this formulation, it is easily shown that (1) unsystematic risk steadily falls (and ultimately vanishes) as the number of securities in the portfolio increases, but (2) the systematic risks do not decrease. This result was also shown in the CAPM, though the intuition was cloudier because the unsystematic risks could be correlated across securities. Also, the APT emphasizes the role of arbitrage in obtaining a linear relationship between expected returns and betas.

DIFFERENCES IN APPLICATION

One advantage of the APT is that it can handle multiple factors while the CAPM ignores them. Although the bulk of our presentation in this chapter focused on the one-factor model, a multifactor model is probably more reflective of reality. That is, we must abstract from many marketwide and industrywide factors before the unsystematic risk of one security becomes uncorrelated with the unsystematic risks of other securities. Under this multifactor version of the APT, the relationship between risk and return can be expressed as:

$$\overline{R} = R_F + (\overline{R}_1 - R_F)\beta_1 + (\overline{R}_2 - R_F)\beta_2 + (\overline{R}_3 - R_F)\beta_3 + \cdots + (\overline{R}_K - R_F)\beta_K \quad (12.6)$$

In this equation, β_1 stands for the security's beta with respect to the first factor, β_2 stands for the security's beta with respect to the second factor, and so on. For example, if the first factor is GNP, β_1 is the security's GNP beta. The term $\overline{R}_1$ is the expected return on a security (or portfolio) whose beta with respect to the first factor is one and whose beta with respect to all other factors is zero. Because the market compensates for risk, $(\overline{R}_1 - R_F)$ will be positive in the normal case.[6] (An analogous interpretation can be given to $\overline{R}_2$, $\overline{R}_3$, and so on.)

The equation states that the security's expected return is related to the security's factor betas. The intuition in Equation 12.6 is straightforward. Each factor represents risk that cannot be diversified away. The higher a security's beta is with regard to a particular factor, the higher the risk that the security bears. In a rational world, the expected return on the security should compensate for this risk. Equation 12.6 states that the expected return is a summation of the risk-free rate plus the compensation for each type of risk that the security bears.

As an example, consider a study where the factors were monthly growth in industrial production (IP), change in expected inflation (ΔEI), unanticipated inflation (UI), unanticipated change in the risk premium between risky bonds and default-free bonds (URP), and unanticipated change in the difference between the return on long-term government bonds and the return on short-term government bonds (UBR).[7] Using the period 1958–1984, the empirical results of the study indicated that the expected monthly return on any stock, $\overline{R}_S$, can be described as:

$$\overline{R}_S = .0041 + .0136\beta_{IP} - .0001\beta_{\Delta EI} - .0006\beta_{UI} + .0072\beta_{URP} - .0052\beta_{UBR}$$

Suppose a particular stock had the following betas: $\beta_{IP} = 1.1$, $\beta_{\Delta EI} = 2$, $\beta_{UI} = 3$, $\beta_{URP} = .1$, $\beta_{UBR} = 1.6$. The expected monthly return on that security would be:

$$\begin{aligned} \overline{R}_S &= .0041 + .0136 \times 1.1 - .0001 \times 2 - .0006 \times 3 + .0072 \times .1 \\ &\quad - .0052 \times 1.6 \\ &= .0095 \end{aligned}$$

Assuming that a firm is unlevered and that one of the firm's projects has risk equivalent to that of the firm, this value of .0095 (i.e., .95%) can be used as the monthly discount rate for the project. (Because annual data are often supplied for capital budgeting purposes, the annual rate of .120 [$= (1.0095)^{12} - 1$] might be used instead.)

Because many factors appear on the right side of Equation 12.6, the APT formulation has the potential to measure expected returns more accurately than does the CAPM. However, as we mentioned earlier, we cannot easily determine which are the appropriate factors. The factors in the preceding study were included for reasons of both common sense and convenience. They were not derived from theory.

By contrast, the use of the market index in the CAPM formulation is implied by the theory of the previous chapter. We suggested in earlier chapters that the S&P

---

[6]Actually, $(\overline{R}_i - R_F)$ could be negative in the case where factor i is perceived as a hedge of some sort.

[7]N. Chen, R. Roll, and S. Ross, "Economic Forces and the Stock Market," *Journal of Business* (July 1986).

500 Index mirrors U.S. stock market movements quite well. Using the Ibbotson-Sinquefield results showing that since 1926 the yearly return on the S&P 500 Index was, on average, about 8.2 percent greater than the risk-free rate, the last chapter easily calculated expected returns on different securities from the CAPM.[8]

12.6 Empirical Approaches to Asset Pricing

EMPIRICAL MODELS

ExcelMaster
coverage online

This section covers multi-factor regression Estimates.

The CAPM and the APT by no means exhaust the models and techniques used in practice to measure the expected return on risky assets. Both the CAPM and the APT are *risk-based models.* They each measure the risk of a security by its beta(s) on some systematic factor(s), and they each argue that the expected excess return must be proportional to the beta(s). Although we have seen that this is intuitively appealing and has a strong basis in theory, there are alternative approaches.

Most of these alternatives can be lumped under the broad heading of parametric or **empirical models.** The word *empirical* refers to the fact that these approaches are based less on some theory of how financial markets work and more on simply looking for regularities and relations in the history of market data. In these approaches, the researcher specifies some parameters or attributes associated with the securities in question and then examines the data directly for a relation between these attributes and expected returns. For example, an extensive amount of research has been done on whether the expected return on a firm is related to its size. Is it true that small firms have higher average returns than large firms? Researchers have also examined a variety of accounting measures such as the ratio of the price of a stock to its accounting earnings, its P/E ratio, and the closely related ratio of the market value of the stock to the book value of the company, the M/B ratio. Here it might be argued that companies with low P/Es or low M/Bs are "undervalued" and can be expected to have higher returns in the future.

To use the empirical approach to determine the expected return, we would estimate the following equation:

$$\overline{R}_i = R_F + k_{P/E}\,(P/E)_i + k_{M/B}\,(M/B)_i + k_{size}\,(size)_i$$

where $\overline{R}_i$ is the expected return of Firm i, and where the k's are coefficients that we estimate from stock market data. Notice that this is the same form as Equation 12.6 with the firm's attributes in place of betas and with the k's in place of the excess factor portfolio returns.

When tested with data, these parametric approaches seem to do quite well. In fact, when comparisons are made between using parameters and using betas to predict stock returns, the parameters, such as P/E and M/B, seem to work better. There are a variety of possible explanations for these results, and the issues have certainly not been settled. Critics of the empirical approach are skeptical of what they call *data mining.* The particular parameters that researchers work with are often chosen because they

---

[8]Going back to 1900 the S&P 500 was on average 7.2 percent greater than the risk-free rate. Though many researchers assume that surrogates for the market portfolio are easily found, Richard Roll, "A Critique of the Asset Pricing Theory's Tests," *Journal of Financial Economics* (March 1977), argues that the absence of a universally acceptable proxy for the market portfolio seriously impairs application of the theory. After all, the market must include real estate, racehorses, and other assets that are not in the stock market.

have been shown to be related to returns. For instance, suppose that you were asked to explain the change in SAT test scores over the past 40 years in some particular state. Suppose that to do this you searched through all of the data series you could find. After much searching, you might discover, for example, that the change in the scores was directly related to the jackrabbit population in Arizona. We know that any such relation is purely accidental; but if you search long enough and have enough choices, you will find something even if it is not really there. It's a bit like staring at clouds. After a while you will see clouds that look like anything you want—clowns, bears, or whatever—but all you are really doing is data mining.

Needless to say, the researchers on these matters defend their work by arguing that they have not mined the data and have been very careful to avoid such traps by not snooping at the data to see what will work.

Of course, as a matter of pure theory, because anyone in the market can easily look up the P/E ratio of a firm, we would certainly not expect to find that firms with low P/Es did better than firms with high P/Es simply because they were undervalued. In an efficient market, such public measures of undervaluation would be quickly exploited and would not last.

Perhaps a better explanation for the success of empirical approaches lies in a synthesis of the risk-based approaches and the empirical methods. In an efficient market, risk and return are related; so perhaps the parameters or attributes that appear to be related to returns are also better measures of risk. For example, if we were to find that low P/E firms outperformed high P/E firms and that this was true even for firms that had the same beta(s), then we would have at least two possible explanations. First, we could simply discard the risk-based theories as incorrect. Furthermore, we could argue that markets are inefficient and that buying low P/E stocks provides us with an opportunity to make higher-than-predicted returns. Second, we could argue that *both* views of the world are correct and that the P/E is really just a better way to measure systematic risk—that is, beta(s)—than directly estimating beta from the data.

STYLE PORTFOLIOS

In addition to their use as a platform for estimating expected returns, stock attributes are also widely used as a way of characterizing money management styles. For example, a portfolio that has a P/E portfolio ratio much in excess of the market average might be characterized as a high P/E or a **growth stock portfolio.** Similarly, a portfolio made up of stocks with an average P/E less than that of a market index might be characterized as a low P/E portfolio or a **value portfolio.**

To evaluate how well portfolio managers are doing, their performance is often compared with the performance of some basic indexes. For example, the portfolio returns of managers who purchase large U.S. stocks might be compared to the performance of the S&P 500 Index. In such a case, the S&P 500 is said to be the **benchmark** against which their performance is measured. Similarly, an international manager might be compared against some common index of international stocks. In choosing an appropriate benchmark, care should be taken to identify a benchmark that contains only those types of stocks that the manager targets as representative of his style and that are also available to be purchased. A manager who was told not to purchase any stocks in the S&P 500 Index would not consider it legitimate to be compared against the S&P 500.

Increasingly, too, managers are compared not only against an index but also against a peer group of similar managers. The performance of a fund that advertises itself

In Their Own Words

KENNETH FRENCH ON THE FAMA–FRENCH THREE-FACTOR MODEL

The Fama–French (1993) three-factor model is an empirically motivated implementation of Ross's (1976) arbitrage pricing theory. When we developed the model, researchers had identified two dominant patterns in the cross-section of average stock returns. Small companies, with relatively little market equity, tend to have higher average stock returns than big companies (Banz, 1981). And value companies, which are often defined as those with a high ratio of book equity to market equity, tend to have higher average returns than growth companies (Fama and French, 1992). Our goal was a simple model that captures these patterns in stock returns.

The three-factor model predicts that the expected excess return on portfolio i, $E(R_i) - R_F$, is determined by its loadings on, well, three factors,

$$E(R_i) - R_F = b_i[E(R_M) - R_F] + s_iE(SMB) + h_iE(HML)$$

The excess return on the market, $E(R_M) - R_F$, plays much the same role here as it does in the capital asset pricing model. The expected compensation investors receive for bearing market risk equals the quantity of market risk, b_i, times the price per unit, $E(R_M) - R_F$.

The second and third factors are aimed at the size and value effect. The size factor, SMB (small minus big), is the difference between the returns on a portfolio of small stocks and a portfolio of big stocks. The value factor, HML (high minus low), is the difference between the returns on a portfolio of high book-to-market stocks and a portfolio of low book-to-market stocks. Because small stocks tend to outperform big stocks and value stocks tend to outperform growth stocks, the expected values of SMB and HML are positive. Thus, the three-factor model predicts that the expected return on a portfolio increases linearly with s_i, its loading on SMB, and with h_i, its loading on HML. A portfolio of small value stocks, for example, is likely to have positive loadings on SMB and HML, so the model predicts the portfolio has a high expected return.

You can estimate a portfolio's loadings on $R_M - R_F$, SMB, and HML by regressing its excess return on the three factors,

$$R_{it} - R_{Ft} = a_i + b_i(R_{Mt} - R_{Ft}) + s_iSMB_t + h_iHML_t + e_{it}$$

The model predicts the intercept a_i in this time series regression is zero. I provide daily, monthly, quarterly, and annual returns for the three factors on my website, www.dartmouth.edu/~kfrench. People typically use monthly returns when estimating the model because they offer a good compromise between market microstructure issues that become important as the interval gets shorter and the loss of observations that occurs as the interval gets longer.

The three-factor model is not perfect, but it does a reasonable job explaining the returns on a wide range of stock portfolios. There is controversy, however, about whether the average premiums on SMB and HML are compensation for risk or the result of mispricing. (For what it is worth, I think they are the result of both risk and mispricing.) Fortunately, the answer to this question is irrelevant for many applications of the model. When evaluating a portfolio manager, for example, we can simply interpret SMB and HML as the returns to passive benchmark portfolios.

as a growth fund might be measured against the performance of a large sample of similar funds. For instance, the performance over some period is commonly assigned to quartiles. The top 25 percent of the funds are said to be in the first quartile, the next 25 percent in the second quartile, the next 25 percent in the third quartile, and the worst-performing 25 percent of the funds in the last quartile. If the fund we are examining happens to have a performance that falls in the second quartile, then we speak of its manager as a second quartile manager.

 ◄ To test your mastery of this material, take a quiz at mhhe.com/rwj

Similarly, we call a fund that purchases low M/B stocks a value fund and would measure its performance against a sample of similar value funds. These approaches to measuring performance are relatively new, and they are part of an active and exciting effort to refine our ability to identify and use investment skills.

Summary and Conclusions

The previous chapter developed the capital asset pricing model (CAPM). As an alternative, this chapter developed the arbitrage pricing theory (APT).

1. The APT assumes that stock returns are generated according to factor models. For example, we might describe a stock's return as:

$$R = \bar{R} + \beta_I F_I + \beta_{GNP} F_{GNP} + \beta_r F_r + \epsilon$$

where I, GNP, and r stand for inflation, gross national product, and the interest rate, respectively. The three factors F_I, F_{GNP}, and F_r represent systematic risk because these factors affect many securities. The term ϵ is considered unsystematic risk because it is unique to each individual security.

2. For convenience, we frequently describe a security's return according to a one-factor model:

$$R = \bar{R} + \beta F + \epsilon$$

3. As securities are added to a portfolio, the unsystematic risks of the individual securities offset each other. A fully diversified portfolio has no unsystematic risk but still has systematic risk. This result indicates that diversification can eliminate some, but not all, of the risk of individual securities.

4. Because of this, the expected return on a stock is positively related to its systematic risk. In a one-factor model, the systematic risk of a security is simply the beta of the CAPM. Thus, the implications of the CAPM and the one-factor APT are identical. However, each security has many risks in a multifactor model. The expected return on a security is positively related to the beta of the security with each factor.

5. Empirical or parametric models that capture the relations between returns and stock attributes such as P/E or M/B ratios can be estimated directly from the data without any appeal to theory. These ratios are also used to measure the styles of portfolio managers and to construct benchmarks and samples against which they are measured.

Concept Questions

1. **Systematic versus Unsystematic Risk** Describe the difference between systematic risk and unsystematic risk.

2. **APT** Consider the following statement: For the APT to be useful, the number of systematic risk factors must be small. Do you agree or disagree with this statement? Why?

3. **APT** David McClemore, the CFO of Ultra Bread, has decided to use an APT model to estimate the required return on the company's stock. The risk factors he plans to use are the risk premium on the stock market, the inflation rate, and the price of wheat. Because wheat is one of the biggest costs Ultra Bread faces, he feels this is a significant risk factor for Ultra Bread. How would you evaluate his choice of risk factors? Are there other risk factors you might suggest?

4. **Systematic and Usystematic Risk** You own stock in the Lewis-Striden Drug Company. Suppose you had expected the following events to occur last month:

   a. The government would announce that real GNP had grown 1.2 percent during the previous quarter. The returns of Lewis-Striden are positively related to real GNP.

394   Part III   Risk

b. The government would announce that inflation over the previous quarter was 3.7 percent. The returns of Lewis-Striden are negatively related to inflation.

c. Interest rates would rise 2.5 percentage points. The returns of Lewis-Striden are negatively related to interest rates.

d. The president of the firm would announce his retirement. The retirement would be effective six months from the announcement day. The president is well liked: In general, he is considered an asset to the firm.

e. Research data would conclusively prove the efficacy of an experimental drug. Completion of the efficacy testing means the drug will be on the market soon.

Suppose the following events actually occurred:

a. The government announced that real GNP grew 2.3 percent during the previous quarter.

b. The government announced that inflation over the previous quarter was 3.7 percent.

c. Interest rates rose 2.1 percentage points.

d. The president of the firm died suddenly of a heart attack.

e. Research results in the efficacy testing were not as strong as expected. The drug must be tested for another six months, and the efficacy results must be resubmitted to the FDA.

f. Lab researchers had a breakthrough with another drug.

g. A competitor announced that it will begin distribution and sale of a medicine that will compete directly with one of Lewis-Striden's top-selling products.

Discuss how each of the actual occurrences affects the return on your Lewis-Striden stock. Which events represent systematic risk? Which events represent unsystematic risk?

5. **Market Model versus APT** What are the differences between a k-factor model and the market model?

6. **APT** In contrast to the CAPM, the APT does not indicate which factors are expected to determine the risk premium of an asset. How can we determine which factors should be included? For example, one risk factor suggested is the company size. Why might this be an important risk factor in an APT model?

7. **CAPM versus APT** What is the relationship between the one-factor model and the CAPM?

8. **Factor Models** How can the return on a portfolio be expressed in terms of a factor model?

9. **Data Mining** What is data mining? Why might it overstate the relation between some stock attribute and returns?

10. **Factor Selection** What is wrong with measuring the performance of a U.S. growth stock manager against a benchmark composed of British stocks?

Questions and Problems

BASIC (Questions 1–4)

1. **Factor Models** A researcher has determined that a two-factor model is appropriate to determine the return on a stock. The factors are the percentage change in GNP and an interest rate. GNP is expected to grow by 3.6 percent, and the interest rate is expected to be 3.1 percent. A stock has a beta of 1.3 on the percentage change in GNP and a beta of −.75 on the interest rate. If the expected rate of return on the stock is 12 percent, what is the revised expected return on the stock if GNP actually grows by 3.2 percent and the interest rate is 3.4 percent?

2. **Factor Models**   Suppose a three-factor model is appropriate to describe the returns of a stock. Information about those three factors is presented in the following chart:

Factor	β	Expected Value	Actual Value
GDP	.006821	$14,011	$13,982
Inflation	−.90	2.80%	2.6%
Interest rates	−.32	4.80%	4.6%

a. What is the systematic risk of the stock return?
b. Suppose unexpected bad news about the firm was announced that causes the stock price to drop by 1.1 percent. If the expected return on the stock is 12.8 percent, what is the total return on this stock?

3. **Factor Models**   Suppose a factor model is appropriate to describe the returns on a stock. The current expected return on the stock is 10.5 percent. Information about those factors is presented in the following chart:

Factor	β	Expected Value	Actual Value
Growth in GNP	1.87	2.1%	2.6%
Inflation	−1.32	4.3	4.8

a. What is the systematic risk of the stock return?
b. The firm announced that its market share had unexpectedly increased from 23 percent to 27 percent. Investors know from past experience that the stock return will increase by .45 percent for every 1 percent increase in its market share. What is the unsystematic risk of the stock?
c. What is the total return on this stock?

4. **Multifactor Models**   Suppose stock returns can be explained by the following three-factor model:

$$R_i = R_F + \beta_1 F_1 + \beta_2 F_2 - \beta_3 F_3$$

Assume there is no firm-specific risk. The information for each stock is presented here:

	β_1	β_2	β_3
Stock A	1.55	.80	.05
Stock B	.81	1.25	−.20
Stock C	.73	−.14	1.24

The risk premiums for the factors are 6.1 percent, 5.3 percent, and 5.7 percent, respectively. If you create a portfolio with 20 percent invested in Stock A, 20 percent invested in Stock B, and the remainder in Stock C, what is the expression for the return on your portfolio? If the risk-free rate is 3.2 percent, what is the expected return on your portfolio?

INTERMEDIATE
(Questions 5–7)

5. **Multifactor Models**   Suppose stock returns can be explained by a two-factor model. The firm-specific risks for all stocks are independent. The following table shows the information for two diversified portfolios:

	β_1	β_2	E(R)
Portfolio A	.85	1.15	16%
Portfolio B	1.45	−.25	12

If the risk-free rate is 4 percent, what are the risk premiums for each factor in this model?

6. **Market Model**   The following three stocks are available in the market:

	E(R)	β
Stock A	10.5%	1.20
Stock B	13.0	.98
Stock C	15.7	1.37
Market	14.2	1.00

Assume the market model is valid.

a. Write the market model equation for each stock.
b. What is the return on a portfolio with weights of 30 percent Stock A, 45 percent Stock B, and 25 percent Stock C?
c. Suppose the return on the market is 15 percent and there are no unsystematic surprises in the returns. What is the return on each stock? What is the return on the portfolio?

7. **Portfolio Risk**   You are forming an equally weighted portfolio of stocks. Many stocks have the same beta of .84 for Factor 1 and the same beta of 1.69 for Factor 2. All stocks also have the same expected return of 11 percent. Assume a two-factor model describes the return on each of these stocks.

a. Write the equation of the returns on your portfolio if you place only five stocks in it.
b. Write the equation of the returns on your portfolio if you place in it a very large number of stocks that all have the same expected returns and the same betas.

CHALLENGE
(Questions 8–10)

8. **APT**   There are two stock markets, each driven by the same common force, F, with an expected value of zero and standard deviation of 10 percent. There are many securities in each market; thus, you can invest in as many stocks as you wish. Due to restrictions, however, you can invest in only one of the two markets. The expected return on every security in both markets is 10 percent.

The returns for each security, i, in the first market are generated by the relationship:

$$R_{1i} = .10 + 1.5F + \epsilon_{1i}$$

where ϵ_{1i} is the term that measures the surprises in the returns of Stock i in Market 1. These surprises are normally distributed; their mean is zero. The returns on Security j in the second market are generated by the relationship:

$$R_{2j} = .10 + .5F + \epsilon_{2j}$$

where ϵ_{2j} is the term that measures the surprises in the returns of Stock j in Market 2. These surprises are normally distributed; their mean is zero. The standard deviation of ϵ_{1i} and ϵ_{2j} for any two stocks, i and j, is 20 percent.

a. If the correlation between the surprises in the returns of any two stocks in the first market is zero, and if the correlation between the surprises in the returns of any two stocks in the second market is zero, in which market would a risk-averse person prefer to invest? (Note: The correlation between ϵ_{1i} and ϵ_{1j} for any i and j is zero, and the correlation between ϵ_{2i} and ϵ_{2j} for any i and j is zero.)

b. If the correlation between ϵ_{1i} and ϵ_{1j} in the first market is .9 and the correlation between ϵ_{2i} and ϵ_{2j} in the second market is zero, in which market would a risk-averse person prefer to invest?

c. If the correlation between ϵ_{1i} and ϵ_{1j} in the first market is zero and the correlation between ϵ_{2i} and ϵ_{2j} in the second market is .5, in which market would a risk-averse person prefer to invest?

d. In general, what is the relationship between the correlations of the disturbances in the two markets that would make a risk-averse person equally willing to invest in either of the two markets?

9. **APT** Assume that the following market model adequately describes the return-generating behavior of risky assets:

$$R_{it} = \alpha_i + \beta_i R_{Mt} + \epsilon_{it}$$

Here:

R_{it} = The return on the ith asset at Time t.

R_{Mt} = The return on a portfolio containing all risky assets in some proportion at Time t.

R_{Mt} and ϵ_{it} are statistically independent.

Short selling (i.e., negative positions) is allowed in the market. You are given the following information:

Asset	β_i	$E(R_i)$	$Var(\epsilon_i)$
A	.7	8.41%	.0100
B	1.2	12.06	.0144
C	1.5	13.95	.0225

The variance of the market is .0121, and there are no transaction costs.

a. Calculate the standard deviation of returns for each asset.

b. Calculate the variance of return of three portfolios containing an infinite number of asset types A, B, or C, respectively.

c. Assume the risk-free rate is 3.3 percent and the expected return on the market is 10.6 percent. Which asset will not be held by rational investors?

d. What equilibrium state will emerge such that no arbitrage opportunities exist? Why?

10. **APT** Assume that the returns on individual securities are generated by the following two-factor model:

$$R_{it} = E(R_{it}) + \beta_{i1}F_{1t} + \beta_{i2}F_{2t}$$

Here:

R_{it} is the return on Security i at Time t.

F_{1t} and F_{2t} are market factors with zero expectation and zero covariance.

In addition, assume that there is a capital market for four securities, and the capital market for these four assets is perfect in the sense that there are no transaction costs and short sales (i.e., negative positions) are permitted. The characteristics of the four securities follow:

Security	β_1	β_2	E(R)
1	1.0	1.5	20%
2	.5	2.0	20
3	1.0	.5	10
4	1.5	.75	10

a. Construct a portfolio containing (long or short) Securities 1 and 2, with a return that does not depend on the market factor, F_1, in any way. (*Hint:* Such a portfolio will have $\beta_1 = 0$.) Compute the expected return and β_2 coefficient for this portfolio.

b. Following the procedure in (a), construct a portfolio containing Securities 3 and 4 with a return that does not depend on the market factor, F_1. Compute the expected return and β_2 coefficient for this portfolio.

c. There is a risk-free asset with an expected return equal to 5 percent, $\beta_1 = 0$, and $\beta_2 = 0$. Describe a possible arbitrage opportunity in such detail that an investor could implement it.

d. What effect would the existence of these kinds of arbitrage opportunities have on the capital markets for these securities in the short run and long run? Graph your analysis.

Excel Master It!

The Fama–French three-factor model has become a popular APT model. However, another model called the Carhart four-factor model has also been proposed (Mark Carhart, 1997, "On Persistence in Mutual Fund Performance," *Journal of Finance* 52, 57–82). In the four-factor model, the first three factors are the same as in the Fama–French three-factor model. The fourth factor is momentum. The momentum factor is constructed by the monthly return difference between the returns on the high and low prior return portfolios.

The factors for the four-factor model are available on Kenneth French's website (http://mba.tuck.dartmouth.edu/pages/faculty/ken.french/index.html). Note that there is a file for the three-factor model as well as a separate file for the momentum factor.

1. The data files are zipped. You will need to open the Zip file, save the text file, and then open the text file in Excel. Make sure you download the monthly factors. The Text Import Wizard in Excel will walk you through the steps necessary to import the text files into columns. When you get the data table set up, estimate the four-factor model and answer the following questions for the stock and mutual fund you selected in the previous chapter.

a. Would you expect the explanatory power of the four-factor regression to be higher or lower than the market model regression from the previous chapter? Why?

b. Are the alpha and betas for each regression statistically different from zero?

c. How do you interpret the betas for each independent variable for the stock and the mutual fund?

d. Which of the two regression estimates has the highest R squared? Is this what you would have expected? Why?

THE FAMA–FRENCH MULTIFACTOR MODEL AND MUTUAL FUND RETURNS

Dawn Browne, an investment broker, has been approached by client Jack Thomas about the risk of his investments. Dawn has recently read several articles concerning the risk factors that can potentially affect asset returns, and she has decided to examine Jack's mutual fund holdings. Jack is currently invested in the Fidelity Magellan Fund (FMAGX), the Fidelity Low-Priced Stock Fund (FLPSX), and the Baron Small Cap Fund (BSCFX).

Dawn would like to estimate the well-known multifactor model proposed by Eugene Fama and Ken French to determine the risk of each mutual fund. Here is the regression equation for the multifactor model she proposes to use:

$$R_{it} - R_{Ft} = \alpha_i + \beta_1(R_{Mt} - R_{Ft}) + \beta_2(SMB_t) + \beta_3(HML_t) + \epsilon_t$$

In the regression equation, R_{it} is the return on Asset i at Time t, R_{Ft} is the risk-free rate at Time t, and R_{Mt} is the return on the market at Time t. Thus, the first risk factor in the Fama–French regression is the market factor often used with the CAPM.

The second risk factor, SMB, or "small minus big," is calculated by taking the difference in the returns on a portfolio of small-cap stocks and a portfolio of big-cap stocks. This factor is intended to pick up the so-called small firm effect. Similarly, the third factor, HML, or "high minus low," is calculated by taking the difference in the returns between a portfolio of "value" stocks and a portfolio of "growth" stocks. Stocks with low market-to-book ratios are classified as value stocks and vice versa for growth stocks. This factor is included because of the historical tendency for value stocks to earn a higher return.

In models such as the one Dawn is considering, the alpha (α) term is of particular interest. It is the regression intercept; but more important, it is also the excess return the asset earned. In other words, if the alpha is positive, the asset earned a return greater than it should have given its level of risk; if the alpha is negative, the asset earned a return lower than it should have given its level of risk. This measure is called "Jensen's alpha," and it is a very widely used tool for mutual fund evaluation.

1. For a large-company stock mutual fund, would you expect the betas to be positive or negative for each of the factors in a Fama–French multifactor model?
2. The Fama–French factors and risk-free rates are available at Ken French's website: www.dartmouth.edu/~kfrench. Download the monthly factors and save the most recent 60 months for each factor. The historical prices for each of the mutual funds can be found on various websites, including finance.yahoo.com. Find the prices of each mutual fund for the same time as the Fama–French factors and calculate the returns for each month. Be sure to include dividends. For each mutual fund, estimate the multifactor regression equation using the Fama–French factors. How well do the regression estimates explain the variation in the return of each mutual fund?
3. What do you observe about the beta coefficients for the different mutual funds? Comment on any similarities or differences.
4. If the market is efficient, what value would you expect for alpha? Do your estimates support market efficiency?
5. Which fund has performed best considering its risk? Why?

CHAPTER 13

Risk, Cost of Capital, and Valuation

▲ For updates on the latest happenings in finance, visit www.rwjcorporatefinance.blogspot.com

With over 95,000 employees on five continents, Germany-based BASF is a major international company. It operates in a variety of industries, including agriculture, oil and gas, chemicals, and plastics. In an attempt to increase value, BASF launched Vision 2020, a comprehensive plan that included all functions within the company and challenged and encouraged all employees to act in an entrepreneurial manner. The major financial component of the strategy was that the company expected to earn its weighted average cost of capital, or WACC, plus a premium. So, what exactly is the WACC?

The WACC is the minimum return a company needs to earn to satisfy all of its investors, including stockholders, bondholders, and preferred stockholders. In 2010, for example, BASF pegged its cost of capital at 9 percent and earned a company record premium of €3.9 billion above its cost of capital. In 2011, the company pegged its WACC at 11 percent. In this chapter, we learn how to compute a firm's cost of capital and find out what it means to the firm and its investors. We will also learn when to use the firm's cost of capital, and, perhaps more important, when not to use it.

The goal of this chapter is to determine the rate at which cash flows of risky projects and firms are to be discounted. Projects and firms are financed with equity, debt, and other sources, and we must estimate the cost of each of these sources in order to determine the appropriate discount rate. We begin with the cost of equity capital. Since the analysis here builds on beta and the capital asset pricing model (CAPM), we discuss beta in depth, including its calculation, its intuition, and its determinants. We next discuss the cost of debt and the cost of preferred stock. These costs serve as building blocks for the weighted average cost of capital (R_{WACC} or, more simply, WACC), which is used to discount cash flows. We calculate the WACC for a real-world company, Eastman Chemical Co. We show how both firms and projects can be valued using WACC. Finally, we introduce flotation costs.

13.1 The Cost of Capital

Whenever a firm has extra cash, it can take one of two actions. It can pay out the cash directly to its investors. Alternatively, the firm can invest the extra cash in a project, paying out the future cash flows of the project. Which action would the investors prefer? If investors can reinvest the cash in a financial asset (a stock or bond) with the same risk as that of the project, the investors would desire the alternative with the highest expected return. In other words, the project should be undertaken only if its expected return is greater than that of a financial asset of comparable risk. This idea is illustrated in Figure 13.1. Our discussion implies a very simple capital budgeting rule:

The discount rate of a project should be the expected return on a financial asset of comparable risk.

400

Figure 13.1
Choices of a Firm
with Extra Cash

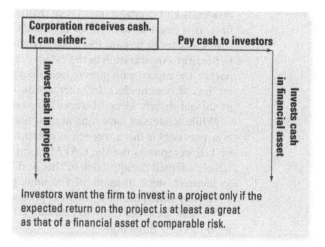

Corporation receives cash.
It can either:

Pay cash to investors

Invest cash in project

Invests cash
in financial asset

Investors want the firm to invest in a project only if the
expected return on the project is at least as great
as that of a financial asset of comparable risk.

There are various synonyms for the discount rate. For example, the discount rate
is often called the *required return* on the project. This is an appropriate name, since
the project should be accepted only if the project generates a return above what is
required. Alternatively, the discount rate of the project is said to be its *cost of capital*.
This name is also appropriate, since the project must earn enough to pay its suppliers
of capital. Our book will use these three terms, the discount rate, the required return,
and the cost of capital, synonymously.

Now imagine that all projects of the firm have the same risk. In that case, one could
say that the discount rate is equal to the cost of capital for the firm as a whole. And, if
the firm is all equity, the discount rate is also equal to the firm's cost of equity capital.

13.2   Estimating the Cost of Equity
Capital with the CAPM

We start with the cost of equity capital, which is the required return on the stockholders' investment in the firm. The problem is that stockholders do not tell the firm what
their required returns are. So, what do we do? Luckily, the capital asset pricing model
(CAPM) can be used to estimate the required return.

Under the CAPM, the expected return on the stock can be written as:

$$R_S = R_F + \beta \times (R_M - R_F) \tag{13.1}$$

where R_F is the risk-free rate and $R_M - R_F$ is the difference between the expected
return on the market portfolio and the riskless rate. This difference is often called the
expected *excess* market return or market risk premium. Note we have dropped the bar
denoting expectations from our expression to simplify the notation, but remember
that we are always thinking about *expected* returns with the CAPM.

The expected return on the stock in Equation 13.1 is based on the stock's risk, as
measured by beta. Alternatively, we could say that this expected return is the required
return on the stock, based on the stock's risk. Similarly, this expected return can be
viewed as the firm's cost of equity capital.

It is important to stress the symmetry between the expected return to the shareholder and the cost of capital to the firm. Imagine a company issuing new equity to
fund a capital budgeting project. The new shareholder's return comes in the form of

402 Part III Risk

dividends and capital gains. These dividends and capital gains represent costs to the firm. It is easier to see this for dividends. Any dividend paid to a new shareholder is cash that cannot be paid to an old shareholder. But capital gains also represent a cost to the firm. Appreciation in the value of a firm's stock is shared by all stockholders. If part of the capital gain goes to new stockholders, only the remainder can be captured by the old stockholders. In other words, the new shareholders dilute the capital gain of the old shareholders. More will be said on this important point a little later.

While academics have long argued for the use of the CAPM in capital budgeting, how prevalent is this approach in practice? One study[1] finds that almost three-fourths of U.S. companies use the CAPM in capital budgeting, indicating that industry has largely adopted the approach of this, and many other, textbooks. This fraction is likely to increase, since so many of the undergraduates and MBAs who were taught the CAPM in school are now reaching positions of power in corporations.

We now have the tools to estimate a firm's cost of equity capital. To do this, we need to know three things:

- The risk-free rate, R_F.
- The market risk premium, $R_M - R_F$.
- The stock beta, β.

EXAMPLE 13.1

Cost of Equity Suppose the stock of the Quatram Company, a publisher of college textbooks, has a beta (β) of 1.3. The firm is 100 percent equity financed; that is, it has no debt. Quatram is considering a number of capital budgeting projects that will double its size. Because these new projects are similar to the firm's existing ones, the average beta on the new projects is assumed to be equal to Quatram's existing beta. The risk-free rate is 5 percent. What is the appropriate discount rate for these new projects, assuming a market risk premium of 8.4 percent?

We estimate the cost of equity, R_S, for Quatram as:

$$R_S = 5\% + (8.4\% \times 1.3)$$
$$= 5\% + 10.92\%$$
$$= 15.92\%$$

Two key assumptions were made in this example: (1) The beta risk of the new projects is the same as the risk of the firm, and (2) the firm is all equity financed. Given these assumptions, it follows that the cash flows of the new projects should be discounted at the 15.92 percent rate.

EXAMPLE 13.2

Project Evaluation and Beta Suppose Alpha Air Freight is an all-equity firm with a beta of 1.21. Further suppose the market risk premium is 9.5 percent, and the risk-free rate is 5 percent. We can determine the expected return on the common stock of Alpha Air Freight from Equation 13.1. We find that the expected return is:

$$5\% + (1.21 \times 9.5\%) = 16.495\%$$

Because this is the return that shareholders can expect in the financial markets on a stock with a β of 1.21, it is the return they expect on Alpha Air Freight's stock.

---

[1]John R. Graham and Campbell R. Harvey, "The Theory and Practice of Corporate Finance: Evidence from the Field," *Journal of Financial Economics* (2001), report in their Table 3 that 73.49 percent of the companies in their sample use the CAPM for capital budgeting.

Further suppose Alpha is evaluating the following non–mutually exclusive projects:

Project	Project's Beta (β)	Project's Expected Cash Flows Next Year	Project's Internal Rate of Return	Project's NPV When Cash Flows Are Discounted at 16.495%	Accept or Reject
A	1.21	$140	40%	$20.2	Accept
B	1.21	120	20	3.0	Accept
C	1.21	110	10	−5.6	Reject

Each project initially costs $100. All projects are assumed to have the same risk as the firm as a whole. Because the cost of equity capital is 16.495 percent, projects in an all-equity firm are discounted at this rate. Projects A and B have positive NPVs, and C has a negative NPV. Thus, only A and B will be accepted. This result is illustrated in Figure 13.2.

Figure 13.2   **Using the Security Market Line to Estimate the Risk-Adjusted Discount Rate for Risky Projects**

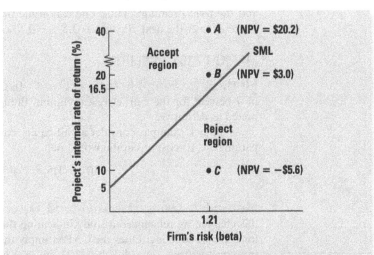

The diagonal line represents the relationship between the cost of equity capital and the firm's beta. An all-equity firm should accept a project whose internal rate of return is greater than the cost of equity capital, and should reject a project whose internal rate of return is less than the cost of equity capital. (This graph assumes that all projects are as risky as the firm.)

In the above two examples, the values for the risk-free rate, the market risk premium, and the firm's beta were *assumed*. How would we go about estimating these parameters in practice? We will investigate each of these parameters in turn.

THE RISK-FREE RATE

While no bond is completely free of the risk of default, Treasury bills and bonds in the United States are about as close to this ideal as possible. No U.S. Treasury instrument has ever defaulted and, at least at the present time, no instrument is considered to be in the slightest danger of a future default. For this reason, Treasury instruments are generally considered to be risk-free.

However, as we learned from Chapter 8, there is a whole term structure of interest rates, where the yield on any Treasury instrument is a function of that instrument's maturity. Which maturity should have its yield serve as the risk-free rate? The CAPM is a period-by-period model, so a short-term rate would be a good place to start. The one-year Treasury bill rate is used frequently and we will adopt this convention. The problem is that some projects have long lives, so the average one-year rate anticipated over the life of the project, rather than today's one-year rate, is preferred.[2]

How can we estimate this expected one-year rate? The anticipated average one-year rate can be estimated from the term structure. Over the period from 1926 to 2011, the average return on 20-year Treasury bonds was 6.1 percent, and the average return on one-year Treasury bills was 3.6 percent. Thus, the term premium, as it is called, was $6.1 - 3.6 = 2.5\%$. This positive term premium is not surprising, since we know that the term structure of interest rates typically slopes upward, reflecting interest rate risk. Suppose the yield on a 20-year Treasury bond is about 3.5 percent. This yield should reflect both the average one-year interest rate over the next 20 years and the term premium. Thus, one can argue that the average one-year interest rate expected over the next 20 years is $3.5\% - 2.5\% = 1.0\%$.

MARKET RISK PREMIUM

Method 1: Using Historical Data   In Chapter 10, we settled on an estimate of 7 percent for the market risk premium, though this number should not be interpreted as definitive.

As a quick example, consider an all-equity company with a beta of 1.5. Given our parameters, its cost of capital would be:

$$1.0\% + 1.5 \times 7\% = 11.5\%$$

Method 2: Using the Dividend Discount Model (DDM)   Earlier in this chapter, we referenced a study indicating that most corporations use the CAPM for capital budgeting. Does the CAPM imply that risk premiums must be calculated from past returns, as we did above? The answer is no. There is another method, based on the dividend discount model of an earlier chapter, for estimating the risk premium.

In Chapter 9, we pointed out that the price of a share of stock can be thought of as equal to the present value of all of its future dividends. Furthermore, we noted in that chapter that, if the firm's dividends are expected to grow at a constant rate, g, the price of a share of stock, P, can be written as:

$$P = \frac{\text{Div}}{R_S - g}$$

---

[2]Another approach is to select a U.S. Treasury security whose maturity matches the maturity of a particular project. The match would need to be exactly correct because while U.S. Treasury securities are probably close to default-free, they have interest rate risk (and so longer term U.S. Treasury securities are not necessarily risk free). Our approach attempts to separate the default risk and interest rate risk elements. In practice both approaches can be used.

where Div is the dividend per share to be received next year, R_S is the discount rate or cost of equity, and g is the constant annual rate of expected growth in dividends. This equation can be rearranged, yielding:

$$R_S = \frac{\text{Div}}{P} + g$$

In words, the annual expected return on a stock is the sum of the dividend yield ($=\text{Div}/P$) over the next year plus the annual expected growth rate in dividends.

Just as this formula can be used to estimate the total expected return on a stock, it can be used to estimate the total expected return on the market as a whole. The first term on the right-hand side is easy to estimate, since a number of print and Internet services calculate the dividend yield for the market. For example, *The Wall Street Journal* recently stated that the average dividend yield across all stocks in the Standard and Poor's (S&P) 500 Index was about 2.1 percent. We will use this number in our forecasts.

Next, we need an estimate of the per-share growth rate in dividends across all companies in the market. Security analysts, who are typically employees of investment banking houses, money management firms, and independent research organizations, study individual securities, industries, and the overall stock market. As part of their work, they forecast dividends and earnings, as well as make stock recommendations. For example, suppose the numbers in the *Value Line (VL) Investment Survey* imply a five-year growth rate in dividends for VL's Industrial Composite Index of about 6 percent per year. With a dividend yield of 2.1 percent, the expected return on the market becomes $2.1\% + 6\% = 8.1\%$. Given our anticipated average one-year yield on Treasury bills of 1.0 percent, the market risk premium would be $8.1\% - 1.0\% = 7.1\%$, almost identical to the 7 percent provided by method 1.

For our firm with a beta of 1.5, the cost of capital becomes:

$$1.0\% + (1.5 \times 7.1\%) = 11.65\%$$

Of course, Value Line is just one source for forecasts. More likely, a firm would either rely on a consensus of many forecasts or use its own subjective growth estimate.

Academics have, nevertheless, long preferred the historical estimated market risk premium for its objectivity. By contrast, estimation of future dividend growth in the DDM seems more subjective. However, the subjective nature of the DDM approach is not meant as a criticism. Proponents of using the DDM point out that returns in the long run can only come from the current dividend yield and future dividend growth. Anyone who thinks that long-run stock returns will exceed the sum of these two components is fooling himself.[3] The expression, "You can't squeeze blood out of a turnip," applies here.

13.3 Estimation of Beta

In the previous section, we assumed that the beta of the company was known. Of course, beta must be estimated in the real world. We pointed out earlier that the beta of a security is the standardized covariance of a security's return with the return on the market portfolio. As we have seen, the formula for security i is:

$$\text{Beta of security } i = \frac{\text{Cov}(R_i, R_M)}{\text{Var}(R_M)} = \frac{\sigma_{i,M}}{\sigma_M^2} \qquad (13.2)$$

---

[3]For example, see Jay Ritter, "The Biggest Mistakes We Teach," *Journal of Financial Research* (Summer 2002); Eugene Fama and Kenneth French, "The Equity Premium," *Journal of Finance* (2002); and R. Jagannathan, E. R. McGrattan, and A. Scherbina, "The Declining U.S. Equity Premium," *Federal Reserve Bank of Minneapolis Quarterly Review* (2000).

Measuring Company Betas

The basic method of measuring company betas is to estimate:

$$\frac{\text{Cov}(R_i, R_M)}{\text{Var}(R_M)}$$

using $t = 1, 2, \ldots, T$ observations.

Problems

1. Betas may vary over time.
2. The sample size may be inadequate.
3. Betas are influenced by changing financial leverage and business risk.

Solutions

1. Problems 1 and 2 can be moderated by more sophisticated statistical techniques.
2. Problem 3 can be lessened by adjusting for changes in business and financial risk.
3. Look at average beta estimates of several comparable firms in the industry.

In words, the beta is the covariance of a security with the market, divided by the variance of the market. Because we calculated both covariance and variance in earlier chapters, calculating beta involves no new material.

REAL-WORLD BETAS

It is instructive to see how betas are determined for actual real-world companies. Figure 13.3 plots monthly returns for four large firms against monthly returns on the S&P 500 Index. Using a standard regression technique, we fit a straight line through the data points. The result is called the "characteristic" line for the security. The slope of the characteristic line is beta. Though we have not shown it in the table, we can also determine the intercept (commonly called alpha) of the characteristic line by regression.

We use five years of monthly data for each plot. Although this choice is arbitrary, it is in line with calculations performed in the real world. Practitioners know that the accuracy of the beta coefficient is suspect when too few observations are used. Conversely, because firms may change their industry over time, observations from the distant past are out of date.

We stated in a previous chapter that the average beta across all stocks in an index is 1. Of course, this need not be true for a subset of the index. For example, of the four securities in our figure, two have betas above 1 and two have betas below 1. Because beta is a measure of the risk of a single security for someone holding a large, diversified portfolio, our results indicate that Procter & Gamble has relatively low risk and Bank of America has relatively high risk.

STABILITY OF BETA

We have stated that the beta of a firm is likely to change if the firm changes its industry. It is also interesting to ask the reverse question: Does the beta of a firm stay the same if its industry stays the same?

Figure 13.3

Plots of Five Years of Monthly Returns (2006–2010) on Four Individual Securities against Five Years of Monthly Returns on the Standard & Poor's (S&P) 500 Index

Take the case of Microsoft, which has remained in the same industry for many decades. Figure 13.4 plots the returns on Microsoft and the returns on the S&P 500 for four successive five-year periods. As can be seen from the figure, Microsoft's beta varies from period to period. However, this movement in beta is probably nothing more than random variation.[4] Thus, for practical purposes, Microsoft's beta has been approximately constant over the two decades covered in the figure. Although Microsoft is just one company, most analysts argue that betas are generally stable for firms remaining in the same industry.

However, this is not to say that, as long as a firm stays in the same industry, its beta will *never* change. Changes in product line, changes in technology, or changes in the market may affect a firm's beta. Furthermore, as we will show in a later section, an increase in the leverage of a firm (i.e., the amount of debt in its capital structure) will increase the firm's beta.

USING AN INDUSTRY BETA

Our approach to estimating the beta of a company from its own past data may seem commonsensical to you. However, it is frequently argued that people can better estimate

---

[4]More precisely, we can say that the beta coefficients over the four periods are not statistically different from each other.

Figure 13.4
Plots of Monthly Returns on Microsoft Corporation against returns on the Standard & Poor's 500 Index for Four Consecutive Five-Year Periods

a firm's beta by involving the whole industry. Consider Table 13.1, which shows the betas of some prominent firms in the software industry. The average beta across all of the firms in the table is .97. Imagine a financial executive at Automatic Data Processing trying to estimate the firm's beta. Because beta estimation is subject to large, random variation in this volatile industry, the executive may be uncomfortable with the estimate of .70. However, the error in beta estimation on a single stock is much higher than the error for a portfolio of securities. Thus, the executive of Automatic Data Processing may prefer the average industry beta of .97 as the estimate of his or her own firm's beta.[5]

Assuming a risk-free rate of 1.0 percent and a risk premium of 7 percent, Automatic Data Processing might estimate its cost of equity capital as:

$$1.0\% + .7 \times 7\% = 5.9\%$$

However, if Automatic Data Processing believed the industry beta contained less estimation error, it could estimate its cost of equity capital as:

$$1.0\% + .97 \times 7\% = 7.79\%$$

The difference is substantial here, presenting a difficult choice for a financial executive at Automatic Data Processing.

---

[5]Actually, one should adjust for leverage before averaging betas, though not much is gained unless leverage ratios differ significantly. Adjustment for leverage will be discussed in later chapters.

Table 13.1
Betas for Firms in the Computer Software Industry

Company	Beta
Microsoft	1.00
Apple, Inc.	1.22
Automatic Data Processing	.70
Oracle Corp.	1.09
Computer Sciences	1.15
CA, Inc.	.97
Fiserv, Inc.	1.07
Accenture, Ltd.	.79
Symantec Corp.	.91
Paychex, Inc.	.84
Equally weighted portfolio	.97

SOURCE: www.reuters.com

While there is no formula for selecting the right beta, there is a very simple guideline. If you believe that the operations of a firm are similar to the operations of the rest of the industry, you should use the industry beta simply to reduce estimation error.[6] However, if an executive believes that the operations of the firm are fundamentally different from those in the rest of the industry, the firm's beta should be used.

When we discussed financial statement analysis in Chapter 3, we noted that a problem frequently comes up in practice—namely, what is the industry? For example, Value Line's *Investment Survey* categorizes Accenture, Ltd., as a computer software company, whereas online financial providers such as www.reuters.com/finance categorize the same company in the business services industry.

13.4 Determinants of Beta

The regression analysis approach in Section 13.3 doesn't tell us where beta comes from. Of course, the beta of a stock does not come out of thin air. Rather, it is determined by the characteristics of the firm. We consider three factors: The cyclical nature of revenues, operating leverage, and financial leverage.

CYCLICALITY OF REVENUES

The revenues of some firms are quite cyclical. That is, these firms do well in the expansion phase of the business cycle and do poorly in the contraction phase. Empirical evidence suggests high-tech firms, retailers, and automotive firms fluctuate with the business cycle. Firms in industries such as utilities, railroads, food, and airlines are less dependent on the cycle. Because beta measures the responsiveness of a stock's return to the market's return, it is not surprising that highly cyclical stocks have high betas.

It is worthwhile to point out that cyclicality is not the same as variability. For example, a moviemaking firm has highly variable revenues because hits and flops are not easily predicted. However, because the revenues of a studio are more dependent

---

[6]As we will see later, an adjustment must be made when the debt level in the industry is different from that of the firm. However, we ignore this adjustment here because firms in the software industry generally have little debt.

on the quality of its releases than the phase of the business cycle, motion picture companies are not particularly cyclical. In other words, stocks with high standard deviations need not have high betas, a point we have stressed before.

OPERATING LEVERAGE

We distinguished fixed costs from variable costs in Chapter 7. At that time, we mentioned that fixed costs do not change as quantity changes. Conversely, variable costs increase as the quantity of output rises. Firms often face a trade-off between fixed and variable costs. For example, a firm can build its own factory, incurring a high level of fixed costs in the process. Alternatively, the firm can outsource production to a supplier, typically generating lower fixed costs but higher variable costs. Fixed costs tend to magnify the impact of sales cyclicality. Fixed costs must be paid, even at a low level of sales, leaving the firm with the possibility of large losses. And with fixed costs replacing variable costs, any additional sales generate low marginal costs, leaving the firm with a substantial increase in profit.

Firms with high fixed costs and low variable costs are generally said to have high **operating leverage.** Conversely, firms with low fixed and high variable costs have low operating leverage. Operating leverage magnifies the effect of the cyclicality of a firm's revenues on beta. That is, a firm with a given sales cyclicality will increase its beta if fixed costs replace variable costs in its production process.

FINANCIAL LEVERAGE AND BETA

As suggested by their names, operating leverage and financial leverage are analogous concepts. Operating leverage refers to the firm's fixed costs of *production*. Financial leverage is the extent to which a firm relies on debt, and a levered firm is a firm with some debt in its capital structure. Because a *levered* firm must make interest payments regardless of the firm's sales, financial leverage refers to the firm's fixed costs of *finance*.

Just as an increase in operating leverage increases beta, an increase in financial leverage (i.e., an increase in debt) increases beta. To see this point, consider a firm with some debt and some equity in its capital structure. Further, imagine an individual who owns all the firm's debt and all its equity. In other words, this individual owns the entire firm. What is the beta of her portfolio of the firm's debt and equity?

As with any portfolio, the beta of this portfolio is a weighted average of the betas of the individual items in the portfolio. Let B stand for the market value of the firm's debt and S stand for the market value of the firm's equity. We have:

$$\beta_{\text{Portfolio}} = \beta_{\text{Asset}} = \frac{S}{B+S} \times \beta_{\text{Equity}} + \frac{B}{B+S} \times \beta_{\text{Debt}} \qquad (13.3)$$

where β_{Equity} is the beta of the stock of the *levered* firm. Notice that the beta of debt, β_{Debt}, is multiplied by $B/(B+S)$, the percentage of debt in the capital structure. Similarly, the beta of equity is multiplied by the percentage of equity in the capital structure. Because the portfolio contains both the debt of the firm and the equity of the firm, the beta of the portfolio can be thought of as the beta of the common stock had the firm been all equity. In practice, this beta is called the **asset beta** because its value is dependent only on the assets of the firm.

The beta of debt is very low in practice. If we make the common assumption that the beta of debt is zero, we have:

$$\beta_{\text{Asset}} = \frac{S}{B+S} \times \beta_{\text{Equity}} \qquad (13.4)$$

Because $S/(B + S)$ must be below 1 for a levered firm, it follows that $\beta_{Asset} < \beta_{Equity}$. Rearranging this equation, we have:

$$\beta_{Equity} = \beta_{Asset}\left(1 + \frac{B}{S}\right)$$

The equity beta will always be greater than the asset beta with financial leverage (assuming the asset beta is positive).[7] In other words, the equity beta of a levered firm will always be greater than the equity beta of an otherwise identical all-equity firm.

Which beta does regression analysis estimate, the asset beta or the equity beta? Regression, as performed in Section 13.3 and also in the real world, provides us with an equity beta because the technique uses *stock* returns as inputs. We must transform this equity beta using Equation 13.4 to arrive at the asset beta. (Of course, the two betas are the same for an all-equity firm.)

EXAMPLE 13.3

Asset versus Equity Betas   Consider a tree growing company, Rapid Cedars, Inc., which is currently all equity and has a beta of .8. The firm has decided to move to a capital structure of one part debt to two parts equity. Because the firm is staying in the same industry, its asset beta should remain at .8. However, assuming a zero beta for its debt, its equity beta would become:

$$\beta_{Equity} = \beta_{Asset}\left(1 + \frac{B}{S}\right)$$

$$1.2 = .8\left(1 + \frac{1}{2}\right)$$

If the firm had one part debt to one part equity in its capital structure, its equity beta would be:

$$1.6 = .8(1 + 1)$$

However, as long as it stayed in the same industry, its asset beta would remain at .8. The effect of leverage, then, is to increase the equity beta.

13.5 The Dividend Discount Model Approach

In Section 13.2, we showed how the CAPM could be used to determine a firm's cost of capital. Among other inputs, we needed an estimate of the market risk premium. One approach used the dividend discount model (DDM) to forecast the expected return on the market as a whole, leading to an estimate of this risk premium. We now use the DDM to estimate the expected return on an individual stock *directly*.

Our discussion in Section 13.2 on the DDM led to the following formula:

$$R_S = \frac{\text{Div}}{P} + g$$

where P is the price per share of a stock, Div is the dividend per share to be received next year, R_S is the discount rate, and g is the expected annual growth rate in dividends per share. The equation tells us that the discount rate on a stock is equal to the sum of

---

[7]It can be shown that the relationship between a firm's asset beta and its equity beta with corporate taxes is:

$$\beta_{Equity} = \beta_{Asset}\left[1 + (1 - t_c)\frac{B}{S}\right]$$

In this expression, t_c is the corporate tax rate. Tax effects are considered in more detail in a later chapter.

the stock's dividend yield ($=\text{Div}/P$) and its expected growth rate of dividends. Thus, in order to apply the DDM to a particular stock, we must estimate both the dividend yield and the expected growth rate.

The dividend yield is relatively easy to forecast. Security analysts routinely provide forecasts of next year's dividend for many stocks. Alternatively, we can set next year's dividend as the product of last year's dividend and $1 + g$, using approaches to estimate g that we describe below. The price per share of any publicly traded stock can generally be determined from either financial newspapers or the Internet.

The expected growth rate of dividends can be estimated in one of three ways. First, we can calculate the firm's historical growth rate in dividends from past data. For some firms, this historical growth rate may be a serviceable, though clearly imperfect, estimate of the future growth rate. Second, in Chapter 9, we argued that the growth rate in dividends can be expressed as:

$$g = \text{Retention ratio} \times \text{ROE}$$

where the retention ratio is the ratio of retained earnings to earnings, and ROE stands for return on equity. Return on equity is the ratio of earnings to the accounting book value of the firm's equity. All the variables needed to estimate both the retention ratio and ROE can be found on a firm's income statement and balance sheet. Third, security analysts commonly provide forecasts of future growth. However, analysts' estimates are generally for five-year growth rates in earnings, while the DDM requires long-term growth rates in dividends.

As an example of the third approach, the consensus five-year forecast for annual earnings growth, as recently reported on finance.yahoo.com, was 7.5 percent for Eastman Chemical Co. The company's dividend yield was 1.04 percent, implying an expected rate of return, and therefore a cost of equity capital, of $1.04 + 7.5 = 8.54\%$ for Eastman.

The above discussion shows how one can use the DDM to estimate a firm's cost of capital. How accurate is this approach compared to the CAPM? We examine this question in the section below.

COMPARISON OF DDM AND CAPM

Both the dividend discount model and the capital asset pricing model are internally consistent models. Nevertheless, academics have generally favored the CAPM over the DDM. In addition, a recent study[8] reported that slightly fewer than three-fourths of companies use the CAPM to estimate the cost of equity capital, while slightly fewer than one-sixth of companies use the dividend discount model to do so. Why has the pendulum swung over to the CAPM? The CAPM has two primary advantages. First, it explicitly adjusts for risk, and second, it is applicable to companies that pay no dividends or whose dividend growth is difficult to estimate. The primary advantage of the DDM is its simplicity. Unfortunately, the DDM is only applicable to firms that pay steady dividends; it is completely useless if companies do not. Another drawback of the DDM is that it does not explicitly consider risk.

While no one, to our knowledge, has done a systematic comparison of the two approaches, the DDM appears to contain more measurement error than does the

[8]John R. Graham and Campbell R. Harvey, "The Theory and Practice of Corporate Finance: Evidence from the Field," *Journal of Financial Economics* (2001), Table 3.

CAPM. The problem is that one is estimating the growth rate of an *individual company* in the DDM, and each of our three suggested approaches to estimate g is fraught with measurement error for single firms. In contrast, consider the calculation of the market risk premium in the CAPM, when the DDM is used to estimate g for the whole market. Though there is clearly measurement error here as well, the error is almost certainly far less; much of the measurement error when estimating g for individual companies is diversified away as we move from individual firms to the market as a whole.[9] Nevertheless, while we have been critical of the DDM's practical application, DDM provides some important intuition, and can be a useful check on the CAPM estimates.

13.6   Cost of Capital for Divisions and Projects

Previous sections of this chapter all assumed that the risk of a potential project is equal to the risk of the existing firm. How should we estimate the discount rate for a project whose risk differs from that of the firm? The answer is that each project should be discounted at a rate commensurate with its own risk. For example, let's assume that we use the CAPM to determine the discount rate.[10] If a project's beta differs from that of the firm, the project's cash flows should be discounted at a rate commensurate with the project's own beta. This is an important point, since firms frequently speak of a *corporate discount rate*. (As mentioned earlier, *required return* and *cost of capital* are frequently used synonymously.) Unless all projects in the corporation are of the same risk, choosing the same discount rate for all projects is incorrect.

The above paragraph considered the discount rates of individual projects. The same message would apply for whole divisions. If a corporation has a number of divisions, each in a different industry, it would be a mistake to assign the same discount rate to each division.

EXAMPLE 13.4

Project Risk   D. D. Ronnelley Co., a publishing firm, may accept a project in computer software. Noting that computer software companies have high betas, the publishing firm views the software venture as more risky than the rest of its business. It should discount the project at a rate commensurate with the risk of software companies. For example, it might use the average beta of a portfolio of publicly traded software firms. Instead, if all projects in D. D. Ronnelley Co. were discounted at the same rate, a bias would result. The firm would accept too many high-risk projects (software ventures) and reject too many low-risk projects (books and magazines). This point is illustrated in Figure 13.5.

(continued)

---

[9]Of course, there is more to the story since we have to estimate three parameters for the CAPM (risk-free rate, market risk premium, and beta), each one of which contains error. Beta estimation is generally considered the problem here, because we need a beta for each company. However, as mentioned earlier in the chapter, analysts frequently calculate average betas across the different companies in an industry in order to reduce measurement error. The presumption is that the betas of different firms in an industry are similar. By contrast, we should not calculate average values of g across the different firms in an industry. Even though these firms are in the same industry, their growth rates can differ widely.

[10]For simplicity, we consider only the CAPM in this section. However, a similar approach would apply if the cost of capital were determined from the DDM.

Figure 13.5   **Relationship between the Firm's Cost of Capital and the Security Market Line (SML)**

A single cost of capital for all projects in a firm, as indicated by the horizontal line in the figure, may lead to incorrect capital budgeting decisions. Projects with high risk, such as the software venture for D. D. Ronnelley Co., should be discounted at a high rate. By using the firm's cost of capital, the firm is likely to accept too many high-risk projects.

Projects with low risk should be discounted at a low rate. By using the firm's cost of capital, the firm is likely to reject too many low-risk projects.

The D. D. Ronnelley (DDR) example points out that we should discount a project at a rate commensurate with the risk of the project's cash flows. However, practitioners should be concerned with three issues here. First, they must choose the appropriate industry. While this may seem to be an easy task, the problem is that companies often have more than one line of business. For example, suppose that DDR was considering a project in the movie industry, not in computer software. Their first thought might be to look at the betas of the largest and most important companies in the film industry. The six biggest studios are Warner Brothers, Columbia, Fox, Universal, Paramount, and Disney. However, the first five studios are owned by Time-Warner, Sony, News Corporation, General Electric, and Viacom, respectively. These parent corporations are all diversified, with movies making up only a small portion of total revenues. And, while the parent of the sixth studio has the same Walt Disney name, it too is quite diversified, with holdings in television, radio, theme parks, and cruise ships. With all this diversification, it would likely be quite difficult to determine the beta of a pure moviemaking company from the betas of the six parents. Analysts often talk about identifying *pure plays* (i.e., other companies that specialize only in projects similar to the project your firm is considering). Pure plays are easier to find in some situations than in others.

Second, even if all companies in a particular industry are pure plays, the beta of a new project may be greater than the beta of existing firms, because a new project is likely to be particularly responsive to economy-wide movements. For example, a start-up computer venture may fail in a recession while IBM, Microsoft, or Oracle will still be around. Conversely, in an expansion, the venture may grow faster than the older computer firms.

Fortunately, a slight adjustment is all that is needed here. The new venture should be assigned a somewhat higher beta than that of the industry to reflect added risk. The adjustment is necessarily ad hoc, so no formula can be given. Our experience indicates that this approach is in widespread practice today.

Third, a problem arises for the rare project constituting its own industry. For example, consider the firms providing consumer shopping by television. Today, we can obtain a reasonable estimate for the beta of this industry because a few of the firms have publicly traded stock. However, when the ventures began in the 1980s, any beta estimate was suspect. At that time, no one knew whether shopping by TV belonged in the television industry, the retail industry, or in an entirely new industry.

What beta should be used when the project constitutes its own industry? Earlier in this chapter we mentioned three determinants of beta: Cyclicality of revenues, operating leverage, and financial leverage. Comparing the values of these three determinants for the project in question to the values for other firms should provide at least a general feel for the project's beta.

13.7 Cost of Fixed Income Securities

In this section, we examine the cost of both debt and preferred stock. We consider the cost of debt first.

COST OF DEBT

The cost of equity is often difficult to estimate. The task generally involves a fair amount of data gathering and the end result is often measured with error. In general, the cost of debt is easier to determine. For bonds with a small risk of defaulting, the current yield to maturity is a good estimate of investor expected returns and the cost of borrowing. The firm can generally obtain this information either by checking the yield on publicly traded bonds or by talking to commercial and investment bankers.

Two years ago, the Ritter Manufacturing Corp. (RMC) issued $100 million of debt with a 7 percent coupon. While the bonds were initially issued at par, rising interest rates over the last two years have caused them to sell at a discount. The yield on the bonds is currently 8 percent. In order to finance expansion, RMC is considering another large issue of bonds. What is the cost of the new debt?

The cost of the new debt should be around 8 percent. If the old bonds are selling at 8 percent, the new debt will not sell at a lower yield. The 7 percent is merely a historical number, often called the *embedded cost* of the debt, with no relevance today.

Alternatively, perhaps a firm is issuing debt for the first time. Here, the firm's investment banker can generally indicate to the firm's managers what the yield on the prospective bonds will be. That yield is the cost of debt. Or, perhaps the company will take out a loan with a commercial bank. Again, the borrowing rate on the prospective loan is the cost of debt.

There is only one complication that needs to be discussed. We have ignored taxes so far, obviously an assumption at odds with reality. Under U.S. tax law, interest payments are *tax deductible*. Consider the following example where two firms, Unlevered

Corp. and Levered Corp., differ only in debt. Unlevered Corp. has no debt and Levered Corp. has $100 of debt, with an interest rate of 10 percent.

Unlevered Corp.		Levered Corp.	
Revenue	$180	Revenue	$180
Expenses	−70	Expenses	−70
Pretax earnings	110	Earnings before interest and taxes	110
Taxes (40% rate)	−44	Interest (10% on $100 borrowed)	−10
Aftertax earnings	$ 66	Pretax earnings	100
		Taxes (40% rate)	−40
		Aftertax earnings	$ 60

While the Levered Corp. must pay $10 of interest per year, its aftertax earnings are only $6 (=66 − 60) less than those of the Unlevered Corp. Why? Because the interest payments are tax deductible. That is, while Levered Corp.'s pretax earnings are $10 (=110 − 100) less than those of Unlevered Corp., Levered Corp. pays $4 (=44 − 40) less in taxes than does Unlevered Corp.

The $6 reduction of aftertax earnings is 6 percent of the $100 that Levered Corp. borrowed. Thus, the aftertax cost of debt is 6 percent. In general, the aftertax cost of debt can be written as:

$$\text{Aftertax cost of debt} = (1 - \text{Tax rate}) \times \text{Borrowing rate}$$
$$6\% = (1 - .40) \times 10\%$$

Why have we tax-adjusted the cost of debt while we did not tax-adjust the cost of equity? Because, while firms can deduct their interest payments before paying taxes, dividends are not tax deductible.

COST OF PREFERRED STOCK

The name preferred stock is an unfortunate one, because preferred stock is probably more similar to bonds than to common stock. Preferred stock pays a constant dividend in perpetuity. Interest payments on bonds are quite similar to dividends on preferred stock, though almost all bonds have a finite maturity. By contrast, dividends on common stock are not constant over time.

Suppose a share of the preferred stock of Polytech, Inc., is selling at $17.16 and pays a dividend of $1.50 per year. Since preferred stocks are perpetuities, they should be priced by the perpetuity formula, $\text{PV} = C/R_p$, where PV is the present value, or price, C is the cash to be received each year, and R_p is the yield, or rate of return. Rearranging, we have:

$$R_p = C/\text{PV}$$

For this preferred issue, the rate of return is 8.7% (=1.50/17.16). The cost of preferred stock is simply this rate of return.

Why don't we tax-adjust the cost of preferred stock the way we did the cost of debt? We don't tax-adjust here, because dividend payments on preferred stock are not tax deductible.

13.8 The Weighted Average Cost of Capital

Sections 13.1 and 13.2 showed how to estimate the discount rate when a project is all equity financed. In this section, we discuss an adjustment when the project is financed with both debt and equity.

Suppose a firm uses both debt and equity to finance its investments. If the firm pays R_B for its debt financing and R_S for its equity, what is the overall or average cost of its capital? The cost of equity is R_S, as discussed in earlier sections. The cost of debt is the firm's borrowing rate, R_B, which we can often observe by looking at the yield to maturity on the firm's debt. If a firm uses both debt and equity, the cost of capital is a weighted average of each. This works out to be:

$$\frac{S}{S + B} \times R_S + \frac{B}{S + B} \times R_B$$

The weights in the formula are, respectively, the proportion of total value represented by equity:

$$\left(\frac{S}{S + B}\right)$$

and the proportion of total value represented by debt:

$$\left(\frac{B}{S + B}\right)$$

This is only natural. If the firm had issued no debt and was therefore an all-equity firm, its average cost of capital would equal its cost of equity, R_S. At the other extreme, if the firm had issued so much debt that its equity was valueless, it would be an all-debt firm, and its average cost of capital would be its cost of debt, R_B.

Interest is tax deductible at the corporate level, as stated in the previous section. The aftertax cost of debt is:

$$\text{Cost of debt (after corporate tax)} = R_B \times (1 - t_C)$$

where t_C is the corporation's tax rate.

Assembling these results, we get the average cost of capital (after tax) for the firm:[11]

$$\text{Average cost of capital} = \left(\frac{S}{S + B}\right) \times R_S + \left(\frac{B}{S + B}\right) \times R_B \times (1 - t_C) \quad (13.5)$$

Because the average cost of capital weighs the cost of equity and the cost of debt, it is usually referred to as the **weighted average cost of capital, R_{WACC},** and from now on we will use this term.

EXAMPLE 13.5

WACC   Consider a firm whose debt has a market value of $40 million and whose stock has a market value of $60 million (3 million outstanding shares of stock, each selling for $20 per share). The firm pays a 5 percent rate of interest on its new debt and has a beta of 1.41. The corporate tax rate is 34 percent. (Assume that the security market line (SML) holds, that the risk premium on

(continued)

---

[11]For simplicity, Equation 13.5 ignores preferred stock financing. With the addition of preferred stock, the formula becomes:

$$\text{Average cost of capital} = \frac{S}{S + B + P} \times R_S + \frac{B}{S + B + P} \times R_B \times (1 - t_C) + \frac{P}{S + B + P} \times R_P$$

where P is the amount of preferred stock in the firm's capital structure and R_P is the cost of preferred stock.

the market is 9.5 percent [somewhat higher than the historical equity risk premium], and that the current Treasury bill rate is 1 percent.) What is this firm's R_{WACC}?

To compute the R_{WACC} using Equation 13.5, we must know (1) the aftertax cost of debt, $R_B \times (1 - t_c)$, (2) the cost of equity, R_s, and (3) the proportions of debt and equity used by the firm. These three values are determined next:

1. The pretax cost of debt is 5 percent, implying an aftertax cost of 3.3 percent [$=5\% \times (1 - .34)$].
2. We calculate the cost of equity capital by using the SML:

$$R_s = R_F + \beta \times [R_M - R_F]$$
$$= 1\% + 1.41 \times 9.5\%$$
$$= 14.40\%$$

3. We compute the proportions of debt and equity from the market values of debt and equity. Because the market value of the firm is $100 million ($=$40 million + $60 million), the proportions of debt and equity are 40 and 60 percent, respectively.

The cost of equity, R_s, is 14.40 percent, and the aftertax cost of debt, $R_B \times (1 - t_c)$, is 3.3 percent. B is $40 million and S is $60 million. Therefore:

$$R_{WACC} = \frac{S}{B + S} \times R_s + \frac{B}{B + S} \times R_B \times (1 - t_c)$$
$$= \left(\frac{60}{100} \times 14.40\%\right) + \left(\frac{40}{100} \times 3.3\%\right) = 9.96\%$$

The above calculations are presented in table form below:

(1) Financing Components	(2) Market Values	(3) Weight	(4) Cost of Capital (after Corporate Tax)	(5) Weighted Cost of Capital
Debt	$ 40,000,000	.40	$5\% \times (1 - .34) = 3.3\%$	1.32%
Equity	60,000,000	.60	$1\% + 1.41 \times 9.5\% = 14.40$	8.64
	$100,000,000	1.00		9.96%

The weights used in the previous example are market value weights. Market value weights are more appropriate than book value weights because the market values of the securities are closer to the actual dollars that would be received from their sale. In fact, it is useful to think in terms of "target" market weights. These are the market weights expected to prevail over the life of the firm or project.

13.9 Valuation with R_{WACC}

Now we are in a position to use the weighted average cost of capital, R_{WACC}, to value both projects and entire firms. Our interpretation of R_{WACC} is that it is the overall expected return the firm must earn on its existing assets to maintain its value. The R_{WACC} reflects the risk and the capital structure of the firm's existing assets. As a result the R_{WACC} is an appropriate discount rate for the firm or for a project that is a replica of the firm.

PROJECT EVALUATION AND THE R_{WACC}

When valuing a project we start by determining the correct discount rate and use discounted cash flow to determine NPV.

Suppose a firm has both a current and a target debt–equity ratio of .6, a cost of debt of 5.15 percent, and a cost of equity of 10 percent. The corporate tax rate is 34 percent. What is the firm's weighted average cost of capital?

Our first step calls for transforming the debt–equity (B/S) ratio to a debt–value ratio. A B/S ratio of .6 implies 6 parts debt for 10 parts equity. Because value is equal to the sum of the debt plus the equity, the debt–value ratio is $6/(6 + 10) = .375$. Similarly, the equity–value ratio is $10/(6 + 10) = .625$. The R_{WACC} will then be:

$$R_{WACC} = \left(\frac{S}{S + B}\right) \times R_S + \left(\frac{B}{S + B}\right) \times R_B \times (1 - t_C)$$
$$= .625 \times 10\% + .375 \times 5.15\% \times .66 = 7.52\%$$

Suppose the firm is considering taking on a warehouse renovation costing $60 million that is expected to yield cost savings of $12 million a year for six years. Using the NPV equation and discounting the six years of expected cash flows from the renovation at the R_{WACC}, we have:

$$NPV = -\$60 + \frac{\$12}{(1 + R_{WACC})} + \cdots + \frac{\$12}{(1 + R_{WACC})^6}$$
$$= -\$60 + \$12 \times \frac{\left[1 - \left(\frac{1}{1.0752}\right)^6\right]}{.0752}$$
$$= -\$60 + (12 \times 4.69)$$
$$= -\$3.71$$

Should the firm take on the warehouse renovation? The project has a negative NPV using the firm's R_{WACC}. This means that the financial markets offer superior investments in the same risk class (namely, the firm's risk class). The answer is clear: The firm should reject the project.

Of course, we are assuming that the project is in the same risk class as the firm and that the project is an integral part of the overall business.

FIRM VALUATION WITH THE R_{WACC}

When valuing a complete business enterprise our approach is the same as the one used for individual capital projects like the warehouse renovation, except that we use a horizon, and this complicates the calculations. Specifically, we use the firm's weighted average cost of capital as our discount rate, and we set up the usual discounted cash flow model by forecasting the firm's entire net cash flow (sometimes called distributable cash flow, free cash flow, or total cash flow of the firm) up to a horizon along with a terminal value of the firm:

$$PV_0 = \frac{CF_1}{1 + R_{WACC}} + \frac{CF_2}{(1 + R_{WACC})^2} + \frac{CF_3}{(1 + R_{WACC})^3} + \cdots + \frac{CF_T + TV_T}{(1 + R_{WACC})^T}$$

Consistent with the differential growth version of the dividend discount model, the terminal value (TV)[12] is estimated by assuming a constant perpetual growth rate for cash flows beyond the horizon, T, so that:

$$TV_T = \frac{CF_{T+1}}{R_{WACC} - g_{CF}} = \frac{CF_T(1 + g_{CF})}{R_{WACC} - g_{CF}}$$

---

[12]The terminal date is often referred to as the horizon. In general, we choose a horizon whenever we can assume cash flow grows at a constant rate perpetually thereafter. By using the word terminal, we do not rule out the firm continuing to exist. Instead, we are attempting to simplify the cash flow estimation process.

where CF is the net cash flows and is equal to earnings before interest and taxes (EBIT), minus taxes, minus capital spending, minus increases in net working capital plus deprecation.[13] g_{CF} is the growth rate of cash flow beyond T, and R_{WACC} is the weighted average cost of capital.

Consider the Good Food Corporation, a public company headquartered in Barstow, California, that is currently a leading global food service retailer. It operates about 10,000 restaurants in 100 countries. Good Food serves a value-based menu focused on hamburgers and french fries. The company has $4 billion in market valued debt and $2 billion in market valued common stock. Its tax rate is 20 percent. Good Food has estimated its cost of debt as 5 percent and its cost of equity as 10 percent. Its weighted average cost of capital is equal to:

Financial Component	Market Values	Weights	Cost of Capital	Weighted Average
Debt	$4 billion	2/3	5%(1−.2) = 4%	2/3 × 4%
Equity	$2 billion	1/3	10%	1/3 × 10%
	$6 billion			6% = the weighted average cost of capital

Good Food is seeking to grow by acquisition and the investment bankers of Good Food have identified a potential acquisition candidate, Happy Meals, Inc. Happy Meals is currently a private firm with no publicly tradable common stock but has the same product mix as Good Food and is a direct competitor to Good Food in many markets. It operates about 4,000 restaurants mostly in North America and Europe. Happy Meals has $1,318.8 million of debt outstanding with its market value the same as the book value.[14] It has 12.5 million shares outstanding. Since Happy Meals is a private firm, we have no stock market price to rely on for our valuation. Happy Meals expects its EBIT to grow 10 percent a year for the next five years. Increases in net working capital and capital spending are both expected to be 24 percent of EBIT. Depreciation will be 8 percent of EBIT. The perpetual growth rate in cash flow after five years is estimated to be 2 percent.

If Good Food acquires Happy Meals, Good Food analysts estimate the net cash flows from Happy Meals (in $ millions) would be (rounding to one decimal):

Year	1	2	3	4	5
Earnings before interest and taxes (EBIT)	150	165	181.5	199.7	219.6
− Taxes (20%)	30	33	36.3	39.9	43.9
= Earnings after taxes	120	132	145.2	159.8	175.7
+ Depreciation	12	13.2	14.5	16	17.6
− Capital spending	36	39.6	43.6	47.9	52.7
− Increases in net working capital	36	39.6	43.6	47.9	52.7
= Net cash flows (CF)	60	66	72.6	80	87.8

---

[13]This definition of cash flow is the same one we used to determine the NPV of capital investments in Chapter 6.

[14]Sometimes analysts refer to a firm's net debt which is the market value of debt minus excess cash. Neither Good Food or Happy Meals has excess cash.

We start our calculations by computing a terminal value of Happy Meals as:

$$TV_5 = \frac{\$87.8 \times 1.02}{.06 - .02} = \$2,238.9$$

Next, we compute the present value of Happy Meals to be:

$$PV_0 = \frac{\$60}{1.06} + \frac{\$66}{(1.06)^2} + \frac{\$72.6}{(1.06)^3} + \frac{\$79.9}{(1.06)^4} + \frac{\$87.8}{(1.06)^5} + \frac{\$2,238.9}{(1.06)^5} = \$1,978.2$$

The present value of net cash flows in Years 1 to 5 is \$305.2, and the present value of the terminal value is:

$$\$2,238.9 \times \left(\frac{1}{1.06}\right)^5 = \$1,673.0$$

so the total value of the company is \$305.2 + \$1,673.0 = \$1,978.2.

To find the value of equity, we subtract the value of debt which gives us \$1,978.2 − \$1,318.8 = \$659.4. To find the equity value per share, we divide the value of equity by the number of shares outstanding: \$659.4/12.5 = \$52.8. Good Food will find Happy Meals an attractive acquisition candidate for payments of less than \$52.8 per share (the less the better).

In doing our valuation of Happy Meals, Inc., it is important to remember that we have assumed that Happy Meals is a pure play for Good Food. Our weighted average cost of capital method only works if Happy Meals has the same business risks as Good Food and the debt-to-equity ratio will remain the same.

The above calculations assume a growing perpetuity after Year 5 (i.e., the horizon). However, we pointed out in Chapter 3 and Chapter 9 that firms as a whole are often valued by multiples. The most common multiple for overall firm valuation is the enterprise value to the EBITDA multiple (i.e., EV/EBITDA). For example, the analysts at Good Food might estimate the terminal value of Happy Meals via an EV/EBITDA multiple, rather than a growing perpetuity. To see how this might work, suppose the EV/EBITDA multiple for comparable firms in the food service industry is 10. The EBITDA for Happy Meals in Year 5 will be equal to EBIT + depreciation or \$237.2 (=\$219.6 + \$17.6). Using the EV/EBITDA multiple of 10, the value of Happy Meals in Year 5 can be estimated as \$2,372.0. The present value of Happy Meals using the EV/EBITDA multiple for terminal value would be:

$$PV_0 = \frac{\$60}{1.06} + \frac{\$66}{(1.06)^2} + \frac{\$72.6}{(1.06)^3} + \frac{\$79.9}{(1.06)^4} + \frac{\$87.8}{(1.06)^5} + \frac{\$2,372}{(1.06)^5} = \$2,077.7$$

The value of the equity of Happy Meals can be estimated as:

$$PV(\text{of entire firm}) \text{ less debt} = \$2,077.7 − \$1,318.8 = \$758.9$$

With 12.5 million shares outstanding, the value of a share of equity would be:

$$\$758.9/12.5 = \$60.7$$

Now we have two estimates of the value of a share of equity in Happy Meals. The different estimates reflect the different ways of calculating terminal value. Using the constant growth discounted cash flow method for terminal value our estimate of the equity value per share of Happy Meals is \$52.8 and using the EV/EBITDA comparable firm method our estimate is \$60.7. As mentioned in Chapter 9, there is no perfect method. If the comparable firms were all identical to Happy Meals, perhaps the EV/EBITDA method would be best. Unfortunately firms are not identical. On the other hand, if we were very sure of the terminal date and the growth in subsequent cash flows, perhaps the constant growth method would be best. Both methods are used.

13.10 Estimating Eastman Chemical's Cost of Capital

ExcelMaster
coverage online

This section introduces the Hyperlink function.

In our previous sections, we calculated the cost of capital in examples. We will now calculate the cost of capital for a real company, Eastman Chemical Co., a leading international chemical company and maker of plastics for soft drink containers and other uses. It was created in 1993, when its former parent company, Eastman Kodak, split off the division as a separate company.

Eastman's Cost of Equity   Our first stop for Eastman is www.reuters.com (ticker: EMN). In October 2011, the website reported the market capitalization of EMN's equity, which is share price times number of shares outstanding, as $5,259.42 million. To estimate Eastman's cost of equity, we will assume a market risk premium of 7 percent, similar to what we calculated in Chapter 11. Eastman's beta on Reuters is 1.88.

In Section 13.2, we estimated the average future riskless rate as the current 20-year Treasury bond yield minus the historical difference between the yield on the 20-year Treasury bond and the yield on the one-year Treasury bill. Since the yield on a Treasury bond was recently 3.5 percent and the historical yield difference between long- and short-term Treasury bonds was 2.5 percent, our estimate of the average riskless rate in the future is $3.5 - 2.5 = 1\%$.

Using Eastman's beta in the CAPM to estimate the cost of equity,[15] we find:

$$R_S = .01 + (1.88 \times .07) = .1416 \text{ or } 14.16\%$$

Eastman's Cost of Debt   Eastman has eight bond issues that account for essentially all of its debt. To calculate the cost of debt, we will have to combine these eight issues and compute a weighted average. We go to www.nasdbondinfo.com to find quotes on the bonds. We should note here that finding the yield to maturity for all of a company's outstanding bond issues on a single day is unusual. In our previous discussion on bonds, we found that the bond market is not as liquid as the stock market, and on many days, individual bond issues may not trade. To find the book value

---

[15]Alternatively, one might use an average beta across all companies in the chemical industry, after properly adjusting for leverage. Some argue this averaging approach provides more accuracy, since errors in beta estimation for a single firm are reduced.

of the bonds, we go to www.sec.gov and find the most recent 10K report. The basic information is as follows:

Coupon Rate	Maturity	Book Value (Face Value in $ Millions)	Price (as % of Par)	Yield to Maturity
7.00%	2012	$150	103.875	1.33%
3.00	2015	250	101.408	2.64
6.30	2018	177	107.500	5.02
5.50	2019	250	111.860	3.78
4.50	2021	250	103.677	4.02
7.25	2024	243	114.840	5.56
7.625	2024	54	122.300	5.20
7.60	2027	222	113.909	6.18

To calculate the weighted average cost of debt, we take the percentage of the total debt represented by each issue and multiply by the yield on the issue. We then add to get the overall weighted average debt cost. We use both book values and market values here for comparison. The results of the calculations are as follows:

Coupon Rate	Book Value (Face value in $ Millions)	Percentage of Total	Market Value (in $ Millions)	Percentage of Total	Yield to Maturity	Book Value Weights	Market Value Weights
7.00%	$ 150	9.40%	$ 155.81	8.97%	1.33%	.12%	.12%
3.00	250	15.66	253.52	14.60	2.64	.41	.39
6.30	177	11.09	190.28	10.96	5.02	.56	.55
5.50	250	15.66	279.65	16.10	3.78	.59	.61
4.50	250	15.66	259.19	14.93	4.02	.63	.60
7.25	243	15.23	279.06	16.07	5.56	.85	.89
7.625	54	3.38	66.04	3.80	5.20	.18	.20
7.60	222	13.91	252.88	14.56	6.18	.86	.90
Total	$1,596	100.00%	$1,736.43	100.00%		4.20%	4.25%

As these calculations show, Eastman's cost of debt is 4.2 percent on a book value basis and 4.25 percent on a market value basis. Thus, for Eastman, whether market values or book values are used makes little difference. The reason is simply that the market values and book values are similar. This will often be the case and explains why companies frequently use book values for debt in WACC calculations. We will, however, use market values in our calculations, because the market reflects current values.

Eastman's WACC   We now have the various pieces necessary to calculate Eastman's WACC. First, we need to calculate the capital structure weights.

The market values of Eastman's debt and equity are $1.736 billion and $5.259 billion, respectively. The total value of the firm is $6.995 billion, implying that the debt and equity percentages are $1.736/6.995 = .248$ and $5.259/6.995 = .752$, respectively. Assuming a tax rate of 35 percent, Eastman's WACC is:

$$R_{WACC} = .248 \times .0425 \times (1 - .35) + .752 \times .1416 = .1133, \text{ or } 11.33\%$$

13.11   Flotation Costs and the Weighted Average Cost of Capital

So far, we have not included issue costs in our discussion of the weighted average cost of capital. When projects are funded by stocks and bonds, the firm will incur these costs, which are commonly called *flotation costs*.

Sometimes it is suggested that the firm's WACC should be adjusted upward to reflect flotation costs. This is really not the best approach because the required return on an investment depends on the risk of the investment, not the source of the funds. This is not to say that flotation costs should be ignored. Since these costs arise as a consequence of the decision to undertake a project, they are relevant cash flows. We therefore briefly discuss how to include them in project analysis.

THE BASIC APPROACH

We start with a simple case. The Spatt Company, an all-equity firm, has a cost of equity of 20 percent. Because this firm is 100 percent equity, its WACC and its cost of equity are the same. Spatt is contemplating a large-scale $100 million expansion of its existing operations. The expansion would be funded by selling new stock.

Based on conversations with its investment banker, Spatt believes its flotation costs will run 10 percent of the amount issued. This means that Spatt's proceeds from the equity sale will be only 90 percent of the amount sold. When flotation costs are considered, what is the cost of the expansion?

Spatt needs to sell enough equity to raise $100 million *after* covering the flotation costs. In other words:

$$\$100 \text{ million} = (1 - .10) \times \text{Amount raised}$$
$$\text{Amount raised} = \$100 \text{ million}/.90 = \$111.11 \text{ million}$$

Spatt's flotation costs are thus $11.11 million, and the true cost of the expansion is $111.11 million including flotation costs.

Things are only slightly more complicated if the firm uses both debt and equity. For example, suppose Spatt's target capital structure is 60 percent equity, 40 percent debt. The flotation costs associated with equity are still 10 percent, but the flotation costs for debt are less—say 5 percent.

Earlier, when we had different capital costs for debt and equity, we calculated a weighted average cost of capital using the target capital structure weights. Here, we will do much the same thing. We can calculate an overall or weighted average flotation cost, f_o, by multiplying the flotation cost for stock, f_S, by the percentage of stock (S/V) and the flotation cost for bonds, f_B, by the percentage of bonds (B/V) and then adding the two together:

$$f_o = (S/V) \times f_S + (B/V) \times f_B$$
$$= 60\% \times .10 + 40\% \times .05 \tag{13.6}$$
$$= 8\%$$

The weighted average flotation cost is thus 8 percent. What this tells us is that for every dollar in outside financing needed for new projects, the firm must actually raise $1/(1 − .08) = 1.087. In our example, the project cost is $100 million when we ignore flotation costs. If we include them, then the true cost is 100 million$/(1 − f_o) =$ 100 million$/.92 = 108.7 million.

In taking issue costs into account, the firm must be careful not to use the wrong weights. The firm should use the target weights, even if it can finance the entire cost of the project with either debt or equity. The fact that a firm can finance a specific project with debt or equity is not directly relevant. If a firm has a target debt–equity ratio of 1, for example, but chooses to finance a particular project with all debt, it will have to raise additional equity later on to maintain its target debt–equity ratio. To take this into account, the firm should always use the target weights in calculating the flotation cost.

EXAMPLE 13.6

Calculating the Weighted Average Flotation Cost   The Weinstein Corporation has a target capital structure of 80 percent equity and 20 percent debt. The flotation costs for equity issues are 20 percent of the amount raised; the flotation costs for debt issues are 6 percent. If Weinstein needs $65 million for a new manufacturing facility, what is the true cost including flotation costs?

We first calculate the weighted average flotation cost, f_o:

$$f_o = S/V \times f_S + B/V \times f_B$$
$$= 80\% \times .20 + 20\% \times .06$$
$$= 17.2\%$$

The weighted average flotation cost is 17.2 percent. The project cost is $65 million without flotation costs. If we include them, then the true cost is 65 million$/(1 − f_o) = 65 million$/.828 = 78.5 million, again illustrating that flotation costs can be a considerable expense.

FLOTATION COSTS AND NPV

To illustrate how flotation costs can be included in an NPV analysis, suppose the Tripleday Printing Company is currently at its target debt–equity ratio of 100 percent. It is considering building a new $500,000 printing plant in Kansas. This new plant is expected to generate aftertax cash flows of $73,150 per year forever. The tax rate is 34 percent. There are two financing options:

1.   A $500,000 new issue of common stock: The issuance costs of the new common stock would be about 10 percent of the amount raised. The required return on the company's new equity is 20 percent.

2.   A $500,000 issue of 30-year bonds: The issuance costs of the new debt would be 2 percent of the proceeds. The company can raise new debt at 10 percent.

What is the NPV of the new printing plant?

To begin, since printing is the company's main line of business, we will use the company's weighted average cost of capital, R_{WACC}, to value the new printing plant:

$$R_{WACC} = S/V \times R_S + B/V \times R_B \times (1 − t_C)$$
$$= .50 \times 20\% + .50 \times 10\% \times (1 − .34)$$
$$= 13.3\%$$

Because the cash flows are $73,150 per year forever, the PV of the cash flows at 13.3 percent per year is:

$$PV = \frac{\$73,150}{.133} = \$550,000$$

If we ignore flotation costs, the NPV is:

$$NPV = \$550,000 - 500,000 = \$50,000$$

With no flotation costs, the project generates an NPV that is greater than zero, so it should be accepted.

What about financing arrangements and issue costs? Because new financing must be raised, the flotation costs are relevant. From the information given, we know that the flotation costs are 2 percent for debt and 10 percent for equity. Because Tripleday uses equal amounts of debt and equity, the weighted average flotation cost, f_o, is:

$$
\begin{aligned}
f_o &= S/V \times f_S + B/V \times f_B \\
&= .50 \times 10\% + .50 \times 2\% \\
&= 6\%
\end{aligned}
$$

Remember, the fact that Tripleday can finance the project with all debt or all equity is irrelevant. Since Tripleday needs $500,000 to fund the new plant, the true cost, once we include flotation costs, is $500,000/(1 − f_o) = $500,000/.94 = $531,915. Because the PV of the cash flows is $550,000, the plant has an NPV of $550,000 − 531,915 = $18,085, so it is still a good investment. However, its value is less than we initially might have thought.

INTERNAL EQUITY AND FLOTATION COSTS

Our discussion of flotation costs to this point implicitly assumed that firms always have to raise the capital needed for new investments. In reality, most firms rarely sell equity at all. Instead, their internally generated cash flow is sufficient to cover the equity portion of their capital spending. Only the debt portion must be raised externally.

The use of internal equity doesn't change our approach. However, we now assign a value of zero to the flotation cost of equity because there is no such cost. In our Tripleday example, the weighted average flotation cost would therefore be:

$$
\begin{aligned}
f_o &= S/V \times f_S + B/V \times f_B \\
&= .50 \times 0\% + .50 \times 2\% \\
&= 1\%
\end{aligned}
$$

◀ To test your mastery of this material, take a quiz at mhhe. com/rwj

Notice that whether equity is generated internally or externally makes a big difference because external equity has a relatively high flotation cost.

Summary and Conclusions

Earlier chapters on capital budgeting assumed that projects generate riskless cash flows. The appropriate discount rate in that case is the riskless interest rate. Of course, most cash flows from real-world capital budgeting projects are risky. This chapter discussed the discount rate when cash flows are risky.

1. A firm with excess cash can either pay a dividend or make a capital expenditure. Because stockholders can reinvest the dividend in risky financial assets, the expected

return on a capital budgeting project should be at least as great as the expected return on a financial asset of comparable risk.

2. The expected return on any asset is dependent on its beta. Thus, we showed how to estimate the beta of a stock. The appropriate procedure employs regression analysis on historical returns.

3. Both beta and covariance measure the responsiveness of a security to movements in the market. Correlation and beta measure different concepts. Beta is the slope of the regression line and correlation is the tightness of fit around the regression line.

4. We considered the case of a project with beta risk equal to that of the firm. If the firm is unlevered, the discount rate on the project is equal to:

$$R_F + \beta \times (R_M - R_F)$$

where R_M is the expected return on the market portfolio and R_F is the risk-free rate. In words, the discount rate on the project is equal to the CAPM's estimate of the expected return on the security.

5. The beta of a company is a function of a number of factors. Perhaps the three most important are:
   • Cyclicality of revenues.
   • Operating leverage.
   • Financial leverage.

6. If the project's beta differs from that of the firm, the discount rate should be based on the project's beta. We can generally estimate the project's beta by determining the average beta of the project's industry.

7. Sometimes we cannot use the average beta of the project's industry as an estimate of the beta of the project. For example, a new project may not fall neatly into any existing industry. In this case, we can estimate the project's beta by considering the project's cyclicality of revenues and its operating leverage. This approach is qualitative.

8. If a firm uses debt, the discount rate to use is the R_{WACC}. To calculate R_{WACC}, we must estimate the cost of equity and the cost of debt applicable to a project. If the project is similar to the firm, the cost of equity can be estimated using the SML for the firm's equity. Conceptually, a dividend growth model could be used as well, though it is likely to be far less accurate in practice.

9. New projects are often funded by bonds and stock. The costs of issuance, generally called flotation costs, should be included in any NPV analysis.

Concept Questions

1. **Project Risk**   If you can borrow all the money you need for a project at 6 percent, doesn't it follow that 6 percent is your cost of capital for the project?

2. **WACC and Taxes**   Why do we use an aftertax figure for cost of debt but not for cost of equity?

3. **SML Cost of Equity Estimation**   If you use the stock beta and the security market line to compute the discount rate for a project, what assumptions are you implicitly making?

4. **SML Cost of Equity Estimation**   What are the advantages of using the SML approach to finding the cost of equity capital? What are the disadvantages? What are the specific pieces of information needed to use this method? Are all of these variables observable, or do they need to be estimated? What are some of the ways in which you could get these estimates?

428   Part III   Risk

5. **Cost of Debt Estimation**   How do you determine the appropriate cost of debt for a company? Does it make a difference if the company's debt is privately placed as opposed to being publicly traded? How would you estimate the cost of debt for a firm whose only debt issues are privately held by institutional investors?

6. **Cost of Capital**   Suppose Tom O'Bedlam, president of Bedlam Products, Inc., has hired you to determine the firm's cost of debt and cost of equity capital.

    a. The stock currently sells for $50 per share, and the dividend per share will probably be about $5. Tom argues, "It will cost us $5 per share to use the stockholders' money this year, so the cost of equity is equal to 10 percent (=$5/50)." What's wrong with this conclusion?

    b. Based on the most recent financial statements, Bedlam Products' total liabilities are $8 million. Total interest expense for the coming year will be about $1 million. Tom therefore reasons, "We owe $8 million, and we will pay $1 million interest. Therefore, our cost of debt is obviously $1 million/8 million = 12.5 percent." What's wrong with this conclusion?

    c. Based on his own analysis, Tom is recommending that the company increase its use of equity financing because, "debt costs 12.5 percent, but equity only costs 10 percent; thus equity is cheaper." Ignoring all the other issues, what do you think about the conclusion that the cost of equity is less than the cost of debt?

7. **Company Risk versus Project Risk**   Both Dow Chemical Company, a large natural gas user, and Superior Oil, a major natural gas producer, are thinking of investing in natural gas wells near Houston. Both are all-equity financed companies. Dow and Superior are looking at identical projects. They've analyzed their respective investments, which would involve a negative cash flow now and positive expected cash flows in the future. These cash flows would be the same for both firms. No debt would be used to finance the projects. Both companies estimate that their projects would have a net present value of $1 million at an 18 percent discount rate and a −$1.1 million NPV at a 22 percent discount rate. Dow has a beta of 1.25, whereas Superior has a beta of .75. The expected risk premium on the market is 8 percent, and risk-free bonds are yielding 12 percent. Should either company proceed? Should both? Explain.

8. **Divisional Cost of Capital**   Under what circumstances would it be appropriate for a firm to use different costs of capital for its different operating divisions? If the overall firm WACC was used as the hurdle rate for all divisions, would the riskier divisions or the more conservative divisions tend to get most of the investment projects? Why? If you were to try to estimate the appropriate cost of capital for different divisions, what problems might you encounter? What are two techniques you could use to develop a rough estimate for each division's cost of capital?

9. **Leverage**   Consider a levered firm's projects that have similar risks to the firm as a whole. Is the discount rate for the projects higher or lower than the rate computed using the security market line? Why?

10. **Beta**   What factors determine the beta of a stock? Define and describe each.

Questions and Problems

BASIC
(Questions 1–15)

1. **Calculating Cost of Equity**   The Dybvig Corporation's common stock has a beta of 1.21. If the risk-free rate is 3.5 percent and the expected return on the market is 11 percent, what is Dybvig's cost of equity capital?

2. **Calculating Cost of Debt**   Advance, Inc., is trying to determine its cost of debt. The firm has a debt issue outstanding with 17 years to maturity that is quoted at 95 percent of face value. The issue makes semiannual payments and has a coupon

rate of 8 percent annually. What is Advance's pretax cost of debt? If the tax rate is 35 percent, what is the aftertax cost of debt?

3. **Calculating Cost of Debt**   Shanken Corp. issued a 30-year, 6.2 percent semiannual bond 7 years ago. The bond currently sells for 108 percent of its face value. The company's tax rate is 35 percent.

   a. What is the pretax cost of debt?
   b. What is the aftertax cost of debt?
   c. Which is more relevant, the pretax or the aftertax cost of debt? Why?

4. **Calculating Cost of Debt**   For the firm in the previous problem, suppose the book value of the debt issue is $70 million. In addition, the company has a second debt issue on the market, a zero coupon bond with 12 years left to maturity; the book value of this issue is $100 million and the bonds sell for 61 percent of par. What is the company's total book value of debt? The total market value? What is your best estimate of the aftertax cost of debt now?

5. **Calculating WACC**   Mullineaux Corporation has a target capital structure of 70 percent common stock and 30 percent debt. Its cost of equity is 13 percent, and the cost of debt is 6 percent. The relevant tax rate is 35 percent. What is Mullineaux's WACC?

6. **Taxes and WACC**   Miller Manufacturing has a target debt–equity ratio of .55. Its cost of equity is 14 percent, and its cost of debt is 7 percent. If the tax rate is 35 percent, what is Miller's WACC?

7. **Finding the Capital Structure**   Fama's Llamas has a weighted average cost of capital of 9.8 percent. The company's cost of equity is 13 percent, and its cost of debt is 6.5 percent. The tax rate is 35 percent. What is Fama's debt–equity ratio?

8. **Book Value versus Market Value**   Filer Manufacturing has 8.3 million shares of common stock outstanding. The current share price is $53, and the book value per share is $4. Filer Manufacturing also has two bond issues outstanding. The first bond issue has a face value of $70 million and a coupon rate of 7 percent and sells for 108.3 percent of par. The second issue has a face value of $60 million and a coupon rate of 7.5 percent and sells for 108.9 percent of par. The first issue matures in 8 years, the second in 27 years.

   a. What are Filer's capital structure weights on a book value basis?
   b. What are Filer's capital structure weights on a market value basis?
   c. Which are more relevant, the book or market value weights? Why?

9. **Calculating the WACC**   In the previous problem, suppose the company's stock has a beta of 1.2. The risk-free rate is 3.1 percent, and the market risk premium is 7 percent. Assume that the overall cost of debt is the weighted average implied by the two outstanding debt issues. Both bonds make semiannual payments. The tax rate is 35 percent. What is the company's WACC?

10. **WACC**   Kose, Inc., has a target debt–equity ratio of .45. Its WACC is 11.2 percent, and the tax rate is 35 percent.

   a. If Kose's cost of equity is 15 percent, what is its pretax cost of debt?
   b. If instead you know that the aftertax cost of debt is 6.4 percent, what is the cost of equity?

11. **Finding the WACC**   Given the following information for Huntington Power Co., find the WACC. Assume the company's tax rate is 35 percent.

Debt:	5,000 6 percent coupon bonds outstanding, $1,000 par value, 25 years to maturity, selling for 105 percent of par; the bonds make semiannual payments.
Common stock:	175,000 shares outstanding, selling for $58 per share; the beta is 1.10.
Market:	7 percent market risk premium and 5 percent risk-free rate.

12. **Finding the WACC** Titan Mining Corporation has 9.3 million shares of common stock outstanding and 260,000 6.8 percent semiannual bonds outstanding, par value $1,000 each. The common stock currently sells for $34 per share and has a beta of 1.20, and the bonds have 20 years to maturity and sell for 104 percent of par. The market risk premium is 7 percent, T-bills are yielding 3.5 percent, and Titan Mining's tax rate is 35 percent.

   a. What is the firm's market value capital structure?

   b. If Titan Mining is evaluating a new investment project that has the same risk as the firm's typical project, what rate should the firm use to discount the project's cash flows?

13. **SML and WACC** An all-equity firm is considering the following projects:

Project	Beta	IRR
W	.80	9.4%
X	.95	10.9
Y	1.15	13.0
Z	1.45	14.2

   The T-bill rate is 3.5 percent, and the expected return on the market is 11 percent.

   a. Which projects have a higher expected return than the firm's 11 percent cost of capital?

   b. Which projects should be accepted?

   c. Which projects would be incorrectly accepted or rejected if the firm's overall cost of capital was used as a hurdle rate?

14. **Calculating Flotation Costs** Suppose your company needs $20 million to build a new assembly line. Your target debt–equity ratio is .75. The flotation cost for new equity is 7 percent, but the flotation cost for debt is only 3 percent. Your boss has decided to fund the project by borrowing money because the flotation costs are lower and the needed funds are relatively small.

   a. What do you think about the rationale behind borrowing the entire amount?

   b. What is your company's weighted average flotation cost, assuming all equity is raised externally?

   c. What is the true cost of building the new assembly line after taking flotation costs into account? Does it matter in this case that the entire amount is being raised from debt?

15. **Calculating Flotation Costs** Southern Alliance Company needs to raise $55 million to start a new project and will raise the money by selling new bonds. The company will generate no internal equity for the foreseeable future. The company has a target capital structure of 65 percent common stock, 5 percent preferred stock, and 30 percent debt. Flotation costs for issuing new common stock are 8 percent, for new preferred stock, 5 percent, and for new debt, 3 percent. What is the true initial cost figure Southern should use when evaluating its project?

16. **WACC and NPV** Och, Inc., is considering a project that will result in initial aftertax cash savings of $3.5 million at the end of the first year, and these savings will grow at a rate of 4 percent per year indefinitely. The firm has a target debt–equity ratio of .55, a cost of equity of 13 percent, and an aftertax cost of debt of 5.5 percent. The cost-saving proposal is somewhat riskier than the usual projects the firm undertakes; management uses the subjective approach and applies an adjustment factor of +2 percent to the cost of capital for such risky projects. Under what circumstances should Och take on the project?

17. **Preferred Stock and WACC** The Saunders Investment Bank has the following financing outstanding. What is the WACC for the company?

Debt:	60,000 bonds with a coupon rate of 6 percent and a current price quote of 109.5; the bonds have 20 years to maturity. 230,000 zero coupon bonds with a price quote of 17.5 and 30 years until maturity.
Preferred stock:	150,000 shares of 4 percent preferred stock with a current price of $79, and a par value of $100.
Common stock:	2,600,000 shares of common stock; the current price is $65, and the beta of the stock is 1.15.
Market:	The corporate tax rate is 40 percent, the market risk premium is 7 percent, and the risk-free rate is 4 percent.

18. **Flotation Costs** Goodbye, Inc., recently issued new securities to finance a new TV show. The project cost $19 million, and the company paid $1,150,000 in flotation costs. In addition, the equity issued had a flotation cost of 7 percent of the amount raised, whereas the debt issued had a flotation cost of 3 percent of the amount raised. If Goodbye issued new securities in the same proportion as its target capital structure, what is the company's target debt–equity ratio?

19. **Calculating the Cost of Equity** Floyd Industries stock has a beta of 1.3. The company just paid a dividend of $.95, and the dividends are expected to grow at 4.5 percent per year. The expected return on the market is 11 percent, and Treasury bills are yielding 4.3 percent. The most recent stock price for Floyd is $64.

   a. Calculate the cost of equity using the DDM method.
   b. Calculate the cost of equity using the SML method.
   c. Why do you think your estimates in (a) and (b) are so different?

20. **Firm Valuation** Schultz Industries is considering the purchase of Arras Manufacturing. Arras is currently a supplier for Schultz, and the acquisition would allow Schultz to better control its material supply. The current cash flow from assets for Arras is $7.5 million. The cash flows are expected to grow at 8 percent for the next five years before leveling off to 4 percent for the indefinite future. The cost of capital for Schultz and Arras is 12 percent and 10 percent, respectively. Arras currently has 3 million shares of stock outstanding and $25 million in debt outstanding. What is the maximum price per share Schultz should pay for Arras?

21. **Firm Valuation** Happy Times, Inc., wants to expand its party stores into the Southeast. In order to establish an immediate presence in the area, the company is considering the purchase of the privately held Joe's Party Supply. Happy Times currently has debt outstanding with a market value of $140 million and a YTM of 6 percent. The company's market capitalization is $380 million, and the required return on equity is 11 percent. Joe's currently has debt outstanding with a market value of $30.5 million. The EBIT for Joe's next year is projected to be $12.5 million. EBIT is expected to grow at 10 percent per year for the next five years before slowing to 3 percent in perpetuity. Net working capital, capital spending, and depreciation as a percentage of EBIT are expected to be 9 percent, 15 percent, and 8 percent, respectively. Joe's has 1.85 million shares outstanding and the tax rate for both companies is 38 percent.

   a. Based on these estimates, what is the maximum share price that Happy Times should be willing to pay for Joe's?
   b. After examining your analysis, the CFO of Happy Times is uncomfortable using the perpetual growth rate in cash flows. Instead, she feels that the terminal value should be estimated using the EV/EBITDA multiple. If the appropriate EV/EBITDA multiple is 8, what is your new estimate of the maximum share price for the purchase?

CHALLENGE
(Questions 22–24)

22. **Flotation Costs and NPV** Photochronograph Corporation (PC) manufactures time series photographic equipment. It is currently at its target debt–equity ratio of .55. It's considering building a new $50 million manufacturing facility. This new plant is expected to generate aftertax cash flows of $6.7 million a year in perpetuity. The company raises all equity from outside financing. There are three financing options:

1. *A new issue of common stock:* The flotation costs of the new common stock would be 8 percent of the amount raised. The required return on the company's new equity is 14 percent.

2. *A new issue of 20-year bonds:* The flotation costs of the new bonds would be 4 percent of the proceeds. If the company issues these new bonds at an annual coupon rate of 8 percent, they will sell at par.

3. *Increased use of accounts payable financing:* Because this financing is part of the company's ongoing daily business, it has no flotation costs, and the company assigns it a cost that is the same as the overall firm WACC. Management has a target ratio of accounts payable to long-term debt of .20. (Assume there is no difference between the pretax and aftertax accounts payable cost.)

What is the NPV of the new plant? Assume that PC has a 35 percent tax rate.

23. **Flotation Costs** Trower Corp. has a debt–equity ratio of .85. The company is considering a new plant that will cost $145 million to build. When the company issues new equity, it incurs a flotation cost of 8 percent. The flotation cost on new debt is 3.5 percent. What is the initial cost of the plant if the company raises all equity externally? What if it typically uses 60 percent retained earnings? What if all equity investments are financed through retained earnings?

24. **Project Evaluation** This is a comprehensive project evaluation problem bringing together much of what you have learned in this and previous chapters. Suppose you have been hired as a financial consultant to Defense Electronics, Inc. (DEI), a large, publicly traded firm that is the market share leader in radar detection systems (RDSs). The company is looking at setting up a manufacturing plant overseas to produce a new line of RDSs. This will be a five-year project. The company bought some land three years ago for $7.5 million in anticipation of using it as a toxic dump site for waste chemicals, but it built a piping system to safely discard the chemicals instead. The land was appraised last week for $7.1 million. In five years, the aftertax value of the land will be $7.4 million, but the company expects to keep the land for a future project. The company wants to build its new manufacturing plant on this land; the plant and equipment will cost $40 million to build. The following market data on DEI's securities is current:

Debt:	260,000 6.8 percent coupon bonds outstanding, 25 years to maturity, selling for 103 percent of par; the bonds have a $1,000 par value each and make semiannual payments.
Common stock:	9,500,000 shares outstanding, selling for $67 per share; the beta is 1.25.
Preferred stock:	450,000 shares of 5.25 percent preferred stock outstanding, selling for $84 per share and having a par value of $100.
Market:	7 percent expected market risk premium; 3.6 percent risk-free rate.

DEI uses G.M. Wharton as its lead underwriter. Wharton charges DEI spreads of 6.5 percent on new common stock issues, 4.5 percent on new preferred stock issues, and 3 percent on new debt issues. Wharton has included all direct and indirect issuance costs (along with its profit) in setting these spreads. Wharton has recommended to DEI that it raise the funds needed to build the plant by issuing new shares of common stock. DEI's tax rate is 35 percent. The project requires $1,400,000 in initial net working capital investment to get operational. Assume Wharton raises all equity for new projects externally.

www.mhhe.com/rwj

a. Calculate the project's initial Time 0 cash flow, taking into account all side effects.
b. The new RDS project is somewhat riskier than a typical project for DEI, primarily because the plant is being located overseas. Management has told you to use an adjustment factor of +2 percent to account for this increased riskiness. Calculate the appropriate discount rate to use when evaluating DEI's project.
c. The manufacturing plant has an eight-year tax life, and DEI uses straight-line depreciation. At the end of the project (that is, the end of Year 5), the plant and equipment can be scrapped for $8.5 million. What is the aftertax salvage value of this plant and equipment?
d. The company will incur $7,900,000 in annual fixed costs. The plan is to manufacture 18,000 RDSs per year and sell them at $10,900 per machine; the variable production costs are $9,450 per RDS. What is the annual operating cash flow (OCF) from this project?
e. DEI's comptroller is primarily interested in the impact of DEI's investments on the bottom line of reported accounting statements. What will you tell her is the accounting break-even quantity of RDSs sold for this project?
f. Finally, DEI's president wants you to throw all your calculations, assumptions, and everything else into the report for the chief financial officer; all he wants to know is what the RDS project's internal rate of return (IRR) and net present value (NPV) are. What will you report?

Mini Case

THE COST OF CAPITAL FOR GOFF COMPUTER, INC.

You have recently been hired by Goff Computer, Inc. (GCI), in the finance area. GCI was founded eight years ago by Chris Goff and currently operates 74 stores in the Southeast. GCI is privately owned by Chris and his family and had sales of $97 million last year.

GCI sells primarily to in-store customers. Customers come to the store and talk with a sales representative. The sales representative assists the customer in determining the type of computer and peripherals that are necessary for the individual customer's computing needs. After the order is taken, the customer pays for the order immediately, and the computer is assembled to fill the order. Delivery of the computer averages 15 days but is guaranteed in 30 days.

GCI's growth to date has been financed from its profits. Whenever the company had sufficient capital, it would open a new store. Relatively little formal analysis has been used in the capital budgeting process. Chris has just read about capital budgeting techniques and has come to you for help. The company has never attempted to determine its cost of capital, and Chris would like you to perform the analysis. Because the company is privately owned, it is difficult to determine the cost of equity for the company. You have determined that to estimate the cost of capital for GCI, you will use Dell as a representative company. The following steps will allow you to calculate this estimate:

1. Most publicly traded corporations are required to submit 10Q (quarterly) and 10K (annual) reports to the SEC detailing their financial operations over the previous quarter or year, respectively. These corporate filings are available on the SEC website at www.sec.gov. Go to the SEC website, follow the "Search for Company Filings" link and the "Companies & Other Filers" link, enter "Dell Computer," and search for SEC filings made by Dell. Find the most recent 10Q and 10K and download the forms. Look on the balance sheet to find the book value of debt and the book value of equity. If you look further down the report, you should find a section titled either "Long-Term Debt" or "Long-Term Debt and Interest Rate Risk Management" that will list a breakdown of Dell's long-term debt.

2. To estimate the cost of equity for Dell, go to finance.yahoo.com and enter the ticker symbol "DELL." Follow the various links to find answers to the following questions:

What is the most recent stock price listed for Dell? What is the market value of equity, or market capitalization? How many shares of stock does Dell have outstanding? What is the beta for Dell? Now go back to finance.yahoo.com and follow the "Bonds" link. What is the yield on 3-month Treasury bills? Using a 7 percent market risk premium, what is the cost of equity for Dell using the CAPM?

3. Go to www.reuters.com and find the list of competitors in the industry. Find the beta for each of these competitors, and then calculate the industry average beta. Using the industry average beta, what is the cost of equity? Does it matter if you use the beta for Dell or the beta for the industry in this case?

4. You now need to calculate the cost of debt for Dell. Go to cxa.marketwatch.com/finra/BondCenter/Default.aspx, enter Dell as the company, and find the yield to maturity for each of Dell's bonds. What is the weighted average cost of debt for Dell using the book value weights and the market value weights? Does it make a difference in this case if you use book value weights or market value weights?

5. You now have all the necessary information to calculate the weighted average cost of capital for Dell. Calculate the weighted average cost of capital for Dell using book value weights and market value weights assuming Dell has a 35 percent marginal tax rate. Which cost of capital number is more relevant?

6. You used Dell as a representative company to estimate the cost of capital for GCI. What are some of the potential problems with this approach in this situation? What improvements might you suggest?

Appendix 13A   Economic Value Added and the Measurement of Financial Performance

To access the appendix for this chapter, please visit www.mhhe.com/rwj.

Appendix 13A Economic Value Added and the Measurement of Financial Performance

Chapter 13 shows how to calculate the appropriate discount rate for capital budgeting and other valuation problems. We now consider the measurement of financial performance. We introduce the concept of economic value added, which uses the same discount rate developed for capital budgeting. We begin with a simple example.

Many years ago, Henry Bodenheimer started Bodie's Blimps, one of the largest high-speed blimp manufacturers. Because growth was so rapid, Henry put most of his effort into capital budgeting. His approach to capital budgeting paralleled that of Chapter 13. He forecast cash flows for various projects and discounted them at the cost of capital appropriate to the beta of the blimp business. However, these projects have grown rapidly, in some cases becoming whole divisions. He now needs to evaluate the performance of these divisions to reward his division managers. How does he perform the appropriate analysis?

Henry is aware that capital budgeting and performance measurement are essentially mirror images of each other. Capital budgeting is forward-looking because we must estimate future cash flows to value a project. By contrast, performance measurement is backward-looking. As Henry stated to a group of his executives, "Capital budgeting is like looking through the windshield while driving a car. You need to know what lies farther down the road to calculate a net present value. Performance measurement is like looking into the rearview mirror. You find out where you have been."

Henry first measured the performance of his various divisions by return on assets (ROA). For example, if a division had earnings after tax of $1,000 and had assets of $10,000, the ROA would be:[1]

$$\frac{\$1,000}{\$10,000} = 10\%$$

He calculated the ROA ratio for each of his divisions, paying a bonus to each of his division managers based on the size of that division's ROA. However, while ROA was generally effective in motivating his managers, there were a number of situations where it appeared that ROA was counterproductive.

For example, Henry always believed that Sharon Smith, head of the supersonic division, was his best manager. The ROA of Smith's division was generally in the high double digits, but the best estimate of the weighted average cost of capital for the division was only 20 percent. Furthermore, the division had been growing rapidly. However, as soon as Henry paid bonuses based on ROA, the division stopped growing. At that time, Smith's division had aftertax earnings of $2,000,000 on an asset base of $2,000,000, for an ROA of 100 percent (= $2 million/$2 million).

Henry found out why the growth stopped when he suggested a project to Smith that would earn $1,000,000 per year on an investment of $2,000,000. This was clearly an attractive project with an ROA of 50 percent (= $1 million/$2 million). He thought that Smith would jump at the chance to place his project into her division because the ROA of the project was much higher than the cost of capital of 20 percent. However, Smith did everything she could to kill the project. And, as Henry later figured out, Smith was rational to do so. Smith must have realized that if the project were accepted, the division's ROA would become:

$$\frac{\$2,000,000 + \$1,000,000}{\$2,000,000 + \$2,000,000} = 75\%$$

---

[1]Earnings after tax is EBIT $(1 - t_c)$ where EBIT is earnings before interest and taxes and t_c is the tax rate.

Thus the ROA of Smith's division would fall from 100 percent to 75 percent if the project were accepted, with Smith's bonus falling in tandem.

Henry was later exposed to the economic value added (EVA) approach,[2] which seems to obviate this particular problem. The formula for EVA is:

$$[\text{ROA} - \text{Weighted average cost of capital}] \times \text{Total capital}$$

Without the new project, the EVA of Smith's division would be:

$$[100\% - 20\%] \times \$2,000,000 = \$1,600,000$$

This is an annual number. That is, the division would bring in $1.6 million above and beyond the cost of capital to the firm each year.

With the new project included, the EVA would jump to:

$$[75\% - 20\%] \times \$4,000,000 = \$2,200,000$$

If Sharon Smith knew that her bonus was based on EVA, she would now have an incentive to accept, not reject, the project. Although ROA appears in the EVA formula, EVA differs substantially from ROA. The big difference is that ROA is a percentage number and EVA is a dollar value. In the preceding example, EVA increased when the new project was added even though the ROA actually decreased. In this situation, EVA correctly incorporates the fact that a high return on a large division may be better than a very high return on a smaller division. The situation here is quite similar to the scale problem in capital budgeting that we discussed in Section 5.5.

Further understanding of EVA can be achieved by rewriting the EVA formula. Because ROA × total capital is equal to earnings after tax, we can write the EVA formula as

$$\text{Earnings after tax} - \text{Weighted average cost of capital} \times \text{Total capital}$$

Thus, EVA can simply be viewed as earnings after capital costs. Although accountants subtract many costs (including depreciation) to get the earnings number shown in financial reports, they do not subtract out capital costs. We can see the logic of accountants because the cost of capital is very subjective. By contrast, costs such as COGS (cost of goods sold), SGA (sales, general, and administration), and even depreciation can be measured more objectively. However, even if the cost of capital is difficult to estimate, it is hard to justify ignoring it completely. After all, this textbook argues that the cost of capital is a necessary input to capital budgeting. Shouldn't it also be a necessary input to performance measurement?

This example argues that EVA can increase investment for firms that are currently underinvesting. However, there are many firms in the reverse situation: The managers are so focused on increasing earnings that they take on projects for which the profits do not justify the capital outlays. These managers either are unaware of capital costs or, knowing these costs, choose to ignore them. Because the cost of capital is right in the middle of the EVA formula, managers will not easily ignore these costs when evaluated on an EVA system.

One other advantage of EVA is that it is so stark: The number is either positive or it is negative. Plenty of divisions have negative EVAs for a number of years. Because these divisions are destroying more value than they are creating, a strong point can be made for liquidating these divisions. Although managers are generally emotionally opposed to this type of action, EVA analysis makes liquidation harder to ignore.

---

[2]Stern Stewart & Company have a copyright on the terms *economic value added* and *EVA*. Details on the Stern Stewart & Company EVA can be found in J. M. Stern, G. B. Stewart, and D. A. Chew, "The EVA Financial Management System," *Journal of Applied Corporate Finance* (Summer 1999).

The preceding discussion puts EVA in a positive light. However, we can certainly find much to criticize with EVA as well. We now focus on two well-known problems with EVA. First, the preceding example uses EVA for performance measurement, where we believe it properly belongs. To us, EVA seems a clear improvement over ROA and other financial ratios. However, EVA has little to offer for capital budgeting because EVA focuses only on current earnings. By contrast, net present value analysis uses projections of all future cash flows, where the cash flows will generally differ from year to year. Thus, as far as capital budgeting is concerned, NPV analysis has a richness that EVA does not have. Although supporters may argue that EVA correctly incorporates the weighted average cost of capital, remember that the discount rate in NPV analysis is the same weighted average cost of capital. That is, both approaches take the cost of equity capital based on beta and combine it with the cost of debt to get an estimate of this weighted average.

A second problem with EVA is that it may increase the shortsightedness of managers. Under EVA, a manager will be well rewarded today if earnings are high today. Future losses may not harm the manager because there is a good chance that she will be promoted or have left the firm by then. Thus, the manager has an incentive to run a division with more regard for short-term than long-term value. By raising prices or cutting quality, the manager may increase current profits (and therefore current EVA). However, to the extent that customer satisfaction is reduced, future profits (and, therefore, future EVA) are likely to fall. But we should not be too harsh with EVA here because the same problem occurs with ROA. A manager who raises prices or cuts quality will increase current ROA at the expense of future ROA. The problem, then, is not EVA per se but with the use of accounting numbers in general. Because stockholders want the discounted present value of all cash flows to be maximized, managers with bonuses based on some function of current profits or current cash flows are likely to behave in a shortsighted way.

EXAMPLE 13A.1

EVA   Assume the following figures for the International Trade Corporation:

$$EBIT = \$2.5 \text{ billion}$$
$$t_c = .4$$
$$R_{WACC} = 11\%$$
$$\text{Total capital contributed} = \text{Total debt} + \text{Equity}$$
$$= \$10 \text{ billion} + \$10 \text{ billion}$$
$$= \$20 \text{ billion}$$

Now we can calculate International Trade's EVA:

$$EVA = EBIT (1 - t_c) - R_{WACC} \times \text{Total capital}$$
$$= (\$2.5 \text{ billion} \times .6) - (.11 \times \$20 \text{ billion})$$
$$= \$1.5 \text{ billion} - \$2.2 \text{ billion}$$
$$= -\$700 \text{ million}$$

Capital Structure and Dividend Policy

CHAPTER 14

Efficient Capital Markets and Behavioral Challenges

The NASDAQ stock market was raging in the late 1990s, gaining about 23 percent, 14 percent, 35 percent, and 62 percent from 1996 to 1999, respectively. Of course, that spectacular run came to a jarring halt, and the NASDAQ lost about 40 percent in 2000, followed by another 30 percent in 2001. The ISDEX, an index of Internet-related stocks, rose from 100 in January 1996 to 1,100 in February 2000, a gain of about 1,000 percent! It then fell like a rock to 600 by May 2000.

Nowhere was the tech bubble more evident than in the initial public offering (IPO) market. In the IPO market, companies offer stock for sale for the first time, and large initial gains are not uncommon. However, during 1999 to 2000, stupendous gains became commonplace. For example, stock in VA Linux shot up 698 percent in the first day of trading! Over this period, a total of 194 IPOs doubled, or more than doubled, in value on the first day. In contrast, only 39 companies had done so in the preceding 24 years.

The performance of the NASDAQ over this period, and particularly the rise and fall of Internet stocks, has been described by many as one of the greatest market "bubbles" in history. The argument is that prices were inflated to economically ridiculous levels before investors came to their senses, which then caused the bubble to pop and prices to plunge. Debate over whether the stock market of the late 1990s really was a bubble has generated much controversy. In this chapter, we discuss the competing ideas, present some evidence on both sides, and then examine the implications for financial managers.

▲ For updates on the latest happenings in finance, visit www.rwjcorporatefinance.blogspot.com

14.1 Can Financing Decisions Create Value?

Earlier parts of the book showed how to evaluate projects according to the net present value criterion. The real world is a competitive one where projects with positive net present value are not always easy to come by. However, through hard work or through good fortune, a firm can identify winning projects. For example, to create value from capital budgeting decisions, the firm is likely to:

1. Locate an unsatisfied demand for a particular product or service.
2. Create a barrier to make it more difficult for other firms to compete.
3. Produce products or services at a lower cost than the competition.
4. Be the first to develop a new product.

The next five chapters concern *financing* decisions. Typical financing decisions include how much and what types of debt and equity to sell, and when to sell them. Just as the net present value criterion was used to evaluate capital budgeting projects, we now want to use the same criterion to evaluate financing decisions.

Though the procedure for evaluating financing decisions is identical to the procedure for evaluating projects, the results are different. It turns out that the typical firm has many more capital expenditure opportunities with positive net present values than financing opportunities with positive net present values. In fact, we later show that some plausible financial models imply that no valuable financial opportunities exist at all.

Though this dearth of profitable financing opportunities will be examined in detail later, a few remarks are in order now. We maintain that there are basically three ways to create valuable financing opportunities:

1. *Fool investors.* Assume that a firm can raise capital either by issuing stock or by issuing a more complex security—say, a combination of stock and warrants. Suppose that, in truth, 100 shares of stock are worth the same as 50 units of our complex security. If investors have a misguided, overly optimistic view of the complex security, perhaps the 50 units can be sold for more than the 100 shares of stock. Clearly, this complex security provides a valuable financing opportunity because the firm is getting more than fair value for it.

   Financial managers try to package securities to receive the greatest value. A cynic might view this as attempting to fool investors.

   However, the theory of efficient capital markets implies that investors cannot easily be fooled. It says that securities are appropriately priced at all times, implying that the market as a whole is shrewd indeed. In our example, 50 units of the complex security would sell for the same price as 100 shares of stock. Thus, corporate managers cannot attempt to create value by fooling investors. Instead, managers must create value in other ways.

2. *Reduce costs or increase subsidies.* We show later in the book that certain forms of financing have greater tax advantages than other forms. Clearly, a firm packaging securities to minimize taxes can increase firm value. In addition, any financing technique involves other costs. For example, investment bankers, lawyers, and accountants must be paid. A firm packaging securities to minimize these costs can also increase its value.

EXAMPLE 14.1

Valuing Financial Subsidies   Suppose Vermont Electronics Company is thinking about relocating its plant to Mexico where labor costs are lower. In the hope that it can stay in Vermont, the company has submitted an application to the state of Vermont to issue $2 million in five-year, tax-exempt industrial bonds. The coupon rate on industrial revenue bonds in Vermont is currently 5 percent. This is an attractive rate because the normal cost of debt capital for Vermont Electronics Company is 10 percent. The firm will pay annual interest of $100,000 (= $2 million × 5%), rather than annual interest of $200,000 (= $2 million × 10%). What is the NPV of this potential financing transaction?

If the application is accepted and the industrial revenue bonds are issued by the Vermont Electronics Company, the NPV (ignoring corporate taxes) is:

$$\text{NPV} = \$2,000,000 - \left[\frac{\$100,000}{1.1} + \frac{\$100,000}{(1.1)^2} + \frac{\$100,000}{(1.1)^3} + \frac{\$100,000}{(1.1)^4} + \frac{\$2,100,000}{(1.1)^5} \right]$$

$$= \$2,000,000 - \$1,620,921$$

$$= \$379,079$$

This transaction has a positive NPV. The Vermont Electronics Company obtains subsidized financing where the value of the subsidy is $379,079.

3. *Create a new security.* There has been a surge in financial innovation in recent decades. For example, in a speech on financial innovation, Nobel laureate Merton Miller asked the rhetorical question, "Can any 20-year period in recorded history have witnessed even a tenth as much new development? Where corporations once issued only straight debt and straight common stock, they now issue zero coupon bonds, adjustable rate notes, floating-rate notes, putable bonds, credit-enhanced debt securities, receivable-backed securities, adjusted-rate preferred stock, convertible adjustable preferred stock, auction rate preferred stock, single-point adjustable rate stock, convertible exchangeable preferred stock, adjustable-rate convertible debt, zero coupon convertible debt, debt with mandatory common stock purchase contracts—to name just a few!"[1] And financial innovation has occurred even more rapidly in the years following Miller's speech.

    Though the advantages of each instrument are different, one general theme is that these new securities cannot easily be duplicated by combinations of existing securities. Thus, previously unsatisfied clientele may pay extra for a specialized security catering to its needs. For example, putable bonds let the purchaser sell the bond at a fixed price back to the firm. This innovation creates a price floor, allowing the investor to reduce her downside risk. Perhaps risk-averse investors or investors with little knowledge of the bond market would find this feature particularly attractive.

    Corporations gain by issuing these unique securities at high prices. However, the value captured by the innovator may well be small in the long run because the innovator usually cannot patent or copyright an idea. Soon many firms are issuing securities of the same kind, forcing prices down as a result.

This brief introduction sets the stage for the next several chapters of the book. Most of the rest of this chapter examines how efficient capital markets work. We show that if capital markets are efficient, corporate managers cannot create value by fooling investors. This is quite important because managers must create value in other, perhaps more difficult, ways. We also describe behavioral challenges to the notion of perfectly efficient capital markets.

14.2 A Description of Efficient Capital Markets

An efficient capital market for stocks is one in which stock prices fully reflect available information about the underlying value of the stock. To illustrate how an efficient market works, suppose the F-stop Camera Corporation (FCC) is attempting to develop a camera that will double the speed of the auto-focusing system now available. FCC believes this research has a positive NPV.

Now consider a share of stock in FCC. What determines the willingness of investors to hold shares of FCC at a particular price? One important factor is the probability that FCC will be the first company to develop the new auto-focusing system. In an efficient market, we would expect the price of the shares of FCC to increase if this probability increases.

---

[1]M. Miller, "Financial Innovation: The Last Twenty Years and the Next," *Journal of Financial and Quantitative Analysis* (December 1986).

Suppose FCC hires a well-known engineer to develop the new auto-focusing system. In an efficient market, what will happen to FCC's share price when this is announced? If the engineer is paid a salary that fully reflects his contribution to the firm, the price of the stock will not necessarily change. Suppose instead that hiring the engineer is a positive NPV transaction. In this case, the price of shares in FCC will increase because the firm can pay the engineer a salary below his true value to the company.

When will the increase in the price of FCC's shares occur? Assume that the hiring announcement is made in a press release on Wednesday morning. In an efficient market, the price of shares in FCC will *immediately* adjust to this new information. Investors should not be able to buy the stock on Wednesday afternoon and make a profit on Thursday. This would imply that it took the stock market a day to realize the implication of the FCC press release. The efficient market hypothesis predicts that the price of shares of FCC stock on Wednesday afternoon will already reflect the information contained in the Wednesday morning press release.

The **efficient market hypothesis** (EMH) has implications for investors and for firms:

- Because information is reflected in prices immediately, investors should only expect to obtain a normal rate of return. Awareness of information when it is released does an investor no good. The price adjusts before the investor has time to trade on it.

- Firms should expect to receive fair value for securities that they sell. *Fair* means that the price they receive from issuing securities is the present value. Thus, valuable financing opportunities that arise from fooling investors are unavailable in efficient capital markets.

Figure 14.1 presents several possible adjustments in stock prices. The solid line represents the path taken by the stock in an efficient market. In this case, the price

Figure 14.1
Reaction of Stock Price to New Information in Efficient and Inefficient Markets

Days before (−) and after (+) announcement

Efficient market response: The price instantaneously adjusts to and fully reflects new information; there is no tendency for subsequent increases and decreases.

Slow response: The price adjusts slowly to the new information; 30 days elapse before the price completely reflects the new information.

Overreaction: The price overadjusts to the new information; there is a bubble in the price sequence.

adjusts immediately to the new information with no further price changes. The dotted line depicts a slow reaction. Here it takes the market 30 days to fully absorb the information. Finally, the broken line illustrates an overreaction and subsequent correction back to the true price. The broken line and the dotted line show the paths that the stock price might take in an inefficient market. If the price of the stock takes several days to adjust, trading profits would be available to investors who suitably timed their purchases and sales.[2]

FOUNDATIONS OF MARKET EFFICIENCY

Figure 14.1 shows the consequences of market efficiency. But what are the conditions that *cause* market efficiency? Andrei Shleifer argues that there are three conditions, any one of which will lead to efficiency:[3] (1) rationality, (2) independent deviations from rationality, and (3) arbitrage. A discussion of these conditions follows.

Rationality   Imagine that all investors are rational. When new information is released in the marketplace, all investors will adjust their estimates of stock prices in a rational way. In our example, investors will use the information in FCC's press release, in conjunction with existing information about the firm, to determine the NPV of FCC's new venture. If the information in the press release implies that the NPV of the venture is $10 million and there are 2 million shares, investors will calculate that the NPV is $5 per share. While FCC's old price might be, say, $40, no one would now transact at that price. Anyone interested in selling would sell only at a price of at least $45 (= $40 + 5). And anyone interested in buying would now be willing to pay up to $45. In other words, the price would rise by $5. And the price would rise immediately because rational investors would see no reason to wait before trading at the new price.

Of course, we all know times when individuals seem to behave less than perfectly rationally. Thus, perhaps it is too much to ask that *all* investors behave rationally. But the market will still be efficient if the following scenario holds.

Independent Deviations from Rationality   Suppose that FCC's press release is not all that clear. How many new cameras are likely to be sold? At what price? What is the likely cost per camera? Will other camera companies be able to develop competing products? How long will the development of these competing products likely take? If these and other questions cannot be answered easily, it will be difficult to estimate NPV.

With so many unanswered questions, many investors may not be thinking clearly. Some investors might get caught up in the romance of a new product, hoping for and ultimately believing in sales projections well above what is rational. They would overpay for new shares. And if they needed to sell shares (perhaps to finance current

---

[2]Now you should appreciate the following short story. A student was walking down the hall with her finance professor when they both saw a $20 bill on the ground. As the student bent down to pick it up, the professor shook his head slowly and, with a look of disappointment on his face, said patiently to the student, "Don't bother. If it was really there, someone else would have already picked it up."

The moral of the story reflects the logic of the efficient market hypothesis: If you think you have found a pattern in stock prices or a simple device for picking winners, you probably have not. If there was such a simple way to make money, someone else would have found it before. Furthermore, if people tried to exploit the information, their efforts would become self-defeating and the pattern would disappear.

[3]Andrei Shleifer, *Inefficient Markets: An Introduction to Behavioral Finance* (Oxford: Oxford University Press, 2000).

consumption), they would do so only at a high price. If these individuals dominate the market, the stock price would likely rise beyond what market efficiency would predict.

However, due to emotional resistance, investors could just as easily react to new information in a pessimistic manner. After all, business historians tell us that investors were initially quite skeptical about the benefits of the telephone, the copier, the automobile, and the motion picture. Certainly, they could be overly skeptical about this new camera. If investors were primarily of this type, the stock price would likely rise less than market efficiency would predict.

But suppose that about as many individuals were irrationally optimistic as were irrationally pessimistic. Prices would likely rise in a manner consistent with market efficiency, even though most investors would be classified as less than fully rational. Thus, market efficiency does not require rational individuals—only countervailing irrationalities.

However, this assumption of offsetting irrationalities at *all* times may be unrealistic. Perhaps at certain times most investors are swept away by excessive optimism and at other times are caught in the throes of extreme pessimism. But even here there is an assumption that will produce efficiency.

Arbitrage Imagine a world with two types of individuals: the irrational amateurs and the rational professionals. The amateurs get caught up in their emotions, at times believing irrationally that a stock is undervalued and at other times believing the opposite. If the passions of the different amateurs do not cancel each other out, these amateurs, by themselves, would tend to carry stocks either above or below their efficient prices.

Now let's bring in the professionals. Suppose professionals go about their business methodically and rationally. They study companies thoroughly, they evaluate the evidence objectively, they estimate stock prices coldly and clearly, and they act accordingly. If a stock is underpriced, they would buy it. If it is overpriced, they would sell it. And their confidence would likely be greater than that of the amateurs. Whereas an amateur might risk only a small sum, these professionals might risk large ones, *knowing* as they do that the stock is mispriced. Furthermore, they would be willing to rearrange their entire portfolio in search of a profit. If they find that General Motors is underpriced, they might sell the Ford stock they own to buy GM. *Arbitrage* is the word that comes to mind here because arbitrage generates profit from the simultaneous purchase and sale of different, but substitute, securities. If the arbitrage of professionals dominates the speculation of amateurs, markets would still be efficient.

14.3 The Different Types of Efficiency

In our previous discussion, we assumed that the market responds immediately to all available information. In actuality, certain information may affect stock prices more quickly than other information. To handle differential response rates, researchers separate information into different types. The most common classification system identifies three types: Information about past prices, publicly available information, and all information. The effect of these three information sets on prices is examined next.

THE WEAK FORM

Imagine a trading strategy that recommends buying a stock after it has gone up three days in a row and recommends selling a stock after it has gone down three days in a row. This strategy uses information based only on past prices. It does not use any other information, such as earnings forecasts, merger announcements, or money supply figures. A capital market is said to be *weakly efficient*, or to satisfy **weak form efficiency,** if it fully incorporates the information in past stock prices. Thus, the preceding strategy would not be able to generate profits if weak form efficiency holds.

Often, weak form efficiency is represented mathematically as:

$$P_t = P_{t-1} + \text{Expected return} + \text{Random error}_t \tag{14.1}$$

Equation 14.1 states that the price today is equal to the sum of the last observed price plus the expected return on the stock (in dollars) plus a random component occurring over the interval. The last observed price could have occurred yesterday, last week, or last month, depending on the sampling interval. The expected return is a function of a security's risk and would be based on the models of risk and return in previous chapters. The random component is due to new information about the stock. It could be either positive or negative and has an expectation of zero. The random component in any period is unrelated to the random component in any past period. Hence, this component is not predictable from past prices. If stock prices follow Equation 14.1 they are said to follow a **random walk.**[4]

Weak form efficiency is about the weakest type of efficiency that we would expect a financial market to display because historical price information is the easiest kind of information about a stock to acquire. If it were possible to make extraordinary profits simply by finding patterns in stock price movements, everyone would do it, and any profits would disappear in the scramble.

This effect of competition can be seen in Figure 14.2. Suppose the price of a stock displays a cyclical pattern, as indicated by the wavy curve. Shrewd investors would buy at the low points, forcing those prices up. Conversely, they would sell at the high points, forcing prices down. Via competition, cyclical regularities would be eliminated, leaving only random fluctuations.

Figure 14.2

Investor Behavior Tends to Eliminate Cyclical Patterns

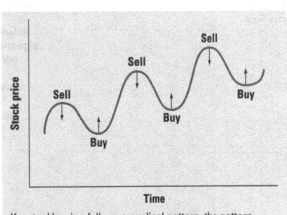

If a stock's price follows a cyclical pattern, the pattern will be quickly eliminated in an efficient market. A random pattern will emerge as investors buy at the trough and sell at the peak of a cycle.

---

[4]For purposes of this text, the random walk can be considered synonymous with weak form efficiency. Technically, the random walk is a slightly more restrictive hypothesis because it assumes that stock returns are identically distributed through time.

THE SEMISTRONG AND STRONG FORMS

If weak form efficiency is controversial, even more contentious are the two stronger types of efficiency, **semistrong form efficiency** and **strong form efficiency.** A market is semistrong form efficient if prices reflect (incorporate) all publicly available information, including information such as published accounting statements for the firm, as well as historical price information. A market is strong form efficient if prices reflect all information, public or private.

The information set of past prices is a subset of the information set of publicly available information, which in turn is a subset of all information. This is shown in Figure 14.3. Thus, strong form efficiency implies semistrong form efficiency, and semistrong form efficiency implies weak form efficiency. The reverse is not true. The distinction between semistrong form efficiency and weak form efficiency is that semistrong form efficiency requires not only that the market be efficient with respect to historical price information, but that *all* of the information available to the public be reflected in prices.

To illustrate the different forms of efficiency, imagine an investor who always sold a particular stock after its price had risen. A market that was only weak form efficient and not semistrong form efficient would still prevent such a strategy from generating excess or abnormal positive profits. According to weak form efficiency, a recent price rise does not imply that the stock is overvalued.

Now consider a firm reporting increased earnings. An individual might consider investing in the stock after reading the news release providing this information. However, if the market is semistrong form efficient, the price should rise immediately upon the news release. Thus, the investor would end up paying the higher price, eliminating all chance for an abnormal return.

Figure 14.3
Relationship among Three Different Information Sets

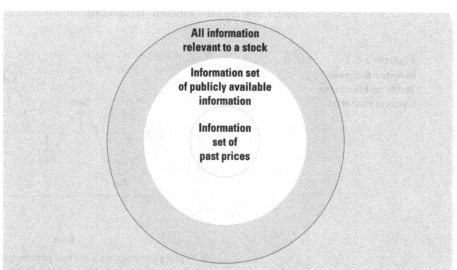

The information set of past prices is a subset of the set of all publicly available information, which in turn is a subset of all information. If today's price reflects only information about past prices, the market is weak form efficient. If today's price reflects all publicly available information, the market is semistrong form efficient. If today's price reflects all information, both public and private, the market is strong form efficient.

Semistrong form efficiency implies weak form efficiency, and strong form efficiency implies semistrong form efficiency.

At the furthest end of the spectrum is strong form efficiency. This form says that anything that is pertinent to the value of the stock and that is known to at least one investor is, in fact, fully incorporated into the stock price. A strict believer in strong form efficiency would deny that an insider who knew whether a company mining operation had struck gold could profit from that information. Such a devotee of the strong form efficient market hypothesis might argue that as soon as the insider tried to trade on his information, the market would recognize what was happening, and the price would shoot up before he could buy any of the stock. Alternatively, believers in strong form efficiency argue that there are no secrets, and as soon as the gold is discovered, the secret gets out.

One reason to expect that markets are weak form efficient is that it is so cheap and easy to find patterns in stock prices. Anyone who can program a computer and knows a little bit of statistics can search for such patterns. It stands to reason that if there were such patterns, people would find and exploit them, in the process causing them to disappear.

Semistrong form efficiency, though, implies more sophisticated investors than does weak form efficiency. An investor must be skilled at economics and statistics and steeped in the idiosyncrasies of individual industries and companies. Furthermore, to acquire and use such skills requires talent, ability, and time. In the jargon of the economist, such an effort is costly, and the ability to be successful at it is probably in scarce supply.

As for strong form efficiency, this is just further down the road than semistrong form efficiency. It is difficult to believe that the market is so efficient that someone with valuable inside information cannot prosper from it. And empirical evidence tends to be unfavorable to this form of market efficiency.

SOME COMMON MISCONCEPTIONS ABOUT THE EFFICIENT MARKET HYPOTHESIS

No idea in finance has attracted as much attention as that of efficient markets, and not all of the attention has been flattering. To a certain extent this is because much of the criticism has been based on a misunderstanding of what the hypothesis does and does not say. We illustrate three misconceptions next.

The Efficacy of Dart Throwing When the notion of market efficiency was first publicized and debated in the popular financial press, it was often characterized by the following quote: ". . . throwing darts at the financial page will produce a portfolio that can be expected to do as well as any managed by professional security analysts."[5,6] This is almost, but not quite, true.

All the efficient market hypothesis really says is that, on average, the manager cannot achieve an abnormal or excess return. The excess return is defined with respect to some benchmark expected return, such as that from the security market line (SML) of Chapter 11. The investor must still decide how risky a portfolio she wants. In addition, a random dart thrower might wind up with all of the darts sticking into one or two high-risk stocks that deal in genetic engineering. Would you really want all of your stock investments in two such stocks?

---

[5]B. G. Malkiel, *A Random Walk Down Wall Street: The Time-Tested Strategy for Successful Investing*, 10th ed. (New York: Norton, 2011).

[6]Older articles often referred to the benchmark of "dart-throwing monkeys." As government involvement in the securities industry grew, the benchmark was often restated as "dart-throwing congressional representatives."

The failure to understand this has often led to confusion about market efficiency. For example, sometimes it is wrongly argued that market efficiency means that it does not matter what you do because the efficiency of the market will protect the unwary. However, someone once remarked, "The efficient market protects the sheep from the wolves, but nothing can protect the sheep from themselves."

What efficiency does say is that the price that a firm obtains when it sells a share of its stock is a fair price in the sense that it reflects the value of that stock given the information that is available about it. Shareholders need not worry that they are paying too much for a stock with a low dividend or some other characteristic because the market has already incorporated it into the price. However, investors still have to worry about such things as their level of risk exposure and their degree of diversification.

Price Fluctuations   Much of the public is skeptical of efficiency because stock prices fluctuate from day to day. However, daily price movement is in no way inconsistent with efficiency; a stock in an efficient market adjusts to new information by changing price. A great deal of new information comes into the stock market each day. In fact, the *absence* of daily price movements in a changing world might suggest an inefficiency.

Stockholder Disinterest   Many laypeople are skeptical that the market price can be efficient if only a fraction of the outstanding shares changes hands on any given day. However, the number of traders in a stock on a given day is generally far less than the number of people following the stock. This is true because an individual will trade only when his appraisal of the value of the stock differs enough from the market price to justify incurring brokerage commissions and other transaction costs. Furthermore, even if the number of traders following a stock is small relative to the number of outstanding shareholders, the stock can be expected to be efficiently priced as long as a number of interested traders use the publicly available information. That is, the stock price can reflect the available information even if many stockholders never follow the stock and are not considering trading in the near future.

14.4   The Evidence

The evidence on the efficient market hypothesis is extensive, with studies covering the broad categories of weak form, semistrong form, and strong form efficiency. In the first category we investigate whether stock price changes are random. We review both *event studies* and studies of the performance of mutual funds in the second category. In the third category, we look at the performance of corporate insiders.

THE WEAK FORM

Weak form efficiency implies that a stock's price movement in the past is unrelated to its price movement in the future. The work of Chapter 11 allows us to test this implication. In that chapter we discussed the concept of correlation between the returns on two different stocks. For example, the correlation between the return on General Motors and the return on Ford is likely to be relatively high because both stocks are in the same industry. Conversely, the correlation between the return on General Motors and the return on the stock of, say, a European fast-food chain is likely to be low.

Financial economists frequently speak of **serial correlation,** which involves only one security. This is the correlation between the current return on a security and the

Chapter 14   Efficient Capital Markets and Behavioral Challenges   **445**

Table 14.1
Serial Correlation Coefficients for Selected Companies, 2010

Company	Serial Correlation Coefficient
Dell	.0034
Eli Lilly	.0411
Medtronic	−.0276
Merck	−.0205
Qualcomm	.0446
Sprint Nextel	−.0469
Time Warner	−.0035
Average for 100 largest companies	−.0153

Dell's coefficient of .0034 is slightly positive, implying that a positive return today makes a positive return tomorrow slightly more likely. Time Warner's coefficient is negative, implying that a positive return today makes a negative return tomorrow slightly more likely. However, the coefficients are so small relative to estimation error and transaction costs that the results are generally considered to be consistent with weak form efficient capital markets.

return on the same security over a later period. A positive coefficient of serial correlation for a particular stock indicates a tendency toward *continuation.* That is, a higher-than-average return today is likely to be followed by higher-than-average returns in the future. Similarly, a lower-than-average return today is likely to be followed by lower-than-average returns in the future.

A negative coefficient of serial correlation for a particular stock indicates a tendency toward *reversal.* A higher-than-average return today is likely to be followed by lower-than-average returns in the future. Similarly, a lower-than-average return today is likely to be followed by higher-than-average returns in the future. Both significantly positive and significantly negative serial correlation coefficients are indications of market inefficiencies; in either case, returns today can be used to predict future returns.

Serial correlation coefficients for stock returns near zero would be consistent with weak form efficiency. Thus, a current stock return that is higher than average is as likely to be followed by lower-than-average returns as by higher-than-average returns. Similarly, a current stock return that is lower than average is as likely to be followed by higher-than-average returns as by lower-than-average returns.

The first seven rows in Table 14.1 show the serial correlation coefficients for daily price changes for seven large U.S. companies. These coefficients indicate whether there are relationships between yesterday's return and today's return. As can be seen, four of the coefficients are negative, implying that a higher-than-average return today makes a lower-than-average return tomorrow more likely. Conversely, three of the coefficients are positive, implying that a higher-than-average return today makes a higher-than-average return tomorrow more likely.

The last line of the table indicates that the average serial correlation coefficient across the 100 largest U.S. stocks is −.0153. Because correlation coefficients can, in principle, vary between −1 and +1, this average coefficient is small. Given both estimation errors and transaction costs, a number of this magnitude is generally considered to be consistent with weak form efficiency.

The weak form of the efficient market hypothesis has been tested in many other ways as well. Our view of the literature is that the evidence, taken as a whole, is consistent with weak form efficiency.

This finding raises an interesting thought: If price changes are truly random, why do so many believe that prices follow patterns? The work of both psychologists and

Figure 14.4
Simulated and
Actual Stock Price
Movements

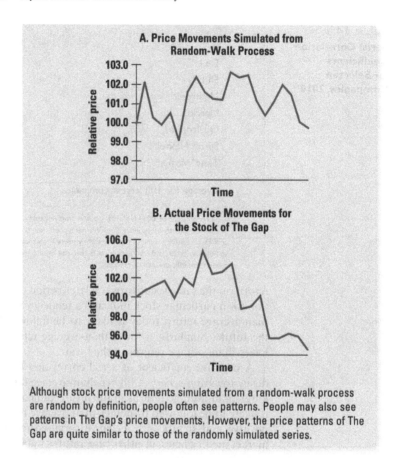

Although stock price movements simulated from a random-walk process are random by definition, people often see patterns. People may also see patterns in The Gap's price movements. However, the price patterns of The Gap are quite similar to those of the randomly simulated series.

statisticians suggests that most people simply do not know what randomness looks like. For example, consider Figure 14.4. The top graph was generated by a computer using random numbers and Equation 14.1. Yet we have found that people examining the chart generally see patterns. Different people see different patterns and forecast different future price movements. However, in our experience, viewers are all quite confident of the patterns they see.

Next, consider the bottom graph, which tracks actual movements in The Gap's stock price. This graph may look quite nonrandom to some, suggesting weak form inefficiency. However, it also bears a close visual resemblance to the simulated series, and statistical tests indicate that it indeed behaves like a purely random series. Thus, in our opinion, people claiming to see patterns in stock price data are probably seeing optical illusions.

THE SEMISTRONG FORM

The semistrong form of the efficient market hypothesis implies that prices should reflect all publicly available information. We present two types of tests of this form.

Event Studies   The *abnormal return* (AR) on a given stock for a particular day can be calculated by subtracting the market's return on the same day (R_m)—as measured by a broad-based index such as the S&P Composite Index—from the actual return (R) on the stock for that day.[7] We write this difference algebraically as:

$$AR = R - R_m$$

The following system will help us understand tests of the semistrong form:

$$\text{Information released at time } t - 1 \rightarrow AR_{t-1}$$
$$\text{Information released at time } t \quad \rightarrow AR_t$$
$$\text{Information released at time } t + 1 \rightarrow AR_{t+1}$$

The arrows indicate that the abnormal return in any time period is related only to the information released during that period.

According to the efficient market hypothesis, a stock's abnormal return at time t, AR_t, should reflect the release of information at the same time, t. Any information released before then should have no effect on abnormal returns in this period because all of its influence should have been felt before. In other words, an efficient market would already have incorporated previous information into prices. Because a stock's return today cannot depend on what the market does not yet know, information that will be known only in the future cannot influence the stock's return either. Hence, the arrows point in the direction that is shown, with information in any period affecting only that period's abnormal return. *Event studies* are statistical studies that examine whether the arrows are as shown or whether the release of information influences returns on other days.

These studies also speak of *cumulative abnormal returns* (CARs), as well as abnormal returns (ARs). As an example, consider a firm with ARs of 1 percent, −3 percent, and 6 percent for Dates −1, 0, and 1, respectively, relative to a corporate announcement. The CARs for Dates −1, 0, and 1 would be 1 percent, −2 percent [=1 percent + (−3 percent)], and 4 percent [=1 percent + (−3 percent) + 6 percent], respectively.

As an example, consider the study by Szewczyk, Tsetsekos, and Zantout[8] on dividend omissions. Figure 14.5 shows the plot of CARs for a sample of companies announcing dividend omissions. Because dividend omissions are generally considered to be bad events, we would expect abnormal returns to be negative around the time of the announcements. They are, as evidenced by a drop in the CAR on both the day before the announcement (Day −1) and the day of the announcement (Day 0).[9] However, note that there is virtually no movement in the CARs in the days following the announcement. This implies that the bad news is fully incorporated into the stock price by the announcement day, a result consistent with market efficiency.

Over the years, this type of methodology has been applied to many events. Announcements of dividends, earnings, mergers, capital expenditures, and new issues

---

[7]We can also measure the abnormal return by using the market model. In this case, the abnormal return is:

$$AR = R - (\alpha + \beta R_m)$$

[8]Samuel H. Szewczyk, George P. Tsetsekos, and Zaher Z. Zantout, "Do Dividend Omissions Signal Future Earnings or Past Earnings?" *Journal of Investing* (Spring 1997).

[9]An astute reader may wonder why the abnormal return is negative on Day −1 as well as on Day 0. To see why, first note that the announcement date is generally taken in academic studies to be the publication date of the story in *The Wall Street Journal* (*WSJ*). Then consider a company announcing a dividend omission via a press release at noon on Tuesday. The stock should fall on Tuesday. The announcement will be reported in the *WSJ* on Wednesday because the Tuesday edition of the *WSJ* has already been printed. For this firm the stock price falls on the day *before* the announcement in the *WSJ*.

Alternatively, imagine another firm announcing a dividend omission via a press release on Tuesday at 8 p.m. Because the stock market is closed at that late hour, the stock price will fall on Wednesday. Because the *WSJ* will report the announcement on Wednesday, the stock price falls on the day of the announcement in the *WSJ*.

Firms may either make announcements during trading hours or after trading hours, so stocks should fall on both Day −1 and Day 0 relative to publication in the *WSJ*.

Figure 14.5   **Cumulative Abnormal Returns for Companies Announcing Dividend Omissions**

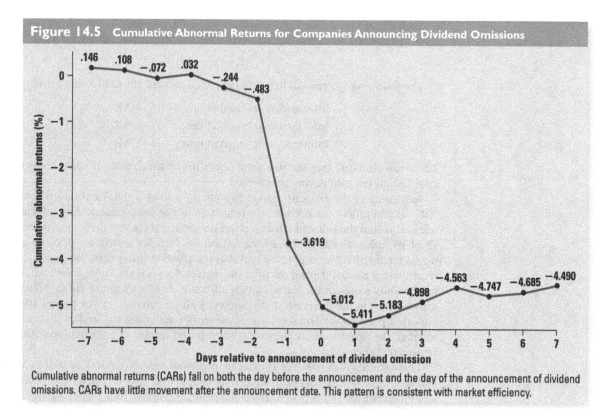

Cumulative abnormal returns (CARs) fall on both the day before the announcement and the day of the announcement of dividend omissions. CARs have little movement after the announcement date. This pattern is consistent with market efficiency.

SOURCE: From Exhibit 2 in Samuel H. Szewczyk, George P. Tsetsekos, and Zaher Z. Zantout, "Do Dividend Omissions Signal Future Earnings or Past Earnings?" *Journal of Investing* (Spring 1997).

of stock are a few examples of the vast literature in the area. The early event study tests generally supported the view that the market is semistrong form (and therefore also weak form) efficient. However, a number of more recent studies present evidence that the market does not impound all relevant information immediately. Some conclude from this that the market is not efficient. Others argue that this conclusion is unwarranted given statistical and methodological problems in the studies. This issue will be addressed in more detail later in the chapter.

The Record of Mutual Funds   If the market is efficient in the semistrong form, then no matter what publicly available information mutual fund managers rely on to pick stocks, their average returns should be the same as those of the average investor in the market as a whole. We can test market efficiency, then, by comparing the performance of actively managed mutual funds to index funds. Actively managed mutual funds try to use publicly available information and certain analytical skills to perform better than the market as a whole. Index funds are passively managed and try to replicate the performance of certain stock market indexes. The Vanguard 500 Index Fund is a well-known example of an index fund that mimics the Standard and Poor's 500 Index. Figure 14.6 is a bar chart that shows the percentage of managed equity funds that beat the Vanguard 500 Index Fund. It uses return data for the previous 10 years (from 1977–1986 through 2000–2009). In only 5 of these 24 investment

Chapter 14   Efficient Capital Markets and Behavioral Challenges   449

Figure 14.6
Percentage of Managed Equity Funds Beating the Vanguard 500 Index Fund, 10-Year Returns

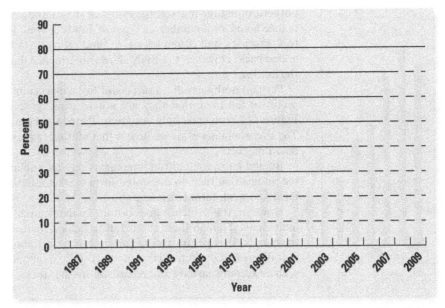

SOURCE: Bradford D. Jordan, Thomas W. Miller, and Steven D. Dolvin, *Fundamentals of Investments*, 6th ed. (New York: McGraw-Hill, 2012).

periods did more than half of the professional money managers beat the Vanguard 500 Index Fund.

Also, consider Figure 14.7, which presents the performance of various types of mutual funds relative to the stock market as a whole. The far left of the figure shows that the universe of all funds covered in the study underperforms the market by 2.13 percent per year after an appropriate adjustment for risk. Thus, rather than

Figure 14.7   Annual Return Performance* of Different Types of U.S. Mutual Funds Relative to a Broad-Based Market Index (1963–1998)

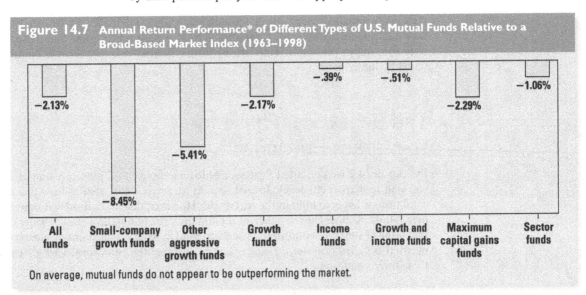

*Performance is relative to the market model.

SOURCE: Taken from Table 2 of Lubos Pastor and Robert F. Stambaugh, "Mutual Fund Performance and Seemingly Unrelated Assets," *Journal of Financial Economics* 63 (2002).

outperforming the market, the evidence shows underperformance. This underperformance holds for a number of types of funds as well. Returns in this study are net of fees, expenses, and commissions, so fund returns would be higher if these costs were added back. However, the study shows no evidence that funds, as a whole, are *beating* the market.

Perhaps nothing rankles successful stock market investors more than to have some professor tell them that they are not necessarily smart, just lucky. However, while Figure 14.7 represents only one study, there have been many papers on mutual funds. The overwhelming evidence here is that mutual funds, on average, do not beat broad-based indexes.

By and large, mutual fund managers rely on publicly available information. Thus the finding that they do not outperform market indexes is consistent with semistrong form and weak form efficiency.

However, this evidence does not imply that mutual funds are bad investments for individuals. Though these funds fail to achieve better returns than some indexes of the market, they permit the investor to buy a portfolio of many stocks (the phrase "a well-diversified portfolio" is often used). They might also provide a variety of services such as keeping custody and records of all the stocks.

THE STRONG FORM

Even the strongest adherents to the efficient market hypothesis would not be surprised to find that markets are inefficient in the strong form. After all, if an individual has information that no one else has, it is likely that she can profit from it.

One group of studies of strong form efficiency investigates insider trading. Insiders in firms have access to information that is not generally available. But if the strong form of the efficient market hypothesis holds, they should not be able to profit by trading on their information. A government agency, the Securities and Exchange Commission, requires insiders in companies to reveal any trading they might do in their own company's stock. By examining records of such trades, we can see whether they made abnormal returns. A number of studies support the view that these trades were abnormally profitable. Thus, strong form efficiency does not seem to be substantiated by the evidence.

14.5 The Behavioral Challenge to Market Efficiency

In Section 14.2 we presented Professor Shleifer's three conditions, any one of which will lead to market efficiency. In that section we made a case that at least one of the conditions is likely to hold in the real world. However, there is definitely disagreement here. Many members of the academic community (including Professor Shleifer) argue that none of the three conditions is likely to hold in reality. This point of view is based on what is called *behavioral finance*. Let us examine the behavioral view of each of these three conditions.

Rationality Are people really rational? Not always. Just travel to Atlantic City or Las Vegas to see people gambling, sometimes with large sums of money. The casino's take implies a negative expected return for the gambler. Because gambling is risky and has a negative expected return, it can never be a rational thing to do. In addition, gamblers will often bet on black at a roulette table after black has occurred a number of consecutive times, thinking that the run will continue. This strategy is faulty because roulette tables have no memory.

But, of course, gambling is only a sideshow as far as finance is concerned. Do we see irrationality in financial markets as well? The answer may well be yes. Many investors do not achieve the degree of diversification that they should. Others trade frequently, generating both commissions and taxes. In fact, taxes can be handled optimally by selling losers and holding onto winners. Although some individuals invest with tax minimization in mind, plenty of them do just the opposite. Many are more likely to sell their winners than their losers, a strategy leading to high tax payments.[10] The behavioral view is not that *all* investors are irrational. Rather, it is that some, perhaps many, investors are.

Independent Deviations from Rationality   Are deviations from rationality generally random, thereby likely to cancel out in a whole population of investors? To the contrary, psychologists have long argued that people deviate from rationality in accordance with a number of basic principles. Not all of these principles have an application to finance and market efficiency, but at least two seem to do so.

The first principle, called *representativeness,* can be explained with the gambling example just used. The gambler believing a run of black will continue is in error, because the probability of a black spin is still only about 50 percent. Gamblers behaving in this way exhibit the psychological trait of representativeness. That is, they draw conclusions from insufficient data. In other words, the gambler believes the small sample he observed is more representative of the population than it really is.

How is this related to finance? Perhaps a market dominated by representativeness leads to bubbles. People see a sector of the market—for example, Internet stocks—having a short history of high revenue growth and extrapolate that it will continue forever. When the growth inevitably stalls, prices have nowhere to go but down.

The second principle is *conservatism,* which means that people are too slow in adjusting their beliefs to new information. Suppose that your goal since childhood was to become a dentist. Perhaps you came from a family of dentists, perhaps you liked the security and relatively high income that come with that profession, or perhaps teeth always fascinated you. As things stand now, you could probably look forward to a long and productive career in that occupation. However, suppose a new drug was developed that would prevent tooth decay. That drug would clearly reduce the demand for dentists. How quickly would you realize the implications as stated here? If you were emotionally attached to dentistry, you might adjust your beliefs slowly. Family and friends could tell you to switch out of predental courses in college, but you just might not be psychologically ready to do that. Instead, you might cling to your rosy view of dentistry's future.

Perhaps there is a relationship to finance here. For example, many studies report that prices seem to adjust slowly to the information contained in earnings announcements.[11] Could it be that because of conservatism, investors are slow in adjusting their beliefs to new information? More will be said about this in the next section.

---

[10]For example, see Brad Barber and Terrance Odean, "The Courage of Misguided Convictions," *Financial Analysts Journal* (November/December 1999).

[11]For example, see Vijay Singal, *Beyond the Random Walk* (New York: Oxford University Press, 2004), Chapter 4.

Arbitrage   In Section 14.2 we suggested that professional investors, knowing that securities are mispriced, could buy the underpriced ones while selling correctly priced (or even overpriced) substitutes. This might undo any mispricing caused by emotional amateurs.

Trading of this sort is likely to be more risky than it appears at first glance. Suppose professionals generally believed that McDonald's stock was underpriced. They would buy it while selling their holdings in, say, Burger King and Wendy's. However, if amateurs were taking opposite positions, prices would adjust to correct levels only if the positions of amateurs were small relative to those of the professionals. In a world of many amateurs, a few professionals would have to take big positions to bring prices into line, perhaps even engaging heavily in short selling. Buying large amounts of one stock and short selling large amounts of other stocks is quite risky, even if the two stocks are in the same industry. Here, unanticipated bad news about McDonald's and unanticipated good news about the other two stocks would cause the professionals to register large losses.

In addition, if amateurs mispriced McDonald's today, what is to prevent McDonald's from being even *more* mispriced tomorrow? This risk of further mispricing, even in the presence of no new information, may also cause professionals to cut back their arbitrage positions. As an example, imagine a shrewd professional who believed Internet stocks were overpriced in 1998. Had he bet on a decline at that time, he would have lost in the near term since prices rose through March 2000. While his position would have eventually made money because prices later fell, near-term risk may reduce the size of arbitrage strategies.

In conclusion, the arguments presented here suggest that the theoretical underpinnings of the efficient capital markets hypothesis, presented in Section 14.2, might not hold in reality. That is, investors may be irrational, irrationality may be related across investors rather than canceling out across investors, and arbitrage strategies may involve too much risk to eliminate market inefficiencies.

14.6   Empirical Challenges to Market Efficiency

Section 14.4 presented empirical evidence supportive of market efficiency. We now present evidence challenging this hypothesis. (Adherents of market efficiency generally refer to results of this type as *anomalies*.)

1.   *Limits to arbitrage:* Royal Dutch Petroleum and Shell Transport agreed to merge their interests in 1907, with all subsequent cash flows being split on a 60 percent–40 percent basis between the two companies. However, both companies continued to be publicly traded. You might imagine that the market value of Royal Dutch would always be 1.5 ($=60/40$) times that of Shell. That is, if Royal Dutch ever became overpriced, rational investors would buy Shell instead of Royal Dutch. If Royal Dutch were underpriced, investors would buy Royal Dutch. In addition, arbitrageurs would go further by buying the underpriced security and selling the overpriced security short.

However, Figure 14.8 shows that Royal Dutch and Shell rarely traded at parity (i.e., 60/40) between 1962 to 2005, at which time the two companies merged. Why would these deviations occur? As stated in the previous section, behavioral finance suggests that there are limits to arbitrage. That is, an investor buying the overpriced asset and selling the underpriced asset does not have a sure thing. Deviations from parity could actually *increase* in the short run, implying losses

Figure 14.8
**Deviations of
the Ratio of the
Market Value of
Royal Dutch to
the Market Value
of Shell from Parity**

Apparently arbitrage is unable to keep the ratio of the market value of Royal Dutch to the market value of Shell at parity.

SOURCE: From Stephen Ross, Randolph Westerfield, and Bradford Jordan, *Fundamentals of Corporate Finance*, 10th ed., Alternate ed., p. 738.

for the arbitrageur. The well-known statement, "Markets can stay irrational longer than you can stay solvent," attributed to John Maynard Keynes, applies here. Thus, risk considerations may force arbitrageurs to take positions that are too small to move prices back to parity.

Academics have documented a number of these deviations from parity. Froot and Dabora show similar results for both the twin companies of Unilever N.V. and Unilever PLC and for two classes of SmithKline Beecham stock.[12] Lamont and Thaler present similar findings for 3Com and its subsidiary Palm, Inc. (see Example 14.2 for more about 3Com and Palm).[13] Other researchers find price behavior in closed-end mutual funds suggestive of parity deviations.

EXAMPLE 14.2

Can Stock Market Investors Add and Subtract?   On March 2, 2000, 3Com, a profitable provider of computer networking products and services, sold 5 percent of one of its subsidiaries, Palm, to the public via an initial public offering (IPO). 3Com planned to distribute the remaining Palm shares to 3Com shareholders at a later date. Under the plan, if you owned one share of 3Com, you would receive 1.5 shares of Palm. So after 3Com sold part of Palm via the IPO, investors could buy Palm shares directly or indirectly by purchasing shares of 3Com and waiting.

(continued)

---

[12]Kenneth A. Froot and Emil M. Dabora, "How Are Stock Prices Affected by the Location of Trade?" *Journal of Financial Economics* 53 (August 1999).

[13]Owen Lamont and Richard Thaler, "Can the Market Add and Subtract? Mispricing in Tech Stock Carve-Outs," *Journal of Political Economy* (April 2003).

What makes this case interesting is what happened in the days that followed the Palm IPO. If you owned one 3Com share, you would be entitled, eventually, to 1.5 shares of Palm. Therefore, each 3Com share should be worth *at least* 1.5 times the value of each Palm share. We say *at least* because the other parts of 3Com were profitable. As a result, each 3Com share should have been worth much more than 1.5 times the value of one Palm share. But as you might guess, things did not work out this way.

The day before the Palm IPO, shares in 3Com sold for $104.13. After the first day of trading, Palm closed at $95.06 per share. Multiplying $95.06 by 1.5 results in $142.59, which is the minimum value we would expect to pay for 3Com. But the day Palm closed at $95.06, 3Com shares closed at $81.81, more than $60 lower than the price implied by Palm.

A 3Com price of $81.81 when Palm was selling for $95.06 implies that the market valued the rest of 3Com's businesses (per share) at $81.81 − 142.59 = −$60.78. Given the number of 3Com shares outstanding at the time, this means the market placed a *negative* value of about $22 billion on the rest of 3Com's businesses. Of course, a stock price cannot be negative. This means that the price of Palm relative to 3Com was much too high.

To profit from this mispricing, investors would purchase shares of 3Com and sell shares of Palm. This trade was a no-brainer. In a well-functioning market arbitrage traders would force the prices into alignment quickly. What happened?

As you can see in the accompanying figure, the market valued 3Com and Palm shares in such a way that the non-Palm part of 3Com had a negative value for about two months from March 2, 2000, until May 8, 2000. Thus, the pricing error was corrected by market forces, but not instantly, which is consistent with the existence of limits to arbitrage.

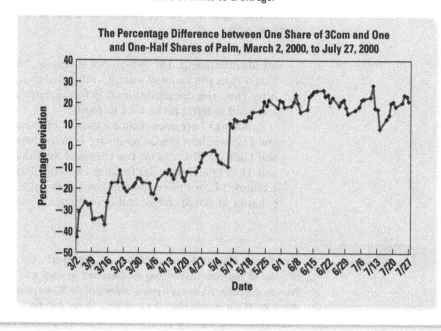

2. *Earnings surprises:* Common sense suggests that prices should rise when earnings are reported to be higher than expected and prices should fall when the reverse occurs. However, market efficiency implies that prices will adjust immediately to the announcement, while behavioral finance would predict another pattern. Kolasinski and Li rank companies by the extent of their *earnings surprise*—that

Figure 14.9

Returns on Two Investment Strategies Based on Earnings Surprise

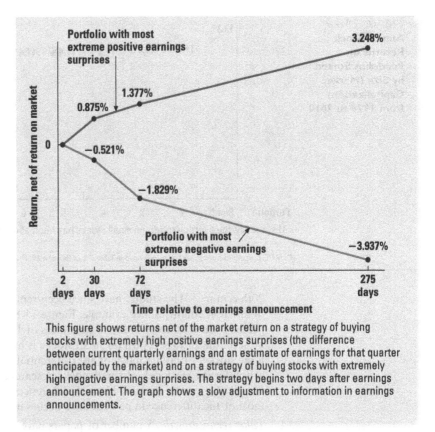

This figure shows returns net of the market return on a strategy of buying stocks with extremely high positive earnings surprises (the difference between current quarterly earnings and an estimate of earnings for that quarter anticipated by the market) and on a strategy of buying stocks with extremely high negative earnings surprises. The strategy begins two days after earnings announcement. The graph shows a slow adjustment to information in earnings announcements.

SOURCE: Adapted from Table 1 of Adam Kolasinski and Xu Li, "Can Rational Learning Explain Underreaction Anomalies? Evidence from Insider Trading after Earnings Announcements," (University of Washington unpublished paper, 2011).

is, the difference between current quarterly earnings and an estimate of earnings for that quarter anticipated by the market.[14] The authors form a portfolio of companies with the most extreme positive surprises and another portfolio of companies with the most extreme negative surprises. Figure 14.9 shows returns from buying the two portfolios, net of the return on the overall market. As can be seen, prices adjust slowly to earnings announcements, with the portfolio with the positive surprises outperforming the portfolio with the negative surprises over the next 275 days. Many other researchers obtain similar results.

Why do prices adjust slowly? Behavioral finance suggests that investors exhibit conservatism because they are slow to adjust to the information contained in the announcements.

3. *Size:* In 1981, two important papers presented evidence that in the United States, the returns on stocks with small market capitalizations were greater than the returns on stocks with large market capitalizations over most of the

---

[14]Adam Kolasinski and Xu Li, "Can Rational Learning Explain Underreaction Anomalies? Evidence from Insider Trading after Earnings Announcements," (University of Washington unpublished paper, 2011). The authors estimated anticipated earnings by a seasonal random walk model.

Figure 14.10
Annual Stock Returns on Portfolios Sorted by Size (Market Capitalization) from 1926 to 2010

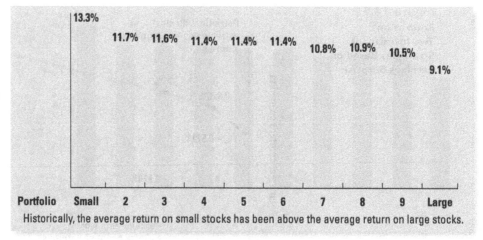

Portfolio	Small	2	3	4	5	6	7	8	9	Large

13.3% 11.7% 11.6% 11.4% 11.4% 11.4% 10.8% 10.9% 10.5% 9.1%

Historically, the average return on small stocks has been above the average return on large stocks.

SOURCE: Calculated from Index Values provided in Table 7.3 of *Ibbotson SBBI® 2011 Classic Yearbook*, Chicago: Morningstar (2011).

20th century.[15] The studies have since been replicated over different periods and in different countries. For example, Figure 14.10 shows average returns over the period from 1926 to 2010 for 10 portfolios of U.S. stocks ranked by size. As can be seen, the average return on small stocks is higher than the average return on large stocks. Although much of the differential performance is merely compensation for the extra risk of small stocks, researchers have generally argued that not all of it can be explained by risk differences. In addition, it appears that most of the difference in performance occurs in the month of January.[16]

4. *Value versus growth:* A number of papers have argued that stocks with high book-value-to-stock-price ratios and/or high earnings-to-price ratios (generally called *value stocks*) outperform stocks with low ratios (*growth stocks*). For example, Fama and French[17] found higher average returns for value stocks than for growth stocks around the world. Figure 14.11 shows the average monthly return differential between value and growth stocks in different geographical regions.

Because the return difference is so large and because these ratios can be obtained so easily for individual stocks, the results may constitute strong evidence against market efficiency. However, a number of papers suggest that the unusual returns are due to differences in risk, not to a true inefficiency.[18] Because the debate revolves around arcane statistical points, we will not pursue the issue further. However, it is safe to say that no conclusion is warranted at this time. As with so many other topics in finance and economics, further research is needed.

---

[15]See R. W. Banz, "The Relationship between Return and Market Value of Common Stocks," *Journal of Financial Economics* (March 1981), and M. R. Reinganum, "Misspecification of Capital Asset Pricing: Empirical Anomalies Based on Earnings Yields and Market Values," *Journal of Financial Economics* (March 1981).

[16]The first paper to document this "January effect," was D. B. Keim, "Size-Related Anomalies and Stock Return Seasonality: Further Empirical Evidence," *Journal of Financial Economics* (June 1983).

[17]Taken from Table I of Eugene F. Fama and Kenneth R. French, "Size, Value, and Momentum in International Stock Returns," [due to be published in the *Critical Finance Review* in 2012].

[18]For example, see E. F. Fama and K. R. French, "Multifactor Explanations of Asset Pricing Anomalies," *Journal of Finance* 51 (March 1996) and Hengjie Ai and Dana Kiku, "Growth to Value: Option Exercise and the Cross Section of Equity Returns," unpublished paper; Wharton School, University of Pennsylvania (2011).

Figure 14.11
Monthly Return Difference Between High Book-to-Price Stocks (value stocks) and Low Book-to-Price Stocks (growth stocks) around the World

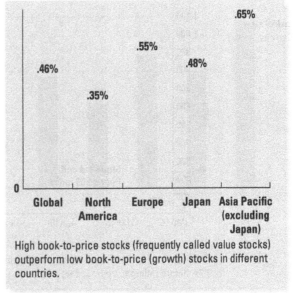

High book-to-price stocks (frequently called value stocks) outperform low book-to-price (growth) stocks in different countries.

SOURCE: Eugene F. Fama, and Kenneth R. French, "Size, Value, and Momentum in International Stock Returns," [due to be published in the *Critical Finance Review* in 2012. Table 1].

5. *Crashes and bubbles*: The stock market crash of October 19, 1987, is extremely puzzling. The market dropped between 20 percent and 25 percent on a Monday following a weekend during which little surprising news was released. A drop of this magnitude for no apparent reason is not consistent with market efficiency. Because the crash of 1929 is still an enigma, it is doubtful that the more recent 1987 debacle will be explained anytime soon—not to mention the crash of 2008, which we discussed in Chapter 10. The recent comments of an eminent historian are apt here: When asked what, in his opinion, the effect of the French Revolution of 1789 was, he replied that it was too early to tell.

Perhaps stock market crashes are evidence consistent with the **bubble theory** of speculative markets. That is, security prices sometimes move wildly above their true values. Eventually, prices fall back to their original level, causing great losses for investors. Consider, for example, the behavior of Internet stocks of the late 1990s. Figure 14.12 shows values of an index of Internet stocks from 1996 through 2002. The index rose over tenfold from January 1996 to its high in March 2000 before retreating to approximately its original level in 2002. For comparison, the figure also shows price movement for the Standard & Poor's 500 Index. While this index rose and fell over the same period, the price movement was quite muted relative to that of Internet stocks.

Many commentators describe the rise and fall of Internet stocks as a *bubble*. Is it correct to do so? Unfortunately, there is no precise definition of the term. Some academics argue that the price movement in the figure is consistent with rationality. Prices rose initially, they say, because it appeared that the Internet would soon capture a large chunk of international commerce. Prices fell when later evidence suggested this would not occur quite so quickly. However, others argue that the initial rosy scenario was never supported by the facts. Rather, prices rose due to nothing more than "irrational exuberance."

458   **Part IV**   Capital Structure and Dividend Policy

Figure 14.12
Value of Index of
Internet Stocks

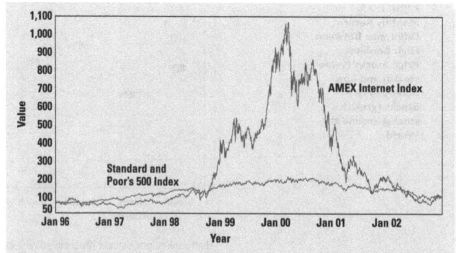

The index of Internet stocks rose over tenfold from the beginning of 1996 to its high in March 2000 before falling to approximately its original level in 2002.

14.7 Reviewing the Differences

It is fair to say that the controversy over efficient capital markets has not yet been resolved. Rather, academic financial economists have sorted themselves into three camps, with some adhering to market efficiency, some believing in behavioral finance, and others (perhaps the majority) not yet convinced that either side has won the argument. This state of affairs is certainly different from, say, 35 years ago, when market efficiency went unchallenged. In addition, the controversy here is perhaps the most contentious of any area of financial economics. Only in this area do grown-up finance professors come close to fisticuffs over an idea.

Adherents of behavioral finance point out, as discussed in Section 14.5, that the three theoretical foundations of market efficiency appear to be violated in the real world. Second, they stress that there are simply too many anomalies, with a number of them having been replicated in out-of-sample tests.[19] Critics of behavioral finance generally make three points in rebuttal:

1. *The file drawer problem:* Scholars generally submit their papers to academic journals, where independent referees judge whether the work is deserving of publication. Papers either get accepted in a journal, leading to potential influence in the field, or they get rejected, leaving the author to, as the phrase goes, bury the paper "in his file drawer." It has been frequently suggested that, holding quality of research constant, referees are more likely to accept a paper with unusual and interesting results. Critics of behavioral finance argue that, since market efficiency has been the received paradigm in finance, any paper challenging efficiency has a higher probability of acceptance than one supporting

---

[19]Excellent reviews of behavioral finance can be found in Andrei Shleifer, *Inefficient Markets: An Introduction to Behavioral Finance*, op. cit., and in Nicholas Barberis and Richard Thaler, "A Survey of Behavioral Finance," in *Handbook of the Economics of Finance*, eds. George Constantinides, Milton Harris, and Rene Stultz (Amsterdam: North Holland, 2003).

efficiency. Thus, the publication process may inadvertently favor behavioral finance research.

2. *Risk:* As indicated in Chapter 11, investors try to maximize expected return per unit of risk. However, risk is not always easy to estimate. Efficient market adherents often suggest that some anomalies might disappear if more sophisticated adjustments for risk were made. As an example, we mentioned in the previous section that a number of researchers have argued that the high returns on value stocks can be explained by their higher risk.

3. *Behavioral finance and market prices:* Critics of behavioral finance *often* argue that, even if the data support certain anomalies, it is not clear that these anomalies support behavioral finance. For example, consider representativeness and conservatism, two psychological principles mentioned earlier in this chapter.

Representativeness implies overweighting the results of small samples, as with the gambler who thinks a few consecutive spins of black on the roulette wheel make black a more likely outcome than red on the next spin. Financial economists argue that representativeness can lead to *overreaction* in stock returns. We mentioned earlier that financial bubbles are likely overreactions to news. Internet companies showed great revenue growth for a short time in the late 1990s, causing many to believe that this growth would continue indefinitely. Stock prices rose (too much) at this point. When at last investors realized that this growth could not be sustained, prices plummeted.

Conservatism states that individuals adjust their beliefs too slowly to new information. A market composed of this type of investor would likely lead to stock prices that *underreact* in the presence of new information. The example concerning earnings surprises may illustrate this underreaction. Prices rose slowly following announcements of positive earnings surprises. Announcements of negative surprises had a similar, but opposite, reaction.

Efficient market believers stress that representativeness and conservatism have opposite implications for stock prices. Which principle, they ask, should dominate in any particular situation? In other words, why should investors overreact to news about Internet stocks but underreact to earnings news? Proponents of market efficiency say that unless behaviorists can answer these two questions satisfactorily, we should not reject market efficiency in favor of behavioral finance.[20]

While we have devoted more space in this section to arguments supporting market efficiency than to arguments supporting behavioral finance, you should not take this difference as evidence in favor of efficiency. Rather, the jury, the community of financial economists in this case, is still out here. It does not appear that our textbook, or any textbook, can easily resolve the differing points of view.

14.8 Implications for Corporate Finance

So far this chapter has examined both theoretical arguments and empirical evidence concerning efficient markets. We now ask whether market efficiency has any relevance for corporate financial managers. The answer is that it does. Next, we consider four implications of efficiency for managers.

---

[20]See, for example, Eugene F. Fama, "Market Efficiency, Long-Term Returns, and Behavioral Finance," *Journal of Financial Economics* 49 (1998).

1. ACCOUNTING CHOICES, FINANCIAL CHOICES, AND MARKET EFFICIENCY

The accounting profession provides firms with a significant amount of leeway in their reporting practices. For example, companies may choose between the last-in, first-out (LIFO) or the first-in, first-out (FIFO) method of valuing inventories. They may choose either the percentage-of-completion or the completed-contract method for construction projects. They may depreciate physical assets by either accelerated or straight-line depreciation.

Managers clearly prefer high stock prices to low stock prices. Should managers use the leeway in accounting choices to report the highest possible income? Not necessarily. That is, accounting choices should not affect stock price if two conditions hold. First, enough information must be provided in the annual report so that financial analysts can construct earnings under the alternative accounting methods. This appears to be the case for many, though not necessarily all, accounting choices. Second, the market must be efficient in the semistrong form. In other words, the market must appropriately use all of this accounting information in determining the market price.

Of course, the issue of whether accounting choices affect stock prices is ultimately an empirical matter. A number of academic papers have addressed this issue. Kaplan and Roll found that the switch from accelerated to straight-line depreciation did not affect stock prices.[21] Kaplan and Roll also looked at changes from the deferral method of accounting for the investment tax credit to the flow-through method.[22] They found that a switch would increase accounting earnings but had no effect on stock prices.

Several other accounting procedures have been studied. Hong, Kaplan, and Mandelker found no evidence that the stock market was affected by the artificially higher earnings reported using the pooling method, compared to the purchase method, for reporting mergers and acquisitions.[23] Biddle and Lindahl found that firms switching to the LIFO method of inventory valuation experienced an increase in stock price.[24] This is to be expected in inflationary environments because LIFO valuation can reduce taxes compared to FIFO. They found that the larger the tax decrease resulting from the use of LIFO, the greater was the increase in stock price. In summary, empirical evidence suggests that accounting changes do not fool the market. Therefore, the evidence does not suggest that managers can boost stock prices through accounting practices. In other words, the market appears efficient enough to see through different accounting choices.

One caveat is called for here. Our discussion specifically assumed that "financial analysts can construct earnings under the alternative accounting methods." However, companies like Enron, WorldCom, Global Crossing, and Xerox simply reported fraudulent numbers in recent years. There was no way for financial analysts to construct alternative earnings numbers because these analysts were unaware how the reported numbers were determined. So it was not surprising that the prices of these

---

[21]R. S. Kaplan and R. Roll, "Investor Evaluation of Accounting Information: Some Empirical Evidence,"*Journal of Business* 45 (April 1972).

[22]Before 1987, U.S. tax law allowed a 10 percent tax credit on the purchase of most kinds of capital equipment.

[23]H. Hong, R. S. Kaplan, and G. Mandelker, "Pooling vs. Purchase: The Effects of Accounting for Mergers on Stock Prices," *Accounting Review* 53 (1978). The pooling method for mergers is no longer allowed under generally accepted accounting principles.

[24]G. C. Biddle and F. W. Lindahl, "Stock Price Reactions to LIFO Adoptions: The Association Between Excess Returns and LIFO Tax Savings," *Journal of Accounting Research* (1982).

stocks initially rose well above fair value. Yes, managers can boost prices in this way—as long as they are willing to serve time once they are caught!

Is there anything else that investors can be expected to see through in an efficient market? Consider stock splits and stock dividends. Today, Amarillo Corporation has 1 million shares outstanding and reports $10 million of earnings. In the hopes of boosting the stock price, the firm's chief financial officer (CFO), Ms. Green, recommends to the board of directors that Amarillo have a 2-for-1 stock split. That is, a shareholder with 100 shares prior to the split would have 200 shares after the split. The CFO contends that each investor would feel richer after the split because he would own more shares.

However, this thinking runs counter to market efficiency. A rational investor knows that he would own the same proportion of the firm after the split as before the split. For example, our investor with 100 shares owns 1/10,000 (=100/1 million) of Amarillo's shares prior to the split. His share of the earnings would be $1,000 (=$10 million/10,000). Although he would own 200 shares after the split, there would now be 2 million shares outstanding. Thus, he still would own 1/10,000 of the firm. His share of the earnings would still be $1,000 because the stock split would not affect the earnings of the entire firm.

2. THE TIMING DECISION

Imagine a firm whose managers are contemplating the date to issue equity. This decision is frequently called the *timing* decision. If managers believe that their stock is overpriced, they are likely to issue equity immediately. Here, they are creating value for their current stockholders because they are selling stock for more than it is worth. Conversely, if the managers believe that their stock is underpriced, they are more likely to wait, hoping that the stock price will eventually rise to its true value.

However, if markets are efficient, securities are always correctly priced. Efficiency implies that stock is sold for its true worth, so the timing decision becomes unimportant. Figure 14.13 shows three possible stock price adjustments to the issuance of new stock.

Of course market efficiency is ultimately an empirical issue. Surprisingly, recent research suggests managers have some timing ability. Ritter presents evidence that annual stock returns over the five years following an initial public offering (IPO) are about 2 percent less for the issuing company than the returns on a non-issuing company of similar book-to-market ratio.[25] Annual stock returns over this period following a seasoned equity offering (SEO) are between 3 percent and 4 percent less for the issuing company than for a comparable nonissuing company. A company's first public offering is called an IPO and all subsequent offerings are termed SEOs. The upper half of Figure 14.14 shows average annual returns of both IPOs and their control group, and the lower half of the figure shows average annual returns of both SEOs and their control group.

The evidence in Ritter's paper suggests that corporate managers issue SEOs when the company's stock is overpriced. In other words, managers appear to time the market successfully. The evidence that managers time their IPOs is less compelling: Returns following IPOs are closer to those of their control group.

---

[25]Jay Ritter, "Investment Banking and Security Issuance," Chapter 9 of *Handbook of the Economics of Finance*, ed. George Constantinides, Milton Harris, and Rene Stulz (Amsterdam: North Holland, 2003).

462   **Part IV**   Capital Structure and Dividend Policy

Figure 14.13
Three Stock Price Adjustments after Issuing Equity

Studies show that stock is more likely to be issued after stock prices have increased. No inferences about market efficiency can be drawn from this result. Rather, market efficiency implies that the stock price of the issuing firm, on average, neither rises nor falls (relative to stock market indexes) after issuance of stock.

Does the ability of a corporate official to issue an SEO when the security is overpriced indicate that the market is inefficient in the semistrong form or the strong form? The answer is actually somewhat more complex than it may first appear. On one hand, managers are likely to have special information that the rest of us do not have, suggesting that the market need only be inefficient in the strong form. On the other hand, if the market were truly semistrong efficient, the price would drop immediately and completely upon the announcement of an upcoming SEO. That is, rational investors would realize that stock is being issued because corporate officials have special information that the stock is overpriced. Indeed, many empirical studies report a price drop on the announcement date. However, Figure 14.14 shows a further price drop in the subsequent years, suggesting that the market is inefficient in the semistrong form.

If firms can time the issuance of common stock, perhaps they can also time the repurchase of stock. Here a firm would like to repurchase when its stock is undervalued. Ikenberry, Lakonishok, and Vermaelen find that stock returns of repurchasing firms are abnormally high in the two years following repurchase, suggesting that timing is effective here.[26]

3. SPECULATION AND EFFICIENT MARKETS

We normally think of individuals and financial institutions as the primary speculators in financial markets. However, industrial corporations speculate as well. For example, many companies make interest rate bets. If the managers of a firm believe that interest rates are likely to rise, they have an incentive to borrow because the present value of the liability will fall with the rate increase. In addition, these managers will have

---

[26]D. Ikenberry, J. Lakonishok, and T. Vermaelen, "Market Underreaction to Open Market Share Repurchases," *Journal of Financial Economics* (October–November 1995).

Figure 14.14
Returns on Initial Public Offerings (IPOs) and Seasoned Equity Offerings (SEOs) in Years Following Issue

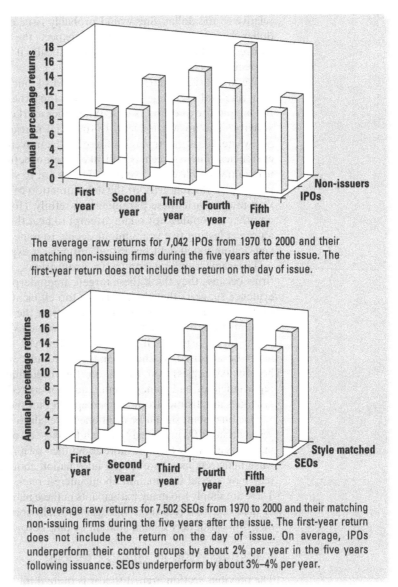

The average raw returns for 7,042 IPOs from 1970 to 2000 and their matching non-issuing firms during the five years after the issue. The first-year return does not include the return on the day of issue.

The average raw returns for 7,502 SEOs from 1970 to 2000 and their matching non-issuing firms during the five years after the issue. The first-year return does not include the return on the day of issue. On average, IPOs underperform their control groups by about 2% per year in the five years following issuance. SEOs underperform by about 3%–4% per year.

SOURCE: Jay Ritter, "Investment Banking and Security Issuance," Chapter 9 of *Handbook of the Economics of Finance*, ed. George Constantinides, Milton Harris, and Rene Stulz (Amsterdam: North Holland, 2003).

an incentive to borrow long term rather than short term in order to lock in the low rates for a longer period. The thinking can get more sophisticated. Suppose that the long-term rate is already higher than the short-term rate. The manager might argue that this differential reflects the market's view that rates will rise. However, perhaps he anticipates a rate increase even greater than what the market anticipates, as implied by the upward-sloping term structure. Again, the manager will want to borrow long term rather than short term.

Firms also speculate in foreign currencies. Suppose that the CFO of a multinational corporation based in the United States believes that the euro will decline relative to the dollar. She would probably issue euro-denominated debt rather than dollar-denominated debt because she expects the value of the foreign liability to fall. Conversely, she would issue debt domestically if she believes foreign currencies will appreciate relative to the dollar.

We are perhaps getting a little ahead of our story: The subtleties of the term structure and exchange rates are treated in other chapters, not this one. However, the big picture question is this: What does market efficiency have to say about such activity? The answer is clear. If financial markets are efficient, managers should not waste their time trying to forecast the movements of interest rates and foreign currencies. Their forecasts will likely be no better than chance. And they will be using up valuable executive time. This is not to say, however, that firms should flippantly pick the maturity or the denomination of their debt in a random fashion. A firm must *choose* these parameters carefully. However, the choice should be based on other rationales, not on an attempt to beat the market. For example, a firm with a project lasting five years might decide to issue five-year debt. A firm might issue yen-denominated debt because it anticipates expanding into Japan in a big way.

The same thinking applies to acquisitions. Many corporations buy up other firms because they think these targets are underpriced. Unfortunately, the empirical evidence suggests that the market is too efficient for this type of speculation to be profitable. And the acquirer never pays just the current market price. The bidding firm must pay a premium above market value to induce a majority of shareholders of the target firm to sell their shares. However, this is not to say that firms should never be acquired. Rather, managers should consider an acquisition if there are benefits (synergies) from the union. Improved marketing, economies in production, replacement of bad management, and even tax reduction are typical synergies. These synergies are distinct from the perception that the acquired firm is underpriced.

One final point should be mentioned. We talked earlier about empirical evidence suggesting that SEOs are timed to take advantage of overpriced stock. This makes sense—managers are likely to know more about their own firms than the market does. However, while managers may have special information about their own firms, it is unlikely that they have special information about interest rates, foreign currencies, and other firms. There are simply too many participants in these markets, many of whom are devoting all of their time to forecasting. Managers typically spend most of their effort running their own firms, with only a small amount of time devoted to studying financial markets.

4. INFORMATION IN MARKET PRICES

The previous section argued that it is quite difficult to forecast future market prices. However, the current and past prices of any asset are known—and of great use. Consider, for example, Becher's study of bank mergers.[27] The author finds that stock prices of acquired banks rise about 23 percent on average upon the first announcement of a merger. This is not surprising because companies are generally bought out at a premium above the current stock price. However, the same study shows that prices of acquiring banks fall almost 5 percent on average upon the same announcement. This is pretty strong evidence that bank mergers do not benefit, and may even hurt, acquiring companies. The reason for this result is unclear, though perhaps acquirers simply overpay for acquisitions. Regardless of the reason, the *implication* is clear. A bank should think deeply before acquiring another bank.

---

[27]David A. Becher, "The Valuation Effects of Bank Mergers," *Journal of Corporate Finance* 6 (2000).

Figure 14.15
Stock Performance
Prior to Forced
Departures of
Management

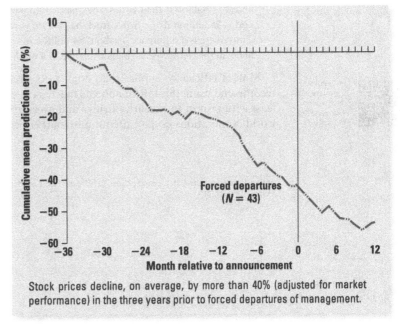

Forced departures
($N = 43$)

Stock prices decline, on average, by more than 40% (adjusted for market performance) in the three years prior to forced departures of management.

SOURCE: Adapted from Figure 1 of Warner, Watts, and Wruck, "Stock Prices and Top Management Changes," *Journal of Financial Economics* 20 (1988).

Furthermore, suppose you are the CFO of a company whose stock price drops significantly upon announcement of an acquisition. The market is telling you that the merger is bad for your firm. Serious consideration should be given to canceling the merger, even if, prior to the announcement, you thought the merger was a good idea.

Of course, mergers are only one type of corporate event. Managers should pay attention to the stock price reaction to any of their announcements, whether it concerns a new venture, a divestiture, a restructuring, or something else.

This is not the only way in which corporations can use the information in market prices. Suppose you are on the board of directors of a company whose stock price has declined precipitously since the current chief executive officer (CEO) was hired. In addition, the stock prices of competitors have risen over the same time. Though there may be extenuating circumstances, this can be viewed as evidence that the CEO is doing a poor job. Perhaps he should be fired. If this seems harsh, consider that Warner, Watts, and Wruck find a strong negative correlation between managerial turnover and prior stock performance.[28] Figure 14.15 shows that stocks fall, on average, about 40 percent in price (relative to market movements) in the three years prior to the forced departure of a top manager.

If managers are fired for bad stock price performance, perhaps they are rewarded for stock price appreciation. Hall and Liebman state,

> Our main empirical finding is that CEO wealth often changes by millions of dollars for typical changes in firm value. For example, the median total compensation for CEOs is

---

[28]Jerold B. Warner, Ross L. Watts, and Karen H. Wruck, "Stock Prices and Top Management Changes," *Journal of Financial Economics* 20 (1988).

about $1 million if their firm's stock has a 30th percentile annual return (-7.0 percent) and is $5 million if the firm's stock has a 70th percentile annual return (20.5 percent). Thus, there is a difference of about $4 million in compensation for achieving a moderately above average performance relative to a moderately below average performance.[29]

◄ To test your mastery of this material, take a quiz at mhhe. com/rwj

Market efficiency implies that stock prices reflect all available information. We recommend using this information as much as possible in corporate decisions. And at least with respect to executive firings and executive compensation, it looks as if real-world corporations do pay attention to market prices.

---

[29]Brian J. Hall and Jeffrey B. Liebman, "Are CEOs Really Paid Like Bureaucrats?" *Quarterly Journal of Economics* (August 1998), p. 654.

Summary and Conclusions

1. An efficient securities market processes the information available to investors about the underlying economic value of the securities and incorporates it into the prices of securities. Market efficiency has two general implications. First, in any given time period, a securities' abnormal return depends on information or news received by the market in that period. Second, an investor who uses the same information as the market cannot expect to earn abnormal returns. In other words, systems for playing the market are doomed to fail.

2. What information does the market use to determine stock prices?
   a. The weak form of the efficient market hypothesis says that the market uses the history of stock prices and is therefore efficient with respect to these past prices. This implies that stock selection based on patterns of past stock price movements is no better than random stock selection.
   b. The semistrong form states that the market uses all publicly available information in setting prices.
   c. Strong form efficiency states that the market uses all of the information that anybody knows about stocks, even inside information.

3. Behavioral finance states that the market is not always efficient. Adherents argue that:
   a. Investors are not rational.
   b. Deviations from rationality are similar across investors.
   c. Arbitrage, being costly, does not eliminate inefficiencies.

4. Behaviorists point to many studies, including those showing that small stocks outperform large stocks, value stocks outperform growth stocks, and stock prices adjust slowly to earnings surprises, as empirical confirmation of their beliefs.

5. Four implications of market efficiency for corporate finance are:
   a. Managers cannot fool the market through creative accounting.
   b. Firms cannot successfully time issues of debt and equity.
   c. Managers cannot profitably speculate in foreign currencies and other instruments.
   d. Managers can reap many benefits by paying attention to market prices.

The following box summarizes some key issues in the efficient markets debate:

Efficient Market Hypothesis: A Summary

Does Not Say:

- Prices are uncaused.
- Investors are foolish and too stupid to be in the market.
- All shares of stock have the same expected returns.
- Investors should throw darts to select stocks.
- There is no upward trend in stock prices.

Does Say:

- Prices reflect underlying value.
- Financial managers cannot time stock and bond sales.
- Managers cannot profitably speculate in foreign currencies.
- Managers cannot boost stock prices through creative accounting.

Why Doesn't Everybody Believe It?

- There are optical illusions, mirages, and apparent patterns in charts of stock market returns.
- The truth is less interesting.
- There is evidence against efficiency:
  - Two different, but financially identical, classes of stock of the same firm selling at different prices.
  - Earnings surprises.
  - Small versus large stocks.
  - Value versus growth stocks.
  - Crashes and bubbles.

Three Forms:

Weak form: Current prices reflect past prices; chartism (technical analysis) is useless.

Semistrong form: Prices reflect all public information; most financial analysis is useless.

Strong form: Prices reflect all that is knowable; nobody consistently makes superior profits.

Concept Questions

1. **Firm Value**   What rule should a firm follow when making financing decisions? How can firms create valuable financing opportunities?

2. **Efficient Market Hypothesis**   Define the three forms of market efficiency.

3. **Efficient Market Hypothesis**   Which of the following statements are true about the efficient market hypothesis?

    a. It implies perfect forecasting ability.
    b. It implies that prices reflect all available information.
    c. It implies an irrational market.
    d. It implies that prices do not fluctuate.
    e. It results from keen competition among investors.

4. **Market Efficiency Implications** Explain why a characteristic of an efficient market is that investments in that market have zero NPVs.

5. **Efficient Market Hypothesis** A stock market analyst is able to identify mispriced stocks by comparing the average price for the last 10 days to the average price for the last 60 days. If this is true, what do you know about the market?

6. **Semistrong Efficiency** If a market is semistrong form efficient, is it also weak form efficient? Explain.

7. **Efficient Market Hypothesis** What are the implications of the efficient market hypothesis for investors who buy and sell stocks in an attempt to "beat the market"?

8. **Stocks versus Gambling** Critically evaluate the following statements: Playing the stock market is like gambling. Such speculative investing has no social value other than the pleasure people get from this form of gambling.

9. **Efficient Market Hypothesis** Several celebrated investors and stock pickers frequently mentioned in the financial press have recorded huge returns on their investments over the past two decades. Does the success of these particular investors invalidate the EMH? Explain.

10. **Efficient Market Hypothesis** For each of the following scenarios, discuss whether profit opportunities exist from trading in the stock of the firm under the conditions that (1) the market is not weak form efficient, (2) the market is weak form but not semistrong form efficient, (3) the market is semistrong form but not strong form efficient, and (4) the market is strong form efficient.

  a. The stock price has risen steadily each day for the past 30 days.
  b. The financial statements for a company were released three days ago, and you believe you've uncovered some anomalies in the company's inventory and cost control reporting techniques that are causing the firm's true liquidity strength to be understated.
  c. You observe that the senior management of a company has been buying a lot of the company's stock on the open market over the past week.

  Use the following information for the next two questions:
  Technical analysis is a controversial investment practice. Technical analysis covers a wide array of techniques, which are all used in an attempt to predict the direction of a particular stock or the market. Technical analysts look at two major types of information: Historical stock prices and investor sentiment. A technical analyst would argue these two information sets provide information about the future direction of a particular stock or the market as a whole.

11. **Technical Analysis** What would a technical analyst say about market efficiency?

12. **Investor Sentiment** A technical analysis tool that is sometimes used to predict market movements is an investor sentiment index. AAII, the American Association of Individual Investors, publishes an investor sentiment index based on a survey of its members. In the following table you will find the percentage of investors who were bullish, bearish, or neutral during a four-week period:

Week	Bullish	Bearish	Neutral
1	37%	25%	38%
2	52	14	34
3	29	35	36
4	43	26	31

What is the investor sentiment index intended to capture? How might it be useful in technical analysis?

13. **Performance of the Pros** In the middle to late 1990s, the performance of the pros was unusually poor—on the order of 90 percent of all equity mutual funds underperformed a passively managed index fund. How does this bear on the issue of market efficiency?

14. **Efficient Markets** A hundred years ago or so, companies did not compile annual reports. Even if you owned stock in a particular company, you were unlikely to be allowed to see the balance sheet and income statement for the company. Assuming the market is semistrong form efficient, what does this say about market efficiency then compared to now?

15. **Efficient Market Hypothesis** Aerotech, an aerospace technology research firm, announced this morning that it has hired the world's most knowledgeable and prolific space researchers. Before today Aerotech's stock had been selling for $100. Assume that no other information is received over the next week and the stock market as a whole does not move.
    a. What do you expect will happen to Aerotech's stock?
    b. Consider the following scenarios:
       i. The stock price jumps to $118 on the day of the announcement. In subsequent days it floats up to $123, then falls back to $116.
       ii. The stock price jumps to $116 and remains at that level.
       iii. The stock price gradually climbs to $116 over the next week.
    Which scenario(s) indicate market efficiency? Which do not? Why?

16. **Efficient Market Hypothesis** When the 56-year-old founder of Gulf & Western, Inc., died of a heart attack, the stock price immediately jumped from $18.00 a share to $20.25, a 12.5 percent increase. This is evidence of market inefficiency because an efficient stock market would have anticipated his death and adjusted the price beforehand. Assume that no other information is received and the stock market as a whole does not move. Is this statement about market efficiency true or false? Explain.

17. **Efficient Market Hypothesis** Today, the following announcement was made: "Early today the Justice Department reached a decision in the Universal Product Care (UPC) case. UPC has been found guilty of discriminatory practices in hiring. For the next five years, UPC must pay $2 million each year to a fund representing victims of UPC's policies." Assuming the market is efficient, should investors not buy UPC stock after the announcement because the litigation will cause an abnormally low rate of return? Explain.

18. **Efficient Market Hypothesis** Newtech Corp. is going to adopt a new chip-testing device that can greatly improve its production efficiency. Do you think the lead engineer can profit from purchasing the firm's stock before the news release on the device? After reading the announcement in *The Wall Street Journal*, should you be able to earn an abnormal return from purchasing the stock if the market is efficient?

19. **Efficient Market Hypothesis** TransTrust Corp. has changed how it accounts for inventory. Taxes are unaffected, although the resulting earnings report released this quarter is 20 percent higher than what it would have been under the old accounting system. There is no other surprise in the earnings report, and the change in the accounting treatment was publicly announced. If the market is efficient, will the stock price be higher when the market learns that the reported earnings are higher?

20. **Efficient Market Hypothesis** The Durkin Investing Agency has been the best stock picker in the country for the past two years. Before this rise to fame occurred, the Durkin newsletter had 200 subscribers. Those subscribers beat the market consistently, earning substantially higher returns after adjustment for risk and transaction costs. Subscriptions have skyrocketed to 10,000. Now, when the Durkin Investing Agency recommends a stock, the price instantly rises several points. The subscribers currently earn only a normal return when they buy recommended stock because the price rises before anybody can act on the information. Briefly explain this phenomenon. Is Durkin's ability to pick stocks consistent with market efficiency?

21. **Efficient Market Hypothesis** Your broker commented that well-managed firms are better investments than poorly managed firms. As evidence your broker cited a recent study examining 100 small manufacturing firms that eight years earlier had been listed in an industry magazine as the best-managed small manufacturers in the country. In the ensuing eight years, the 100 firms listed have not earned more than the normal market return. Your broker continued to say that if the firms were well managed, they should have produced better-than-average returns. If the market is efficient, do you agree with your broker?

22. **Efficient Market Hypothesis** A famous economist just announced in *The Wall Street Journal* his findings that the recession is over and the economy is again entering an expansion. Assume market efficiency. Can you profit from investing in the stock market after you read this announcement?

23. **Efficient Market Hypothesis** Suppose the market is semistrong form efficient. Can you expect to earn excess returns if you make trades based on:
    a. Your broker's information about record earnings for a stock?
    b. Rumors about a merger of a firm?
    c. Yesterday's announcement of a successful new product test?

24. **Efficient Market Hypothesis** Imagine that a particular macroeconomic variable that influences your firm's net earnings is positively serially correlated. Assume market efficiency. Would you expect price changes in your stock to be serially correlated? Why or why not?

25. **Efficient Market Hypothesis** The efficient market hypothesis implies that all mutual funds should obtain the same expected risk-adjusted returns. Therefore, we can simply pick mutual funds at random. Is this statement true or false? Explain.

26. **Efficient Market Hypothesis** Assume that markets are efficient. During a trading day American Golf Inc. announces that it has lost a contract for a large golfing project that, prior to the news, it was widely believed to have secured. If the market is efficient, how should the stock price react to this information if no additional information is released?

27. **Efficient Market Hypothesis** Prospectors, Inc., is a publicly traded gold prospecting company in Alaska. Although the firm's searches for gold usually fail, the prospectors occasionally find a rich vein of ore. What pattern would you expect to observe for Prospectors' cumulative abnormal returns if the market is efficient?

28. **Evidence on Market Efficiency** Some people argue that the efficient market hypothesis cannot explain the 1987 market crash or the high price-to-earnings ratios of Internet stocks during the late 1990s. What alternative hypothesis is currently used for these two phenomena?

Chapter 14 Efficient Capital Markets and Behavioral Challenges **471**

Questions and Problems

1. **Cumulative Abnormal Returns** Delta, United, and American Airlines announced purchases of planes on July 18 (7/18), February 12 (2/12), and October 7 (10/7), respectively. Given the following information, calculate the cumulative abnormal return (CAR) for these stocks as a group. Graph the result and provide an explanation. All of the stocks have a beta of 1, and no other announcements are made.

	Delta			United			American	
Date	Market Return	Company Return	Date	Market Return	Company Return	Date	Market Return	Company Return
7/12	−.3	−.5	2/8	−.9	−1.1	10/1	.5	.3
7/13	.0	.2	2/9	−1.0	−1.1	10/2	.4	.6
7/16	.5	.7	2/10	.4	.2	10/3	1.1	1.1
7/17	−.5	−.3	2/11	.6	.8	10/6	.1	−.3
7/18	−2.2	1.1	2/12	−.3	−.1	10/7	−2.2	−.3
7/19	−.9	−.7	2/15	1.1	1.2	10/8	.5	.5
7/20	−1.0	−1.1	2/16	.5	.5	10/9	−.3	−.2
7/23	.7	.5	2/17	−.3	−.2	10/10	.3	.1
7/24	.2	.1	2/18	.3	.2	10/13	.0	−.1

2. **Cumulative Abnormal Returns** The following diagram shows the cumulative abnormal returns (CAR) for 386 oil exploration companies announcing oil discoveries between 1950 and 1980. Month 0 in the diagram is the announcement month. Assume that no other information is received and the stock market as a whole does not move. Is the diagram consistent with market efficiency? Why or why not?

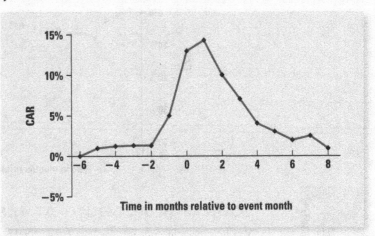

3. **Cumulative Abnormal Returns** The following figures present the results of four cumulative abnormal returns (CAR) studies. Indicate whether the results of each study support, reject, or are inconclusive about the semistrong form of the efficient market hypothesis. In each figure, Time 0 is the date of an event.

4. **Cumulative Abnormal Returns**   A study analyzed the behavior of the stock prices of firms that had lost antitrust cases. Included in the diagram are all firms that lost the initial court decision, even if the decision was later overturned on appeal. The event at Time 0 is the initial, pre-appeal court decision. Assume no other information was released, aside from that disclosed in the initial trial. The stock prices all have a beta of 1. Is the diagram consistent with market efficiency? Why or why not?

YOUR 401(k) ACCOUNT AT EAST COAST YACHTS

You have been at your job for East Coast Yachts for a week now and have decided you need to sign up for the company's 401(k) plan. Even after your discussion with Sarah Brown, the Bledsoe Financial Services representative, you are still unsure which investment option you should choose. Recall that the options available to you are stock in East Coast Yachts, the Bledsoe S&P 500 Index Fund, the Bledsoe Small-Cap Fund, the Bledsoe Large-Company Stock Fund, the Bledsoe Bond Fund, and the Bledsoe Money Market Fund. You have decided that you should invest in a diversified portfolio, with 70 percent of

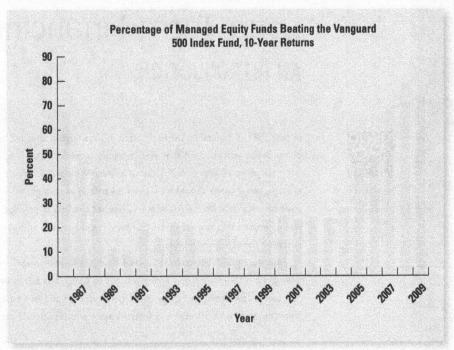

SOURCE: From Bradford Jordan, Thomas Miller, and Steven Dolvin, *Fundamentals of Investments*, 6th ed., p. 237. McGraw-Hill, New York, 2012.

your investment in equities, 25 percent in bonds, and 5 percent in the money market fund. You have also decided to focus your equity investment on large-cap stocks, but you are debating whether to select the S&P 500 Index Fund or the Large-Company Stock Fund.

In thinking it over, you understand the basic difference in the two funds. One is a purely passive fund that replicates a widely followed large-cap index, the S&P 500, and has low fees. The other is actively managed with the intention that the skill of the portfolio manager will result in improved performance relative to an index. Fees are higher in the latter fund. You're just not certain which way to go, so you ask Dan Ervin, who works in the company's finance area, for advice.

After discussing your concerns, Dan gives you some information comparing the performance of equity mutual funds and the Vanguard 500 Index Fund. The Vanguard 500 is the world's largest equity index mutual fund. It replicates the S&P 500, and its return is only negligibly different from the S&P 500. Fees are very low. As a result, the Vanguard 500 is essentially identical to the Bledsoe S&P 500 Index Fund offered in the 401(k) plan, but it has been in existence for much longer, so you can study its track record for over two decades. The graph shown above summarizes Dan's comments by showing the percentage of equity mutual funds that outperformed the Vanguard 500 Fund over the previous 22 years.[30] So, for example, from January 1977 to December 1986, about 70 percent of equity mutual funds outperformed the Vanguard 500. Dan suggests that you study the graph and answer the following questions:

1. What implications do you draw from the graph for mutual fund investors?

2. Is the graph consistent or inconsistent with market efficiency? Explain carefully.

3. What investment decision would you make for the equity portion of your 401(k) account? Why?

---

[30]Note that this graph is not hypothetical; it reflects the actual performance of the Vanguard 500 Index Fund relative to a very large population of diversified equity mutual funds. Specialty funds, such as international funds, are excluded. All returns are net of management fees but do not include sales charges (which are known as "loads"), if any. As a result, the performance of actively managed funds is overstated.

CHAPTER 15

Long-Term Financing

AN INTRODUCTION

▲ For updates on the latest happenings in finance, visit www.rwjcorporatefinance.blogspot.com

In July 2011, a budget battle took place in Washington that left few, if any, winners. In the end, a compromise was reached that was designed to reduce the federal budget deficit by $2.1 trillion over 10 years. However, bond rating agency Standard & Poor's felt that the cuts weren't deep enough, saying there should have been $4 trillion in savings. As a result, S&P downgraded the U.S. government's debt from AAA to AA+. Besides the loss of prestige resulting from the downgrade, it was estimated that the lower credit rating could result in an increase of $100 billion in borrowing costs for the U.S. government.

Also during 2011, Italy, Spain, Ireland, Portugal, Cyprus, and Greece all saw their sovereign debts downgraded. Greece's credit rating was cut to CCC, just a step or two above default. In large part due to the low credit rating, investors demanded a yield of 14 percent on Greek bonds at a time when the yield on a 10-year U.S Treasury note was less than 3 percent.

15.1 Some Features of Common and Preferred Stocks

In this chapter, we examine specific features of both stocks and bonds. We begin with stock, both common and preferred. In discussing common stock features, we focus on shareholder rights and dividend payments. For preferred stock, we explain what the "preferred" means, and we also debate whether preferred stock is really debt or equity.

COMMON STOCK FEATURES

The term **common stock** means different things to different people, but it is usually applied to stock that has no special preference either in receiving dividends or in bankruptcy.

Shareholder Rights A corporation's shareholders elect directors who, in turn, hire management to carry out their directives. Shareholders, therefore, control the corporation through the right to elect the directors. Generally, only shareholders have this right.

Directors are elected each year at an annual meeting. Although there are exceptions (discussed next), the general idea is "one share, one vote" (*not* one *shareholder,* one vote). Corporate democracy is thus very different from our political democracy. With corporate democracy, the "golden rule" prevails absolutely.[1]

---

[1]The golden rule: Whosoever has the gold makes the rules.

Directors are elected at an annual shareholders' meeting by a vote of the holders of a majority of shares who are present and entitled to vote. However, the exact mechanism for electing directors differs across companies. The most important difference is whether shares must be voted cumulatively or voted straight.

To illustrate the two different voting procedures, imagine that a corporation has two shareholders: Smith with 20 shares and Jones with 80 shares. Both want to be a director. Jones does not want Smith, however. We assume there are a total of four directors to be elected.

The effect of **cumulative voting** is to permit minority participation.[2] If cumulative voting is permitted, the total number of votes that each shareholder may cast is determined first. This is usually calculated as the number of shares (owned or controlled) multiplied by the number of directors to be elected.

With cumulative voting, the directors are elected all at once. In our example, this means that the top four vote getters will be the new directors. A shareholder can distribute votes however she wishes.

Will Smith get a seat on the board? If we ignore the possibility of a five-way tie, then the answer is yes. Smith will cast $20 \times 4 = 80$ votes, and Jones will cast $80 \times 4 = 320$ votes. If Smith gives all his votes to himself, he is assured of a directorship. The reason is that Jones can't divide 320 votes among four candidates in such a way as to give all of them more than 80 votes, so Smith will finish fourth at worst.

In general, if there are $\mathcal{N}$ directors up for election, then $1/(\mathcal{N} + 1)$ percent of the stock plus one share will guarantee you a seat. In our current example, this is $1/(4 + 1) = 20$ percent. So the more seats that are up for election at one time, the easier (and cheaper) it is to win one.

With **straight voting**, the directors are elected one at a time. Each time, Smith can cast 20 votes and Jones can cast 80. As a consequence, Jones will elect all of the candidates. The only way to guarantee a seat is to own 50 percent plus one share. This also guarantees that you will win every seat, so it's really all or nothing.

EXAMPLE 15.1

Buying the Election   Stock in JRJ Corporation sells for $20 per share and features cumulative voting. There are 10,000 shares outstanding. If three directors are up for election, how much does it cost to ensure yourself a seat on the board?

The question here is how many shares of stock it will take to get a seat. The answer is 2,501, so the cost is $2,501 \times \$20 = \$50,020$. Why 2,501? Because there is no way the remaining 7,499 votes can be divided among three people to give all of them more than 2,501 votes. For example, suppose two people receive 2,502 votes and the first two seats. A third person can receive at most $10,000 - 2,502 - 2,502 - 2,501 = 2,495$, so the third seat is yours.

As we've illustrated, straight voting can "freeze out" minority shareholders, which is why many states have mandatory cumulative voting. However, in states where cumulative voting is mandatory, corporations have ways to minimize its impact.

One such way is to stagger the voting for the board of directors. With staggered elections, only a fraction of the directorships are up for election at a particular time. For example, if only two directors are up for election at any one time, it will take $1/(2 + 1) = 33.33$ percent of the stock plus one share to guarantee a seat.

---

[2] By minority participation, we mean participation by shareholders with relatively small amounts of stock.

Overall, staggering has two basic effects:

1. Staggering makes it more difficult for a minority to elect a director under cumulative voting because fewer directors are elected at one time.
2. Staggering deters takeover attempts because of the difficulty of voting in a majority of new directors.

However, staggering can also serve a beneficial purpose. It provides "institutional memory" from continuity on the board of directors. Continuity may be important for corporations with significant long-range plans and projects.

Proxy Voting   At the annual meeting shareholders can vote in person, or they can transfer their right to vote to another party. A **proxy** is the grant of authority by a shareholder to someone else to vote her shares. For convenience, much of the voting in large public corporations is actually done by proxy.

Obviously, management wants to accumulate as many proxies as possible. However, an "outside" group of shareholders can try to obtain proxies in an attempt to replace management by electing enough directors. The resulting battle is called a *proxy fight*.

Classes of Stock   Some firms have more than one class of common stock. Often, the classes are created with unequal voting rights. For example, Ford Motor Company's Class B common stock is held by Ford family interests and trusts and not publicly traded. This class has 40 percent of the voting power, even though it represents less than 10 percent of the total number of shares outstanding.

There are many other cases of corporations with different classes of stock. Berkshire Hathaway Class B shares have 1/200th vote of Class A shares, though each Class A share can be converted to only 30 Class B shares. The CEO of cable TV giant Comcast, Brian Roberts, owns about .4 percent of the company's equity, but he has a third of all the votes, thanks to a special class of stock. Google has two classes of common stock, A and B. The Class A shares are held by the public, and each share has one vote. The Class B shares are held by company insiders, with each Class B share having 10 votes. As a result, Google's founders and management control the company.

Historically, the New York Stock Exchange did not allow companies to create classes of publicly traded common stock with unequal voting rights. However, exceptions (e.g., Ford) appear to have been made. In addition, many non-NYSE companies have dual classes of common stock. Limited-voting stock allows management of a firm to raise equity capital while maintaining control.

The subject of unequal voting rights is controversial in the United States, and the idea of one share, one vote, has a strong following and a long history. Interestingly, however, shares with unequal voting rights are quite common around the world.

Other Rights   The value of a share of common stock in a corporation is directly related to the general rights of shareholders. In addition to the right to vote for directors, shareholders usually have the following rights:

1. The right to share proportionally in dividends.
2. The right to share proportionally in assets remaining after liabilities have been paid in a liquidation.
3. The right to vote on stockholder matters of great importance, such as a merger. Voting usually occurs at the annual meeting or a special meeting.

In addition, corporations sometimes give the *preemptive right* to their stockholders. A preemptive right forces a company to sell stock to its existing stockholders before offering the stock to the general public. The right lets each stockholder protect his proportionate ownership in the corporation.

Dividends Corporations are legally authorized to pay **dividends** to their shareholders. The payment of dividends is at the discretion of the board of directors.

Some important characteristics of dividends include the following:

1. Unless a dividend is declared by the board of directors of a corporation, it is not a liability of the corporation. A corporation cannot default on an undeclared dividend. As a consequence, corporations cannot become bankrupt because of nonpayment of dividends. The amount of the dividend and even whether it is paid are decisions based on the business judgment of the board of directors.

2. Dividends are paid out of the corporation's aftertax cash flow. They are not business expenses and are not deductible for corporate tax purposes.

3. Dividends received by individual shareholders are taxable. However, corporations are permitted to exclude 70 percent of the dividends they receive from other corporations and are taxed only on the remaining 30 percent.[3]

PREFERRED STOCK FEATURES

Preferred stock pays a cash dividend expressed in terms of dollars per share. Preferred stock has a preference over common stock in the payment of dividends and in the distribution of corporation assets in the event of liquidation. *Preference* means only that holders of preferred shares must receive a dividend (in the case of an ongoing firm) before holders of common shares are entitled to anything. Preferred stock typically has no maturity date.

Preferred stock is a form of equity from a legal and tax standpoint. It is important to note, however, that holders of preferred stock usually have no voting privileges.

Stated Value Preferred shares have a stated liquidating value, usually $100 per share. For example, General Motors' "$5 preferred," paying an annual dividend of $5, translates into a dividend yield of 5 percent of stated value.

Cumulative and Noncumulative Dividends A preferred dividend is *not* like interest on a bond. The decision of the board of directors not to pay the dividends on preferred shares may have nothing to do with the current net income of the corporation.

Dividends payable on preferred stock are either *cumulative* or *noncumulative;* most are cumulative. If preferred dividends are cumulative and are not paid in a particular year, they will be carried forward as an *arrearage*. Usually, both the accumulated (past) preferred dividends and the current preferred dividends must be paid before the common shareholders can receive anything.

Unpaid preferred dividends are *not* debts of the firm. Directors elected by the common shareholders can defer preferred dividends indefinitely. However, in such cases, common shareholders must also forgo dividends. In addition, holders of preferred

---

[3]More specifically, the 70 percent exclusion applies when the recipient owns less than 20 percent of the outstanding stock in a corporation. If a corporation owns more than 20 percent but less than 80 percent, the exclusion is 80 percent. If more than 80 percent is owned, the corporation can file a single "consolidated" return and the exclusion is effectively 100 percent.

shares are sometimes granted voting and other rights if preferred dividends have not been paid for some time.

Is Preferred Stock Really Debt? A good case can be made that preferred stock is really debt in disguise. Preferred shareholders receive a stated dividend only, and, if the corporation is liquidated, preferred shareholders get a stated value. Often, preferred stocks carry credit ratings much like those of bonds. Preferred stock is sometimes convertible into common stock. In addition, preferred stocks are often callable, which allows the issuer to repurchase, or "call," part or all of the issue at a stated price. More will be said about the call feature in the next section.

Though preferred stock typically has no maturity date, many issues have obligatory sinking funds. A sinking fund requires a company to retire a portion of its preferred stock each year. A sinking fund effectively creates a final maturity, since the entire issue will ultimately be retired. More will be said on sinking funds in the next section. For these reasons, preferred stock seems to be a lot like debt. However, for tax purposes, preferred dividends are treated like common stock dividends.

In the 1990s, firms began to sell securities that looked a lot like preferred stock but were treated as debt for tax purposes. The new securities were given interesting acronyms like TOPrS (trust-originated preferred securities, or toppers), MIPS (monthly income preferred securities), and QUIPS (quarterly income preferred securities), among others. Because of various specific features, these instruments can be counted as debt for tax purposes, making the interest payments tax deductible. Payments made to investors in these instruments are treated as interest for personal income taxes for individuals. Until 2003, interest payments and dividends were taxed at the same marginal tax rate. When the tax rate on dividend payments was reduced, these instruments were not included, so individuals must still pay their higher income tax rate on dividend payments received from these instruments.

15.2 Corporate Long-Term Debt

In this section, we describe in some detail the basic terms and features of a typical long-term corporate bond. We discuss additional issues associated with long-term debt in subsequent sections.

Securities issued by corporations may be classified roughly as *equity securities* or *debt securities*. A debt represents something that must be repaid; it is the result of borrowing money. When corporations borrow, they generally promise to make regularly scheduled interest payments and to repay the original amount borrowed (that is, the principal). The person or firm making the loan is called the *creditor*, or *lender*. The corporation borrowing the money is called the *debtor*, or *borrower*.

From a financial point of view, the main differences between debt and equity are:

Information for bond investors can be found at **www. investinginbonds. com**.

1. Debt is not an ownership interest in the firm. Creditors generally do not have voting power.

2. The corporation's payment of interest on debt is considered a cost of doing business and is fully tax deductible. Dividends paid to stockholders are *not* tax deductible.

3. Unpaid debt is a liability of the firm. If it is not paid, the creditors can legally claim the assets of the firm. This action can result in liquidation or reorganization, two of the possible consequences of bankruptcy. Thus, one of the costs of

issuing debt is the possibility of financial failure. This possibility does not arise when equity is issued.

IS IT DEBT OR EQUITY?

Sometimes it is not clear if a particular security is debt or equity. For example, suppose a corporation issues a perpetual bond with interest payable solely from corporate income if, and only if, earned. Whether or not this is really a debt is hard to say and is primarily a legal and semantic issue. Courts and taxing authorities would have the final say.

Corporations are very adept at creating exotic, hybrid securities that have many features of equity but are treated as debt. Obviously, the distinction between debt and equity is very important for tax purposes. So, one reason that corporations try to create a debt security that is really equity is to obtain the tax benefits of debt and the bankruptcy benefits of equity.

As a general rule, equity represents an ownership interest and is a residual claim. This means that equityholders are paid after debtholders. As a result, the risks and benefits associated with owning debt and equity are different. To give just one example, note that the maximum reward for owning a debt security is ultimately fixed by the amount of the loan, whereas there is no upper limit to the potential reward from owning an equity interest.

Equity versus Debt

Feature	Equity	Debt
Income	Dividends	Interest
Tax status	Dividends are taxed as personal income, although currently capped at 15%. Dividends are not a business expense.	Interest is taxed as personal income. Interest is a business expense, and corporations can deduct interest when computing their corporate tax liability.
Control	Common stock usually has voting rights.	Control is exercised with loan agreement.
Default	Firms cannot be forced into bankruptcy for nonpayment of dividends.	Unpaid debt is a liability of the firm. Nonpayment results in bankruptcy.

Bottom line: Tax status favors debt, but default favors equity. Control features of debt and equity are different, but one is not better than the other.

LONG-TERM DEBT: THE BASICS

Ultimately, all long-term debt securities are promises made by the issuing firm to pay principal when due and to make timely interest payments on the unpaid balance. Beyond this, there are a number of features that distinguish these securities from one another. We discuss some of these features next.

The maturity of a long-term debt instrument is the length of time the debt remains outstanding with some unpaid balance. Debt securities can be short term (with maturities of one year or less) or long term (with maturities of more than one year).[4] Short-term debt is sometimes referred to as *unfunded debt*.[5]

Debt securities are typically called *notes, debentures,* or *bonds*. Strictly speaking, a bond is a secured debt, meaning that certain property is pledged as security for repayment of the debt. However, in common usage, the word *bond* refers to all kinds of secured and unsecured debt. We will therefore continue to use the term generically to refer to long-term debt. Also, usually, the only difference between a note and a bond is the original maturity. Issues with an original maturity of 10 years or less are often called notes. Longer-term issues are called bonds.

Long-term debt can be issued to the public or privately placed. Privately placed debt is issued to a lender and not offered to the public. Because this is a private transaction, the specific terms are up to the parties involved. We concentrate on public-issue bonds. However, most of what we say about them holds true for private-issue, long-term debt as well.

There are many other aspects to long-term debt, including such terms as security, call features, sinking funds, ratings, and protective covenants. The following table illustrates these features for a bond issued by Intel. If some of these terms are unfamiliar, have no fear. We will discuss them all presently.

Information on individual bonds can be found at **www.nasdbondinfo.com**.

Features of an Intel Bond		
Term		**Explanation**
Amount of issue	$1.5 billion	The company issued $1.5 billion worth of bonds.
Date of issue	09/19/2011	The bonds were sold on 09/19/2011.
Maturity	10/01/2041	The bonds mature on 10/01/2041.
Face value	$2,000	The denomination of the bonds is $2,000.
Annual coupon	4.80	Each bondholder will receive $96 per bond per year (4.80% of face value).
Offer price	99.258	The offer price will be 99.258% of the $2,000 face value, or $1,985.16, per bond.
Coupon payment dates	04/01, 10/01	Coupons of $96/2 = $48 will be paid on these dates.
Security	None	The bonds are not secured by specific assets.
Sinking fund	None	The bonds have no sinking fund.
Call provision	At any time	The bonds do not have a deferred call.
Call price	Treasury rate plus .25%	The bonds have a "make whole" call price.
Rating	Moody's A1, S&P A+	The bonds have relatively high credit rating (but not the best possible rating).

Many of these features will be detailed in the bond indenture, so we discuss this first.

---

[4]There is no universally agreed-upon distinction between short-term and long-term debt. In addition, people often refer to intermediate-term debt, which has a maturity of more than 1 year and less than 3 to 5, or even 10, years.

[5]The word *funding* is part of the jargon of finance. It generally refers to the long term. Thus, a firm planning to "fund" its debt requirements may be replacing short-term debt with long-term debt.

THE INDENTURE

The **indenture** is the written agreement between the corporation (the borrower) and its creditors. It is sometimes referred to as the *deed of trust*.[6] Usually, a trustee (a bank perhaps) is appointed by the corporation to represent the bondholders. The trust company must (1) make sure the terms of the indenture are obeyed, (2) manage the sinking fund (described in the following pages), and (3) represent the bondholders in default, that is, if the company defaults on its payments to them.

The bond indenture is a legal document. It can run several hundred pages and generally makes for very tedious reading. It is an important document, however, because it generally includes the following provisions:

1. The basic terms of the bonds.
2. A description of property used as security.
3. Seniority.
4. The repayment arrangements.
5. The call provisions.
6. Details of the protective covenants.

We discuss these features next.

Terms of a Bond   Corporate bonds usually have a face value (that is, a denomination) of $1,000. This is called the *principal value* and it is stated on the bond certificate. So, if a corporation wanted to borrow $1 million, 1,000 bonds would have to be sold. The par value (that is, initial accounting value) of a bond is almost always the same as the face value, and the terms are used interchangeably in practice. Although a par value of $1,000 is most common, essentially any par value is possible. For example, looking at our Intel bonds, the par value is $2,000.

Corporate bonds are usually in **registered form.** For example, the indenture might read as follows:

Interest is payable semiannually on July 1 and January 1 of each year to the person in whose name the bond is registered at the close of business on June 15 or December 15, respectively.

This means that the company has a registrar who will record the initial ownership of each bond, as well as any changes in ownership. The company will pay the interest and principal by check mailed directly to the address of the owner of record. A corporate bond may be registered and have attached "coupons." To obtain an interest payment, the owner must separate a coupon from the bond certificate and send it to the company registrar (the paying agent).

Alternatively, the bond could be in **bearer form.** This means that the certificate is the basic evidence of ownership, and the corporation will "pay the bearer." Ownership is not otherwise recorded, and, as with a registered bond with attached coupons, the holder of the bond certificate detaches the coupons and sends them to the company to receive payment.

There are two drawbacks to bearer bonds. First, they are difficult to recover if they are lost or stolen. Second, because the company does not know who owns its

---

[6]The phrases *loan agreement,* or *loan contract* are usually used for privately placed debt and term loans.

bonds, it cannot notify bondholders of important events. Bearer bonds were once the dominant type, but they are now much less common (in the United States) than registered bonds.

Security   Debt securities are classified according to the collateral and mortgages used to protect the bondholder.

Collateral is a general term that frequently means securities (for example, bonds and stocks) that are pledged as security for payment of debt. For example, collateral trust bonds often involve a pledge of common stock held by the corporation. However, the term *collateral* is commonly used to refer to any asset pledged on a debt.

Mortgage securities are secured by a mortgage on the real property of the borrower. The property involved is usually real estate, such as land or buildings. The legal document that describes the mortgage is called a *mortgage trust indenture* or *trust deed*.

Sometimes mortgages are on specific property, such as a railroad car. More often, blanket mortgages are used. A blanket mortgage pledges all the real property owned by the company.[7]

Bonds frequently represent unsecured obligations of the company. A **debenture** is an unsecured bond for which no specific pledge of property is made. The term **note** is generally used for such instruments if the maturity of the unsecured bond is less than 10 or so years from the date when the bond was originally issued. Debenture holders have a claim only on property not otherwise pledged, in other words, the property that remains after mortgages and collateral trusts are taken into account.

The terminology that we use here and elsewhere in this chapter is standard in the United States. Outside the United States, these same terms can have different meanings. For example, bonds issued by the British government ("gilts") are called treasury "stock." Also, in the United Kingdom, a debenture is a *secured* obligation.

At the current time, public bonds issued in the United States by industrial and financial companies are typically debentures. However, most utility and railroad bonds are secured by a pledge of assets.

The Securities Industry and Financial Markets Association (SIFMA) site is www.sifma.org.

Seniority   In general terms, *seniority* indicates preference in position over other lenders, and debts are sometimes labeled as *senior* or *junior* to indicate seniority. Some debt is *subordinated,* as in, for example, a subordinated debenture.

In the event of default, holders of subordinated debt must give preference to other specified creditors. Usually, this means that the subordinated lenders will be paid off only after the specified creditors have been compensated. However, debt cannot be subordinated to equity.

Repayment   Bonds can be repaid entirely at maturity, at which time the bondholder receives the stated, or face, value of the bond, or they may be repaid in part or in entirety before maturity. Early repayment in some form is more typical and is often handled through a sinking fund.

A **sinking fund** is an account managed by the bond trustee for the purpose of repaying the bonds. The company makes annual payments to the trustee, who then uses the funds to retire a portion of the debt. The trustee does this by either buying up some of the bonds in the market or calling in a fraction of the outstanding bonds. This second option is discussed in the next section.

---

[7]Real property includes land and things "affixed thereto." It does not include cash or inventories.

There are many different kinds of sinking fund arrangements, and the details are spelled out in the indenture. For example:

1. Some sinking funds start about 10 years after the initial issuance.
2. Some sinking funds establish equal payments over the life of the bond.
3. Some high-quality bond issues establish payments to the sinking fund that are not sufficient to redeem the entire issue. As a consequence, there may be a large "balloon payment" at maturity.

The Call Provision   A **call provision** allows the company to repurchase, or "call," part or all of the bond issue at stated prices over a specific period. Corporate bonds are usually callable.

Generally, the call price is above the bond's stated value (that is, the par value). The difference between the call price and the stated value is the **call premium.** The amount of the call premium may become smaller over time. One arrangement is to initially set the call premium equal to the annual coupon payment and then make it decline to zero as the call date moves closer to the time of maturity.

Call provisions are often not operative during the first part of a bond's life, making the call provision less of a worry for bondholders in the bond's early years. For example, a company might be prohibited from calling its bonds for the first 10 years. This is a **deferred call provision.** During the period of prohibition, the bond is said to be **call protected.**

In just the last few years, a new type of call provision, a "make-whole" call, has become widespread in the corporate bond market. With such a feature, bondholders receive approximately what the bonds are worth if they are called. Because bondholders don't suffer a loss in the event of a call, they are "made whole."

To determine the make-whole call price, we calculate the present value of the remaining interest and principal payments at a rate specified in the indenture. For example, looking at our Intel issue, we see that the discount rate is "Treasury rate plus .25%." What this means is that we determine the discount rate by first finding a U.S. Treasury issue with the same maturity. We calculate the yield to maturity on the Treasury issue and then add on an additional .25 percent to get the discount rate we use.

Notice that, with a make-whole call provision, the call price is higher when interest rates are lower and vice versa (why?). Also notice that, as is common with a make-whole call, the Intel issue does not have a deferred call feature. Why might investors not be too concerned about the absence of this feature?

Protective Covenants   A **protective covenant** in the indenture or loan agreement affects certain corporate actions. Protective covenants can be classified into two types: negative covenants and positive (or affirmative) covenants.

A *negative covenant* is a "thou shalt not" type of covenant. It limits or prohibits actions that the company might take. For example, the firm must limit the amount of dividends it pays according to some formula.

A *positive covenant* is a "thou shalt" type of covenant. It specifies an action that the company must take or a condition that the company must abide by. For example, the company must maintain its working capital at or above some specified minimum level.

A particular indenture may feature many different negative and positive covenants.

Want detailed information on the amount and terms of the debt issued by a particular firm? Check out its latest financial statements by searching SEC filings at **www.sec.gov**.

15.3 Some Different Types of Bonds

Thus far, we have considered only "plain vanilla" corporate bonds. In this section, we look at corporate bonds with unusual features.

FLOATING-RATE BONDS

The conventional bonds we have talked about in this chapter have fixed-dollar obligations because the coupon rate is set as a fixed percentage of the par value and the principal is set equal to the par value. With *floating-rate bonds (floaters)*, the coupon payments are adjustable. The adjustments are tied to an interest rate index such as the Treasury bill interest rate or the London Interbank Offered Rate (LIBOR).

The value of a floating-rate bond depends on how the coupon payment adjustments are defined. In most cases, the coupon adjusts with a lag to some base rate. For example, suppose a coupon rate adjustment is made on June 1. The adjustment might be based on the simple average of Treasury bond yields during the previous three months.

In addition, the majority of floaters have the following features:

1. The holder has the right to redeem his note at par on the coupon payment date after some specified amount of time. This is called a *put* provision, and it is discussed in the following section.

2. The coupon rate has a floor and a ceiling, meaning that the coupon is subject to a minimum and a maximum. In this case, the coupon rate is said to be "capped," and the upper and lower rates are sometimes called the *collar*.

OTHER TYPES OF BONDS

Many bonds have unusual or exotic features. One such feature is called a warrant. For a bond with warrants attached, the buyers also receive the right to purchase shares of stock in the company at a fixed price per share over the subsequent life of the bond. Such a right can be very valuable if the stock price climbs substantially. (A later chapter discusses this subject in greater depth.) Bonds with warrants differ from convertible bonds because the warrants can be sold separately from the bond.

Bond features are really only limited by the imaginations of the parties involved. Unfortunately, there are far too many variations for us to cover in detail here. We therefore close out this section by mentioning only a few of the more common types.

Income bonds are similar to conventional bonds, except that coupon payments are dependent on company income. Specifically, coupons are paid to bondholders only if the firm's income is sufficient. This would appear to be an attractive feature, but income bonds are not very common.

A *convertible bond* can be swapped for a fixed number of shares of stock anytime before maturity at the holder's option. Convertibles are relatively common, but the number has been decreasing in recent years.

A *put bond* allows the *holder* to force the issuer to buy the bond back at a stated price. For example, International Paper Co. has bonds outstanding that allow the holder to force International Paper to buy the bonds back at 100 percent of face value given that certain "risk" events happen. One such event is a change in credit rating from investment grade to lower than investment grade by Moody's or S&P. The put feature is therefore just the reverse of the call provision.

A given bond may have many unusual features. Two of the most recent exotic bonds are CoCo bonds, which have a coupon payment, and NoNo bonds, which are zero coupon bonds. CoCo and NoNo bonds are contingent convertible, putable, callable, subordinated bonds. The contingent convertible clause is similar to the normal conversion feature, except the contingent feature must be met. For example, a contingent feature may require that the company stock trade at 110 percent of the conversion price for 20 out of the most recent 30 days. Valuing a bond of this sort can be quite complex, and the yield to maturity calculation is often meaningless. For example, in 2011, a NoNo issued by the American International Group (AIG) was selling at a price of $1,032.50, with a yield to maturity of negative 1.6 percent. At the same time, a NoNo issued by Merrill Lynch was selling for $1,205, which implied a yield to maturity of negative 107 percent!

15.4 Bank Loans

In addition to issuing bonds, a firm may simply borrow from a bank. Two important features of bank loans are lines of credit and syndication.

Lines of Credit   Banks often provide a business customer with a line of credit, setting the maximum amount that the bank is willing to lend to the business. The business can then borrow the money according to its need for funds. If the bank is legally obligated, the credit line is generally referred to as a revolving line of credit or a *revolver*. As an example, imagine a revolver for $75 million with a three-year commitment, implying that the business could borrow part or all of the $75 million anytime within the next three years. A commitment fee is generally charged on the unused portion of the revolver. Suppose the commitment fee is .20% and the corporation borrows $25 million in a particular year, leaving $50 million unborrowed. The dollar commitment fee would be $100,000 (= .20% × $50 million) for that year, in addition to the interest on the $25 million actually borrowed.

Syndicated Loans   Very large banks such as Citigroup typically have a larger demand for loans than they can supply, and small regional banks frequently have more funds on hand than they can profitably lend to existing customers. Basically, they cannot generate enough good loans with the funds they have available. As a result, a very large bank may arrange a syndicated loan with a firm or country and then sell portions of it to a syndicate of other banks. With a syndicated loan, each bank has a separate loan agreement with the borrowers.

The syndicate is generally composed of a lead arranger and participant lenders. As the name suggests, the lead arranger takes the lead, creating the relationship with the borrower and negotiating the specifics of the loan. The participant lenders are typically not involved in the negotiation process. The lead arranger works with the participant lenders to determine shares of the loan, and generally lends the most. While all lenders receive interest and principal payments, the lead arranger also receives an up-front fee as compensation for his additional responsibilities.

A syndicated loan may be publicly traded. It may be a line of credit and be "undrawn," or it may be drawn and used by a firm. Syndicated loans are always rated investment grade. However, a *leveraged* syndicated loan is rated speculative grade (i.e., it is "junk").

15.5 International Bonds

A **Eurobond** is a bond issued in multiple countries but denominated in a single currency, usually the issuer's home currency. For example, an American firm may issue a dollar-denominated bond in a number of foreign countries. Such bonds have become an important way to raise capital for many international companies and governments. Eurobonds are issued outside the restrictions that apply to domestic offerings and are syndicated and traded mostly from London. However, trading can and does take place anywhere there are buyers and sellers. Eurobonds had been trading for many years before the euro, the single currency across many European countries, was created in 1999. However, because the two terms are so similar, people mistakenly think Eurobonds must be denominated in euros. To avoid confusion, many refer to Eurobonds as international bonds.

Foreign bonds, unlike Eurobonds, are issued in a single country and are usually denominated in that country's currency. For example, a Canadian firm might issue yen-denominated bonds in Japan. Often, the country in which these bonds are issued will draw distinctions between them and bonds issued by domestic issuers—including different tax laws, restrictions on the amount issued, and tougher disclosure rules.

Foreign bonds often are nicknamed for the country where they are issued: Yankee bonds (United States), Samurai bonds (Japan), Rembrandt bonds (the Netherlands), Bulldog bonds (Britain). Partly because of tougher regulations and disclosure requirements, the foreign bond market hasn't grown in past years with the vigor of the Eurobond market.

15.6 Patterns of Financing

The previous sections of this chapter discussed some institutional details related to long-term financing. We now consider the relationship between long-term financing and investments. As we have seen in earlier chapters, firms want to spend on capital projects with positive NPV. How can these firms get the cash to fund investments in positive NPV projects? First, firms generating positive cash flow internally can use that flow for positive NPV investments. In accounting terms, this cash flow is net income plus depreciation minus dividends. Second, firms can fund positive NPV capital spending through external financing, i.e., by issuing debt and equity.

This relationship between investment and financing is described in Figure 15.1. The left-hand side of the figure shows that cash flow can fund both capital spending and investment in net working capital. As indicated in the figure, U.S. firms have historically used about 80 percent of cash flow on capital spending and about 20 percent on investment in net working capital. The right-hand side of the figure shows the two sources of cash flow, internal and external financing. In the figure, uses of cash flow exceed internal financing. Thus, stocks and bonds must be issued to fill the *financial deficit.*

In practice, what has been the split between internal and external financing? Figure 15.2 breaks down total financing for U.S. businesses into internal financing, financing through new equity, and financing through new debt for each year from 1995 to 2010. Consider 1995, for example. Internal financing in the U.S. was about 75 percent of the total, new debt was somewhat above 25 percent of the total, and new equity was a slightly negative number. Notice that in this year, as in all the years, the

Chapter 15   Long-Term Financing   487

Figure 15.1
The Long-Term
Financial Deficit

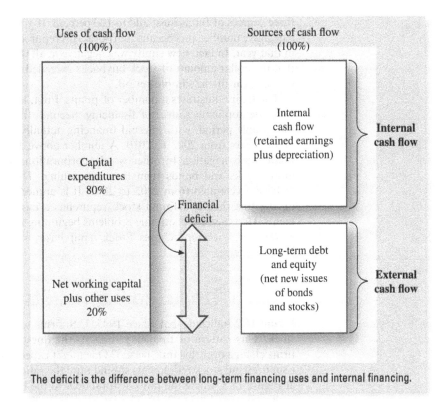

The deficit is the difference between long-term financing uses and internal financing.

Figure 15.2
Financing Decisions
by U.S. Nonfinancial
Corporations

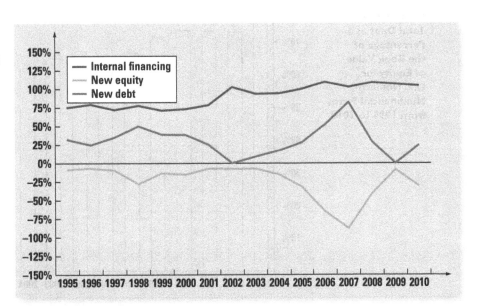

three sources of funds must add to 100 percent. If you are wondering why net equity is a negative number, it is because corporations repurchased more stock than they issued in that year. In fact, new equity was negative in all the years of our sample, indicating that the dollar amount of stock buybacks exceeded the dollar amount of stock issues in each year of the sample period.

The figure illustrates a number of points. First, internally generated cash flow has been the dominant source of financing. Second, this dominance has increased over the sample period, with internal financing actually exceeding 100 percent for most of the years from 2002 to 2010. A number above 100 percent implies that external financing is negative. In other words, corporations are, in dollar terms, redeeming more stocks and bonds than they are issuing. Third, net stock buybacks appear to have accelerated from 2002 to 2007. It is argued that firms were flush with cash during this time and found stock repurchases more attractive than dividend payments. However, the economic problems beginning in 2008 greatly reduced the dollar amount of stock repurchases. Stock repurchases will be discussed in more detail in later chapters.

15.7 Recent Trends in Capital Structure

Figure 15.2 indicates that, since 1995, U.S. firms tended to issue debt while retiring stock. This pattern of financing suggests the question: Did the capital structure of firms change over this time period? One might expect the answer to be yes, since debt issuances and stock retirements should raise the ratio of debt to equity. However, look at Figure 15.3, where the ratio of total debt to the book value of equity is shown for each year from 1995 to 2010. The ratio was actually lower in 2010 than it was in 1995,

Figure 15.3
**Book Debt Ratio:
Total Debt as a
Percentage of
the Book Value
of Equity for
U.S. Nonfarm,
Nonfinancial Firms
from 1995 to 2010**

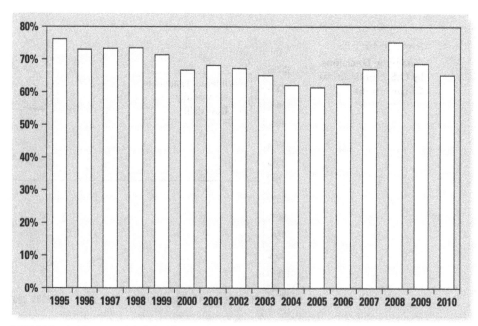

SOURCE: Board of Governors of the Federal Reserve System. "Flow of Funds Accounts of the United States." Federal Reserve Statistical Release. June 9, 2011, <http://www.federalreserve.gov/releases/z1/20110609.

Chapter 15   Long-Term Financing   **489**

Figure 15.4
Market Debt
Ratio: Total Debt
as a Percentage
of the Market
Value of Equity
for U.S. Nonfarm,
Nonfinancial Firms
from 1995 to 2010

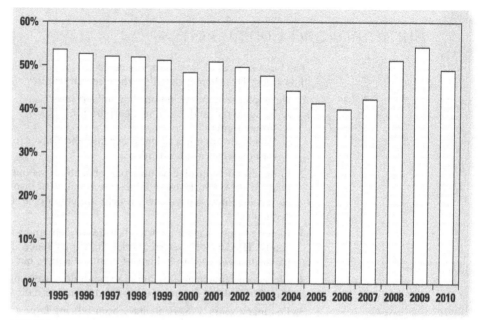

SOURCE: Board of Governors of the Federal Reserve System. "Flow of Funds Accounts of the United States." Federal Reserve Statistical Release. June 9, 2011, <http://www.federalreserve.gov/releases/z1/20110609.

though the decline was modest. This result is not surprising once retained earnings are considered. As long as net income exceeds dividends, retained earnings will be positive, raising the book value of equity.

Of course, equity can be measured in terms of market value, rather than book value. Figure 15.4 shows the ratio of total debt to the market value of equity for U.S. firms for each year since 1995. While the ratio here has also fallen slightly over the 15-year period, the pattern is somewhat different. This is not surprising, since movements in the stock market affect market values of individual firms. Taken together, both figures suggest that the ratio of debt to equity has changed little, in spite of the pattern exhibited in Figure 15.2 of debt issuance funding equity retirements.

WHICH ARE BEST: BOOK OR MARKET VALUES?

Financial economists generally prefer market values when calculating debt ratios, since, as Chapter 14 indicates, market prices reflect current information. However, the use of market values contrasts with the perspective of many corporate practitioners.

Our conversations with corporate treasurers suggest to us that the use of book values is popular because of the volatility of the stock market. It is frequently claimed that the inherent volatility of the stock market makes market-based debt ratios move around too much. In addition, restrictions of debt in bond covenants are usually expressed in book values rather than market values. Moreover, firms such as Standard & Poor's and Moody's use debt ratios expressed in book values to measure credit-worthiness.

A key fact is that whether we use book or market values, debt ratios for U.S. non-financial firms generally have been well below 100 percent of total equity in recent years; that is, firms generally use less debt than equity.

◄ To test your mastery of this material, take a quiz at mhhe. com/rwj

Summary and Conclusions

The basic sources of long-term financing are long-term debt, preferred stock, and common stock. This chapter described the essential features of each.

1. We emphasized that common shareholders have:
   a. Residual risk and return in a corporation.
   b. Voting rights.
   c. Dividends are not a business expense and firms cannot be forced into bankruptcy for non payment of a dividend.

2. Long-term debt involves contractual obligations set out in indentures. There are many kinds of debt, but the essential feature is that debt involves a stated amount that must be repaid. Interest payments on debt are considered a business expense and are tax deductible.

3. Preferred stock has some of the features of debt and some of the features of common equity. Holders of preferred stock have preference in liquidation and in dividend payments compared to holders of common equity, but often hold no voting rights.

4. Firms need financing for capital expenditures, working capital, and other long-term uses. Most of the financing is provided from internally generated cash flow.

5. For many years, U.S. firms have been retiring large amounts of equity. These share buybacks have been financed with new debt.

Concept Questions

1. **Bond Features**   What are the main features of a corporate bond that would be listed in the indenture?

2. **Preferred Stock and Debt**   What are the differences between preferred stock and debt?

3. **Preferred Stock**   Preferred stock doesn't offer a corporate tax shield on the dividends paid. Why do we still observe some firms issuing preferred stock?

4. **Preferred Stock and Bond Yields**   The yields on nonconvertible preferred stock are lower than the yields on corporate bonds. Why is there a difference? Which investors are the primary holders of preferred stock? Why?

5. **Corporate Financing**   What are the main differences between corporate debt and equity? Why do some firms try to issue equity in the guise of debt?

6. **Call Provisions**   A company is contemplating a long-term bond issue. It is debating whether to include a call provision. What are the benefits to the company from including a call provision? What are the costs? How do these answers change for a put provision?

7. **Proxy**   What is a proxy?

8. **Preferred Stock**   Do you think preferred stock is more like debt or equity? Why?

9. **Long-Term Financing**   As was mentioned in the chapter, new equity issues are generally only a small portion of all new issues. At the same time, companies continue to issue new debt. Why do companies tend to issue little new equity but continue to issue new debt?

10. **Internal versus External Financing**   What is the difference between internal financing and external financing?

11. **Internal versus External Financing**   What factors influence a firm's choice of external versus internal equity financing?

12. **Classes of Stock**   Several publicly traded companies have issued more than one class of stock. Why might a company issue more than one class of stock?

13. **Callable Bonds**   Do you agree or disagree with the following statement: In an efficient market, callable and noncallable bonds will be priced in such a way that there will be no advantage or disadvantage to the call provision. Why?

14. **Bond Prices**   If interest rates fall, will the price of noncallable bonds move up higher than that of callable bonds? Why or why not?

15. **Sinking Funds**   Sinking funds have both positive and negative characteristics for bondholders. Why?

Questions and Problems

BASIC
(Questions 1–6)

1. **Corporate Voting**   The shareholders of the Stackhouse Company need to elect seven new directors. There are 850,000 shares outstanding currently trading at $43 per share. You would like to serve on the board of directors; unfortunately no one else will be voting for you. How much will it cost you to be certain that you can be elected if the company uses straight voting? How much will it cost you if the company uses cumulative voting?

2. **Cumulative Voting**   An election is being held to fill three seats on the board of directors of a firm in which you hold stock. The company has 7,600 shares outstanding. If the election is conducted under cumulative voting and you own 300 shares, how many more shares must you buy to be assured of earning a seat on the board?

3. **Cumulative Voting**   The shareholders of Motive Power Corp. need to elect three new directors to the board. There are 13,000,000 shares of common stock outstanding, and the current share price is $10.50. If the company uses cumulative voting procedures, how much will it cost to guarantee yourself one seat on the board of directors?

4. **Corporate Voting**   Candle box Inc. is going to elect six board members next month. Betty Brown owns 17.4 percent of the total shares outstanding. How confident can she be of having one of her candidate friends elected under the cumulative voting rule? Will her friend be elected for certain if the voting procedure is changed to the staggering rule, under which shareholders vote on two board members at a time?

INTERMEDIATE
(Questions 5–10)

5. **Valuing Callable Bonds**   KIC, Inc., plans to issue $5 million of bonds with a coupon rate of 8 percent and 30 years to maturity. The current market interest rates on these bonds are 7 percent. In one year, the interest rate on the bonds will be either 10 percent or 6 percent with equal probability. Assume investors are risk-neutral.
   a. If the bonds are noncallable, what is the price of the bonds today?
   b. If the bonds are callable one year from today at $1,080, will their price be greater or less than the price you computed in (a)? Why?

6. **Valuing Callable Bonds**   New Business Ventures, Inc., has an outstanding perpetual bond with a 10 percent coupon rate that can be called in one year. The bond makes annual coupon payments. The call premium is set at $150 over par value. There is a 60 percent chance that the interest rate in one year will be 12 percent, and a 40 percent chance that the interest rate will be 7 percent. If the current interest rate is 10 percent, what is the current market price of the bond?

7. **Valuing Callable Bonds** Bowdeen Manufacturing intends to issue callable, perpetual bonds with annual coupon payments. The bonds are callable at $1,175. One-year interest rates are 9 percent. There is a 60 percent probability that long-term interest rates one year from today will be 10 percent, and a 40 percent probability that they will be 8 percent. Assume that if interest rates fall the bonds will be called. What coupon rate should the bonds have in order to sell at par value?

8. **Valuing Callable Bonds** Illinois Industries has decided to borrow money by issuing perpetual bonds with a coupon rate of 7 percent, payable annually. The one-year interest rate is 7 percent. Next year, there is a 35 percent probability that interest rates will increase to 9 percent, and there is a 65 percent probability that they will fall to 6 percent.

   a. What will the market value of these bonds be if they are noncallable?
   b. If the company decides instead to make the bonds callable in one year, what coupon will be demanded by the bondholders for the bonds to sell at par? Assume that the bonds will be called if interest rates rise and that the call premium is equal to the annual coupon.
   c. What will be the value of the call provision to the company?

9. **Bond Refunding** An outstanding issue of Public Express Airlines debentures has a call provision attached. The total principal value of the bonds is $250 million, and the bonds have an annual coupon rate of 9 percent. The company is considering refunding the bond issue. Refunding means that the company would issue new bonds and use the proceeds from the new bond issuance to repurchase the outstanding bonds. The total cost of refunding would be 10 percent of the principal amount raised. The appropriate tax rate for the company is 35 percent. How low does the borrowing cost need to drop to justify refunding with a new bond issue?

10. **Bond Refunding** Charles River Associates is considering whether to call either of the two perpetual bond issues the company currently has outstanding. If the bond is called, it will be refunded, that is, a new bond issue will be made with a lower coupon rate. The proceeds from the new bond issue will be used to repurchase one of the existing bond issues. The information about the two currently outstanding bond issues is:

	Bond A	Bond B
Coupon rate	7.00%	8.00%
Value outstanding	$125,000,000	$132,000,000
Call premium	7.50%	8.50%
Transaction cost of refunding	$ 11,500,000	$ 13,000,000
Current YTM	6.25%	7.10%

The corporate tax rate is 35 percent. What is the NPV of the refunding for each bond? Which, if either, bond should the company refinance? Assume the call premium is tax deductible.

CHALLENGE
(Questions 11–12)

11. **Valuing the Call Feature** Consider the prices of the following three Treasury issues as of February 24, 2012:

6.500	May 16	106.31250	106.37500	−13	5.28
8.250	May 16	103.43750	103.5000	−3	5.24
12.000	May 16	134.78125	134.96875	−15	5.32

The bond in the middle is callable in February 2013. What is the implied value of the call feature? (*Hint:* Is there a way to combine the two noncallable issues to create an issue that has the same coupon as the callable bond?)

12. **Treasury Bonds** The following Treasury bond quote appeared in *The Wall Street Journal* on May 11, 2004:

| 9.125 | May 09 | 100.09375 | 100.12500 | ... | −2.15 |

Why would anyone buy this Treasury bond with a negative yield to maturity? How is this possible?

CHAPTER 16

Capital Structure

BASIC CONCEPTS

▲ For updates on the latest happenings in finance, visit www. rwjcorporatefinance. blogspot.com

On June 27, 2011, the Los Angeles Dodgers baseball team filed for bankruptcy. A bankruptcy filing by a major sports franchise is unusual, to say the least, especially when the list of creditors is examined. For example, the Dodgers owed former players Manny Ramirez and Andruw Jones $21 million and $11 million, respectively. Other creditors included the Chicago White Sox ($3.5 million), concession operator Levy restaurants ($588,322), and famed announcer Vin Scully ($152,778), who has been the team's announcer since its move to Los Angeles in 1958.

Of course, in bankruptcy, customers can also be involved in the process. In this case, Dodgers' season ticket holders filed to be part of the bankruptcy, since the value of Dodgers' tickets could be affected by how the club came out of bankruptcy. In fact, the ticket holders argued that the value may have already been damaged due to "understaffed and inefficient concession stands that cause ticket holders to miss one or more innings while standing in insufferable lines for food." In bankruptcy, firms usually pay no taxes because they have no taxable income. It turns out that taxes can play a central role in capital structure decisions, as demonstrated in Chapter 16.

16.1 The Capital Structure Question and the Pie Theory

How should a firm choose its debt–equity ratio? We call our approach to the capital structure question the **pie model.** If you are wondering why we chose this name, just take a look at Figure 16.1. The pie in question is the sum of the financial claims of the firm, debt and equity in this case. We *define* the value of the firm to be this sum. Hence the value of the firm, V, is:

$$V \equiv B + S \qquad (16.1)$$

where B is the market value of the debt and S is the market value of the equity. Figure 16.1 presents two possible ways of slicing this pie between stock and debt: 40 percent–60 percent and 60 percent–40 percent. If the goal of the management of the firm is to make the firm as valuable as possible, then the firm should pick the debt–equity ratio that makes the pie—the total value—as big as possible.

This discussion begs two important questions:

1. Why should the stockholders in the firm care about maximizing the value of the entire firm?

2. What ratio of debt to equity maximizes the shareholders' interests?

Let us examine each of the two questions in turn.

Figure 16.1
Two Pie Models of
Capital Structure

16.2 Maximizing Firm Value versus Maximizing Stockholder Interests

The following example illustrates that the capital structure that maximizes the value of the firm is the one that financial managers should choose for the shareholders.

EXAMPLE 16.1

Debt and Firm Value   Suppose the market value of the J. J. Sprint Company is $1,000. The company currently has no debt, and each of J. J. Sprint's 100 shares of stock sells for $10. A company such as J. J. Sprint with no debt is called an *unlevered* company. Further suppose that J. J. Sprint plans to borrow $500 and pay the $500 proceeds to shareholders as an extra cash dividend of $5 per share. After the issuance of debt, the firm becomes *levered*. The investments of the firm will not change as a result of this transaction. What will the value of the firm be after the proposed restructuring?

Management recognizes that, by definition, only one of three outcomes can occur from restructuring. Firm value after restructuring can be (1) greater than the original firm value of $1,000, (2) equal to $1,000, or (3) less than $1,000. After consulting with investment bankers, management believes that restructuring will not change firm value more than $250 in either direction. Thus it views firm values of $1,250, $1,000, and $750 as the relevant range. The original capital structure and these three possibilities under the new capital structure are presented next:

	No Debt (Original Capital Structure)	Value of Debt plus Equity after Payment of Dividend (Three Possibilities)		
		I	II	III
Debt	$ 0	$ 500	$ 500	$500
Equity	1,000	750	500	250
Firm value	$1,000	$1,250	$1,000	$750

Note that the value of equity is below $1,000 under any of the three possibilities. This can be explained in one of two ways. First, the table shows the value of the equity *after* the extra cash dividend is paid. Because cash is paid out, a dividend represents a partial liquidation of

(continued)

the firm. Consequently there is less value in the firm for the equityholders after the dividend payment. Second, in the event of a future liquidation, stockholders will be paid only after bondholders have been paid in full. Thus the debt is an encumbrance of the firm, reducing the value of the equity.

Of course management recognizes that there are infinite possible outcomes. These three are to be viewed as *representative* outcomes only. We can now determine the payoff to stockholders under the three possibilities:

	Payoff to Shareholders after Restructuring		
	I	II	III
Capital gains	−$250	−$500	−$750
Dividends	500	500	500
Net gain or loss to stockholders	$250	$ 0	−$250

No one can be sure ahead of time which of the three outcomes will occur. However, imagine that managers believe that Outcome I is most likely. They should definitely restructure the firm because the stockholders would gain $250. That is, although the price of the stock declines by $250 to $750, they receive $500 in dividends. Their net gain is $250 = −$250 + $500. Also, notice that the value of the firm would rise by $250 = $1,250 − $1,000.

Alternatively, imagine that managers believe that Outcome III is most likely. In this case they should not restructure the firm because the stockholders would expect a $250 loss. That is, the stock falls by $750 to $250 and they receive $500 in dividends. Their net loss is −$250 = −$750 + $500. Also, notice that the value of the firm would change by −$250 = $750 − $1,000.

Finally, imagine that the managers believe that Outcome II is most likely. Restructuring would not affect the stockholders' interest because the net gain to stockholders in this case is zero. Also notice that the value of the firm is unchanged if Outcome II occurs.

This example explains why managers should attempt to maximize the value of the firm. In other words, it answers question (1) in Section 16.1. We find in this example the following wisdom:

Managers should choose the capital structure that they believe will have the highest firm value because this capital structure will be most beneficial to the firm's stockholders.[1]

Clearly, J. J. Sprint should borrow $500 if it expects Outcome I. The crucial question in determining a firm's capital structure is, of course, which outcome is likely to occur. However, this example does not tell us which of the three outcomes is most likely to occur. Thus it does not tell us whether debt should be added to J. J. Sprint's capital structure. In other words, it does not answer question (2) in Section 16.1. This second question is treated in the next section.

---

[1]This result may not hold exactly in a more complex case where debt has a significant possibility of default. Issues of default are treated in the next chapter.

Chapter 16   Capital Structure   497

16.3 Financial Leverage and Firm Value: An Example

ExcelMaster
coverage online

This section covers scroll
bars and pie charts.

LEVERAGE AND RETURNS TO SHAREHOLDERS

The previous section shows that the capital structure producing the highest firm value is the one that maximizes shareholder wealth. In this section, we wish to determine that optimal capital structure. We begin by illustrating the effect of capital structure on returns to stockholders. We will use a detailed example that we encourage students to study carefully. Once we have this example under our belts, we will be ready to determine the optimal capital structure.

Trans Am Corporation currently has no debt in its capital structure. The firm is considering issuing debt to buy back some of its equity. Both its current and proposed capital structures are presented in Table 16.1. The firm's assets are $8,000. There are 400 shares of the all-equity firm, implying a market value per share of $20. The proposed debt issue is for $4,000, leaving $4,000 in equity. The interest rate is 10 percent.

The effect of economic conditions on earnings per share is shown in Table 16.2 for the current capital structure (all equity). Consider first the middle column where earnings are expected to be $1,200. Because assets are $8,000, the return on assets (ROA) is 15 percent (=$1,200/$8,000). Assets equal equity for this all-equity firm, so return on equity (ROE) is also 15 percent. Earnings per share (EPS) is $3.00 (=$1,200/400). Similar calculations yield EPS of $1.00 and $5.00 in the cases of recession and expansion, respectively.

The case of leverage is presented in Table 16.3. ROA in the three economic states is identical in Tables 16.2 and 16.3 because this ratio is calculated before interest is considered. Debt is $4,000 here, so interest is $400 (=.10 × $4,000). Thus earnings after interest are $800 (=$1,200 − $400) in the middle (expected) case. Because equity is $4,000, ROE is 20 percent (=$800/$4,000). Earnings per share are $4.00 (=$800/200). Similar calculations yield earnings of $0 and $8.00 for recession and expansion, respectively.

Tables 16.2 and 16.3 show that the effect of financial leverage depends on the company's earnings before interest. If earnings before interest are equal to $1,200,

Table 16.1

Financial Structure of Trans Am Corporation

	Current	Proposed
Assets	$8,000	$8,000
Debt	$ 0	$4,000
Equity (market and book)	$8,000	$4,000
Interest rate	10%	10%
Market value/share	$ 20	$ 20
Shares outstanding	400	200

The proposed capital structure has leverage, whereas the current structure is all equity.

Table 16.2

Trans Am's Current Capital Structure: No Debt

	Recession	Expected	Expansion
Return on assets (ROA)	5%	15%	25%
Earnings	$400	$1,200	$2,000
Return on equity (ROE) = Earnings/Equity	5%	15%	25%
Earnings per share (EPS)	$1.00	$3.00	$5.00

Table 16.3
Trans Am's Proposed Capital Structure: Debt = $4,000

	Recession	Expected	Expansion
Return on assets (ROA)	5%	15%	25%
Earnings before interest (EBI)	$400	$1,200	$2,000
Interest	−400	−400	−400
Earnings after interest	$ 0	$ 800	$1,600
Return on equity (ROE) = Earnings after interest/Equity	0	20%	40%
Earnings per share (EPS)	0	$ 4.00	$ 8.00

the return on equity (ROE) is higher under the proposed structure. If earnings before interest are equal to $400, the ROE is higher under the current structure.

This idea is represented in Figure 16.2. The solid line represents the case of no leverage. The line begins at the origin, indicating that earnings per share (EPS) would be zero if earnings before interest (EBI) was zero. The EPS rises in tandem with a rise in EBI.

The dotted line represents the case of $4,000 of debt. Here EPS is negative if EBI is zero. This follows because $400 of interest must be paid regardless of the firm's profits.

Now consider the slopes of the two lines. The slope of the dotted line (the line with debt) is higher than the slope of the solid line. This occurs because the levered firm has *fewer* shares of stock outstanding than the unlevered firm. Therefore, any increase in EBI leads to a greater rise in EPS for the levered firm because the earnings increase is distributed over fewer shares of stock.

Because the dotted line has a lower intercept but a higher slope, the two lines must intersect. The *break-even* point occurs at $800 of EBI. Were earnings before interest

Figure 16.2
Financial Leverage: EPS and EBI for the Trans Am Corporation

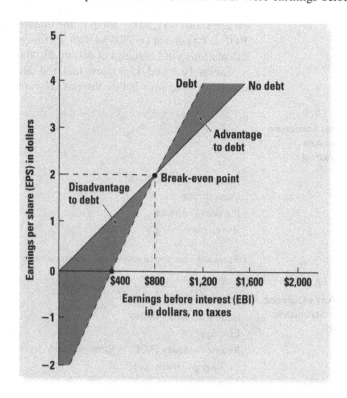

Chapter 16   Capital Structure   **499**

Table 16.4   Payoff and Cost to Shareholders of Trans Am Corporation under the Proposed Structure and under the Current Structure with Homemade Leverage

	Recession	Expected	Expansion
Strategy A: Buy 100 Shares of Levered Equity			
EPS of *levered* equity (taken from last line of Table 16.3)	$0	$ 4	$ 8
Earnings per 100 shares	0	400	800
Initial cost = 100 shares @ $20/share = $2,000			
Strategy B: Homemade Leverage			
Earnings per 200 shares in current	$1 × 200 =	$3 × 200 =	$5 × 200 =
unlevered Trans Am	200	600	1,000
Interest at 10% on $2,000	−200	−200	−200
Net earnings	$ 0	$ 400	$ 800
Initial cost = 200 shares @ $20/share − $2,000 = $2,000			

Initial cost = 200 shares @ $20/share − $2,000 = $2,000
       Cost of stock   Amount
                            borrowed

Investor receives the same payoff whether she (1) buys shares in a levered corporation or (2) buys shares in an unlevered firm and borrows on personal account. Her initial investment is the same in either case. Thus the firm neither helps nor hurts her by adding debt to capital structure.

to be $800, both firms would produce $2 of earnings per share (EPS). Because $800 is breakeven, earnings above $800 lead to a greater EPS for the levered firm. Earnings below $800 lead to a greater EPS for the unlevered firm.

THE CHOICE BETWEEN DEBT AND EQUITY

Tables 16.2 and 16.3 and Figure 16.2 are important because they show the effect of leverage on earnings per share. Students should study the tables and figure until they feel comfortable with the calculation of each number in them. However, we have not yet presented the punch line. That is, we have not yet stated which capital structure is better for Trans Am.

At this point many students believe that leverage is beneficial because EPS is expected to be $4.00 with leverage and only $3.00 without leverage. However, leverage also creates *risk*. Note that in a recession, EPS is higher ($1.00 versus $0) for the unlevered firm. Thus a risk-averse investor might prefer the all-equity firm, whereas a risk-neutral (or less risk-averse) investor might prefer leverage. Given this ambiguity, which capital structure *is* better?

Modigliani and Miller (MM or M & M) have a convincing argument that a firm cannot change the total value of its outstanding securities by changing the proportions of its capital structure. In other words, the value of the firm is always the same under different capital structures. In still other words, no capital structure is any better or worse than any other capital structure for the firm's stockholders. This rather pessimistic result is the famous **MM Proposition I.**[2]

Their argument compares a simple strategy, which we call Strategy *A*, with a two-part strategy, which we call Strategy *B*. Both of these strategies for shareholders of Trans Am are illuminated in Table 16.4. Let us now examine the first strategy.

---

[2]The original paper is F. Modigliani and M. Miller, "The Cost of Capital, Corporation Finance and the Theory of Investment," *American Economic Review* (June 1958).

Strategy A: Buy 100 shares of the levered equity

The first line in the top panel of Table 16.4 shows EPS for the proposed levered equity in the three economic states. The second line shows the earnings in the three states for an individual buying 100 shares. The next line shows that the cost of these 100 shares is $2,000.

Let us now consider the second strategy, which has two parts to it.

Strategy B: Homemade leverage

1. Borrow $2,000 from either a bank or, more likely, a brokerage house. (If the brokerage house is the lender, we say that this activity is *going on margin.*)

2. Use the borrowed proceeds plus your own investment of $2,000 (a total of $4,000) to buy 200 shares of the current unlevered equity at $20 per share.

The bottom panel of Table 16.4 shows payoffs under Strategy *B,* which we call the *homemade leverage* strategy. First observe the middle column, which indicates that 200 shares of the unlevered equity are expected to generate $600 of earnings. Assuming that the $2,000 is borrowed at a 10 percent interest rate, the interest expense is $200 ($=.10 \times \$2,000$). Thus the net earnings are expected to be $400. A similar calculation generates net earnings of either $0 or $800 in recession or expansion, respectively.

Now let us compare these two strategies, both in terms of earnings per year and in terms of initial cost. The top panel of the table shows that Strategy *A* generates earnings of $0, $400, and $800 in the three states. The bottom panel of the table shows that Strategy *B* generates the *same* net earnings in the three states.

The top panel of the table shows that Strategy *A* involves an initial cost of $2,000. Similarly, the bottom panel shows an *identical* net cost of $2,000 for Strategy *B.*

This shows a very important result. Both the cost and the payoff from the two strategies are the same. Thus we must conclude that Trans Am is neither helping nor hurting its stockholders by restructuring. In other words, an investor is not receiving anything from corporate leverage that she could not receive on her own.

Note that, as shown in Table 16.1, the equity of the unlevered firm is valued at $8,000. Because the equity of the levered firm is $4,000 and its debt is $4,000, the value of the levered firm is also $8,000. Now suppose that, for whatever reason, the value of the levered firm were actually greater than the value of the unlevered firm. Here Strategy *A* would cost more than Strategy *B.* In this case an investor would prefer to borrow on his own account and invest in the stock of the unlevered firm. He would get the same net earnings each year as if he had invested in the stock of the levered firm. However, his cost would be less. The strategy would not be unique to our investor. Given the higher value of the levered firm, no rational investor would invest in the stock of the levered firm. Anyone desiring shares in the levered firm would get the same dollar return more cheaply by borrowing to finance a purchase of the unlevered firm's shares. The equilibrium result would be, of course, that the value of the levered firm would fall and the value of the unlevered firm would rise until they became equal. At this point individuals would be indifferent between Strategy *A* and Strategy *B.*

This example illustrates the basic result of Modigliani–Miller (MM) and is, as we have noted, commonly called their Proposition I. We restate this proposition as follows:

MM Proposition I (no taxes): The value of the levered firm is the same as the value of the unlevered firm.

This is one of the most important results in all of corporate finance. In fact, it is generally considered the beginning point of modern managerial finance. Before MM, the effect of leverage on the value of the firm was considered complex and convoluted. Modigliani and Miller showed a blindingly simple result: If levered firms are priced too high, rational investors will simply borrow on their personal accounts to buy shares in unlevered firms. This substitution is often called *homemade leverage*. As long as individuals borrow (and lend) on the same terms as the firms, they can duplicate the effects of corporate leverage on their own.

The example of Trans Am Corporation shows that leverage does not affect the value of the firm. Because we showed earlier that stockholders' welfare is directly related to the firm's value, the example indicates that changes in capital structure cannot affect the stockholders' welfare.

A KEY ASSUMPTION

The MM result hinges on the assumption that individuals can borrow as cheaply as corporations. If, alternatively, individuals can borrow only at a higher rate, we can easily show that corporations can increase firm value by borrowing.

Is this assumption of equal borrowing costs a good one? Individuals who want to buy stock and borrow can do so by establishing a margin account with a broker. Under this arrangement the broker lends the individual a portion of the purchase price. For example, the individual might buy $10,000 of stock by investing $6,000 of her own funds and borrowing $4,000 from the broker. Should the stock be worth $9,000 on the next day, the individual's net worth or equity in the account would be $5,000 = $9,000 − $4,000.[3]

The broker fears that a sudden price drop will cause the equity in the individual's account to be negative, implying that the broker may not get her loan repaid in full. To guard against this possibility, stock exchange rules require that the individual make additional cash contributions (replenish her margin account) as the stock price falls. Because (1) the procedures for replenishing the account have developed over many years and (2) the broker holds the stock as collateral, there is little default risk to the broker.[4] In particular, if margin contributions are not made on time, the broker can sell the stock to satisfy her loan. Therefore, brokers generally charge low interest, with many rates being only slightly above the risk-free rate.

By contrast, corporations frequently borrow using illiquid assets (e.g., plant and equipment) as collateral. The costs to the lender of initial negotiation and ongoing supervision, as well as of working out arrangements in the event of financial distress, can be quite substantial. Thus it is difficult to argue that individuals must borrow at higher rates than corporations.

16.4 Modigliani and Miller: Proposition II (No Taxes)

RISK TO EQUITYHOLDERS RISES WITH LEVERAGE

At a Trans Am corporate meeting, a corporate officer said, "Well, maybe it does not matter whether the corporation or the individual levers—as long as some leverage takes place. Leverage benefits investors. After all, an investor's expected return rises with the amount of the leverage present." He then pointed out that, as shown in Tables 16.2 and 16.3, the expected return on unlevered equity is 15 percent whereas the expected return on levered equity is 20 percent.

---

[3]We are ignoring the one-day interest charge on the loan.

[4]Had this text been published before October 19, 1987, when stock prices declined by more than 20 percent in a single day, we might have used the phrase "virtually no" risk instead of "little" risk.

However, another officer replied, "Not necessarily. Though the expected return rises with leverage, the *risk* rises as well." This point can be seen from an examination of Tables 16.2 and 16.3. With earnings before interest (EBI) varying between $400 and $2,000, earnings per share (EPS) for the stockholders of the unlevered firm vary between $1.00 and $5.00. EPS for the stockholders of the levered firm varies between $0 and $8.00. This greater range for the EPS of the levered firm implies greater risk for the levered firm's stockholders. In other words, levered stockholders have better returns in good times than do unlevered stockholders but have worse returns in bad times. The two tables also show greater range for the ROE of the levered firm's stockholders. The earlier interpretation concerning risk applies here as well.

The same insight can be taken from Figure 16.2. The slope of the line for the levered firm is greater than the slope of the line for the unlevered firm. This means that the levered stockholders have better returns in good times than do unlevered stockholders but have worse returns in bad times, implying greater risk with leverage. In other words, the slope of the line measures the risk to stockholders because the slope indicates the responsiveness of ROE to changes in firm performance (earnings before interest).

PROPOSITION II: REQUIRED RETURN TO EQUITYHOLDERS RISES WITH LEVERAGE

Because levered equity has greater risk, it should have a greater expected return as compensation. In our example, the market *requires* only a 15 percent expected return for the unlevered equity, but it requires a 20 percent expected return for the levered equity.

This type of reasoning allows us to develop **MM Proposition II.** Here MM argue that the expected return on equity is positively related to leverage because the risk to equityholders increases with leverage.

To develop this position recall that the firm's weighted average cost of capital, R_{WACC}, can be written as:[5]

$$R_{WACC} = \frac{S}{B + S} \times R_S + \frac{B}{B + S} \times R_B \tag{16.2}$$

where:

R_B is the cost of debt.

R_S is the expected return on equity or stock, also called the *cost of equity* or the *required return on equity.*

R_{WACC} is the firm's weighted average cost of capital.

B is the value of the firm's bonds or debt.

S is the value of the firm's stock or equity.

Equation 16.2 is quite intuitive. It simply says that a firm's weighted average cost of capital is a weighted average of its cost of debt and its cost of equity. The weight applied to debt is the proportion of debt in the capital structure, and the weight applied to equity is the proportion of equity in the capital structure. Calculations of R_{WACC} from Equation 16.2 for both the unlevered and the levered firm are presented in Table 16.5.

An implication of MM Proposition I is that R_{WACC} is a constant for a given firm, regardless of the capital structure.[6] For example, Table 16.5 shows that R_{WACC} for Trans Am is 15 percent, with or without leverage.

---

[5]Because we do not have taxes here, the cost of debt is R_B, not $R_B(1 - t_c)$ as it was in Chapter 13.

[6]This statement holds in a world of no taxes. It does not hold in a world with taxes, a point to be brought out later in this chapter (see Figure 16.6).

Table 16.5
Cost of Capital
Calculations for
Trans Am

$$R_{WACC} = \frac{B}{B+S} \times R_B + \frac{S}{B+S} \times R_S$$

Unlevered firm: $15\% = \dfrac{0}{\$8,000} \times 10\%^* + \dfrac{\$8,000}{\$8,000} \times 15\%^\dagger$

Levered firm: $15\% = \dfrac{\$4,000}{\$8,000} \times 10\%^* + \dfrac{\$4,000}{\$8,000} \times 20\%^\ddagger$

*10% is the cost of debt.

†From the "Expected" column in Table 16.2, we learn that expected earnings for the unlevered firm are $1,200. From Table 16.1 we learn that equity for the unlevered firm is $8,000. Thus R_S for the unlevered firm is:

$$\frac{\text{Expected earnings}}{\text{Equity}} = \frac{\$1,200}{\$8,000} = 15\%$$

‡From the "Expected" column in Table 16.3, we learn that expected earnings after interest for the levered firm are $800. From Table 16.1 we learn that equity for the levered firm is $4,000. Thus R_S for the levered firm is:

$$\frac{\text{Expected earnings after interest}}{\text{Equity}} = \frac{\$800}{\$4,000} = 20\%$$

Let us now define R_0 to be the *cost of capital for an all-equity firm*. For the Trans Am Corp., R_0 is calculated as:

$$R_0 = \frac{\text{Expected earnings to unlevered firm}}{\text{Unlevered equity}} = \frac{\$1,200}{\$8,000} = 15\%$$

As can be seen from Table 16.5, R_{WACC} is equal to R_0 for Trans Am. In fact, R_{WACC} must *always* equal R_0 in a world without corporate taxes.[7]

Proposition II states the expected return on equity, R_S, in terms of leverage. The exact relationship, derived by setting $R_{WACC} = R_0$ and then rearranging Equation 16.2, is:[8]

MM Proposition II (No Taxes)

$$R_S = R_0 + \frac{B}{S}(R_0 - R_B) \tag{16.3}$$

Equation 16.3 implies that the required return on equity is a linear function of the firm's debt–equity ratio. Examining Equation 16.3, we see that if R_0 exceeds the cost of debt, R_B, then the cost of equity rises with increases in the debt–equity ratio, B/S. Normally R_0 should exceed R_B. That is, because even unlevered equity is risky, it should have an expected return greater than that of less risky debt. Note that Equation 16.3 holds for Trans Am in its levered state:

$$.20 = .15 + \frac{\$4,000}{\$4,000}(.15 - .10)$$

---

[7]This statement holds in a world of no taxes. It does not hold in a world with taxes, a point to be brought out later in this chapter (see Figure 16.6).

[8]This can be derived from Equation 16.2 by setting $R_{WACC} = R_0$, yielding:

$$\frac{B}{B+S}R_B + \frac{S}{B+S}R_S = R_0$$

Multiplying both sides by $(B + S)/S$ yields:

$$\frac{B}{S}R_B + R_S = \frac{B+S}{S}R_0$$

We can rewrite the right side as:

$$\frac{B}{S}R_B + R_S = \frac{B}{S}R_0 + R_0$$

Moving $(B/S)R_B$ to the right side and rearranging yields:

$$R_S = R_0 + \frac{B}{S}(R_0 - R_B)$$

Figure 16.3
The Cost of Equity, the Cost of Debt, and the Weighted Average Cost of Capital: MM Proposition II with No Corporate Taxes

$$R_S = R_0 + (R_0 - R_B)B/S$$

  R_S is the cost of equity.

  R_B is the cost of debt.

  R_0 is the cost of capital for an all-equity firm.

  R_{WACC} is a firm's weighted average cost of capital. In a world with no taxes, R_{WACC} for a levered firm is equal to R_0.

  R_0 is a single point whereas R_S, R_B, and R_{WACC} are all entire lines.

The cost of equity capital, R_S, is positively related to the firm's debt–equity ratio. The firm's weighted average cost of capital, R_{WACC}, is invariant to the firm's debt–equity ratio.

Figure 16.3 graphs Equation 16.3. As you can see, we have plotted the relation between the cost of equity, R_S, and the debt–equity ratio, B/S, as a straight line. What we witness in Equation 16.3 and illustrate in Figure 16.3 is the effect of leverage on the cost of equity. As the firm raises the debt–equity ratio, each dollar of equity is levered with additional debt. This raises the risk of equity and therefore the required return, R_S, on the equity.

Figure 16.3 also shows that R_{WACC} is unaffected by leverage, a point we have already made. (It is important for students to realize that R_0, the cost of capital for an all-equity firm, is represented by a single dot on the graph. By contrast, R_{WACC} is an entire line.)

EXAMPLE 16.2

MM Propositions I and II   Luteran Motors, an all-equity firm, has expected earnings of $10 million per year in perpetuity. The firm pays all of its earnings out as dividends, so the $10 million may also be viewed as the stockholders' expected cash flow. There are 10 million shares outstanding, implying expected annual cash flow of $1 per share. The cost of capital for this unlevered firm is 10 percent. In addition, the firm will soon build a new plant for $4 million. The plant is expected to generate additional cash flow of $1 million per year. These figures can be described as follows:

Current Company	New Plant
Cash flow: $10 million	Initial outlay: $4 million
Number of outstanding shares: 10 million	Additional annual cash flow: $1 million

The project's net present value is:

$$-\$4 \text{ million} + \frac{\$1 \text{ million}}{.1} = \$6 \text{ million}$$

Chapter 16 Capital Structure **505**

assuming that the project is discounted at the same rate as the firm as a whole. Before the market knows of the project, the *market value* balance sheet of the firm is this:

LUTERAN MOTORS Balance Sheet (All Equity)	
Old assets: $\dfrac{\$10 \text{ million}}{.1} = \$100 \text{ million}$	Equity: $100 million (10 million shares of stock)

The value of the firm is $100 million because the cash flow of $10 million per year is capitalized (discounted) at 10 percent. A share of stock sells for $10 (=$100 million/10 million) because there are 10 million shares outstanding.

The market value balance sheet is a useful tool for financial analysis. Because students are often thrown off guard by it initially, we recommend extra study here. The key is that the market value balance sheet has the same form as the balance sheet that accountants use. That is, assets are placed on the left side whereas liabilities and owners' equity are placed on the right side. In addition, the left and right sides must be equal. The difference between a market value balance sheet and the accountant's balance sheet is in the numbers. Accountants value items in terms of historical cost (original purchase price less depreciation), whereas financial analysts value items in terms of market value.

The firm will issue $4 million of either equity or debt. Let us consider the effect of equity and debt financing in turn.

Stock Financing   Imagine that the firm announces that in the near future it will raise $4 million in equity to build a new plant. The stock price, and therefore the value of the firm, will rise to reflect the positive net present value of the plant. According to efficient markets, the increase occurs immediately. That is, the rise occurs on the day of the announcement, not on the date of either the onset of construction of the plant or the forthcoming stock offering. The market value balance sheet becomes this:

LUTERAN MOTORS Balance Sheet (upon Announcement of Equity Issue to Construct Plant)			
Old assets	$100 million	Equity	$106 million (10 million shares of stock)
NPV of plant $-4 \text{ million} + \dfrac{\$1 \text{ million}}{.1} = 6 \text{ million}$			
Total assets	$106 million		

Note that the NPV of the plant is included in the market value balance sheet. Because the new shares have not yet been issued, the number of outstanding shares remains 10 million. The price per share has now risen to $10.60 (=$106 million/10 million) to reflect news concerning the plant.

Shortly thereafter, $4 million of stock is issued or *floated*. Because the stock is selling at $10.60 per share, 377,358 (=$4 million/$10.60) shares of stock are issued. Imagine that the funds are

(continued)

put in the bank *temporarily* before being used to build the plant. The market value balance sheet becomes this:

LUTERAN MOTORS Balance Sheet (upon Issuance of Stock but Before Construction Begins on Plant)			
Old assets	$100 million	Equity	$110 million
			(10,377,358 shares of stock)
NPV of plant	6 million		
Proceeds from new issue of stock (currently placed in bank)	4 million		
Total assets	$110 million		

The number of shares outstanding is now 10,377,358 because 377,358 new shares were issued. The price per share is $10.60 (=$110,000,000/10,377,358). Note that the price has not changed. This is consistent with efficient capital markets because the stock price should move due only to new information.

Of course the funds are placed in the bank only temporarily. Shortly after the new issue, the $4 million is given to a contractor who builds the plant. To avoid problems in discounting, we assume that the plant is built immediately. The balance sheet then looks like this:

LUTERAN MOTORS Balance Sheet (upon Completion of the Plant)			
Old assets	$100 million	Equity	$110 million
			(10,377,358 shares of stock)
PV of plant: $\dfrac{\$1\ \text{million}}{.1} =$	10 million		
Total assets	$110 million		

Though total assets do not change, the composition of the assets does change. The bank account has been emptied to pay the contractor. The present value of cash flows of $1 million a year from the plant is reflected as an asset worth $10 million. Because the building expenditures of $4 million have already been paid, they no longer represent a future cost. Hence they no longer reduce the value of the plant. According to efficient capital markets, the price per share of stock remains $10.60.

Expected yearly cash flow from the firm is $11 million, $10 million of which comes from the old assets and $1 million from the new. The expected return to equityholders is:

$$R_S = \frac{\$11\ \text{million}}{\$110\ \text{million}} = .10$$

Because the firm is all equity, $R_S = R_0 = .10$.

Debt Financing   Alternatively, imagine the firm announces that in the near future it will borrow $4 million at 6 percent to build a new plant. This implies yearly interest payments of $240,000

($=\$4,000,000 \times 6\%$). Again the stock price rises immediately to reflect the positive net present value of the plant. Thus we have the following:

LUTERAN MOTORS **Balance Sheet** **(upon Announcement of Debt Issue to Construct Plant)**			
Old assets	$100 million	Equity	$106 million
			(10 million shares of stock)
NPV of plant:			
$-\$4 \text{ million} + \dfrac{\$1 \text{ million}}{.1} =$ 6 million			
Total assets	$106 million		

The value of the firm is the same as in the equity financing case because (1) the same plant is to be built and (2) MM proved that debt financing is neither better nor worse than equity financing.

At some point $4 million of debt is issued. As before, the funds are placed in the bank temporarily. The market value balance sheet becomes this:

LUTERAN MOTORS **Balance Sheet** **(upon Debt Issuance but Before Construction Begins on Plant)**			
Old assets	$100 million	Debt	$ 4 million
NPV of plant	6 million	Equity	106 million
			(10 million shares of stock)
Proceeds from debt issue (currently invested in bank)	4 million		
Total assets	$110 million	Debt plus equity	$110 million

Note that debt appears on the right side of the balance sheet. The stock price is still $10.60 in accordance with our discussion of efficient capital markets.

Finally, the contractor receives $4 million and builds the plant. The market value balance sheet turns into this:

LUTERAN MOTORS **Balance Sheet** **(upon Completion of the Plant)**			
Old assets	$100 million	Debt	$ 4 million
PV of plant	10 million	Equity	106 million
			(10 million shares of stock)
Total assets	$110 million	Debt plus equity	$110 million

The only change here is that the bank account has been depleted to pay the contractor. The equityholders expect yearly cash flow after interest of:

$$\underset{\substack{\text{Cash flow on} \\ \text{old assets}}}{\$10,000,000} + \underset{\substack{\text{Cash flow on} \\ \text{new assets}}}{\$1,000,000} - \underset{\substack{\text{Interest:} \\ \$4 \text{ million} \times 6\%}}{\$240,000} = \$10,760,000$$

(continued)

The equityholders expect to earn a return of:

$$\frac{\$10{,}760{,}000}{\$106{,}000{,}000} = 10.15\%$$

This return of 10.15 percent for levered equityholders is higher than the 10 percent return for the unlevered equityholders. This result is sensible because, as we argued earlier, levered equity is riskier. In fact, the return of 10.15 percent should be exactly what MM Proposition II predicts. This prediction can be verified by plugging the values into:

$$R_s = R_0 + \frac{B}{S} \times (R_0 - R_B)$$

We obtain:

$$10.15\% = 10\% + \frac{\$4{,}000{,}000}{\$106{,}000{,}000} \times (10\% - 6\%)$$

This example was useful for two reasons. First, we wanted to introduce the concept of market value balance sheets, a tool that will prove useful elsewhere in the text. Among other things, this technique allows us to calculate the price per share of a new issue of stock. Second, the example illustrates three aspects of Modigliani and Miller:

1. The example is consistent with MM Proposition I because the value of the firm is $110 million after either equity or debt financing.

2. Students are often more interested in stock price than in firm value. We show that the stock price is always $10.60, regardless of whether debt or equity financing is used.

3. The example is consistent with MM Proposition II. The expected return to equityholders rises from 10 to 10.15 percent, just as MM Proposition II states. This rise occurs because the equityholders of a levered firm face more risk than do the equityholders of an unlevered firm.

MM: AN INTERPRETATION

The Modigliani–Miller results indicate that managers cannot change the value of a firm by repackaging the firm's securities. Though this idea was considered revolutionary when it was originally proposed in the late 1950s, the MM approach and proof have since met with wide acclaim.[9]

MM argue that the firm's overall cost of capital cannot be reduced as debt is substituted for equity, even though debt appears to be cheaper than equity. The reason for this is that as the firm adds debt, the remaining equity becomes more risky. As this risk rises, the cost of equity capital rises as a result. The increase in the cost of the remaining equity capital offsets the higher proportion of the firm financed by low-cost debt. In fact, MM prove that the two effects exactly offset each other, so that both the value of the firm and the firm's overall cost of capital are invariant to leverage.

MM use an interesting analogy to food. They consider a dairy farmer with two choices. On the one hand, he can sell whole milk. On the other hand, by skimming he can sell a combination of cream and lowfat milk. Though the farmer can get a high price for the cream, he gets a low price for the lowfat milk, implying no net gain. In fact, imagine that the proceeds from the whole-milk strategy were less than those from the cream–lowfat milk strategy. Arbitrageurs would buy the whole milk, perform the skimming operation themselves, and resell the cream and lowfat milk separately.

---

[9]Both Merton Miller and Franco Modigliani were awarded separate Nobel Prizes, in part for their work on capital structure.

In Their Own Words

IN PROFESSOR MILLER'S WORDS . . .

The Modigliani–Miller results are not easy to understand fully. This point is related in a story told by Merton Miller.*

"How difficult it is to summarize briefly the contribution of the [Modigliani–Miller] papers was brought home to me very clearly last October after Franco Modigliani was awarded the Nobel Prize in Economics in part—but, of course, only in part—for the work in finance. The television camera crews from our local stations in Chicago immediately descended upon me. 'We understand,' they said, 'that you worked with Modigliani some years back in developing these M and M theorems and we wonder if you could explain them briefly to our television viewers.'

" 'How briefly?' I asked.

" 'Oh, take ten seconds,' was the reply.

"Ten seconds to explain the work of a lifetime! Ten seconds to describe two carefully reasoned articles, each running to more than thirty printed pages and each with sixty or so long footnotes! When they saw the look of dismay on my face, they said, 'You don't have to go into details. Just give us the main points in simple, commonsense terms.'

"The main point of the first or cost-of-capital article was, in principle at least, simple enough to make. It said that in an economist's ideal world of complete and perfect capital markets and with full and symmetric information among all market participants, the total market value of all the securities issued by a firm was governed by the earning power and risk of its underlying real assets and was independent of how the mix of securities issued to finance it was divided between debt instruments and equity capital. . . .

"Such a summary, however, uses too many shorthanded terms and concepts, like perfect capital markets, that are rich in connotations to economists but hardly so to the general public. So I thought, instead, of an analogy that we ourselves had invoked in the original paper. . . .

" 'Think of the firm,' I said, 'as a gigantic tub of whole milk. The farmer can sell the whole milk as is.

Or he can separate out the cream and sell it at a considerably higher price than the whole milk would bring. (That's the analogy of a firm selling low-yield and hence high-priced debt securities.) But, of course, what the farmer would have left would be skim milk with low butterfat content and that would sell for much less than whole milk. That corresponds to the levered equity. The M and M proposition says that if there were no costs of separation (and, of course, no government dairy support programs), the cream plus the skim milk would bring the same price as the whole milk.'

"The television people conferred among themselves and came back to inform me that it was too long, too complicated, and too academic.

" 'Don't you have anything simpler?' they asked. I thought of another way that the M and M proposition is presented these days, which emphasizes the notion of market completeness and stresses the role of securities as devices for 'partitioning' a firm's payoffs in each possible state of the world among the group of its capital suppliers.

" 'Think of the firm,' I said, 'as a gigantic pizza, divided into quarters. If now you cut each quarter in half into eighths, the M and M proposition says that you will have more pieces but not more pizza.'

"Again there was a whispered conference among the camera crew, and the director came back and said:

" 'Professor, we understand from the press releases that there were two M and M propositions. Can we try the other one?' "

[Professor Miller tried valiantly to explain the second proposition, though this was apparently even more difficult to get across. After his attempt:]

"Once again there was a whispered conversation. They shut the lights off. They folded up their equipment. They thanked me for giving them the time. They said that they'd get back to me. But I knew that I had somehow lost my chance to start a new career as a packager of economic wisdom for TV viewers in convenient ten-second bites. Some have the talent for it . . . and some just don't."

*Taken from GSB Chicago, University of Chicago (Autumn 1986).

Competition between arbitrageurs would tend to boost the price of whole milk until proceeds from the two strategies became equal. Thus the value of the farmer's milk is invariant to the way in which the milk is packaged.

Food found its way into this chapter earlier when we viewed the firm as a pie. MM argue that the size of the pie does not change no matter how stockholders and bondholders divide it. MM say that a firm's capital structure is irrelevant; it is what it

---

Summary of Modigliani–Miller Propositions without Taxes

Assumptions

- No taxes.
- No transaction costs.
- Individuals and corporations borrow at same rate.

Results

Proposition I: $V_L = V_U$ (Value of levered firm equals value of unlevered firm)

Proposition II: $R_S = R_0 + \frac{B}{S}(R_0 - R_B)$

Intuition

Proposition I: Through homemade leverage individuals can either duplicate or undo the effects of corporate leverage.

Proposition II: The cost of equity rises with leverage because the risk to equity rises with leverage.

---

is by some historical accident. The theory implies that firms' debt–equity ratios could be anything. They are what they are because of whimsical and random managerial decisions about how much to borrow and how much stock to issue.

Although scholars are always fascinated with far-reaching theories, students are perhaps more concerned with real-world applications. Do real-world managers follow MM by treating capital structure decisions with indifference? Unfortunately for the theory, virtually all companies in certain industries, such as banking, choose high debt–equity ratios. Conversely, companies in other industries, such as pharmaceuticals, choose low debt–equity ratios. In fact, almost any industry has a debt–equity ratio to which companies in that industry tend to adhere. Thus companies do not appear to be selecting their degree of leverage in a frivolous or random manner. Because of this, financial economists (including MM themselves) have argued that real-world factors may have been left out of the theory.

Though many of our students have argued that individuals can borrow only at rates above the corporate borrowing rate, we disagreed with this argument earlier in the chapter. But when we look elsewhere for unrealistic assumptions in the theory, we find two:[10]

1. Taxes were ignored.
2. Bankruptcy costs and other agency costs were not considered.

We turn to taxes in the next section. Bankruptcy costs and other agency costs will be treated in the next chapter. A summary of the main Modigliani–Miller results without taxes is presented in the nearby boxed section.

16.5 Taxes

THE BASIC INSIGHT

The previous part of this chapter showed that firm value is unrelated to debt in a world without taxes. We now show that in the presence of corporate taxes, the firm's value is positively related to its debt. The basic intuition can be seen from a pie chart,

---

[10]MM were aware of both of these issues, as can be seen in their original paper.

Figure 16.4
Two Pie Models of Capital Structure under Corporate Taxes

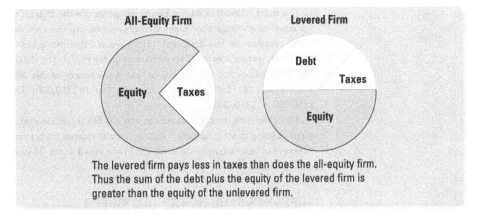

The levered firm pays less in taxes than does the all-equity firm. Thus the sum of the debt plus the equity of the levered firm is greater than the equity of the unlevered firm.

such as the one in Figure 16.4. Consider the all-equity firm on the left. Here both equityholders and the IRS have claims on the firm. The value of the all-equity firm is, of course, that part of the pie owned by the equityholders. The proportion going to taxes is simply a cost.

The pie on the right for the levered firm shows three claims: Equityholders, debtholders, and taxes. The value of the levered firm is the sum of the value of the debt and the value of the equity. In selecting between the two capital structures in the picture, a financial manager should select the one with the higher value. Assuming that the total area is the same for both pies,[11] value is maximized for the capital structure paying the least in taxes. In other words, the manager should choose the capital structure that the IRS hates the most.

We will show that due to a quirk in U.S. tax law, the proportion of the pie allocated to taxes is less for the levered firm than it is for the unlevered firm. Thus, managers should select high leverage.

EXAMPLE 16.3

Taxes and Cash Flow   The Water Products Company has a corporate tax rate, t_C, of 35 percent and expected earnings before interest and taxes (EBIT) of $1 million each year. Its entire earnings after taxes are paid out as dividends.

The firm is considering two alternative capital structures. Under Plan I, Water Products would have no debt in its capital structure. Under Plan II, the company would have $4,000,000 of debt, B. The cost of debt, R_B, is 10 percent.

The chief financial officer for Water Products makes the following calculations:

	Plan I	Plan II
Earnings before interest and corporate taxes (EBIT)	$1,000,000	$1,000,000
Interest ($R_B B$)	0	400,000
Earnings before taxes (EBT) = (EBIT − $R_B B$)	1,000,000	600,000
Taxes (t_C = .35)	350,000	210,000
Earnings after corporate taxes	650,000	390,000
(EAT) = [(EBIT − $R_B B$) × (1 − t_C)]		
Total cash flow to both stockholders and bondholders	$ 650,000	$ 790,000
[EBIT × (1 − t_C) + $t_C R_B B$]		

(continued)

---

[11]Under the MM propositions developed earlier, the two pies should be of the same size.

> The most relevant numbers for our purposes are the two on the bottom line. Dividends, which are equal to earnings after taxes in this example, are the cash flow to stockholders, and interest is the cash flow to bondholders.[12] Here we see that more cash flow reaches the owners of the firm (both stockholders and bondholders) under Plan II. The difference is $140,000 = $790,000 − $650,000. It does not take us long to realize the source of this difference. The IRS receives less tax under Plan II ($210,000) than it does under Plan I ($350,000). The difference here is $140,000 = $350,000 − $210,000.
>
> This difference occurs because the way the IRS treats interest is different from the way it treats earnings going to stockholders.[13] Interest totally escapes corporate taxation, whereas earnings after interest but before corporate taxes (EBT) are taxed at the 35 percent rate.

PRESENT VALUE OF THE TAX SHIELD

The previous discussion shows a tax advantage to debt or, equivalently, a tax disadvantage to equity. We now want to value this advantage. The dollar interest is:

$$\text{Interest} = \underbrace{R_B}_{\text{Interest rate}} \times \underbrace{B}_{\text{Amount borrowed}}$$

This interest is $400,000 (=10 percent × $4,000,000) for Water Products. All this interest is tax deductible. That is, whatever the taxable income of Water Products would have been without the debt, the taxable income is now $400,000 *less* with the debt.

Because the corporate tax rate is .35 in our example, the reduction in corporate taxes is $140,000 (=.35 × $400,000). This number is identical to the reduction in corporate taxes calculated previously.

Algebraically, the reduction in corporate taxes is:

$$\underbrace{t_C}_{\text{Corporate tax rate}} \times \underbrace{R_B \times B}_{\text{Dollar amount of interest}} \tag{16.4}$$

That is, whatever the taxes that a firm would pay each year without debt, the firm will pay $t_C R_B B$ less with the debt of B. Equation 16.4 is often called the *tax shield from debt*. Note that it is an *annual* amount.

As long as the firm expects to be in a positive tax bracket, we can assume that the cash flow in Equation 16.4 has the same risk as the interest on the debt. Thus its value can be determined by discounting at the cost of debt, R_B. Assuming that the cash flows are perpetual, the present value of the tax shield is:

$$\frac{t_C R_B B}{R_B} = t_C B$$

VALUE OF THE LEVERED FIRM

We have just calculated the present value of the tax shield from debt. Our next step is to calculate the value of the levered firm. The annual aftertax cash flow of an unlevered firm is:

$$\text{EBIT} \times (1 - t_C)$$

---

[12]The reader may wonder why the "total cash flow to both stockholders and bondholders" in this example does not include adjustments for depreciation, capital spending, and working capital that we emphasized in Chapters 2 and 6. It is because we are implicitly assuming that depreciation is equal to capital spending. We are also assuming that the changes in net working capital are zero. These assumptions make sense because the projected cash flows for the Water Products Company are perpetual.

[13]Note that stockholders actually receive more under Plan I ($650,000) than under Plan II ($390,000). Students are often bothered by this because it seems to imply that stockholders are better off without leverage. However, remember that there are more shares outstanding in Plan I than in Plan II. A full-blown model would show that earnings *per share* are higher with leverage.

where EBIT is earnings before interest and taxes. The value of an unlevered firm (that is, a firm with no debt) is the present value of EBIT $\times (1 - t_C)$:

$$V_U = \frac{\text{EBIT} \times (1 - t_C)}{R_0}$$

Here:

V_U = Present value of an unlevered firm.

EBIT $\times (1 - t_C)$ = Firm cash flows after corporate taxes.

t_C = Corporate tax rate.

R_0 = The cost of capital to an all-equity firm. As can be seen from the formula, R_0 now discounts *aftertax* cash flows.

As shown previously, leverage increases the value of the firm by the tax shield, which is $t_C B$ for perpetual debt. Thus we merely add this tax shield to the value of the unlevered firm to get the value of the levered firm.

We can write this algebraically as follows:[14]

MM Proposition I (Corporate Taxes)

$$V_L = \frac{\text{EBIT} \times (1 - t_C)}{R_0} + \frac{t_C R_B B}{R_B} = V_U + t_C B \qquad (16.5)$$

Equation 16.5 is MM Proposition I under corporate taxes. The first term in Equation 16.5 is the value of the cash flows of the firm with no debt tax shield. In other words, this term is equal to V_U, the value of the all-equity firm. The value of the levered firm is the value of an all-equity firm plus $t_C B$, the tax rate times the value of the debt. $t_C B$ is the present value of the tax shield in the case of perpetual cash flows.[15] Because the tax shield increases with the amount of debt, the firm can raise its total cash flow and its value by substituting debt for equity.

---

[14]This relationship holds when the debt level is assumed to be constant through time. A different formula would apply if the debt–equity ratio was assumed to be nonconstant over time. For a deeper treatment of this point, see J. A. Miles and J. R. Ezzell, "The Weighted Average Cost of Capital, Perfect Capital Markets and Project Life: A Clarification," *Journal of Financial and Quantitative Analysis* (September 1980).

[15]The following example calculates the present value if we assume the debt has a finite life. Suppose the Maxwell Company has $1 million in debt with an 8 percent coupon rate. If the debt matures in two years and the cost of debt capital, R_B, is 10 percent, what is the present value of the tax shields if the corporate tax rate is 35 percent? The debt is amortized in equal installments over two years.

Year	Loan Balance	Interest	Tax Shield	Present Value of Tax Shield
0	$1,000,000			
1	500,000	$80,000	.35 × $80,000	$25,454.54
2	0	40,000	.35 × $40,000	11,570.25
				$37,024.79

The present value of the tax saving is:

$$\text{PV} = \frac{.35 \times \$80,000}{1.10} + \frac{.35 \times \$40,000}{(1.10)^2} = \$37,024.79$$

The Maxwell Company's value is higher than that of a comparable unlevered firm by $37,024.79.

EXAMPLE 16.4

MM with Corporate Taxes   Divided Airlines is currently an unlevered firm. The company expects to generate $153.85 in earnings before interest and taxes (EBIT) in perpetuity. The corporate tax rate is 35 percent, implying aftertax earnings of $100. All earnings after tax are paid out as dividends.

The firm is considering a capital restructuring to allow $200 of debt. Its cost of debt capital is 10 percent. Unlevered firms in the same industry have a cost of equity capital of 20 percent. What will the new value of Divided Airlines be?

The value of Divided Airlines will be equal to:

$$
\begin{aligned}
V_L &= \frac{\text{EBIT} \times (1 - t_c)}{R_0} + t_c B \\
&= \frac{\$100}{.20} + (.35 \times \$200) \\
&= \$500 + \$70 = \$570
\end{aligned}
$$

The value of the levered firm is $570, which is greater than the unlevered value of $500. Because $V_L = B + S$, the value of levered equity, S, is equal to $570 - \$200 = \$370$. The value of Divided Airlines as a function of leverage is illustrated in Figure 16.5.

Figure 16.5   **The Effect of Financial Leverage on Firm Value: MM with Corporate Taxes in the Case of Divided Airlines**

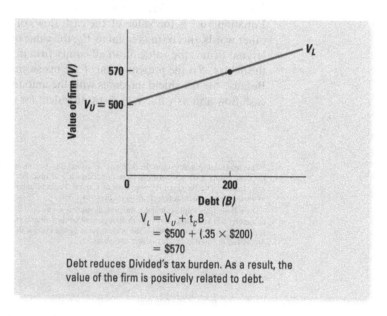

$$
\begin{aligned}
V_L &= V_U + t_c B \\
&= \$500 + (.35 \times \$200) \\
&= \$570
\end{aligned}
$$

Debt reduces Divided's tax burden. As a result, the value of the firm is positively related to debt.

EXPECTED RETURN AND LEVERAGE UNDER CORPORATE TAXES

MM Proposition II under no taxes posits a positive relationship between the expected return on equity and leverage. This result occurs because the risk of equity increases with leverage. The same intuition also holds in a world of corporate taxes. The exact formula in a world of corporate taxes is this:[16]

MM Proposition II (Corporate Taxes)

$$R_S = R_0 + \frac{B}{S} \times (1 - t_C) \times (R_0 - R_B) \qquad (16.6)$$

Applying the formula to Divided Airlines, we get:

$$R_S = .2351 = .20 + \frac{200}{370} \times (1 - .35) \times (.20 - .10)$$

This calculation is illustrated in Figure 16.6.

Whenever $R_0 > R_B$, R_S increases with leverage, a result that we also found in the no-tax case. As stated earlier in this chapter, R_0 should exceed R_B. That is, because equity (even unlevered equity) is risky, it should have an expected return greater than that on the less risky debt.

Let's check our calculations by determining the value of the levered equity in another way. The algebraic formula for the value of levered equity is:

$$S = \frac{(\text{EBIT} - R_B B) \times (1 - t_C)}{R_S}$$

---

[16]This relationship can be shown as follows: Given MM Proposition I under taxes, a levered firm's market value balance sheet can be written as:

$t_C B$ = Tax shield	S = Equity
V_U = Value of unlevered firm	B = Debt

The value of the unlevered firm is simply the value of the assets without benefit of leverage. The balance sheet indicates that the firm's value increases by $t_C B$ when debt of B is added. The expected cash flow *from* the left side of the balance sheet can be written as:

$$V_U R_0 + t_C B R_B \qquad (a)$$

Because assets are risky, their expected rate of return is R_0. The tax shield has the same risk as the debt, so its expected rate of return is R_B.

The expected cash *to* bondholders and stockholders together is:

$$S R_S + B R_B \qquad (b)$$

Expression (b) reflects the fact that stock earns an expected return of R_S and debt earns the interest rate R_B.

Because all cash flows are paid out as dividends in our no-growth perpetuity model, the cash flows going into the firm equal those going to stockholders. Hence (a) and (b) are equal:

$$S R_S + B R_B = V_U R_0 + t_C B R_B \qquad (c)$$

Dividing both sides of (c) by S, subtracting $B R_B$ from both sides, and rearranging yields:

$$R_S = \frac{V_U}{S} \times R_0 - (1 - t_C) \times \frac{B}{S} R_B \qquad (d)$$

Because the value of the levered firm, V_L, equals $V_U + t_C B = B + S$, it follows that $V_U = S + (1 - t_C) \times B$. Thus (d) can be rewritten as:

$$R_S = \frac{S + (1 - t_C) \times B}{S} \times R_0 - (1 - t_C) \times \frac{B}{S} R_B \qquad (e)$$

Bringing the terms involving $(1 - t_C) \times (B/S)$ together produces Equation 16.6.

Figure 16.6
The Effect of Financial Leverage on the Cost of Debt and Equity Capital

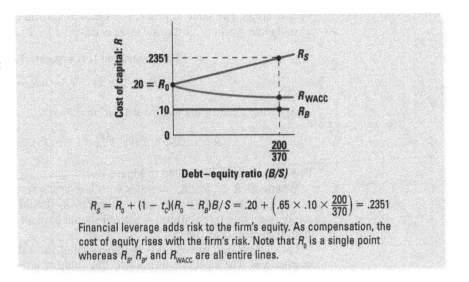

$$R_S = R_0 + (1 - t_C)(R_0 - R_B)B/S = .20 + \left(.65 \times .10 \times \frac{200}{370}\right) = .2351$$

Financial leverage adds risk to the firm's equity. As compensation, the cost of equity rises with the firm's risk. Note that R_0 is a single point whereas R_S, R_B, and R_{WACC} are all entire lines.

The numerator is the expected cash flow to levered equity after interest and taxes. The denominator is the rate at which the cash flow to equity is discounted.

For Divided Airlines we get:

$$\frac{(\$153.85 - .10 \times \$200)(1 - .35)}{.2351} = \$370$$

This is the same result we obtained earlier (ignoring a small rounding error).

THE WEIGHTED AVERAGE COST OF CAPITAL, R_{WACC}, AND CORPORATE TAXES

In Chapter 13, we defined the weighted average cost of capital (with corporate taxes) as follows (note that $V_L = S + B$):

$$R_{WACC} = \frac{S}{V_L}R_S + \frac{B}{V_L}R_B(1 - t_C)$$

Note that the cost of debt capital, R_B, is multiplied by $(1 - t_C)$ because interest is tax deductible at the corporate level. However, the cost of equity, R_S, is not multiplied by this factor because dividends are not deductible. In the no-tax case, R_{WACC} is not affected by leverage. This result is reflected in Figure 16.3, which we discussed earlier. However, because debt is tax-advantaged relative to equity, it can be shown that R_{WACC} declines with leverage in a world with corporate taxes. This result can be seen in Figure 16.6.

For Divided Airlines, R_{WACC} is equal to:

$$R_{WACC} = \left(\frac{370}{570} \times .2351\right) + \left(\frac{200}{570} \times .10 \times .65\right) = .1754$$

Divided Airlines has reduced its R_{WACC} from .20 (with no debt) to .1754 with reliance on debt. This result is intuitively pleasing because it suggests that when a firm lowers its R_{WACC}, the firm's value will increase. Using the R_{WACC} approach, we can confirm that the value of Divided Airlines is $570:

$$V_L = \frac{EBIT \times (1 - t_C)}{R_{WACC}} = \frac{\$100}{.1754} = \$570$$

STOCK PRICE AND LEVERAGE UNDER CORPORATE TAXES

At this point students often believe the numbers—or at least are too intimidated to dispute them. However, they sometimes think we have asked the wrong question. "Why are we choosing to maximize the value of the firm?" they will say. "If managers are looking out for the stockholders' interest, why aren't they trying to maximize stock price?" If this question occurred to you, you have come to the right section.

Our response is twofold: First, we showed in the first section of this chapter that the capital structure that maximizes firm value is also the one that most benefits the interests of the stockholders.

However, that general explanation is not always convincing to students. As a second procedure, we calculate the stock price of Divided Airlines both before and after the exchange of debt for stock. We do this by presenting a set of market value balance sheets. The market value balance sheet for the company in its all-equity form can be represented as follows:

DIVIDED AIRLINES Balance Sheet (All-Equity Firm)			
Physical assets	$\frac{\$153.85}{.20} \times (1 - .35) = \$500$	Equity	$500 (100 shares)

Assuming that there are 100 shares outstanding, each share is worth $5 = $500/100.

Next, imagine the company announces that in the near future it will issue $200 of debt to buy back $200 of stock. We know from our previous discussion that the value of the firm will rise to reflect the tax shield of debt. If we assume that capital markets efficiently price securities, the increase occurs immediately. That is, the rise occurs on the day of the announcement, not on the date of the debt-for-equity exchange. The market value balance sheet now becomes this:

DIVIDED AIRLINES Balance Sheet (upon Announcement of Debt Issue)			
Physical assets	$500	Equity	$570 (100 shares)
Present value of tax shield: $t_c B = 35\% \times \$200 =$	70		
Total assets	$570		

Note that the debt has not yet been issued. Therefore, only equity appears on the right side of the balance sheet. Each share is now worth $570/100 = $5.70, implying that the stockholders have benefited by $70. The equityholders gain because they are the owners of a firm that has improved its financial policy.

The introduction of the tax shield to the balance sheet is perplexing to many students. Although physical assets are tangible, the ethereal nature of the tax shield bothers these students. However, remember that an asset is any item with value. The tax shield has value because it reduces the stream of future taxes. The fact that one cannot touch the shield in the way that one can touch a physical asset is a philosophical, not financial, consideration.

At some point the exchange of debt for equity occurs. Debt of $200 is issued, and the proceeds are used to buy back shares. How many shares of stock are repurchased? Because shares are now selling at $5.70 each, the number of shares that the firm acquires is $200/$5.70 = 35.09. This leaves 64.91 (=100 − 35.09) shares of stock outstanding. The market value balance sheet is now this:

DIVIDED AIRLINES Balance Sheet (after Exchange Has Taken Place)			
Physical assets	$500	Equity	$370
		(100 − 35.09 = 64.91 shares)	
Present value of tax shield	70	Debt	200
Total assets	$570	Debt plus equity	$570

Each share of stock is worth $370/64.91 = $5.70 after the exchange. Notice that the stock price does not change on the exchange date. As we mentioned, the stock price moves on the date of the announcement only. Because the shareholders participating in the exchange receive a price equal to the market price per share after the exchange, they do not care whether they exchange their stock.

This example was provided for two reasons. First, it shows that an increase in the value of the firm from debt financing leads to an increase in the price of the stock. In fact, the stockholders capture the entire $70 tax shield. Second, we wanted to provide more work with market value balance sheets.

A summary of the main results of Modigliani–Miller with corporate taxes is presented in the following boxed section:

Summary of Modigliani–Miller Propositions with Corporate Taxes

Assumptions

- Corporations are taxed at the rate t_C, on earnings after interest.
- No transaction costs.
- Individuals and corporations borrow at the same rate.

Results

Proposition I: $V_L = V_U + t_C B$ (for a firm with perpetual debt)

Proposition II: $R_S = R_0 + \dfrac{B}{S}(1 - t_C)(R_0 - R_B)$

Intuition

Proposition I: Because corporations can deduct interest payments but not dividend payments, corporate leverage lowers tax payments.

Proposition II: The cost of equity rises with leverage because the risk to equity rises with leverage.

◄ To test your mastery of this material, take a quiz at mhhe. com/rwj

Summary and Conclusions

1. We began our discussion of the capital structure decision by arguing that the particular capital structure that maximizes the value of the firm is also the one that provides the most benefit to the stockholders.

2. In a world of no taxes, the famous Proposition I of Modigliani and Miller proves that the value of the firm is unaffected by the debt–equity ratio. In other words, a firm's capital structure is a matter of indifference in that world. The authors obtain their results by showing that either a high or a low corporate ratio of debt to equity can be offset by homemade leverage. The result hinges on the assumption that individuals can borrow at the same rate as corporations, an assumption we believe to be quite plausible.

3. MM's Proposition II in a world without taxes states that:

$$R_S = R_0 + \frac{B}{S}(R_0 - R_B)$$

This implies that the expected rate of return on equity (also called the *cost of equity* or the *required return on equity*) is positively related to the firm's leverage. This makes intuitive sense because the risk of equity rises with leverage, a point illustrated by Figure 16.2.

4. Although the above work of MM is quite elegant, it does not explain the empirical findings on capital structure very well. MM imply that the capital structure decision is a matter of indifference, whereas the decision appears to be a weighty one in the real world. To achieve real-world applicability, we next considered corporate taxes.

5. In a world with corporate taxes but no bankruptcy costs, firm value is an increasing function of leverage. The formula for the value of the firm is:

$$V_L = V_U + t_C B$$

Expected return on levered equity can be expressed as:

$$R_S = R_0 + (1 - t_C) \times (R_0 - R_B) \times \frac{B}{S}$$

Here, value is positively related to leverage. This result implies that firms should have a capital structure almost entirely composed of debt. Because real-world firms select more moderate levels of debt, the next chapter considers modifications to the results of this chapter.

Concept Questions

1. **MM Assumptions** List the three assumptions that lie behind the Modigliani–Miller theory in a world without taxes. Are these assumptions reasonable in the real world? Explain.

2. **MM Propositions** In a world with no taxes, no transaction costs, and no costs of financial distress, is the following statement true, false, or uncertain? If a firm issues equity to repurchase some of its debt, the price per share of the firm's stock will rise because the shares are less risky. Explain.

3. **MM Propositions** In a world with no taxes, no transaction costs, and no costs of financial distress, is the following statement true, false, or uncertain? Moderate borrowing will not increase the required return on a firm's equity. Explain.

4. **MM Propositions** What is the quirk in the tax code that makes a levered firm more valuable than an otherwise identical unlevered firm?

5. **Business Risk versus Financial Risk** Explain what is meant by business and financial risk. Suppose Firm *A* has greater business risk than Firm *B*. Is it true that Firm *A* also has a higher cost of equity capital? Explain.

6. **MM Propositions** How would you answer in the following debate?

    Q: Isn't it true that the riskiness of a firm's equity will rise if the firm increases its use of debt financing?

    A: Yes, that's the essence of MM Proposition II.

    Q: And isn't it true that, as a firm increases its use of borrowing, the likelihood of default increases, thereby increasing the risk of the firm's debt?

    A: Yes.

    Q: In other words, increased borrowing increases the risk of the equity *and* the debt?

    A: That's right.

    Q: Well, given that the firm uses only debt and equity financing, and given that the risks of both are increased by increased borrowing, does it not follow that increasing debt increases the overall risk of the firm and therefore decreases the value of the firm?

    A: ?

7. **Optimal Capital Structure** Is there an easily identifiable debt–equity ratio that will maximize the value of a firm? Why or why not?

8. **Financial Leverage** Why is the use of debt financing referred to as financial "leverage"?

9. **Homemade Leverage** What is homemade leverage?

10. **Capital Structure Goal** What is the basic goal of financial management with regard to capital structure?

Questions and Problems

www.mhhe.com/rwj

BASIC (Questions 1–16)

1. **EBIT and Leverage** Money, Inc., has no debt outstanding and a total market value of $275,000. Earnings before interest and taxes, EBIT, are projected to be $21,000 if economic conditions are normal. If there is strong expansion in the economy, then EBIT will be 25 percent higher. If there is a recession, then EBIT will be 40 percent lower. Money is considering a $99,000 debt issue with an interest rate of 8 percent. The proceeds will be used to repurchase shares of stock. There are currently 5,000 shares outstanding. Ignore taxes for this problem.

    a. Calculate earnings per share, EPS, under each of the three economic scenarios before any debt is issued. Also calculate the percentage changes in EPS when the economy expands or enters a recession.

    b. Repeat part (a) assuming that Money goes through with recapitalization. What do you observe?

2. **EBIT, Taxes, and Leverage** Repeat parts (a) and (b) in Problem 1 assuming Money has a tax rate of 35 percent.

3. **ROE and Leverage** Suppose the company in Problem 1 has a market-to-book ratio of 1.0.

    a. Calculate return on equity, ROE, under each of the three economic scenarios before any debt is issued. Also calculate the percentage changes in ROE for economic expansion and recession, assuming no taxes.

b. Repeat part (a) assuming the firm goes through with the proposed recapitalization.

c. Repeat parts (a) and (b) of this problem assuming the firm has a tax rate of 35 percent.

4. **Break-Even EBIT** Rolston Corporation is comparing two different capital structures, an all-equity plan (Plan I) and a levered plan (Plan II). Under Plan I, Rolston would have 265,000 shares of stock outstanding. Under Plan II, there would be 185,000 shares of stock outstanding and $2.8 million in debt outstanding. The interest rate on the debt is 10 percent and there are no taxes.

   a. If EBIT is $750,000, which plan will result in the higher EPS?

   b. If EBIT is $1,500,000, which plan will result in the higher EPS?

   c. What is the break-even EBIT?

5. **MM and Stock Value** In Problem 4, use MM Proposition I to find the price per share of equity under each of the two proposed plans. What is the value of the firm?

 6. **Break-Even EBIT and Leverage** Kolby Corp. is comparing two different capital structures. Plan I would result in 900 shares of stock and $65,700 in debt. Plan II would result in 1,900 shares of stock and $29,200 in debt. The interest rate on the debt is 10 percent.

   a. Ignoring taxes, compare both of these plans to an all-equity plan assuming that EBIT will be $8,500. The all-equity plan would result in 2,700 shares of stock outstanding. Which of the three plans has the highest EPS? The lowest?

   b. In part (a) what are the break-even levels of EBIT for each plan as compared to that for an all-equity plan? Is one higher than the other? Why?

   c. Ignoring taxes, when will EPS be identical for Plans I and II?

   d. Repeat parts (a), (b), and (c) assuming that the corporate tax rate is 40 percent. Are the break-even levels of EBIT different from before? Why or why not?

7. **Leverage and Stock Value** Ignoring taxes in Problem 6, what is the price per share of equity under Plan I? Plan II? What principle is illustrated by your answers?

8. **Homemade Leverage** Star, Inc., a prominent consumer products firm, is debating whether or not to convert its all-equity capital structure to one that is 35 percent debt. Currently there are 6,000 shares outstanding and the price per share is $58. EBIT is expected to remain at $33,000 per year forever. The interest rate on new debt is 8 percent, and there are no taxes.

   a. Ms. Brown, a shareholder of the firm, owns 100 shares of stock. What is her cash flow under the current capital structure, assuming the firm has a dividend payout rate of 100 percent?

   b. What will Ms. Brown's cash flow be under the proposed capital structure of the firm? Assume that she keeps all 100 of her shares.

   c. Suppose Star does convert, but Ms. Brown prefers the current all-equity capital structure. Show how she could unlever her shares of stock to recreate the original capital structure.

   d. Using your answer to part (c), explain why Star's choice of capital structure is irrelevant.

9. **Homemade Leverage and WACC** ABC Co. and XYZ Co. are identical firms in all respects except for their capital structure. ABC is all equity financed with $750,000 in stock. XYZ uses both stock and perpetual debt; its stock is worth $375,000 and the interest rate on its debt is 8 percent. Both firms expect EBIT to be $86,000. Ignore taxes.

   a. Richard owns $30,000 worth of XYZ's stock. What rate of return is he expecting?

   b. Show how Richard could generate exactly the same cash flows and rate of return by investing in ABC and using homemade leverage.

   c. What is the cost of equity for ABC? What is it for XYZ?

   d. What is the WACC for ABC? For XYZ? What principle have you illustrated?

522

10. **MM**   Nina Corp. uses no debt. The weighted average cost of capital is 9 percent. If the current market value of the equity is $37 million and there are no taxes, what is EBIT?

11. **MM and Taxes**   In the previous question, suppose the corporate tax rate is 35 percent. What is EBIT in this case? What is the WACC? Explain.

12. **Calculating WACC**   Weston Industries has a debt–equity ratio of 1.5. Its WACC is 11 percent, and its cost of debt is 7 percent. The corporate tax rate is 35 percent.

    a. What is Weston's cost of equity capital?
    b. What is Weston's unlevered cost of equity capital?
    c. What would the cost of equity be if the debt–equity ratio were 2? What if it were 1.0? What if it were zero?

13. **Calculating WACC**   Shadow Corp. has no debt but can borrow at 8 percent. The firm's WACC is currently 11 percent, and the tax rate is 35 percent.

    a. What is Shadow's cost of equity?
    b. If the firm converts to 25 percent debt, what will its cost of equity be?
    c. If the firm converts to 50 percent debt, what will its cost of equity be?
    d. What is Shadow's WACC in part (b)? In part (c)?

14. **MM and Taxes**   Bruce & Co. expects its EBIT to be $185,000 every year forever. The firm can borrow at 9 percent. Bruce currently has no debt, and its cost of equity is 16 percent. If the tax rate is 35 percent, what is the value of the firm? What will the value be if Bruce borrows $135,000 and uses the proceeds to repurchase shares?

15. **MM and Taxes**   In Problem 14, what is the cost of equity after recapitalization? What is the WACC? What are the implications for the firm's capital structure decision?

16. **MM Proposition I**   Levered, Inc., and Unlevered, Inc., are identical in every way except their capital structures. Each company expects to earn $29 million before interest per year in perpetuity, with each company distributing all its earnings as dividends. Levered's perpetual debt has a market value of $91 million and costs 8 percent per year. Levered has 2.3 million shares outstanding, currently worth $105 per share. Unlevered has no debt and 4.5 million shares outstanding, currently worth $80 per share. Neither firm pays taxes. Is Levered's stock a better buy than Unlevered's stock?

INTERMEDIATE
(Questions 17–25)

17. **MM**   Tool Manufacturing has an expected EBIT of $57,000 in perpetuity and a tax rate of 35 percent. The firm has $90,000 in outstanding debt at an interest rate of 8 percent, and its unlevered cost of capital is 15 percent. What is the value of the firm according to MM Proposition I with taxes? Should Tool change its debt–equity ratio if the goal is to maximize the value of the firm? Explain.

18. **Firm Value**   Cavo Corporation expects an EBIT of $19,750 every year forever. The company currently has no debt, and its cost of equity is 15 percent.

    a. What is the current value of the company?
    b. Suppose the company can borrow at 10 percent. If the corporate tax rate is 35 percent, what will the value of the firm be if the company takes on debt equal to 50 percent of its unlevered value? What if it takes on debt equal to 100 percent of its unlevered value?
    c. What will the value of the firm be if the company takes on debt equal to 50 percent of its levered value? What if the company takes on debt equal to 100 percent of its levered value?

19. **MM Proposition I with Taxes**   The Maxwell Company is financed entirely with equity. The company is considering a loan of $1.8 million. The loan will be repaid in equal installments over the next two years, and it has an interest rate of 8 percent. The company's tax rate is 35 percent. According to MM Proposition I with taxes, what would be the increase in the value of the company after the loan?

20. **MM Proposition I without Taxes**   Alpha Corporation and Beta Corporation are identical in every way except their capital structures. Alpha Corporation, an all-equity firm, has 15,000 shares of stock outstanding, currently worth $30 per share. Beta Corporation uses leverage in its capital structure. The market value of Beta's debt is $65,000, and its cost of debt is 9 percent. Each firm is expected to have earnings before interest of $75,000 in perpetuity. Neither firm pays taxes. Assume that every investor can borrow at 9 percent per year.

a. What is the value of Alpha Corporation?
b. What is the value of Beta Corporation?
c. What is the market value of Beta Corporation's equity?
d. How much will it cost to purchase 20 percent of each firm's equity?
e. Assuming each firm meets its earnings estimates, what will be the dollar return to each position in part (d) over the next year?
f. Construct an investment strategy in which an investor purchases 20 percent of Alpha's equity and replicates both the cost and dollar return of purchasing 20 percent of Beta's equity.
g. Is Alpha's equity more or less risky than Beta's equity? Explain.

21. **Cost of Capital**   Acetate, Inc., has equity with a market value of $23 million and debt with a market value of $7 million. Treasury bills that mature in one year yield 5 percent per year, and the expected return on the market portfolio is 12 percent. The beta of Acetate's equity is 1.15. The firm pays no taxes.

a. What is Acetate's debt–equity ratio?
b. What is the firm's weighted average cost of capital?
c. What is the cost of capital for an otherwise identical all-equity firm?

22. **Homemade Leverage**   The Veblen Company and the Knight Company are identical in every respect except that Veblen is not levered. The market value of Knight Company's 6 percent bonds is $1.4 million. Financial information for the two firms appears here. All earnings streams are perpetuities. Neither firm pays taxes. Both firms distribute all earnings available to common stockholders immediately.

	Veblen	Knight
Projected operating income	$ 550,000	$ 550,000
Year-end interest on debt	—	84,000
Market value of stock	4,300,000	3,140,000
Market value of debt	—	1,400,000

a. An investor who can borrow at 6 percent per year wishes to purchase 5 percent of Knight's equity. Can he increase his dollar return by purchasing 5 percent of Veblen's equity if he borrows so that the initial net costs of the two strategies are the same?
b. Given the two investment strategies in (a), which will investors choose? When will this process cease?

23. **MM Propositions**   Locomotive Corporation is planning to repurchase part of its common stock by issuing corporate debt. As a result, the firm's debt–equity ratio is expected to rise from 35 percent to 50 percent. The firm currently has $3.6 million worth of debt outstanding. The cost of this debt is 8 percent per year. Locomotive expects to have an EBIT of $1.35 million per year in perpetuity. Locomotive pays no taxes.

a. What is the market value of Locomotive Corporation before and after the repurchase announcement?
b. What is the expected return on the firm's equity before the announcement of the stock repurchase plan?

   c. What is the expected return on the equity of an otherwise identical all-equity firm?

   d. What is the expected return on the firm's equity after the announcement of the stock repurchase plan?

24. **Stock Value and Leverage** Green Manufacturing, Inc., plans to announce that it will issue $2 million of perpetual debt and use the proceeds to repurchase common stock. The bonds will sell at par with a coupon rate of 6 percent. Green is currently an all-equity firm worth $6.3 million with 400,000 shares of common stock outstanding. After the sale of the bonds, Green will maintain the new capital structure indefinitely. Green currently generates annual pretax earnings of $1.5 million. This level of earnings is expected to remain constant in perpetuity. Green is subject to a corporate tax rate of 40 percent.

   a. What is the expected return on Green's equity before the announcement of the debt issue?

   b. Construct Green's market value balance sheet before the announcement of the debt issue. What is the price per share of the firm's equity?

   c. Construct Green's market value balance sheet immediately after the announcement of the debt issue.

   d. What is Green's stock price per share immediately after the repurchase announcement?

   e. How many shares will Green repurchase as a result of the debt issue? How many shares of common stock will remain after the repurchase?

   f. Construct the market value balance sheet after the restructuring.

   g. What is the required return on Green's equity after the restructuring?

25. **MM with Taxes** Williamson, Inc., has a debt–equity ratio of 2.5. The firm's weighted average cost of capital is 10 percent, and its pretax cost of debt is 6 percent. Williamson is subject to a corporate tax rate of 35 percent.

   a. What is Williamson's cost of equity capital?

   b. What is Williamson's unlevered cost of equity capital?

   c. What would Williamson's weighted average cost of capital be if the firm's debt–equity ratio were .75? What if it were 1.5?

26. **Weighted Average Cost of Capital** In a world of corporate taxes only, show that the R_{WACC} can be written as $R_{WACC} = R_0 \times [1 - t_C(B/V)]$.

27. **Cost of Equity and Leverage** Assuming a world of corporate taxes only, show that the cost of equity, R_S, is as given in the chapter by MM Proposition II with corporate taxes.

28. **Business and Financial Risk** Assume a firm's debt is risk-free, so that the cost of debt equals the risk-free rate, R_f. Define β_A as the firm's *asset* beta—that is, the systematic risk of the firm's assets. Define β_S to be the beta of the firm's equity. Use the capital asset pricing model, CAPM, along with MM Proposition II to show that $\beta_S = \beta_A \times (1 + B/S)$, where B/S is the debt–equity ratio. Assume the tax rate is zero.

29. **Stockholder Risk** Suppose a firm's business operations mirror movements in the economy as a whole very closely—that is, the firm's asset beta is 1.0. Use the result of previous problem to find the equity beta for this firm for debt–equity ratios of 0, 1, 5, and 20. What does this tell you about the relationship between capital structure and shareholder risk? How is the shareholders' required return on equity affected? Explain.

30. **Unlevered Cost of Equity** Beginning with the cost of capital equation—that is:

$$R_{WACC} = \frac{S}{B+S}R_S + \frac{B}{B+S}R_B$$

show that the cost of equity capital for a levered firm can be written as follows:

$$R_S = R_0 + \frac{B}{S}(R_0 - R_B)$$

Mini Case

STEPHENSON REAL ESTATE RECAPITALIZATION

Stephenson Real Estate Company was founded 25 years ago by the current CEO, Robert Stephenson. The company purchases real estate, including land and buildings, and rents the property to tenants. The company has shown a profit every year for the past 18 years, and the shareholders are satisfied with the company's management. Prior to founding Stephenson Real Estate, Robert was the founder and CEO of a failed alpaca farming operation. The resulting bankruptcy made him extremely averse to debt financing. As a result, the company is entirely equity financed, with 12 million shares of common stock outstanding. The stock currently trades at $48.50 per share.

Stephenson is evaluating a plan to purchase a huge tract of land in the southeastern United States for $45 million. The land will subsequently be leased to tenant farmers. This purchase is expected to increase Stephenson's annual pretax earnings by $11 million in perpetuity. Kim Weyand, the company's new CFO, has been put in charge of the project. Kim has determined that the company's current cost of capital is 11.5 percent. She feels that the company would be more valuable if it included debt in its capital structure, so she is evaluating whether the company should issue debt to entirely finance the project. Based on some conversations with investment banks, she thinks that the company can issue bonds at par value with a coupon rate of 7 percent. Based on her analysis, she also believes that a capital structure in the range of 70 percent equity/30 percent debt would be optimal. If the company goes beyond 30 percent debt, its bonds would carry a lower rating and a much higher coupon because the possibility of financial distress and the associated costs would rise sharply. Stephenson has a 40 percent corporate tax rate (state and federal).

1. If Stephenson wishes to maximize its total market value, would you recommend that it issue debt or equity to finance the land purchase? Explain.

2. Construct Stephenson's market value balance sheet before it announces the purchase.

3. Suppose Stephenson decides to issue equity to finance the purchase.
   a. What is the net present value of the project?
   b. Construct Stephenson's market value balance sheet after it announces that the firm will finance the purchase using equity. What would be the new price per share of the firm's stock? How many shares will Stephenson need to issue to finance the purchase?
   c. Construct Stephenson's market value balance sheet after the equity issue but before the purchase has been made. How many shares of common stock does Stephenson have outstanding? What is the price per share of the firm's stock?
   d. Construct Stephenson's market value balance sheet after the purchase has been made.

4. Suppose Stephenson decides to issue debt to finance the purchase.
   a. What will the market value of the Stephenson company be if the purchase is financed with debt?
   b. Construct Stephenson's market value balance sheet after both the debt issue and the land purchase. What is the price per share of the firm's stock?

5. Which method of financing maximizes the per-share stock price of Stephenson's equity?

CHAPTER 17

Capital Structure

LIMITS TO THE USE OF DEBT

▲ For updates on the latest happenings in finance, visit www.rwjcorporatefinance.blogspot.com

On February 16, 2011, famed bookseller Borders Group began a new chapter in its corporate life—Chapter 11 bankruptcy. The company had been faced with intense competition from rivals Amazon.com and Barnes & Noble. As a part of the bankruptcy process, the company planned to shut down about 200 of its 462 stores and change its focus to e-books and nonbook products. The company's biggest unsecured creditors were publishing companies. In fact, the six largest publishers were owed a combined $182 million and expected to get back only 25 cents on the dollar. Of course, Borders was not alone. The Honolulu Symphony Orchestra sounded a sour note, filing for Chapter 11 bankruptcy to reorganize its finances in 2009. It was later forced to switch to a Chapter 7 liquidation in February 2011. The assets to be auctioned included two grand pianos, a harpsichord, and 11 cowbells. Even pizza was not immune to bankruptcy. Round Table Pizza, which promised to serve "The Last Honest Pizza," and famed Chicago pizzeria Giordano's, home of "world famous" deep-dish pizza, both filed for bankruptcy within a week of each other in February 2011.

The previous chapter began with the question, "How should a firm choose its debt–equity ratio?" We first presented the Modigliani-Miller (MM) result that, in a world without taxes, the value of the levered firm is the same as the value of the unlevered firm. In other words, the choice of the debt–equity ratio is unimportant here.

We next showed the MM result that, in a world with corporate taxes, the value of the firm increases with leverage, implying that firms should take on as much debt as possible. But this result leaves one with a number of questions. Is this the whole story? Should financial managers really set their firms' debt-to-value ratios near 100 percent? If so, why do real-world companies have, as we show later in this chapter, rather modest levels of debt?

The current chapter bridges the gap between theory and practice. We show that there are good reasons for modest capital structures in practice, even in a world with taxes. We begin with the concept of bankruptcy costs. These costs increase with debt, offsetting the tax advantage of leverage.

17.1 Costs of Financial Distress

BANKRUPTCY RISK OR BANKRUPTCY COST?

As mentioned throughout the previous chapter, debt provides tax benefits to the firm. However, debt puts pressure on the firm because interest and principal payments are obligations. If these obligations are not met, the firm may risk some sort of financial distress. The ultimate distress is *bankruptcy*, where ownership of the firm's assets is legally transferred from the stockholders to the bondholders. These debt obligations are fundamentally different from stock obligations. Although stockholders like and expect dividends, they are not legally entitled to dividends in the way bondholders are legally entitled to interest and principal payments.

We show next that bankruptcy costs, or more generally financial distress costs, tend to offset the advantages to debt. We begin by positing a simple example of bankruptcy. Taxes are ignored to focus only on the costs of debt.

EXAMPLE 17.1

Bankruptcy Costs   The Knight Corporation plans to be in business for one more year. It forecasts a cash flow of either $100 or $50 in the coming year, each occurring with 50 percent probability. The firm has no other assets. Previously issued debt requires payments of $49 of interest and principal. The Day Corporation has identical cash flow prospects but has $60 of interest and principal obligations. The cash flows of these two firms can be represented as follows:

	Knight Corporation		Day Corporation	
	Boom Times (prob. 50%)	Recession (prob. 50%)	Boom Times (prob. 50%)	Recession (prob. 50%)
Cash flow	$100	$50	$100	$50
Payment of interest and principal on debt	49	49	60	50
Distribution to stockholders	$ 51	$ 1	$ 40	$ 0

For Knight Corporation in both boom times and recession and for Day Corporation in boom times, cash flow exceeds interest and principal payments. In these situations the bondholders are paid in full, and the stockholders receive any residual. However, the most interesting of the four columns involves Day Corporation in a recession. Here the bondholders are owed $60, but the firm has only $50 in cash. Because we assume that the firm has no other assets, the bondholders cannot be satisfied in full. Bankruptcy occurs, implying that the bondholders will receive all of the firm's cash, and the stockholders will receive nothing. Importantly, the stockholders do not have to come up with the additional $10 (=$60 − $50). Corporations have limited liability in America and most other countries, implying that bondholders cannot sue the stockholders for the extra $10.[1]

Let's compare the two companies in recession. The bondholders of Knight receive $49 and the stockholders receive $1, for a total of $50. The bondholders of Day receive $50 and the stockholders receive $0, also for a total of $50. There is an important point here. While Day goes bankrupt but Knight does not, the investors of both firms receive $50. In other words, bankruptcy does not reduce the firm's cash flows. One often hears that bankruptcy causes a reduction in value or cash flow. But that is not the case. In our example, it is a recession causing the reduction, not bankruptcy.

(continued)

---

[1]There are situations where the limited liability of corporations can be "pierced." Typically, fraud or misrepresentation must be present.

However, we have left something out. Day's example is not realistic because it ignores an important cash flow. A more realistic set of numbers might be:

Day Corporation

	Boom Times (prob. 50%)	Recession (prob. 50%)
Earnings	$100	$50
Debt repayment	60	35
Distribution to stockholders	$ 40	$ 0

Why do the bondholders receive only $35 in a recession? If cash flow is only $50, bondholders will be informed that they will not be paid in full. These bondholders are likely to hire lawyers to negotiate or even to sue the company. Similarly, the firm is likely to hire lawyers to defend itself. Further costs will be incurred if the case gets to a bankruptcy court. These fees are always paid before the bondholders get paid. In this example, we are assuming that bankruptcy costs total $15 (=$50 − $35).

Let's compare the example with bankruptcy costs to the example without these costs. Because of its greater leverage, Day Corporation faces the possibility of bankruptcy, while Knight Corporation does not. Nevertheless, as we saw earlier, total cash flow to investors is the same for both firms in a world without bankruptcy costs. However, once we introduce bankruptcy costs, total cash flow to investors becomes lower for the bankrupt company, Day. In a recession, Knight's bondholders receive $49 and the stockholders receive $1, for a total of $50. In a recession, Day's bondholders receive $35 and the stockholders receive $0, for a total of only $35. Thus, we can conclude the following:

Leverage increases the likelihood of bankruptcy. However, bankruptcy does not, by itself, lower the cash flows to investors. Rather, it is the costs associated with bankruptcy that lower cash flows.

Our pie example can provide an explanation. In a world without bankruptcy costs, the bondholders and the stockholders share the entire pie. However, bankruptcy costs eat up some of the pie in the real world, leaving less for the stockholders and bondholders.

17.2 Description of Financial Distress Costs

The preceding example showed that bankruptcy costs can lower the value of the firm. In fact, the same general result holds even if a legal bankruptcy is prevented. Thus *financial distress costs* may be a better phrase than *bankruptcy costs*. It is worthwhile to describe these costs in more detail.

DIRECT COSTS OF FINANCIAL DISTRESS: LEGAL AND ADMINISTRATIVE COSTS OF LIQUIDATION OR REORGANIZATION

As mentioned earlier, lawyers are involved throughout all the stages before and during bankruptcy. With fees often in the hundreds of dollars an hour, these costs can add up quickly. A wag once remarked that bankruptcies are to lawyers what blood is to sharks. In addition, administrative and accounting fees can substantially add to the total bill. And if a trial takes place, we must not forget expert witnesses. Each side may hire a number of these witnesses to testify about the fairness of a proposed settlement. Their fees can easily rival those of lawyers or accountants. (However, we personally look upon these witnesses kindly because they are frequently drawn from the ranks of finance professors.)

One of the most well-publicized bankruptcies in recent years concerned a municipality, Orange County, California, not a corporation. This bankruptcy followed large bond trading losses in the county's financial portfolio. The *Los Angeles Times* stated:

> Orange County taxpayers lost $1.69 billion, and their government, one year ago today, sank into bankruptcy. Now they are spending millions more to get out of it.
>
> Accountants pore over fiscal ledgers at $325 an hour. Lawyers toil into the night—at $385 an hour. Financial advisers from one of the nation's most prominent investment houses labor for the taxpayers at $150,000 a month. Clerks stand by the photocopy machines, running up bills that sometimes exceed $3,000.
>
> Total so far: $29 million. And it's nowhere near over.
>
> The multipronged effort to lift Orange County out of the nation's worst municipal bankruptcy has become a money-eating machine, gobbling up taxpayer funds at a rate of $2.4 million a month. That's $115,000 a day.
>
> County administrators are not alarmed.
>
> They say Orange County's bankruptcy was an epic disaster that will require equally dramatic expenditures of taxpayer cash to help it survive. While they have refused to pay several thousand dollars worth of claimed expenses—lavish dinners, big hotel bills—they have rarely questioned the sky-high hourly fees. They predict the costs could climb much higher.
>
> Indeed, participants in the county's investment pool have agreed to create a separate $50 million fund to pay the costs of doing legal battle with Wall Street.[2]

Bankruptcy costs in the private sector are often far larger than those in Orange County. For example, the direct costs of Enron's and WorldCom's bankruptcies were commonly estimated to exceed $1 billion and $600 million, respectively. The costs of Lehman Brothers' bankruptcy are larger still. While Lehman filed for bankruptcy in 2008, the bankruptcy had not been completed by early 2011. As of that time, the direct costs of Lehman's bankruptcy were expected to total almost $2 billion. This number is the sum of many large costs. For example, one law firm billed $200,000 for business meals, $439,000 for computerized and other research, $115,000 for local transportation, and $287,000 for copying charges at 10 cents per page. The other costs of the bankruptcy may have been even larger. Some experts estimated that because Lehman rushed into bankruptcy it lost out on $75 billion that it could have earned if the sale of many of its assets had been better planned.

A number of academic studies have measured the direct costs of financial distress. Although large in absolute amount, these costs are actually small as a percentage of firm value. White, Altman, and Weiss estimate the direct costs of financial distress to be about 3 percent of the market value of the firm.[3] In a study of direct financial distress costs of 20 railroad bankruptcies, Warner finds that net financial distress

[2]"The High Cost of Going Bankrupt," *Los Angeles Times Orange County Edition*, December 6, 1995. Taken from Lexis/Nexis.
[3]M. J. White, "Bankruptcy Costs and the New Bankruptcy Code," *Journal of Finance* (May 1983); E. I. Altman, "A Further Empirical Investigation of the Bankruptcy Cost Question," *Journal of Finance* (September 1984); and Lawrence A. Weiss, "Bankruptcy Resolution: Direct Costs and Violation of Priority of Claims," *Journal of Financial Economics* 27 (1990).

costs were, on average, 1 percent of the market value of the firm seven years before bankruptcy and were somewhat larger percentages as bankruptcy approached (for example, 2.5 percent of the market value of the firm three years before bankruptcy).[4] Lubben estimates the average cost of legal fees alone to be about 1.5 percent of total assets for bankrupt firms.[5] Bris, Welch, and Zhu find bankruptcy expenses as measured against asset values to be in the 2 to 10 percent range.[6]

INDIRECT COSTS OF FINANCIAL DISTRESS

Impaired Ability to Conduct Business   Bankruptcy hampers conduct with customers and suppliers. Sales are frequently lost because of both fear of impaired service and loss of trust. For example, in 2008, both General Motors and Chrysler were experiencing significant financial difficulties, and many people felt that one or both companies would eventually file for bankruptcy (both later did). As a result of the bad news surrounding the companies, there was a loss of confidence in their automobiles. A study showed that 75 percent of Americans would not purchase an automobile from a bankrupt company because the company might not honor the warranty, and it might be difficult to obtain replacement parts. This concern resulted in lost potential sales for both companies, which only added to their financial distress. Chrysler actually found itself in a similar situation when it skirted insolvency in the 1970s. Many previously loyal Chrysler customers, fearing the loss of parts and servicing in a bankruptcy, switched to other manufacturers. As another example, gamblers avoided Atlantis casino in Atlantic City after it became technically insolvent. Gamblers are a superstitious bunch. Many wondered, "If the casino itself cannot make money, how can I expect to make money there?" A particularly outrageous story concerned two unrelated stores both named Mitchells in New York City. When one Mitchells declared bankruptcy, customers stayed away from both stores. In time, the second store was forced to declare bankruptcy as well.

Though these costs clearly exist, it is quite difficult to measure them. Altman estimates that both direct and indirect costs of financial distress are frequently greater than 20 percent of firm value.[7] Andrade and Kaplan estimate total distress costs to be between 10 percent and 20 percent of firm value.[8] Bar-Or estimates expected future distress costs for firms that are currently healthy to be 8 to 10 percent of operating value, a number below the estimates of either Altman or Andrade and Kaplan.[9] However, unlike Bar-Or, these authors consider distress costs for firms already in distress, not expected distress costs for currently healthy firms.

Cutler and Summers examine the costs of the well-publicized Texaco bankruptcy.[10] In January 1984, Pennzoil reached what it believed to be a binding agreement to acquire three-sevenths of Getty Oil. However, less than a week later, Texaco acquired all of Getty at a higher per-share price. Pennzoil then sued Getty for breach of

[4]J. B. Warner, "Bankruptcy Costs: Some Evidence," *Journal of Finance* (May 1977).

[5]Stephen J. Lubben, "The Direct Costs of Corporate Reorganization: An Empirical Examination of Professional Fees in Large Chapter 11 Cases," *American Bankruptcy Law Journal* (2000).

[6]Arturo Bris, Ivo Welch, and Ning Zhu, "The Costs of Bankruptcy: Chapter 7 Liquidation versus Chapter 11 Reorganization," *Journal of Finance* (June 2006).

[7]E. I. Altman, *op. cit.*

[8]Gregor Andrade and Steven N. Kaplan, "How Costly Is Financial (Not Economic) Distress? Evidence from Highly Leveraged Transactions That Became Distressed," *Journal of Finance* (October 1998).

[9]Yuval Bar-Or, "An Investigation of Expected Financial Distress Costs," unpublished paper, Wharton School, University of Pennsylvania (March 2000).

[10]David M. Cutler and Lawrence H. Summers, "The Costs of Conflict Resolution and Financial Distress: Evidence from the Texaco–Pennzoil Litigation," *Rand Journal of Economics* (Summer 1988).

contract. Because Texaco had previously indemnified Getty against litigation, Texaco became liable for damages.

In November 1985, the Texas State Court awarded damages of $12 billion to Pennzoil, although this amount was later reduced. As a result, Texaco filed for bankruptcy. Cutler and Summers identify nine important events over the course of the litigation. They find that Texaco's market value (stock price times number of shares outstanding) fell a cumulative $4.1 billion over these events, whereas Pennzoil's rose only $682 million. Thus, Pennzoil gained about one-sixth of what Texaco lost, resulting in a net loss to the two firms of almost $3.5 billion.

What could explain this net loss? Cutler and Summers suggest that it is likely due to costs that Texaco and Pennzoil incurred from the litigation and subsequent bankruptcy. The authors argue that direct bankruptcy fees represent only a small part of these costs, estimating Texaco's aftertax legal expenses as about $165 million. Legal costs to Pennzoil were more difficult to assess because Pennzoil's lead lawyer, Joe Jamail, stated publicly that he had no set fee. However, using a clever statistical analysis, the authors estimate his fee was about $200 million. Thus we must search elsewhere for the bulk of the costs.

Indirect costs of financial distress may be the culprit. An affidavit by Texaco stated that, following the lawsuit, some of its suppliers were demanding cash payments. Other suppliers halted or canceled shipments of crude oil. Certain banks restricted Texaco's use of futures contracts on foreign exchange. The affidavit stressed that these constraints were reducing Texaco's ability to run its business, leading to deterioration of its financial condition. Could these sorts of indirect costs explain the $3.5 billion disparity between Texaco's drop and Pennzoil's rise in market value? Unfortunately, although indirect costs likely played a large role here; there is simply no way to obtain a decent quantitative estimate for them.

AGENCY COSTS

When a firm has debt, conflicts of interest arise between stockholders and bondholders. Because of this, stockholders are tempted to pursue selfish strategies. These conflicts of interest, which are magnified when financial distress is incurred, impose **agency costs** on the firm. We describe three kinds of selfish strategies that stockholders use to hurt the bondholders and help themselves. These strategies are costly because they will lower the market value of the whole firm.

Selfish Investment Strategy I: *Incentive to Take Large Risks* Firms near bankruptcy often take great chances because they believe that they are playing with someone else's money. To see this, imagine a levered firm considering two *mutually exclusive* projects, a low-risk one and a high-risk one. There are two equally likely outcomes, recession and boom. The firm is in such dire straits that should a recession hit, it will come near to bankruptcy with one project and actually fall into bankruptcy with the other. The cash flows for the entire firm if the low-risk project is taken can be described as follows:

Value of Entire Firm if Low-Risk Project Is Chosen

	Probability	Value of Firm	=	Stock	+	Bonds
Recession	.5	$100	=	$ 0	+	$100
Boom	.5	200	=	100	+	100

If a recession occurs, the value of the firm will be $100; if a boom occurs, the value of the firm will be $200. The expected value of the firm is $150 (=.5 × $100 + .5 × $200).

The firm has promised to pay bondholders $100. Shareholders will obtain the difference between the total payoff and the amount paid to the bondholders. In other words, the bondholders have the prior claim on the payoffs, and the shareholders have the residual claim.

Now suppose that the riskier project can be substituted for the low-risk project. The payoffs and probabilities are as follows:

Value of Entire Firm if High-Risk Project Is Chosen

	Probability	Value of Firm	=	Stock	+	Bonds
Recession	.5	$ 50	=	$ 0	+	$ 50
Boom	.5	240	=	140	+	100

The expected value of the *firm* is $145 (=.5 × $50 + .5 × $240), which is lower than the expected value of the firm with the low-risk project. Thus the low-risk project would be accepted if the firm were all equity. However, note that the expected value of the *stock* is $70 (=.5 × 0 + .5 × $140) with the high-risk project, but only $50 (=.5 × 0 + .5 × $100) with the low-risk project. Given the firm's present levered state, stockholders will select the high-risk project, even though the high-risk project has a *lower* NPV.

The key is that relative to the low-risk project, the high-risk project increases firm value in a boom and decreases firm value in a recession. The increase in value in a boom is captured by the stockholders because the bondholders are paid in full (they receive $100) regardless of which project is accepted. Conversely, the drop in value in a recession is lost by the bondholders because they are paid in full with the low-risk project but receive only $50 with the high-risk one. The stockholders will receive nothing in a recession anyway, whether the high-risk or low-risk project is selected. Thus, financial economists argue that stockholders expropriate value from the bondholders by selecting high-risk projects.

A story, perhaps apocryphal, illustrates this idea. It seems that Federal Express was near financial collapse within a few years of its inception. The founder, Frederick Smith, took $20,000 of corporate funds to Las Vegas in despair. He won at the gaming tables, providing enough capital to allow the firm to survive. Had he lost, the banks would simply have received $20,000 less when the firm reached bankruptcy.

Selfish Investment Strategy 2: *Incentive toward Underinvestment* Stockholders of a firm with a significant probability of bankruptcy often find that new investment helps the bondholders at the stockholders' expense. The simplest case might be a real estate owner facing imminent bankruptcy. If he takes $100,000 out of his own pocket to refurbish the building, he could increase the building's value by, say, $150,000. Though this investment has a positive net present value, he will turn it down if the increase in value cannot prevent bankruptcy. "Why," he asks, "should I use my own funds to improve the value of a building that the bank will soon repossess?"

This idea is formalized by the following simple example. Consider the firm in Table 17.1, which must decide whether to accept or reject a new project. The project's cost is $1,000. The first two columns in the table show cash flows without the project. The firm receives cash inflows of $5,000 and $2,400 under a boom and a recession, respectively. However, the firm must pay principal and interest of $4,000, implying that the firm will default in a recession.

Table 17.1

Example
Illustrating
Incentive to
Underinvest

	Firm without Project		Firm with Project Costing $1,000	
	Boom	**Recession**	**Boom**	**Recession**
Firm cash flows	$5,000	$2,400	$6,700	$4,100
Bondholders' claim	4,000	2,400	4,000	4,000
Stockholders' claim	$1,000	$ 0	$2,700	$ 100

The project has positive NPV. However, much of its value is captured by bondholders. Rational managers, acting in the stockholders' interest, will reject the project.

Alternatively, as indicated in the next two columns of the table, the firm could raise equity to invest in the new project. Assume that the project generates cash flow of $1,700 in either state, bringing the firm's cash flow to $6,700 (= $5,000 + $1,700) in a boom and $4,100 (= $2,400 + $1,700) in a recession. Since the firm's cash flow of $4,100 in a recession exceeds the bondholders' claim of $4,000, bankruptcy is avoided. Because $1,700 is much greater than the project's cost of $1,000, the project has a positive NPV at any plausible interest rate. Clearly, an all-equity firm would accept the project.

However, the project hurts the stockholders of the levered firm. To see this, imagine the old stockholders contribute the $1,000 *themselves*.[11] Assuming that a boom and a recession are equally likely, the expected value of the stockholders' interest without the project is $500 (=.5 × $1,000 + .5 × 0). The expected value with the project is $1,400 (=.5 × $2,700 + .5 × $100). The stockholders' interest rises by only $900 (= $1,400 − $500) while costing $1,000.

Why does a project with a positive NPV hurt the stockholders? The key is that the stockholders contribute the full $1,000 investment, but the stockholders and bondholders *share* the benefits. The stockholders take the entire gain if a boom occurs. Conversely, the bondholders reap most of the cash flow from the project in a recession.

The discussion of selfish Strategy 1 is quite similar to the discussion of selfish Strategy 2. In both cases, an investment strategy for the levered firm is different from the one for the unlevered firm. Thus, leverage results in distorted investment policy. Whereas the unlevered corporation always chooses projects with positive net present value, the levered firm may deviate from this policy.

Selfish Investment Strategy 3: *Milking the Property* Another strategy is to pay out extra dividends or other distributions in times of financial distress, leaving less in the firm for the bondholders. This is known as *milking the property*, a phrase taken from real estate. Strategies 2 and 3 are very similar. In Strategy 2, the firm chooses not to raise new equity. Strategy 3 goes one step further because equity is actually withdrawn through the dividend.

Summary of Selfish Strategies The distortions just discussed occur only when there is a significant probability of bankruptcy or financial distress. Thus, distortions are unlikely to affect, say, utilities regulated by state commissions, since financial distress is rare among these firms. By contrast, small firms in risky industries, such as the computer field, are more likely to experience financial distress and, in turn, to be affected by such distortions.

Who pays for the cost of selfish investment strategies? We argue that it is ultimately the stockholders. Rational bondholders know that when financial distress is

---

[11]The same qualitative results will be obtained if the $1,000 is raised from new stockholders. However, the arithmetic becomes much more difficult because we must determine how many new shares are issued.

imminent, they cannot expect help from stockholders. Rather, stockholders are likely to choose investment strategies that reduce the value of the bonds. Bondholders protect themselves accordingly by raising the interest rate that they require on the bonds. Because the stockholders must pay these high rates, they ultimately bear the costs of selfish strategies. For firms that face these distortions, debt will be difficult and costly to obtain. These firms will have low leverage ratios.

The relationship between stockholders and bondholders is very similar to the relationship between Errol Flynn and David Niven, good friends and movie stars in the 1930s. Niven reportedly said that the good thing about Flynn was that you knew exactly where you stood with him. When you needed his help, you could always count on him to let you down.

17.3 Can Costs of Debt Be Reduced?

As U.S. senators are prone to say, "A billion here, a billion there. Pretty soon it all adds up." Each of the costs of financial distress we have mentioned is substantial in its own right. The sum of them may well affect debt financing severely. Thus, managers have an incentive to reduce these costs. We now turn to some of their methods. However, it should be mentioned at the outset that the methods here can, at most, reduce the costs of debt. They cannot *eliminate* them entirely.

PROTECTIVE COVENANTS

Because the stockholders must pay higher interest rates as insurance against their own selfish strategies, they frequently make agreements with bondholders in hopes of lower rates. These agreements, called **protective covenants,** are incorporated as part of the loan document (or *indenture*) between stockholders and bondholders. The covenants must be taken seriously because a broken covenant can lead to default. Protective covenants can be classified into two types: negative covenants and positive covenants.

A **negative covenant** limits or prohibits actions that the company may take. Here are some typical negative covenants:

1. Limitations are placed on the amount of dividends a company may pay.
2. The firm may not pledge any of its assets to other lenders.
3. The firm may not merge with another firm.
4. The firm may not sell or lease its major assets without approval by the lender.
5. The firm may not issue additional long-term debt.

A **positive covenant** specifies an action that the company agrees to take or a condition the company must abide by. Here are some examples:

1. The company agrees to maintain its working capital at a minimum level.
2. The company must furnish periodic financial statements to the lender.

These lists of covenants are not exhaustive. The authors have seen loan agreements with more than 30 covenants.

Smith and Warner examined public issues of debt and found that 91 percent of the bond indentures included covenants that restricted the issuance of additional debt, 23 percent restricted dividends, 39 percent restricted mergers, and 36 percent limited the sale of assets.[12]

---

[12]C. W. Smith and J. B. Warner, "On Financial Contracting: An Analysis of Bond Covenants," *Journal of Financial Economics* 7 (1979).

Table 17.2   Loan Covenants

Shareholder Action or Firm Circumstances	Covenant Type	Reason for Covenant
As firm approaches financial distress, shareholders may want firm to make high-risk investments.	Financial statement restrictions 1. Minimum working capital 2. Minimum interest coverage 3. Minimum net worth	High-risk investments transfer value from bondholders to stockholders when financial distress is a realistic possibility. Covenants reduce probability of financial distress.
Shareholders may attempt to transfer corporate assets to themselves.	Restrictions on asset disposition 1. Limit on dividends 2. Limit on sale of assets 3. Collateral and mortgages	Covenants limit the ability of shareholders to transfer assets to themselves and to *underinvest*.
Shareholders may attempt to increase risk of firm.	Restrictions on switching assets	Increased firm risk helps shareholders and hurts bondholders.
Shareholders may attempt to issue new debt of equal or greater priority.	Dilution restrictions 1. Limit on leasing 2. Limit on further borrowing	Covenants restrict *dilution of the claim of existing bondholders*.

Protective covenants should reduce the costs of bankruptcy, ultimately increasing the value of the firm. Thus, stockholders are likely to favor all reasonable covenants. To see this, consider three choices by stockholders to reduce bankruptcy costs:

1. *Issue no debt.* Because of the tax advantages to debt, this is a very costly way of avoiding conflicts.

2. *Issue debt with no restrictive and protective covenants.* In this case, bondholders will demand high interest rates to compensate for the unprotected status of their debt.

3. *Write protective and restrictive covenants into the loan contracts.* If the covenants are reasonable and are clearly written, the creditors may receive protection without large costs being imposed on the shareholders. With this protection, the creditors are likely to accept a lower interest rate than they would accept without the covenants.

Thus, bond covenants, even if they reduce flexibility, can increase the value of the firm. They can be the lowest-cost solution to the stockholder–bondholder conflict. A list of typical bond covenants and their uses appears in Table 17.2.

CONSOLIDATION OF DEBT

One reason bankruptcy costs are so high is that different creditors (and their lawyers) contend with each other. This problem can be alleviated by proper coordination between bondholders and stockholders. For example, perhaps one, or at most a few, lenders can shoulder the entire debt. Should financial distress occur, negotiating costs are minimized under this arrangement. In addition, bondholders can purchase stock as well. In this way, stockholders and debtholders are not pitted against each other because they are not separate entities. This appears to be the approach in Japan, where large banks generally take significant stock positions in the firms to which they lend money. Debt–equity ratios in Japan are far higher than those in the United States.

17.4 Integration of Tax Effects and Financial Distress Costs

Modigliani and Miller argue that the firm's value rises with leverage in the presence of corporate taxes. Because this relationship implies that all firms should choose maximum debt, the theory does not predict the behavior of firms in the real world.

Other authors have suggested that bankruptcy and related costs reduce the value of the levered firm. The integration of tax effects and distress costs appears in Figure 17.1. In the top graph of the figure, the diagonal straight line represents the value of the firm in a world without bankruptcy costs. The ∩-shaped curve represents the value of the firm with these costs. This curve rises as the firm moves from all equity to a small amount of debt. Here, the present value of the distress costs is minimal because the probability of distress is so small. However, as more and more debt is added, the present value of these costs rises at an *increasing* rate. At some point, the increase in the present value of these costs from an additional dollar of debt equals

Figure 17.1
The Optimal Amount of Debt and the Value of the Firm

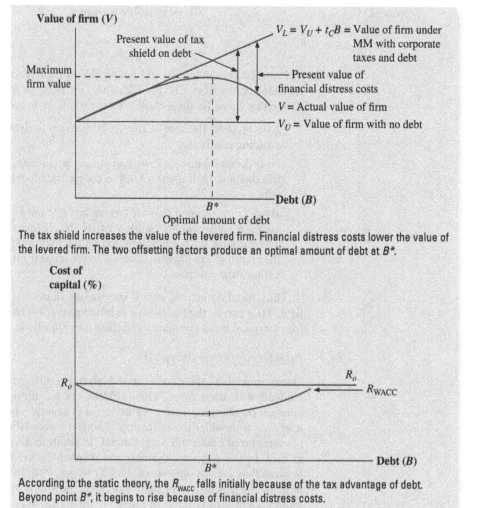

The tax shield increases the value of the levered firm. Financial distress costs lower the value of the levered firm. The two offsetting factors produce an optimal amount of debt at B^*.

According to the static theory, the R_{WACC} falls initially because of the tax advantage of debt. Beyond point B^*, it begins to rise because of financial distress costs.

the increase in the present value of the tax shield. This is the debt level maximizing the value of the firm and is represented by B^* in Figure 17.1. In other words, B^* is the optimal amount of debt. Bankruptcy costs increase faster than the tax shield beyond this point, implying a reduction in firm value from further leverage.

In the bottom graph of Figure 17.1, the weighted average cost of capital (R_{WACC}) falls as debt is added to the capital structure. After reaching B^*, the weighted average cost of capital rises. The optimal amount of debt produces the lowest weighted average cost of capital.

Our discussion implies that a firm's capital structure decision involves a trade-off between the tax benefits of debt and the costs of financial distress. In fact, this approach is frequently called the *trade-off* or the *static trade-off* theory of capital structure. The implication is that there is an optimal amount of debt for any individual firm. This amount of debt becomes the firm's target debt level. Because financial distress costs cannot be expressed in a precise way, no formula has yet been developed to determine a firm's optimal debt level exactly. However, the last section of this chapter offers some rules of thumb for selecting a debt–equity ratio in the real world. Our situation reminds us of a quote from John Maynard Keynes. He reputedly said that although most historians would agree that Queen Elizabeth I was both a better monarch and an unhappier woman than Queen Victoria, no one has yet been able to express the statement in a precise and rigorous formula.

PIE AGAIN

Now that we have considered bankruptcy costs, let's return to the pie approach of the previous chapter. The cash flows (CF) of the firm go to four different claimants: Stockholders, bondholders, the government (in the form of taxes), and, during the bankruptcy process, lawyers (and others). We can express this idea algebraically as:

$$CF = \text{Payments to stockholders}$$
$$+$$
$$\text{Payments to bondholders}$$
$$+$$
$$\text{Payments to the government}$$
$$+$$
$$\text{Payments to lawyers (and others)}$$

It follows that the total value of the firm, V_T, equals the sum of the following four components:

$$V_T = S + B + G + L$$

where S is the value of the equity, B is the value of the bonds, G is the value of the government claims from taxes, and L stands for the value that lawyers and others receive when the firm is under financial distress. This relationship is illustrated in Figure 17.2.

Nor have we begun to exhaust the list of financial claims to the firm's cash flows. To give an unusual example, everyone reading this book has an economic claim to the cash flows of General Motors. After all, if you are injured in an accident, you might sue GM. Win or lose, GM will expend resources dealing with the matter. If you think this is far-fetched and unimportant, ask yourself how much GM might be willing to pay every man, woman, and child in the country to have them promise that they would never sue GM, no matter what happened. The law does not permit such payments, but that does not mean that a value to all of those potential claims does

Figure 17.2
The Pie Model with
Real-World Factors

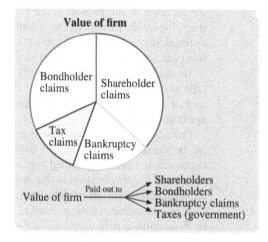

not exist. We guess that it would run into the billions of dollars, and, for GM or any other company, there should be a slice of the pie labeled *LS* for "potential lawsuits."

Figure 17.2 illustrates the essence of MM's intuition. While V_T is determined by the firm's cash flows, the firm's capital structure merely cuts V_T into slices. Capital structure does *not* affect the total value, V_T.

There is, however, a difference between claims such as those of stockholders and bondholders on the one hand and those of government and potential litigants in lawsuits on the other. The first set of claims are **marketable claims,** and the second set are **nonmarketable claims.** Marketable claims can be bought and sold in financial markets, and the nonmarketable claims cannot. This distinction between marketable and nonmarketable claims is important. When stock is issued, stockholders pay cash to the firm for the privilege of later receiving dividends. Similarly, bondholders pay cash to the firm for the privilege of receiving interest in the future. However, the IRS pays nothing to the firm for the privilege of receiving taxes in the future. Similarly, lawyers pay nothing to the firm for the privilege of receiving fees from the firm in the future.

When we speak of the *value of the firm,* we are referring just to the value of the marketable claims, V_M, and not the value of nonmarketable claims, V_N. What we have shown is that capital structure does not affect the total value:

$$V_T = S + B + G + L$$
$$= V_M + V_N$$

But as we saw, the value of the marketable claims, V_M, can change with changes in the capital structure.

By the pie theory, any increase in V_M must imply an identical decrease in V_N. Rational financial managers will choose a capital structure to maximize the value of the marketable claims, V_M. Equivalently, rational managers will work to minimize the value of the nonmarketable claims, V_N. These are taxes and bankruptcy costs in the previous example, but they also include all the other nonmarketable claims such as the *LS* claim.

17.5 Signaling

The previous section pointed out that the corporate leverage decision involves a trade-off between a tax subsidy and financial distress costs. This idea was graphed in Figure 17.1, where the marginal tax subsidy exceeds the distress costs for low levels of debt. The reverse holds for high levels of debt. The firm's capital structure is optimized where the marginal subsidy to debt equals the marginal cost.

Let's explore this idea a little more. What is the relationship between a company's profitability and its debt level? A firm with low anticipated profits will likely take on a low level of debt. A small interest deduction is all that is needed to offset all of this firm's pretax profits. And too much debt would raise the firm's expected distress costs. A more successful firm would probably take on more debt. This firm could use the extra interest to reduce the taxes from its greater earnings. Being more financially secure, this firm would find its extra debt increasing the risk of bankruptcy only slightly. In other words, rational firms raise debt levels (and the concomitant interest payments) when profits are expected to increase.

How do investors react to an increase in debt? Rational investors are likely to infer a higher firm value from a higher debt level. Thus, these investors are likely to bid up a firm's stock price after the firm has, say, issued debt in order to buy back equity. We say that investors view debt as a *signal* of firm value.

Now we get to the incentives of managers to fool the public. Consider a firm whose level of debt is optimal. That is, the marginal tax benefit of debt equals the marginal distress costs of debt. However, imagine that the firm's manager desires to increase the firm's current stock price, perhaps because he knows that many of his stockholders want to sell their stock soon. This manager might want to increase the level of debt just to make investors *think* that the firm is more valuable than it really is. If the strategy works, investors will push up the price of the stock.

This implies that firms can fool investors by taking on *some* additional leverage. Now let's ask the big question. Are there benefits to extra debt but no costs, implying that all firms will take on as much debt as possible? The answer, fortunately, is that there are costs as well. Imagine that a firm has issued extra debt just to fool the public. At some point, the market will learn that the company is not that valuable after all. At this time the stock price should actually fall *below* what it would have been had the debt never been increased. Why? Because the firm's debt level is now above the optimal level. That is, the marginal tax benefit of debt is below the marginal cost of debt. Thus if the current stockholders plan to sell, say, half of their shares now and retain the other half, an increase in debt will help them on immediate sales but likely hurt them on later ones.

Now here is the important point: We said that in a world where managers do not attempt to fool investors, valuable firms issue more debt than less valuable ones. It turns out that even when managers attempt to fool investors, the more valuable firms will still want to issue more debt than the less valuable firms. That is, while all firms will increase debt levels somewhat to fool investors, the costs of extra debt prevent the less valuable firms from issuing more debt than the more valuable firms issue. Thus, investors can still treat debt level as a signal of firm value. In other words, investors can still view an announcement of debt as a positive sign for the firm.

The foregoing is a simplified example of debt signaling, and you might argue that it is too simplified. For example, perhaps the stockholders of some firms want to sell most of their stock immediately, whereas the stockholders of other firms want to sell only a little of theirs now. It is impossible to tell here whether the firms with the most debt are the most valuable or merely the ones with the most impatient stockholders. Because other objections can be brought up as well, signaling theory is best validated by empirical evidence. And fortunately, the empirical evidence tends to support the theory.

For example, consider the evidence concerning **exchange offers.** Firms often change their debt levels through exchange offers, of which there are two types. The first type of offer allows stockholders to exchange some of their stock for debt, thereby increasing leverage. The second type allows bondholders to exchange some of their debt for

572

Corporate Finance

540   *Part IV* Capital Structure and Dividend Policy

Figure 17.3
Stock Returns at the Time of Announcements of Exchange Offers

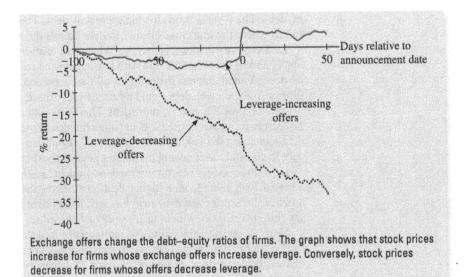

Exchange offers change the debt–equity ratios of firms. The graph shows that stock prices increase for firms whose exchange offers increase leverage. Conversely, stock prices decrease for firms whose offers decrease leverage.

SOURCE: K. Shah, "The Nature of Information Conveyed by Pure Capital Structure Changes," *Journal of Financial Economics* 36 (August 1994).

stock, decreasing leverage. Figure 17.3 shows the stock price behavior of firms that change their proportions of debt and equity via exchange offers. The solid line in the figure indicates that stock prices rise substantially on the date when an exchange offering increasing leverage is announced. (This date is referred to as date 0 in the figure.) Conversely, the dotted line in the figure indicates that stock price falls substantially when an offer decreasing leverage is announced.

The market infers from an increase in debt that the firm is better off, leading to a stock price rise. Conversely, the market infers the reverse from a decrease in debt, implying a stock price fall. Thus, we say that managers signal information when they change leverage.

17.6 Shirking, Perquisites, and Bad Investments: A Note on Agency Cost of Equity

A previous section introduced the static trade-off model, where a rise in debt increases both the tax shield and the costs of distress. We now extend the trade-off model by considering an important agency cost of equity. A discussion of this cost of equity is contained in a well-known quote from Adam Smith:[13]

> The directors of such [joint-stock] companies, however, being the managers of other people's money than of their own, it cannot well be expected that they should watch over it with the same anxious vigilance with which the partners in a private copartnery frequently watch over their own. Like the stewards of a rich man, they are apt to consider attention to small matters as not for their master's honor, and very easily give themselves a dispensation from having it. Negligence and profusion, therefore, must always prevail, more or less, in the management of the affairs of such a company.

[13]Adam Smith, *The Wealth of Nations* [1776], Cannon edition (New York: Modern Library, 1937), p. 700, as quoted in M. C. Jensen and W. Meckling, "Theory of the Firm: Managerial Behavior, Agency Costs, and Ownership Structure," *Journal of Financial Economics* 3 (1976).

This elegant prose can be restated in modern vocabulary. An individual will work harder for a firm if she is one of its owners than if she is just an employee. In addition, the individual will work harder if she owns a large percentage of the company than if she owns a small percentage. This idea has an important implication for capital structure, which we illustrate with the following example.

EXAMPLE 17.2

Agency Costs   Ms. Pagell is an owner–entrepreneur running a computer services firm worth $1 million. She currently owns 100 percent of the firm. Because of the need to expand, she must raise another $2 million. She can either issue $2 million of debt at 12 percent interest or issue $2 million in stock. The cash flows under the two alternatives are presented here:

	Debt Issue				Stock Issue			
Work Intensity	Cash Flow	Interest	Cash Flow to Equity	Cash Flow to Ms. Pagell (100% of equity)	Cash Flow	Interest	Cash Flow to Equity	Cash Flow to Ms. Pagell ($33\frac{1}{3}$% of equity)
6-hour days	$300,000	$240,000	$ 60,000	$ 60,000	$300,000	0	$300,000	$100,000
10-hour days	400,000	240,000	160,000	160,000	400,000	0	400,000	133,333

Like any entrepreneur, Ms. Pagell can choose the degree of intensity with which she works. In our example, she can work either a 6- or a 10-hour day. With the debt issue, the extra work brings her $100,000 (=$160,000 − $60,000) more income. However, let's assume that with a stock issue she retains only a one-third interest in the equity. Here, the extra work brings her merely $33,333 (=$133,333 − $100,000). Being human, she is likely to work harder if she issues debt. In other words, she has more incentive to *shirk* if she issues equity.

In addition, she is likely to obtain more *perquisites* (a big office, a company car, more expense account meals) if she issues stock. If she is a one-third stockholder, two-thirds of these costs are paid for by the other stockholders. If she is the sole owner, any additional perquisites reduce her equity stake alone.

Finally, she is more likely to take on capital budgeting projects with negative net present values. It might seem surprising that a manager with any equity interest at all would take on negative NPV projects, since the stock price would clearly fall here. However, managerial salaries generally rise with firm size, providing managers with an incentive to accept some unprofitable projects after all the profitable ones have been taken on. That is, when an unprofitable project is accepted, the loss in stock value to a manager with only a small equity interest may be less than the increase in salary. In fact, it is our opinion that losses from accepting bad projects are far greater than losses from either shirking or excessive perquisites. Hugely unprofitable projects have bankrupted whole firms, something that even the largest expense account is unlikely to do.

Thus, as the firm issues more equity, our entrepreneur will likely increase leisure time, work-related perquisites, and unprofitable investments. These three items are called *agency costs* because managers of the firm are agents of the stockholders.[14]

---

[14]As previously discussed, *agency costs* are generally defined as the costs from the conflicts of interest among stockholders, bondholders, and managers.

This example is quite applicable to a small company considering a large stock offering. Because a manager–owner will greatly dilute his or her share of the total equity in this case, a significant drop in work intensity or a significant increase in fringe benefits is possible. However, the example may be less applicable for a large corporation with many stockholders. For example, consider a large company such as General Electric issuing stock for the umpteenth time. The typical manager there already has such a small percentage stake in the firm that any temptation for negligence has probably been experienced before. An additional offering cannot be expected to increase this temptation.

Who bears the burden of these agency costs, the current owner, i.e., Ms. Pagell, or the new stockholders? The new stockholders do not bear these costs as long as they invest with their eyes open. Knowing that Ms. Pagell may work shorter hours, they will pay only a low price for the stock. Thus, it is the owner who is hurt by agency costs. However, Ms. Pagell can protect herself to some extent. Just as stockholders reduce bankruptcy costs through protective covenants, an owner may allow monitoring by new stockholders. However, though proper reporting and surveillance may reduce the agency costs of equity, these techniques are unlikely to eliminate them.

It is commonly suggested that leveraged buyouts (LBOs) significantly reduce these costs of equity. In an LBO, a purchaser (usually a team of existing management) buys out the stockholders at a price above the current market. In other words, the company goes private: The stock is placed in the hands of only a few people. Because the managers now own a substantial chunk of the business, they are likely to work harder than when they were simply hired hands.[15]

EFFECT OF AGENCY COSTS OF EQUITY ON DEBT–EQUITY FINANCING

The preceding discussion of the agency costs of equity should be viewed as an extension of the static trade-off model. That is, we stated in Section 17.4 that the change in the value of the firm when debt is substituted for equity is the difference between (1) the tax shield on debt, and (2) the increase in the costs of financial distress (including the agency costs of debt). Now the change in the value of the firm is (1) the tax shield on debt, plus (2) the reduction in the agency costs of equity, minus (3) the increase in the costs of financial distress (including the agency costs of debt). The optimal debt–equity ratio would be higher in a world with agency costs of equity than in a world without these costs. However, because costs of financial distress are so significant, the costs of equity do not imply 100 percent debt financing.

FREE CASH FLOW

Any reader of murder mysteries knows that a criminal must have both motive and opportunity. The discussion thus far has been about motive. Managers with only a small ownership interest have an incentive for wasteful behavior. For example, they bear only a small portion of the costs of, say, excessive expense accounts, and they reap all of the benefits.

Now let's talk about opportunity. A manager can pad his expense account only if the firm has the cash flow to cover it. Thus, we might expect to see more wasteful activity in a firm with a capacity to generate large cash flows than in one with a capacity to generate only small cash flows. This simple idea, which is formally called

---

[15]One professor we know introduces his classes to LBOs by asking the students three questions:
  1. How many of you have ever owned a car?
  2. How many of you have ever rented a car?
  3. How many of you took better care of the car you owned than the car you rented?
Just as it is human nature to take better care of your own car, it is human nature to work harder when you own more of the company.

the *free cash flow hypothesis*,[16] is backed by a fair amount of empirical research. For example, a frequently cited paper found that firms with high free cash flow are more likely to make bad acquisitions than firms with low free cash flow.[17]

The hypothesis has important implications for capital structure. Since dividends leave the firm, they reduce free cash flow. Thus, according to the free cash flow hypothesis, an increase in dividends should benefit the stockholders by reducing the ability of managers to pursue wasteful activities. Furthermore, since interest and principal also leave the firm, debt reduces free cash flow as well. In fact, firms are legally obligated to pay interest and principal, implying that creditors can push the company into bankruptcy if these payments are withheld. By contrast, firms have no legal obligation to continue paying dividends. Thus, bond payments should have a greater effect than dividends on the free-spending ways of managers. Because of this, the free cash flow hypothesis argues that a shift from equity to debt will boost firm value.

In summary, the free cash flow hypothesis provides still another reason for firms to issue debt. We previously discussed the cost of equity; new equity dilutes the holdings of managers with equity interests, increasing their *motive* to waste corporate resources. We now state that debt reduces free cash flow, because the firm must make interest and principal payments. The free cash flow hypothesis implies that debt reduces the *opportunity* for managers to waste resources.

17.7 The Pecking-Order Theory

Although the trade-off theory has dominated corporate finance circles for a long time, attention is also being paid to the *pecking-order theory*.[18] To understand this view of the world, let's put ourselves in the position of a corporate financial manager whose firm needs new capital. The manager faces a choice between issuing debt and issuing equity. Previously, we evaluated the choice in terms of tax benefits, distress costs, and agency costs. However, there is one consideration that we have so far neglected: timing.

Imagine the manager saying:

> I want to issue stock in one situation only—when it is overvalued. If the stock of my firm is selling at $50 per share, but I think that it is actually worth $60, I will not issue stock. I would actually be giving new stockholders a gift because they would receive stock worth $60 but would only have to pay $50 for it. More important, my current stockholders would be upset because the firm would be receiving $50 in cash but giving away something worth $60. So if I believe that my stock is undervalued, I would issue bonds. Bonds, particularly those with little or no risk of default, are likely to be priced correctly. Their value is determined primarily by the marketwide interest rate, a variable that is publicly known.
>
> But suppose our stock is selling at $70. Now I'd like to issue stock. If I can get some fool to buy our stock for $70 while the stock is really worth only $60, I will be making $10 for our current shareholders.

Although this may strike you as a cynical view, it seems to square well with reality. Before the United States adopted insider trading and disclosure laws, many managers were alleged to have unfairly trumpeted their firm's prospects prior to equity issuance. And even today, managers seem more willing to issue equity after the price of their

---

[16]The seminal theoretical article is Michael C. Jensen, "The Agency Costs of Free Cash Flow, Corporate Finance and Takeovers," *American Economic Review* (May 1986), pp. 323–39.

[17]L. Lang, R. Stulz, and R. Walkling, "Managerial Performance, Tobin's Q and the Gains from Successful Tender Offers," *Journal of Financial Economics* (1989).

[18]The pecking-order theory is generally attributed to S. C. Myers, "The Capital Structure Puzzle," *Journal of Finance* 39 (July 1984).

stock has risen than after their stock has fallen in price. Thus, timing might be an important motive in equity issuance, perhaps even more important than the motives in the trade-off model. After all, the firm in the preceding example *immediately* makes $10 by properly timing the issuance of equity. Ten dollars' worth of agency costs and bankruptcy cost reduction might take many years to realize.

The key that makes the example work is asymmetric information: The manager must know more about his firm's prospects than does the typical investor. If the manager's estimate of the true worth of the company is no better than the estimate of a typical investor, any attempts by the manager to time will fail. This assumption of asymmetry is quite plausible. Managers should know more about their company than do outsiders because managers work at the company every day. (One caveat is that some managers are perpetually optimistic about their firm, blurring good judgment.)

But we are not done with this example yet; we must consider the investor. Imagine an investor saying:

> I make investments carefully because they involve my hard-earned money. However, even with all the time I put into studying stocks, I can't possibly know what the managers themselves know. After all, I've got a day job to be concerned with. So I watch what the managers do. If a firm issues stock, the firm was likely overvalued beforehand. If a firm issues debt, the firm was likely undervalued.

When we look at both issuers and investors, we see a kind of poker game, with each side trying to outwit the other. What should the issuing firm do in this poker game? Clearly, the firm should issue debt if the equity is undervalued. But what if the equity is overvalued? Here it gets tricky because a first thought is that the firm should issue equity. However, if a firm issues equity, investors will infer that the stock is overvalued. They will not buy it until the stock has fallen enough to eliminate any advantage from equity issuance. In fact, it can be shown that only the most overvalued firms have any incentive to issue equity. Should even a moderately overpriced firm issue equity, investors will infer that this firm is among the *most* overpriced, causing the stock to fall more than is deserved. Thus, the end result is that virtually no one will issue equity.[19]

This result that essentially all firms should issue debt is clearly an extreme one. It is as extreme as (1) the Modigliani–Miller (MM) result that in a world without taxes, firms are indifferent to capital structure and (2) the MM result that in a world of corporate taxes but no financial distress costs, all firms should be 100 percent debt-financed. Perhaps we in finance have a penchant for extreme models!

But just as we can temper MM's conclusions by combining financial distress costs with corporate taxes, we can temper those of the pure pecking-order theory. This pure version assumes that timing is the financial manager's only consideration. In reality, a manager must consider taxes, financial distress costs, and agency costs as well. Thus, a firm may issue debt only up to a point. If financial distress becomes a real possibility beyond that point, the firm may issue equity instead.

RULES OF THE PECKING ORDER

The previous discussion presented the basic ideas behind the pecking-order theory. What are the practical implications of the theory for financial managers? The theory provides the following two rules for the real world.

---

[19]In the interest of simplicity, we have not presented our results in the form of a rigorous model. To the extent that a reader wants a deeper explanation, we refer him or her to S. C. Myers, "The Capital Structure Puzzle," *Journal of Finance* 39 (July 1984).

Rule #1: Use Internal Financing For expository purposes, we have oversimplified by comparing equity to *riskless* debt. Managers cannot use special knowledge of their firm to determine if this type of debt is mispriced because the rate of interest is the same for all issuers of riskless debt. However, in reality, corporate debt has the possibility of default. Thus, just as managers tend to issue equity when they think it is overvalued, managers also tend to issue debt when they think it is overvalued.

When would managers view their debt as overvalued? Probably in the same situations when they think their equity is overvalued. For example, if the public thinks that the firm's prospects are rosy but the managers see trouble ahead, these managers would view their debt—as well as their equity—as being overvalued. That is, the public might see the debt as nearly risk-free, whereas the managers see a strong possibility of default.

Thus, investors are likely to price a debt issue with the same skepticism that they have when pricing an equity issue. The way managers get out of this box is to finance projects out of retained earnings. You don't have to worry about investor skepticism if you can avoid going to investors in the first place. So the first rule of the pecking order is this:

Use internal financing.

Rule #2: Issue Safe Securities First Although investors fear mispricing of both debt and equity, the fear is much greater for equity. Corporate debt still has relatively little risk compared to equity because if financial distress is avoided, investors receive a fixed return. Thus, the pecking-order theory implies that if outside financing is required, debt should be issued before equity. Only when the firm's debt capacity is reached should the firm consider equity.

Of course, there are many types of debt. For example, because convertible debt is more risky than straight debt, the pecking-order theory implies that managers should issue straight debt before issuing convertibles. So, the second rule of pecking-order theory is this:

Issue the safest securities first.

IMPLICATIONS

A number of implications associated with the pecking-order theory are at odds with those of the trade-off theory.

1. *There is no target amount of leverage.* According to the trade-off model, each firm balances the benefits of debt, such as the tax shield, with the costs of debt, such as distress costs. The optimal amount of leverage occurs where the marginal benefit of debt equals the marginal cost of debt.

   By contrast, the pecking-order theory does not imply a target amount of leverage. Rather, each firm chooses its leverage ratio based on financing needs. Firms first fund projects out of retained earnings. This should lower the percentage of debt in the capital structure, because profitable, internally funded projects raise both the book value and the market value of equity. Additional projects are funded with debt, clearly raising the debt level. However, at some point the debt capacity of the firm becomes exhausted, giving way to equity issuance. Thus, the amount of leverage is determined by the happenstance of available projects. Firms do not pursue a target debt-to-equity ratio.

2. *Profitable firms use less debt.* Profitable firms generate cash internally, implying less need for outside financing. Because firms desiring outside capital turn to debt first, profitable firms end up relying on less debt. The trade-off model does not have this implication. Here the greater cash flow of more profitable firms

creates greater debt capacity. These firms will use that debt capacity to capture the tax shield and the other benefits of leverage.

3. *Companies like financial slack.* The pecking-order theory is based on the difficulties of obtaining financing at a reasonable cost. A skeptical investing public thinks a stock is overvalued if the managers try to issue more of it, thereby leading to a stock price decline. Because this happens with bonds only to a lesser extent, managers rely first on bond financing. However, firms can only issue so much debt before encountering the potential costs of financial distress.

   Wouldn't it be easier to have the cash ahead of time? This is the idea behind *financial slack.* Because firms know that they will have to fund profitable projects at various times in the future, they accumulate cash today. They are then not forced to go to the capital markets when a project comes up. However, there is a limit to the amount of cash a firm will want to accumulate. As mentioned earlier in this chapter, too much free cash may tempt managers to pursue wasteful activities.

17.8 Personal Taxes

So far in this chapter, we have considered corporate taxes only. Because interest on debt is tax deductible whereas dividends on stock are not deductible, we argued that the tax code gives firms an incentive to issue debt. But corporations are not the only ones paying taxes; individuals must pay taxes on both the dividends and the interest that they receive. We cannot fully understand the effect of taxes on capital structure until all taxes, both corporate and personal, are considered.

THE BASICS OF PERSONAL TAXES

Let's begin by examining an all-equity firm that receives $1 of pretax earnings. If the corporate tax rate is t_C, the firm pays taxes of t_C, leaving itself with earnings after taxes of $1 - t_C$. Let's assume that this entire amount is distributed to the stockholders as dividends. If the personal tax rate on stock dividends is t_S, the stockholders pay taxes of $(1 - t_C) \times t_S$, leaving them with $(1 - t_C) \times (1 - t_S)$ after taxes.

Alternatively, imagine that the firm is financed with debt. Here, the entire $1 of earnings will be paid out as interest because interest is deductible at the corporate level. If the personal tax rate on interest is t_B, the bondholders pay taxes of t_B, leaving them with $1 - t_B$ after taxes.

THE EFFECT OF PERSONAL TAXES ON CAPITAL STRUCTURE

To explore the effect of personal taxes on capital structure, let's consider three questions:

1. Ignoring costs of financial distress, what is the firm's optimal capital structure if dividends and interest are taxed at the same personal rate—that is, $t_S = t_B$?

   The firm should select the capital structure that gets the most cash into the hands of its investors. This is tantamount to selecting a capital structure that minimizes the total amount of taxes at both the corporate and personal levels.

   As we have said, beginning with $1 of pretax corporate earnings, stockholders receive $(1 - t_C) \times (1 - t_S)$, and bondholders receive $1 - t_B$. We can see that if $t_S = t_B$, bondholders receive more than stockholders. Thus, the firm should issue debt, not equity, in this situation. Intuitively, income is taxed twice—once at the corporate level and once at the personal level—if it is paid to stockholders. Conversely, income is taxed only at the personal level if it is paid to bondholders.

Note that the assumption of no personal taxes, which we used in the previous chapter, is a special case of the assumption that both interest and dividends are taxed at the same rate. Without personal taxes, the stockholders receive $1 - t_C$ while the bondholders receive \$1. Thus, as we stated in a previous chapter, firms should issue debt in a world without personal taxes.

2. Under what conditions will the firm be indifferent between issuing equity or debt?

    The firm will be indifferent if the cash flow to stockholders equals the cash flow to bondholders. That is, the firm is indifferent when:

$$(1 - t_C) \times (1 - t_S) = 1 - t_B \qquad (17.1)$$

3. What should companies do in the real world?

    Although this is clearly an important question, it is, unfortunately, a hard one—perhaps too hard to answer definitively. Nevertheless, let's begin by working with the highest tax rates. As of 2011, the corporate tax rate was 35 percent. For investors in the highest marginal tax bracket, interest income was also taxed at 35 percent. Investors in this highest bracket faced a 15 percent tax rate on dividends.

    At these rates, the left side of Equation 17.1 becomes $(1 - .35) \times (1 - .15)$, which equals .55. The right side of the equation becomes $1 - .35$, which equals .65. Starting with \$1 of pretax income, any rational firm would rather put \$.65 instead of \$.55 into its investors' hands. Thus, it appears at first glance that firms should prefer debt over equity, just as we argued in the previous chapter.

    Does anything else in the real world alter this conclusion? Perhaps: Our discussion on equity income is not yet complete. Firms can repurchase shares with excess cash instead of paying a dividend. Although capital gains are also taxed at a maximum of 15 percent, the shareholder pays a capital gains tax only on the gain from sale, not on the entire proceeds from the repurchase. Thus, the *effective* tax rate on capital gains is actually lower than 15 percent. Because firms both pay dividends and repurchase shares, the effective personal tax rate on *stock distributions* must be below 15 percent.

    This lower effective tax rate makes equity issuance less burdensome, but the lower rate will not induce any firm to choose stocks over bonds. For example, suppose that the effective tax rate on stock distributions is 10 percent. From every dollar of pretax corporate income, stockholders receive $(1 - .35) \times (1 - .10)$, which equals \$.59. This amount is less than the \$.65 that bondholders receive. In fact, as long as the effective tax rate on stock income is positive, bondholders will still receive more than stockholders from a dollar of pretax corporate income. And we have assumed that all bondholders face a tax rate of .35 on interest income. In reality, plenty of bondholders are in lower tax brackets, further tipping the scales toward bond financing.

    Was there ever a time when stocks had a tax advantage over bonds? Very likely, yes. Consider the 1970s, when the marginal tax rate on interest income was as high as 70 percent. While dividends were taxed at the same rate as interest, capital gains were taxed at a much lower rate. Corporate income was taxed at 46 percent. Thus, both the effective tax rate on equity income and the corporate tax rate were well below the maximum rate on interest. Under reasonable assumptions we can make a case that stocks had the tax advantage at that time.[20]

---

[20]Actually, a well-known model of capital structure argues that an equilibrium would have occurred with firms issuing both debt and equity. Investors in low-tax brackets would buy the debt and investors in high-tax brackets would buy the equity. See Merton Miller, "Debt and Taxes," *Journal of Finance* (May 1977).

However, given that bonds appear to have the tax advantage today, is there anything that might cause firms to issue stock rather than bonds? Yes—the same costs of financial distress we discussed earlier in the chapter. We previously said that these costs are an offset to debt's tax advantage, causing firms to employ less than 100 percent leverage. The same point applies in the presence of personal taxes. And as long as the personal tax rate on equity income is below the personal tax rate on interest, the tax advantage to debt is smaller in a world with personal taxes than in a world without personal taxes. Thus, the optimal amount of debt will be lower in a world with personal taxes than in a world without them.

17.9   How Firms Establish Capital Structure

The theories of capital structure are among the most elegant and sophisticated in the field of finance. Financial economists should (and do!) pat themselves on the back for contributions in this area. However, the practical applications of the theories are less than fully satisfying. Consider that our work on net present value produced an *exact* formula for evaluating projects. Prescriptions for capital structure under either the trade-off model or the pecking-order theory are vague by comparison. No exact formula is available for evaluating the optimal debt–equity ratio. Because of this, we turn to evidence from the real world.

The following empirical regularities are worth considering when formulating capital structure policy.

1. *Most nonfinancial corporations have low debt–asset ratios.* How much debt is used in the real world? Figure 17.4 shows the median debt-to-value ratio, defined as book value of debt to market value of the firm, in each of 39 different countries. This ratio ranges from slightly over 50 percent for Korea to slightly under 10 percent for Australia. The ratio for U.S. companies is the fourth lowest.

   Should we view these ratios as being high or low? Because academics generally see corporate tax reduction as a chief motivation for debt, we might wonder if real-world companies issue enough debt to greatly reduce, if not downright eliminate, corporate taxes. The empirical evidence suggests that this is not the case. For example, corporate taxes in the United States for 2010 were over $400 billion. Thus, it is clear that corporations do not issue debt up to the point where tax shelters are completely used up.[21] There are clearly limits to the amount of debt corporations can issue, perhaps because of the financial distress costs discussed earlier in this chapter.

2. *A number of firms use no debt.* In a fascinating study, Agrawal and Nagarajan examined approximately 100 firms on the New York Stock Exchange without long-term debt.[22] They found that these firms are averse to leverage of any kind, with little short-term debt as well. In addition, they have levels of cash and marketable securities well above their levered counterparts. Typically, the managers of these firms have high equity ownership. Furthermore, there is significantly greater family involvement in all-equity firms than in levered firms.

---

[21]For further insight, see John Graham, "How Big Are the Tax Benefits of Debt?" *Journal of Finance* (2000).

[22]Anup Agrawal and Nandu Nagarajan, "Corporate Capital Structure, Agency Costs, and Ownership Control: The Case of All-Equity Firms," *Journal of Finance* 45 (September 1990).

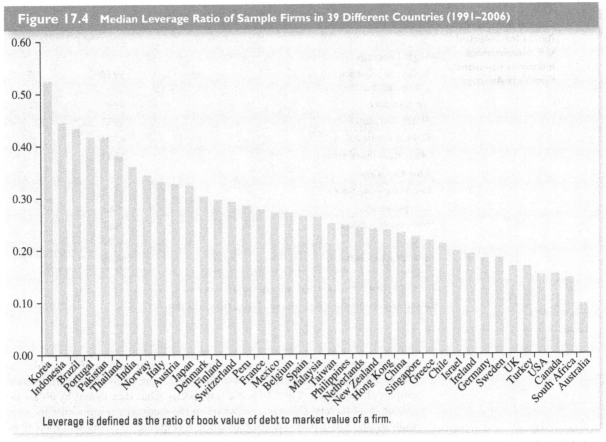

Figure 17.4   Median Leverage Ratio of Sample Firms in 39 Different Countries (1991–2006)

Leverage is defined as the ratio of book value of debt to market value of a firm.

SOURCE: Joseph P. H. Fan, Sheridan Titman, and Garry Twite, "An International Comparison of Capital Structure and Debt Maturity Choices," unpublished paper, University of Texas at Austin (September 2010), Figure 1.

Thus, a story emerges. Managers of all-equity firms are less diversified than the managers of similar, but levered, firms. Because of this, significant leverage represents an added risk that the managers of all-equity firms are loath to accept.

3. *There are differences in the capital structures of different industries.* There are significant interindustry differences in debt ratios that persist over time. As can be seen in Table 17.3, debt ratios tend to be quite low in high-growth industries with ample future investment opportunities, such as the drug and electronics industries. This is true even when the need for external financing is great. Industries with large investments in tangible assets, such as building construction, tend to have high leverage.

4. *Most corporations employ target debt–equity ratios.* Graham and Harvey asked 392 chief financial officers (CFOs) whether their firms use target debt–equity ratios, with the results being presented in Figure 17.5.[23] As can be seen, the great majority of the firms use targets, though the strictness of the targets varies

---

[23]John Graham and Campbell Harvey, "The Theory and Practice of Corporate Finance," *Journal of Financial Economics* (May/June 2001).

550

Table 17.3
Capital Structure Ratios for Selected U.S. Nonfinancial Industries (medians), Five-Year Average

	Debt as a Percentage of the Market Value of Equity and Debt (Industry Medians)
High Leverage	
Radio and television broadcasting stations	59.60
Air transport	45.89
Hotels and motels	45.55
Building construction	42.31
Natural gas distribution	33.11
Low Leverage	
Electronic equipment	10.58
Computers	9.53
Educational services	8.93
Drugs	8.79
Biological products	8.05

DEFINITION: Debt is the total of short-term debt and long-term debt.

SOURCE: Ibbotson 2011 *Cost of Capital Yearbook* (Chicago: Morningstar, 2011).

across companies. Only 19 percent of the firms avoid target ratios. Results elsewhere in the paper indicate that large firms are more likely than small firms to employ these targets. The CFOs did not specify what they meant by either *flexible* or *strict* targets. However, elsewhere in the study, the respondents indicated that, by and large, they did not rebalance in response to changes in their firm's stock price, suggesting flexibility in target ratios.

Figure 17.5
Survey Results on the Use of Target Debt–Equity Ratios

This figure shows the survey responses of 392 CFOs concerning their use of target debt–equity ratios.

SOURCE: Figure 6 of John Graham and Campbell Harvey, "The Theory and Practice of Corporate Finance," *Journal of Financial Economics* (May/June 2001).

How should companies establish target debt–equity ratios? While there is no mathematical formula for establishing a target ratio, we present three important factors affecting the ratio:

- *Taxes:* As we pointed out earlier, firms can deduct interest for tax purposes only to the extent of their profits before interest. Thus, highly profitable firms are more likely to have larger target ratios than less profitable firms.[24]

- *Types of assets:* Financial distress is costly with or without formal bankruptcy proceedings. The costs of financial distress depend on the types of assets that the firm has. For example, if a firm has a large investment in land, buildings, and other tangible assets, it will have smaller costs of financial distress than a firm with a large investment in research and development. Research and development typically has less resale value than land; thus, most of its value disappears in financial distress. Therefore, firms with large investments in tangible assets are likely to have higher target debt–equity ratios than firms with large investments in research and development.

- *Uncertainty of operating income:* Firms with uncertain operating income have a high probability of experiencing financial distress, even without debt. Thus, these firms must finance mostly with equity. For example, pharmaceutical firms have uncertain operating income because no one can predict whether today's research will generate new, profitable drugs. Consequently, these firms issue little debt. By contrast, the operating income of firms in regulated industries, such as utilities, generally has low volatility. Relative to other industries, utilities use a great deal of debt.

5. *Capital structures of individual firms can vary significantly over time.* While Graham and Harvey report that most firms use target leverage ratios, a recent paper nevertheless concludes that capital structures of individual firms often vary widely over time.[25] For example, consider Figure 17.6, which presents leverage ratios for General Motors, IBM, and Eastman Kodak since 1926. Both book leverage (total book value of debt divided by total assets) and market leverage (total book value of debt divided by total book debt plus market value of common stock) are shown. Regardless of the measure, all three companies display significant variations in leverage. Large variations in individual firm leverage over time is evidence that variations in individual firm investment opportunities and the need for financing are important determinants of capital structure and the importance of financial slack (i.e., firms borrow money when they have projects worth spending it on).

One final note is in order. Because no formula supports them, the preceding points may seem too nebulous to assist financial decision making. Instead, many real-world firms simply base their capital structure decisions on industry averages and the need for a certain amount of financial slack. This may strike some as a cowardly approach, but it at least keeps firms from deviating far from accepted practice. After all, the existing firms in any industry are the survivors. Therefore we should pay at least some attention to their decisions.

 ◄ To test your mastery of this material, take a quiz at mhhe.com/rwj

---

[24]By contrast, the pecking-order theory argues that profitable firms will employ less debt because they can invest out of retained earnings. However, the pecking-order theory argues against the use of target ratios in the first place.

[25]Harry DeAngelo and Richard Roll, "How Stable Are Corporate Capital Structures?" Unpublished paper, Marshall School of Business, University of Southern California (July 2011).

552   **Part IV**   Capital Structure and Dividend Policy

Figure 17.6
Leverage Ratios of General Motors, IBM, and Eastman Kodak over Time

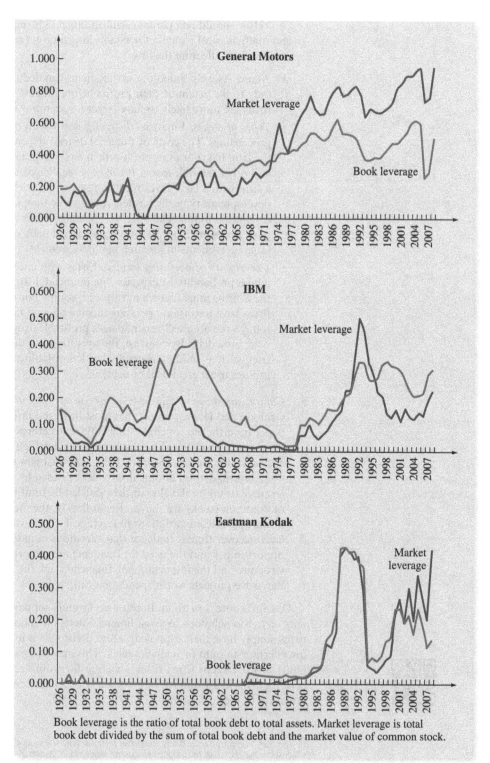

Book leverage is the ratio of total book debt to total assets. Market leverage is total book debt divided by the sum of total book debt and the market value of common stock.

SOURCE: Harry DeAngelo and Richard Roll, "How Stable are Corporate Capital Structures?" Unpublished paper, Marshall School of Business, University of Southern California (July 2011), Figure 1.

Summary and Conclusions

1. We mentioned in the last chapter that according to theory, firms should create all-debt capital structures under corporate taxation. Because firms generally employ moderate amounts of debt in the real world, the theory must have been missing something at that point. We stated in this chapter that costs of financial distress cause firms to restrain their issuance of debt. These costs are of two types: Direct and indirect. Lawyers' and accountants' fees during the bankruptcy process are examples of direct costs. We mentioned four examples of indirect costs:

    Impaired ability to conduct business.
    Incentive to take on risky projects.
    Incentive toward underinvestment.
    Distribution of funds to stockholders prior to bankruptcy.

2. Because financial distress costs are substantial and the stockholders ultimately bear them, firms have an incentive to reduce costs. Protective covenants and debt consolidation are two common cost reduction techniques.

3. Because costs of financial distress can be reduced but not eliminated, firms will not finance entirely with debt. Figure 17.1 illustrates the relationship between firm value and debt. In the figure, firms select the debt–equity ratio at which firm value is maximized.

4. Signaling theory argues that profitable firms are likely to increase their leverage because the extra interest payments will offset some of the pretax profits. Rational stockholders will infer higher firm value from a higher debt level. Thus investors view debt as a signal of firm value.

5. Managers owning a small proportion of a firm's equity can be expected to work less, maintain more lavish expense accounts, and accept more pet projects with negative NPVs than managers owning a large proportion of equity. Because new issues of equity dilute a manager's percentage interest in the firm, such agency costs are likely to increase when a firm's growth is financed through new equity rather than through new debt.

6. The pecking-order theory implies that managers prefer internal to external financing. If external financing is required, managers tend to choose the safest securities, such as debt. Firms may accumulate slack to avoid external equity.

7. The results so far have ignored personal taxes. If distributions to equityholders are taxed at a lower effective personal tax rate than are interest payments, the tax advantage to debt at the corporate level is partially offset.

8. Debt–equity ratios vary across industries. We present three factors determining the target debt–equity ratio:

    a. *Taxes:* Firms with high taxable income should rely more on debt than firms with low taxable income.

    b. *Types of assets:* Firms with a high percentage of intangible assets such as research and development should have low debt. Firms with primarily tangible assets should have higher debt.

    c. *Uncertainty of operating income:* Firms with high uncertainty of operating income should rely mostly on equity.

Concept Questions

1. **Bankruptcy Costs** What are the direct and indirect costs of bankruptcy? Briefly explain each.

2. **Stockholder Incentives** Do you agree or disagree with the following statement? A firm's stockholders will never want the firm to invest in projects with negative net present values. Why?

3. **Capital Structure Decisions**   Due to large losses incurred in the past several years, a firm has $2 billion in tax loss carryforwards. This means that the next $2 billion of the firm's income will be free from corporate income taxes. Security analysts estimate that it will take many years for the firm to generate $2 billion in earnings. The firm has a moderate amount of debt in its capital structure. The firm's CEO is deciding whether to issue debt or equity to raise the funds needed to finance an upcoming project. Which method of financing would you recommend? Why?

4. **Cost of Debt**   What steps can stockholders take to reduce the costs of debt?

5. **M&M and Bankruptcy Costs**   How does the existence of financial distress costs and agency costs affect Modigliani and Miller's theory in a world where corporations pay taxes?

6. **Agency Costs of Equity**   What are the sources of agency costs of equity?

7. **Observed Capital Structures**   Refer to the observed capital structures given in Table 17.3 of the text. What do you notice about the types of industries with respect to their average debt–equity ratios? Are certain types of industries more likely to be highly leveraged than others? What are some possible reasons for this observed segmentation? Do the operating results and tax history of the firms play a role? How about their future earnings prospects? Explain.

8. **Bankruptcy and Corporate Ethics**   As mentioned in the text, some firms have filed for bankruptcy because of actual or likely litigation-related losses. Is this a proper use of the bankruptcy process?

9. **Bankruptcy and Corporate Ethics**   Firms sometimes use the threat of a bankruptcy filing to force creditors to renegotiate terms. Critics argue that in such cases the firm is using bankruptcy laws "as a sword rather than a shield." Is this an ethical tactic?

10. **Bankruptcy and Corporate Ethics**   Continental Airlines once filed for bankruptcy, at least in part, as a means of reducing labor costs. Whether this move was ethical or proper was hotly debated. Give both sides of the argument.

Questions and Problems

BASIC
(Questions 1–4)

1. **Firm Value**   Janetta Corp. has an EBIT rate of $975,000 per year that is expected to continue in perpetuity. The unlevered cost of equity for the company is 14 percent, and the corporate tax rate is 35 percent. The company also has a perpetual bond issue outstanding with a market value of $1.9 million.

   a. What is the value of the company?

   b. The CFO of the company informs the company president that the value of the company is $4.8 million. Is the CFO correct?

2. **Agency Costs**   Tom Scott is the owner, president, and primary salesperson for Scott Manufacturing. Because of this, the company's profits are driven by the amount of work Tom does. If he works 40 hours each week, the company's EBIT will be $550,000 per year; if he works a 50-hour week, the company's EBIT will be $625,000 per year. The company is currently worth $3.2 million. The company needs a cash infusion of $1.3 million, and it can issue equity or issue debt with an interest rate of 8 percent. Assume there are no corporate taxes.

   a. What are the cash flows to Tom under each scenario?

   b. Under which form of financing is Tom likely to work harder?

   c. What specific new costs will occur with each form of financing?

3. **Nonmarketed Claims** Dream, Inc., has debt outstanding with a face value of $6 million. The value of the firm if it were entirely financed by equity would be $17.85 million. The company also has 350,000 shares of stock outstanding that sell at a price of $38 per share. The corporate tax rate is 35 percent. What is the decrease in the value of the company due to expected bankruptcy costs?

4. **Capital Structure and Nonmarketed Claims** Suppose the president of the company in the previous problem stated that the company should increase the amount of debt in its capital structure because of the tax-advantaged status of its interest payments. His argument is that this action would increase the value of the company. How would you respond?

5. **Capital Structure and Growth** Edwards Construction currently has debt outstanding with a market value of $85,000 and a cost of 9 percent. The company has EBIT of $7,650 that is expected to continue in perpetuity. Assume there are no taxes.

   a. What is the value of the company's equity? What is the debt-to-value ratio?
   b. What are the equity value and debt-to-value ratio if the company's growth rate is 3 percent?
   c. What are the equity value and debt-to-value ratio if the company's growth rate is 7 percent?

6. **Costs of Financial Distress** Steinberg Corporation and Dietrich Corporation are identical firms except that Dietrich is more levered. Both companies will remain in business for one more year. The companies' economists agree that the probability of the continuation of the current expansion is 80 percent for the next year, and the probability of a recession is 20 percent. If the expansion continues, each firm will generate earnings before interest and taxes (EBIT) of $2.7 million. If a recession occurs, each firm will generate earnings before interest and taxes (EBIT) of $1.1 million. Steinberg's debt obligation requires the firm to pay $900,000 at the end of the year. Dietrich's debt obligation requires the firm to pay $1.2 million at the end of the year. Neither firm pays taxes. Assume a discount rate of 13 percent.

   a. What is the value today of Steinberg's debt and equity? What about that for Dietrich's?
   b. Steinberg's CEO recently stated that Steinberg's value should be higher than Dietrich's because the firm has less debt and therefore less bankruptcy risk. Do you agree or disagree with this statement?

7. **Agency Costs** Fountain Corporation's economists estimate that a good business environment and a bad business environment are equally likely for the coming year. The managers of Fountain must choose between two mutually exclusive projects. Assume that the project Fountain chooses will be the firm's only activity and that the firm will close one year from today. Fountain is obligated to make a $3,500 payment to bondholders at the end of the year. The projects have the same systematic risk but different volatilities. Consider the following information pertaining to the two projects:

Economy	Probability	Low-Volatility Project Payoff	High-Volatility Project Payoff
Bad	.50	$3,500	$2,900
Good	.50	3,700	4,300

   a. What is the expected value of the firm if the low-volatility project is undertaken? What if the high-volatility project is undertaken? Which of the two strategies maximizes the expected value of the firm?
   b. What is the expected value of the firm's equity if the low-volatility project is undertaken? What is it if the high-volatility project is undertaken?

c. Which project would Fountain's stockholders prefer? Explain.

d. Suppose bondholders are fully aware that stockholders might choose to maximize equity value rather than total firm value and opt for the high-volatility project. To minimize this agency cost, the firm's bondholders decide to use a bond covenant to stipulate that the bondholders can demand a higher payment if Fountain chooses to take on the high-volatility project. What payment to bondholders would make stockholders indifferent between the two projects?

8. Financial Distress   Good Time Company is a regional chain department store. It will remain in business for one more year. The probability of a boom year is 60 percent and the probability of a recession is 40 percent. It is projected that the company will generate a total cash flow of $185 million in a boom year and $76 million in a recession. The company's required debt payment at the end of the year is $110 million. The market value of the company's outstanding debt is $83 million. The company pays no taxes.

a. What payoff do bondholders expect to receive in the event of a recession?

b. What is the promised return on the company's debt?

c. What is the expected return on the company's debt?

CHALLENGE
(Questions 9–10)

9. Personal Taxes, Bankruptcy Costs, and Firm Value   When personal taxes on interest income and bankruptcy costs are considered, the general expression for the value of a levered firm in a world in which the tax rate on equity distributions equals zero is:

$$V_L = V_U + \{1 - [(1 - t_C)/(1 - t_B)]\} \times B - C(B)$$

where:

V_L = The value of a levered firm.
V_U = The value of an unlevered firm.
B = The value of the firm's debt.
t_C = The tax rate on corporate income.
t_B = The personal tax rate on interest income.
$C(B)$ = The present value of the costs of financial distress.

a. In their no-tax model, what do Modigliani and Miller assume about t_C, t_B, and $C(B)$? What do these assumptions imply about a firm's optimal debt–equity ratio?

b. In their model with corporate taxes, what do Modigliani and Miller assume about t_C, t_B, and $C(B)$? What do these assumptions imply about a firm's optimal debt–equity ratio?

c. Consider an all-equity firm that is certain to be able to use interest deductions to reduce its corporate tax bill. If the corporate tax rate is 34 percent, the personal tax rate on interest income is 20 percent, and there are no costs of financial distress, by how much will the value of the firm change if it issues $1 million in debt and uses the proceeds to repurchase equity?

d. Consider another all-equity firm that does not pay taxes due to large tax loss carryforwards from previous years. The personal tax rate on interest income is 20 percent, and there are no costs of financial distress. What would be the change in the value of this firm from adding $1 of perpetual debt rather than $1 of equity?

10. Personal Taxes, Bankruptcy Costs, and Firm Value   Overnight Publishing Company (OPC) has $2.5 million in excess cash. The firm plans to use this cash either to retire all of its outstanding debt or to repurchase equity. The firm's debt is held by one institution that is willing to sell it back to OPC for $2.5 million. The institution will not charge OPC any transaction costs. Once OPC becomes an all-equity firm, it will

www.mhhe.com/rwj

remain unlevered forever. If OPC does not retire the debt, the company will use the $2.5 million in cash to buy back some of its stock on the open market. Repurchasing stock also has no transaction costs. The company will generate $1,300,000 of annual earnings before interest and taxes in perpetuity regardless of its capital structure. The firm immediately pays out all earnings as dividends at the end of each year. OPC is subject to a corporate tax rate of 35 percent, and the required rate of return on the firm's unlevered equity is 20 percent. The personal tax rate on interest income is 25 percent, and there are no taxes on equity distribution. Assume there are no bankruptcy costs.

a. What is the value of OPC if it chooses to retire all of its debt and become an unlevered firm?

b. What is the value of OPC if is decides to repurchase stock instead of retiring its debt?

(*Hint:* Use the equation for the value of a levered firm with personal tax on interest income from the previous problem.)

c. Assume that expected bankruptcy costs have a present value of $400,000. How does this influence OPC's decision?

McKENZIE CORPORATION'S CAPITAL BUDGETING

Sam McKenzie is the founder and CEO of McKenzie Restaurants, Inc., a regional company. Sam is considering opening several new restaurants. Sally Thornton, the company's CFO, has been put in charge of the capital budgeting analysis. She has examined the potential for the company's expansion and determined that the success of the new restaurants will depend critically on the state of the economy over the next few years.

McKenzie currently has a bond issue outstanding with a face value of $29 million that is due in one year. Covenants associated with this bond issue prohibit the issuance of any additional debt. This restriction means that the expansion will be entirely financed with equity at a cost of $5.7 million. Sally has summarized her analysis in the following table, which shows the value of the company in each state of the economy next year, both with and without expansion:

Economic Growth	Probability	Without Expansion	With Expansion
Low	.30	$25,000,000	$27,000,000
Normal	.50	30,000,000	37,000,000
High	.20	48,000,000	57,000,000

1. What is the expected value of the company in one year, with and without expansion? Would the company's stockholders be better off with or without expansion? Why?

2. What is the expected value of the company's debt in one year, with and without the expansion?

3. One year from now, how much value creation is expected from the expansion? How much value is expected for stockholders? Bondholders?

4. If the company announces that it is not expanding, what do you think will happen to the price of its bonds? What will happen to the price of the bonds if the company does expand?

5. If the company opts not to expand, what are the implications for the company's future borrowing needs? What are the implications if the company does expand?

6. Because of the bond covenant, the expansion would have to be financed with equity. How would it affect your answer if the expansion were financed with cash on hand instead of new equity?

Appendix 17A　Some Useful Formulas of Financial Structure

Appendix 17B　The Miller Model and the Graduated Income Tax

To access the appendixes for this chapter, please visit www.mhhe.com/rwj.

Appendix 17A Some Useful Formulas of Financial Structure

Definitions:

$E(EBIT)$ = A perpetual expectation of cash operating income before interest and taxes.

V_U = Value of an unlevered firm.

V_L = Value of levered firm.

B = Present value of debt.

S = Present value of equity.

R_S = Cost of equity.

R_B = Cost of debt capital.

R_0 = Cost of capital to an all-equity firm. In a world of no corporate taxes, the weighted average cost of capital to a levered firm, R_{WACC}, is also equal to R_0. However, with corporate taxes, R_0 is above R_{WACC} for a levered firm.

Model I (No Tax):

$$V_L = V_U = \frac{E(EBIT)}{R_0}$$

$$R_S = R_0 + (R_0 - R_B) \times B/S$$

Model II (Corporate Tax, $t_C > 0$; No Personal Taxes, $t_S = t_B = 0$):

$$V_L = \frac{E[EBIT] \times (1 - t_C)}{R_0} + \frac{t_C R_B B}{R_B} = V_U + t_C B$$

$$R_S = R_0 + (1 - t_C) \times (R_0 - R_B) \times B/S$$

Model III (Corporate Tax, $t_C > 0$; Personal Tax, $t_B > 0$; $t_S > 0$):

$$V_L = V_U + \left[1 - \frac{(1 - t_C) \times (1 - t_S)}{(1 - t_B)}\right] \times B$$

Appendix 17B   The Miller Model and the Graduated Income Tax

In Section 16.9, we assumed a flat personal income tax on interest income. In other words, we assumed that all individuals are subject to the same personal tax rate on interest income. Merton Miller derived the results of this section in a classic paper.[1] However, the genius of his paper was to consider the implications of personal taxes when tax rates differ across individuals.

This *graduated* income tax is consistent with the real world. For example, individuals are currently taxed at rates from 0 to 35 percent in the United States, depending on income. In addition, other entities, such as corporate pension funds, individual retirement accounts (IRAs), and universities, are tax exempt.

To illustrate Miller's model with graduated taxes, we consider a world where *all* firms initially only issue equity. We assume that $t_c = 35$ percent and $t_s = 0$.[2] The required return on stock, R_s, is 10 percent. In addition, we posit a graduated personal income tax, where tax rates vary between 0 and 50 percent. All individuals are risk-neutral.

Now consider a courageous firm contemplating a $1,000 issue of debt. What is the interest rate that the firm can pay and still be as well off as if it issued equity? Because debt is tax deductible, the after–corporate tax cost of debt is $(1 - t_c) \times R_B$. However, equity is not deductible at the corporate level, so the aftertax cost of equity is R_S. Thus, the firm is indifferent to whether it issues debt or equity when

$$(1 - t_C) \times R_B = R_S \tag{17B.1}$$

Because $t_C = 35$ percent and $R_S = 10$ percent, the firm could afford to pay a rate on debt as high as 15.38 percent.

Miller argues that those in the lowest tax brackets (tax exempt in our example) will buy the debt because they pay the least personal tax on interest. These tax-exempt investors will be indifferent to whether they buy the stock or purchase bonds also yielding 10 percent. Thus, if this firm is the *only* one issuing debt, it can pay an interest rate well below its break-even rate of 15.38 percent.

Noticing the gain to the first firm, many other firms are likely to issue debt. However, if there are only a fixed number of tax-exempt investors, new debt issues must attract people in higher brackets. Because these individuals are taxed on interest at a higher rate than they are taxed on equity distributions, they will buy debt only if its yield is greater than 10 percent. For example, an individual in the 15 percent bracket has an interest rate after personal tax of $R_B \times (1 - 0.15)$. He will be indifferent to whether he buys bonds or stock if $R_B = 11.765$ percent because $0.11765 \times 0.85 = 10$ percent. Because 11.765 percent is less than the 15.38 percent rate of Equation 17.1, corporations gain by issuing debt to investors in the 15 percent bracket.

Now consider investors in the 35 percent bracket. A return on bonds of 15.38 percent provides them with a 10 percent = 15.38 percent $\times (1 - 0.35)$ interest rate after personal tax. Thus, they are indifferent to whether they earn a 15.38 percent return on bonds or a 10 percent return on stock. Miller argues that in equilibrium, corporations will issue enough debt so that investors with personal tax brackets up to and including 35 percent

---

[1] M. Miller, "Debt and Taxes," *Journal of Finance* (May 1977). Yes, this is the same Miller of MM.

[2] The assumption that $t_S = 0$ is perhaps an extreme one. However, it is commonly made in the literature, justified by the investor's ability to defer realization of capital gains indefinitely. Besides, the same qualitative conclusions hold if $t_S > 0$, though the explanation would be more involved.

www.mhhe.com/rwj

will hold debt.[3] Additional debt will not be issued because the interest rate needed to attract investors in higher tax brackets is above the 15.38 percent rate that corporations can afford to pay.

The beauty of competition is that other companies can so capitalize on someone's innovation that all value to the courageous first entrant is eliminated. According to the Miller model, firms will issue enough debt so that individuals up to and including the 35 percent bracket hold it. To induce these investors to hold bonds, the competitive interest rate becomes 15.38 percent. No firm profits from issuing debt in equilibrium. Rather, all firms are indifferent to whether they issue debt or equity in equilibrium.

Miller's work produces three results:

1. In aggregate, the corporate sector will issue just enough debt so that individuals with tax brackets equal to and below the corporate tax rate, t_C, will hold debt, and individuals with higher tax brackets will not hold debt. Thus, individuals in these higher brackets will hold stock.

2. Because people in tax brackets equal to the corporate rate hold debt, there is no gain or loss to corporate leverage. Therefore, the capital structure decision is a matter of indifference to an individual firm. Though the Miller model is quite sophisticated, this conclusion is identical to that reached by MM in a world without any taxes.

3. As given in Equation 16.1, the return on bonds will be higher than the return on stocks of comparable risk. [An adjustment to Equation 16.4 must be made to reflect the greater risk of stocks in the real world.]

EXAMPLE 17B.1

Miller's Model   Consider an economy in which there are four groups of investors and no others:

Group	Marginal Tax Rate (%) on Bonds (t_B)	Personal Wealth (in $ millions)
Finance majors	50%	$1,200
Accounting majors	35	300
Marketing majors	20	150
Management majors	0	50

We assume that investors are risk-neutral and that equity income is untaxed at the personal level for all investors (i.e., $t_S = 0$). All investors can earn a tax-free return of 5.4 percent by investing in foreign real estate; therefore, this is the return on equity. The corporate tax rate is 35 percent. Interest payments are tax deductible at the corporate level and taxable at the individual level. Corporations receive a total of $120 million in cash flow before tax and interest. There are no growth opportunities, and every year is the same in perpetuity. What is the range of possible debt–equity ratios?

The return on equity, r_S, will be set equal to the return on foreign real estate, which is 0.054. In a Miller equilibrium, $R_S = (1 - t_C) \times R_B$. Therefore,

$$R_B = \frac{0.054}{1 - 0.35} = 0.0831$$

(continued)

[3]All investors with $t_B <$ 35 percent hold bonds. Because investors with $t_B =$ 35 percent are indifferent to whether they hold stocks or bonds, only some of them are likely to choose bonds.

Given the tax brackets of the different groups of investors, we would expect that finance majors would hold equity and foreign real estate, and accounting majors would be indifferent to whether they held equity or debt. Marketing and management majors would hold bonds because their personal tax rates are below 0.35. Because accounting majors are indifferent to whether they hold bonds or stocks, we must learn what happens if they invest in bonds or equity. If accounting majors use their $300 to buy bonds, $B = \$300 + \$150 + \$50 = \$500$. Then the following calculations can be made:

$$S = \frac{(\text{EBIT} - R_B B) \times (1 - t_C)}{R_S}$$

$$= \frac{[\$120 - (0.0831 \times \$500)] \times (1 - 0.35)}{0.054}$$

$$= \$944$$

$$B = \frac{R_B B}{R_B} = \$500$$

$$V_L = S + B = \$944 + \$500 = \$1,444$$

$$\frac{B}{S} = \frac{\$500}{\$944} = 0.530$$

If accounting majors buy stocks and foreign real estate ($B = \$150 + \$50 = \$200$),

$$S = \frac{(\text{EBIT} - R_B B) \times (1 - t_C)}{R_S}$$

$$= \frac{[\$120 - (0.0831 \times \$200)] \times (1 - 0.35)}{0.054}$$

$$= \$1,244$$

$$B = \$200$$

$$V_L = S + B = \$1,244 + \$200 = \$1,444$$

$$\frac{B}{S} = \frac{\$200}{\$1,244} = 0.161$$

Thus, depending on the amount of bonds held by accounting majors, the debt–equity ratio in the economy can lie in the range of 0.161 to 0.530.

CHAPTER 18

Valuation and Capital Budgeting for the Levered Firm

In May 2011, Volkswagen opened its newest auto plant in Chattanooga, Tennessee, at a cost of $1 billion. So why did Volkswagen pick Tennessee? One of the reasons was a package granted to the firm consisting of $570 million in state and local tax credits, including tax breaks, infrastructure work, and other incentives. The package was the largest ever offered to a foreign automaker and beat out the $385 million package offered by the state of Alabama.

▲ For updates on the latest happenings in finance, visit www.rwjcorporatefinance.blogspot.com

When a corporation opens a major plant or considers relocation, municipalities often create packages loaded with subsidies such as these. Other common subsidies include subsidized debt, educational training, and road and infrastructure creation.

With subsidized debt, a state or municipality guarantees the debt, which allows the company to borrow at a much lower interest rate. If the interest rate on the debt is lower than the company's normal cost of debt, how does the firm evaluate the financial benefits of this and other such subsidies? In this chapter, we illustrate how to evaluate projects using the adjusted present value and flows to equity approaches to valuation to answer this and related questions.

18.1 Adjusted Present Value Approach

In this chapter, we describe three approaches to valuation for the levered firm. In particular, we describe the adjusted present value (APV) approach, the flow to equity (FTE) approach, and the weighted average cost of capital (WACC) approach. As you may recognize, we have discussed each of these approaches in previous chapters. The analysis of these approaches is relevant for entire firms as well as projects. The specific purpose of this chapter is to tie things together and show that each of the approaches is logically consistent with each other and can give the same answer. However, at times, one approach might be easier to implement than another, and we suggest guidelines for selecting between the approaches. We start with the adjusted present value method.

The **adjusted present value (APV)** method is best described by the following formula:

$$APV = NPV + NPVF$$

In words, the value of a project to a levered firm (APV) is equal to the value of the project to an unlevered firm (NPV) plus the net present value of the financing side effects (NPVF). We can generally think of four side effects:

1. *The tax subsidy to debt*: This was discussed in Chapter 16, where we pointed out that for perpetual debt the value of the tax subsidy is $t_C B$. (t_C is the corporate tax rate, and B is the value of the debt.) The material about valuation under corporate taxes in Chapter 16 is actually an application of the APV approach.

2. *The costs of issuing new securities*: As we will discuss in detail in Chapter 20, investment bankers participate in the public issuance of corporate debt. These bankers must be compensated for their time and effort, a cost that lowers the value of the project.

3. *The costs of financial distress*: The possibility of financial distress, and bankruptcy in particular, arises with debt financing. As stated in the previous chapter, financial distress imposes costs, thereby lowering value.

4. *Subsidies to debt financing*: The interest on debt issued by state and local governments is not taxable to the investor. Because of this, the yield on tax-exempt debt is generally substantially below the yield on taxable debt. Frequently corporations can obtain financing from a municipality at the tax-exempt rate because the municipality can borrow at that rate as well. As with any subsidy, this subsidy adds value.

Although each of the preceding four side effects is important, the tax deduction to debt almost certainly has the highest dollar value in most actual situations. For this reason, the following example considers the tax subsidy but not the other three side effects.[1]

Consider a project of the P. B. Singer Co. with the following characteristics:

Cash inflows: $500,000 per year for the indefinite future.

Cash costs: 72% of sales.

Initial investment: $475,000.

$t_C = 34\%$

$R_0 = 20\%$, where R_0 is the cost of capital for a project of an all-equity firm.

If both the project and the firm are financed with only equity, the project's cash flow is as follows:

Cash inflows	$500,000
Cash costs	−360,000
Operating income	140,000
Corporate tax (34% tax rate)	−47,600
Unlevered cash flow (UCF)	$ 92,400

The distinction between present value and net present value is important for this example. The *present value* of a project is determined before the initial investment at Date 0 is subtracted. The initial investment is subtracted for the calculation of *net present value*.

Given a discount rate of 20 percent, the present value of the project is:

$$\frac{\$92,400}{.20} = \$462,000$$

The net present value (NPV) of the project—that is, the value of the project to an all-equity firm—is:

$$\$462,000 - \$475,000 = -\$13,000$$

Because the NPV is negative, the project would be rejected by an all-equity firm.

Now imagine that the firm finances the project with exactly $126,229.50 in debt, so that the remaining investment of $348,770.50 (= $475,000 − $126,229.50) is financed

---

[1]The Bicksler Enterprises example in Section 18.6 handles both flotation costs and interest subsidies.

with equity. The net present value of the project under leverage, which we call the adjusted present value, or the APV, is:

$$\text{APV} = \text{NPV} + t_C \times B$$
$$\$29,918 = -\$13,000 + .34 \times \$126,229.50$$

That is, the value of the project when financed with some leverage is equal to the value of the project when financed with all equity plus the tax shield from the debt. Because this number is positive, the project should be accepted.[2]

You may be wondering why we chose such a precise amount of debt. Actually, we chose it so that the ratio of debt to the present value of the project under leverage is .25.[3]

In this example, debt is a fixed proportion of the present value of the project, not a fixed proportion of the initial investment of \$475,000. This is consistent with the goal of a target debt-to-*market*-value ratio, which we find in the real world. For example, commercial banks typically lend to real estate developers a fixed percentage of the appraised market value of a project, not a fixed percentage of the initial investment.

18.2 Flow to Equity Approach

The **flow to equity (FTE)** approach is an alternative valuation approach. The formula simply calls for discounting the cash flow from the project to the equityholders of the levered firm at the cost of equity capital, R_S. For a perpetuity this becomes:

$$\frac{\text{Cash flow from project to equityholders of the levered firm}}{R_S}$$

There are three steps to the FTE approach.

STEP 1: CALCULATING LEVERED CASH FLOW (LCF)[4]

Assuming an interest rate of 10 percent, the perpetual cash flow to equityholders in our P. B. Singer Co. example is:

Cash inflows	\$500,000.00
Cash costs	−360,000.00
Interest (10% × \$126,229.50)	−12,622.95
Income after interest	127,377.05
Corporate tax (34% tax rate)	−43,308.20
Levered cash flow (LCF)	\$ 84,068.85

---

[2]This example is meant to dramatize the potential importance of the tax benefits of debt. In practice, the firm will likely find the value of a project to an all-equity firm to have at least an NPV of zero.

[3]That is, the present value of the project after the initial investment has been made is \$504,918 (= \$29,918 + \$475,000). Thus, the debt-to-value ratio of the project is .25 (= \$126,229.50/\$504,918).

This level of debt can be calculated directly. Note that:

$$\text{Present value of levered project} = \text{Present value of unlevered project} + t_C \times B$$
$$V_{\text{With debt}} = \$462,000 \qquad\qquad + .34 \times .25 \times V_{\text{With debt}}$$

Rearranging the last line, we have:

$$V_{\text{With debt}} \times (1 - .34 \times .25) = \$462,000$$
$$V_{\text{With debt}} = \$504,918$$

Debt is .25 of value: \$126,229.50 = .25 × \$504,918.

[4]We use the term *levered cash flow* (LCF) for simplicity. A more complete term would be *distributable cash flow (a.k.a. free cash flow) from the project to the equityholders of a levered firm*. Similarly, a more complete term for *unlevered cash flow* (UCF) would be *distributable cash flow (a.k.a. free cash flow) from the project to the equityholders of an unlevered firm*.

Alternatively, we can calculate levered cash flow (LCF) directly from unlevered cash flow (UCF). The key here is that the difference between the cash flow that equityholders receive in an unlevered firm and the cash flow that equityholders receive in a levered firm is the aftertax interest payment. (Repayment of principal does not appear in this example because the debt is perpetual.) We write this algebraically as:

$$\text{UCF} - \text{LCF} = (1 - t_C)R_B B$$

The term on the right side of this expression is the aftertax interest payment. Thus, because cash flow to the unlevered equityholders (UCF) is \$92,400 and the aftertax interest payment is \$8,331.15 ($=.66 \times .10 \times \$126{,}229.50$), cash flow to the levered equityholders (LCF) is:

$$\$92{,}400 - \$8{,}331.15 = \$84{,}068.85$$

which is exactly the number we calculated earlier.

STEP 2: CALCULATING R_S

The next step is to calculate the discount rate, R_S. Note that we assumed that the discount rate on unlevered equity, R_0, is .20. As we saw in an earlier chapter, the formula for R_S is:

$$R_S = R_0 + \frac{B}{S}(1 - t_C)(R_0 - R_B)$$

Note that our target debt-to-value ratio of 1/4 implies a target debt-to-equity ratio of 1/3. Applying the preceding formula to this example, we have:

$$R_S = .222 = .20 + \frac{1}{3}(.66)(.20 - .10)$$

STEP 3: VALUATION

The present value of the project's LCF is:

$$\frac{\text{LCF}}{R_S} = \frac{\$84{,}068.85}{.222} = \$378{,}688.50$$

Because the initial investment is \$475,000 and \$126,229.50 is borrowed, the firm must advance the project \$348,770.50 ($=\$475{,}000 - \$126{,}229.50$) out of its own cash reserves. The *net* present value of the project is simply the difference between the present value of the project's LCF and the investment not borrowed. Thus, the NPV is:

$$\$378{,}688.50 - \$348{,}770.50 = \$29{,}918$$

which is identical to the result found with the APV approach.

18.3   Weighted Average Cost of Capital Method

Finally, we can value a project or a firm using the **weighted average cost of capital** (WACC) method. Although this method was discussed in earlier chapters, it is worthwhile to review it here. The WACC approach begins with the insight that projects of levered firms are simultaneously financed with both debt and equity. The cost of capital is a weighted average of the cost of debt and the cost of equity. The cost of equity is R_S. Ignoring taxes, the cost of debt is simply the borrowing rate, R_B. However, with corporate taxes, the appropriate cost of debt is $(1 - t_C)R_B$, the aftertax cost of debt.

The formula for determining the weighted average cost of capital, R_{WACC}, is:

$$R_{WACC} = \frac{S}{S + B} R_S + \frac{B}{S + B} R_B(1 - t_C)$$

The weight for equity, $S/(S + B)$, and the weight for debt, $B/(S + B)$, are target ratios. Target ratios are generally expressed in terms of market values, not accounting values. (Recall that another phrase for accounting value is *book value.*)

The formula calls for discounting the *unlevered* cash flow of the project (UCF) at the weighted average cost of capital, R_{WACC}. The net present value of the project can be written algebraically as:

$$\sum_{t=1}^{\infty} \frac{UCF_t}{(1 + R_{WACC})^t} - \text{Initial investment}$$

If the project is a perpetuity, the net present value is:

$$\frac{UCF}{R_{WACC}} - \text{Initial investment}$$

We previously stated that the target debt-to-value ratio of our project is 1/4 and the corporate tax rate is .34, implying that the weighted average cost of capital is:

$$R_{WACC} = \frac{3}{4} \times .222 + \frac{1}{4} \times .10 \times .66 = .183$$

Note that R_{WACC}, .183, is lower than the cost of equity capital for an all-equity firm, .20. This must always be the case because debt financing provides a tax subsidy that lowers the average cost of capital.

We previously determined the UCF of the project to be \$92,400, implying that the present value of the project is:

$$\frac{\$92,400}{.183} = \$504,918$$

The initial investment is \$475,000, so the NPV of the project is:

$$\$504,918 - \$475,000 = \$29,918$$

Note that all three approaches yield the same value.

18.4 A Comparison of the APV, FTE, and WACC Approaches

In this chapter, we provide three approaches to valuation for projects of a levered firm. The adjusted present value (APV) approach first values the project on an all-equity basis. That is, the project's aftertax cash flows under all-equity financing (called unlevered cash flows, or UCF) are placed in the numerator of the capital budgeting equation. The discount rate, assuming all-equity financing, appears in the denominator. At this point, the calculation is identical to that performed in the early chapters of this book. We then add the net present value of the debt. We point out that the net present value of the debt is likely to be the sum of four parameters: Tax effects, flotation costs, bankruptcy costs, and interest subsidies.

The flow to equity (FTE) approach discounts the aftertax cash flow from a project going to the equityholders of a levered firm (LCF). LCF, which stands for levered cash flow, is the residual to equityholders after interest has been deducted. The discount rate is R_S, the cost of capital to the equityholders of a levered firm. For a firm with leverage, R_S must be greater than R_0, the cost of capital for an unlevered firm.

This follows from our material in Chapter 16 showing that leverage raises the risk to the equityholders.

The last approach is the weighted average cost of capital (WACC) method. This technique calculates the project's aftertax cash flows assuming all-equity financing (UCF). The UCF is placed in the numerator of the capital budgeting equation. The denominator, R_{WACC}, is a weighted average of the cost of equity capital and the cost of debt capital. The tax advantage of debt is reflected in the denominator because the cost of debt capital is determined net of corporate tax. The numerator does not reflect debt at all.

All three approaches perform the same task: Valuation in the presence of debt financing. And as illustrated by the previous example, all three provide the same valuation estimate. However, as we saw before, the approaches are markedly different in technique. Because of this, students often ask questions of the following sort: "How can this be? How can the three approaches look so different and yet give the same answer?" We believe that the best way to handle questions like these is through the following two points:

1. *APV versus WACC:* Of the three approaches, APV and WACC display the greatest similarity. After all, both approaches put the unlevered cash flow (UCF) in the numerator. However, the APV approach discounts these flows at R_0, yielding the value of the unlevered project. Adding the present value of the tax shield gives the value of the project under leverage. The WACC approach discounts UCF at R_{WACC}, which is lower than R_0.

   Thus, both approaches adjust the basic NPV formula for unlevered firms to reflect the tax benefit of leverage. The APV approach makes this adjustment directly. It simply adds in the present value of the tax shield as a separate term. The WACC approach makes the adjustment in a more subtle way. Here, the discount rate is lowered below R_0. Although we do not provide a proof in this book, it can be shown that these two adjustments always have the same quantitative effect.

2. *Entity being valued*: The FTE approach appears at first glance to be far different from the other two. For both the APV and the WACC approaches, the initial investment is subtracted out in the final step ($475,000 in our example). However, for the FTE approach, only the firm's contribution to the initial investment ($348,770.50 = $475,000 − $126,229.50) is subtracted out. This occurs because under the FTE approach only the future cash flows to the levered equityholders (LCF) are valued. By contrast, future cash flows to the unlevered equityholders (UCF) are valued in both the APV and WACC approaches. Thus, because LCFs are net of interest payments, whereas UCFs are not, the initial investment under the FTE approach is correspondingly reduced by debt financing. In this way, the FTE approach produces the same answer that the other two approaches do.

A SUGGESTED GUIDELINE

The net present value of our project is exactly the same under each of the three methods. In theory, this should always be the case.[5] However, one method usually provides an easier computation than another, and, in many cases, one or more of the methods are virtually impossible computationally. We first consider when it is best to use the WACC and FTE approaches.

---

[5]See I. Inselbag and H. Kaufold, "Two DCF Approaches for Valuing Companies under Alternative Financial Strategies (and How to Choose between Them)," *Journal of Applied Corporate Finance* (Spring 1997).

If the risk of a project stays constant throughout its life, it is plausible to assume that R_0 remains constant throughout the project's life. This assumption of constant risk appears to be reasonable for most real-world projects. In addition, if the debt-to-value ratio remains constant over the life of the project, both R_S and R_{WACC} will remain constant as well. Under this latter assumption, either the FTE or the WACC approach is easy to apply. However, if the debt-to-value ratio varies from year to year, both R_S and R_{WACC} vary from year to year as well. Using the FTE or the WACC approach when the denominator changes every year is computationally quite complex, and when computations become complex, the error rate rises. Thus, both the FTE and WACC approaches present difficulties when the debt-to-value *ratio* changes over time.

The APV approach is based on the *level* of debt in each future period. Consequently, when the debt level can be specified precisely for future periods, the APV approach is quite easy to use. However, when the debt level is uncertain, the APV approach becomes more problematic. For example, when the debt-to-value ratio is constant, the debt level varies with the value of the project. Because the value of the project in a future year cannot be easily forecast, the level of debt cannot be easily forecast either.

Thus, we suggest the following guideline:

Use WACC or FTE if the firm's target debt-to-value *ratio* applies to the project over its life. Use APV if the project's *level* of debt is known over the life of the project.

There are a number of situations where the APV approach is preferred. For example, in a leveraged buyout (LBO) the firm begins with a large amount of debt but rapidly pays down the debt over a number of years. Because the schedule of debt reduction in the future is known when the LBO is arranged, tax shields in every future year can be easily forecast. Thus, the APV approach is easy to use here. (An illustration of the APV approach applied to LBOs is provided in the appendix to this chapter.) By contrast, the WACC and FTE approaches are virtually impossible to apply here because the debt-to-equity value cannot be expected to be constant over time. In addition, situations involving interest subsidies and flotation costs are much easier to handle with the APV approach. (The Bicksler Enterprises example in Section 18.6 applies the APV approach to subsidies and flotation costs.) Finally, the APV approach handles the lease-versus-buy decision much more easily than does either the FTE or the WACC approach. (A full treatment of the lease-versus-buy decision appears in a later chapter.)

The preceding examples are special cases. Typical capital budgeting situations are more amenable to either the WACC or the FTE approach than to the APV approach. Financial managers generally think in terms of target debt-to-value *ratios*. If a project does better than expected, both its value and its debt capacity will likely rise. The manager will increase debt correspondingly here. Conversely, the manager would be likely to reduce debt if the value of the project were to decline unexpectedly. Of course, because financing is a time-consuming task, the ratio cannot be adjusted daily or monthly. Rather, the adjustment can be expected to occur over the long run. As mentioned before, the WACC and FTE approaches are more appropriate than is the APV approach when a firm focuses on a target debt-to-value ratio.

Because of this, we recommend that the WACC and the FTE approaches, rather than the APV approach, be used in most real-world situations. In addition, frequent discussions with business executives have convinced us that the WACC is by far the most widely used method in the real world. Thus, practitioners seem to agree with us that, outside of the special situations mentioned, the APV approach is a less important method of capital budgeting.

The Three Methods of Valuation with Leverage

1. Adjusted present value (APV) method:

$$\sum_{t=1}^{\infty} \frac{\text{UCF}_t}{(1+R_0)^t} + \text{Additional effects of debt} - \text{Initial investment}$$

UCF_t = The project's cash flow at date t to the equityholders of an unlevered firm.
R_0 = Cost of capital for project in an unlevered firm.

2. Flow to equity (FTE) method:

$$\sum_{t=1}^{\infty} \frac{\text{LCF}_t}{(1+R_S)^t} - (\text{Initial investment} - \text{Amount borrowed})$$

LCF_t = The project's cash flow at date t to the equityholders of a levered firm.
R_S = Cost of equity capital with leverage.

3. Weighted average cost of capital (WACC) method:

$$\sum_{t=1}^{\infty} \frac{\text{UCF}_t}{(1+R_{\text{WACC}})^t} - \text{Initial investment}$$

R_{WACC} = Weighted average cost of capital.

Notes

1. The middle term in the APV formula implies that the value of a project with leverage is greater than the value of the project without leverage. Because $R_{\text{WACC}} < R_0$, the WACC formula implies that the value of a project with leverage is greater than the value of the project without leverage.
2. In the FTE method, cash flow *after interest* (LCF) is used. Initial investment is reduced by *amount borrowed* as well.

Guidelines

1. Use WACC or FTE if the firm's target debt-to-value *ratio* applies to the project over its life.
2. Use APV if the project's *level* of debt is known over the life of the project.

18.5 Valuation When the Discount Rate Must Be Estimated

The previous sections of this chapter introduced APV, FTE, and WACC—the three basic approaches to valuation of a firm with leverage. However, one important detail remains. The example in Sections 18.1 through 18.3 *assumed* a discount rate. We now want to show how this rate is determined for firms with leverage, with an application to the three preceding approaches. The example in this section adds to the work in Chapters 9–13 on the discount rate for levered and unlevered firms along with that in Chapter 16 on the effect of leverage on the cost of capital.

EXAMPLE 18.1

Cost of Capital World-Wide Enterprises (WWE) is a large conglomerate thinking of entering the widget business, where it plans to finance projects with a debt-to-value ratio of 25 percent (or a debt-to-equity ratio of 1/3). There is currently one firm in the widget industry, American Widgets (AW). This firm is financed with 40 percent debt and 60 percent equity. The beta of AW's equity is 1.5. AW, has a borrowing rate of 12 percent, and WWE expects to borrow for its widget venture at 10 percent. The corporate tax rate for both firms is .40, the market risk premium is 8.5 percent, and the riskless interest rate is 8 percent. What is the appropriate discount rate for WWE to use for its widget venture?

As shown in Sections 18.1–18.3, a corporation may use one of three capital budgeting approaches: APV, FTE, or WACC. The appropriate discount rates for these three approaches are R_0, R_S, and R_{WACC}, respectively. Because AW is WWE's only competitor in widgets, we look at AW's cost of capital to calculate R_0, R_S, and R_{WACC} for WWE's widget venture. The following four-step procedure will allow us to calculate all three discount rates:

1. *Determining AW's cost of equity capital:* First, we determine AW's cost of equity capital using the security market line (SML):

AW's Cost of Equity Capital

$$R_S = R_F + \beta \times (\bar{R}_M - R_F)$$
$$20.75\% = 8\% + 1.5 \times 8.5\%$$

where $\bar{R}_M$ is the expected return on the market portfolio and R_F is the risk-free rate.

2. *Determining AW's hypothetical all-equity cost of capital:* We must standardize the preceding number in some way because AW's and WWE's widget ventures have different target debt-to-value ratios. The easiest approach is to calculate the hypothetical cost of equity capital for AW, assuming all-equity financing. This can be determined from MM's Proposition II under taxes:

AW's Cost of Capital if All Equity

$$R_S = R_0 + \frac{B}{S}(1 - t_c)(R_0 - R_B)$$
$$20.75\% = R_0 + \frac{.4}{.6}(.60)(R_0 - 12\%)$$

By solving the equation, we find that $R_0 = .1825$. Of course, R_0 is less than R_S because the cost of equity capital would be less when the firm employs no leverage.

At this point, firms in the real world generally make the assumption that the business risk of their venture is about equal to the business risk of the firms already in the business. Applying this assumption to our problem, we assert that the hypothetical discount rate of WWE's widget venture if all equity financed is also .1825.[6] This discount rate would be employed if WWE uses the APV approach because the APV approach calls for R_0, the project's cost of capital in a firm with no leverage.

3. *Determining R_S for WWE's widget venture:* Alternatively, WWE might use the FTE approach, where the discount rate for levered equity is determined like this:

Cost of Equity Capital for WWE's Widget Venture

$$R_S = R_0 + \frac{B}{S}(1 - t_c)(R_0 - R_B)$$
$$19.9\% = 18.25\% + \frac{1}{3}(.60)(18.25\% - 10\%)$$

(continued)

---

[6]Alternatively, a firm might assume that its venture would be somewhat riskier because it is a new entrant. Thus, the firm might select a discount rate slightly higher than .1825. Of course, no exact formula exists for adjusting the discount rate upward.

Note that the cost of equity capital for WWE's widget venture, .199, is less than the cost of equity capital for AW, .2075. This occurs because AW has a higher debt-to-equity ratio. (As mentioned, both firms are assumed to have the same business risk.)

4. *Determining R_{WACC} for WWE's widget venture:* Finally, WWE might use the WACC approach. Here is the appropriate calculation:

$$R_{WACC} \text{ for WWE's Widget Venture}$$

$$R_{WACC} = \frac{B}{S+B}R_B(1-t_c) + \frac{S}{S+B}R_S$$

$$16.425\% = \frac{1}{4}10\%(.60) + \frac{3}{4}19.9\%$$

The preceding example shows how the three discount rates, R_0, R_S, and R_{WACC}, are determined in the real world. These are the appropriate rates for the APV, FTE, and WACC approaches, respectively. Note that R_S for American Widgets is determined first because the cost of equity capital can be determined from the beta of the firm's stock. As discussed in an earlier chapter, beta can easily be estimated for any publicly traded firm such as AW.

18.6 APV Example

As mentioned earlier in this chapter, firms generally set a target debt-to-equity ratio, allowing the use of WACC and FTE for capital budgeting. APV does not work as well here. However, as we also mentioned earlier, APV is the preferred approach when there are side benefits and side costs to debt. Because the analysis here can be tricky, we now devote an entire section to an example where, in addition to the tax subsidy to debt, both flotation costs and interest subsidies come into play.

EXAMPLE 18.2

APV   Bicksler Enterprises is considering a $10 million project that will last five years, implying straight-line depreciation per year of $2 million. The cash revenues less cash expenses per year are $3,500,000. The corporate tax bracket is 34 percent. The risk-free rate is 10 percent, and the cost of unlevered equity is 20 percent.

The cash flow projections each year are these:

	CF_0	CF_1	CF_2	CF_3	CF_4	CF_5
Initial outlay	−$10,000,000					
Depreciation tax shield		.34 × $2,000,000 = $680,000	$ 680,000	$ 680,000	$ 680,000	$ 680,000
Revenue less expenses		(1 − .34) × $3,500,000 = $2,310,000	$2,310,000	$2,310,000	$2,310,000	$2,310,000

We stated before that the APV of a project is the sum of its all-equity value plus the additional effects of debt. We examine each in turn.

All-Equity Value   Assuming the project is financed with all equity, the value of the project is:

$$-\$10,000,000 + \frac{\$680,000}{.10} \times \left[1 - \left(\frac{1}{1.10}\right)^5 \right] + \frac{\$2,310,000}{.20} \times \left[1 - \left(\frac{1}{1.20}\right)^5 \right] = -\$513,951$$

Initial cost + Depreciation tax shield + Present value of (Cash revenues − Cash expenses)

This calculation uses the techniques presented in the early chapters of this book. Notice that the depreciation tax shield is discounted at the riskless rate of 10 percent. The revenues and expenses are discounted at the higher rate of 20 percent.

An all-equity firm would clearly *reject* this project because the NPV is −$513,951. And equity flotation costs (not mentioned yet) would only make the NPV more negative. However, debt financing may add enough value to the project to justify acceptance. We consider the effects of debt next.

Additional Effects of Debt   Bicksler Enterprises can obtain a five-year, nonamortizing loan for $7,500,000 after flotation costs at the risk-free rate of 10 percent. Flotation costs are fees paid when stock or debt is issued. These fees may go to printers, lawyers, and investment bankers, among others. Bicksler Enterprises is informed that flotation costs will be 1 percent of the gross proceeds of its loan. The previous chapter indicates that debt financing alters the NPV of a typical project. We look at the effects of debt next.

Flotation Costs   Given that flotation costs are 1 percent of the gross proceeds, we have:

$$\$7,500,000 = (1 - .01) \times \text{Gross proceeds} = .99 \times \text{Gross proceeds}$$

Thus, the gross proceeds are:

$$\frac{\$7,500,000}{1 - .01} = \frac{\$7,500,000}{.99} = \$7,575,758$$

This implies flotation costs of $75,758 (=1% × $7,575,758). To check the calculation, note that net proceeds are $7,500,000 (=$7,575,758 − $75,758). In other words, Bicksler Enterprises receives only $7,500,000. The flotation costs of $75,758 are received by intermediaries such as investment bankers.

Flotation costs are paid immediately but are deducted from taxes by amortizing on a straight-line basis over the life of the loan. The cash flows from flotation costs are as follows:

	Date 0	Date 1	Date 2	Date 3	Date 4	Date 5
Flotation costs	−$75,758					
Deduction		$\frac{\$75,758}{5} = \$15,152$	$15,152	$15,152	$15,152	$15,152
Tax shield from flotation costs		$.34 \times \$15,152$ $= \$5,152$	$5,152	$5,152	$5,152	$5,152

The relevant cash flows from flotation costs are in boldface. When we discount at 10 percent, the tax shield has a net present value of:

$$\$5,152 \times A^5_{.10} = \$19,530$$

This implies a net cost of flotation of:

$$-\$75,758 + \$19,530 = -\$56,228$$

(continued)

The net present value of the project after the flotation costs of debt but before the benefits of debt is:

$$-\$513,951 - \$56,228 = -\$570,179$$

Tax Subsidy   Interest must be paid on the gross proceeds of the loan, even though intermediaries receive the flotation costs. Because the gross proceeds of the loan are $7,575,758, annual interest is $757,576 (= $7,575,758 × .10). The interest cost after taxes is $500,000 [= $757,576 × (1 − .34)]. Because the loan is nonamortizing, the entire debt of $7,575,758 is repaid at Date 5. These terms are indicated here:

	Date 0	Date 1	Date 2	Date 3	Date 4	Date 5
Loan (gross proceeds)	**$7,575,758**					
Interest paid		10% × $7,575,758 = $757,576	$ 757,576	$ 757,576	$ 757,576	$ 757,576
Interest cost after taxes		(1 − .34) × $757,576 = **$500,000**	**$500,000**	**$500,000**	**$500,000**	**$ 500,000**
Repayment of debt						**$7,575,758**

The relevant cash flows are listed in boldface in the preceding table. They are (1) loan received, (2) annual interest cost after taxes, and (3) repayment of debt. Note that we include the *gross* proceeds of the loan as an inflow because the flotation costs have previously been subtracted.

In Chapter 16 we mentioned that the financing decision can be evaluated in terms of net present value. The net present value of the loan is simply the sum of the net present values of each of the three cash flows. This can be represented as follows:

$$\text{NPV (loan)} = + \frac{\text{Amount}}{\text{borrowed}} - \frac{\text{Present value}}{\text{of aftertax interest payments}} - \frac{\text{Present value}}{\text{of loan repayments}} \qquad (18.1)$$

The calculations for this example are:

$$\$976,415 = +\$7,575,758 - \frac{\$500,000}{.10} \times \left[1 - \left(\frac{1}{1.10}\right)^5\right] - \frac{\$7,575,758}{(1.10)^5} \qquad (18.1')$$

The NPV (loan) is positive, reflecting the interest tax shield.[7]

The adjusted present value of the project with this financing is:

$$\text{APV} = \text{All-equity value} - \text{Flotation costs of debt} + \text{NPV (loan)} \qquad (18.2)$$

$$\$406,236 = -\$513,951 \quad - \quad \$56,228 \quad + \quad \$976,415 \qquad (18.2')$$

Though we previously saw that an all-equity firm would reject the project, a firm would *accept* the project if a $7,500,000 (net) loan could be obtained.

Because the loan just discussed was at the market rate of 10 percent, we have considered only two of the three additional effects of debt (flotation costs and tax subsidy) so far. We now examine another loan where the third effect arises.

---

[7]The NPV (loan) must be zero in a no-tax world because interest provides no tax shield there. To check this intuition, we calculate:

$$\text{No-tax case: } 0 = +\$7,575,758 - \frac{\$757,576}{.10} \times \left[1 - \left(\frac{1}{1.10}\right)^5\right] - \frac{\$7,575,758}{(1.10)^5}$$

Non–Market-Rate Financing A number of companies are fortunate enough to obtain subsidized financing from a governmental authority. Suppose that the project of Bicksler Enterprises is deemed socially beneficial and the state of New Jersey grants the firm a $7,500,000 loan at 8 percent interest. In addition, all flotation costs are absorbed by the state. Clearly, the company will choose this loan over the one we previously calculated. Here are the cash flows from the loan:

	Date 0	Date 1	Date 2	Date 3	Date 4	Date 5
Loan received	**$7,500,000**					
Interest paid		8% × $7,500,000 = $600,000	$ 600,000	$ 600,000	$ 600,000	$ 600,000
Aftertax interest		(1 − .34) × $600,000 = **$396,000**	**$396,000**	**$396,000**	**$396,000**	**$ 396,000**
Repayment of debt						**$7,500,000**

The relevant cash flows are listed in boldface in the preceding table. Using Equation 18.1, the NPV (loan) is:

$$\$1,341,939 = +\$7,500,000 - \frac{\$396,000}{.10} \times \left[1 - \left(\frac{1}{1.10}\right)^5\right] - \frac{\$7,500,000}{(1.10)^5} \qquad (18.1''')$$

Why do we discount the cash flows in Equation 18.1‴ at 10 percent when the firm is borrowing at 8 percent? We discount at 10 percent because that is the fair or marketwide rate. That is, 10 percent is the rate at which the firm could borrow *without* benefit of subsidization. The net present value of the subsidized loan is larger than the net present value of the earlier loan because the firm is now borrowing at the below-market rate of 8 percent. Note that the NPV (loan) calculation in Equation 18.1‴ captures both the tax effect *and* the non–market-rate effect.

The net present value of the project with subsidized debt financing is:

$$\text{APV} = \text{All-equity value} - \text{Flotation costs of debt} + \text{NPV (loan)} \qquad (18.2)$$

$$+\$827,988 = -\$513,951 \quad - \qquad 0 \qquad + \$1,341,939 \qquad (18.2''')$$

The preceding example illustrates the adjusted present value (APV) approach. The approach begins with the present value of a project for the all-equity firm. Next, the effects of debt are added in. The approach has much to recommend it. It is intuitively appealing because individual components are calculated separately and added together in a simple way. And, if the debt from the project can be specified precisely, the present value of the debt can be calculated precisely.

18.7 Beta and Leverage

A previous chapter provides the formula for the relationship between the beta of the common stock and leverage of the firm in a world without taxes. We reproduce this formula here:

The No-Tax Case

$$\beta_{\text{Equity}} = \beta_{\text{Asset}}\left(1 + \frac{\text{Debt}}{\text{Equity}}\right) \qquad (18.3)$$

As pointed out earlier, this relationship holds under the assumption that the beta of debt is zero.

Because firms must pay corporate taxes in practice, it is worthwhile to provide the relationship in a world with corporate taxes. It can be shown that the relationship between the beta of the unlevered firm and the beta of the levered equity is this:[8]

The Corporate Tax Case

$$\beta_{\text{Equity}} = \left(1 + \frac{(1 - t_C)\text{Debt}}{\text{Equity}}\right)\beta_{\text{Unlevered firm}} \qquad (18.4)$$

when (1) the corporation is taxed at the rate of t_C and (2) the debt has a zero beta.

Because $[1 + (1 - t_C) \text{Debt/Equity}]$ must be more than 1 for a levered firm, it follows that $\beta_{\text{Unlevered firm}} < \beta_{\text{Equity}}$. The corporate tax case of Equation 18.4 is quite similar to the no-tax case of Equation 18.3 because the beta of levered equity must be greater than the beta of the unlevered firm in either case. The intuition that leverage increases the risk of equity applies in both cases.

However, notice that the two equations are not equal. It can be shown that leverage increases the equity beta less rapidly under corporate taxes. This occurs because, under taxes, leverage creates a *riskless* tax shield, thereby lowering the risk of the entire firm.

---

[8]This result holds only if the beta of debt equals zero. To see this, note that:

$$V_U + t_C B = V_L = B + S \qquad \text{(a)}$$

where:

V_U = Value of unlevered firm.
V_L = Value of levered firm.
B = Value of debt in a levered firm.
S = Value of equity in a levered firm.

As we stated in the text, the beta of the levered firm is a weighted average of the debt beta and the equity beta:

$$\frac{B}{B + S} \times \beta_B + \frac{S}{B + S} \times \beta_S$$

where β_B and β_S are the betas of the debt and the equity of the levered firm, respectively. Because $V_L = B + S$, we have:

$$\frac{B}{V_L} \times \beta_B + \frac{S}{V_L} \times \beta_S \qquad \text{(b)}$$

The beta of the levered firm can *also* be expressed as a weighted average of the beta of the unlevered firm and the beta of the tax shield:

$$\frac{V_U}{V_U + t_C B} \times \beta_U + \frac{t_C B}{V_U + t_C B} \times \beta_B$$

where β_U is the beta of the unlevered firm. This follows from Equation (a). Because $V_L = V_U + t_C B$, we have:

$$\frac{V_U}{V_L} \times \beta_U + \frac{t_C B}{V_L} \times \beta_B \qquad \text{(c)}$$

We can equate (b) and (c) because both represent the beta of a levered firm. Equation (a) tells us that $V_U = S + (1 - t_C) \times B$. Under the assumption that $\beta_B = 0$, equating (b) and (c) and using Equation (a) yields Equation 18.4.

The generalized formula for the levered beta (where β_B is not zero) is:

$$\beta_S = \beta_U + (1 - t_C)(\beta_U - \beta_B)\frac{B}{S}$$

and:

$$\beta_U = \frac{S}{B(1 - t_C) + S}\beta_S + \frac{B(1 - t_C)}{B(1 - t_C) + S}\beta_B$$

EXAMPLE 18.3

Unlevered Betas C. F. Lee, Incorporated is considering a scale-enhancing project. The market value of the firm's debt is $100 million, and the market value of the firm's equity is $200 million. The debt is considered riskless. The corporate tax rate is 34 percent. Regression analysis indicates that the beta of the firm's equity is 2. The risk-free rate is 10 percent, and the expected market premium is 8.5 percent. What would the project's discount rate be in the hypothetical case that C. F. Lee, Inc., is all equity?

We can answer this question in two steps.

1. *Determining beta of hypothetical all-equity firm:* Rearranging Equation 18.4, we have this:

$$\text{Unlevered Beta}$$

$$\frac{\text{Equity}}{\text{Equity} + (1 - t_c) \times \text{Debt}} \times \beta_{\text{Equity}} = \beta_{\text{Unlevered firm}} \qquad (18.5)$$

$$\frac{\$200 \text{ million}}{\$200 \text{ million} + (1 - .34) \times \$100 \text{ million}} \times 2 = 1.50$$

2. *Determining discount rate:* We calculate the discount rate from the security market line (SML) as follows:

$$\text{Discount Rate}$$

$$R_S = R_F + \beta \times [\bar{R}_M - R_F]$$

$$22.75\% = 10\% + 1.50 \times 8.5\%$$

THE PROJECT IS NOT SCALE ENHANCING

Because the previous example assumed that the project is scale enhancing, we began with the beta of the firm's equity. If the project is not scale enhancing, we could begin with the equity betas of firms in the industry of the project. For each firm, we could calculate the hypothetical beta of the unlevered equity by Equation 18.5. The SML could then be used to determine the project's discount rate from the average of these betas.

 ◄ To test your mastery of this material, take a quiz at mhhe. com/rwj

EXAMPLE 18.4

More Unlevered Betas The J. Lowes Corporation, which currently manufactures staples, is considering a $1 million investment in a project in the aircraft adhesives industry. The corporation estimates unlevered aftertax cash flows (UCF) of $300,000 per year into perpetuity from the project. The firm will finance the project with a debt-to-value ratio of .5 (or, equivalently, a debt-to-equity ratio of 1.0).

The three competitors in this new industry are currently unlevered, with betas of 1.2, 1.3, and 1.4. Assuming a risk-free rate of 5 percent, a market risk premium of 9 percent, and a corporate tax rate of 34 percent, what is the net present value of the project?

We can answer this question in five steps.

1. *Calculating the average unlevered beta in the industry:* The average unlevered beta across all three existing competitors in the aircraft adhesives industry is:

$$\frac{1.2 + 1.3 + 1.4}{3} = 1.3$$

(continued)

2. *Calculating the levered beta for J. Lowes's new project:* Assuming the same unlevered beta for this new project as for the existing competitors, we have, from Equation 18.4:

Levered Beta

$$\beta_{Equity} = \left(1 + \frac{(1 - t_c)\, Debt}{Equity}\right)\beta_{Unlevered\ firm}$$

$$2.16 = \left(1 + \frac{.66 \times 1}{1}\right) \times 1.3$$

3. *Calculating the cost of levered equity for the new project:* We calculate the discount rate from the security market line (SML) as follows:

Discount Rate

$$R_s = R_F + \beta \times [\bar{R}_M - R_F]$$

$$.244 = .05 + 2.16 \times .09$$

4. *Calculating the WACC for the new project:* The formula for determining the weighted average cost of capital, R_{WACC}, is:

$$R_{WACC} = \frac{B}{V}R_B(1 - t_c) + \frac{S}{V}R_s$$

$$.139 = \frac{1}{2} \times .05 \times .66 + \frac{1}{2} \times .244$$

5. *Determining the project's value:* Because the cash flows are perpetual, the NPV of the project is:

$$\frac{Unlevered\ cash\ flows\ (UCF)}{R_{WACC}} - Initial\ investment$$

$$\frac{\$300,000}{.139} - \$1\ million = \$1.16\ million$$

Summary and Conclusions

Earlier chapters of this text showed how to value projects and entire firms with and without leverage. In the last three chapters we discuss how to determine the optimal amount of leverage. We pointed out that the introduction of taxes and bankruptcy costs changes a firm's financing decisions. Most rational corporations should employ some debt in a world of this type. The present chapter has discussed three methods for valuation by levered firms: the adjusted present value (APV), flow to equity (FTE), and weighted average cost of capital (WACC) approaches.

Concept Questions

1. **APV** How is the APV of a project calculated?
2. **WACC and APV** What is the main difference between the WACC and APV methods?
3. **FTE** What is the main difference between the FTE approach and the other two approaches?

Chapter 18   Valuation and Capital Budgeting for the Levered Firm   **575**

4. **Capital Budgeting**   You are determining whether your company should undertake a new project and have calculated the NPV of the project using the WACC method when the CFO, a former accountant, notices that you did not use the interest payments in calculating the cash flows of the project. What should you tell him? If he insists that you include the interest payments in calculating the cash flows, what method can you use?

5. **Beta and Leverage**   What are the two types of risk that are measured by a levered beta?

Questions and Problems

www.mhhe.com/rwj

BASIC
(Questions 1–9)

1. **NPV and APV**   Zoso is a rental car company that is trying to determine whether to add 25 cars to its fleet. The company fully depreciates all its rental cars over five years using the straight-line method. The new cars are expected to generate $175,000 per year in earnings before taxes and depreciation for five years. The company is entirely financed by equity and has a 35 percent tax rate. The required return on the company's unlevered equity is 13 percent, and the new fleet will not change the risk of the company.

    a. What is the maximum price that the company should be willing to pay for the new fleet of cars if it remains an all-equity company?

    b. Suppose the company can purchase the fleet of cars for $480,000. Additionally, assume the company can issue $390,000 of five-year, 8 percent debt to finance the project. All principal will be repaid in one balloon payment at the end of the fifth year. What is the adjusted present value (APV) of the project?

2. **APV**   Gemini, Inc., an all-equity firm, is considering a $1.7 million investment that will be depreciated according to the straight-line method over its four-year life. The project is expected to generate earnings before taxes and depreciation of $595,000 per year for four years. The investment will not change the risk level of the firm. The company can obtain a four-year, 9.5 percent loan to finance the project from a local bank. All principal will be repaid in one balloon payment at the end of the fourth year. The bank will charge the firm $45,000 in flotation fees, which will be amortized over the four-year life of the loan. If the company financed the project entirely with equity, the firm's cost of capital would be 13 percent. The corporate tax rate is 30 percent. Using the adjusted present value method, determine whether the company should undertake the project.

3. **FTE**   Milano Pizza Club owns three identical restaurants popular for their specialty pizzas. Each restaurant has a debt–equity ratio of 40 percent and makes interest payments of $41,000 at the end of each year. The cost of the firm's levered equity is 19 percent. Each store estimates that annual sales will be $1.3 million; annual cost of goods sold will be $670,000; and annual general and administrative costs will be $405,000. These cash flows are expected to remain the same forever. The corporate tax rate is 40 percent.

    a. Use the flow to equity approach to determine the value of the company's equity.

    b. What is the total value of the company?

4. **WACC**   If Wild Widgets, Inc., were an all-equity company, it would have a beta of .85. The company has a target debt–equity ratio of .40. The expected return on the market portfolio is 11 percent, and Treasury bills currently yield 4 percent. The company has one bond issue outstanding that matures in 20 years and has a coupon

rate of 7 percent. The bond currently sells for $1,080. The corporate tax rate is 34 percent.

a. What is the company's cost of debt?
b. What is the company's cost of equity?
c. What is the company's weighted average cost of capital?

5. Beta and Leverage   North Pole Fishing Equipment Corporation and South Pole Fishing Equipment Corporation would have identical equity betas of 1.10 if both were all equity financed. The market value information for each company is shown here:

	North Pole	South Pole
Debt	$2,900,000	$3,800,000
Equity	$3,800,000	$2,900,000

The expected return on the market portfolio is 10.9 percent, and the risk-free rate is 3.2 percent. Both companies are subject to a corporate tax rate of 35 percent. Assume the beta of debt is zero.

a. What is the equity beta of each of the two companies?
b. What is the required rate of return on each of the two companies' equity?

6. NPV of Loans   Daniel Kaffe, CFO of Kendrick Enterprises, is evaluating a 10-year, 8 percent loan with gross proceeds of $5,850,000. The interest payments on the loan will be made annually. Flotation costs are estimated to be 2.5 percent of gross proceeds and will be amortized using a straight-line schedule over the 10-year life of the loan. The company has a tax rate of 40 percent, and the loan will not increase the risk of financial distress for the company.

a. Calculate the net present value of the loan excluding flotation costs.
b. Calculate the net present value of the loan including flotation costs.

7. NPV for an All-Equity Company   Shattered Glass, Inc., is an all-equity firm. The cost of the company's equity is currently 11 percent, and the risk-free rate is 3.5 percent. The company is currently considering a project that will cost $11.4 million and last six years. The project will generate revenues minus expenses each year in the amount of $3.2 million. If the company has a tax rate of 40 percent, should it accept the project?

8. WACC   National Electric Company (NEC) is considering a $45 million project in its power systems division. Tom Edison, the company's chief financial officer, has evaluated the project and determined that the project's unlevered cash flows will be $3.1 million per year in perpetuity. Mr. Edison has devised two possibilities for raising the initial investment: Issuing 10-year bonds or issuing common stock. NEC's pretax cost of debt is 6.9 percent, and its cost of equity is 10.8 percent. The company's target debt-to-value ratio is 80 percent. The project has the same risk as NEC's existing businesses, and it will support the same amount of debt. NEC is in the 34 percent tax bracket. Should NEC accept the project?

9. WACC   Bolero, Inc., has compiled the following information on its financing costs:

Type of Financing	Book Value	Market Value	Cost
Short-term debt	$10,000,000	$11,000,000	4.1%
Long-term debt	3,000,000	3,000,000	7.2
Common stock	6,000,000	26,000,000	13.8
Total	$19,000,000	$40,000,000	

Chapter 18 Valuation and Capital Budgeting for the Levered Firm **577**

The company is in the 35 percent tax bracket and has a target debt–equity ratio of 60 percent. The target short-term debt/long-term debt ratio is 20 percent.

a. What is the company's weighted average cost of capital using book value weights?

b. What is the company's weighted average cost of capital using market value weights?

c. What is the company's weighted average cost of capital using target capital structure weights?

d. What is the difference between WACCs? Which is the correct WACC to use for project evaluation?

INTERMEDIATE
(Questions 10–14)

10. APV Triad Corporation has established a joint venture with Tobacco Road Construction, Inc., to build a toll road in North Carolina. The initial investment in paving equipment is $80 million. The equipment will be fully depreciated using the straight-line method over its economic life of five years. Earnings before interest, taxes, and depreciation collected from the toll road are projected to be $12.1 million per annum for 20 years starting from the end of the first year. The corporate tax rate is 35 percent. The required rate of return for the project under all-equity financing is 13 percent. The pretax cost of debt for the joint partnership is 8.5 percent. To encourage investment in the country's infrastructure, the U.S. government will subsidize the project with a $25 million, 15-year loan at an interest rate of 5 percent per year. All principal will be repaid in one balloon payment at the end of Year 15. What is the adjusted present value of this project?

11. APV For the company in the previous problem, what is the value of being able to issue subsidized debt instead of having to issue debt at the terms it would normally receive? Assume the face amount and maturity of the debt issue are the same.

12. APV MVP, Inc., has produced rodeo supplies for over 20 years. The company currently has a debt–equity ratio of 50 percent and is in the 40 percent tax bracket. The required return on the firm's levered equity is 16 percent. MVP is planning to expand its production capacity. The equipment to be purchased is expected to generate the following unlevered cash flows:

Year	Cash Flow
0	–$18,000,000
1	5,700,000
2	9,500,000
3	8,800,000

The company has arranged a $9.3 million debt issue to partially finance the expansion. Under the loan, the company would pay interest of 9 percent at the end of each year on the outstanding balance at the beginning of the year. The company would also make year-end principal payments of $3,100,000 per year, completely retiring the issue by the end of the third year. Using the adjusted present value method, should the company proceed with the expansion?

13. WACC Neon Corporation's stock returns have a covariance with the market portfolio of .0415. The standard deviation of the returns on the market portfolio is 20 percent, and the expected market risk premium is 7.5 percent. The company has bonds outstanding with a total market value of $55 million and a yield to maturity of 6.5 percent. The company also has 4.5 million shares of common stock outstanding, each selling for $25. The company's CEO considers the firm's current debt–equity ratio optimal. The corporate tax rate is 35 percent, and Treasury bills currently yield 3.4 percent. The company is considering the purchase of additional equipment that would cost $42 million. The expected unlevered cash flows from the equipment are $11.8 million per year for five years. Purchasing the equipment will not change the risk level of the firm.

    a. Use the weighted average cost of capital approach to determine whether Neon should purchase the equipment.

    b. Suppose the company decides to fund the purchase of the equipment entirely with debt. What is the cost of capital for the project now? Explain.

14.   **Beta and Leverage**   Stackhouse Industries has a new project available that requires an initial investment of $4.5 million. The project will provide unlevered cash flows of $675,000 per year for the next 20 years. The company will finance the project with a debt-to-value ratio of .40. The company's bonds have a YTM of 6.8 percent. The companies with operations comparable to this project have unlevered betas of 1.15, 1.08, 1.30, and 1.25. The risk-free rate is 3.8 percent, and the market risk premium is 7 percent. The company has a tax rate of 34 percent. What is the NPV of this project?

CHALLENGE
(Questions 15–18)

15.   **APV, FTE, and WACC**   Seger, Inc., is an unlevered firm with expected annual earnings before taxes of $21 million in perpetuity. The current required return on the firm's equity is 16 percent, and the firm distributes all of its earnings as dividends at the end of each year. The company has 1.3 million shares of common stock outstanding and is subject to a corporate tax rate of 35 percent. The firm is planning a recapitalization under which it will issue $30 million of perpetual 9 percent debt and use the proceeds to buy back shares.

    a. Calculate the value of the company before the recapitalization plan is announced. What is the value of equity before the announcement? What is the price per share?

    b. Use the APV method to calculate the company value after the recapitalization plan is announced. What is the value of equity after the announcement? What is the price per share?

    c. How many shares will be repurchased? What is the value of equity after the repurchase has been completed? What is the price per share?

    d. Use the flow to equity method to calculate the value of the company's equity after the recapitalization.

16.   **APV, FTE, and WACC**   Mojito Mint Company has a debt–equity ratio of .35. The required return on the company's unlevered equity is 13 percent, and the pretax cost of the firm's debt is 7 percent. Sales revenue for the company is expected to remain stable indefinitely at last year's level of $17,500,000. Variable costs amount to 60 percent of sales. The tax rate is 40 percent, and the company distributes all its earnings as dividends at the end of each year.

    a. If the company were financed entirely by equity, how much would it be worth?

    b. What is the required return on the firm's levered equity?

    c. Use the weighted average cost of capital method to calculate the value of the company. What is the value of the company's equity? What is the value of the company's debt?

    d. Use the flow to equity method to calculate the value of the company's equity.

17.   **APV, FTE, and WACC**   Lone Star Industries just issued $235,000 of perpetual 8 percent debt and used the proceeds to repurchase stock. The company expects to generate $118,000 of earnings before interest and taxes in perpetuity. The company distributes all its earnings as dividends at the end of each year. The firm's unlevered cost of capital is 14 percent, and the corporate tax rate is 40 percent.

    a. What is the value of the company as an unlevered firm?

    b. Use the adjusted present value method to calculate the value of the company with leverage.

    c. What is the required return on the firm's levered equity?

    d. Use the flow to equity method to calculate the value of the company's equity.

18. **Projects That Are Not Scale Enhancing**   Blue Angel, Inc., a private firm in the holiday gift industry, is considering a new project. The company currently has a target debt–equity ratio of .40, but the industry target debt–equity ratio is .35. The industry average beta is 1.2. The market risk premium is 7 percent, and the risk-free rate is 5 percent. Assume all companies in this industry can issue debt at the risk-free rate. The corporate tax rate is 40 percent. The project requires an initial outlay of $675,000 and is expected to result in a $95,000 cash inflow at the end of the first year. The project will be financed at Blue Angel's target debt–equity ratio. Annual cash flows from the project will grow at an constant rate of 5 percent until the end of the fifth year and remain constant forever thereafter. Should Blue Angel invest in the project?

THE LEVERAGED BUYOUT OF CHEEK PRODUCTS, INC.

Cheek Products, Inc. (CPI) was founded 53 years ago by Joe Cheek and originally sold snack foods such as potato chips and pretzels. Through acquisitions, the company has grown into a conglomerate with major divisions in the snack food industry, home security systems, cosmetics, and plastics. Additionally, the company has several smaller divisions. In recent years, the company has been underperforming, but the company's management doesn't seem to be aggressively pursuing opportunities to improve operations (or the stock price).

Meg Whalen is a financial analyst specializing in identifying potential buyout targets. She believes that two major changes are needed at Cheek. First, she thinks that the company would be better off if it sold several divisions and concentrated on its core competencies in snack foods and home security systems. Second, the company is financed entirely with equity. Because the cash flows of the company are relatively steady, Meg thinks the company's debt–equity ratio should be at least .25. She believes these changes would significantly enhance shareholder wealth, but she also believes that the existing board and company management are unlikely to take the necessary actions. As a result, Meg thinks the company is a good candidate for a leveraged buyout.

A leveraged buyout (LBO) is the acquisition by a small group of equity investors of a public or private company. Generally, an LBO is financed primarily with debt. The new shareholders service the heavy interest and principal payments with cash from operations and/or asset sales. Shareholders generally hope to reverse the LBO within three to seven years by way of a public offering or sale of the company to another firm. A buyout is therefore likely to be successful only if the firm generates enough cash to service the debt in the early years and if the company is attractive to other buyers a few years down the road.

Meg has suggested the potential LBO to her partners, Ben Feller and Brenton Flynn. Ben and Brenton have asked Meg to provide projections of the cash flows for the company. Meg has provided the following estimates (in millions):

	2012	2013	2014	2015	2016
Sales	$2,749	$3,083	$3,322	$3,400	$3,539
Costs	731	959	1,009	1,091	1,149
Depreciation	485	516	537	564	575
EBT	$1,533	$1,608	$1,776	$1,745	$1,815
Capital expenditures	$ 279	$ 242	304	308	$ 304
Change in NWC	$ (122)	$ (186)	101	95	$ 108
Asset sales	$1,419	$1,028			

At the end of five years, Meg estimates that the growth rate in cash flows will be 3.5 percent per year. The capital expenditures are for new projects and the replacement of equipment that wears out. Additionally, the company would realize cash flow from the sale of several divisions. Even though the company will sell these divisions, overall sales should increase because of a more concentrated effort on the remaining divisions.

After plowing through the company's financials and various pro forma scenarios, Ben and Brenton feel that in five years they will be able to sell the company to another party or take it public again. They are also aware that they will have to borrow a considerable amount of the purchase price. The interest payments on the debt for each of the next five years if the LBO is undertaken will be these (in millions):

	2012	2013	2014	2015	2016
Interest payments	$1,927	$1,859	$2,592	$2,526	$2,614

The company currently has a required return on assets of 14 percent. Because of the high debt level, the debt will carry a yield to maturity of 12.5 percent for the next five years. When the debt is refinanced in five years, they believe the new yield to maturity will be 8 percent.

CPI currently has 425 million shares of stock outstanding that sell for $29 per share. The corporate tax rate is 40 percent. If Meg, Ben, and Brenton decide to undertake the LBO, what is the most they should offer per share?

Appendix 18A   The Adjusted Present Value Approach to Valuing Leveraged Buyouts

To access the appendix for this chapter, please visit www.mhhe.com/rwj.

Appendix 18A   The Adjusted Present Value Approach to Valuing Leveraged Buyouts[1]

Introduction

A leveraged buyout (LBO) is the acquisition by a small group of equity investors of a public or private company financed primarily with debt. The equityholders service the heavy interest and principal payments with cash from operations and/or asset sales. The shareholders generally hope to reverse the LBO within three to seven years by way of a public offering or sale of the company to another firm. A buyout is therefore likely to be successful only if the firm generates enough cash to serve the debt in the early years, and if the company is attractive to other buyers as the buyout matures.

In a leveraged buyout, the equity investors are expected to pay off outstanding principal according to a specific timetable. The owners know that the firm's debt–equity ratio will fall and can forecast the dollar amount of debt needed to finance future operations. Under these circumstances, the adjusted present value (APV) approach is more practical than the weighted average cost of capital (WACC) approach because the capital structure is changing. In this appendix, we illustrate the use of this procedure in valuing the RJR Nabisco transaction, the largest LBO in history.

The RJR Nabisco Buyout   In the summer of 1988, the price of RJR stock was hovering around $55 a share. The firm had $5 billion of debt. The firm's CEO, acting in concert with some other senior managers of the firm, announced a bid of $75 per share to take the firm private in a management buyout. Within days of management's offer, Kohlberg, Kravis, and Roberts (KKR) entered the fray with a $90 bid of their own. By the end of November, KKR emerged from the ensuing bidding process with an offer of $109 a share, or $25 billion total. We now use the APV technique to analyze KKR's winning strategy.

The APV method as described in this chapter can be used to value companies as well as projects. Applied in this way, the maximum value of a levered firm (V_L) is its value as an all-equity entity (V_U) plus the discounted value of the interest tax shields from the debt its assets will support (PVTS).[2] This relation can be stated as:

$$V_L = V_U + \text{PVTS}$$
$$= \sum_{t=1}^{\infty} \frac{\text{UCF}_t}{(1+R_0)^t} + \sum_{t=1}^{\infty} \frac{t_C R_B B_{t-1}}{(1+R_B)^t}$$

In the second part of this equation, UCF_t is the unlevered cash flow from operations for year t. Discounting these cash flows by the required return on assets, R_0, yields the all-equity value of the company. B_{t-1} represents the debt balance remaining at the end of year $(t-1)$. Because interest in a given year is based on the debt balance remaining at the end of the previous year, the interest paid in year t is $R_B B_{t-1}$. The numerator of the second

---

[1]This appendix has been adapted by Isik Inselbag and Howard Kaufold, The Wharton School, University of Pennsylvania, from their unpublished manuscript titled "Analyzing the RJR Nabisco Buyout: An Adjusted Present Value Approach."

[2]We should also deduct from this value any costs of financial distress. However, we would expect these costs to be small in the case of RJR for two reasons. As a firm in the tobacco and food industries, its cash flows are relatively stable and recession resistant. Furthermore, the firm's assets are divisible and attractive to a number of potential buyers, allowing the firm to receive full value if disposition is required.

**Table 18A.1
RJR Operating
Cash Flows
(in $ millions)**

	1989	1990	1991	1992	1993
Operating income	$2,620	$3,410	$3,645	$3,950	$4,310
Tax on operating income	891	1,142	1,222	1,326	1,448
Aftertax operating income	1,729	2,268	2,423	2,624	2,862
Add back depreciation	449	475	475	475	475
Less capital expenditures	522	512	525	538	551
Less change in working capital	(203)	(275)	200	225	250
Add proceeds from asset sales	3,545	1,805			
Unlevered cash flow (UCF)	$5,404	$4,311	$2,173	$2,336	$2,536

**Table 18A.2
Projected Interest
Expenses and
Tax Shields
(in $ millions)**

	1989	1990	1991	1992	1993
Interest expenses	$3,384	$3,004	$3,111	$3,294	$3,483
Interest tax shields ($t_c = 34\%$)	1,151	1,021	1,058	1,120	1,184

term, $t_c R_B B_{t-1}$, is therefore the tax shield for year t. We discount this series of annual tax shields using the rate at which the firm borrows, R_B.[3]

KKR planned to sell several of RJR's food divisions and operate the remaining parts of the firm more efficiently. Table 18A.1 presents KKR's projected unlevered cash flows for RJR under the buyout, adjusting for planned asset sales and operational efficiencies.

With respect to financial strategy, KKR planned a significant increase in leverage with accompanying tax benefits. Specifically, KKR issued almost $24 billion of new debt to complete the buyout, raising annual interest costs to more than $3 billion.[4] Table 18A.2 presents the projected interest expense and tax shields for the transaction.

We now use the data from Tables 18A.1 and 18A.2 to calculate the APV of the RJR buyout. This valuation process is presented in Table 18A.3.

The valuation presented in Table 18A.3 involves four steps.

Step 1: *Calculating the present value of unlevered cash flows for 1989–1993* The unlevered cash flows for 1989–1993 are shown in the last line of Table 18A.1 and the first line of Table 18A.3. These flows are discounted by the required asset return, R_0, which at the time of the buyout was approximately 14 percent. The value as of the end of 1988 of the unlevered cash flows expected from 1989 through 1993 is:

$$\frac{5.404}{1.14} + \frac{4.311}{1.14^2} + \frac{2.173}{1.14^3} + \frac{2.336}{1.14^4} + \frac{2.536}{1.14^5} = \$12.224 \text{ billion}$$

---

[3]The pretax borrowing rate, R_B, represents the appropriate discount rate for the interest tax shields when there is a precommitment to a specific debt repayment schedule under the terms of the LBO. If debt covenants require that the entire free cash flow be dedicated to debt service, the amount of debt outstanding and, therefore, the interest tax shield at any point in time are a direct function of the operating cash flows of the firm. Because the debt balance is then as risky as the cash flows, the required return on assets should be used to discount the interest tax shields.

[4]A significant portion of this debt was of the payment in kind (PIK) variety, which offers lenders additional bonds instead of cash interest. This PIK debt financing provided KKR with significant tax shields while allowing it to postpone the cash burden of debt service to future years. For simplicity of presentation, Table 18A.2 does not separately show cash versus noncash interest charges.

Chapter 18 Valuation and Capital Budgeting for the Levered Firm   **18A-3**

Table 18A.3
RJR LBO Valuation
(in $ millions
except share data)

	1989	1990	1991	1992	1993
Unlevered cash flow (UCF)	$ 5,404	$4,311	$2,173	$2,336	$ 2,536
Terminal value: (3% growth after 1993)					
Unlevered terminal value (UTV)					23,746
Terminal value at target debt					26,654
Tax shield in terminal value					2,908
Interest tax shields	1,151	1,021	1,058	1,120	1,184
PV of UCF 1989–1993 at 14%	12,224				
PV of UTV at 14%	12,333				
Total unlevered value	$24,557				
PV of tax shields 1989–1993 at 13.5%	3,834				
PV of tax shield in TV at 13.5%	1,544				
Total value of tax shields	5,378				
Total value	29,935				
Less value of assumed debt	5,000				
Value of equity	$24,935				
Number of shares	229 million				
Value per share	$ 108.9				

Step 2: *Calculating the present value of the unlevered cash flows beyond 1993 (unlevered terminal value)*   We assume the unlevered cash flows grow at the modest annual rate of 3 percent after 1993. The value, as of the end of 1993, of these cash flows is equal to the following discounted value of a growing perpetuity:

$$\frac{2.536(1.03)}{0.14 - 0.03} = \$23.746 \text{ billion}$$

This translates to a 1988 value of:

$$\frac{23.746}{1.14^5} = \$12.333 \text{ billion}$$

As in Step 1, the discount rate is the required asset rate of 14 percent.

The total unlevered value of the firm is therefore $12.224 + $12.333 = $24.557 billion.

To calculate the total buyout value, we must add the interest tax shields expected to be realized by debt financing.

Step 3: *Calculating the present value of interest tax shields for 1989–1993*   Under the prevailing U.S. tax laws in 1989, every dollar of interest reduced taxes by 34 cents. The present value of the interest tax shield for the period from 1989–1993 can be calculated by discounting the annual tax savings at the pretax average cost of debt, which was approximately 13.5 percent. Using the tax shields from Table 18A.2, the discounted value of these tax shields is calculated as:

$$\frac{1.151}{1.135} + \frac{1.021}{1.135^2} + \frac{1.058}{1.135^3} + \frac{1.120}{1.135^4} + \frac{1.184}{1.135^5} = \$3.834 \text{ billion}$$

Step 4: *Calculating the present value of interest tax shields beyond 1993*   Finally, we must calculate the value of tax shields associated with debt used to finance the operations of the company after 1993. We assume that debt will be reduced and maintained at 25 percent of the value of the firm from that date forward.[5] Under this assumption it is appropriate to use the WACC method to calculate a terminal value for the firm at the target capital structure. This in turn can be decomposed into an all-equity value and a value from tax shields.

If, after 1993, RJR uses 25 percent debt in its capital structure, its WACC at this target capital structure would be approximately 12.8 percent.[6] Then the levered terminal value as of the end of 1993 can be estimated as:

$$\frac{2.536(1.03)}{0.128 - 0.03} = \$26.654 \text{ billion}$$

Because the levered value of the company is the sum of the unlevered value plus the value of interest tax shields, it is the case that:

$$\text{Value of tax shields (end 1993)} = V_L \text{ (end 1993)} - V_U \text{ (end 1993)}$$
$$= \$26.654 \text{ billion} - \$23.746 \text{ billion}$$
$$= \$2.908 \text{ billion}$$

To calculate the value, as of the end of 1988, of these future tax shields, we again discount by the borrowing rate of 13.5 percent to get:[7]

$$\frac{2.908}{1.135^5} = \$1.544 \text{ billion}$$

The total value of interest tax shields therefore equals $\$3.834 + \$1.544 = \$5.378$ billion.

Adding all of these components together, the total value of RJR under the buyout proposal is $29.935 billion. Deducting the $5 billion market value of assumed debt yields a value for equity of $24.935 billion, or $108.9 per share.

---

[5]This 25 percent figure is consistent with the debt utilization in industries in which RJR Nabisco is involved. In fact, that was the debt-to-total-market-value ratio for RJR immediately before management's initial buyout proposal. The firm can achieve this target by 1993 if a significant portion of the convertible debt used to finance the buyout is exchanged for equity by that time. Alternatively, KKR could issue new equity (as would occur, for example, if the firm were taken public) and use the proceeds to retire some of the outstanding debt.

[6]To calculate this rate, use the weighted average cost of capital from this chapter:

$$R_{\text{WACC}} = \frac{S}{S + B} R_S + \frac{B}{S + B} R_B (1 - t_C)$$

and substitute the appropriate values for the proportions of debt and equity used, as well as their respective costs. Specifically, at the target debt-to-value ratio, $B/(S + B) = 25$ percent, and $S/(S + B) = (1 - B/(S + B)) = 75$ percent. Given this blend:

$$R_S = R_0 + \frac{B}{S}(1 - t_C)(R_0 - R_B)$$
$$= 0.14 = \frac{0.25}{0.75}(1 - 0.34)(0.14 - 0.135)$$
$$= 0.141$$

Using these findings plus the borrowing rate of 13.5 percent in R_{WACC}, we find:
$$R_{\text{WACC}} = 0.75(0.141) + 0.25(0.135)(1 - 0.34)$$
$$= 0.128$$

In fact, this value is an approximation to the true weighted average cost of capital when the market debt-to-value blend is constant or when the cash flows are growing. For a detailed discussion of this issue, see Isik Inselbag and Howard Kaufold, "A Comparison of Alternative Discounted Cash Flow Approaches to Firm Valuation," The Wharton School, University of Pennsylvania (June 1990), unpublished paper.

[7]A good argument can be made that because post-1993 debt levels are proportional to firm value, the tax shields are as risky as the firm and should be discounted at the rate R_0.

Concluding Comments about LBO Valuation Methods As mentioned in this chapter, the WACC method is by far the most widely applied approach to capital budgeting. We could analyze an LBO and generate the results of the second section of this appendix using this technique, but it would be a much more difficult process. We have tried to show that the APV approach is the preferred way to analyze a transaction in which the capital structure is not stable over time.

Consider the WACC approach to valuing the KKR bid for RJR. We could discount the operating cash flows of RJR by a set of weighted average costs of capital and arrive at the same $30 billion total value for the company. To do this, we would need to calculate the appropriate rate for each year because the WACC rises as the buyout proceeds. This occurs because the value of the tax subsidy declines as debt principal is repaid. In other words, no single return represents the cost of capital when the firm's capital structure is changing.

There is also a theoretical problem with the WACC approach to valuing a buyout. To calculate the changing WACC, we must know the market value of a firm's debt and equity. But if the debt and equity values are already known, the total market value of the company is also known. That is, we must know the value of the company to calculate the WACC. We must therefore resort to using book value measures for debt and equity, or make assumptions about the evolution of their market values, to implement the WACC method.

CHAPTER 19

Dividends and Other Payouts

On February 16, 2011, cable TV and Internet provider Comcast announced a broad plan to reward stockholders for the recent success of the firm's business. Under the plan, Comcast would (1) boost its annual dividend by 18 percent from 38 cents per share to 45 cents per share; and (2) increase its planned repurchase of Comcast's common stock from $1.2 billion the previous year to $2.1 billion in shares. Investors cheered, bidding up the stock price by about 4 percent on the day of the announcement. Why were investors so pleased? To find out, this chapter explores these types of actions and their implications for shareholders.

▲ For updates on the latest happenings in finance, visit www.rwjcorporatefinance.blogspot.com

19.1 Different Types of Payouts

The term *dividend* usually refers to a cash distribution of earnings. If a distribution is made from sources other than current or accumulated retained earnings, the term *distribution* rather than dividend is used. However, it is acceptable to refer to a distribution from earnings as a *dividend* and a distribution from capital as a *liquidating dividend.*

The most common type of dividend is in the form of cash. When public companies pay dividends, they usually pay **regular cash dividends** four times a year. Sometimes firms will pay a regular cash dividend and an *extra cash dividend.* Paying a cash dividend reduces corporate cash and retained earnings—except in the case of a liquidating dividend (where paid-in capital may be reduced).

Another type of dividend is paid out in shares of stock. This dividend is referred to as a **stock dividend.** It is not a true dividend because no cash leaves the firm. Rather, a stock dividend increases the number of shares outstanding, thereby reducing the value of each share. A stock dividend is commonly expressed as a ratio; for example, with a 2 percent stock dividend a shareholder receives 1 new share for every 50 currently owned.

When a firm declares a **stock split,** it increases the number of shares outstanding. Because each share is now entitled to a smaller percentage of the firm's cash flow, the stock price should fall. For example, if the managers of a firm whose stock is selling at $90 declare a three-for-one stock split, the price of a share of stock should fall to about $30. A stock split strongly resembles a stock dividend except that it is usually much larger.

An alternative form of cash payout is a **stock repurchase.** Just as a firm may use cash to pay dividends, it may use cash to buy back shares of its stock. The shares are held by the corporation and accounted for as treasury stock.

19.2 Standard Method of Cash Dividend Payment

The decision to pay a dividend rests in the hands of the board of directors of the corporation. A dividend is distributable to shareholders of record on a specific date. When a dividend has been declared, it becomes a liability of the firm and cannot be easily rescinded by the corporation. The amount of the dividend is expressed as dollars per share (*dividend per share*), as a percentage of the market price (*dividend yield*), or as a percentage of earnings per share (*dividend payout*).

Figure 19.1
Example of Procedure for Dividend Payment

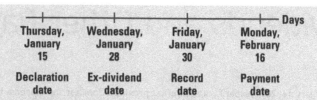

1. *Declaration date:* The board of directors declares a payment of dividends.
2. *Record date:* The declared dividends are distributable to shareholders of record on a specific date.
3. *Ex-dividend date:* A share of stock becomes ex dividend on the date the seller is entitled to keep the dividend; under NYSE rules, shares are traded ex dividend on and after the second business day before the record date.
4. *Payment date:* The dividend checks are mailed to shareholders of record.

For a list of today's dividends, go to **www.earnings.com**.

The mechanics of a dividend payment can be illustrated by the example in Figure 19.1 and the following chronology:

1. *Declaration date:* On January 15 (the declaration date), the board of directors passes a resolution to pay a dividend of $1 per share on February 16 to all holders of record on January 30.

2. *Date of record:* The corporation prepares a list on January 30 of all individuals believed to be stockholders as of this date. The word *believed* is important here: The dividend will not be paid to individuals whose notification of purchase is received by the company after January 30.

3. *Ex-dividend date:* The procedure for the date of record would be unfair if efficient brokerage houses could notify the corporation by January 30 of a trade occurring on January 29, whereas the same trade might not reach the corporation until February 2 if executed by a less efficient house. To eliminate this problem, all brokerage firms entitle stockholders to receive the dividend if they purchased the stock three business days before the date of record. The second day before the date of record, which is Wednesday, January 28, in our example, is called the *ex-dividend date.* Before this date the stock is said to trade *cum dividend.*

4. *Date of payment:* The dividend checks are mailed to the stockholders on February 16.

Obviously, the ex-dividend date is important because an individual purchasing the security before the ex-dividend date will receive the current dividend, whereas another individual purchasing the security on or after this date will not receive the dividend. The stock price will therefore fall on the ex-dividend date (assuming no other events occur). It is worthwhile to note that this drop is an indication of efficiency, not inefficiency, because the market rationally attaches value to a cash dividend. In a world with neither taxes nor transaction costs, the stock price would be expected to fall by the amount of the dividend:

Before ex-dividend date	Price = $(P + 1)$
On or after ex-dividend date	Price = P

This is illustrated in Figure 19.2.

The amount of the price drop may depend on tax rates. For example, consider the case with no capital gains taxes. On the day before a stock goes ex dividend, a

Figure 19.2
Price Behavior around the Ex-Dividend Date for a $1 Cash Dividend

In a world without taxes, the stock price will fall by the amount of the dividend on the ex-date (time 0). If the dividend is $1 per share, the price will be equal to P on the ex-date.

Before ex-date (-1)	Price $= \$(P+1)$
Ex-date (0)	Price $= \$P$

purchaser must decide either: (1) To buy the stock immediately and pay tax on the forthcoming dividend or (2) To buy the stock tomorrow, thereby missing the dividend. If all investors are in the 15 percent tax bracket and the quarterly dividend is $1, the stock price should fall by $.85 on the ex-dividend date. That is, if the stock price falls by this amount on the ex-dividend date, purchasers will receive the same return from either strategy.

As an example of the price drop on the ex-dividend date, we examine the relatively enormous dividend paid by investment advisory company Diamond Hill Investment Group in December 2010. The dividend was $13 per share at a time when the stock price was around $85, so the dividend was about 15 percent of the total stock price.

The stock went ex dividend on November 29, 2010. The stock price chart here shows the change in Diamond Hill stock four days prior to the ex-dividend date and on the ex-dividend date.

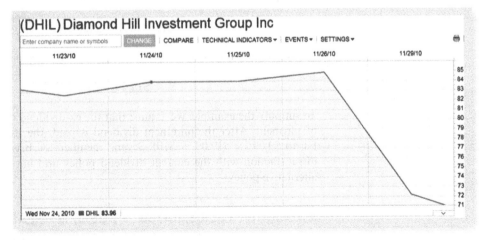

The stock closed at $84.86 on November 26 (a Friday) and closed at $72.19 on November 29–a drop of $12.67. With a 15 percent tax rate on dividends, we would have expected a drop of $11.05, so the actual price dropped slightly more than we would have expected. We discuss dividends and taxes in more detail in a subsequent section.

19.3 The Benchmark Case: An Illustration of the Irrelevance of Dividend Policy

We have stated in previous chapters that the value of a firm stems from its ability to generate and pay out its distributable (i.e., free) cash flow. Specially, we put forth the idea that the value of a share of stock should be equal to the present value of its future expected dividend payouts (and share repurchases, which we treat in the next section). This still stands. In this section, we discuss dividend policy, which we define as the timing of a firm's dividend payouts given the level of its distributable cash flow.

A powerful argument can be made that the timing of dividends when cash flows do not change does not matter. This will be illustrated with the Bristol Corporation. Bristol is an all-equity firm that started 10 years ago. The current financial managers know at the present time (Date 0) that the firm will dissolve in one year (Date 1). At Date 0 the managers are able to forecast cash flows with perfect certainty. The managers know that the firm will receive a cash flow of $10,000 immediately and another $10,000 next year. Bristol has no additional positive NPV projects.

CURRENT POLICY: DIVIDENDS SET EQUAL TO CASH FLOW

At the present time, dividends (Div) at each date are set equal to the available cash flow of $10,000. The value of the firm can be calculated by discounting these dividends. This value is expressed as:

$$V_0 = \text{Div}_0 + \frac{\text{Div}_1}{1 + R_S}$$

where Div_0 and Div_1 are the cash flows paid out in dividends, and R_S is the discount rate. The first dividend is not discounted because it will be paid immediately.

Assuming $R_S = 10$ percent, the value of the firm is:

$$\$19,090.91 = \$10,000 + \frac{\$10,000}{1.1}$$

If 1,000 shares are outstanding, the value of each share is:

$$\$19.09 = \$10 + \frac{\$10}{1.1} \tag{19.1}$$

To simplify the example, we assume that the ex-dividend date is the same as the date of payment. After the imminent dividend is paid, the stock price will immediately fall to $9.09 (= $19.09 − $10). Several members of Bristol's board have expressed dissatisfaction with the current dividend policy and have asked you to analyze an alternative policy.

ALTERNATIVE POLICY: INITIAL DIVIDEND IS GREATER THAN CASH FLOW

Another policy is for the firm to pay a dividend of $11 per share immediately, which is, of course, a total dividend payout of $11,000. Because the available cash flow is only $10,000, the extra $1,000 must be raised in one of a few ways. Perhaps the simplest would be to issue $1,000 of bonds or stock now (at Date 0). Assume that stock is issued and the new stockholders will desire enough cash flow at Date 1 to let them earn the required 10 percent return on their Date 0 investment. The new stockholders will demand $1,100 of the Date 1 cash flow, leaving only $8,900 to the old stockholders. The dividends to the old stockholders will be these:

	Date 0	Date 1
Aggregate dividends to old stockholders	$11,000	$8,900
Dividends per share	$ 11.00	$ 8.90

The present value of the dividends per share is therefore:

$$\$19.09 = \$11 + \frac{\$8.90}{1.1} \qquad (19.2)$$

Students often find it instructive to determine the price at which the new stock is issued. Because the new stockholders are not entitled to the immediate dividend, they would pay $8.09 (= $8.90/1.1) per share. Thus, 123.61 (= $1,000/$8.09) new shares are issued.

THE INDIFFERENCE PROPOSITION

Note that the values in Equations 19.1 and 19.2 are equal. This leads to the initially surprising conclusion that the change in dividend policy did not affect the value of a share of stock as long as all distributable cash flow is paid out. However, on reflection, the result seems sensible. The new stockholders are parting with their money at Date 0 and receiving it back with the appropriate return at Date 1. In other words, they are taking on a zero NPV investment.

HOMEMADE DIVIDENDS

To illustrate the indifference investors have toward dividend policy in our example, we used present value equations. An alternative and perhaps more intuitively appealing explanation avoids the mathematics of discounted cash flows.

Suppose individual investor X prefers dividends per share of $10 at both Dates 0 and 1. Would she be disappointed when informed that the firm's management is adopting the alternative dividend policy (dividends of $11 and $8.90 on the two dates, respectively)? Not necessarily: She could easily reinvest the $1 of unneeded funds received on Date 0, yielding an incremental return of $1.10 at Date 1. Thus, she would receive her desired net cash flow of $11 − $1 = $10 at Date 0 and $8.90 + $1.10 = $10 at Date 1.

Conversely, imagine investor Z preferring $11 of cash flow at Date 0 and $8.90 of cash flow at Date 1, who finds that management will pay dividends of $10 at both Dates 0 and 1. He can sell off shares of stock at Date 0 to receive the desired amount of cash flow. That is, if he sells off shares (or fractions of shares) at Date 0 totaling $1, his cash flow at Date 0 becomes $10 + $1 = $11. Because a $1 sale of stock at Date 0 will reduce his dividends by $1.10 at Date 1, his net cash flow at Date 1 would be $10 − $1.10 = $8.90.

The example illustrates how investors can make **homemade dividends.** In this instance, corporate dividend policy is being undone by a potentially dissatisfied stockholder. This homemade dividend is illustrated by Figure 19.3. Here the firm's cash flows of $10 per share at both Dates 0 and 1 are represented by Point A. This point also represents the initial dividend payout. However, as we just saw, the firm could alternatively pay out $11 per share at Date 0 and $8.90 per share at Date 1, a strategy

Figure 19.3
Homemade
Dividends: A
Trade-off between
Dividends per
Share at Date 0
and Dividends per
Share at Date 1

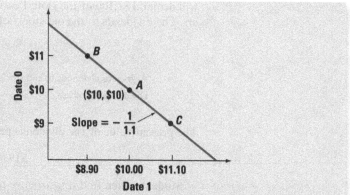

The graph illustrates both (1) how managers can vary dividend policy and (2) how individuals can undo the firm's dividend policy.

Managers varying dividend policy: A firm paying out all cash flows immediately is at Point *A* on the graph. The firm could achieve Point *B* by issuing stock to pay extra dividends or achieve Point *C* by buying back old stock with some of its cash.

Individuals undoing the firm's dividend policy: Suppose the firm adopts the dividend policy represented by Point *B*: dividends per share of $11 at Date 0 and $8.90 at Date 1. An investor can reinvest $1 of the dividends at 10 percent, which will place her at Point *A*. Suppose, alternatively, the firm adopts the dividend policy represented by Point *A*. An investor can sell off $1 of stock at Date 0, placing him at Point *B*. No matter what dividend policy the firm establishes, a shareholder can undo it.

represented by Point *B*. Similarly, by either issuing new stock or buying back old stock, the firm could achieve a dividend payout represented by any point on the diagonal line.

The previous paragraph describes the choices available to the managers of the firm. The same diagonal line also represents the choices available to the shareholder. For example, if the shareholder receives a per-share dividend distribution of ($11, $8.90), he or she can either reinvest some of the dividends to move down and to the right on the graph or sell off shares of stock and move up and to the left.

The implications of the graph can be summarized in two sentences:

1. By varying dividend policy, managers can achieve any payout along the diagonal line in Figure 19.3.

2. Either by reinvesting excess dividends at Date 0 or by selling off shares of stock at this date, an individual investor can achieve any net cash payout along the diagonal line.

Thus, because both the corporation and the individual investor can move only along the diagonal line, dividend policy in this model is irrelevant. The changes the managers make in dividend policy can be undone by an individual who, by either reinvesting dividends or selling off stock, can move to a desired point on the diagonal line.

A TEST

You can test your knowledge of this material by examining these true statements:

1. Dividends are relevant.

2. Dividend policy is irrelevant.

The first statement follows from common sense. Clearly, investors prefer higher dividends to lower dividends at any single date if the dividend level is held constant at every other date. In other words, if the dividend per share at a given date is raised while the dividend per share for each other date is held constant, the stock price will rise. This act can be accomplished by management decisions that improve productivity, increase tax savings, or strengthen product marketing. In fact, you may recall that in Chapter 9 we argued that the value of a firm's equity is equal to the discounted present value of all its future dividends.

The second statement is understandable once we realize that dividend policy cannot raise the dividend per share at one date while holding the dividend level per share constant at all other dates. Rather, dividend policy merely establishes the trade-off between dividends at one date and dividends at another date. As we saw in Figure 19.3, holding cash flows constant, an increase in Date 0 dividends can be accomplished only by a decrease in Date 1 dividends. The extent of the decrease is such that the present value of all dividends is not affected.

DIVIDENDS AND INVESTMENT POLICY

The preceding argument shows that an increase in dividends through issuance of new shares neither helps nor hurts the stockholders. Similarly, a reduction in dividends through share repurchase neither helps nor hurts stockholders. The key to this result is understanding that the overall level of cash flows is assumed to be fixed and that we are not changing the available positive net present value projects.

What about reducing capital expenditures to increase dividends? Earlier chapters show that a firm should accept all positive net present value projects. To do otherwise would reduce the value of the firm. Thus, we have an important point:

Firms should never give up a positive NPV project to increase a dividend (or to pay a dividend for the first time).

This idea was implicitly considered by Miller and Modigliani. One of the assumptions underlying their dividend irrelevance proposition was this: "The investment policy of the firm is set ahead of time and is not altered by changes in dividend policy."

19.4 Repurchase of Stock

Instead of paying dividends, a firm may use cash to repurchase shares of its own stock. Share repurchases have taken on increased importance in recent years. Consider Figure 19.4, which shows the aggregate dollar amounts of dividends, repurchases, and earnings for large U.S. firms in the years from 2004 to 2011. As can be seen, the amount of repurchases was more than the amount of dividends up to 2008. However, the amount of dividends exceeded the amount of repurchases in late 2008 and 2009. This trend reversed after 2009. Notice also from Figure 19.4 that there is "stickiness" to repurchases and dividend payouts. In late 2008 when aggregate corporate earnings turned negative, the level of dividends and share repurchases did not change much. More generally, the volatility of aggregate earnings has been greater than that of dividends and share repurchases.

Share repurchases are typically accomplished in one of three ways. First, companies may simply purchase their own stock, just as anyone would buy shares of a particular stock. In these *open market purchases*, the firm does not reveal itself as the

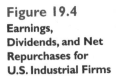

Figure 19.4
Earnings, Dividends, and Net Repurchases for U.S. Industrial Firms

SOURCE: Standard & Poor's Financial Services at www.standardandpoors.com/indices/market-attributes/en/us.

buyer. Thus, the seller does not know whether the shares were sold back to the firm or to just another investor.

Second, the firm could institute a *tender offer.* Here, the firm announces to all of its stockholders that it is willing to buy a fixed number of shares at a specific price. For example, suppose Arts and Crafts (A&C), Inc., has 1 million shares of stock outstanding, with a stock price of $50 per share. The firm makes a tender offer to buy back 300,000 shares at $60 per share. A&C chooses a price above $50 to induce shareholders to sell—that is, tender—their shares. In fact, if the tender price is set high enough, shareholders may want to sell more than the 300,000 shares. In the extreme case where all outstanding shares are tendered, A&C will buy back 3 out of every 10 shares that a shareholder has. On the other hand, if shareholders do not tender enough shares, the offer can be canceled. A method related to a tender offer is the *Dutch auction.* Here the firm does not set a fixed price for the shares to be sold. Instead, the firm conducts an auction in which it bids for shares. The firm announces the number of shares it is willing to buy back at various prices, and shareholders indicate how many shares they are willing to sell at the various prices. The firm will then pay the lowest price that will achieve its goal.

Finally, firms may repurchase shares from specific individual stockholders, a procedure called a *targeted repurchase.* For example, suppose the International Biotechnology Corporation purchased approximately 10 percent of the outstanding stock of the Prime Robotics Company (P-R Co.) in April at around $38 per share. At that time, International Biotechnology announced to the Securities and Exchange Commission that it might eventually try to take control of P-R Co. In May, P-R Co. repurchased the International Biotechnology holdings at $48 per share, well above the market price at that time. This offer was not extended to other shareholders.

Companies engage in targeted repurchases for a variety of reasons. In some rare cases, a single large stockholder can be bought out at a price lower than that in a tender offer. The legal fees in a targeted repurchase may also be lower than those in a more typical buyback. In addition, the shares of large stockholders are often repurchased to avoid a takeover unfavorable to management.

We now consider an example of a repurchase presented in the theoretical world of a perfect capital market. We next discuss real-world factors involved in the repurchase decision.

DIVIDEND VERSUS REPURCHASE: CONCEPTUAL EXAMPLE

Imagine that Telephonic Industries has excess cash of $300,000 (or $3 per share) and is considering an immediate payment of this amount as an extra dividend. The firm forecasts that, after the dividend, earnings will be $450,000 per year, or $4.50 for each of the 100,000 shares outstanding. Because the price–earnings ratio is 6 for comparable companies, the shares of the firm should sell for $27 (=$4.50 × 6) after the dividend is paid. These figures are presented in the top half of Table 19.1. Because the dividend is $3 per share, the stock would have sold for $30 a share *before* payment of the dividend.

Alternatively, the firm could use the excess cash to repurchase some of its own stock. Imagine that a tender offer of $30 per share is made. Here, 10,000 shares are repurchased so that the total number of shares remaining is 90,000. With fewer shares outstanding, the earnings per share will rise to $5 (=$450,000/90,000). The price–earnings ratio remains at 6 because both the business and financial risks of the firm are the same in the repurchase case as they were in the dividend case. Thus, the price of a share after the repurchase is $30 (=$5 × 6). These results are presented in the bottom half of Table 19.1.

If commissions, taxes, and other imperfections are ignored in our example, the stockholders are indifferent between a dividend and a repurchase. With dividends each stockholder owns a share worth $27 and receives $3 in dividends, so that the total value is $30. This figure is the same as both the amount received by the selling stockholders and the value of the stock for the remaining stockholders in the repurchase case.

This example illustrates the important point that, in a perfect market, the firm is indifferent between a dividend payment and a share repurchase. This result is quite similar to the indifference propositions established by MM for debt versus equity financing and for dividends versus capital gains.

Table 19.1

Dividend versus Repurchase Example for Telephonic Industries

	For Entire Firm	Per Share
Extra Dividend		**(100,000 shares outstanding)**
Proposed dividend	$ 300,000	$ 3.00
Forecasted annual earnings after dividend	450,000	4.50
Market value of stock after dividend	2,700,000	27.00
Repurchase		**(90,000 shares outstanding)**
Forecasted annual earnings after repurchase	$ 450,000	$ 5.00
Market value of stock after repurchase	2,700,000	30.00

You may often read in the popular financial press that a repurchase agreement is beneficial because earnings per share increase. Earnings per share do rise for Telephonic Industries if a repurchase is substituted for a cash dividend: The EPS is $4.50 after a dividend and $5 after the repurchase. This result holds because the drop in shares after a repurchase implies a reduction in the denominator of the EPS ratio.

However, the financial press frequently places undue emphasis on EPS figures in a repurchase agreement. Given the irrelevance propositions we have discussed, the increase in EPS here is not beneficial. Table 19.1 shows that, in a perfect capital market, the total value to the stockholder is the same under the dividend payment strategy as under the repurchase strategy.

DIVIDENDS VERSUS REPURCHASES: REAL-WORLD CONSIDERATIONS

We previously referred to Figure 19.4, which showed growth in share repurchases relative to dividends. In fact, most firms that pay dividends also repurchase shares of stock. This suggests that repurchasing shares of stock is not always a substitute for paying dividends but rather a complement to it. For example, recently the number of U.S. industrial firms that pay dividends only or repurchase only is about the same as the number of firms paying both dividends and repurchasing shares. Why do some firms choose repurchases over dividends? Here are perhaps five of the most common reasons.

1. Flexibility Firms often view dividends as a commitment to their stockholders and are quite hesitant to reduce an existing dividend. Repurchases do not represent a similar commitment. Thus, a firm with a permanent increase in cash flow is likely to increase its dividend. Conversely, a firm whose cash flow increase is only temporary is likely to repurchase shares of stock.

2. Executive Compensation Executives are frequently given stock options as part of their overall compensation. Let's revisit the Telephonic Industries example of Table 19.1, where the firm's stock was selling at $30 when the firm was considering either a dividend or a repurchase. Further imagine that Telephonic had granted 1,000 stock options to its CEO, Ralph Taylor, two years earlier. At that time, the stock price was, say, only $20. This means that Mr. Taylor can buy 1,000 shares for $20 a share at any time between the grant of the options and their expiration, a procedure called *exercising* the options. His gain from exercising is directly proportional to the rise in the stock price above $20. As we saw in the example, the price of the stock would fall to $27 following a dividend but would remain at $30 following a repurchase. The CEO would clearly prefer a repurchase to a dividend because the difference between the stock price and the exercise price of $20 would be $10 (= $30 − $20) following the repurchase but only $7 (= $27 − $20) following the dividend. Existing stock options will always have greater value when the firm repurchases shares instead of paying a dividend because the stock price will be greater after a repurchase than after a dividend.

3. Offset to Dilution In addition, the exercise of stock options increases the number of shares outstanding. In other words, exercise causes dilution of the stock. Firms frequently buy back shares of stock to offset this dilution. However, it is hard to argue that this is a valid reason for repurchase. As we showed in

Table 19.1, repurchase is neither better nor worse for the stockholders than a dividend. Our argument holds whether or not stock options have been exercised previously.

4. Undervaluation Many companies buy back stock because they believe that a repurchase is their best investment. This occurs more frequently when managers believe that the stock price is temporarily depressed.

The fact that some companies repurchase their stock when they believe it is undervalued does not imply that the management of the company must be correct; only empirical studies can make this determination. The immediate stock market reaction to the announcement of a stock repurchase is usually quite favorable. In addition, some empirical work has shown that the long-term stock price performance of securities after a buyback is better than the stock price performance of comparable companies that do not repurchase.

5. Taxes Because taxes for both dividends and share repurchases are treated in depth in the next section, suffice it to say at this point that repurchases provide a tax advantage over dividends.

19.5 Personal Taxes, Dividends, and Stock Repurchases

Section 19.3 asserted that in a world without taxes and other frictions, the timing of dividend payout does not matter if distributable cash flows do not change. Similarly, Section 19.4 concluded that the choice between a share repurchase and a dividend is irrelevant in a world of this type. This section examines the effect of taxes on both dividends and repurchases. Our discussion is facilitated by classifying firms into two types: Those without sufficient cash to pay a dividend and those with sufficient cash to do so.

FIRMS WITHOUT SUFFICIENT CASH TO PAY A DIVIDEND

It is simplest to begin with a firm without cash that is owned by a single entrepreneur. If this firm should decide to pay a dividend of $100, it must raise capital. The firm might choose among a number of different stock and bond issues to pay the dividend. However, for simplicity, we assume that the entrepreneur contributes cash to the firm by issuing stock to himself. This transaction, diagrammed in the left side of Figure 19.5, would clearly be a *wash* in a world of no taxes. $100 cash goes into the firm when stock is issued and is immediately paid out as a dividend. Thus, the entrepreneur neither benefits nor loses when the dividend is paid, a result consistent with Miller–Modigliani.

Now assume that dividends are taxed at the owner's personal tax rate of 15 percent. The firm still receives $100 upon issuance of stock. However, the entrepreneur does not get to keep the full $100 dividend. Instead the dividend payment is taxed, implying that the owner receives only $85 net after tax. Thus, the entrepreneur loses $15.

Though the example is clearly contrived and unrealistic, similar results can be reached for more plausible situations. Thus, financial economists generally agree that in a world of personal taxes, firms should not issue stock to pay dividends.

Figure 19.5
Firm Issues Stock
to Pay a Dividend

In the no-tax case, the entrepreneur receives the $100 in dividends that he gave to the firm when purchasing stock. The entire operation is called a *wash;* in other words, it has no economic effect. With taxes, the entrepreneur still receives $100 in dividends. However, he must pay $15 in taxes to the IRS. The entrepreneur loses and the IRS wins when a firm issues stock to pay a dividend.

The direct costs of issuance will add to this effect. Investment bankers must be paid when new capital is raised. Thus, the net receipts due to the firm from a new issue are less than 100 percent of total capital raised. Because the size of new issues can be lowered by a reduction in dividends, we have another argument in favor of a low-dividend policy.

Of course, our advice not to finance dividends through new stock issues might need to be modified somewhat in the real world. A company with a large and steady cash flow for many years in the past might be paying a regular dividend. If the cash flow unexpectedly dried up for a single year, should new stock be issued so that dividends could be continued? Although our previous discussion would imply that new stock should not be issued, many managers might issue the stock anyway for practical reasons. In particular, stockholders appear to prefer dividend stability. Thus, managers might be forced to issue stock to achieve this stability, knowing full well the adverse tax consequences.

FIRMS WITH SUFFICIENT CASH TO PAY A DIVIDEND

The previous discussion argued that in a world with personal taxes, a firm should not issue stock to pay a dividend. Does the tax disadvantage of dividends imply the stronger policy, "Never, under any circumstances, pay dividends in a world with personal taxes"?

We argue next that this prescription does not necessarily apply to firms with excess cash. To see this, imagine a firm with $1 million in extra cash after selecting all positive NPV projects and determining the level of prudent cash balances. The firm might consider the following alternatives to a dividend:

1. *Select additional capital budgeting projects.* Because the firm has taken all the available positive NPV projects already, it must invest its excess cash in negative NPV projects. This is clearly a policy at variance with the principles of corporate finance.

In spite of our distaste for this policy, researchers have suggested that many managers purposely take on negative NPV projects in lieu of paying dividends.[1] The idea here is that managers would rather keep the funds in the firm because their prestige, pay, and perquisites are often tied to the firm's size. Although managers may help themselves here, they are hurting stockholders. We broached this subject in the section titled "Free Cash Flow" in Chapter 17, and we will have more to say about it later in this chapter.

2. *Acquire other companies.* To avoid the payment of dividends, a firm might use excess cash to acquire another company. This strategy has the advantage of acquiring profitable assets. However, a firm often incurs heavy costs when it embarks on an acquisition program. In addition, acquisitions are invariably made above the market price. Premiums of 20 to 80 percent are not uncommon. Because of this, a number of researchers have argued that mergers are not generally profitable to the acquiring company, even when firms are merged for a valid business purpose. Therefore, a company making an acquisition merely to avoid a dividend is unlikely to succeed.

3. *Purchase financial assets.* The strategy of purchasing financial assets in lieu of a dividend payment can be illustrated with the following example.

EXAMPLE 19.1

Dividends and Taxes   The Regional Electric Company has $1,000 of extra cash. It can retain the cash and invest it in Treasury bills yielding 10 percent, or it can pay the cash to shareholders as a dividend. Shareholders can also invest in Treasury bills with the same yield. Suppose the corporate tax rate is 34 percent, and the personal tax rate is 28 percent for all individuals. However, the maximum tax rate on dividends is 15 percent. How much cash will investors have after five years under each policy?

If dividends are paid now, shareholders will receive:

$$\$1,000 \times (1 - .15) = \$850$$

today after taxes. Because their return after personal tax on Treasury bills is 7.2 [$=10 \times (1 - .28)$] percent, shareholders will have:

$$\$850 \times (1.072)^5 = \$1,203.35 \tag{19.3}$$

in five years. Note that interest income is taxed at the personal tax rate (28 percent in this example), but dividends are taxed at the lower rate of 15 percent.

If Regional Electric Company retains the cash to invest in Treasury bills, its aftertax interest rate will be .066 [$=.10 \times (1 - .34)$]. At the end of five years, the firm will have:

$$\$1,000 \times (1.066)^5 = \$1,376.53$$

If these proceeds are then paid as a dividend, the stockholders will receive:

$$\$1,376.53 \times (1 - .15) = \$1,170.05 \tag{19.4}$$

after personal taxes at Date 5. The value in Equation 19.3 is greater than that in Equation 19.4, implying that cash to stockholders will be greater if the firm pays the dividend now.

This example shows that for a firm with extra cash, the dividend payout decision will depend on personal and corporate tax rates. If personal tax rates are higher than corporate tax rates, a firm will have an incentive to reduce dividend payouts. However, if personal tax rates are lower than corporate tax rates, a firm will have an incentive to pay out any excess cash as dividends.

---

[1] See, for example, M. C. Jensen, "Agency Costs of Free Cash Flow, Corporate Finance, and Takeovers," *American Economic Review* (May 1986).

In the United States, both the highest marginal tax rate for individuals and the corporate tax rate were 35 percent in 2012. Because many investors face marginal tax rates well below the maximum, it appears that firms have an incentive not to hoard cash.

However, a quirk in the tax code provides an offsetting incentive. In particular, 70 percent of the dividends that one corporation receives from another corporation are excluded from corporate tax.[2] Individuals are not granted this exclusion. The quirk increases the likelihood that proceeds will be higher if the firm invests cash in other dividend-paying stocks rather than paying out cash as a dividend.

The firm's decision to invest in financial assets or to pay a dividend is a complex one, depending on the tax rate of the firm, the marginal tax rates of its investors, and the application of the dividend exclusion. While there are likely many real-world situations where the numbers favor investment in financial assets, few companies actually seem to hoard cash in this manner without limit. The reason is that Section 532 of the Internal Revenue Code penalizes firms exhibiting "improper accumulation of surplus." Thus, in the final analysis, the purchase of financial assets, like selecting negative NPV projects and acquiring other companies, does not obviate the need for companies with excess cash to pay dividends.

4. *Repurchase shares.* The example we described in the previous section showed that investors are indifferent between share repurchases and dividends in a world without taxes and transaction costs. However, under current tax law, stockholders generally prefer a repurchase to a dividend.

As an example, consider an individual receiving a dividend of $1 on each of 100 shares of a stock. With a 15 percent tax rate, that individual would pay taxes of $15 on the dividend. Selling shareholders would pay lower taxes if the firm repurchased $100 of existing shares. This occurs because taxes are paid only on the *profit* from a sale. The individual's gain on a sale would be only $40 if the shares sold for $100 were originally purchased for, say, $60. The capital gains tax would be $6 ($=.15 \times \$40$), a number below the tax on dividends of $15. Note that the tax from a repurchase is less than the tax on a dividend even though the same 15 percent tax rate applies to both the repurchase and the dividend.

Of all the alternatives to dividends mentioned in this section, the strongest case can be made for repurchases. In fact, academics have long wondered why firms *ever* pay a dividend instead of repurchasing stock. There have been at least two possible reasons for avoiding repurchases. First, Grullon and Michaely point out that in the past the Securities and Exchange Commission (SEC) had accused some firms undergoing share repurchase programs of illegal price manipulation.[3] However, these authors indicate that SEC Rule 10b-18, adopted in 1982, provides guidelines for firms to avoid the charge of price manipulation. These guidelines are relatively easy to follow, so firms should not have to worry about this charge today. In fact, Grullon and Michaely believe that the large increase in buyback programs in recent years is at least partially the result

---

[2]This exclusion applies if the firm owns less than 20 percent of the stock in the other company. The exclusion rises to 80 percent if the firm owns more than 20 percent of the stock of the other company and is 100 percent if the firm owns more than 80 percent of the stock of the other company. Corporations are not granted an exclusion for interest earned on bonds.

[3]See Gustavo Grullon and Roni Michaely, "Dividends, Share Repurchases, and the Substitution Hypothesis," *Journal of Finance* (August 2002), p. 1677.

of 10b-18. Second, the IRS can penalize firms repurchasing their own stocks if the only reason is to avoid the taxes that would be levied on dividends. However, this threat has not materialized with the growth in corporate repurchases. Thus, these two reasons do not seem to justify the avoidance of repurchases.

SUMMARY OF PERSONAL TAXES

This section suggests that because of personal taxes, firms have an incentive to reduce dividends. For example, they might increase capital expenditures, acquire other companies, or purchase financial assets. However, due to financial considerations and legal constraints, rational firms with large cash flows will likely exhaust these activities with plenty of cash left over for dividends.

It is harder to explain why firms pay dividends instead of repurchasing shares. The tax savings from repurchases can be significant, and fear of either the SEC or the IRS seems overblown. Academics are of two minds here. Some argue that corporations were simply slow to grasp the benefits from repurchases. However, since the idea has firmly caught on, the trend toward replacement of dividends with repurchases could continue. Others argue that companies have paid dividends all along for good reasons. We consider potential benefits of dividends in the next section.

19.6 Real-World Factors Favoring a High-Dividend Policy

The previous section pointed out that because individuals pay taxes on dividends, financial managers might seek ways to reduce dividends. While we discussed the problems with taking on more capital budgeting projects, acquiring other firms, and hoarding cash, we stated that a share repurchase has many of the benefits of a dividend with less of a tax disadvantage. This section considers reasons why a firm might pay its shareholders high dividends even in the presence of personal taxes on these dividends.

DESIRE FOR CURRENT INCOME

It has been argued that many individuals desire current income. The classic example is the group of retired people and others living on a fixed income. The argument further states that these individuals would bid up the stock price should dividends rise and bid down the stock price should dividends fall.

This argument does not hold in perfect capital markets because an individual preferring high current cash flow but holding low-dividend securities could easily sell off shares to provide the necessary funds. Thus in a world of no transaction costs, a high–current-dividend policy would be of no value to the stockholder.

However, the current income argument is relevant in the real world. Stock sales involve brokerage fees and other transaction costs—direct cash expenses that could be avoided by an investment in high-dividend securities. In addition, stock sales are time-consuming, further leading investors to buy high-dividend securities.

To put this argument in perspective, remember that financial intermediaries such as mutual funds can perform repackaging transactions at low cost. Such intermediaries could buy low-dividend stocks and, by a controlled policy of realizing gains, pay their investors at a higher rate.

BEHAVIORAL FINANCE

Suppose it turned out that the transaction costs in selling no-dividend securities could not account for the preference of investors for dividends. Would there still be a reason for high dividends? We introduced the topic of behavioral finance in Chapter 14, pointing out that the ideas of behaviorists represent a strong challenge to the theory of efficient capital markets. It turns out that behavioral finance also has an argument for high dividends.

The basic idea here concerns *self-control,* a concept that, though quite important in psychology, has received virtually no emphasis in finance. Although we cannot review all that psychology has to say about self-control, let's focus on one example—losing weight. Suppose Al Martin, a college student, just got back from the Christmas break more than a few pounds heavier than he would like. Everyone would probably agree that diet and exercise are the two ways to lose weight. But how should Al put this approach into practice? (We'll focus on exercise, though the same principle would apply to diet as well.) One way—let's call it the economists' way—would involve trying to make rational decisions. Each day Al would balance the costs and the benefits of exercising. Perhaps he would choose to exercise on most days because losing the weight is important to him. However, when he is too busy with exams, he might rationally choose not to exercise because he cannot afford the time. And he wants to be socially active as well. So he may rationally choose to avoid exercise on days when parties and other social commitments become too time-consuming.

This seems sensible—at first glance. The problem is that he must make a choice every day, and there may simply be too many days when his lack of self-control gets the better of him. He may tell himself that he doesn't have the time to exercise on a particular day, simply because he is starting to find exercise boring, not because he really doesn't have the time. Before long, he is avoiding exercise on most days—and overeating in reaction to the guilt from not exercising!

Is there an alternative? One way would be to set rigid rules. Perhaps Al decides to exercise five days a week *no matter what.* This is not necessarily the best approach for everyone, but there is no question that many of us (perhaps most of us) live by a set of rules. For example, Shefrin and Statman[4] suggest some typical rules:

- Jog at least two miles a day.
- Do not consume more than 1,200 calories per day.
- Bank the wife's salary and spend from only the husband's paycheck.
- Save at least 2 percent of every paycheck for children's college education and never withdraw from this fund.
- Never touch a drop of alcohol.

What does this have to do with dividends? Investors must also deal with self-control. Suppose a retiree wants to consume $20,000 a year from savings, in addition to Social Security and her pension. On one hand, she could buy stocks with a dividend yield high enough to generate $20,000 in dividends. On the other hand, she could place her savings in no-dividend stocks, selling off $20,000 each year for consumption. Though these two approaches seem equivalent financially, the second one may allow for too much leeway. If lack of self-control gets the better of her, she might sell off too

---

[4]Hersh M. Shefrin and Meir Statman, "Explaining Investor Preference for Cash Dividends," *Journal of Financial Economics* 13 (1984).

much, leaving little for her later years. Better, perhaps, to short-circuit this possibility by investing in dividend-paying stocks with a firm personal rule of *never* "dipping into principal." Although behaviorists do not claim that this approach is for everyone, they argue that enough people think this way to explain why firms pay dividends—even though, as we said earlier, dividends are tax disadvantaged.

Does behavioral finance argue for increased stock repurchases as well as increased dividends? The answer is no, because investors will sell the stock that firms repurchase. As we have said, selling stock involves too much leeway. Investors might sell too many shares of stock, leaving little for later years. Thus, the behaviorist argument may explain why companies pay dividends in a world with personal taxes.

AGENCY COSTS

Although stockholders, bondholders, and management form firms for mutually beneficial reasons, one party may later gain at the other's expense. For example, take the potential conflict between bondholders and stockholders. Bondholders would like stockholders to leave as much cash as possible in the firm so that this cash would be available to pay the bondholders during times of financial distress. Conversely, stockholders would like to keep this extra cash for themselves. That's where dividends come in. Managers, acting on behalf of the stockholders, may pay dividends simply to keep the cash away from the bondholders. In other words, a dividend can be viewed as a wealth transfer from bondholders to stockholders. There is empirical evidence for this view of things. For example, DeAngelo and DeAngelo find that firms in financial distress are reluctant to cut dividends.[5] Of course, bondholders know about the propensity of stockholders to transfer money out of the firm. To protect themselves, bondholders frequently create loan agreements stating that dividends can be paid only if the firm has earnings, cash flow, and working capital above specified levels.

Although managers may be looking out for stockholders in any conflict with bondholders, managers may pursue selfish goals at the expense of stockholders in other situations. For example, as discussed in a previous chapter, managers might pad expense accounts, take on pet projects with negative NPVs, or simply not work hard. Managers find it easier to pursue these selfish goals when the firm has plenty of free cash flow. After all, one cannot squander funds if the funds are not available in the first place. And that is where dividends come in. Several scholars have suggested that the board of directors can use dividends to reduce agency costs.[6] By paying dividends equal to the amount of "surplus" cash flow, a firm can reduce management's ability to squander the firm's resources.

This discussion suggests a reason for increased dividends, but the same argument applies to share repurchases as well. Managers, acting on behalf of stockholders, can just as easily keep cash from bondholders through repurchases as through dividends. And the board of directors, also acting on behalf of stockholders, can reduce the cash available to spendthrift managers just as easily through repurchases as through dividends. Thus, the presence of agency costs is not an argument for dividends over repurchases. Rather, agency costs imply firms may increase either dividends or share repurchases rather than hoard large amounts of cash.

---

[5]H. DeAngelo and L. DeAngelo, "Dividend Policy and Financial Distress: An Empirical Investigation of Troubled NYSE Firms," *Journal of Finance* 45 (1990).

[6]Michael Rozeff, "How Companies Set Their Dividend Payout Ratios," in *The Revolution in Corporate Finance,* edited by Joel M. Stern and Donald H. Chew (New York: Basil Blackwell, 1986). See also Robert S. Hansen, Raman Kumar, and Dilip K. Shome, "Dividend Policy and Corporate Monitoring: Evidence from the Regulated Electric Utility Industry," *Financial Management* (Spring 1994).

INFORMATION CONTENT OF DIVIDENDS AND DIVIDEND SIGNALING

Information Content   While there are many things researchers do not know about dividends, we know one thing for sure: The stock price of a firm generally rises when the firm announces a dividend increase and generally falls when a dividend reduction is announced. For example, Asquith and Mullins estimate that stock prices rise about 3 percent following announcements of dividend initiations.[7] Michaely, Thaler, and Womack find that stock prices fall about 7 percent following announcements of dividend omissions.[8]

The question is how we should *interpret* this empirical evidence. Consider the following three positions on dividends:

1.   From the homemade dividend argument of MM, dividend policy is irrelevant, given that future earnings (and cash flow) are held constant.

2.   Because of tax effects, a firm's stock price is negatively related to the current dividend when future earnings (or cash flow) are held constant.

3.   Because of stockholders' desire for current income, a firm's stock price is positively related to its current dividend, even when future earnings (or cash flow) are held constant.

At first glance, the empirical evidence that stock prices rise when dividend increases are announced may seem consistent with Position 3 and inconsistent with Positions 1 and 2. In fact, many writers have said this. However, other authors have countered that the observation itself is consistent with all three positions. They point out that companies do not like to cut a dividend. Thus, firms will raise the dividend only when future earnings, cash flow, and so on are expected to rise enough so that the dividend is not likely to be reduced later to its original level. A dividend increase is management's *signal* to the market that the firm is expected to do well.

It is the expectation of good times, and not only the stockholders' affinity for current income, that raises the stock price. The rise in the stock price following the dividend signal is called the **information content effect** of the dividend. To recapitulate, imagine that the stock price is unaffected or even negatively affected by the level of dividends, given that future earnings (or cash flow) are held constant. Nevertheless, the information content effect implies that the stock price may rise when dividends are raised—if dividends simultaneously cause stockholders to *increase* their expectations of future earnings and cash flow.

Dividend Signaling   We just argued that the market infers a rise in earnings and cash flows from a dividend increase, leading to a higher stock price. Conversely, the market infers a decrease in cash flows from a dividend reduction, leading to a fall in stock price. This raises an interesting corporate strategy: Could management increase dividends just to make the market *think* that cash flows will be higher, even when management knows that cash flows will not rise?

While this strategy may seem dishonest, academics take the position that managers frequently attempt the strategy. Academics begin with the following accounting identity for an all-equity firm:

$$\text{Cash flow}^9 = \text{Capital expenditures} + \text{Dividends} \tag{19.5}$$

[7]P. Asquith and D. Mullins, Jr., "The Impact of Initiating Dividend Payments on Shareholders' Wealth," *Journal of Business* (January 1983).

[8]R. Michaely, R. H. Thaler, and K. Womack, "Price Reactions to Dividend Initiations and Omissions: Overreactions or Drift?" *Journal of Finance* 50 (1995).

[9]The correct representation of Equation 19.5 involves cash flow, not earnings. However, with little loss of understanding, we could discuss dividend signaling in terms of earnings, not cash flow.

Equation 19.5 must hold if a firm is neither issuing nor repurchasing stock. That is, the cash flow from the firm must go somewhere. If it is not paid out in dividends, it must be used in some expenditure. Whether the expenditure involves a capital budgeting project or a purchase of Treasury bills, it is still an expenditure.

Imagine that we are in the middle of the year and investors are trying to make some forecast of cash flow over the entire year. These investors may use Equation 19.5 to estimate cash flow. For example, suppose the firm announces that current dividends will be $50 million and the market believes that capital expenditures are $80 million. The market would then determine cash flow to be $130 million (=$50 + $80).

Now, suppose that the firm had, alternatively, announced a dividend of $70 million. The market might assume that cash flow remains at $130 million, implying capital expenditures of $60 million (=$130 − $70). Here, the increase in dividends would hurt stock price because the market anticipates valuable capital expenditures will be crowded out. Alternatively, the market might assume that capital expenditures remain at $80 million, implying the estimate of cash flow to be $150 million (=$70 + $80). Stock price would likely rise here because stock prices usually increase with cash flow. In general, academics believe that models where investors assume capital expenditures remain the same are more realistic. Thus, an increase in dividends raises stock price.

Now we come to the incentives of managers to fool the public. Suppose you are a manager who wants to boost stock price, perhaps because you are planning to sell some of your personal holdings of the company's stock immediately. You might increase dividends so that the market would raise its estimate of the firm's cash flow, thereby also boosting the current stock price.

If this strategy is appealing, would anything prevent you from raising dividends without limit? The answer is yes because there is also a *cost* to raising dividends. That is, the firm will have to forgo some of its profitable projects. Remember that cash flow in Equation 19.5 is a constant, so an increase in dividends is obtained only by a reduction in capital expenditures. At some point the market will learn that cash flow has not increased, but instead profitable capital expenditures have been cut. Once the market absorbs this information, stock price should fall below what it would have been had dividends never been raised. Thus, if you plan to sell, say, half of your shares and retain the other half, an increase in dividends should help you on the immediate sale but hurt you when you sell your remaining shares years later. So your decision on the level of dividends will be based, among other things, on the timing of your personal stock sales.

This is a simplified example of dividend signaling, where the manager sets dividend policy based on maximum benefit for himself.[10] Alternatively, a given manager may have no desire to sell his shares immediately but knows that, at any one time, plenty of ordinary shareholders will want to do so. Thus, for the benefit of shareholders in general, a manager will always be aware of the trade-off between current and future stock price. And this, then, is the essence of signaling with dividends. It is not enough for a manager to set dividend policy to maximize the true (or intrinsic) value of the firm. He must also consider the effect of dividend policy on the current stock price, even if the current stock price does not reflect true value.

Does a motive to signal imply that managers will increase dividends rather than share repurchases? The answer is likely no: Most academic models imply that

---

[10]Papers examining fully developed models of signaling include S. Bhattacharya, "Imperfect Information, Dividend Policy, and 'the Bird in the Hand' Fallacy," *Bell Journal of Economics* 10 (1979); S. Bhattacharya, "Non-dissipative Signaling Structure and Dividend Policy," *Quarterly Journal of Economics* 95 (1980), p. 1; S. Ross, "The Determination of Financial Structure: The Incentive Signalling Approach," *Bell Journal of Economics* 8 (1977), p. 1; M. Miller and K. Rock, "Dividend Policy under Asymmetric Information," *Journal of Finance* (1985).

dividends and share repurchases are perfect substitutes.[11] Rather, these models indicate that managers will consider reducing capital spending (even on projects with positive NPVs) to increase either dividends or share repurchases.

19.7 The Clientele Effect: A Resolution of Real-World Factors?

In the previous two sections, we pointed out that the existence of personal taxes favors a low-dividend policy, whereas other factors favor high dividends. The financial profession had hoped that it would be easy to determine which of these sets of factors dominates. Unfortunately, after years of research, no one has been able to conclude which of the two is more important. This is surprising: we might be skeptical that the two sets of factors would cancel each other out so perfectly.

However, one particular idea, known as the *clientele effect,* implies that the two sets of factors are likely to cancel each other out after all. To understand this idea, let's separate investors in high tax brackets from those in low tax brackets. Individuals in high tax brackets likely prefer either no or low dividends. Low tax bracket investors generally fall into three categories. First, there are individual investors in low brackets. They are likely to prefer some dividends if they desire current income. Second, pension funds pay no taxes on either dividends or capital gains. Because they face no tax consequences, pension funds will also prefer dividends if they have a preference for current income. Finally, corporations can exclude at least 70 percent of their dividend income but cannot exclude any of their capital gains. Thus, corporations are likely to prefer high-dividend stocks, even without a preference for current income.

Suppose that 40 percent of all investors prefer high dividends and 60 percent prefer low dividends, yet only 20 percent of firms pay high dividends while 80 percent pay low dividends. Here, the high-dividend firms will be in short supply, implying that their stock should be bid up while the stock of low-dividend firms should be bid down.

However, the dividend policies of all firms need not be fixed in the long run. In this example, we would expect enough low-dividend firms to increase their payout so that 40 percent of the firms pay high dividends and 60 percent of the firms pay low dividends. After this adjustment, no firm will gain from changing its dividend policy. Once payouts of corporations conform to the desires of stockholders, no single firm can affect its market value by switching from one dividend strategy to another.

Clienteles are likely to form in the following way:

Group	Stocks
Individuals in high tax brackets	Zero- to low-payout stocks
Individuals in low tax brackets	Low- to medium-payout stocks
Tax-free institutions	Medium-payout stocks
Corporations	High-payout stocks

---

[11]Signaling models where dividends and repurchases are not perfect substitutes are contained in Franklin Allen, Antonio Bernardo, and Ivo Welch, "A Theory of Dividends Based on Tax Clienteles," *Journal of Finance* (2002) and Kose John and Joseph Williams, "Dividends, Dilution and Taxes: A Signalling Equilibrium," *Journal of Finance* (1985).

Figure 19.6
**Preferences of
Investors for
Dividend Yield**

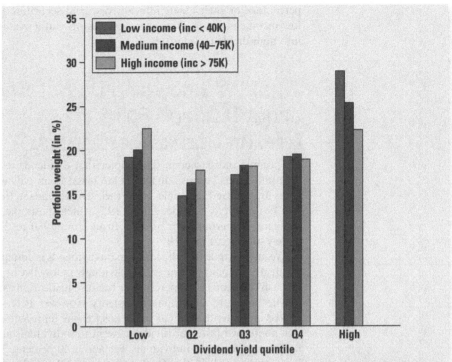

All stocks are ranked on their dividend yields and placed into five quintile portfolios. The figure shows the weight of each quintile in the portfolios of low-, medium-, and high-income investors. Relative to those with lower income, high-income investors place a greater percentage of their assets in low-dividend stocks and a smaller percentage in high-dividend stocks.

SOURCE: Adapted from Figure 2 of John Graham and Alok Kumar, "Do Dividend Clienteles Exist? Evidence on Dividend Preferences of Retail Investors," *Journal of Finance* 61 (2006), pp. 1305–36.

To see if you understand the clientele effect, consider the following statement: "In a world where many investors like high dividends, a firm can boost its share price by increasing its dividend payout ratio." True or false?

The statement is likely to be false. As long as there are already enough high-dividend firms to satisfy dividend-loving investors, a firm will not be able to boost its share price by paying high dividends. A firm can boost its stock price only if an *unsatisfied* clientele exists.

Our discussion of clienteles followed from the fact that tax brackets vary across investors. If shareholders care about taxes, stocks should attract clienteles based on dividend yield. Is there any evidence that this is the case?

Consider Figure 19.6. Here, John Graham and Alok Kumar[12] rank common stocks by their dividend yields (the ratio of dividend to stock price) and place them into five portfolios, called quintiles. The bottom quintile contains the 20 percent of stocks with the lowest dividend yields; the next quintile contains the 20 percent of stocks with the next lowest dividend yields; and so on. The figure shows the weight of each quintile in the portfolios of low-, medium-, and high-income investors. As can be seen, relative to low-income investors, high-income investors put a greater

---

[12]John Graham and Alok Kumar, "Do Dividend Clienteles Exist? Evidence on Dividend Preferences of Retail Investors," *Journal of Finance* (June 2006).

602   **Part IV**   Capital Structure and Dividend Policy

percentage of their assets into low-dividend securities. Conversely, again relative to low-income investors, high-income investors put a smaller percentage of their assets into high-dividend securities.

19.8 What We Know and Do Not Know about Dividend Policy

CORPORATE DIVIDENDS ARE SUBSTANTIAL

We pointed out earlier in the chapter that dividends are tax disadvantaged relative to capital gains because dividends are taxed upon payment whereas taxes on capital gains are deferred until sale. Nevertheless, dividends in the U.S. economy are substantial. For example, consider Figure 19.7, which shows the ratio of aggregate dividends to aggregate earnings for all U.S. firms from 1980 to 2010. The ratio was approximately 61 percent in 2010.

We might argue that the taxation on dividends is actually minimal, perhaps because dividends are paid primarily to individuals in low tax brackets (currently the tax rate on cash dividends is 15 percent) or because institutions such as pension funds, which pay no taxes, are the primary recipients. However, Peterson, Peterson, and Ang conducted an in-depth study of dividends for one representative year, 1979.[13] They found that about two-thirds of dividends went to individuals and that the average marginal tax bracket for these individuals was about 40 percent. Thus, we must conclude that large amounts of dividends are paid, even in the presence of substantial taxation.

Figure 19.7
Ratio of Aggregate Dividends to Aggregate Earnings for All U.S. Firms: 1980 to 2010

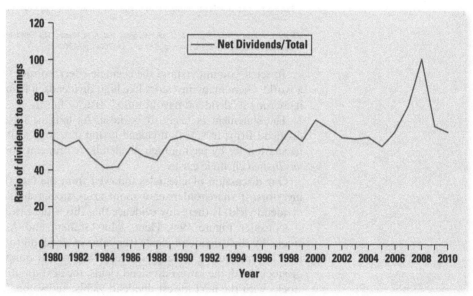

SOURCE: *The Economic Report of the President*, February 2008, Table B-90.

---

[13]P. Peterson, D. Peterson, and J. Ang, "Direct Evidence on the Marginal Rate of Taxation on Dividend Income," *Journal of Financial Economics* 14 (1985).

Chapter 19 Dividends and Other Payouts | **603**

FEWER COMPANIES PAY DIVIDENDS

Although dividends are substantial, Fama and French (FF) point out that the percentage of companies paying dividends has fallen over the last few decades.[14] FF argue that the decline was caused primarily by an explosion of small, currently unprofitable companies that have recently listed on various stock exchanges. For the most part, firms of this type do not pay dividends. Figure 19.8 shows that the proportion of dividend payers among U.S. industrial firms dropped substantially from 1973 to 2002.

This figure, presented in a paper by DeAngelo, DeAngelo, and Skinner[15] also shows an *increase* in the proportion of dividend payers from 2002 to 2010. One obvious explanation is the cut in the maximum tax rate on dividends to 15 percent, signed into law in May 2003. However, DeAngelo, DeAngelo, and Skinner downplay the effect of the tax cut, suggesting a number of other reasons. It should be noted, the resurgence in dividend payers has been observed only over the two-year period from 2002 to 2004.

Figure 19.8 does not imply that dividends across *all* firms declined from 1973 to 2002. DeAngelo, DeAngelo, and Skinner[16] point out that while small firms have shied away from dividends, the largest firms have substantially increased their dividends over recent decades. This increase has created such concentration in dividends

Figure 19.8
Proportion of Dividend Payers among All U.S. Industrial Firms

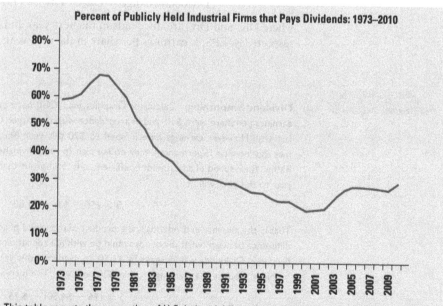

This table reports the proportion of U.S. industrial firms that paid dividends over the years from 1973 to 2010. The proportion dropped significantly from 1973 to 2002, with a rebound over the next two years.

SOURCE: Harry DeAngelo, Linda DeAngelo, and Douglas J. Skinner, "Corporate Payout Policy," in *Foundations and Trends in Finance*, vol. 3 (2008). Data updated by DeAngelo, DeAngelo, and Skinner.

---

[14]E. F. Fama and K. R. French, "Disappearing Dividends: Changing Firm Characteristics or Lower Propensity to Pay?" *Journal of Financial Economics* (April 2001).

[15]Harry DeAngelo, Linda DeAngelo, and Douglas J. Skinner, "Corporate Payout Policy," in *Foundations and Trends in Finance*, vol. 3 (2008). Data updated by the authors.

[16]Harry DeAngelo, Linda DeAngelo, and Douglas J. Skinner, "Are Dividends Disappearing? Dividend Concentration and the Consolidation of Earnings," *Journal of Financial Economics* (2004).

that the 25 top dividend-paying firms accounted for more than 50 percent of aggregate dividends in the United States in 2000. DeAngelo and colleagues suggest that "Industrial firms exhibit a two-tier structure in which a small number of firms with very high earnings generates the majority of earnings and dominates the dividend supply, while the majority of firms has at best a modest impact on aggregate earnings and dividends."

CORPORATIONS SMOOTH DIVIDENDS

In 1956, John Lintner made two important observations concerning dividend policy that still ring true.[17] First, real-world companies typically set long-term target ratios of dividends to earnings. A firm is likely to set a low target ratio if it has many positive NPV projects relative to available cash flow and a high ratio if it has few positive NPV projects. Second, managers know that only part of any change in earnings is likely to be permanent. Because managers need time to assess the permanence of any earnings rise, dividend changes appear to lag earnings changes by a number of periods.

Taken together, Lintner's observations suggest that two parameters describe dividend policy: the target payout ratio (t) and the speed of adjustment of current dividends to the target (s). Dividend changes will tend to conform to the following model:

$$\text{Dividend change} \equiv \text{Div}_1 - \text{Div}_0 = s \cdot (t\text{EPS}_1 - \text{Div}_0) \tag{19.6}$$

where Div_1 and Div_0 are dividends in the next year and dividends in the current year, respectively. EPS_1 is earnings per share in the next year.

EXAMPLE 19.2

Dividend Smoothing Calculator Graphics, Inc., (CGI) has a target payout ratio of .30. Last year's earnings per share were $10, and in accordance with the target, CGI paid dividends of $3 per share last year. However, earnings have jumped to $20 this year. Because the managers do not believe that this increase is permanent, they do *not* plan to raise dividends all the way to $6 (=.30 × $20). Rather, their speed of adjustment coefficient, s, is .5, implying that the *increase* in dividends from last year to this year will be:

$$.5 \times (\$6 - \$3) = \$1.50$$

That is, the increase in dividends is the product of the speed of adjustment coefficient, .50, times the difference between what dividends would be with full adjustment [$6 (=.30 × $20)] and last year's dividends. Dividends will increase by $1.50, so dividends this year will be $4.50 (=$3 + $1.50).

Now, suppose that earnings stay at $20 next year. The increase in dividends next year will be:

$$.5 \times (\$6 - \$4.50) = \$.75$$

In words, the increase in dividends from this year to next year will be the speed of adjustment coefficient (.50) times the difference between what dividends would have been next year with full adjustment ($6) and this year's dividends ($4.50). Because dividends will increase by $.75, dividends next year will be $5.25 (=$4.50 + $.75). In this way, dividends will slowly rise every year if earnings in all future years remain at $20. However, dividends will reach $6 only at infinity.

---

[17]J. Lintner, "Distribution of Incomes of Corporations among Dividends, Retained Earnings, and Taxes," *American Economic Review* (May 1956).

The limiting cases in Equation 19.6 occur when $s = 1$ and $s = 0$. If $s = 1$, the actual change in dividends will be equal to the target change in dividends. Here, full adjustment occurs immediately. If $s = 0$, $\text{Div}_1 = \text{Div}_0$. In other words, there is no change in dividends at all. Real-world companies can be expected to set s between 0 and 1.

An implication of Lintner's model is that the dividends-to-earnings ratio rises when a company begins a period of bad times, and the ratio falls when a company starts a period of good times. Thus, dividends display less variability than do earnings. In other words, firms *smooth* dividends.

The Pros and Cons of Paying Dividends

Pros	Cons
1. Dividends may appeal to investors who desire stable cash flow but do not want to incur the transaction costs from periodically selling shares of stock.	1. Dividends have been traditionally taxed as ordinary income.
2. Behavioral finance argues that investors with limited self-control can meet current consumption needs with high-dividend stocks while adhering to the policy of never dipping into principal.	2. Dividends can reduce internal sources of financing. Dividends may force the firm to forgo positive NPV projects or to rely on costly external equity financing.
3. Managers, acting on behalf of stockholders, can pay dividends in order to keep cash from bondholders.	3. Once established, dividend cuts are hard to make without adversely affecting a firm's stock price.
4. The board of directors, acting on behalf of stockholders, can use dividends to reduce the cash available to spendthrift managers.	
5. Managers may increase dividends to signal their optimism concerning future cash flow.	

SOME SURVEY EVIDENCE ABOUT DIVIDENDS

A recent study surveyed a large number of financial executives regarding dividend policy. One of the questions asked was this: "Do these statements describe factors that affect your company's dividend decisions?" Table 19.2 shows some of the results.

As shown in Table 19.2, financial managers are very disinclined to cut dividends. Moreover, they are very conscious of their previous dividends and desire to maintain a relatively steady dividend. In contrast, the cost of external capital and the desire to attract "prudent man" investors (those with fiduciary duties) are less important.

Table 19.3 is drawn from the same survey, but here the responses are to the question, "How important are the following factors to your company's dividend decisions?" Not surprisingly given the responses in Table 19.2 and our earlier discussion,

Table 19.2
Survey Responses on Dividend Decisions*

Policy Statements	Percentage Who Agree or Strongly Agree
1. We try to avoid reducing dividends per share.	93.8%
2. We try to maintain a smooth dividend from year to year.	89.6
3. We consider the level of dividends per share that we have paid in recent quarters.	88.2
4. We are reluctant to make dividend changes that might have to be reversed in the future.	77.9
5. We consider the change or growth in dividends per share.	66.7
6. We consider the cost of raising external capital to be smaller than the cost of cutting dividends.	42.8
7. We pay dividends to attract investors subject to "prudent man" investment restrictions.	41.7

*Survey respondents were asked the question, "Do these statements describe factors that affect your company's dividend decisions?"

SOURCE: Adapted from Table 4 of A. Brav, J. R. Graham, C. R. Harvey, and R. Michaely, "Payout Policy in the 21st Century," *Journal of Financial Economics* (2005).

the highest priority is maintaining a consistent dividend policy. The next several items are also consistent with our previous analysis. Financial managers are very concerned about earnings stability and future earnings levels in making dividend decisions, and they consider the availability of good investment opportunities. Survey respondents also believed that attracting both institutional and individual (retail) investors was relatively important.

In contrast to our discussion in the earlier part of this chapter of taxes and flotation costs, the financial managers in this survey did not think that personal taxes paid on dividends by shareholders are very important. And even fewer think that equity flotation costs are relevant.

Table 19.3
Survey Responses on Dividend Decisions*

Policy Statements	Percentage Who Think This Is Important or Very Important
1. Maintaining consistency with our historic dividend policy.	84.1%
2. Stability of future earnings.	71.9
3. A sustainable change in earnings.	67.1
4. Attracting institutional investors to purchase our stock.	52.5
5. The availability of good investment opportunities for our firm to pursue.	47.6
6. Attracting retail investors to purchase our stock.	44.5
7. Personal taxes our stockholders pay when receiving dividends.	21.1
8. Flotation costs to issuing new equity.	9.3

*Survey respondents were asked the question, "How important are the following factors to your company's dividend decisions?"

SOURCE: Adapted from Table 5 of A. Brav, J. R. Graham, C. R. Harvey, and R. Michaely, "Payout Policy in the 21st Century," *Journal of Financial Economics* (2005).

19.9 Putting It All Together

Much of what we have discussed in this chapter (and much of what we know about dividends from decades of research) can be pulled together and summarized in the following six points:[18]

1. Aggregate dividend and stock repurchases are massive, and they have increased steadily in nominal and real terms over the years.

2. Cash dividends and repurchases are heavily concentrated among a relatively small number of large, mature firms.

3. Managers are very reluctant to cut dividends, normally doing so only due to firm-specific problems.

4. Managers smooth dividends, raising them slowly and incrementally as earnings grow.

5. Stock prices react to unanticipated changes in dividends.

6. The magnitude of stock repurchases tends to vary with transitory earnings.

The challenge now is to fit these six pieces into a reasonably coherent picture. With regard to payouts in general, meaning the combination of stock repurchases and cash dividends, a simple life cycle theory fits Points 1 and 2. The key ideas are straightforward. First, relatively young firms with less available cash generally should not make cash distributions. They need the cash to fund positive NPV projects (and flotation costs discourage the raising of outside cash).

However, as a firm survives and matures, it begins to generate free cash flow (which, you will recall, is internally generated cash flow beyond that needed to fund profitable investment activities). Significant free cash flow can lead to agency problems if it is not distributed. Managers may become tempted to pursue empire building or otherwise spend the excess cash in ways not in the shareholders' best interests. Thus, firms come under shareholder pressure to make distributions rather than hoard cash. And, consistent with what we observe, we expect large firms with a history of profitability to make large distributions.

Thus, the life cycle theory says that firms trade off the agency costs of excess cash retention against the potential future costs of external equity financing. A firm should begin making distributions when it generates sufficient internal cash flow to fund its investment needs now and into the foreseeable future.

The more complex issue concerns the type of distribution, cash dividends versus repurchase. The tax argument in favor of repurchases is a clear and strong one. Repurchases are a much more flexible option (and managers greatly value financial flexibility), so the question is: Why would firms ever choose a cash dividend?

If we are to answer this question, we have to ask a different question. What can a cash dividend accomplish that a share repurchase cannot? One answer is that when a firm makes a commitment to pay a cash dividend now and into the future, it sends a two-part signal to the markets. As we have already discussed, one signal is that the firm anticipates being profitable, with the ability to make the payments on an ongoing basis. Note that a firm cannot benefit by trying to fool the market in this regard because the firm would ultimately be punished when it couldn't make the dividend

---

[18]This list is distilled in part from a longer list in Harry DeAngelo and Linda DeAngelo, "Payout Policy Pedagogy: What Matters and Why," *European Financial Management* 13 (2007).

payment (or couldn't make it without relying on external financing). Thus, a cash dividend may let a firm distinguish itself from less profitable rivals.

A second, and more subtle, signal takes us back to the agency problem of free cash flow. By committing to pay cash dividends now and in the future, the firm signals that it won't be hoarding cash (or at least not as much cash), thereby reducing agency costs and enhancing shareholder wealth.

This two-part signaling story is consistent with Points 3 to 5 on the previous page, but an obvious objection remains. Why don't firms just commit to a policy of setting aside whatever money would be used to pay dividends and use it instead to buy back shares? After all, either way, a firm is committing to pay out cash to shareholders.

A fixed repurchase strategy suffers from two drawbacks. The first is verifiability. A firm could announce an open market repurchase and then simply not do it. By suitably fudging its books, it would be some time before the deception was discovered. Thus, it would be necessary for shareholders to develop a monitoring mechanism, meaning some sort of way for stockholders to know for sure that the repurchase was in fact done. Such a mechanism wouldn't be difficult to build (it could be a simple trustee relationship such as we observe in the bond markets), but it currently does not exist. Of course, a tender offer repurchase needs little or no verification, but such offers have expenses associated with them. The beauty of a cash dividend is that it needs no monitoring. A firm is forced to cut and mail checks four times a year, year in and year out.

Characteristics of a Sensible Payout Policy

- Over time pay out all free cash flows.
- Avoid cutting positive NPV projects to pay dividends or buy back shares.
- Do not initiate dividends until the firm is generating substantial free cash flow.
- Set the current regular dividend consistent with a long-run target payout ratio.
- Set the level of dividends low enough to avoid expensive future external financing.
- Use repurchases to distribute transitory cash flow increases.

A second objection to a fixed repurchase strategy is more controversial. Suppose managers, as insiders, are better able than stockholders to judge whether their stock price is too high or too low. (Note that this idea does not conflict with semistrong market efficiency if inside information is the reason.) In this case, a fixed repurchase commitment forces management to buy back stock even in circumstances when the stock is overvalued. In other words, it forces management into making negative NPV investments.

More research on the cash dividend versus share repurchase question is needed, but the historical trend seems to be favoring continued growth in repurchases relative to dividends. Total corporate payouts seem to be relatively stable over time at roughly 20 percent of aggregate earnings, but repurchases are becoming a larger portion of that total. The split reached about 50−50 in the latter part of the 1990s, but it looks like aggregate repurchases have recently passed aggregate dividends.

One aspect of aggregate cash dividends that has not received much attention is that there may be a strong legacy effect. Before 1982, the regulatory status of stock repurchases was somewhat murky, creating a significant disincentive. In 1982, the SEC, after years of debate, created a clear set of guidelines for firms to follow, thereby making repurchases much more attractive.

The legacy effect arises because many of the giant firms that pay such a large portion of aggregate dividends were paying dividends before (and perhaps long before) 1982. To the extent that these firms are unwilling to cut their dividends, aggregate cash dividends will be large, but only because of a "lock-in" effect for older firms. If locked-in, legacy payers account for much of the aggregate dividend, what we should observe is (1) a sharply reduced tendency for maturing firms to initiate dividends and (2) a growth in repurchases relative to cash dividends over time. We actually do see evidence of both of these trends; however, as the case of Microsoft clearly shows, legacy effects alone can't account for all cash dividend payers.

19.10 Stock Dividends and Stock Splits

Another type of dividend is paid out in shares of stock. This type of dividend is called a **stock dividend.** A stock dividend is not a true dividend because it is not paid in cash. The effect of a stock dividend is to increase the number of shares that each owner holds. Because there are more shares outstanding, each is simply worth less.

A stock dividend is commonly expressed as a percentage; for example, a 20 percent stock dividend means that a shareholder receives one new share for every five currently owned (a 20 percent increase). Because every shareholder receives 20 percent more stock, the total number of shares outstanding rises by 20 percent. As we will see in a moment, the result is that each share of stock is worth about 20 percent less.

A **stock split** is essentially the same thing as a stock dividend, except that a split is expressed as a ratio instead of a percentage. When a split is declared, each share is split up to create additional shares. For example, in a three-for-one stock split, each old share is split into three new shares.

Information on upcoming stock splits is available on the splits calendar at **www. investmenthouse. com** and **finance.yahoo.com**.

SOME DETAILS ABOUT STOCK SPLITS AND STOCK DIVIDENDS

Stock splits and stock dividends have essentially the same impacts on the corporation and the shareholder. They increase the number of shares outstanding and reduce the value per share. The accounting treatment is not the same, however, and it depends on two things: (1) whether the distribution is a stock split or a stock dividend and (2) the size of the stock dividend if it is called a dividend.

By convention, stock dividends of less than 20 to 25 percent are called *small stock dividends.* The accounting procedure for such a dividend is discussed next. A stock dividend greater than this value of 20 to 25 percent is called a *large stock dividend.* Large stock dividends are not uncommon. For example, in October 2010, water heater manufacturer A.O. Smith announced a three-for-two stock split in the form of a 50 percent stock dividend. The same month, automotive supplier Magna International announced a two-for-one stock split in the form of a 100 percent stock dividend. Except for some relatively minor accounting differences, this has the same effect as a two-for-one stock split.

Example of a Small Stock Dividend   The Peterson Co., a consulting firm specializing in difficult accounting problems, has 10,000 shares of stock outstanding, each selling at $66. The total market value of the equity is $66 × 10,000 = $660,000. With a 10 percent stock dividend, each stockholder receives one additional share for each 10 owned, and the total number of shares outstanding after the dividend is 11,000.

Before the stock dividend, the equity portion of Peterson's balance sheet might look like this:

Common stock ($1 par, 10,000 shares outstanding)	$ 10,000
Capital in excess of par value	200,000
Retained earnings	290,000
Total owners' equity	$500,000

A seemingly arbitrary accounting procedure is used to adjust the balance sheet after a small stock dividend. Because 1,000 new shares are issued, the common stock account is increased by $1,000 (1,000 shares at $1 par value each), for a total of $11,000. The market price of $66 is $65 greater than the par value, so the "excess" of $65 × 1,000 shares = $65,000 is added to the capital surplus account (capital in excess of par value), producing a total of $265,000.

Total owners' equity is unaffected by the stock dividend because no cash has come in or out, so retained earnings are reduced by the entire $66,000, leaving $224,000. The net effect of these machinations is that Peterson's equity accounts now look like this:

Common stock ($1 par, 11,000 shares outstanding)	$ 11,000
Capital in excess of par value	265,000
Retained earnings	224,000
Total owners' equity	$500,000

Example of a Stock Split   A stock split is conceptually similar to a stock dividend, but it is commonly expressed as a ratio. For example, in a three-for-two split, each shareholder receives one additional share of stock for each two held originally, so a three-for-two split amounts to a 50 percent stock dividend. Again, no cash is paid out, and the percentage of the entire firm that each shareholder owns is unaffected.

The accounting treatment of a stock split is a little different from (and simpler than) that of a stock dividend. Suppose Peterson decides to declare a two-for-one stock split. The number of shares outstanding will double to 20,000, and the par value will be halved to $.50 per share. The owners' equity after the split is represented as follows:

For a list of recent stock splits, try **www.stocksplits. net**.

Common stock ($.50 par, 20,000 shares outstanding)	$ 10,000
Capital in excess of par value	200,000
Retained earnings	290,000
Total owners' equity	$500,000

Note that for all three of the categories, the figures on the right are completely unaffected by the split. The only changes are in the par value per share and the number of shares outstanding. Because the number of shares has doubled, the par value of each is cut in half.

Example of a Large Stock Dividend   In our example, if a 100 percent stock dividend were declared, 10,000 new shares would be distributed, so 20,000 shares would be outstanding. At a $1 par value per share, the common stock account would rise by $10,000, for a total of $20,000. The retained earnings account would be reduced by $10,000, leaving $280,000. The result would be the following:

Common stock ($1 par, 20,000 shares outstanding)	$ 20,000
Capital in excess of par value	200,000
Retained earnings	280,000
Total owners' equity	$500,000

VALUE OF STOCK SPLITS AND STOCK DIVIDENDS

The laws of logic tell us that stock splits and stock dividends can (1) leave the value of the firm unaffected, (2) increase its value, or (3) decrease its value. Unfortunately, the issues are complex enough that we cannot easily determine which of the three relationships holds.

The Benchmark Case   A strong case can be made that stock dividends and splits do not change either the wealth of any shareholder or the wealth of the firm as a whole. In our preceding example, the equity had a total market value of $660,000. With the small stock dividend, the number of shares increased to 11,000, so it seems that each would be worth $660,000/11,000 = $60.

For example, a shareholder who had 100 shares worth $66 each before the dividend would have 110 shares worth $60 each afterward. The total value of the stock is $6,600 either way; so the stock dividend doesn't really have any economic effect.

After the stock split, there are 20,000 shares outstanding, so each should be worth $660,000/20,000 = $33. In other words, the number of shares doubles and the price halves. From these calculations, it appears that stock dividends and splits are just paper transactions.

Although these results are relatively obvious, there are reasons that are often given to suggest that there may be some benefits to these actions. The typical financial manager is aware of many real-world complexities, and for that reason the stock split or stock dividend decision is not treated lightly in practice.

Popular Trading Range   Proponents of stock dividends and stock splits frequently argue that a security has a proper **trading range.** When the security is priced above this level, many investors do not have the funds to buy the common trading unit of 100 shares, called a *round lot.* Although securities can be purchased in *odd-lot* form (fewer than 100 shares), the commissions are greater. Thus, firms will split the stock to keep the price in this trading range.

For example, in early 2003, Microsoft announced a two-for-one stock split. This was the ninth split for Microsoft since the company went public in 1986. The stock had split three-for-two on two occasions and two-for-one a total of seven times. So for every share of Microsoft you owned in 1986 when the company first went public, you would own 288 shares as of the most recent stock split in 2003. Similarly, since Walmart went public in 1970, it has split its stock two-for-one 11 times, and Dell Computer has split three-for-two once and two-for-one 6 times since going public in 1988.

Although this argument of a trading range is a popular one, its validity is questionable for a number of reasons. Mutual funds, pension funds, and other institutions have steadily increased their trading activity since World War II and now handle a sizable percentage of total trading volume (on the order of 80 percent of NYSE trading volume, for example). Because these institutions buy and sell in huge amounts, the individual share price is of little concern.

Furthermore, we sometimes observe share prices that are quite large that do not appear to cause problems. To take an extreme case, consider the Swiss chocolatier Lindt. In July 2011, Lindt shares were selling for around 26,387 Swiss francs each, or about $37,247. A round lot would have cost a cool $3.72 million. This is fairly expensive, but also consider Berkshire-Hathaway, the company run by legendary investor Warren Buffett. In July 2011, each share in the company sold for about $113,000, down from a high of $151,650 in December 2007.

Finally, there is evidence that stock splits may actually decrease the liquidity of the company's shares. Following a two-for-one split, the number of shares traded should more than double if liquidity is increased by the split. This doesn't appear to happen, and the reverse is sometimes observed.

REVERSE SPLITS

A less frequently encountered financial maneuver is the **reverse split.** For example, in January 2011, solar power company Evergreen Solar underwent a 1-for-6 reverse stock split, and, in February 2011, PremierWest Bancorp underwent a 1-for-10 reverse split. In a 1-for-10 reverse split, each investor exchanges 10 old shares for 1 new share. The par value is increased by a factor of 10 in the process. In what is one of the biggest reverse splits ever (in terms of market cap), banking giant Citigroup announced in March 2011 that it would do a 1-for-10 reverse split, thereby reducing the number of its shares outstanding from 29 billion to 2.9 billion. As with stock splits and stock dividends, a case can be made that a reverse split has no real effect.

Given real-world imperfections, three related reasons are cited for reverse splits. First, transaction costs to shareholders may be less after the reverse split. Second, the liquidity and marketability of a company's stock might be improved when its price is raised to the popular trading range. Third, stocks selling at prices below a certain level are not considered respectable, meaning that investors underestimate these firms' earnings, cash flow, growth, and stability. Some financial analysts argue that a reverse split can achieve instant respectability. As was the case with stock splits, none of these reasons is particularly compelling, especially not the third one.

There are two other reasons for reverse splits. First, stock exchanges have minimum price per share requirements. A reverse split may bring the stock price up to such a minimum. In 2001–2002, in the wake of a bear market, this motive became an increasingly important one. In 2001, 106 companies asked their shareholders to approve reverse splits. There were 111 reverse splits in 2002 and 75 in 2003, but only 14 by mid-year 2004. The most common reason for these reverse splits is that NASDAQ delists companies whose stock price drops below $1 per share for 30 days. Many companies, particularly Internet-related technology companies, found themselves in danger of being delisted and used reverse splits to boost their stock prices. Second, companies sometimes perform reverse splits and, at the same time, buy out any stockholders who end up with less than a certain number of shares.

For example, in January 2011, Phoenix Footwear Group, Inc. completed a reverse/forward split. In this case, the company first did a 1-for-200 reverse stock split. The company repurchased all shares held by stockholders with less than one share of stock, thereby eliminating small shareholders (and reducing the total number of shareholders). The purpose of the reverse split was to allow the company to "go dark." The reverse split and share repurchase left the company with fewer than 300 shareholders, so it would no longer be required to file periodic reports with the SEC. What made the proposal especially imaginative was that immediately after the reverse split, the company did a 200-for-1 ordinary split to restore the stock to its original cost!

◄ To test your mastery of this material, take a quiz at mhhe. com/rwj

Summary and Conclusions

1. The dividend policy of a firm is irrelevant in a perfect capital market because the shareholder can effectively undo the firm's dividend strategy. If a shareholder receives a greater dividend than desired, he or she can reinvest the excess. Conversely, if the shareholder receives a smaller dividend than desired, he or she can sell off extra shares of stock. This argument is due to MM and is similar to their homemade leverage concept, discussed in a previous chapter.

2. Stockholders will be indifferent between dividends and share repurchases in a perfect capital market.

3. Because dividends in the United States are taxed, companies should not issue stock to pay out a dividend.

4. Also because of taxes, firms have an incentive to reduce dividends. For example, they might consider increasing capital expenditures, acquiring other companies, or purchasing financial assets. However, due to financial considerations and legal constraints, rational firms with large cash flows will likely exhaust these activities with plenty of cash left over for dividends.

5. In a world with personal taxes, a strong case can be made for repurchasing shares instead of paying dividends.

6. Nevertheless, there are a number of justifications for dividends even in a world with personal taxes:
   a. Investors in no-dividend stocks incur transaction costs when selling off shares for current consumption.
   b. Behavioral finance argues that investors with limited self-control can meet current consumption needs via high-dividend stocks while adhering to a policy of "never dipping into principal."
   c. Managers, acting on behalf of stockholders, can pay dividends to keep cash from bondholders. The board of directors, also acting on behalf of stockholders, can use dividends to reduce the cash available to spendthrift managers.

7. The stock market reacts positively to increases in dividends (or an initial payment) and negatively to decreases in dividends. This suggests that there is information content in dividend payments.

8. High (low) dividend firms should arise to meet the demands of dividend-preferring (capital gains–preferring) investors. Because of these clienteles, it is not clear that a firm can create value by changing its dividend policy.

www.mhhe.com/rwj

Concept Questions

1. **Dividend Policy Irrelevance**   How is it possible that dividends are so important, but at the same time dividend policy is irrelevant?

2. **Stock Repurchases**   What is the impact of a stock repurchase on a company's debt ratio? Does this suggest another use for excess cash?

3. **Dividend Policy**   It is sometimes suggested that firms should follow a "residual" dividend policy. With such a policy, the main idea is that a firm should focus on meeting its investment needs and maintaining its desired debt–equity ratio. Having done so, a firm pays out any leftover, or residual, income as dividends. What do you think would be the chief drawback to a residual dividend policy?

4. **Dividend Chronology**   On Tuesday, December 8, Hometown Power Co.'s board of directors declares a dividend of 75 cents per share payable on Wednesday, January 17, to shareholders of record as of Wednesday, January 3. When is the ex-dividend date? If a shareholder buys stock before that date, who gets the dividends on those shares—the buyer or the seller?

5. **Alternative Dividends**   Some corporations, like one British company that offers its large shareholders free crematorium use, pay dividends in kind (that is, offer their services to shareholders at below-market cost). Should mutual funds invest in stocks that pay these dividends in kind? (The fundholders do not receive these services.)

6. **Dividends and Stock Price**   If increases in dividends tend to be followed by (immediate) increases in share prices, how can it be said that dividend policy is irrelevant?

7. **Dividends and Stock Price**   Last month, Central Virginia Power Company, which had been having trouble with cost overruns on a nuclear power plant that it had been building, announced that it was "temporarily suspending dividend payments due to the cash flow crunch associated with its investment program." The company's stock price dropped from $28.50 to $25 when this announcement was made. How would you interpret this change in the stock price? (That is, what would you say caused it?)

8. **Dividend Reinvestment Plans**   The DRK Corporation has recently developed a dividend reinvestment plan, or DRIP. The plan allows investors to reinvest cash dividends automatically in DRK in exchange for new shares of stock. Over time, investors in DRK will be able to build their holdings by reinvesting dividends to purchase additional shares of the company.

    Over 1,000 companies offer dividend reinvestment plans. Most companies with DRIPs charge no brokerage or service fees. In fact, the shares of DRK will be purchased at a 10 percent discount from the market price.

    A consultant for DRK estimates that about 75 percent of DRK's shareholders will take part in this plan. This is somewhat higher than the average.

    Evaluate DRK's dividend reinvestment plan. Will it increase shareholder wealth? Discuss the advantages and disadvantages involved here.

9. **Dividend Policy**   For initial public offerings of common stock, 2007 was a relatively slow year, with only about $35.6 billion raised by the process. Relatively few of the 159 firms involved paid cash dividends. Why do you think that most chose not to pay cash dividends?

10. **Investment and Dividends**   The Phew Charitable Trust pays no taxes on its capital gains or on its dividend income or interest income. Would it be irrational for it to have low-dividend, high-growth stocks in its portfolio? Would it be irrational for it to have municipal bonds in its portfolio? Explain.

    Use the following information to answer the next two questions:
    Historically, the U.S. tax code treated dividend payments made to shareholders as ordinary income. Thus, dividends were taxed at the investor's marginal tax rate, which was as high as 38.6 percent in 2002. Capital gains were taxed at a capital gains tax rate, which was the same for most investors and fluctuated through the years. In 2002, the capital gains tax rate stood at 20 percent. In an effort to stimulate the economy, President George W. Bush presided over a tax plan overhaul that included changes in dividend and capital gains tax rates. The new tax plan, which was implemented in 2003, called for a 15 percent tax rate on both dividends and capital gains for investors in higher tax brackets. For lower tax bracket investors, the tax rate on dividends and capital gains was set at 5 percent through 2007, dropping to zero in 2008.

11. **Ex-Dividend Stock Prices**   How do you think this tax law change affects ex-dividend stock prices?

Chapter 19   Dividends and Other Payouts   **615**

12. **Stock Repurchases**   How do you think this tax law change affected the relative attractiveness of stock repurchases compared to dividend payments?

13. **Dividends and Stock Value**   The growing perpetuity model expresses the value of a share of stock as the present value of the expected dividends from that stock. How can you conclude that dividend policy is irrelevant when this model is valid?

14. **Bird-in-the-Hand Argument**   The bird-in-the-hand argument, which states that a dividend today is safer than the uncertain prospect of a capital gain tomorrow, is often used to justify high dividend payout ratios. Explain the fallacy behind this argument.

15. **Dividends and Income Preference**   The desire for current income is not a valid explanation of preference for high current dividend policy because investors can always create homemade dividends by selling a portion of their stocks. Is this statement true or false? Why?

16. **Dividends and Clientele**   Cap Henderson owns Neotech stock because its price has been steadily rising over the past few years and he expects this performance to continue. Cap is trying to convince Sarah Jones to purchase some Neotech stock, but she is reluctant because Neotech has never paid a dividend. She depends on steady dividends to provide her with income.
    a. What preferences are these two investors demonstrating?
    b. What argument should Cap use to convince Sarah that Neotech stock is the stock for her?
    c. Why might Cap's argument not convince Sarah?

17. **Dividends and Taxes**   Your aunt is in a high tax bracket and would like to minimize the tax burden of her investment portfolio. She is willing to buy and sell to maximize her aftertax returns, and she has asked for your advice. What would you suggest she do?

18. **Dividends versus Capital Gains**   If the market places the same value on $1 of dividends as on $1 of capital gains, then firms with different payout ratios will appeal to different clienteles of investors. One clientele is as good as another; therefore, a firm cannot increase its value by changing its dividend policy. Yet empirical investigations reveal a strong correlation between dividend payout ratios and other firm characteristics. For example, small, rapidly growing firms that have recently gone public almost always have payout ratios that are zero; all earnings are reinvested in the business. Explain this phenomenon if dividend policy is irrelevant.

19. **Dividend Irrelevancy**   In spite of the theoretical argument that dividend policy should be irrelevant, the fact remains that many investors like high dividends. If this preference exists, a firm can boost its share price by increasing its dividend payout ratio. Explain the fallacy in this argument.

20. **Dividends and Stock Price**   Empirical research has found that there have been significant increases in stock price on the day an initial dividend (i.e., the first time a firm pays a cash dividend) is announced. What does this finding imply about the information content of initial dividends?

Questions and Problems

BASIC
(Questions 1–10)

1. **Dividends and Taxes**   Lee Ann, Inc., has declared a $9.50 per-share dividend. Suppose capital gains are not taxed, but dividends are taxed at 15 percent. New IRS regulations require that taxes be withheld when the dividend is paid. Lee Ann sells for $115 per share, and the stock is about to go exdividend. What do you think the ex-dividend price will be?

2. **Stock Dividends** The owners' equity accounts for Hexagon International are shown here:

Common stock ($1 par value)	$ 30,000
Capital surplus	185,000
Retained earnings	627,500
Total owners' equity	$842,500

     a. If Hexagon stock currently sells for $37 per share and a 10 percent stock dividend is declared, how many new shares will be distributed? Show how the equity accounts would change.

     b. If Hexagon declared a 25 percent stock dividend, how would the accounts change?

3. **Stock Splits** For the company in Problem 2, show how the equity accounts will change if:

     a. Hexagon declares a four-for-one stock split. How many shares are outstanding now? What is the new par value per share?

     b. Hexagon declares a one-for-five reverse stock split. How many shares are outstanding now? What is the new par value per share?

4. **Stock Splits and Stock Dividends** Roll Corporation (RC) currently has 330,000 shares of stock outstanding that sell for $64 per share. Assuming no market imperfections or tax effects exist, what will the share price be after:

     a. RC has a five-for-three stock split?

     b. RC has a 15 percent stock dividend?

     c. RC has a 42.5 percent stock dividend?

     d. RC has a four-for-seven reverse stock split?

     Determine the new number of shares outstanding in parts (a) through (d).

5. **Regular Dividends** The balance sheet for Levy Corp. is shown here in market value terms. There are 12,000 shares of stock outstanding.

Market Value Balance Sheet			
Cash	$ 55,000	Equity	$465,000
Fixed assets	410,000		
Total	$465,000	Total	$465,000

     The company has declared a dividend of $1.90 per share. The stock goes ex dividend tomorrow. Ignoring any tax effects, what is the stock selling for today? What will it sell for tomorrow? What will the balance sheet look like after the dividends are paid?

6. **Share Repurchase** In the previous problem, suppose Levy has announced it is going to repurchase $22,800 worth of stock. What effect will this transaction have on the equity of the firm? How many shares will be outstanding? What will the price per share be after the repurchase? Ignoring tax effects, show how the share repurchase is effectively the same as a cash dividend.

7. **Stock Dividends** The market value balance sheet for Outbox Manufacturing is shown here. Outbox has declared a stock dividend of 25 percent. The stock goes exdividend tomorrow (the chronology for a stock dividend is similar to that for a cash dividend). There are 20,000 shares of stock outstanding. What will the ex-dividend price be?

Market Value Balance Sheet			
Cash	$295,000	Debt	$180,000
Fixed assets	540,000	Equity	655,000
Total	$835,000	Total	$835,000

8. **Stock Dividends**   The company with the common equity accounts shown here has declared a stock dividend of 15 percent when the market value of its stock is $45 per share. What effects on the equity accounts will the distribution of the stock dividend have?

Common stock ($1 par value)	$ 410,000
Capital surplus	2,150,000
Retained earnings	5,320,000
Total owners' equity	$7,880,000

9. **Stock Splits**   In the previous problem, suppose the company instead decides on a five-for-one stock split. The firm's 45 cent per share cash dividend on the new (postsplit) shares represents an increase of 10 percent over last year's dividend on the presplit stock. What effect does this have on the equity accounts? What was last year's dividend per share?

10. **Dividends and Stock Price**   The Mann Company belongs to a risk class for which the appropriate discount rate is 10 percent. Mann currently has 220,000 outstanding shares selling at $110 each. The firm is contemplating the declaration of a $4 dividend at the end of the fiscal year that just began. Assume there are no taxes on dividends. Answer the following questions based on the Miller and Modigliani model, which is discussed in the text.

    a. What will be the price of the stock on the ex-dividend date if the dividend is declared?

    b. What will be the price of the stock at the end of the year if the dividend is not declared?

    c. If Mann makes $4.5 million of new investments at the beginning of the period, earns net income of $1.9 million, and pays the dividend at the end of the year, how many shares of new stock must the firm issue to meet its funding needs?

    d. Is it realistic to use the MM model in the real world to value stock? Why or why not?

INTERMEDIATE
(Questions 11–16)

11. **Homemade Dividends**   You own 1,000 shares of stock in Avondale Corporation. You will receive a dividend of $1.10 per share in one year. In two years, Avondale will pay a liquidating dividend of $56 per share. The required return on Avondale stock is 14 percent. What is the current share price of your stock (ignoring taxes)? If you would rather have equal dividends in each of the next two years, show how you can accomplish this by creating homemade dividends. (*Hint:* Dividends will be in the form of an annuity.)

12. **Homemade Dividends**   In the previous problem, suppose you want only $500 total in dividends the first year. What will your homemade dividend be in two years?

13. **Stock Repurchase**   Flychucker Corporation is evaluating an extra dividend versus a share repurchase. In either case $4,000 would be spent. Current earnings are $2.10 per share, and the stock currently sells for $46 per share. There are 800 shares outstanding. Ignore taxes and other imperfections in answering parts (a) and (b).

    a. Evaluate the two alternatives in terms of the effect on the price per share of the stock and shareholder wealth.

   b. What will be the effect on Flychucker's EPS and PE ratio under the two different scenarios?

   c. In the real world, which of these actions would you recommend? Why?

14. **Dividends and Firm Value** The net income of Novis Corporation is $85,000. The company has 25,000 outstanding shares and a 100 percent payout policy. The expected value of the firm one year from now is $1,725,000. The appropriate discount rate for Novis is 12 percent, and the dividend tax rate is zero.

   a. What is the current value of the firm assuming the current dividend has not yet been paid?

   b. What is the ex-dividend price of Novis's stock if the board follows its current policy?

   c. At the dividend declaration meeting, several board members claimed that the dividend is too meager and is probably depressing Novis's price. They proposed that Novis sell enough new shares to finance a $4.60 dividend.

     i. Comment on the claim that the low dividend is depressing the stock price. Support your argument with calculations.

     ii. If the proposal is adopted, at what price will the new shares sell? How many will be sold?

15. **Dividend Policy** Gibson Co. has a current period cash flow of $1.1 million and pays no dividends. The present value of the company's future cash flows is $15 million. The company is entirely financed with equity and has 600,000 shares outstanding. Assume the dividend tax rate is zero.

   a. What is the share price of the Gibson stock?

   b. Suppose the board of directors of Gibson Co. announces its plan to pay out 50 percent of its current cash flow as cash dividends to its shareholders. How can Jeff Miller, who owns 1,000 shares of Gibson stock, achieve a zero payout policy on his own?

16. **Dividend Smoothing** The Sharpe Co. just paid a dividend of $1.80 per share of stock. Its target payout ratio is 40 percent. The company expects to have an earnings per share of $4.95 one year from now.

   a. If the adjustment rate is .3 as defined in the Lintner model, what is the dividend one year from now?

   b. If the adjustment rate is .6 instead, what is the dividend one year from now?

   c. Which adjustment rate is more conservative? Why?

CHALLENGE
(Questions 17–20)

17. **Expected Return, Dividends, and Taxes** The Gecko Company and the Gordon Company are two firms whose business risk is the same but that have different dividend policies. Gecko pays no dividend, whereas Gordon has an expected dividend yield of 5.5 percent. Suppose the capital gains tax rate is zero, whereas the dividend tax rate is 35 percent. Gecko has an expected earnings growth rate of 13 percent annually, and its stock price is expected to grow at this same rate. If the aftertax expected returns on the two stocks are equal (because they are in the same risk class), what is the pretax required return on Gordon's stock?

18. **Dividends and Taxes** As discussed in the text, in the absence of market imperfections and tax effects, we would expect the share price to decline by the amount of the dividend payment when the stock goes ex dividend. Once we consider the role of taxes, however, this is not necessarily true. One model has been proposed that incorporates tax effects into determining the ex-dividend price:[19]

$$(P_0 - P_X)/D = (1 - t_P)/(1 - t_G)$$

---

[19]E. Elton and M. Gruber, "Marginal Stockholder Tax Rates and the Clientele Effect," *Review of Economics and Statistics* 52 (February 1970).

Here P_0 is the price just before the stock goes ex, P_X is the ex-dividend share price, D is the amount of the dividend per share, t_P is the relevant marginal personal tax rate on dividends, and t_G is the effective marginal tax rate on capital gains.

a. If $t_P = t_G = 0$, how much will the share price fall when the stock goes ex?
b. If $t_P = 15$ percent and $t_G = 0$, how much will the share price fall?
c. If $t_P = 15$ percent and $t_G = 20$ percent, how much will the share price fall?
d. Suppose the only owners of stock are corporations. Recall that corporations get at least a 70 percent exemption from taxation on the dividend income they receive, but they do not get such an exemption on capital gains. If the corporation's income and capital gains tax rates are both 35 percent, what does this model predict the ex-dividend share price will be?
e. What does this problem tell you about real-world tax considerations and the dividend policy of the firm?

19. **Dividends versus Reinvestment** National Business Machine Co. (NBM) has $4 million of extra cash after taxes have been paid. NBM has two choices to make use of this cash. One alternative is to invest the cash in financial assets. The resulting investment income will be paid out as a special dividend at the end of three years. In this case, the firm can invest in either Treasury bills yielding 3 percent or 5 percent preferred stock. IRS regulations allow the company to exclude from taxable income 70 percent of the dividends received from investing in another company's stock. Another alternative is to pay out the cash now as dividends. This would allow the shareholders to invest on their own in Treasury bills with the same yield or in preferred stock. The corporate tax rate is 35 percent. Assume the investor has a 31 percent personal income tax rate, which is applied to interest income and preferred stock dividends. The personal dividend tax rate is 15 percent on common stock dividends. Should the cash be paid today or in three years? Which of the two options generates the highest aftertax income for the shareholders?

20. **Dividends versus Reinvestment** After completing its capital spending for the year, Carlson Manufacturing has $1,000 extra cash. Carlson's managers must choose between investing the cash in Treasury bonds that yield 8 percent or paying the cash out to investors who would invest in the bonds themselves.

a. If the corporate tax rate is 35 percent, what personal tax rate would make the investors equally willing to receive the dividend or to let Carlson invest the money?
b. Is the answer to (a) reasonable? Why or why not?
c. Suppose the only investment choice is a preferred stock that yields 12 percent. The corporate dividend exclusion of 70 percent applies. What personal tax rate will make the stockholders indifferent to the outcome of Carlson's dividend decision?
d. Is this a compelling argument for a low dividend payout ratio? Why or why not?

www.mhhe.com/rwj

Mini Case

ELECTRONIC TIMING, INC.

Electronic Timing, Inc. (ETI), is a small company founded 15 years ago by electronics engineers Tom Miller and Jessica Kerr. ETI manufactures integrated circuits to capitalize on the complex mixed-signal design technology and has recently entered the market for frequency timing generators, or silicon timing devices, which provide the timing signals or "clocks" necessary to synchronize electronic systems. Its clock products originally were used in PC video graphics applications, but the market subsequently expanded to include motherboards, PC peripheral devices, and other digital consumer electronics, such as digital television boxes and game consoles. ETI also designs and markets custom application-specific integrated circuits (ASICs) for industrial customers. The ASIC's design combines analog and digital, or mixed-signal, technology. In addition to Tom and Jessica, Nolan

Pittman, who provided capital for the company, is the third primary owner. Each owns 25 percent of the $1 million shares outstanding. Several other individuals, including current employees, own the remaining company shares.

Recently, the company designed a new computer motherboard. The company's new design is both more efficient and less expensive to manufacture, and the ETI design is expected to become standard in many personal computers. After investigating the possibility of manufacturing the new motherboard, ETI determined that the costs involved in building a new plant would be prohibitive. The owners also decided that they were unwilling to bring in another large outside owner. Instead, ETI sold the design to an outside firm. The sale of the motherboard design was completed for an aftertax payment of $30 million.

1. Tom believes the company should use the extra cash to pay a special one-time dividend. How will this proposal affect the stock price? How will it affect the value of the company?

2. Jessica believes that the company should use the extra cash to pay off debt and upgrade and expand its existing manufacturing capability. How would Jessica's proposals affect the company?

3. Nolan is in favor of a share repurchase. He argues that a repurchase will increase the company's P/E ratio, return on assets, and return on equity. Are his arguments correct? How will a share repurchase affect the value of the company?

4. Another option discussed by Tom, Jessica, and Nolan would be to begin a regular dividend payment to shareholders. How would you evaluate this proposal?

5. One way to value a share of stock is the dividend growth, or growing perpetuity, model. Consider the following: The dividend payout ratio is 1 minus b, where b is the "retention" or "plowback" ratio. So, the dividend next year will be the earnings next year, E_1, times 1 minus the retention ratio. The most commonly used equation to calculate the sustainable growth rate is the return on equity times the retention ratio. Substituting these relationships into the dividend growth model, we get the following equation to calculate the price of a share of stock today:

$$P_0 = \frac{E_1(1-b)}{R_S - \text{ROE} \times b}$$

What are the implications of this result in terms of whether the company should pay a dividend or upgrade and expand its manufacturing capability? Explain.

6. Does the question of whether the company should pay a dividend depend on whether the company is organized as a corporation or an LLC?